THE NEW MARITIME HISTORY OF DEVON

Volume II

THE NEW
MARITIME HISTORY
of
DEVON

Volume II: From the Late Eigthteenth Century to the Present Day

Edited by

MICHAEL DUFFY
STEPHEN FISHER
BASIL GREENHILL
DAVID J STARKEY
JOYCE YOUINGS

CONWAY MARITIME PRESS

in association with

THE UNIVERSITY OF EXETER

Frontispiece: Plymouth Pier from the Hoe, painted in 1923 by Charles Ginner. It was destroyed in 1941. (*Plymouth City Museum and Art Gallery*)

© The University of Exeter and the contributors 1994

First published in Great Britain 1994 by
Conway Maritime Press
an imprint of Brassey's (UK) Ltd,
33 John Street, London WC1N 2AT
in association with the University of Exeter

British Library Cataloguing in Publication Data
The New Maritime History of Devon – Vol. 2:
From the Late Eigthteenth Century to the Present Day
I. Duffy, Michael *et al.*
387.509423

ISBN 0 85177 633 7

Maps drawn by Rodney Fry, Department of Geography, University of Exeter
Designed and typeset by The Word Shop, Bury, Lancashire
Printed and bound in Great Britain by The Bath Press

Contents

List of Contributors

PETER ALLINGTON, Master (HT), Shipkeeper and Skipper of the Tamar sailing barge *Shamrock*, National Maritime Museum, Cotehele Quay, Cornwall.

MARK BRAYSHAY, BA, PhD, Senior Lecturer in Goegraphy, University of Plymouth.

JOHN CHANNON, BA, PhD, Senior Lecturer in Russian Economic and Social History, University of London, author of many papers on the economic, social and environmental aspects of resort development.

The late E A G CLARK, BA, PhD, lately Professor of Education, Rhodes University, South Africa, author of *The Ports of the Exe Estuary* (1960).

JONATHAN COAD, MA, FSA, Inspector of Ancient Monuments and Historic Buildings, English Heritage, author of *The Royal Dockyards, 1690–1850* (1989).

ROBIN CRAIG, BSc (Econ), FRHistS, formerly Senior Lecturer in Economic and Social History, University of London, editor of *Maritime History*, author (with R Jarvis) of *Liverpool Registry of Merchant Ships* (1967) and many papers on Britain's shipping and shipbuilding industries.

MICHAEL DUFFY, MA, DPhil, Senior Lecturer in History and co-Director of the Centre for Maritime Historical Studies, University of Exeter, editor of *Mariner's Mirror* and author of *Soldiers, Sugar and Seapower: the British Expedition to the West Indies and the War against Revolutionary France* (1987).

STEPHEN FISHER, BSc (Econ), PhD, FRHistS, Senior Lecturer in Economic History and co-Director of the Centre for Maritime Historical Studies, University of Exeter, author of *The Portugal Trade: a Study of Anglo-Portugese Commerce, 1700–1770* (1971 and Portugese edn, 1984), editor of *Innovation in Shipping and Trade* (1989).

ANN GIFFARD, NDD, author (with Basil Greenhill) of *Steam, Politics and Patronage: the Transformation of the Royal Navy 1815–1854* (1994).

CRISPIN GILL, OBE, FSA, formerly assistant editor of *The Western Morning News* and editor of *The Countryman*, author of *Plymouth: a New History* (new edn 1993).

BASIL GREENHILL, CB, CMG, BA, PhD, FRHistS, FSA, formerly Director, National Maritime Museum, Honorary Research Fellow, University of Exeter, author (with Ann Giffard) of *Steam, Politics and Patronage: the Transformation of the Royal Navy 1815–1854* (1994).

PETER HILDITCH, BA, PhD, Research Fellow, University of Exeter, author of many papers on the British shipbuilding and maritime defence industries.

ALSTON KENNERLEY, Master Mariner, MA, PhD, FNI, Principal Lecturer in the Institute of Marine Studies, University of Plymouth, author of many papers on the education and welfare of nineteenth-century seafarers.

ANDREW D LAMBERT, MA, PhD, Lecturer in War Studies, University of London, author of *The Last Sailing Battlefleet* (1991).

NIGEL J MORGAN, BA, PhD, Communications Officer, Torfaen Council, Pontypool, author of *Participation in Sport and Leisure in Wales* (1991).

DAVID MURCH, MBIM, Chairman of Salcombe Museum Society, author of many papers on the history of Salcombe trade and shipping.

MICHAEL NIX, BA, PhD, Curator of Tiverton Museum, author of *The Cruel Coast of North Devon* (1982).

ANTHONY NORTHWAY, BSc (Econ), MA, MSc, formerly Senior Lecturer in History, Newcastle-upon-Tyne Polytechnic.

DEREK OAKLEY, MBE, Captain, Royal Marines, author of *A Pictorial History of the Royal Marines* (1988).

AMBER PATRICK, BA, MPhil, Civil Servant, author of *Morwellham Quay: a History of a Tamar Valley Mining Quay 1140–1900* (1990).

PHILIP PAYTON, BSc, PhD, FRHistS, Director of the Institute of Cornish Studies, University of Exeter, author of *The Making of Modern Cornwall: Historical Experience and the Persistence of 'Difference'* (1992).

J H PORTER, BA, PhD, FRHistS, formerly Senior Lecturer in Economic and Social History, University of Exeter, author of many papers on social history.

MARK PORTER, MA, Lecturer at Somerset College of Art and Technology.

ANTHONY REDFERN, ExC, BA, PhD, Head of the Institute of Marine Studies, University of Plymouth, author of *Watchkeeper Collision Avoidance Behaviour* (1993).

IAN SKINNER, BA, PhD, Civil Servant, States of Jersey, author of papers on naval operations in the Channel Approaches during the Second World War.

DAVID J STARKEY, MA, PhD, Leverhulme Research Fellow in Maritime History, University of Exeter, author of *British Privateering Enterprise in the Eighteenth Century* (1990).

LESLIE J TAYLOR, BSc, MIEE, Chartered Engineer.

JOHN TRAVIS, BA, PhD, Tutor in the Department of Adult and Continuing Education, University of Exeter, author of *The Rise of the Devon Seaside Resorts 1750–1900* (1993).

List of Figures

List of Figures

The Editors are grateful to the many individuals and institutions cited in the captions to these figures for kindly assenting to the reproduction of material. Devonport Management Limited generously subsidised the cost of illustrating the volume.

Lists of Tables, Maps and Abbreviations

List of Tables

List of Maps

Abbreviations

Acknowledgements

The Editors would like to express their gratitude to all those who have contributed towards the preparation and completion of the second volume of *The New Maritime History of Devon*. As with volume I, a substantial grant from the Leverhulme Trust largely sustained the research costs of the venture. Necessary additional funding was provided by the British Academy, Devon County Council, the Devonshire Association, Bideford Town Council, Devonport Management Ltd and the University of Exeter. The project as a whole was administered by a Steering Committee (see below), which offered valuable guidance in the design of the work. Once the investigation was under way, each of the research fellows and contributors benefited from the ready assistance of countless librarians and archivists, without whose vital support their efforts would not have been possible. To these custodians of records we offer a collective and heartfelt vote of thanks.

In bringing the fruits of this research to publication, the Editors have incurred many other debts. Generous contributions towards the costs of printing were made by Claude D Pike, J Paul Getty jr, John Holman and Sons Ltd, John Swire & Sons Ltd, Watts Blake Bearne & Co plc, Plymouth City Museums and Art Gallery, and the Scouloudi Foundation in association with the Institute of Historical Research. Permission to use illustrative material was granted by the Trustees of the National Maritime Museum, Greenwich; the Imperial War Museum; HM Naval Base Museum, Devonport; RMCTC Lympstone; RNEC Manadon; RNC Dartmouth; Devonport Management Ltd; Devon Record Office; Devon Library Services; Devon Property Department; the City of Plymouth Museums and Art Gallery; the Devon and Exeter Institution; the *Western Morning News*, the *Express and Echo* (Exeter) and the *Herald Express* (Torquay); and by numerous individuals as cited in the captions. The expertise of John Saunders and Tony Fisher, of the University of Exeter's Photographic Department, proved invaluable in the preparation of many of the volume's illustrations, while all of the maps were drawn with great skill by Rodney Fry of the Department of Geography at Exeter. The final typescript was the work of many hands, though a large proportion of it was undertaken efficiently and accurately by Celia Manning, Loveday Metcalfe and Sue Murch. Lastly our warm thanks are offered to Ray Blackmore, Julian Mannering and their colleagues at Conway Maritime Press who have assisted greatly in bringing this project to a successful conclusion.

EXETER   MICHAEL DUFFY
JULY 1994   STEPHEN FISHER
                    BASIL GREENHILL
                    DAVID J STARKEY
                    JOYCE YOUINGS

MEMBERS OF THE STEERING COMMITTEE

BENEFACTORS

The following made grants towards the cost of research:

Bideford Town Council

The British Academy

Devon County Council

Devonport Management Ltd

The Devonshire Association

The Leverhulme Trust

University of Exeter

and towards the cost of printing Volume II:

J Paul Getty jr

Claude D Pike

John Holman and Sons Ltd

John Swire & Sons Ltd

Watts Blake Bearne & Co plc

Plymouth City Museums and Art Gallery

The Scouloudi Foundation in association with the Institute of Historical Research.

Introduction

THIS SECOND VOLUME OF *The New Maritime History of Devon* covers the last two hundred years or so of the county's maritime past, from about 1780 to the 1990s. Relatively short as this period is compared with the long reaches of time covered in Volume I, it nevertheless contains a rich and diverse range of maritime activities, for which the documentary source material and pictorial illustration is much more abundant. Devon's maritime interests in these two modern centuries were full of contrast and change, offering instances of both significant growth and innovation as well as relative and absolute decline.

As is shown in detail in the contributions listed below, the traditional maritime interest of Devon in trade – coastal and foreign – did undergo further expansion from the late eighteenth century to the onset of the First World War. Merchant shipowning and shipbuilding in Devon, however, both reached a peak in the 1860s and 1870s and then underwent absolute decline in the tonnages owned and launched. The commercial transactions carried on between Devon ports and other parts of the United Kingdom and abroad, inwards and outwards, had great variety and exhibited considerable change over the period to 1914, shipments of woollen textiles in particular falling away as exports in both coastal and foreign trade, with ball clay emerging as a notable export and coastwise coal imports growing vigorously. Such commerce required substantial volumes of shipping, and up to the 1860s the county's shipowners built up and maintained fleets of wooden sailing vessels for such business, although a significant proportion of Devon's trade was carried in vessels owned elsewhere. Devon-owned merchant shipping was also employed in the trades of other ports, both British and foreign, a business which was a source of much invisible income. Most notable amongst these carrying or cross trades, as far as Devon shipping was concerned, were the movement of vast quantities of Quebec timber across the Atlantic, the freighting of Newfoundland cod to Southern Europe, and the fruit trade from thence to British ports serving the growing markets of the nation. In this period to the 1860s Devon's principal rivers and estuaries had numerous small shipyards, specialising in the construction and repair of the wooden schooners, brigs and sloops favoured by the county's shipowners.

From the 1870s, however, Devon's merchant shipowning and shipbuilding contracted absolutely as the county's shipowners and shipbuilders generally declined to make the transition from wooden sailing vessels to iron- and steel-hulled vessels driven by steam. Moreover, Devon's seaborne trade, shipowning and shipbuilding came to be increasingly overshadowed by the focusing of the fast-expanding national trade and shipowning on a relatively few major ports – London, Liverpool, Hull and Glasgow, for example – and the associated concentration of an impressively expanding national ship-building industry, especially those companies producing the newer kinds of vessels, on the rivers of northeast and northwest England and the Clyde. Until the First World War Devon's mercantile shipowners continued to deploy their diminishing stock of schooners and other vessels in various niches of the tonnage market, while the county's mercantile shipbuilding was reduced to a core of small-scale but increasingly efficient yards, largely concerned with wooden sailing vessels, although some modern steamship building was undertaken. The later nineteenth century, in fact, was to see a significant migration of Devon shipowning enterprise outwards to the rising maritime areas. Holmans of Topsham, for instance, moved their base of operations to London, while Reardon Smith of Bideford shifted to Cardiff.

The actual decline in Devon's seaborne trading appears to date from the First World War, the risks at sea discouraging maritime commerce. Moreover, enemy action had a devastating effect on the remaining stock of mercantile shipping. In the interwar years movements in maritime trading activity more or less responded to the timing of the United Kingdom trade cycle, with Plymouth standing out in terms of tonnages of cargo handled and their variety as it had done over the previous century. Neither merchant shipowning nor shipbuilding, however, showed any real sign of revival in Devon between the wars, although some shipyards, notably in Dartmouth, continued to produce significant numbers of vessels, modern in design but invariably of relatively small tonnage, while others concentrated on ship repair and maintenance. After the Second World War, and especially in the 1960s and 1970s, there was some recovery in Devon's maritime trade, notably in the expanding ball clay shipments from Teignmouth and Plymouth, in the development of 'roll-on, roll-off' traffic with Brittany and Spain at Plymouth, and in agricultural products and fertilisers at various ports. In mercantile shipbuilding the outstanding growth point was the establishment of a highly successful modern shipyard at Appledore in North Devon in the 1970s, which for a number of years was a world leader in its covered and assembly system of production.

Devon's other notable traditional pursuit in earlier times had been the fishing industry, both offshore and in distant waters. Here the modern story is one of marked vicissitudes but of essential continuity and even success. In the mid and later nineteenth century, Devon's local fisheries underwent significant growth, the leading fishing centres of Plymouth and Brixham enjoying much prosperity. The interwar years, however, were generally difficult for all fishing communities in the county, as were the immediate post-Second World War decades, but in the 1970s there was a return to high levels of activity and prosperity. Devon's other historic fishing interest was cod fishing off the Grand Banks of Newfoundland. Here, the involvement of Devon-based fishermen in the actual fishing for the codfish virtually ceased in the Napoleonic Wars as the Newfoundlanders themselves came to man their own fishery. Instead, for a hundred years or so, until just after the First World War, Devon's merchants and shipowners, notably in Dart-mouth, Salcombe and Bideford, maintained the Devon-Newfoundland connection in the dried cod carrying trade to Southern Europe.

In contrast to the mixed fortunes of the mercantile and fishing interests of the county over the nineteenth and twentieth centuries, stand the two maritime and maritime-related growth stories of the period since 1780. The first was the continuing and indeed generally increasing interest of the British Admiralty in Devon, and most particularly in Plymouth, both as a base and as a shipbuilding and repair facility for the Royal Navy. Repeated expansion and modernisation of Plymouth's facilities occurred over the nineteenth and twentieth centuries. Plymouth Dock (renamed Devonport in 1824) began the period as one of the three principal Royal Navy dockyards, alongside Portsmouth and Chatham, but by the 1980s Plymouth/Devonport had assumed a clear position of primacy – indeed, it became the most notable West European naval base. Admiralty interest in Devon is also seen in its choice as a fitting location for advanced naval education and training, for officer cadets at Dartmouth from the 1860s, and shortly after for naval engineering training in Plymouth, at Keyham and later at Manadon. Increasingly over the twentieth century basic training for the Royal Marines (at Lympstone on the Exe) and naval ratings (at Plymouth) has been concentrated in Devon too.

The other outstanding Devon maritime growth story of modern times, seaside tourism and other sea-related leisure activities, had its beginnings in the royal and aristocratic patronage of Sidmouth and Dawlish, Teignmouth and Torquay in the second half of the eighteenth century. Through the nineteenth century the social basis of seaside tourism broadened as the middle classes began to travel to the Devon coasts in growing numbers, from Bristol, the Midlands and London. From the later nineteenth century, too, the south Devon resorts began to be rivalled by the later-developing north Devon resorts, particularly Ilfracombe. The twentieth century has seen a further broadening of the tourist clientele, and, especially from the 1920s and even more the 1950s, a diversification of this activity into leisure yachting and other forms of small-boat pursuits. Devon in the last two centuries, then, was in the van of English maritime counties, although in a rather more socially select way than most, in developing and responding to the Englishman's and his family's modern liking for the sea – that is, in the exploitation of the sea, the coastline and maritime communities as a leisure resource. Seaside tourism after 1945 became a key growth point in the Devon economy.

As the contributors in the following pages also reveal, these varied developments in Devon's maritime history in modern times have been the product of a number of factors. They may be summed up broadly as technological, economic, social and political, operating both within the county and in other areas of the British economy. Devon in the nineteenth century, it may be said, did not play a leading part in the Industrial Revolution and the continuing industrialisation of Britain. Its previously important woollen textile industries declined greatly from the 1830s with the competition from more technologically innovative regions in the north, and from the 1870s the copper mining interests in West Devon severely contracted, in response to rising costs as the most accessible lodes were exhausted and competition from copper producers elsewhere in Britain and abroad. The virtual absence of any significant new industry in the county requiring large volumes of shipping for the transport of its products to home or foreign markets (the one exception is the clay extraction undertaken in the Teign valley, at Lee Moor near Plymouth, and at Marland in North Devon) or significantly bulky raw material imports (the exception here is coal) meant that the economic mainstay for a vigorously expansive, as opposed to a steady, growth of local commerce and the shipowning industry disappeared. This loss of a great productive base for local trade and shipping, compared with the stimuli operating in certain select industrial regions and ports elsewhere in Britain, was reinforced by the relatively slow growth of Devon's population, its internal market – the one exception was Plymouth – particularly because of heavy migration out of the county, within England and overseas. Indeed, it was very much the traditional enterprise and skill of Devon shipowners and seafarers, and particularly their initiatives in creating a significant carrying fleet for other British ports, that ensured that a vital Devon shipping interest was maintained for as long as it was.

The classic Industrial Revolution of the late eighteenth to the mid-nineteenth centuries and continuing industrialisation, however, was to bring further transformation of Devon's maritime world. The mid-nineteenth century and later change to iron and steel vessels and the use of steam power for propulsion was, for various reasons, not adopted by Devon's mercantile shipowners and shipbuilders, although there were a number of attempts and successful enterprises. The reasons lie mainly in the continuing profitability of the traditional vessels in the case of local shipowning, and, in the case of shipbuilding, in cost factors including poor external economies of scale. So Devon's mercantile shipowning and shipbuilding remained attached to the gradually but inexorably declining technology of the wooden sailing vessel. Moreover, steam, this time in the form of the railways, which came to Devon in the 1840s, was also, in general and gradually, to re-order and eventually undermine the local trading world in the competition it brought to coastal traffic, although the damage done to the coastal trades did not become decisive until the advent of another and complementary major transport innovation, the motor lorry of the 1920s.

There were two prime exceptions to the generally debilitating effects of British technological change in the nineteenth century on the Devon maritime world. One was the benefits granted to the county's fishing industry by the relatively speedy access the railway system gave to markets in the industrial towns and regions of the Midlands and in London. The second was the constant technological modernisation of Devonport Dockyard through large-scale state investment, which is discussed more below as a political factor. Mention could also be made of the growing passenger traffic the railway brought to and carried from Plymouth for the developing transatlantic liner services.

Whilst the onset and earlier phases of the British Industrial Revolution were essentially stultifying or even damaging to traditional mercantile maritime Devon, the county's sea-related economy has benefited greatly from the later stages of industrialisation, from the maturing industrial economy and society. The rising real incomes of all classes in Britain associated with productivity advance, and the coming of increased leisure, of 'holidays with pay', have sustained the impressive growth of Devon's sea-related leisure industries, seaside tourism and boating of all kinds. Here Devon's broadly 'missing out', as it might be put, on the classic Industrial Revolution, the escaping of its traditional seaside communities and ports, and its beautiful and varied coastline, from the despoiling effects of industrial and urban (including dockland) growth, has proved to be a real bonus for the county.

The last fundamental factor shaping Devon's maritime story in this period was political in nature, and relates to the major and continuing naval involvement with the county. For the Admiralty's persisting need for a major naval base close to the 'Western Approaches' to the English Channel, with significant warshipbuilding and repair facilities, stems from national political decisions, or, more exactly, strategic considerations.

Over the nineteenth century, as Britain's imperial interests and foreign trade expanded, and as sea power came to be even more crucial in the conduct of British foreign policy, so naval thinking rated bases with ready access to the Atlantic as of prime importance. Continuing Anglo-French rivalry for much of the century also gave priority to this westward focus in naval planning. Rising international tension from the close of the century, two world wars, and the 'cold war' after 1945 to the 1980s have all maintained the Admiralty's interest in its great naval base and facility at Devonport. So, too, has the quite recent ending of the age of the large warship, at least for the British, and the turn strategically to more emphasis on submarine means of warfare. In this latest era of naval weaponry a southwestern base with easy access into the open, broad Atlantic, which Devonport eminently provides, remains paramount. Nevertheless, strategy did not require that British warships in the later nineteenth century and into the interwar years should be built at Devonport, as many of them were, instead of in arguably more efficient and better-located regions for modern shipbuilding, such as the North East or the North West. The decision to do so, which meant that iron and steam-propelled vessels were constructed in number at Devonport, contrasts remarkably with the limited extent of modern mercantile shipbuilding elsewhere in Devon. It can only be ascribed to deliberate decision-taking by central government and the Admiralty, to the acceptance of the need for substantial subsidy for political and strategic ends. As a result, from the 1780s to the early 1990s Devonport Dockyard has remained Devon's largest industrial enterprise, a great factory and workshop sustained by political and maritime factors.

The contributions in this volume deal with these broad issues and developments in Devon's maritime affairs over the last two hundred years or more in full and often fascinating detail. For the first time for many aspects of this wide-ranging story we have a clear idea of what actually happened and an understanding of scale and trend. Thus, the overall movements in trade and mercantile shipowning are treated for the North Devon ports to the Second World War by Basil Greenhill and Michael Nix, and for the South Devon ports by David Starkey. The twentieth-century developments in the Devon ports and their commercial activities are also examined by Mark Porter, who is especially interesting on the role played by individual ports, notably Plymouth, in attempting to generate their own business, that is supply-led growth. In a related area, Crispin Gill, in a short contribution, is revealing on the way in which a management take-over of the harbour facilities at Teignmouth in 1979 led to the revitalisation of that port. There are also valuable studies of the maritime traffic of two of the most important navigable rivers in Devon involved in coastal and foreign trade. Amber Patrick traces the nineteenth-century mining-related shipping and trade of the Tamar, giving special attention to the heyday of Morwellham and the other river ports and quays in the 1850s and 1860s, while the late Arthur Clark offers a long-term profile of the rise and fall of commercial traffic on the Exe estuary and the historic Exeter canal, which ran from the port basin in Exeter to below Topsham where it enters the Exe estuary.

Amongst its varied nineteenth-century trades, Plymouth came to be an important emigration embarkation port for Australia for two or three decades, for Devon folk but mainly for up-country people. The shipping employed and the organisation of this sizeable business is treated well by Mark Brayshay. In another contribution on Devon emigration, this time from North Devon to Canada, Ann Giffard presents much vivid first-hand evidence, especially of conditions on board the emigrant vessels.

The central question of why Devon mercantile shipbuilding did not make a successful adjustment to the new age of iron and steam shipping is treated by David Starkey in his chapter on the county's merchant shipbuilding, and by Robin Craig in his contribution on such mercantile steamship enterprise as was initiated in the county. Leslie Taylor presents some fascinating pages on William Froude, one-time assistant to Isambard Kingdom Brunel, and the ship design investigations conducted in his pioneering Torquay ship-model testing tank. Especial note needs to be taken of David Starkey's further piece on the successful and highly modern, not to say innovative, commercial shipbuilding carried on at Appledore from the 1970s, a remarkable indication of what can be done in a seemingly difficult regional and national context given excellent productive and business enterprise.

Basil Greenhill has compiled two chapters offering lively, first-hand impressions of the Devon maritime world. The first gives a perceptive account of the seaman's life, including some rare material on Devon women who went to sea, while the second, with contributions also by Robin Craig and Jeffrey Porter, deals with shipping as a business, focusing on three notable Devon shipping families. Handling and navigating the sailing vessels of the nineteenth century in the English Channel and off the North Devon coast, in their commercial employments with Devon ports, posed special problems and challenges to seafarers. This hitherto little-discussed subject is closely examined by Peter Allington and Basil Greenhill, who draw on past as well as present-day first-hand experience of the sea in all its movements and vagaries. The perils of the sea are evident at all times, and the record of maritime casualties off the Devon coasts, and the evolution of search and rescue organisations, is reviewed by Alston Kennerley. In another contribution Kennerley also considers one of the prime ways by which the sea has become safer for seafarers – through improvements in mercantile education and training, in which advance Plymouth became a leading centre from the mid-nineteenth century onwards. Since the Second World War remarkable progress has been made in ensuring greater safety at sea through advances in navigational methods. Here, Anthony Redfern

provides an engrossing discussion with special reference to the navigation of mercantile shipping along the Devon coasts, including how the growing flows of often very large vessels indeed, moving up and down the English Channel, are safely organised.

The expansion and later vicissitudes of Devon's inshore fisheries receive attention in two chapters. The first, by Anthony Northway, analyses this enterprise from the mid-eighteenth century to the later decades of the nineteenth, in terms of catches, employment of men and capital, techniques and technological innovation. The twentieth-century developments are treated by Mark Porter, from the 'Golden Age' of the pre-1900 decades to the contraction and difficulties of the First World War period and the interwar years, on to the distinct recovery that marked the 1970s.

There is, naturally enough, a group of contributions dealing with various aspects of the major theme that is the Royal Navy and Devon. Plymouth's continuing strategic importance as an operational naval base over the nineteenth and twentieth centuries is discussed by Peter Hilditch, while Ian Skinner explores its important but often overlooked role in the Second World War. The power of Plymouth's maritime striking arm has depended on the extent and depth of its support facilities, and these are also investigated. Jonathan Coad shows how the Dockyard itself was subjected to repeated surges of modernisation, to keep pace with the evolving needs of naval warfare, while the impressive story of naval technological innovation from 1815 to the opening of the frigate complex in 1977 and the submarine refit facility in 1980 is investigated by Andrew Lambert. While these facilities have remained centred on Devonport, the base's function as a reservoir of naval manpower has been extended to other parts of Devon, as Philip Payton shows in his examination of the training of officers, engineers and seamen, and Derek Oakley indicates in his study of the marines. Finally, the economic and social impact of such a vast naval arsenal in Devon, on Plymouth itself, and more widely in the county as well as the South West region, is considered in another essay by Peter Hilditch.

There is also a small group of papers concerned with Devon's rise as a centre of seaside tourism. This subject has only fairly recently begun to be investigated by historians, and our contributions are very much in a pioneering vein. John Travis offers a broad description and analysis of the growth of both the south and north Devon coastal resorts from the mid-eighteenth century to 1900. Nigel Morgan reviews the twentieth-century experience, analysing the further development of seaside tourism in the county; his themes include the role of 'image' advertising so successfully employed by Torquay, in its focusing on the concept of an 'English Riviera'. Crispin Gill has some interesting reflections on the expansion of yachting and the linked development of boat-building yards, marinas and other facilities that have characterised recent years. John Channon rounds off this theme of sea-related leisure activities in the twentieth century with a treatment of the sea as an environment, on the relationship between man's pollution of the coastal seas and foreshores and the growth of and 'selling' of Devon seaside holidaymaking. It is especially clear in these issues of the recreational uses of Devon's coastal beaches and seas, and 'environmental' questions to do with their natural state and cleanliness and the control of pollution, that further historical investigation is necessary to develop our understanding and perspective.

Stephen Fisher

1 *Shiphandling and Hazards on the Devon Coast*

Peter Allington, Basil Greenhill and Alston Kennerley

The sea has always been the greatest highway of mankind, though when shipping was dependent on wind power, and navigational aids were primitive, it was subject to far more hazards than land travel. Since each of the world's coasts is unique in its particular topography and in wind and tidal conditions, to survive their passage sailors were dependent on the application of knowledge acquired by personal experience. Devon's coasts, with their considerable indigenous trade and the heavy use of the English and Bristol Channels by vessels in transit, were amongst Europe's major points of landfall and departure. If the coastal lore was understood, then the hazards of the elements encountered while negotiating these coasts might be ameliorated, if never totally mastered. Moreover, as was demonstrated many times, tired or careless crews, failings in the ship itself or in its equipment, or unexpectedly severe weather meant that the possibility of shipwreck was never more than a wind or a fog or a tide away. It has been said with some justice that the wooden sailing ship was probably the most dangerous vehicle ever put to regular commercial use.

The South Coast

Before the middle of the twentieth century the safe conduct of any sailing vessel in areas of changeable winds with land or shoals close at hand warranted a close study of the weather at all times. The success or failure of a voyage depended on the accuracy of the predicted strength and direction of the wind, relying on the master's judgement based on his own observations of the sky and cloud formations, particularly at dawn and dusk, along with the rate of rise or fall in barometric pressure and any tendency for the wind to back or veer. There were certain rough and ready rules to

1.1 The consequences of errors of judgement. These battered fragments are all that remains of the schooner *Agnes* of Bideford after she went ashore in December 1911. (*Royal Institution of Cornwall*)

guide him, but every few years there could be dangerous exceptions, such as in 1588, when the Spanish Armada was subjected to winds in July as severe as one would expect in mid-winter, or the more recent example of the Fastnet Race in 1979.

In a *Seaman's Guide* of 1847 it is stated in the section 'Directions for sailing from the Atlantic Ocean into and up the British Channel' that,

> Although the winds at the entrance to the English Channel are various, and subject to uncertain directions, at all times of the year; yet there is a general, and somewhat uniform course of them to be expected, which will most commonly be found to prevail at certain periods of the year; thus, from January to May, they are observed to come from the north and north-east, although sometimes in January, they may incline to the south and south-westward; and from January to May, south-westers will occasionally occur; yet it will seldom be found to blow long from that quarter; but shifts round to the westward, and sometimes to the north and north-east. But from May to December, westerly and south westerly winds may be said most commonly to prevail.[1]

In the fine settled weather often found in May and June the land heats up during the day, and the rising hot air creates an onshore breeze in the afternoon. At night and early morning the opposite occurs, the wind coming off the land. This condition can augment or diminish the established wind direction. For example, a light southerly blowing in from the sea can freshen considerably in the afternoon, while a northerly airflow off the English coast can become calm by late morning, and a light southerly towards evening. Should the established weather pattern result in a calm state at sea, then large areas in mid-channel could have no wind, but along the English and French coasts these onshore/offshore breezes created by the heating/cooling of the land mass will be blowing.

Strong headwinds were to be avoided if at all possible, as most of the vessels under consideration could make little or no progress in these circumstances, especially when clear of any lee the land might provide. Offshore, depending on the severity of the blow and amount of uninterrupted sea room to build up in, the waves will increase in height. In addition, in the English and Bristol Channels strong tides can further cause these waves to steepen and break, particularly off headlands that experience a 'race', or in the vicinity of shoals. Depending on the circumstances, the vessel may 'lie-to', that is, under much reduced canvas, making slight headway but drifting bodily to leeward and no longer fighting the sea, or, if a good harbour or sheltered anchorage were not far to leeward, the ship can be run off before the wind and a safe haven made for. By comparison, the north coast of Devon is less well provided than the south in this respect, many of the harbours drying out at low water or having a bar at their entrance. This was a very dangerous coast for sailing vessels.

Plymouth Sound is described in the 'Sailing Directions for the English and Bristol Channels 1879' as 'being generally considered, and not without reason, the most capacious and secure rendezvous in Great Britain'.[2] Furthermore, the *Seaman's Guide* of 1847 states in the sailing directions that,

> Plymouth may be considered the best port in the Channel to run for in a storm, or in case of distress, having two entrances, as well as two inner harbours, in both ships may be run on the mud, should they have lost their anchors; those from the westward may proceed to Catwater and those from the eastward to Hamoaze.[3]

This extract mentions a very important point, that is, a safe place in which to put a vessel ashore. The older wooden vessels often leaked, and in bad weather could be making water faster than the pumps were able to cope with it – in other words, the vessel could be sinking. The one chance left of saving both the vessel and crew was to beach her, if possible in a sheltered location. The whereabouts of bays, creeks or harbours which offered this facility was therefore common knowledge to the coasting seaman.

Start Bay and Torbay are considered good anchorages when the wind is offshore, and both are easily identified from seaward by either Start Point or the bold high land of Berry Head marking the southern limits of Torbay. Although open to the eastward, and though southeasterly gales send in a heavy sea, there is shelter in Torbay from all winds from northeast-northerly through to south by west and even to south-southeast if a berth be taken up close to the southwestern shore. The entrance is wide and relatively free of dangers, and the whole bay affords good anchorage with a mud or clay bottom except for a patch in the southwestern corner. The nature of the sea bed and depth of water are important factors in selecting a safe anchorage.

The wind's strength and direction, which may remain fairly constant out at sea, is often influenced by high land along the shore creating sudden gusts of varied strength and direction. Thus the mariner is faced with an added difficulty, his source of energy being even less predictable. Certain harbours suffered badly in this respect. Sailing directions, for instance, describe Dartmouth as,

difficult to enter, and also to leave, in consequence of sudden gusts of wind descend from the high lands with great force. So great is the inconvenience occasioned by these gusts, that Captain Martin White, RN, says no square rigged vessel should attempt to enter or leave the harbour except with leading winds. These eddy winds are strongest when the wind is westward of NW, at which time a vessel requires all the attention of a skilful pilot. Those from the NW and SE are the true winds; and, as a general rule, it may be said that in moderate weather, with the wind between NW by N and NNE, or SW and SE a vessel will be found pretty well under command.[4]

Surface currents and the tides are also affected by the winds and the barometric pressure. The changes can be considerable, and are difficult to prejudge. The following extract is from 'Sailing Directions for the English and Bristol Channels 1879':

Currents, etc — a current of considerable strength frequently sets across the Channel, at some distance from the westward of Ouessant and Scilly, in a NW and WNW direction, the breadth and velocity of which is greatly dependent upon the wind most prevalent, and proportioned to its strength and direction; winds blowing from the W and SW quarter will be found very much to accelerate its force, and render it an object of serious attention. A strong SW wind constantly throws a great accumulation of water into the Channel, which tends greatly to increase the force of the flood tide, while it considerably retards the ebb, and augments the rise of water fully 10 feet above its ordinary elevation; therefore, vessels having entered the Channel with a strong SW gale, are liable to be driven ahead of their reckoning, and by taking the first of the flood, will have 10 or 11 hours' tide, which at 8 or 10 knots, will carry them from Start Point to Beachy Head, or even so far as Dungeness.[5]

More locally, the wind direction and barometric pressure will raise or lower the predicted height of the tide along the coast and more importantly in the harbours, estuaries and tidal section of the rivers. This can make a great difference. For example, a strong northerly wind and a barometric pressure of 30.9in can cut the height of tide in the Tamar River by as much as 3ft; a low pressure of 28.2in combined with a

southerly gale will have the opposite effect – a higher tide than expected will occur. Should there have been heavy rain inland, the amount of fresh water coming down in this situation can result in depths 3ft greater than the predicted high water.

Sailing vessels will, of course, experience periods of calm, but according to the 'Channel Sailing Directions' these

. . . are of rare occurences, and do not last long, except in summer. When they occur during winter, it is regarded as a precursor of bad weather. The most certain indications of bad weather are, swell in the offing during a calm, and surf on the coast.[6]

All vessels of whatever means of propulsion face an increased hazard in poor visibility. In this part of the world it is usually caused by mist, fog, heavy rain, hail or snow, and in the days before radar, was much worse at night.

If the deep-water sailing ship was enveloped in fog with plenty of sea room and clear of ice and regular trade routes, the increase in the risk of collision was small compared with the same situation if she were in the Western Approaches or the English or Bristol Channels. Here, with a high density of shipping, a very real possibility of collision existed. Fog is often accompanied by calms or light variable winds, so all sailing vessels in these circumstances would either be drifting, moving slowly, or perhaps, if the water was shallow enough, lying at anchor. Most collisions would therefore not be serious, but the danger of being run down and sunk increased dramatically once power driven vessels became common. Unable to get out of the way, the sailing ship was a 'sitting duck', and the approaching steamer, perhaps unable to hear, or wrongly interpreting her fog signal, often ploughed on with fatal consequences.

Snow, as well as affecting visibility, continually changes the direction in which the wind blows, and very sudden shifts occur during hail showers. Consequently, when sailing along the coast in these conditions, there was a danger of being driven ashore.

In clear weather, fixing the vessel's position should not be a problem, either with bearings of shore marks or features, or, away from land, with sights of the Sun, Moon, stars and planets. Even if an accurate longitude was not obtained, at least a precise latitude should be known. However, this not only required the heavenly body to be visible, but a good horizon was needed as well, to enable the altitude to be measured. With overcast sky or hazy weather this was not possible, and ships were often in the Western Approaches homeward bound not having been able to take sights for several days. Their position was reckoned by the various courses and distances from the last known fix, and was thus subject to considerable error. Closing the land it was vital to verify the distance off, and this was done with the help of soundings both for depth of water and the nature of the sea bed. Even if sounding did not give a definite position, at least the use of the lead told the mariner where he was not.

1.2 More than fifty vessels are setting sail after lying windbound in a sheltered roadstead. (*Postcard*)

1.3   Going through the wind. (*Bristol City Museum*)

The following remarks on entering the Channel are from Captain White's valuable *Book of Directions for the English Channel*:

During the winter season, however, when the almost total absence of the sun and stars preclude the possibility of ascertaining a correct parallel by astronomical means, the approaches to Scilly and Ushant should always be contemplated with caution; because, in that case, the course steered, the distance measured, depth of water, and quality of ground, are the only elements that can be resorted to. Many vessels, by neglect of this precaution, have been found actually within Scilly, unconscious of their situation; and numerous, indeed are the instances of those who have ended their voyages and their lives among Les Minquires Rocks, or on the iron-bound coast of France, by not sounding at all; while others have been 3, 4 or 5 degrees out of their reckoning, even when eastward of the meridian of Cape Clear; which never would have been the case, had common-place attention alone been given to the lead progressively. When running for the English Channel, the ground should invariably be sought for in good time; nor should the use of the lead in any case be intermitted, after the ground has been once obtained, especially during the night.

He goes on to say,

In entering the Channel from the NW or W, ships should always endeavour to obtain soundings as early as possible, getting between the latitudes of 49° 15′ and 49° 25′, according to the inclination of the wind; because it is between these limits that your relative situation can, with greater certainty, be ascertained, as well as in respect to depth of water as to quality of ground, or the distinction between ooze and sand, and which cannot be so well defined in any other latitude on making an approach to the Channel.[7]

The deep-sea-lead (pronounced dipsey) weighs from 14lb to 18lb, and is cone shaped with a concave hollow bottom which is armed with tallow so that a sample of the sea bed will stick to it on contact; and the deep-sea-line is from 90 to 110 fathoms (540ft) long with various marks attached to indicate the depth. To obtain soundings, the ship would be 'hove to' so that she had little or no way, and the long line held by several seamen spaced out along the ship's side, each with part of the line coiled ready to let go. Books of sailing directions go into great detail as to the depths and nature of the bottom for the various latitudes and positions in relation to the land in the Approaches to the English Channel, and such soundings and samples of the bottom obtained related to the chart.

When proceeding up the Channel in thick weather, the Eddystone is an obvious hazard to be avoided. Specific instructions are given:

From the Lizard to the Start: The course from the Lizard to the Start is E by S, 20½ leagues. In running up, go not into less water than 40 fathoms, for 35 fathoms is in the stream of the Eddystone; neither go without the depth of 50, for in this depth of water you will have black sand, with small brown stones and shells, abreast of Scilly.

From the Eddystone to the Start, you may stand towards the shore into 32 fathoms, and off 46. Within ½ mile of the Start Point are 15 fathoms of water. Eight miles to the southward of the Start, lies Start Knoll, with 29 fathoms on it, and 37 fathoms very near it, on both sides.[8]

On a more general nature, the following passage is taken from the *Seaman's Guide* of 1847:

Having entered the Channel, it is not considered safe to keep over towards the French shore, for the whole length of this coast is full of sunken rocks and dangers, so that the mariner ought never to approach it nearer than just to discover the land from the mast-head; but should you happen to make any of the lights on this part of the coast, you will, at once, determine your situation, by the different periods of their revolution; and, it is to be observed, that along this shore, and among the rocks and islands, the flood tide, at the distance of 10 or 12 leagues off the land sets to the SE, while the ebb does not set NW, but west along shore; so that vessels driven off the coast with north-westerly gales, will not have the tide to help them off, and are most liable to be driven on shore.

"Strangers", says Mr Dechamps, "looking upon the charts will observe many inlets that appear like harbours, sufficiently capacious to admit ships, in case of distress or stormy weather; but this is an error, for there is no safe harbour, easy of access, on the whole coast of Brittany and Normandy, excepting Guernsey and Jersey, where a vessel can take refuge in safety, before they reach Cherbourg; while the opposite coast of England affords safe and commodious ports and roadsteads throughout."

The mariner will easily know when he is to the southward, by the courseness of the ground and the over-whelming of the tide, which whirls round in several places, with breakers; and, it has frequently been observed, that much larger quantities of black weeds are to be met with on the south side of the Channel, than on the north. Therefore, he should endeavour to keep upon the English coast at from 5 to 7 leagues distance, till he gets up as high as Portland.[9]

These directions serve to underline the unhandiness of many sailing vessels, which in adverse conditions could not make good a course relative to the wind better than 90°. The danger of drifting on to the French coast by the nature of the tidal flow in that area, should the vessel face a northwest gale or prolonged calm, is also apparent, the resultant direction of both flood and ebb being roughly south-southwest.

Peter Allington

Going Through the Wind

This unique photograph (Fig. 1.3) illustrates a particular aspect of shiphandling. It shows the schooner *Troubadour* starting to come round on to the port tack off Portishead Point, possibly to stand inshore and anchor to await the next flood tide, before proceeding further up the Bristol Channel. The helm has only recently been put down, as the ship's boat is still towing right astern. She has reached a position where the very light breeze is about two points on the starboard bow, round enough for the upper topsail and weather leech of the lower topsail to be coming aback. The man standing aft on the weather side could be rounding in the main sheet, as there appears to be no slack in the heavy purchase, and, unlike the foresail, the luff of the mainsail has not started to lift.

Well before she has come head to wind, the square topsails will be fully aback, helping to swing the bows round on to the new track, making this manoeuvre much more certain in these conditions than in a purely fore and aft rigged vessel. In vessels without square topsails, both schooners and ketches, a backed headsail would be effective only if the vessel were virtually pointing at the eye of the wind. Up to that point the whole momentum of the swing is maintained by the rudder, once the sails have lost 'forward drive'. For this to work effectively a good flow past the blade is required. In the conditions shown, the vessel's initial speed would not be much, and of course she would slow even further as she came round. It was therefore not uncommon, especially if she were on a light draught and in a light breeze, for the windage of hull and rig to prevent a vessel without square

1.4 Ketches outward bound towards Bideford Bar.
West Appledore or Irsha is to the left. The structure in
the foreground is the last remains of the Cock family's
first shipbuilding yard, the Churchfield Yard,
established in the 1850s. (*Postcard*)

topsails from tacking, forcing the vessel to wear
round.

Therefore, especially in these light wind conditions, the topsail schooner had the advantage of
being certain of tacking once the square sails
were aback, and this point is reached well before
the vessel is head to wind. This was one of the
reasons why the schooner with square topsails
was very popular with seamen and shipowners in
British waters, even though she required an
additional man in the crew.

The *Troubadour*, 86 tons, of Bristol, was built
by M'Gill at Mount Stewart, Prince Edward Island, Canada, in 1867. She
measured 83.7 × 21.1 × 9.5ft, and at the time the photograph was taken
she was owned by John Downs of South View, Portishead, Somerset, and
worked frequently out of ports and harbours in Devon.

Peter Allington

The North Coast

The Report of the Commissioners on Harbours of Refuge, 1858.
In August 1858 a Royal Commission was appointed to enquire into the
matter of harbours of refuge. Under the chairmanship of Rear-Admiral
James Hope, CB, its members included W S Lindsay, the shipowner,
publicist and historian; Captain John Washington, who three years before
had succeeded the great Admiral Beaufort as Hydrographer of the Navy;
and Captain, later Admiral Sir B J Sulivan, who had emerged from the
Crimean War as perhaps the most competent of all the naval officers
involved in it and who in 1858 held the appointment of Professional Officer
at the Board of Trade. The Commissioners' Report (which made no
recommendations for harbour works in Devon) was published by HM
Stationery Office in two volumes in 1859.

The Commissioners were concerned with 'such parts of the coast as, being
much frequented, are without any adequate place of safety into which vessels
can run if overtaken by storms'.[10] They pointed out the importance of such
safe harbours (such as Plymouth), and that 'all vessels and especially that
class by which the coast is chiefly frequented, should have harbours in which
they can take shelter, for the purpose of avoiding the risks and wear and
tear incurred by keeping the sea'.[11] These terms of reference meant that they
considered the north coast of Devon, but not the south.

The Commission's appointment was the consequence of Parliamentary
concern with marine casualties generally. According to the report, in the
years 1852 to 1857 inclusive, 4,680 people had died on the British coast,
1,549 of them in 1854. The annual loss of property was estimated at
£1,500,000 (say one hundred million pounds in early 1990's values). In
1856–7 alone there were 187 marine casualties in the Bristol Channel (east
of a line drawn from the Scilly Isles to Milford) involving the loss of 114
lives. Eight vessels were totally lost on the coast of North Devon, and
another four off Lundy.[12] There emerges from the Commission's report a
very detailed picture of contemporary pilotage practices and a great deal of
detail about the problems of shiphandling out of North Devon ports. There
also emerges very clearly a conclusion summarised in the Report in the
following words, '. . . that by far the larger proportion of losses occur
among the comparatively inferior vessels frequenting the coasts, and that
few happen amongst the generally superior class of vessels proceeding
foreign'.[13]

The Commission's evidence in North Devon was taken at Bideford on 29
September 1858, in what must have been a marathon session involving a
record of some 18,000 words. A selection from it is reproduced here with
its original use of the term 'back' where a later generation might have said
'rear', and with the interesting local spelling of Sker-weather for Scar-
weather. The evidence is recorded on pages 291 to 302 of volume 2 of the
Report and is perhaps the more valuable because of its spontaneity. The
local shipping community was given less than 24hr notice of the Commissioners' arrival. The Commission chose its witnesses well. Their experience
covered a wide range of types of seafaring from North Devon. It is perhaps
not surprising that the principal examination was of William Yeo of
Appledore (see Chapter 9), who, two years before, had opened the
Richmond Dry Dock and who was already a man of great influence in North
Devon. He was able to tell the Commission that he had 'crossed the Western
Ocean 45 times as Master'. Others examined were Captain Joshua Williams,
an Appledore master mariner of vast experience who had been forty years
in command under sail before settling down as a shipowner; John Dunsford,
who had been master of smaller vessels in the Mediterranean trade for thirty-
eight years; Richard Yeo, who had been in command of coasting vessels out
of Bideford for more than thirty years; and a local pilot, Joseph Cox.

William Yeo summarised the first and last stages of a passage out of the
Bristol Channel:

Question
No

10,416 Ships outward-bound during the prevalence of westerly
winds, that is, in winds from south-west to west-north-west,
do they, in working down channel, keep either shore by
preference? – They keep the south shore until they get to
Hartland Point.

10,417 After they weather Hartland Point do they reach to the
westward immediately? – Do you mean to the north-west?

10,418 Yes? – They do. Generally the wind comes south-west, and
they cannot weather Hartland Point; they are driven up
channel; but by keeping Lundy Island they keep the channel
open, and are ready to take advantage of a change of wind.

10,419 And homeward-bound ships, what part of the land do they
make? – They generally come in at the parallel of latitude of
Lundy Island. They try to make Lundy or Hartland. If the
wind is south-west they make the land above Hartland Point
a mile or so; if north-west they try to make Lundy Island.

10,420 But always with a north-west wind they try to make Lundy
Island; they do not go outside? – They never go on the other
side unless they are obliged to go to the north of Lundy
Island and Hartland point.

10,421 Have you ever taken shelter under Lundy in strong south-
west or west gales? – Yes; I was there in 1838 for three days;
it was blowing very strong. The water is very deep there,
and we dragged off considerably.

10,422 What do you call very deep for a ship of 1,000 tons? – We
first brought up in fifteen fathoms of water, and then we
could just see a glimmer of the light.

10,423 And while you lay in Lundy Roads did the wind back round
to the north-west and blow hard? – No; it blew hard from

10,423
cont.   the south-west and west-south-west, and then died away a calm; but all at once it went round to the east. We managed to get our anchors, but a ship which lay alongside of us could not; she went ashore and went to pieces. It was a ship belonging to Shields.

10,424   Then you have an objection to state to Lundy Island as a place of shelter? – Lundy Island is a place of shelter when you are well in; when you are close in you are protected from winds from the south-west round to north-west.

10,425   Did you state that a ship went ashore on Rat Island? – Not Rat Island. She went ashore on Lundy Island.

10,426   Is it a state of things which often happens, ships having a difficulty to get away? – If the wind shifts suddenly so that you cannot get your anchors.

10,427   And as it dies away to the south you cannot fetch out? – If the wind shifts the vessel goes ashore. The tide runs right in on the island.

10,428   You are well acquainted with the Bristol Channel, and the prevailing winds there? – Yes.

10,429   Are these sudden shifts of wind of common occurrence? – Yes. In the winter, very often it blows from the south-west, goes round to the west-south-west, and then flies round to the north-west.

10,430   And from the north-west does it die away, and an east wind come in? – Yes.

10,431   Have ships in an east wind a chance of getting away? – Not generally; only sometimes. We find that the wind backs round to the south-south-east and south-east, then you are ashore.

10,432   With the wind south-east, can you get away from Lundy Island easily enough? – Yes; you can fetch away.

A selection of the rest of his evidence gives in detail the local experience of North Devon seamen:

10,437   Do you know Penarth Roads? – I do.

10,438   What kind of anchorage is that? – The anchorage is very good in the roads, but it is very narrow for large ships. If a ship drives between Penarth Head and the grounds only a very little, she is ashore on the grounds.

10,439   But is it a place to lie in during any wind or weather, with good ground tackle? – We do not hear of any damage; but I myself prefer lying above Penarth Roads.

10,440   Could a harbour of refuge be made in that part of the Bristol Channel, where ships, if so disposed, could run in, drop their anchor, and lay in safety? – I do not see any place below Penarth Roads. You must go to Penarth or the Holmes.

10,441   The holding ground all over the channel is, I presume, good? – Not all over the channel; it is rocky in some parts.

10,442   Are you of opinion that harbours of refuge, in general are necessary? – Well, I think they are, in localities of this sort, where we have no harbour that a ship can run for from the Land's End to Penarth Roads; not on the west coast.

10,452   What course would a vessel going from Bristol to America take down channel in favourable weather? – We keep the south side.

10,453   Why? It is more clear of danger.

10,454   But have you not a rocky coast in case of adverse winds? – Rocky, but bold on the south side. On the north side we have sands.

10,471   That makes a good case for a harbour of refuge at Lundy Island, if you can get one, does it not? – Not a fortnight ago I saw 300 vessels leave Penarth Roads.

10,472   What became of them? – They had a fair wind, and made their passage.

10,473   If they had had an adverse wind what would they have done? – Probably they might have got ten or fifteen miles below Lundy Island, and then they would have been driven back to Penarth Roads.

10,474   Would they have hesitated to go to Lundy Island, if it had been capable of receiving them? – Oh yes.

10,475   Do you doubt the capacity of Lundy Island? – Yes. The tide sets right in on the island, and there is not sufficient room for a quantity of ships. Very often a great number of ships from all parts stop at Lundy Island. We have had several ships wrecked in this bay; ships coming from Liverpool, and driven up the channel.

10,476   Then Lundy Island is available? – Yes.

10,477   Supposing you had the disposal of the public money, and might apply it either to Lundy Island or Clovelly, to which would you give the preference, for the benefit of trade generally? – I think I should give the preference to Clovelly, because at Clovelly you can form a harbour which will hold a whole fleet going up this channel, or to the north, and you have a clean bottom of clay, and an anchorage of twelve fathoms into three fathoms off shore.

10,478   And Clovelly is protected from what wind? – West-north-west and west, east-north-east, north-west, and by north.

10,479   Would it be easy to get out of the harbour if it were so constructed as to have two entrances? – Yes.

10,499   You have known 300 vessels leave Penarth Roads in one tide. Do you know of any case where those vessels, after they had got out to the chops of the channel, had been obliged to put back? – Frequently I have known it.

10,500   Where did they run for? – Lundy Island or Penarth Roads; and a few that know the place will run to Milford Haven.

10,501   Would they be able to reach Milford Haven in a north-west gale at all? – No; in a north-west gale they are driven back to Penarth Roads.

10,502   Would it not be a great convenience if there were a harbour on the south coast that they could run for in north-west gales? – Yes.

Joshua Williams also came down strongly in favour of a harbour of refuge at Clovelly:

10,579   Will you state to the Commissioners the reasons why you entertain that opinion? – In the first place, it is a very eligible place to make a harbour of refuge in. There is the best anchorage in the world there. You can go three or more miles off and not get more than eleven fathoms of water. You could shoot a marble at low water into three fathoms.

10,580   Do you consider that the most preferable point of the coast at which to place a harbour of refuge? – Yes, I do. When it blows strong from the south-west, after you round Hartland Point you are in the harbour itself. It is smooth water.

10,581   Is it much made use of at present? – Yes: I have been riding there in heavy gales of wind myself.

10,582   From what direction do the north winds blow? – West-south-west and west.

10,583   And if the winds back round to the north-west, what happens then? – I can ride there; there is a roadstead.

10,590   Is the holding ground bad at Lundy Island? – I know it is, because I have been riding there or driving.

10,591   Is it owing to the great depth of water? – The ground is bad. When you are in 13 fathoms the best anchors will not hold. They drag about a mile, and then you get a sandbank, which is good holding ground, but there is a very heavy sea.

10,592   Is it your opinion that it is unadvisable to spend any of the public money in attempting to make a harbour at Lundy Island? – Yes. Running up with a west or south-west or a west-south-west wind a vessel can never get there. When the wind goes round it would blow the topmast off. I have been there myself when I could not carry a bit of canvas. If you could fetch into the roads it would be very well.

Captain Williams went on to say that he had frequently seen as many as 300 vessels, windbound, in Swansea Bay.

John Dunsford shared the views of the previous examinees:

10,682   Outward-bound, how do you make the passage down with the wind westerly? – We generally keep round to the south side.

10,683   And after passing Lundy Island you take your departure? – It all depends upon the wind. We generally steer west with a fair wind, or reach to the north if we have a head wind.

10,684   And with the wind right up the channel below Lundy Island you do not think of working along the south shore, I suppose? – No; we work away, and we take the ship according to how the wind is.

1.5 On the morning of 16 September 1936, the crew of the Braunton-owned, Barnstaple-registered, ketch *Didoc*, ex *Jules Claes*, built at Lysekil in Sweden in 1921, made an error of judgement of a type most unusual among local seamen so familiar with the tides, rocks and mudbanks of the Bristol Channel. Cutting inside the outer reefs off the wild coast of North Devon in hazy weather, they grounded on one of the ledges off Morte Point. The sea was calm, the vessel without cargo. She floated off, undamaged, on the next tide. (*Knight, Barnstaple*)

Question No

10,685   You are aware of the objects of this inquiry? – Yes.

10,686   Will you state to the Commissioners any opinion which you entertain upon the subject? – I believe Clovelly Road one of the best places in the channel for a harbour of refuge.

10,687   Give us the reasons why? – In the most common gales we find that the roadstead has the advantage of a tide always making to the windward, which is a great help for ships getting out of the bay.

10,688   Any other reason? – That would save a great many lives. I have known many lost in this bay in my time, which would have been saved if there had been a harbour of refuge here.

10,689   Do you know the anchorage under Lundy Island? – Yes.

10,690   What is it good for? – The anchorage is not very good. It is all hard ground and deep water. If a ship drives away, and brings her anchor home, she is off in deep water immediately.

10,691   In what winds do you find shelter under Lundy Island? – West-south-west and south-west; but with the wind north-west, it is right along the island.

Richard Yeo demonstrated the kind of intimate local knowledge that meant the difference between success and failure as a coasting shipmaster:

Question No

10,833   Would not vessels find good anchorage at Morte Bay in north-east winds? – No; the strength of the tide is very great in Morte Bay.

10,834   Is the tide stronger in Morte Bay than at Clovelly? – No; but there is a heavy ground western swell in Morte Bay; vessels would be exposed very much more in Morte Bay than at Clovelly.

10,835   If you merely want refuge above Lundy Island would you not rather have such a harbour on the north shore, that when the wind came round you would be to windward, and able to run out with a fair wind, than on the south shore, where you would have to work out off a lee shore? – I would prefer the south shore. Vessels on the north shore going back to get shelter would be running through dangerous sands. There are the Mixons, very dangerous in thick weather, and the operation of the tide is strong just above the Sker-weather. If there was a harbour inside Hartland Point it would be an advantage to get in upon a winter's night; when the wind came fair vessels might make their course. Even in Plymouth Sound they must wait till they get an opportunity; they cannot get out at all times.

Question No

10,836   When the wind is fair, can they not go? – Oh yes.

10,837   Have you ever anchored at Lundy Island? – Not many times. I have always been very timid of anchoring at Lundy Island.

10,838   Have you ever been well in under the shore at Lundy Island? – Yes.

10,839   Is the anchorage better there than out farther? – I should think it was.

10,840   Have you held on well there? – Yes.

10,841   If the wind came round to north, would you think that a fair wind to go from under Lundy Island? – Yes.

10,842   Do vessels frequently anchor in Morte Bay? – When the wind is east they have no place.

10,843   Do they anchor then in good numbers? – Yes, because of the wind off the back.

10,844   I want merely to know the fact, whether vessels in great numbers do or do not anchor in Morte Bay? – When the wind is east, blowing strong, and they cannot get up the Bristol Channel; but the ground swell round the head renders it impossible to anchor except with chain cables, and even then they generally part. It is all very well when there is no ground swell.

The Commission, however, did not recommend the construction of a harbour of refuge at Clovelly, though they considered Lundy. And in their final report the Commission said:[14]

The trade of the Bristol Channel comprises nearly one sixth of the shipping and one tenth of the tonnage of the entire United Kingdom, and its exportation of coal amounting to five million of tons, is daily on the increase. Its foreign trade, including the importation of copper ore, is one of very considerable value. Wind-bound vessels accumulate in its principal anchorages in large numbers; at the Mumbles, we hear of 300 vessels; in Penarth Roads, of 500 vessels; off Lundy Island, of 100 vessels; and in Whitesand Bay of 200 vessels.

The consideration of the refuge question in the Bristol Channel leads to its division into two districts; one, the Bristol Channel proper, lying to the eastward of Lundy Island, the other comprising the coast from Hartland point to the Land's End. In the former of these, the upper part of the Channel, supplying safe anchorage throughout, we are of opinion no Life harbour is required, – a view of the case confirmed by the returns, which show no wrecks from stress of weather above the Holmes; but it is unquestionable that a Refuge harbour at the entrance of this channel would confer a great benefit on the trade, at all the ports from Cardiff and Bridgwater upwards, and that at Lundy Island is to be found a site in every respect well adapted for such a harbour, except the important one of expense – the depth of water, and consequent cost being so great as to preclude the possibility of our recommending it at present.

To the general trade bound to the westward, and unable to make head against heavy contrary winds, a harbour at Lundy Island would afford shelter, with less risk than one at the Mumbles, and with much less loss of distance than running back to Penarth or King Road. To it, as a port of departure from which they could get to sea with the first favourable slant of wind, the larger and more valuable vessels from the ports above named would be towed down, and the smaller vessels, taking advantage of the tide, would work down as opportunities, brief but favourable, offered. For the collection of convoys, and for a naval station to watch the Channel, it is well suited. Being subject to no violence from sea to the eastward, the breakwater would be of the cheapest description, a mere rubble mound, the construction of which requiring little skilled labour, would be well adapted for the employment of convicts, for the safe custody of whom the island would afford every facility.

But with all these advantages, the depth of water in which the breakwater must be necessarily placed, as appears on the plan we have given, is so great as to occasion a cost of construction not to be thought of until those harbours which are of more urgent necessity shall have been completed, and practical proofs of the benefit which is expected to accrue from them shall have been obtained; or unless a field for convict labour is required; and for these objects we recommend that it should be kept in view.

The Commission also came up with an interesting recommendation to improve Padstow, which, had it been implemented, would have had considerable advantages for North Devon coasting vessels bound (as many were until well into the present century) for the beaches and small harbours of the north Cornish coast and round the land.[15]

Basil Greenhill

Clearing the North Devon Coast in a Four-masted Barque in 1937 – A Personal Reminiscence

The steel four-masted barque *Viking*, 4,000 tons deadweight, was built at Copenhagen in 1906 as a cargo-carrying cadet ship run on a commercial basis. In 1929 she was bought by Gustaf Erikson of Mariehamn, Åland,

1.6   A big square-rigged vessel in restricted waters. The Åland Finnish four-masted barque *Viking* of Mariehamn beating out of the Bristol Channel in 1937, the North Devon coast visible in the background. (*Basil Greenhill*)

Finland, and operated in the Australian grain trade to British ports and the timber trade from Finland. In July 1937 I joined her in Sharpness, Gloucestershire, where she had discharged a grain cargo and been dry-docked, for a passage towards Kotka in the eastern part of the Gulf of Finland where she was to load timber. We had some difficulty in clearing the coast of North Devon of a type typical of hundreds of similar passages under sail in the preceding century.

Viking looked out of Sharpness at 0725hrs behind the tugs *Triton* and *Steeleopolis*. Two Braunton ketches, the *Bessie* and the *Bessie Ellen*, and one from Appledore, the *Ade*, ex *Annie Christian*, came down the estuary with us under sail and power. They had loaded coal in Lydney, Gloucestershire, for North Devon. At 1335hrs we reached Barry Roads; we had already dropped *Steeleopolis* off Avonmouth, Port of Bristol. In the face of a southwesterly breeze and a flowing tide we dropped anchor in the roadstead. In the evening the wind came round northwesterly, with heavy squalls, and the wisdom of the delay was obvious. All next day we lay in Barry Roads. In the harbour a mile or so away we could see the masts of another four-masted barque, the *Archibald Russel*, also hailing from Mariehamn. In the evening the three-masted schooner *Brooklands*, ex *Susan Vittery*, which had no engine, sailed across our bows on her way up channel.

The weather reports, picked up on the little domestic receiver in the captain's stateroom, which was the only radio in use on board, were not encouraging, but at 2000hrs the wind veered north-northwest and the master, Ivar Hägerstrand, a veteran of thirty roundings of Cape Horn, who had become more and more impatient as the day wore on, gave the order to make sail. His decision was a difficult one, for the *Viking* was a poor performer to windward, especially in ballast.

Viking was set on the starboard tack, with everything set except royals and mainsail. Aided by the ebb we cleared Breaksea Lightship by midnight, and in the early hours of the morning we were becalmed a little east of the Foreland Light, just west of the boundary between Somerset and Devon. Here we lay to a single anchor in eleven fathoms, the glass falling. The sky looked angry and there was always the danger of a strong southwesterly springing up. But at dawn the wind rose to a moderate gale from the north-northwest. As the ebb was making again, at 0900hrs, the anchor was hove up and all sail set except the royals, the mainsail and the cross-jack. On the starboard tack we made westing as far as Bull Point a few miles from Ilfracombe (North Devon). The ebb was now slackening and, with a heading south of west the flood tide was setting her in towards a lee shore. Braces and sheets were slackened off and a slightly more southerly course took us into Bideford (North Devon) Bay, where there was sea room to go round through the wind on to the port tack. The next ebb found *Viking* off Swansea Bay, where we put about once more, heading between Hartland Point and the south of Lundy. By midnight we had reached well over to the English shore, but with the wind a little more westerly the westward offing from Hartland was hardly safe, so we put about once more on the port tack to stand off before sailing down the coast of Cornwall.

Next morning, at 0600hrs, all sail was set with the vessel on the starboard tack. The wind was blowing a moderate gale and *Viking* travelled at ten or eleven knots, heeling over to the breeze, a bone in her teeth which rose sometimes to the hawse holes. We sailed down the Cornish coast with an offing of about ten miles. There were white horses on the wave crests and the sea turned from the grey of the estuary to deep blue. Later the wind began to back southwesterly and, as we passed the Wolf Rock and rounded the land, we were very glad to be out of the Bristol Channel before the change took place. We squared away for the run up the English Channel with a fair wind and a moderate sky.

Basil Greenhill

Maritime Casualties and Search and Rescue

Seafaring has always been a most hazardous occupation, perhaps lying second only to mining in the incidence of injury and mortality. A great many of these human casualties have occurred when ships have succumbed to the marine environment to become total or partial losses, and a great many ship casualties have taken place at the interface between land and sea. Maritime casualties have occurred at some time or another in all areas of the open seas and along all the world's coastlines.

The number of casualties along a particular section of coast is a function not only of the nature of the topography and natural phenomena, but also of the density of shipping in the area. Devon's coasts certainly have been amongst the most hazardous and busiest of the world, and in recent centuries at least they have seen significant numbers of casualties. Because known shipwrecks have often been dramatic events, some have been etched more deeply into local, and sometimes national consciousness, and thus have probably been recorded more fully than other maritime events. Shipwrecks have certainly been subjected to considerable research and published listing, and this interest has been extended through the development of underwater archaeology, which has turned the remains of wrecks into valuable sources for maritime historians.

Despite technological advances and regulatory measures to improve safety at sea, marine casualties still happen, but modern technology has made possible improvements in the response from the land. To the attempt in the past to rescue survivors and salvage property has been added the ability to use sophisticated search techniques to locate casualties, thus extending the area of response well beyond the immediate vicinity of the coastline. To take account of this wider context, the term 'maritime casualty' will often be used in this contribution in preference to the term 'wreck', which has been defined as ' . . . the hull of a ship which has become a total loss through stress of weather, stranding, collision, or any other cause, whether it lies on the bottom of the sea or on the shore'.[16] Maritime casualties may include any 'vessels in distress and in need of assistance'. Some will have become shipwrecks, but others, through the efforts of their own crews or with the support of other vessels or the rescue services, will have survived to make port.

The Context of Maritime Casualties

Most of the commonly used attributes for maritime casualties describe the final state of vessels when crews are forced to abandon ship or assistance is given by others. These terms include stranded (grounded, ran ashore), foundered, sunk, explosion, burnt (on fire), collision, dismasted, broke up, break down (engines). Descriptions of casualties employing such terms usually refer to bad weather conditions but nearly always fail to explore the range of underlying factors, internal and external, which might lead to a ship getting into difficulty. The list is extensive, and in some cases a cumulative series of failures, individually capable of being overcome, has led to disaster. Amongst the internal factors are those which relate to the ship itself. In operational conditions the hull, masts, rigging, sails, steering, rudder, engines or hatch covers, for example, may have failed owing to poor design, the use of inappropriate materials, inadequate maintenance or negligence. Another set concerns the cargo (and ballast and fuel), its nature, distribution and the method of stowage, and this is closely connected to the stability of ships and the strength of their hulls. Some cargoes are subject to spontaneous combustion, some carry the risk of explosion, some behave like liquids if proper precautions are not taken during loading. Then there is the human element: the numbers and experience of seamen and the education, experience and leadership ability of masters and officers. A key element here may well be fatigue; the final drama of a maritime casualty has often been preceded by days or weeks of continuous activity in which the crew has become exhausted, and possibly the judgment of the master has become clouded through continuous duty and lack of rest. The external factors concern the environments in which ships must be operated: geographic, meteorological, oceanographic and demographic. All decisions made by masters impinge on the safety of their ships, and in reaching a particular decision a master has usually to weigh many of the factors indicated above.

1.7 The wreck of the East Indiaman *Dutton* in Plymouth Sound, January 1796, painted by Nicholas Pocock. (*City of Plymouth Museums & Art Gallery*)

The geographic location of the South West peninsula, and of Devon as part of it, has long meant that its position has been of concern to shipping passing along its coasts as well as to those bound to or from its ports. In particular the shape of Devon, with the headlands of Hartland Point and Start Point 'bulging' northwards and southwards, has always brought shipping trading with the ports higher up the Bristol Channel, or with London and the other ports in North West Europe, into a relationship with its coasts. These headlands have provided many a ship inward bound from the Atlantic Ocean with perhaps the first positive position after several days of uncertainty because of overcast skies in the Western Approaches. Despite the dangers of the Devon and South West coasts most shipping has tended to favour the English rather than the French side of the Channel, excluding those principally concerned with the French or southward coast, and thus the charting and marking of its main features has been of interest to all European shipping. The greatest danger from the local geography comes when ships attempt to enter port. Until the advent of accurate large-scale charts of harbours and their approaches, local knowledge acquired by experience was essential for guiding ships in and out of ports. Thus pilotage, providing geographical knowledge and the understanding of local tides and currents, was an early and important service to the safe movement of ships.

Ships' log books or the reports of shipwrecks rarely reveal the drawn-out dramas faced by ships in long periods of adverse weather, or the stress faced by their crews. For an understanding of this it is useful to turn to informed fiction. F C Hendry (Shalimar) provides such an insight in his short story 'Their Hopes and Fears'.[17] The *Lindores* was homeward bound from San Francisco to Cardiff and was now

> . . .rushing at eleven knots towards the deep gash in the west coast of Britain that is known as the Bristol Channel - rushing blindfold and without certainty, for still no observations had been obtained . . . "Can't go on much farther . . . ought to be inside the Bristol Channel by now . . . should be up to Lundy before daybreak by my reckoning," he [the captain] cried, and the words seemed to be wrung from him in his anguished uncertainty. "Dead reckoning at that; seven days dead reckoning," he added bitterly.

Three days later, by then completely lost, the ship encounters a tug, and the captain learns that his ship is close to Skokholm Island, west of Milford Haven, some sixty miles north of where it should be. A tow is offered, and the master is suddenly faced with a commercial decision with his ship now on a lee shore:

> Captain Bowie suddenly went limp; the mental trials and pyhsical hardships of the last few days had been too much for him; his legs were trembling and from sheer weakness he had to hang on to the poop rail. The temptation to give the tug-boat skipper any price he demanded was overwhelming . . . he might even get a rest in his room . . .

A fee of £70 was agreed, the tow rope was taken and the ship's sails furled. During the night the tow parted, and although the captain attempted to sail his ship clear of the Welsh coast, she eventually stranded, the crew, excepting the master, being saved by the Coastguard lifesaving apparatus.

Three aspects of the general meteorology of the area of the world in which Devon is located have clearly been significant in many of the cases of maritime casualty.[18] The prevailing southwesterly air stream produces mainly cloudy and damp weather, obscuring the sky and preventing the fixing of a position by the Sun or stars perhaps for several days at a time. The most frequent directions for gales is also from the west and southwest, and they may likewise persist for several days. The shape of the land in coastal areas may modify the general direction and strength of the winds, in some cases increasing the strength by up to 20 per cent, with 'funnel' effects particularly affecting some port areas. The passage of depressions, with their frontal troughs and associated squalls, may produce sudden and unexpected changes of wind direction, perhaps turning a sheltered bay into a hazardous lee shore. In such conditions visibility at sea may be reduced close to zero, eliminating any hope of fixing position by shore marks. Visibility may also be severely reduced in fairly calm weather owing to the formation of sea fog, which can persist for two or three days. Poor visibility not only prevents fixing, but also greatly increases the risk of collision between ships. The

combination of the shape of Devon's coasts and the prevailing westerly winds has produced a concentration of shipwrecks on the west-facing sections of the coastlines and at the entrances to harbours. The prevailing weather caused difficulties for all ships heading west, but those in the Bristol Channel had less room to manoeuvre than those in the English Channel. Forced to tack back and forth in order to make westerly progress, they were vulnerable to both the weather and tides, particularly at the ends of each tack. In 1859 the barque *Lochlibo* spent thirteen days in such manoeuvres, finally stranding in the vicinity of Hartland Point.[19]

Although there is some residual easterly drift in the English Channel from the North Atlantic current, the predominant oceanographic feature of the waters off Devon's coasts are the tidal streams and the rise and fall of the tides, both being predominantly semi-diurnal.[20] The dominant directions for the tidal streams in the Channel are easterly and westerly, but with a tendency to run parallel with coastlines and with local physical features producing special effects. The spring rate offshore reaches about one knot. Greater rates are found off headlands, the spring rate off Start Point, for example, reaching 2.5 knots. In rivers and harbours stronger tidal streams may occur; that in the narrows off Exmouth may run at three or four knots. Off Morte Point the spring rate reaches 3 knots. The tendency in certain conditions for the tidal stream to flow into bays may lead to ships becoming 'embayed' or trapped and unable to sail out again. Bideford Bay was particularly notorious for this.

The last of the external factors impinging on ship safety is the density of shipping in the area. The amount of sea room available for manoeuvring decreases, and the risk of collision increases, wherever focal points occur on shipping routes and where ships congregate in sheltered anchorages and harbours. Off South Devon the focal points are off Start Point, in the vicinity of the Eddystone Rocks, and in the approaches to the main ports, especially Plymouth, while Torbay has long been a major sheltered anchorage. Off the north coast, focal points are off Hartland Point, Morte Point and in the vicinity of Lundy Island, and the approaches to the Taw/Torridge estuary, with Lundy offering some shelter. By the nineteenth century the growth of British trade, both coastal and overseas, meant an increasing number of ships off the coasts of Devon. Numbers of ships belonging to other countries would also appear in the area. In adverse conditions the favoured areas for shelter could become very crowded. Some reports have referred to hundreds of vessels. Seventy-four were counted in Torbay on 10 January 1866, and were caught in a hurricane which blew up from the east and veered to east-northeast; perhaps two-thirds of them became casualties that night.[21]

It is very difficult to produce a meaningful quantification of maritime casualties for a particular area, even for recent times. For earlier periods it is impossible. There are problems of definition. Ships stranding on the coast in question, providing they have been correctly identified, present few problems except that of multiple reporting. But casualties occurring some distance off the coast raise doubts as to their inclusion. Those 'off Lundy' should no doubt be counted, but to what extent should those 'off Eddystone' be included? The returns compiled by the Board of Trade and Lloyds for the Royal Commission on Unseaworthy Ships, 1873/1874, include only British ships.[22] Lists relating to the lifesaving organisations may only include vessels actually helped. Ships lost out at sea may never be recorded, or their presence in the area may only be deduced long after they have sunk. The examples of mass destruction such as that in 1866, or the series of gales in November 1859, said to have claimed 248 ships and 686 lives, serve well to illustrate the vulnerability of shipping in this area given such conditions.[23] The lists in the books on shipwrecks, cumulating known casualties over decades or centuries, also give an impression of quantity, as well as concentration, and they do show that casualties have continued to occur in the area. In contrast, the returns to the Royal Commission on Unseaworthy Ships seem sparse. The lists for 1870, 1871, and 1872 show only 9, 14 and 9 casualties respectively occurring in the vicinity of Devon, out of national totals of 1,140, 1,076 and 1,070. A separate return for 1868, giving ports of registry, showed five ships registered in Devon ports which became casualties elsewhere and a further six ships missing.[24] Even if these figures are fairly accurate, they must still be related to the annual number of ship movements in the area. The estimate by the Lundy Cable Company of some

80,000 ships passing the island in 1883 (over 200 per day), gives some indication of the population to which maritime casualties in the area belonged, and accounts perhaps for the large numbers of casualties which could occur in a single storm.[25]

Assistance for Maritime Casualties

For ships in difficulty, the first and perhaps most important form of assistance has always been the ability of crews to help themselves. The quality of leadership and the extent of training and discipline may enable the situation to be turned round through temporary measures, or may enable full advantage of external help to be taken when it arrives. The second form of assistance, weather and location permitting, similarly has always been that offered by other ships. In the nineteenth century the development of steam propulsion added a commercial aspect to the traditional free rendering of help by one ship to another. Tugs cruised in the vicinity of Lundy Island, for example, hoping to negotiate tows with ships who judged themselves at risk. It was only when vessels in distress came very close to land, by which time stranding was probably inevitable, that people on shore might be in a position to render assistance. In tolerable weather conditions local boats might be able to reach the casualty, or it might be reached from the shore. But a great many ships were wrecked at the height of storms, and well into the nineteenth century those on shore might well be unable to do more than succour those seafarers who survived the struggle from ship to land. The ability to provide effective help at even one wreck location required equipment, manpower and effective leadership; to make it available anywhere along a coastline required systematic organisation and significant finance. An example of an effective rescue before the development of the rescue services concerned the *Dutton*, an East-Indiaman bound for the West Indies with troops, which ran ashore under the Plymouth Hoe in January 1796.[26] Sir Edward Pellew provided the leadership, organising rescue boats and getting hawsers ashore. He even supervised the evacuation of the ship, and nearly 600 persons were rescued.

Amongst the earliest of the measures taken ashore to improve the safety of shipping was the provision of coastal marking: beacons, buoys and lighthouses. The chapel lighthouse at Ilfracombe is a surviving medieval example, and it is possible that there were medieval lights on the south coast of Devon.[27] Plymouth financed a beacon on Rame Head in the sixteenth century, and the Eddystone Rocks were first marked in 1698.[28] But the provision and continuous showing of lights on all of the significant locations on Devon's coasts had to wait until well into the nineteenth century, when Trinity House was finally given control of all English lights, and technology, finance and organisation made a proper coverage of the coasts possible.[29] These developments, and those leading towards the provision of organised rescue services, were spurred on by the increasing public concern at the growing number of maritime casualties and the rising level of loss of life. No doubt this was in part related to the growth of seaborne trade and to the increasing numbers of British ships, and to the rapidly changing technology. Many of the parliamentary investigations, from that on Shipwrecks (1836) to that on Loss of Life at Sea (1884/87), were directed at shipping safety, while much of the large amount of shipping legislation was also concerned with safety.

The organised response from on shore to the needs of maritime casualties took the form of stationing lifeboats and lifesaving apparatus at strategic points around the coasts, with a heavy emphasis on volunteer manning. Locally-run lifeboats existed in the latter part of the eigthteenth century, and investigations into lifeboat design and lifesaving apparatus were already under way at the start of the nineteenth century. The first lifeboats provided in Devon, at Plymouth and Exmouth in 1803, were presumably under local management and may not have proved effective, as nothing is known of them after their arrival.[30] Following the formation of the National Institution for the Preservation of Life from Shipwreck in 1824, boats were established at Appledore, Plymouth and Ilfracombe, though by 1851 there were no lifeboats being maintained on the south coast of Devon.[31] That year the Institution was virtually refounded and, with the revival of public interest, during the third quarter of the century existing boats in North Devon were brought under the wing of the Royal National Lifeboat Institution, decayed ones were refounded and new boats were established to provide five locations on the north coast of Devon and eight on the south coast. Since then redundancy, the introduction of motor lifeboats and rationalisation

1.8 The breeches buoy in action. A customs official on his way to board the Finnish four-masted barque *Herzogin Cecilie*, grounded at Soar Hill Cove, South Devon, April 1936. (*Western Morning News*) ▶

1.9 Coastguards waiting for the fog to clear before firing a line by rocket aboard the Finnish four-masted barque *Herzogin Cecilie*, grounded at Soar Hill Cove, South Devon, April 1936. (*Betty Yeoman*) ▼

have led to the closure of a number of stations. Brixham received the first power driven boat in 1922, but the last of the rowing and sailing boats, at Lynmouth, was not withdrawn until 1944.

Although members of the Coastguard are closely indentified with life-saving, this did not become their primary function until well into the twentieth century, though they have always assisted in lifesaving and usually taken charge.[32] Their origins lie with the attempts of the Customs and Excise to curtail smuggling through the use of riding officers and Revenue cruisers for patrolling the coasts. In 1809 a Preventive Water Guard was formed to augment the Customs patrols. As a secondary duty it was instructed to assist in saving life and issued with Manby's mortar apparatus. The various coastal watch services were reorganised as the Coastguards in 1822, the anti-smuggling role remaining the first priority. In 1831 its manpower was designated as a reserve for the Royal Navy, and by 1839 the long-standing subdivision of the British coastline had been further refined into local command districts. In 1851 at least six sets of mortar lifesaving apparatus were distributed along the south coast of Devon. Under the Merchant Shipping Act of 1854, the Board of Trade became responsible for issuing the apparatus to the Coastguard and to the volunteer lifesaving brigades which were being formed. In North Devon in 1908 there were three volunteer lifesaving companies, and a further five sets of apparatus were held by the Coastguard. The primary role of the Coastguard as a coast watching and life saving force did not emerge until the Coastguard Act of 1925, which sanctioned the transfer of the service from the control of the Admiralty to that of the Board of Trade.

Communications have always been a key element in the provision of assistance to maritime casualties. Before the advent of radio, ships had to rely on visual signals to indicate their distress. General signals include flares and rockets and flying the ensign upside down, in the hope that they would be noticed. Semaphore, code flags and the Morse light all contributed to the refinement of distress communications by ships. Ashore, such signals, or the vessel itself, might be sighted equally by the casual onlooker or by the coastal watch. Before the coming of telephones a considerable lapse of time could occur before messages reached the nearest coastguard or lifeboat station, and even longer before equipment might be in position at a coastal wreck or the lifeboat reach a vessel at sea. By the end of the nineteenth century the spread of the telephone was beginning to ease communications ashore; in particular the coastguard stations were linked by a coastal telephone line. Both ships at sea and the Coastguard benefited from the introduction of wireless telegraphy, the latter being so equipped just before the First World War. Communications were further improved not only with respect to receiving distress messages, but also between the various rescue services, through the development of VHF radio telephony equipment. The coastguard received its first sets in 1963, and through continuing technological development, and reviews of the communications needs of the rescue services, this has become the dominant mode, with even the smallest vessels carrying the equipment.

Alston Kennerley

1: Shiphandling and Hazards on the Devon Coast

1 J W Norie, *The Seaman's New Guide and Coaster's Companion* (1847), 133.

2 James F Imray, *Sailing Directions for the English and Bristol Channels* (1879), 75.

3 Norie, *Seaman's New Guide*, 41.

4 Imray, *Sailing Directions*, 70.

5 Imray, *Sailing Directions*, 109.

6 Imray, *Sailing Directions*, 109.

7 Quoted in Norie, *Seaman's New Guide*, 133.

8 Norie, *Seaman's New Guide*, 135.

9 Norie, *Seaman's New Guide*, 135.

10 *Report of the Commissioners on Harbours of Refuge* (BPP, 1859, I), v.

11 *Report* (BPP, 1859, I), v.

12 *Report* (BPP, 1859, I), 76–81.

13 *Report* (BPP, 1859, I), vi.

14 *Report* (BPP, 1859, I), xii.

15 *Report* (BPP, 1859, I), xiii.

16 P Kemp, (ed.), *The Oxford Companion to Ships and the Sea* (Oxford, 1976), 945.

17 F C Hendry (Shalimar), *Land and Sea* (1939), 240–70.

18 Hydrographic Department, Great Britain, *Channel Pilot* (NP 28, Hydrographer of the Navy, 2nd edn., 1977, revised 1984); and *West Coasts of England and Wales Pilot* (NP 38, Hydrographer of the Navy, 1974) especially Chapter 1 in each volume.

19 M Nix, *The Cruel Coast of North Devon* (Bideford, 1982), 10.

20 See *Channel Pilot* and *West Coasts of England and Wales Pilot*.

21 G Farr, *Wreck and Rescue on the Coast of Devon. The Story of the South Devon Lifeboats* (Truro, 1968), 108.

22 BPP, 1873, XXXVI; 1874, XXXIV.

23 O Warner, *The Lifeboat Service. A History of the Royal National Lifeboat Institution, 1824–1974* (1974), 43. See also R Larn, *Devon Shipwrecks* (Newton Abbot, 1974).

24 BPP, 1874, XXXIV, Appendix LXXXV to the Minutes of Evidence, 682–765, and Appendix LIX to the Minutes of Evidence, 442–9.

25 Nix, *Cruel Coast*, 9.

26 Farr, *Wreck and Rescue*, 20–1.

27 D B Hague & R Christie, *Lighthouses* (1975), 20–1.

28 Hague & Christie, *Lighthouses*, 39.

29 H P Mead, *Trinity House* (1947), 115.

30 Farr, *Wreck and Rescue*, 22, 173.

31 See also Warner, *Lifeboat Service*, and G Farr, *Wreck and Rescue in the Bristol Channel, I: The Story of the English Lifeboats* (Truro, 1966).

32 The following paragraphs are based on W Webb, *Coastguard. An Official History of HM Coastguard* (HMSO, 1976); and Nix, *Cruel Coast*.

2 The Seaman's Life in His Own Words

COMPILED BY BASIL GREENHILL

TWO PARTICULAR DIFFICULTIES face those who seek to take account of the maritime dimension of history, and both concern the life of the seaman. The first is the consequence of the demise of the sailing ship, which presents us with a cultural break more complete than almost any other of the numerous similar breaks which have accompanied the development of technology and the consequent changes in occupation, standard of living, and outlook on life in the twentieth century. Until well into the 1980s there were men alive who had lived in what Sir Alan Moore called 'the blaze of the old tradition'[1] of the technology of the sailing vessel and the social structures that went with it. This technology, and the limitations it imposed on the operation of vessels, both merchant and war, and, perhaps even more important, the attitudes of mind that followed from the processes of its absorption, which had to begin in the earliest youth, are very important for historical understanding. First-hand knowledge of them is now inevitably totally lost.

The wooden sailing vessel was the only kind of merchant or fighting ship for more than six-and-a-half of the eight centuries since ships and shipping in anything like a modern sense began to be important in European waters. Only by total immersion in the profession of seafaring could the skills be acquired to manage, maintain and sail a structure made up of hundreds, if not thousands, of relatively small pieces of wood fastened together with wooden, copper alloy or iron pins, bearing a heavy cargo under economically competitive conditions, or bearing heavy guns and overmanned with their gunners and overladen with their supplies and under threat from the enemy. These vessels had as their motive power only the wind, working through the energy-collecting agency of sails, masts, rigging and deck gear, which together comprised equipment no more sophisticated than could be made by a foundry, a blacksmith or a carpenter, and simple ropework of the type seen in Newfoundland by Mrs Robert Adams and described later in this chapter.

More than two thousand years ago, Thucidides wrote 'Seamanship is a skill just like anything else, and it is impossible to perform it proficiently as a haphazard spare time activity. In fact it leaves no spare time for anything else.'[2]

A Russian, Ivan Goncharov, later to become famous as the author of the novel *Oblomov*, wrote in 1852 of the introduction of auxiliary steam engines driving screws in the Royal Navy, 'Woe to the seaman of the old school whose whole mind, science and art backed by his self-esteem and ambition are contained in the rigging. The conclusion is foregone . . . while we were at Portsmouth Naval docks they half dismantled a completely finished ship and put a steam engine in.'[3]

The men of the sailing ships, merchant or naval — which effectively means almost all seamen until 1870 or so — were trained for little except the all-absorbing mystery of their craft. On its proper practice depended physical as well as economic survival. The seaman's mobile combined workplace and place of residence took him to places both exotic and sordid, which, at a time when travel for most people was very limited, gave his occupation an aura of spurious mystery and romance. But at the same time this occupation, and the craft absorbtion necessary for survival, cut him off from normal human life and society to a degree which did not occur with most other occupations which employed large numbers of men. Sailing ships moved slowly, and their loading and discharge in distant ports took a long time. Naval commissions might last three years with no shore leave, for fear

of desertion. The seaman was denied normal home and community life, a regular sexual life, and participation in social affairs with men and women of other disciplines.

In consequence of their situation seamen became remote from their fellow men and women, speaking even their own language, using different words of nautical origin for everyday things, finding nautical similes for use in the, to them, strange world of everyday life ashore. They became obsessed with their own culture because they were isolated from all others. I have known many such men, the men of the sailing vessels which survived in odd economic backwaters of Europe and North America well into the twentieth century, and to a man they showed the scars of their isolation from society ashore and their intense specialism, so vital to survival.

Indeed, it was more than isolation. The strange world of the seaman, the rigorous and back-breaking labour imposed by the nature of his work, handling heavy sails and gear whose disposition owed more to tradition than to science; his outlandish speech and his inability to relate to life ashore; his too-often desperate attempts to solve the unsolvable by seeking oblivion in alcohol, sex and violence; all of this alienated the seaman, seafaring, ships and the whole strange maritime world from the majority of the human race. As a result a complex relationship developed, full of contradictions, of fantasy on both sides, of fear, of guilt on the part of the landsman, and of strong mutual rejection.

It was a consequence of this situation that, as the archaeologist T C

2.1 The complexities of the seamanship of the sailing vessel had to be assimilated from the earliest youth. Here a boy who, at 12 years of age may well be already working, takes a boat out, sculling with one oar, across the ebb tide towards anchored local sailing barges from Appledore Quay. (*W C Fox*)

2.2 Seamen working aloft in the rigging, making fast the square topsails of the three-masted schooner *Brooklands*, ex *Susan Vittery*, built at Dartmouth in 1859 for the Azores fruit trade and subsequently employed in the Newfoundland trade. (*Douglas Bennet*)

Lethbridge pointed out in 1952,[4] agricultural and seafaring communities in the days when people sailed for a living really faced in opposite directions. They stood back to back, rather than face to face, the one regarding the sea, the other the land. Even the class structures of the two types of community tended to be different. Hazardous though sea enterprise was, there was much more chance of generating capital and moving upwards in the economic scale in a shipping place.

The second of the two difficulties to which I referred in the first paragraph comprises the silence of the seaman. He is a remarkably elusive creature. He has left relatively few accounts of himself at first hand – for very good reasons which are apparent from what has already been said. As far as Devon is concerned we are fortunate in that there are autobiographical accounts from the nineteenth and twentieth centuries, some of which have been published.

W J Slade's *Out of Appledore* and *West Country Coasting Ketches* give a

2.3 North Devon seamen photographed at Appledore about the year 1900. All but two have been identified. They are: Hartree Harding (second from left); William Gregory (third from left); Archie Ross (front), who is known to have sailed in the Newfoundland trade; William Screech (fifth from left), who was mate of the ketch *Emu*; and Harry Sussex (far right), a ship's carpenter. (*W C Fox*)

first-hand account of the life of a Devon seaman, shipmaster and, eventually, shipowner in the home trade which is unique in its completeness and its attention to social and business detail.[5] There is nothing romantic in Captain Slade's account of a very hardworking life, culminating however, in his case, in early financial independence. Thus, writing of the fitting of auxiliary oil engines into the schooners and ketches working from Appledore just after the First World War, he says,

> I consider these voyages early in 1920 were really the start of my life in an auxiliary motor vessel, bearing in mind that the Master was also the engineer it can be understood that life was no bed of roses. Whilst in harbour there was always plenty to do in the engine room besides having to work the cargoes in and out. The accommodation aft was crude and living conditions miserable because half the cabin was taken for the engine room space and the smell of diesel oil was everywhere. There was no sleep at sea because of the excessive vibration and noise. Often the top of the flimsy deckhouse leaked like a colander, in fact for twenty years, I hardly knew what it was to have a dry bed to sleep in when away from home. In addition, being rather addicted to seasickness I suffered badly from this for all the remainder of my life at sea, so how could I be expected to love it? To me it was my living, and I did what I could to make it successful, but only I know how miserable I often felt during the time at sea and how I fought against the desire to lay windbound as often as I could.
>
> But I did make a success of it all the way through and never allowed anyone to leave me behind, and I certainly didn't allow my seasickness to hinder my chances of making a passage. There was one difference made through having motor power. It was not necessary to buy stocks of food and instead of salt beef our diet could be improved. The days of hunger had gradually passed, and even though conditions were so crude, there was plenty of good substantial food.[6]

Stephen Reynolds graduated in chemistry at Manchester University. His inclinations, however, were literary, and he worked in Paris as sub-editor of an Anglo-French review. In the early years of this century, during or after a bout of ill health, he settled in Sidmouth and became so absorbed in the life of its beach fishermen that he entered into partnership with two of them, Bob and Tom Woolley, in the ownership of boats and gear. He eventually became Resident Inspector of Fisheries for the South West Area, but not before he had published a series of books which take the reader into the very guts and soul of the Devon small boat fisherman's life a century ago. In the best of these, *A Poor Man's House*, he wrote of the domestic lives of the fishermen (he lodged with the Woolley family), of eating and sleeping and bringing up children and of marital relations. There was much that was gentle and kindly in the fishermen's background, but Reynold's also relates what poverty and disease and hunger meant, and of the life of watching and waiting for fish which, when they came, did so, often enough, in such numbers that the price to the fishermen, always low, became almost derisory. He tells especially of the work of boat handling and net handling and of the men themselves, and at its best his writing acquires a kind of brooding visual magic which earned him high praise from such giants in the contemporary literary world as Joseph Conrad, Arnold Bennett and John Galsworthy. Reynolds died at Sidmouth in the great influenza epidemic of 1919 at the early age of 37, but he left behind a record of unique quality and value. One extract must suffice.

> The early hours were a long-drawn nightmare of discomfort. About three o'clock we started hauling in for another thousand of fish, and by four o'clock we were ready to take the ebb tide homewards. There was nothing to eat aboard, nothing to drink, and very little tobacco. We had drifted to a dozen miles from home, and had scarcely wind enough to fill the sail. We took perforce to the sweeps. The boat had no life in her. There was not much life in us. With eyes that closed of themselves, and parched, lumpy throats, we rowed — rowed like machines, using pain for fuel. The sun dawned late.
>
> Until nearly eight in the morning we rocked at the sweeps. Finally, as if to mock us, after rowing all that way, a breeze sprang up from the south-east, and we sailed the short mile home. Had we waited, the wind would have done all our work. But we weren't to know.[7]

By way of contrast with the literary Stephen Reynolds, Richard Behenna, a Cornishman by birth, sailed in a number of Devon vessels including the Northam-built *Peter & Sarah* and the *Bellona* of Bideford. His simple, semi-literate account of the life gives a picture of hardship and squalor which he

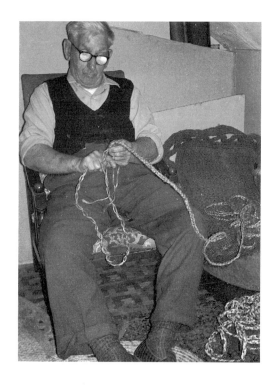

2.4   Devon sailing vessels in the home trade, like all others, had from time to time to lie windbound in distant harbours for long periods in the winter months. At such times one of the principal occupations of the crew was the making of rope mats for domestic use and for sale. In this photograph Captain William Lamey of the ketch *Hobah* of Bideford is working at the plaiting of hemp line into a rope, the first stage of making a mat. (*Basil Greenhill*)

2.5   The cabin of the three-masted schooner *Kathleen & May* of Bideford. The vessel is now preserved in dock at St Mary Overy in London. (*A C Littlejohns*)

took completely for granted. Take the *Bellona*, of which Behenna wrote,

1854, I left plymouth in the brigg "Bellona" of Bideford with government stors for Malta. We had fine whether the most of the way. We took 11 days to go ther. We lay a month in Malta, and then we was sent to alexandra to load wheat for detford dockyard. Ther was no docks at alexandra then; the men that loaded us was hall arabs. I thought thay wher like a lot wild pepal. The whether was hot, and thay wor very little close. We left alexandra after been ther 4 weeks for detford in London river. We had a long passag down the Medetrian, light wind or head wind most of the time untill we got to the gut of gibaltar. Then we took a fair wind, but the mate wanted the capt to go into gibaltar to get some provisions and watter as we was geting short, but the capt would not. He said that we might get to england a week and we had planty for eight or nine days, so we pass gibalter with strong breeze of wind, but it only last ed for day, and then we got beclmed of the spanish coast. Then the capt wished he put in at gibalter, for we found out by this we was one cask of watter short. We was swarm with rats and they had cut from the bung of the cask half down the cask, and with the rol of the ship, nearly hall the watter was lost. The little wind that was blowing was of the land. We was getting out of sight of land and no like of wind to work the ship. It is a week now since we pass gibalter, and hall our Provisions geting short, so we was now put on half allowance. Three days after this, we was cut to tow biskits a man per day . . . spok tow ships, both short of Provisions. Tow days latter, we was cut to one biskit a day per man and one half pint of watter a day for each man. Hall our stores was getting done, and making very little head way with the ship. We often wish it would come to rain to get a good drink. The rats was bad on us by night; they would get in our beads, and eat our toe nails right down to the flesh, and sometimes, they would draw blood from us. We was nine days on 1 biskit and half a pint of watter per day when we put into queenstown and got suplied fresh stors. We was nice looking lot when we got to queenstown, half starved and no watter to wash our skin for the last tow weeks. We was not left to get mor than half as much as we could eate for three days, then we was let to get our full. Then we sailed for detford in London river. The whether was fine an fair, and we arrived in London river after been 72 days out from Alexandra.[8]

Edmund Eglinton in *The Mary Fletcher* has given us an account of one week in the working life of a Devon coasting ketch of the 1920s which again is unique in the hour-by-hour detailed account it presents of the work of the seamen and of the relationships which existed between them. Eglinton was one of life's happy men, and the picture he paints is of a well adjusted team of highly skilled men working together to the common end of grinding a living out of the old vessel. This picture, based very closely on his own

experience at sea, is representative of the better type of small Devon merchant shipping operation of the early years of this century.[9]

Herbert Callard (1876–1965) left a narrative of his first voyage – in the Newfoundland trade from Salcombe – in the summer of 1892. This is now in the Salcombe Maritime and Local History Museum and, together with the two diaries which follow, has been made available for publication here through the good offices of David and Muriel Murch of Salcombe. Herbert Callard wrote,

Against Mother's wishes and not yet sixteen, I went to sign on the *Lord Devon*,[10] a topsail schooner, for two years "full and plenty" the day for sailing was to be in June 1892. I was listed as cook and seaman and I was on board long before it was time to cast off.

Having got well clear of the harbour on a course SW by W, I was given the helm and had difficulty keeping her head right because the wind had dropped. The other four members of the crew were getting their tea. They were Captain W Smith, the Mate William Boyce, Edward Hannaford and Sam Creber, AB's.

Presently Captain Smith came on deck with a tumbler half full of what I thought was cold tea. "Drink this" he said. I gulped it down and then knew it was rum. Hardly had it reached my stomach before it was on its way up again. "You won't get any more of that for a long time," said Captain Smith, "if that's what you are going to do with it."

Soon it was the first dogwatch and he took me aside and began telling me what I had to learn before I became entitled to my pound of tobacco and pipe. I would have to box the compass, make fast the top-gallant sail, the main topmast staysail, the flying jib, the gaff topsail and a hundred and one other things. It was two months before I got my pipe.

The first night I had the first watch with "Ted" Hannaford and was pumping out the bilge until midnight. Then I turned in but no sleep came, instead the fleas came out of my straw mattress in their hundreds. Eventually I took it up on deck and heaved it overboard. I slept in the sail locker after that, a bit cramped but dry and clean.

Next morning we had a fair wind from the east and in ten days we were at Cadiz, discharging ballast and loading salt for St John's, Newfoundland. On Sunday 19 July we spoke with the full-rigged ship, *Regland Castle*, but she gave us no news of interest. We arrived at St John's after 34 days and were surprised to discover that a great part of the town had been destroyed by fire and that thousands were homeless.

My first day ashore was a bit of a disaster. I was eagerly looking about at the disaster from my vantage point at the corner of Water Street near Dender's Wharf when two policemen came and one of them gave me such a clout on the head that I ran back on board as fast as my legs would carry me. If this was Newfoundland, I thought, they could lose it again as soon as they liked.

2.6 Beaching a small boat through a very light surf at Sidmouth. (*Postcard*)

We were there about three weeks before getting orders to go to Twilingate where we discharged our salt. A fortnight or so later we were back at St John's loading a general cargo for Greenspond, Bonavista Bay. This time we had three lady passengers who slept in the captain's quarters. It was a very short passage but we had a lengthy stay at Greenspond and I made some good friends there. I was so sad at leaving them that the mate used to "chaff" me about it during the first few days of our eastward voyage. We were bound for Lisbon with salt cod and within a few hours of arriving we had orders to discharge it elsewhere, so all I remember of Lisbon that time was that it was the only place we had to keep an anchor watch. My birthday, 5 November, was our day for sailing and we spent it trying to beat out of the harbour and failing to make it. As eight bells struck midnight I was furling the topgallant sail. What a birthday!

Next day we got clear, bound for Naples and arrived just before Christmas. On Christmas Eve, the mate and two AB's were in the forecastle with a five gallon jar of vino they had bought. I was in the sail locker trying to sleep when along came the mate and grabbed one of my seaboots and hit me hard in the stomach with it. He then ordered me to go to the Captain and ask for two extra loaves an a Dutch cheese. When I took them back to the forecastle the mate poured out a tumbler of wine for me, but when I said I did not want it he swore and shouted, "Drink that or I will break your skull". So I drank it and a lot more besides. Next morning I was feeling pretty miserable when I was sent aloft to loose the topgallant, in fact I was not very well all Christmas Day.

Soon after Christmas we were under sail for Marathonesa in Greece, a short passage. Only the Captain went ashore there. We discharged the ballast we had loaded in Naples and took on a cargo of valonia, acorn cups for use in the tanneries. There were acorns with it and our pig, "Dinnis" used to relish them. It was quite usual in the days of sail when voyages could be quite long to carry live stock as extra provisions.

On 13 January 1893 we sailed for our home port, Salcombe, and had a rough passage of 73 days before arriving on 2 April, Easter Sunder. We were hove-to in the Malta Channel for 15 days and later passed Gibraltar during the night when it was blowing a gale. Nothing else worth telling until we were becalmed just south of the isles of Scilly. "Ted" Hannaford and I had just taken over the deck, my first task was to light the galley fire. While I was thus engaged I heard a mighty wind approaching and realised that having been becalmed we were still under full sail. The next moment the wind struck the ship, and I thought the mast was going to go. All hands were soon on deck and the Captain was trying to shorten sail. My job was to furl the topgallant, the main topsail staysail, the flying jib and the gaff topsail. It was bitterly cold and the canvas was as stiff as a board. I am not ashamed to admit that I was crying long before I had finished, while the crew were cursing and swearing. The squall passed as quickly as it had come so the sails had to be spread once more.

I recall that it was then a pleasant day and remained so until we were off the Lizard but then the wind increased to a full gale offshore. We took in the kites at once, that is the sails I mentioned earlier, and while we were doing so all the crockery in the galley was smashed. The skipper was very angry with me when I came down from aloft. He even said that I would have to pay for it. Well, the dog-watches over, I was relieved at eight bells and went below but no sleep because at times the starboard gunwale was under water and the sea rushed into the forecastle.

We were under reefed topsail and the Captain was eager to close-reef. On a larger vessel he would have just given the orders, but with only a small crew all from the same town there was a discussion about it and we were all gathered aft as it was impossible to get to the forecastle. I must confess I had visions of a watery grave that night but we came in safely past Plymouth at about midnight on 1 April, and about 2am Easter Sunday we were off Bolt Head. I was relieved from the helm and sent aloft to burn a flare for a pilot. We were not heavily laden, having only about a 100 tons of cargo, so there was no problem about getting in over the Bar. It was not long before Mr Peter Foale the pilot had us anchored off the old castle near the Blackstone Rocks. All the crew went ashore and I was left in full charge for the first time in my life.

I soon had company, my brother Bill and other school mates, but we had very little food and not much water. The *Lord Devon* carried only one ton of fresh water in a tank in the captain's cabin, and on deck abaft the galley there were two casks which got brakish in due course. The casks supplied the water for our cooking and was eked out when possible with rain water caught in the canvas cover of the lifeboat. However, for my guests I managed to scrape up a little flour and a few currants which with a little Russian tallow I made into pancakes.

About 4pm that day we lifted the anchor and came up with the tide to anchor off the pier where I came ashore in time to hear the church bell ringing for Evensong at five oclock. I received ten golden sovereigns for my pay and I had never been so well off in my life before.

A diary included as part of letter written by John T Hill to his elder brother from Cadiz, dated 11 April 1892, describing a voyage on the Salcombe Shipowning Co's vessel the *Lady Bertha*,[11] under the command of Captain R W Adams, is also in the Salcombe Maritime and Local History Museum in the F W Hill Collection.

Friday 25th March:- Started to haul off at 2pm, passed through the dock gates at 3pm, towed down as far as Barry Docks, and let-go the tug *Kingfisher* at 6pm. Passed the Breaksea lightship at 7pm. My hands and the ropes dont agree very well.

Saturday 26th:- Turn out at 7am, raining with light wind and there is a strong flood tide, so drop the anchor. 6pm get in the anchor and 30 fathoms of chain, I have done cooler work than heaving up anchors; fresh breeze from the WNW 7.30pm. off Ilfracombe.

Sunday 27th:- 1pm. wind shifts to the N, we are off Bull Point with a rising sea. 4.15pm cast the log off Lundy. A very high sea breaking aboard, one forced me to my knees, when I was hauling round the gallant sail braces and it came in and shut out the daylight. 6.15pm. shortened sail. 9.30pm. I have the notion that I shall sleep better without the pilchards that I had for tea, so I just empty them out the way they went in.

Monday 28th:- Awake nearly all night, with the wind howling and seas breaking on board. 8am. checked the log and find 110 mls from Lundy or 22 mls West of Scilly and we alter course to the SW 4pm. put on the sails we took off yesterday. 8.30pm. get sick and cut up some tobacco and smoke a pipeful to take away the tastes and go to bed.

Tuesday 29th:- Fish and taties for breakfast. Take sights with Robert, (the captain) each of us have a sextant. Noon 166½ mls by log. 4pm. alter course SW by S to SSW.

Wednesday 30th:- Everything tame but the sea and wind. 4pm. Reefed the mainsail, took in gaff topsail and the staysail, and 11pm. the gallant sail. 170 mls at noon, sea running mountain high, sky very cloudy.

Thursday 31st:- A shocking night — seas breaking over and around us in fine style. Take in squaresail and double reefed mainsail. Cloudy and "small" rain. 7am. Alter course to S by W ½W. sea rising again, and breaking on deck. 8.30pm. turn in. 11pm. woke up, went up on deck and found that we are becalmed but with strong lightning, the ship rolling and kicking with the sails flapping. I thought I had better finish dressing, I put on my new sea-boots (I bought them in Newport. They come right up and fasten on to my braces). 11.30pm. Took in square sail, a few puffs of wind from the SE.

Friday 1st April:- Very strong and quick lightning from the E. Take in gallant sail and main topmast stay sail, wind freshening and shifted suddenly to S. The main boom went whiz and struck me on the head which sent me sprawling, as it was my hat went overboard. I can still feel the bruise now. It rained dreadfully and the seas washed over us as if they would sink her. At 3pm called all hands on deck and took in the upper and lower topsails, 2 reefs in the main, 1 reef in the foresail. I stood for some time on the fore hatch clinging to the topsail halliards, on the look out. The sea looked like one mass of blue fire, the phosphorescence was so brilliant. There was 2 to 3 feet of water rushing from the side to the other as we rolled. I was afraid it would break out the side above deck. 3am. the wind dropped as suddenly as it came, in less than five minutes we were in the second calm. 6am. wind came from the E. the weather clearing a bit with the sunrise which was really grand. At 7am. turned in and slept until 12.30pm. 8pm. set fore staysail and set lower topsail. 9pm. set the upper topsail and reef out of the foresail. I slept from 2.30 until 4am. It had been cloudy all day with heavy seas.

Saturday 2nd:- At 7.30am the sea was full of porpoises and the water was so clear that I watched them swim under the ship. 3pm. 37 mls off Lisbon Rock and can see it quite plain for nearly 7 hours. A splendid day.

Sunday 3rd:- When I got up at 7.30am Cape St Vincent was in sight and we passed close to it at 11.30am. It did look pretty with the old convent built on the edge of the high cliff, all in ruins now. There is a lighthouse near by and a great hole through the Cape large enough for a ship to pass through. We passed several steamers, great beauties. At 9.30pm we passed Santa Maria light and saw several others, but could

2.7   The food for the crews of Devon schooners was cooked in the galley on deck and, whatever the weather, had to be carried along the slippery wet deck and down below to the cabin, where it was the custom for all the crew to eat together. Here the cook of the three-master *Kathleen & May* of Bideford is beginning his hazardous journey from the galley. (*Basil Greenhill*)

not make out what they were. A better day than yesterday. I put our cigars in the bread tank.

Monday 4th:- A lovely morning. I put a line out but caught no fish. Very little wind at noon we are only 20mls off Cadiz. The heat is something immense. 4.30pm. sight Cadiz, hoist the Union Jack for a pilot who comes on board at 6pm and at 7.15pm we are anchored in the harbour and the pilot leaves. The city looked very pretty and strange to me.

Tuesday 5th:- Rise at 6am. Officers come on board at 7.30 and leave a blooming soldier with a rifle on board. He came down to breakfast with us but I bundled on deck to wait until we had finished, he eats as much as two of us.

Here the diary ends.

Devon women, of course, have gone to sea in one capacity or another throughout the centuries. W J Slade's mother, Annie Harding, was born in 1865, the daughter of the master of an aged trading smack called the *Dahlia*[12] working in the Bristol Channel. Her brothers having gone away to sea in other vessels, Annie was pressed into service as one of the *Dahlia*'s crew of three as soon as she left school. In W J Slade's words,

She was taught the compass and how to steer by it, how to trim the sails by the wind or going off the wind, but better still she knew the land and sets of tides according to the time it ebbed or flowed. She also became a good judge of weather conditions. In fact she knew enough to be left in charge of the watch while her father slept.

In those days most of the old ships were veritable death traps. When at sea they were generally kept floating by continual pumping. The first stop after leaving Lydney [with coal for North Devon] was Penarth Mud. There the crew would rest from the pump because the mud would get in the leaks to stop the water flowing in. Often I have heard mother talk of the hours she stood at the pump in her high laced up boots with hardly any time to rest or make a cup of tea till she eventually arrived at the port of discharge. Then all her spare time was taken up in cooking and feeding the crew including herself.[13]

At the opposite end of the social scale of a Devon seafaring community

2.8   The *Lady St Johns* loading saltfish by way of a plank over her stern direct from the flakes at Burin, Newfoundland, on her maiden voyage in 1898. (*Peggy Cleave*)

was Lavinia Catherine, wife of Captain Robert Wilson Adams, master of the brand new schooner *Lady St John's* of Salcombe.[14] We are again indebted to David and Muriel Murch of Salcombe for drawing our attention to her diary, which is also in the F W Hill Collection of personal papers in the Salcombe Maritime and Local History Museum.

The 114–ton schooner *Lady St John's* was built by W Date and Sons at Kingsbridge, South Devon, for F W Hill and Co. F W Hill held twenty-eight shares, while his son-in-law, Captain Robert Wilson Adams, master of the *Lady St John's*, held ten shares and the remainder were held by other members of the family and by the ship's builder, W Date, by the ship smith and a banker. The vessel was launched in April 1898, the ceremony being performed by the captain's wife. Her diary starts on 18 May;

We left Salcombe for Cadiz . . . Daddy [F W Hill] and Moll went off with us. When we got on board we found . . . numerous friends and relations . . . When the anchor was up Daddy and the ladies went ashore. After we got outside (the harbour) we cruised about a bit and the male friends and relations were very pleased with the way the vessel behaved. We waited for the *Kingsbridge Packet* . . . we sent a boat to stop her to get some Cornish butter, and to take our visitors back to Salcombe. Each vessel dipped their flags as a token of farewell.

We had a nice breese, but were becalmed for two days off Cape Finisterre, and one or two days rough [weather] off the coast of Portugal. We arrived at Cadiz on 28 May, 10 days after leaving England. We loaded salt and were ready to sail first thing 3 June but there was no wind, a vessel that tried had to bring up. A breeze sprang up about dinner time and we got under way at once, although the wind was light we made fairly good progress and soon overhauled some of the vessels that had got out before us.

While we were off the Portuguese coast a fishing boat came alongside and we bought a nice lot of fish which lasted us for two days teas, and me for several days more . . . We had a very pleasant passage across until we got to the Banks when we ran into fog and did not get a sight for five or six days. On 28 June we were able to get the sun to verify our position and on the evening of the next day we saw the high land at the entrance of St Johns. We had to lay to until morning when a tug came and towed us in. We anchored about 6.30am. Had fresh meat for breakfast and dinner together with what fresh vegetables that could be got.

To our satisfaction we had beaten several vessels that had left before us, and had the best passage of the season only 28 days . . . We found that the *Lord Devon* had got the freight intended for us and had sailed for the Straights.

A day or two after our arrival we hauled down to John's warf to take out our salt. Captain Bains of the ss *Leopard* came on board and invited us to his steamer next day . . . On Friday 22 July we sailed and arrived at Burin on the 25 and began taking out ballast for the fish. They commenced loading as soon as there was room to work in the hold as it was not safe laying in the roads with cargo. Robert told

me that I would have to do the cooking as all the hands were needed about the cargo, so that kept me pretty busy as it is no joke cooking for half a dozen men with appetites like horses.

On Thursday afternoon Robert took me ashore, but the tide was so far out that our boat could not get into the steps, so I had to get into a dory and even then one of the men carried me on shore. On the beach the women were busy drying fish and we went through a rope walk and saw them curing flax, and then saw a man with the flax twisted round his body, at one end the flax was fastened to a wheel which a boy was turning and as the man worked the flax he walked backwards putting the made up strands over rests as he went. I was told that the strands would again be twisted together until a rope of sufficient thickness was made.

Next day Friday 5 August we finished taking in what fish they had and left for Fortune where we were able to take in the remainder of our cargo . . . It blew very hard one night, and as it was an open roadstead, Robert got every thing ready in case we had to slip our anchor and put to sea. We did not go to bed until 4am when he called Mr Collings to keep watch in his place.

On Friday 12 August 1898 the *Lady St John's* sailed for Portugal, but without the writer of the diary because her husband would not allow his wife to make a westward autumn passage across the Atlantic, as it would be too stormy. Mrs Adams stayed in Burin until mid October, then travelled by the ss *Alert* to Placentia and then by train to St John's. The *Lady St John's* arrived back at St John's on Monday 24 October 1898. The diary continues,

Robert told me that the first part of the return passage from Oporto had been very fine and that they had made good speed but the latter part had been very stormy, or as he had said 'regular up hill work' but there had been no injuries and no damage.

A few days later we were chartered to load for Carthagina and came alongside the warf to discharge the salt and to load at Goodridges. On the 8 November we were once more on our way eastwards with a fair wind.

Here the diary ends.

The *Lady St John's* was to be the last of the Devon Newfoundland traders. Between 1924 and 1926 she made five easterly passages of twenty-nine days on average, including one from St John's to Oporto in only fourteen days. In 1927 she was twenty-seven days westward, and in 1928 her three eastward passages averaged eighteen and a half days. She was sold to French owners in 1930. Thus she closed four and a half centuries of Devon involvement in the Newfoundland trade.

Small wooden sailing vessels of the types owned in the ports of Devon were, as has already been indicated, dangerous vehicles of transport. Great numbers of them were lost at sea or on the coasts. Quite apart from the losses of vessels, many seamen were killed or injured in the normal course of their work in the rigging or on deck. Seafaring was, indeed, a hazardous occupation. Of all the thousands upon thousands of incidents affecting Devon seamen which occurred over the centuries covered by this history, two, at opposite ends of the scales of seafaring and disaster, must suffice as illustrations. The following account is based on information given to me by Robert Ellis of Tideford many years ago.

From 9–12 March 1891 a great gale accompanied by heavy snow blew over southwest Britain. Countless trees were blown down, roads blocked and outlying settlements cut off for days. Rail services were disrupted by the snow, telegraph lines were brought down all over Devon, and much damage was done to seaside property, shore installations, and vessels at sea and in harbour, though there were surprisingly few losses. On 9 March the Tamar sailing barge *Elizabeth Jane*[15] was bound for Tideford on the St German's River from Plymouth. The crew comprised Captain Ellis, who had shares in the vessel, and his ten- or eleven-year-old son, Robert John.

The gale came with little warning and solid driving snow. They managed to make the shelter of Wacker Creek on the south side of the Lynher, near Anthony. They lay off the tide mill there for a week, unable to get ashore and with food and fuel only for the day's trip from Plymouth. The snow drove into the tiny cabin, which had only sitting head room, and it was unbelievably cold. Robert Ellis never forgot the experience, nor the relief of his mother when the *Elizabeth Jane* was eventually able to make her way up to Tideford, where the family lived.

At the other end of the seafaring scale of hazard is the loss of the *William Anning* of Plymouth. The events are recorded in the Official Log. Robin Craig has prepared the following extracts from it, correcting spelling, grammar and punctuation.

The *William Anning* of Plymouth was a wooden brigantine of 177 tons register. She had been built in Rye, Sussex, in 1863. She measured a little over 100ft in length, 23½ft in breadth, and something over 12ft in depth. She had voyaged from London to Cardiff, sailed to Rio de Janeiro, then set course for Philadelphia, where she loaded a cargo of wheat, bound to Penarth Roads, for orders. She sailed from Delaware Breakwater on 5 February 1874.

7 February: wind variable, rain, sky looking dirty. Midnight: strong gales. Mainstaysail blown away. Shipping great quantity of water and labouring heavily, wind WNW.
8 February: Weather carried away middlestay; replaced it.
10 February: sky looking dirty, wind ESE and increasing. 8pm: strong gale and heavy sea; ship labouring heavily and shipping a quantity of water.
11 February: 8am, strong gale WSW: noon, complete hurricane NW, ship under balance close-reefed mainsail. Ship full of water on deck. Bulwarks gone, fore and aft spars washed adrift, two watercasks, spare anchors and boat chocks and other things [washed overboard]. Sea making a complete breach over her. Ship making more water than usual. Awful weather, expecting ship to go down with us often. Lat 36 degrees 44′N, Long 67 degrees 37′W.
12 February: heavy gale, still sea going right over her; everything on deck adrift and ship full of water.
13 February: ship making no more water, a little grain coming up the pumps.
22 February: Strong gale and heavy sea, ship rolling and labouring heavily, sea going right over her.
23 February: wind increasing all the time, taking in sail as required: pumps carefully attended to.
25 February: thick rain with strong gale and heavy sea from the westward. Shipping quantity of water. At 8pm, looking worse — not intending to run ship any longer, hove to heading northward under close-reefed mainsail.
Midnight: a heavy sea struck her on the port bow, knocking away bulwarks and bowsprit and the two jibstays carried away and washed boom jib adrift — saved the jib, (but) ship's headgear a complete wreck.
26 February: heavy gale NW with heavy snow and hail. Squally with a tremendous sea. Ship labouring heavily and shipping a great quantity of water.
27 February: 2am, heavy sea struck her on the port bow and started rail and cathead, stove in the galley with other damage. 10pm. wind freshening, stowed all sail but close-reefed mainsail.
28 February: 8am, (wind) still increasing, a complete hurricane. 10am. balance close-reefed mainsail went from the leach and blew to pieces. Sea struck her and filling her up; stove in longboat, bulwarks gone, sea making a clean (breach) over her. Give her up for a lost ship for we are awfully situated. Noon: complete hurricane, galley gone. Lat 43 degrees 57′N, Long 36 degrees 47′W.
  A heavy sea struck on the port bow and knocked away the cutwater and false stem, bulwarks, mainrail, stanchions: vessel a complete wreck and on her beam ends. Cut away the mainsail to try to save her. Found ship had sprung a leak. Took several hours with all hands to the pumps to get [them] to suck. Kept almost constantly at the pumps to keep her from foundering. Cut away jibbom and topgallant-mast to ease the ship forward. Set forestaysail aft on mainmast to keep ship to. We have no means to find our position, suppose to be in Lat 43 degrees 57′ N Long 35 degrees 37′W.
1 March: Blowing terrific [*sic*] and mountains of sea. Keep almost constantly at pumps except time to get something to eat. Sea making right over. Hard job to keep to pumps. We know we must pump or sink. No one knows but ourselves what we have to go through, wet and cold, washed about, nothing warm to make use of and not knowing the moment she may go down with us expecting every sea to take her down. Took all hands in cabin yesterday as water running all through decks of forecastle cabin: very little better. Ship strained and knocked to pieces. Butts in deck forward opened: found that the wooden ends from the seam were started, and no way to stop the leaking. Nothing for us but to pump so long as strength can hold out. Noon: tremendous sea still and washing over her; can't stand it much longer. Lat 44 degrees 21′N Long 35 degrees 23′W, wind NW, strong gale.
2 March: Tremendous sea and a strong gale NW. Sea making right over her. Leak increasing. Kept almost constantly at the pumps and crew nearly exhausted. Hove the bower anchor overboard to lighten her forward.
3 March: at daylight a sail in sight to the eastward standing to WSW. Made small sail and bore down on her as we saw there was a chance of saving *William Anning*. The sail we bore down on was the Barque *Columbia* of Bremen bound to New York. We asked the Captain to take us off as our vessel was in a sinking state, which he kindly consented to do, but try to do it if possible with the ship's boat. Wind lessening all time, and sea gone down smoother. We got ship's boat out and took part of crew on board, and came back after the rest which was about noon. We abandoned the *William Anning* of Plymouth and got safe on board the Barque *Columbia* of Bremen, Captain Henry Glustien [?], Bremen.

2: The Seaman's Life in His Own Words

1 A Moore, *Last Days of Mast and Sail* (Oxford, 1925), 241.
2 Thucidides, 1 – 142–9.
3 I Goncharov, *The Voyage of the Frigate 'Pallada'* (1965), 28.
4 T C Lethbridge, *Boats and Boatmen* (1952), 23.
5 W J Slade, *Out of Appledore. The Autobiography of a Coasting Shipmaster and Shipowner in the Last Days of Wooden Sailing Ships* (4th edn., 1980); W J Slade and B Greenhill, *Westcountry Coasting Ketches* (1974).
6 Slade, *Out of Appledore*, 58.
7 S Reynolds, *A Poor Man's House* (1908).
8 R B Behenna, ed., *A Victorian Sailor's Diary* (Truro, 1981), 14.
9 E Eglinton, *The Mary Fletcher* (Exeter, 1990).
10 *Lord Devon*: Wood Schooner, 98 tons register, built 1885 Salcombe, owned by the Salcombe Shipowning Co Ltd and registered at Salcombe.
11 *Lady Bertha*: Wood Schooner, 98 tons register, built 1878 at Salcombe, owned by the Salcombe Shipowning Co Ltd and registered at Salcombe.
12 *Dahlia*: Wood Smack, 35 tons register, built 1838 at Newport, Mon., owned, 1890, by Richard Cann of Appledore and registered at Caernarfon.
13 'My Mother. The story of Annie Slade, 1865–1964' in B Greenhill and A Giffard, eds, *Women Under Sail* (1971), 110–11.
14 *Lady St John's*: Wood Schooner, 95 tons register, built 1898 at Kingsbridge, owned 1927 by John Lidecome of Kingsbridge and Norman Furneave of Penryn, Cornwall, and registered in Salcombe.
15 *Elizabeth Jane*: an unregistered inside barge. She was left derelict and completely worn out off Anthony Passage in the 1950s.

3 The Ports, Seaborne Trade and Shipping Industry of South Devon, 1786–1914

DAVID J STARKEY

PORTS, SEABORNE TRADE, AND THE SHIPPING INDUSTRY are variously concerned with perhaps the most important facet of human maritime activity, the transportation of goods and people. While ports exist to facilitate the landing and loading, and the collection and distribution, of commodities conveyed by sea, the shipping industry provides the vessels which carry such cargoes around the coasts or across the oceans. The demand for both of these services is conditioned by the level of seaborne trade, by the capacity of one nation, region or other economic unit to exchange its products for those generated in another. Though distinct, these three areas of the transportation business are clearly interdependent, together forming the central features of what might be termed a 'maritime economy'.

Between 1786 and 1914 – that is, between the Act of General Registry[1] and the outbreak of the First World War – Britain's maritime economy underwent profound change. By the 1780s, technical and organisational innovations had begun to transform the manufacturing and extractive sectors of the economy at large, setting in motion the process of industrialisation which was to permeate every part of the nation's economic life. As levels of production and consumption increased over the course of the nineteenth century, so the volume and value of Britain's seaborne commerce expanded, with a much greater range of goods carried to and from an ever-widening network of trading partners. Quantitative and qualitative change was also evident in the port and shipping industries. Ports could handle much greater volumes of traffic as substantial amounts of capital were invested in naviga-

3.1   The quay and town ferry at Exeter in 1885. Three schooners are discharging cargo. The middle vessel, bigger and more loftily rigged than the others and without square topsails, is the *Swordfish*, built in 1885 by John Ramsay at Summerside, Prince Edward Island, Canada, for James Richards of New Bideford. (*Postcard*)

3.2   Sutton Pool and the Barbican in winter, by William Gibbons, 1881. (City of Plymouth Museums & Art Gallery)

tional improvements, deep-water docks, rail connections, and steam-powered lifting equipment. The English shipping industry, which comprised some 9,360 wooden sailing craft measuring an aggregate of 1.05 million tons on 30 September 1788,[2] had extended to 16,001 vessels totalling 8.9 million tons by 31 December 1913; meanwhile, the character of the mercantile marine had altered radically, for 92.9 per cent of this tonnage was now driven by steam.[3]

Such developments, like the industrialisation process at large, were not evenly spread over time or space. The pace of change quickened as the nineteenth century proceeded, with the most rapid increase in trade, the principal dock-building works, and the widespread introduction of the steamship occurring in the late Victorian age. Spatially, trading activity and vessel ownership became increasingly concentrated at ports which served the manufacturing districts, notably Liverpool, Hull, and Glasgow, at the coal ports of South Wales and the North East, and at London, the chief centre of consumption as well as a major manufacturing location. Moreover, as traffic levels and ship size grew inexorably from the 1880s, it was at these major ports that cargo- and ship-handling provisions were extended, exacerbating the centripetal tendencies of commercial and shipping operations. A considerable volume of trade, however, was handled at the numerous relatively small ports which served regions such as East Anglia, North Wales, and the West Country. Indeed, in certain respects – notably the coastwise carriage of bulky, low-value commodities – the nineteenth century witnessed a marked increase in the seaborne trade of these and other non-industrial areas.[4]

The experience of such 'minor' ports in the industrial age is well illustrated by the case of the harbours and havens of Devon's English Channel coast. Because they served an area of comparatively slow economic growth (hereafter termed the 'region' of 'South Devon'), long-term relative decline was apparent in the volumes of trade handled and shipping owned at most of the region's ports. Yet there were also significant growth points as the locality felt many of the influences which stimulated the development of ports, trade, and shipping nationally. In examining the character and administration of the region's ports, the extent and nature of its seaborne trade, and the scale and deployment of the local shipping industry, the present chapter indentifies these areas of expansion in tracing the overall developmental pattern of South Devon's maritime economy in the 1786–1914 period.

'Harbours, Ports, or Rivers'

The hinterland served by South Devon's ports was comparatively productive in the pre-industrial age. Agriculture was the principal economic activity, especially in the low-lying and relatively fertile area to the east of Exeter, and in the South Hams. The extractive industries were prominent, with clay produced in the Bovey Basin, stone hewn from the southern reaches of Dartmoor, and a range of ores mined in the Tamar Valley. Various goods were manufactured for local consumption, though the region was particu-larly noted for the production and export of woollen and worsted cloth. Orga-nised on a domestic, 'putting out' basis, this industry was chiefly conducted in the Exe, Creedy, and Culm valleys, and thus it was mainly through the port of Exeter that large quantities of cloth were transported overseas.[5]

By the late eighteenth century, however, growth in the local economy was clearly less dynamic than that evident in other regions, notably in respect of the textile industry. With this 'leading sector' settling in Lancashire and the West Riding of Yorkshire, it was there and in other northern districts that the industrialisation process became centred. While those areas experienced relatively high rates of income and population growth as manufacturing output increased and diversified over the nineteenth century, such indicators exhibited only modest rises for much of southern England, including Devon. To some degree, this divergence reflected the 'de-industrialisation' of the county's economy as competition from more efficient producers led to the long-term decline of the manufacturing sector, particularly the cloth industry.[6] Chiefly, however, it was a function of the dynamics of the industrialisation process. Accordingly, once an industry was established in a certain region, cost factors determined that industrial growth agglomerated in that locality, while in outlying areas a reverse spiral was apparent. With resources attracted from the less productive to the faster-growing regions, the industrial 'core' fed off the emergent 'periphery', and areas like Devon, which were once economically autonomous, became increasingly dependent on distant centres of production, consuming their fuel and manufactures and supplying food and raw materials in return.[7]

Transport was basic to this relationship. On land, the distance between Devon and the industrial heartlands rendered communication by road difficult and expensive. While this problem was mitigated by the extension of the rail network into the county during the 1840s, transportation by sea remained significant, not only for the carriage of goods overseas, but also (indeed, especially) for the shipment of commodities to and from other regions. This had been the case for many centuries, of course, with shipping activity concentrated at various locations along South Devon's coastline. Extending from the eastern bank of the River Axe to the western side of the Tamar, this long stretch of coast is indented by numerous sheltered, navigable estuaries – notably the Exe, Teign, Dart, Kingsbridge River, Plym, and Tamar. It was at such favourable sites that shipmasters sought safe accommodation for their vessels, and it was there that the landing places established from the earliest times evolved into the Legal and Sufferance Quays of the medieval period and the Customs Ports of the modern age.[8]

First delimited in 1558, the Customs Port was an administrative unit rather than a specific location where goods were landed or loaded, or where vessels were built and owned. By 1786 the shores of England and Wales were divided into seventy-four Customs Ports, each comprising a 'head port' to which were subject 'creeks' or 'member ports' as appropriate.[9] Devon's south coast was covered by three Customs Ports until the mid-nineteenth century, with Exeter serving as the administrative centre for Exmouth, Teignmouth, Topsham and various other creeks between the Axe and Teign estuaries, the port of Dartmouth embracing its chief members of Brixham, Salcombe and Torquay, and Plymouth's jurisdiction extending westwards from Challaborough, near the Avon estuary, to the River Seaton in Cornwall. In September 1852, much to the delight of the town's populace, Teignmouth was granted 'independence' from Exeter and elevated to the status of Customs Port.[10] Although Salcombe and Brixham were severed from Dartmouth and established as ports of registry in 1863 and 1864 respectively, there were no further changes in the region's trading port limits before the First World War.

Vessels might be discharged or laden at various sites within these Customs Ports. Although coasting ketches and sloops sometimes discharged small consignments of goods into horse-drawn carts on open beaches, most craft sought the safety and convenience of a quay, pier, wharf or dock. Such provisions were generally concentrated in the more navigable estuaries; thus, in the late 1840s, quay, pier or harbour dues on coastal shipments of coal were levied at Exeter, Topsham, Teignmouth, Dartmouth, Salcombe, and at nine different landing places in 'Plymouth and its district', while similar charges were made at Brixham and Torquay harbours.[11] Thirty years later, the Customs Board identified eighteen separate 'harbours, ports, or rivers' between and including Axmouth, at the eastern extremity of Devon, and the river port of Calstock, on the Cornish bank of the Tamar. Seven of these sites lay within the Customs Port of Plymouth – Calstock, Cattewater, Devonport, Millbay, Mutton Cove, Plymouth Harbour and Sutton Harbour – while Axmouth, Beer,

Exmouth Dock, and Topsham were members of the Port of Exeter, Teignmouth administered Paignton and Torquay, and Brixham and Salcombe were both listed as creeks of Dartmouth.[12]

Different types of authority exercised rights over these ports. The Lords Commissioners of the Admiralty not only controlled Devonport Dockyard but also Plymouth Harbour, and therefore possessed the right to veto developments in the commercial port on strategic grounds. Private landowners held a significant interest in South Devon's harbours, especially in the early nineteenth century. Thus, ancient property grants entitled the Lord of the Manor of Kenton to exact tolls upon cargoes discharged in the Bight of the Exe,[13] while the Duchy of Cornwall owned 'all the water, soil and pool of Sutton situate near the Borough of Plymouth' as well as the waters of the Port of Dartmouth.[14] Some of the region's lesser port provisions were also in private hands, with Axmouth, Beer, and Torquay under the respective proprietorships of W F Hallet, Esq., the Honourable Mark Rolle (also the proprietor of Rolle Quay, Barnstaple) and Lord Haldon. In contrast, municipal authority held sway at Exeter, where the 'Mayor, Aldermen and Burgesses' controlled the Exeter Canal as well as the quays in the city and at Topsham.[15]

Although the situation at Exeter remained largely unaltered, change was apparent in the administration of most South Devon ports during the nineteenth century. In the early 1800s, for example, there was much agitation at Plymouth as the merchants, shipowners and seafarers who used Sutton Pool pressed the owners of the site, the Duchy of Cornwall, to improve the facilities available. After a decade of friction in which dues were withheld, petitions and public meetings organised and various schemes proposed, the Duchy agreed to lease the harbour to the Sutton Pool Company, a joint-stock venture instituted by Act of Parliament. Authorised to raise £50,000 for the building of quays, wet and dry docks, and warehouses, the Company assumed full managerial responsibility for the site, its successor, the Sutton Harbour Improvement Company, eventually purchasing the lease from the Duchy in 1891.[16] Similar transitions occurred at Teignmouth and Dartmouth, though here, and in Brixham, Salcombe and the Cattewater, port users exercised control through the medium of the Harbour Commission. Established by privately-promoted Acts of Parliament, these self-elected bodies were established to obviate the institutional restrictions which sometimes hampered port development. Teignmouth Harbour Commission, for instance, was created in 1836 to represent local interests dissatisfied with the apathetic efforts of Exeter's city fathers to assist the port,[17] while Dartmouth Harbour Commission was founded in 1864 by parties exasperated at the counter-productive wrangling between the Duchy of Cornwall and its lessees, the Town Council, over the administration of the 'waterbaileywick' of Dartmouth.[18]

Such organisational tensions imply that pressure upon South Devon's port provision was generally increasing in the nineteenth century. At the same time, the nature of this demand was changing as various forces combined to shape port development. To landward, the establishment of linkages

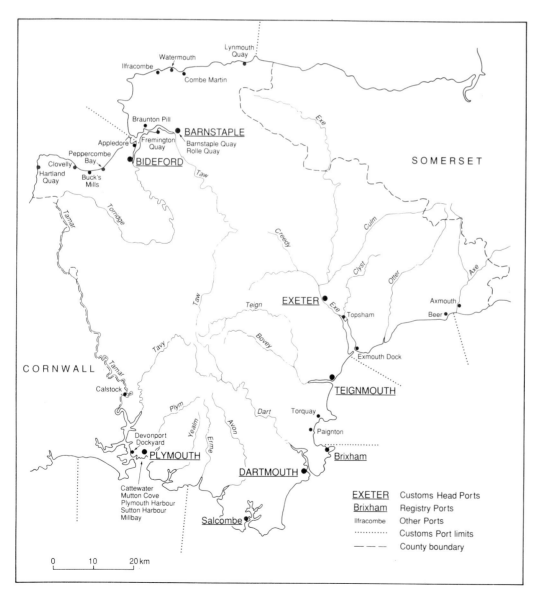

Map 3.1 Port Authorities in Devon according to the Customs Board Return of 1881. (Accounts and Papers [BPP, 1882, LXII, 409])

3.3 The graving dock, Great Western Docks, Millbay, Plymouth. Designed by I K Brunel, the Docks were built at a cost of £250,000 and opened for traffic on 11 February 1857. Willoughby Bros Ltd repaired vessels at the graving dock until 1969. (Illustrated London News, *28 February, 1857*)

In this changing context, Plymouth was the most favourably endowed of South Devon's ports. Although Dartmouth presided over a deep-water site, and relatively large ships could enter the Teign, Plymouth Sound could safely accommodate the most substantial of vessels. With a long waterfront, moreover, there was ample space in which berthing and cargo-handling facilities, warehousing and railway linkages could be developed. Although this space was administered by three separate authorities, a strong degree of complementarity was evident. Sutton Harbour specialised in handling fishing craft and wooden sailing vessels, while, in the second half of the nineteenth century, Millbay Docks serviced the great steamships which visited Plymouth, including the passenger liners, and the wharves in the Cattewater dealt with much of the port's petroleum, clay and fertiliser business.[30] Plymouth also enjoyed significant economic advantages over its South Devon rivals. The town's population, unlike that of the rest of the region, expanded rapidly during the nineteenth century – by some 345 per cent between 1801 and 1901[31] – vastly increasing the demand for seaborne imports. Plymouth was also well situated in relation to South Devon's main export trades; thus, while Exeter's port function declined with the demise of the export-oriented woollen industry, and Dartmouth served a highly restricted, rural hinterland, the mineral and agricultural produce of the Tamar Valley, the stone of Dartmoor, and the china clay of Lee Moor were largely shipped through Plymouth.

Most of the factors governing port development therefore favoured Plymouth rather than its neighbours. Accordingly, just as Britain's trade became increasingly concentrated at the major ports, so a growing proportion of South Devon's seaborne traffic passed through Plymouth as the nineteenth century progressed. Nevertheless, as an analysis of the trade and shipping of South Devon indicates, there was still a role for the region's lesser ports to perform.

with the interior became increasingly important. At Teignmouth, for instance, the Haytor Granite Tramway and the Stover Canal were constructed in the late eighteenth century to connect the port with the productive parts of its hinterland.[19] Similarly, the navigable Tamar provided Plymouth with an important inland channel of communication, while granite was conveyed from Dartmoor to Sutton Harbour by a horse-drawn railway opened in 1823.[20] Steam railways, however, had a much greater impact on port growth in South Devon. The two new ports established in the region during the nineteenth century, both operating as joint-stock concerns, depended to a large degree upon physical and financial connections with the railways. Thus, at Millbay in Plymouth, it was the capital of the South Devon Railway Company and the extension of its line to the waterfront in 1848 which explained the rapid growth of business and facilities at the site,[21] while Exmouth Dock was founded in 1864 by a group of 'courageous and far-seeing men' who identified the profitable potential of a river-mouth site linked to Exeter by rail.[22] Similarly, the revival of Sutton Harbour in the 1870s and the emergence of the Cattewater as Plymouth's third major harbour in the 1880s was largely due to the arrival of the London and South Western Railway's line.[23]

Developments in navigation and shipping further affected demands upon the port industry. For example, concern for the safety of ships and seafarers led to widespread navigational improvements. In South Devon this was perhaps best reflected in the construction of Plymouth Breakwater, an Admiralty project which not only enhanced the Sound's utility as a harbour of refuge, but also gave rise to a considerable local trade in the carriage of limestone.[24] Along the coast, obstructions in the approaches to Salcombe Harbour and the Dart were identified and removed in mid-century,[25] and at Brixham a substantial breakwater was started in 1843 though not completed until 1912.[26] Improvements to navigation also resulted from positive attempts to enhance the commercial viability of ports. Thus, the navigational problems posed by the Exe were bypassed to some degree by the extension of Exeter Canal in 1827, while Teignmouth Harbour Commission rendered the Teign more passable by building the Hackney Channel in the 1840s,[27] and 'Squire' Hallet resurrected the decayed port of Axmouth for a while in the 1860s by digging out the ruins of the ancient harbour and erecting a small pier.[28] Of great significance to port development, moreover, was the increase in the size of the average merchant ship. This was particularly marked from the 1860s, when substantial steam-driven vessels were increasingly deployed in the transoceanic trades. With such craft restricted to deep-water sites which offered extensive berthing and cargo-handling facilities, the late nineteenth century witnessed the decline of many ports – especially in terms of foreign trade – which now lacked the physical capacity to handle the typical trading vessel of the day.[29]

Seaborne Trade: Statistical Profile

The level of Britain's seaborne trade increased markedly during the nineteenth century. This was true in terms of value; the aggregate worth of exports rose from £14.1 million in 1790 to £470.9 million in 1913, while imports experienced an increase of similar proportions during the same period.[32] It was also true with respect to the volume of trade. In many ways this was a more accurate measure, for it could be applied to coastal as well as foreign trade, while it indicated the quantity of goods shipped and therefore the level of traffic handled by a port. Such demand intensified during 1789–1910 as the total tonnage of vessels entering British ports from foreign and colonial countries expanded from 1.2 million to 66.7 million tons, a rise broadly mirrored in the tonnage clearing for overseas destinations.[33] Similarly, coastal trade, despite the competition provided by the railways, continued to grow throughout the nineteenth century. Indeed, with tonnage employed expanding at a rate of 1.5 per cent annually, the Victorian period represented a veritable 'golden age' for coastwise transportation in Britain.[34]

South Devon's part in this sustained growth can be gauged from the national returns compiled by the Board of Customs. These data are arranged according to Customs Ports, and offer a thorough account of the volume and character of the shipping engaged in both foreign and coastal trade. Vessels are quantified in terms of their number and tonnage, their ownership, whether British or foreign, and the predominant method of propulsion: sail or steam. Trade is divided into foreign, colonial, and coastal, its direction considered by reference to entrances and clearances into and from particular ports, while its character is treated simply as 'with cargoes and in ballast', 'with cargoes only', or 'in ballast'. Such returns are relatively sparse for the first half of the nineteenth century, especially for the coasting trade, which lacks a port-by-port account between 1796 and 1841, though from 1853 they exist in an annual series. Significant changes in categorisation occurred during this time. In 1824, for instance, vessels entering from, or clearing for, Ireland were reclassified as coastal, as opposed to foreign, traders.[35] In 1873, low-value goods such as chalk, flint and clay were designated as cargo rather than ballast, creating an illusory increase in the coastal trade.[36] In 1907, vessels 'calling off' ports to deliver mail and passengers were considered as entering the port, a recategorisation which rendered Plymouth the fastest-growing British port in the decade

before the First World War,[37] while in 1910 arrivals and departures replaced entrances and clearances in the foreign trade, an accounting change which saw Dartmouth's outward-bound shipping 'increase' in volume from 5,721 tons in 1905 to 847,881 tons in 1913.[38]

In spite of such complexities, a clear outline of the development and distribution of seaborne trade emerges from the returns. Tables 3.1 and 3.2 trace the pattern of South Devon's foreign and coastal trade during the 1789–1913 period. At the regional level it is evident that the aggregate tonnage of vessels entering and clearing South Devon increased absolutely between the 1780s and the First World War, with entrances generally eclipsing clearances by a significant margin. This expansion occurred in both foreign-going and coastwise ship movements, and in terms of 'traffic' handled (vessels with cargoes and in ballast) as well as 'trade' conducted in craft laden with cargoes only. The volume of coastal shipping was substantially greater than that engaged in foreign trade at each of the region's Customs Ports. In 1789, for instance, coastwise entrances with cargoes engaged two-and-a-half times the tonnage entering from overseas, while in 1895 roughly 80 per cent of South Devon's seaborne traffic – entrances and clearances, with cargoes and in ballast – was coastal in orientation. In relative terms, moreover, coastwise shipping was much the more significant of the two branches of the region's seaborne transportation. While foreign-going tonnage progressively diminished as a proportion of the national total during the nineteenth century, South Devon kept pace with the general growth of the English coastal trade throughout the period, reaching a relative peak in 1905, when 5.3 per cent of England's coastwise entrances and 3.4 per cent of clearances were handled at the region's Customs Ports.

There were important differences in the trade patterns of the four South Devon Customs Ports. Plymouth's seaborne commerce expanded considerably during the 1789–1905 period, with foreign-going entrances and clearances increasing by factors of twenty-two and thirty-six respectively, coastal entries displaying a twenty-fold rise, and the volume of shipping clearing coastwise expanding from 7,000 tons in 1789 to 191,300 tons in 1845 and 778,200 tons in 1913. This growth largely accounted for the absolute increase in the volume of South Devon's seaborne trade; Plymouth

Table 3.1

Tonnage entering and clearing South Devon Customs Ports from and for foreign parts, 1789–1905

('000 tons)

a) with cargoes and in ballast, 1789–1905

		Dh	Er	Ph	Th	England & Wales	% South Devon
1789*	Ent	11.8	11.0	14.2	–	1,177.8	3.1
	Cl	10.6	7.5	3.1	–	1,036.7	2.0
1826	Ent	8.8	8.7	44.1	–	2,189.0	2.8
	Cl	10.8	8.6	42.3	–	2,010.1	3.1
1845	Ent	13.3	13.1	55.1	–	5,220.3	1.6
	Cl	16.1	6.1	51.2	–	5,272.8	1.4
1855	Ent	5.9	8.1	74.9	4.1	7,994.8	1.2
	Cl	10.3	3.4	57.6	3.8	8,580.9	0.9
1865	Ent	9.9	12.8	86.6	6.9	12,524.2	0.9
	Cl	7.3	5.8	50.2	6.4	12,914.2	0.5
1875	Ent	10.7	17.8	154.2	4.7	19,485.0	1.0
	Cl	17.0	15.4	99.7	8.4	20,449.5	0.7
1885	Ent	10.1	20.0	240.5	2.5	27,609.4	1.0
	Cl	5.0	10.2	119.4	6.1	28,341.8	0.5
1895	Ent	3.7	17.2	216.2	8.7	34,388.8	0.7
	Cl	24.1	8.0	133.0	13.6	34,797.8	0.5
1905	Ent	2.9	13.3	312.0	13.6	48,376.1	0.7
	Cl	5.7	6.2	113.2	17.8	48,575.8	0.3

* For compatibility with subsequent years, Irish trade is excluded from the 1789 figures.

b) with cargoes only, 1875–1905

		Dh	Er	Ph	Th	England & Wales	% South Devon
1875	Ent	9.1	17.8	151.2	3.9	16,126.6	1.1
	Cl	0.9	0.6	23.4	4.9	17,874.8	0.2
1885	Ent	9.6	20.0	230.0	2.0	21,863.8	1.0
	Cl	0.4	0.3	52.7	5.2	25,725.4	0.2
1895	Ent	3.1	17.2	204.9	7.5	26,862.3	0.9
	Cl	0.2	0.6	79.9	9.2	31,393.9	0.3
1905	Ent	2.7	13.2	307.2	12.0	34,770.3	1.0
	Cl	0.3	0.3	50.0	12.5	42,575.0	0.1

Key to ports: Bm – Brixham;   Dh – Dartmouth;   Er – Exeter;
Ph – Plymouth;   Se – Salcombe;   Th – Teignmouth

Sources: 1789 – PRO, CUST 17/11; 1826 – *Accounts and Papers* (BPP, 1826–7, XVIII, 202); 1845 – *Accounts and Papers* (BPP, 1846, XLV, 307); 1855–65 – *Annual Statements of Trade and Navigation*; 1875–1905 – *Annual Statements of Navigation and Shipping*.

Table 3.2

Tonnage entering and clearing South Devon Customs Ports coastwise, 1789–1913

(with cargoes only; '000 tons)

		Dh	Er	Ph	Th	England & Wales	% South Devon
1789*	Ent	18.2	36.3	39.7	–	2,564.3	3.7
	Cl	7.5	19.9	7.0	–	3,398.3	1.0
1845	Ent	73.9	86.8	284.2	–	10,414.3	4.3
	Cl	16.9	45.4	191.3	–	11,093.8	2.3
1855	Ent	36.8	63.6	362.0	48.9	10,103.8	5.1
	Cl	10.1	9.9	219.0	33.6	10,818.9	2.5
1865	Ent	39.1	58.4	422.0	56.9	11,894.6	4.8
	Cl	23.1	6.9	249.5	7.8	12,684.4	2.3
1875	Ent	48.2	34.0	515.1	48.3	13,883.3	4.7
	Cl	16.9	8.1	344.1	38.8	13,360.0	3.1
1885	Ent	76.7	44.8	602.9	71.3	16,552.9	4.8
	Cl	27.8	14.0	435.0	39.7	16,508.3	3.1
1895	Ent	118.6	47.9	613.1	91.4	18,605.5	4.7
	Cl	16.2	15.8	453.7	87.6	19,158.6	3.0
1905	Ent	115.1	42.6	778.3	94.8	19,360.7	5.3
	Cl	14.7	13.1	590.7	84.4	20,595.9	3.4
1913	Ent	113.0	28.1	778.2	89.3	21,238.1	4.7
	Cl	16.1	6.0	450.3	73.6	22,332.6	2.4

* For compatibility with subsequent years, the 1789 figures include Irish trade originally tabulated with foreign trade.

Key to ports: see Table 3.1

Sources: 1789 – PRO, CUST 17/11; 1845 – *Accounts and Papers* (BPP, 1846, XLV, 307); 1855–65 – *Annual Statements of Trade and Navigation*; 1875–1913 – *Annual Statements of Navigation and Shipping*.

handled 38.4 per cent of the tonnage entering the region from overseas in 1789, and 42.1 per cent of coastal entries, shares which had grown to 91.3 and 75.5 per cent respectively by 1905. Conversely, the traffic handled at Dartmouth, Exeter, and Teignmouth tended to decline in relative terms, though there were notable areas of absolute expansion. Dartmouth's coastal trade, for instance, increased rapidly in the early nineteenth century, entries rising from 18,200 to 68,200 tons between 1789 and 1826.[39] Coastwise shipments into and out of Exeter more than doubled over the same period, and remained buoyant until a steady demise set in during the mid-1840s.[40] Later in the century, a marked expansion was apparent in the level of Dartmouth's coastwise imports, while Teignmouth's foreign trade increased steadily, with the tonnage of vessels clearing with cargoes exceeding that entering – a 'positive' balance unparalleled in the region, save for a brief spell in the early 1820s when a surge occurred in Dartmouth's exports.[41] Teignmouth's coastal trade was also characterised by a high level of clearances relative to entries, while in contrast to the other South Devon ports coasters entering the Teign in ballast outnumbered those clearing unladen.

Intra-regional contrasts were likewise apparent in respect of the vessels engaged in South Devon's trade. In 1900, for instance, over 86 per cent of the tonnage entering Plymouth from overseas was steam-driven, while 91.1 per cent of the port's coastwise entries – compared with the national mean of 82.3 per cent – was similarly powered. Sailing vessels, on the other hand, accounted for 85.9 and 72.6 per cent of the foreign-going tonnage entering Dartmouth and Exeter respectively in 1900, though steamships represented some 81.8 per cent of the coastal shipping entering the Dart. Teignmouth's trade was largely conveyed in steam vessels at this juncture, but there was still a place for sailing craft as almost 40 per cent of entries from abroad and nearly 25 per cent of those in the coastal trade were propelled by the wind. In terms of vessel size, it is clear that the steamships using South Devon's ports were generally much larger than the sailing vessels, the typical foreign-going steamer entering Teignmouth in 1900, for instance, measuring 326.1 tons as against the 113.2 tons of the average sailing vessel. Furthermore, steamships entering Plymouth were, on average, of a greater tonnage than those handled at Dartmouth, Exeter or Teignmouth. Accordingly, the mean Plymouth coaster, at 418.6 tons, was nearly 60 tons larger than its Teignmouth equivalent in 1900, while in the foreign trade the average steamer entering Plymouth measured 511.2 tons, over 150 tons larger than its Exeter counterpart.[42]

It is therefore evident that the volume of South Devon's seaborne trade expanded during the 1789–1913 period; that coastwise shipments were more significant than those to and from overseas, both absolutely and relatively; that inward traffic was generally more important than outward; and that much of the region's trade growth was concentrated at Plymouth, which tended to accommodate larger vessels, and a greater proportion of steamships, than its neighbours. Such a profile reflects broad developments in British trade and shipping activity as well as the nature of the regional economy served by South Devon ports. Foreign trade became increasingly focused on major ports as the Victorian age progressed, a trend apparent, in a local context, in the growing significance of Plymouth. Coastal shipping was more widely dispersed, increasing in volume at lesser harbours such as Dartmouth and Teignmouth as well as at the major ports. There was a clear distinction, however, between the ports serving the relatively productive, industrial areas clustered around the coalfields and those with

rural hinterlands. Whereas clearances vastly outstripped entries at coal ports such as Cardiff, Newport, Newcastle and Sunderland, the reverse was generally true in the more 'peripheral' areas. In the long run, therefore, South Devon's predominant trade flows, as befitting a region experiencing low rates of economic growth relative to the centres of industrial development, were inward and coastal.

Seaborne Trade: Commodities and Directions

The relatively high volume of coastal shipping handled at South Devon ports during the nineteenth century suggests that inter- and intra-regional trade was of greater significance to the local economy than international commerce. Perhaps the most important facet of this buoyant coastal trade was the import of coal, a contention that applied to many other areas of the British Isles distant from the coalfields. For centuries, the spine of this business had been the shipment of coal from northeast England to London. So it remained throughout the nineteenth century, with the capital accounting for 62.6 per cent of the duties paid on coastwise coal imports into England and Wales during 1818, and 61.3 per cent of the coal, by volume, received coastways in 1900.[43] There were various other flows, however. South Walian coal, for instance, not only inspired the rapid growth of exports, both coastal and foreign, from ports such as Cardiff, Newport and Swansea, but also fired a great proportion of hearths, furnaces, and engines on both sides of the Irish Sea. Cumbrian and Scottish coal conveyed through Whitehaven and Maryport, Irvine and Saltcoats, also supplied the extensive west coast and Irish markets, while in east Scotland the coastal trades of Aberdeen and Grangemouth were respectively founded on substantial imports and exports of this steam-age fuel.[44]

The shipment of supplies to the various small- and medium-sized ports in southern England was a further significant dimension of the coastwise coal trade. Devon was prominent in this respect, ranking as the fourth most important county in England and Wales in 1829 – after London, Norfolk and Kent – in terms of the total duty charged on landings of coal, cinders and culm.[45] That the bulk of these imports entered the south of the county is suggested by a similar account for 1818, by which Dartmouth, Exeter and Plymouth together collected just over £30,000 on coals received – 3.4 per cent of the total for England and Wales – as against a sum of nearly £4,000 levied at Barnstaple, Bideford and Ilfracombe.[46] By 1874 this difference had narrowed, with 424,327 tons of coal passing through South Devon's ports and 96,985 tons landed at Barnstaple and Bideford, though, as a proportion of English coal imports, South Devon's aggregate receipts now stood at 6.2

3.4 Coal being discharged from a steam coaster at Beacon Quay, Torquay, c1880. (*Torquay Library*)

per cent.[47] As Table 3.3(a) indicates, this relative level declined slightly in the last quarter of the nineteenth century, despite an absolute increase in the region's coal imports from 449,700 tons in 1870 to 637,700 tons in 1895. In the Edwardian era a faster than average rate of expansion was discernible locally; in 1913, 965,000 tons of coal were handled at South Devon's ports, some 6.3 per cent of English coastal importations.

This long-term expansion was not evenly distributed between the region's ports. Teignmouth's coal imports increased from just over 60,000 tons in 1870 to fluctuate around a mean of approximately 68,000 tons in the subsequent half-century, though a growing proportion was landed at the member port of Torquay.[48] The volume of coal landed in Exeter Customs Port (which included Teignmouth until 1853) more than doubled to just over 64,000 tons between 1784 and 1818, a level of importation that was still evident in the late 1840s.[49] However, from 1870 onwards, with Teignmouth by now 'independent', a downward trend held sway so that in the immediate prewar years less than 30,000 tons of coal were landed annually, most being discharged at Exmouth Dock. Coal imports to the Dart, in contrast, expanded five-fold in the 1870–1913 period. Growth was particularly marked in the 1880s and in the decade prior to the First World War, by which time Dartmouth was England's tenth most significant coal importer. Plymouth ranked higher still, as Table 3.3(b) shows. With coal receipts rising from just under 80,000 tons in 1818[50] to over 280,000 tons in 1870 and 653,000 tons in 1913, the port was consistently among the five leading destinations for coastal colliers throughout the 1870–1913 period.

Table 3.3
Coastwise imports of coal at South Devon Customs Ports, 1870–1913

('000 tons)

a) Coal Received Coastwise, 1870–1913

	Dh	Er	Ph	Th	England & Wales	% South Devon
1870	45.4	61.9	282.3	60.1	7,275.8	6.2
1875	46.3	37.8	352.7	68.4	7,055.1	7.2
1880	55.5	30.8	294.2	79.6	7,736.3	5.9
1885	93.7	39.2	362.0	73.5	8,790.9	6.5
1890	164.8	39.4	397.0	67.6	9,782.6	6.8
1895	150.9	49.8	375.0	62.0	12,719.1	5.0
1900	161.3	32.9	464.3	57.6	13,044.5	5.5
1905	151.7	45.9	520.7	83.0	14,553.6	5.5
1910	176.1	28.9	630.2	70.1	15,334.2	5.9
1913	225.6	29.9	653.8	55.7	15,224.4	6.3

b) Principal English Coal Importing Ports, 1875–1913

	1875			1895			1913	
1	London	3,134.8	1	London	6,856.9	1	London	9,061.2
2	Rochester	457.6	2	Rochester	611.8	2	Southampton	780.2
3	Plymouth	352.7	3	Southampton	462.7	3	Plymouth	653.8
4	Bristol	330.0	4	Plymouth	375.0	4	Rochester	576.5
5	Bridgwater	264.1	5	Portsmouth	302.3	5	Portsmouth	456.0
6	Southampton	219.2	6	Bristol	274.3	6	Bristol	430.2
7	Portsmouth	185.1	7	Liverpool	224.5	7	Liverpool	343.2
8	Hayle	152.1	8	Penzance	215.4	8	Weymouth	282.3
9	Faversham	139.9	9	Bridgwater	213.7	9	Penzance	259.1
10	Liverpool	100.8	10	Faversham	193.0	10	Dartmouth	225.6

Key to ports: see Table 3.1

Sources: *Accounts and Papers* (BPP, 1871, LXII, 13; 1876, LXVIII, 67; 1881, LXXXIII, 133; 1886, LX, 207; 1890–91, LXXVII, 77; 1897, LXXIX, 181; 1902, CXVI (2), 438; 1906, CXXXIV, 953; 1911, CI, 756; 1914–16, LXXX, 730).

Underlying these divergent patterns of coal importation in South Devon were two sets of factors. In the first place, the physical characteristics of the region's ports and their hinterlands in relation to the provision of rival transportation services – determinants which applied to seaborne traffic generally – conditioned the volume of coal landed. Such considerations were especially pertinent to Exeter, where the latent disadvantages of the port's situation became increasingly clear as the nineteenth century progressed. While the utilisation of larger, steam-powered colliers in the last quarter of the century emphasised the navigational difficulties posed by the Exe estuary, the prohibition of such craft from the Exeter Canal until 1880 further isolated the city from its customary seaborne supply of coal, notwithstanding the development of Exmouth Dock. Exeter's coal market, moreover, was vulnerable to competition. Ports with superior facilities and rail linkages were able to supply areas formerly served by the city's coal merchants. Large quantities of coal were shipped across the Bristol Channel to Bridgwater or to Fremington Quay, near Barnstaple, built by the London and South Western Railway in 1855, and thence by rail to consumers in all parts of Somerset and much of Devon.[51] Suppliers in Plymouth and, more especially, Teignmouth, also encroached upon Exeter's hinterland. In 1855, for instance, Crediton Gas Company, Tiverton Gas Company, and consumers in Bradninch and Broadclyst bought coal landed in the Teign.[52]

Direct shipments by rail, which accounted for approximately one-eighth of Devon's supply in 1903,[53] further impinged upon Exeter's coal trade. Richard Bussell, a Topsham coal dealer of long standing, was keenly aware of this fact as early as November 1845, when he advised the Tidal Harbours Commission that

. . . before the Bristol and Exeter railway opened [in 1844] his sale of coals alone amounted to nearly six thousand tons per annum: it is now reduced to one thousand. Used to employ twenty sail of ships a year; navigated, probably, by 150 men. Now five ships, not employing more than 40 men, are sufficient for this trade. The trade of almost all the other coal-dealers is reduced in the same scale.[54]

Secondly, the demand for coal in Devon changed both in degree and in kind during the nineteenth century. Like most other places, the county's fuel requirements increased greatly as the century wore on. In the agrarian sector, large quantities of culm – small, hard pieces of anthracite coal – fired the kilns which produced that ubiquitous fertilizer, lime. Indeed, Devon was the leading importer of culm in 1829,[55] indicating not only the vitality of this branch of the coastal trade, but also the significance of agriculture to the county's economy. The demand for household coal expanded in line with population growth and improvements in the standard of living. Furthermore, the application of steam power to an ever-widening range of production processes stimulated industrial consumption. Coal landed at Plymouth fired the engines deployed in the mines of the Tamar Valley, Teignmouth's imports were purchased by concerns like the Bovey Pottery Company and various clay producers, and Exeter's trade served the town gasworks and the paper mills of the Exe Valley.[56]

While coal had been used in agriculture, home and industry for many centuries, a new source of demand emerged in the second half of the nineteenth century. With steamships forming a rapidly growing part of the tonnage employed in seaborne trade, bunkering depots were established in the major ports and at strategic points along the principal shipping routes. As in so many aspects of its maritime past, Devon's location was highly significant. As the county was adjacent to one of the world's busiest thoroughfares, and in close proximity to the Western Approaches, it was logical that deep-water sites along Devon's English Channel coast should develop coaling facilities for steamers approaching or leaving home waters. Accordingly, Plymouth served as a refuelling station for commercial as well as naval vessels, with more than 10,000 tons of bunker coal shipped in foreign-going merchantmen during 1896.[57] However, Dartmouth emerged as South Devon's principal bunkering port, at least as far as merchant shipping was concerned. From 1868, when three coal hulks were moored in the Dart, until 1914, the supply of fuel to passing steamships represented the port's main 'trade'. Nearly 750 ships called for coal in the peak year of 1890, and even in the depressed year of 1896 some 404 steamers were replenished with 35,108 tons of coal laboriously trans-shipped by gangs of casually-employed 'lumpers' paid at the rate of 2d per ton.[58] Dominated by three firms, Collins, Wiltons, and the Channel Coaling Co, this business explained the idiosyncrasies apparent in Dartmouth's trade statistics. Coal imports accounted for the vast excess of coastwise entrances over clearances from the 1870s, while bunkering led to a marked discrepancy between

3.5   Millbay Docks, Plymouth: the inner basin, *c*1865. (*City of Plymouth Museums & Art Gallery*)

foreign-going 'arrivals' and 'entrances'. In 1910, for example, 535 steamers of 598,313 tons 'arrived', but only five, measuring 1,795 tons, 'entered' the port.[59]

South Devon's coal imports originated largely in South Wales and northeast England. In 1810, for instance, 136 of the 253 shipments discharged in the Bight of the Exe were conveyed from the North East, while a further 106 arrived from South Wales. This balance shifted as the century progressed, with northeastern coal constituting 63, 84 and 88 per cent of the totals trans-shipped in 1830, 1855 and 1860 respectively. Whereas Sunderland had supplied most of Exeter's coal in the late eighteenth and early nineteenth centuries, Newcastle shared the trade by 1830, though both had given way to Teesside by 1860, with Hartlepool and Middlesborough now predominant.[60] Northeastern coal was also ascendant in the Teignmouth market, though Newcastle was chief amongst the ports of despatch here, accounting for four-fifths of the 151 shipments entering the Teign in 1855.[61] Dartmouth and Plymouth relied more heavily upon South Walian supplies of coal and culm. In 1811, for instance, no fewer than 374 vessels, measuring 25,736 tons, cleared Neath for Dartmouth, while a further 61 craft departed Cardiff, Newport and Swansea for the same destination. Twelve years later, 397 vessels left South Wales for Plymouth, the majority – 212 craft of 25,121 tons – clearing from Swansea.[62] With Welsh coal exchanged for the copper ore of the Tamar Valley,[63] and sold from the bunkering hulks moored in the Dart, these lines of supply remained important throughout the nineteenth century.

After coal, the 'London trade' was South Devon's principal inter-regional linkage. A vast range of goods was imported from the Thames, in line with the capital's redistributive role in Britain's coastal trade. In 1855, for instance, thirty shipments were landed at Teignmouth, comprising commodities as diverse as candles and kippers, grease and guano, mahogany and superphosphate.[64] Typically, these cargoes (together with passengers, of course) were carried in vessels engaged solely in the London trade. Such 'constant traders' had long been a feature of the business, suggesting that a high and persistent demand existed for this channel of communication. By 1815, for example, Exeter-bound goods and passengers might be embarked at Beal's, Chamberlain's, or Topping's Wharf, with rival shippers pledging that consignments would depart 'with the utmost dispatch' every fourteen or sixteen days, and pointing out the particular handling or lading qualities of their craft.[65] Price competition was likewise apparent at this juncture, with reductions in freight rates introduced successively at each of the wharves. If this was due largely to the ending of the Napoleonic War – rates had risen in 1803 'in consequence of the great advance of seamens' wages'[66] – it also

reflected the intrinsic worth of the London trade to coastal shipowners. This was generally a high-value, low-bulk business in which speed was of the essence. Accordingly, steamships were introduced into the trade at a relatively early stage, while it was this element of South Devon's inter-regional traffic which shifted rapidly and almost entirely to the railways in the mid-nineteenth century.[67]

South Devon's ports also traded with regions in the western parts of the British Isles. Apart from the flow of coal from South Wales, goods were transported from various ports between the Severn and the Clyde. Liverpool was a notable source of imports. In 1811, for example, some 43 vessels cleared thence for South Devon, while in 1823 the total had risen to 119, with 38 sailing from Plymouth, 21 for Dartmouth, and 60 coasters, measuring 5,622 tons, destined for the Exe.[68] Thirty years later, cargoes of Lancashire coal and Cheshire salt were shipped from the Mersey to South Devon, together with foreign-produced goods such as rice, sugar, tea and timber; consignments which attested to Liverpool's growing entrepôt function.[69] Bristol had assumed a similar role in the eighteenth century, and fifty-eight vessels cleared for South Devon in 1808. However, this figure had not risen by 1823, in contrast to the marked increase in Liverpool clearances, implying that Bristol was losing its place in the coastal trading network of western Britain.[70] South Devon also imported goods by sea from Scotland and Ireland, with shipments arriving occasionally from the Clyde and more frequently from Cork, Youghal and, most especially, Waterford. Dublin, too, maintained strong trading connections with the region, perhaps the most notable being the delivery of porter in 'constant traders' like the *Mary Jane*, which entered Teignmouth from the Liffey four or five times a year in the 1850s.[71]

Intra-regional trade flows formed an important part of South Devon's coastal traffic. Large quantities of goods, chiefly high-bulk, low-value cargoes, were transported by sea 'within' the area, as well as between local ports and others in Dorset, Cornwall, and along the Bristol Channel coast. Indeed, in terms of vessels entering, such trade represented nearly half of Exeter's coastwise shipping in 1804, and over a quarter in 1820,[72] while it formed the most significant facet of Teignmouth's incoming traffic, save for the import of coal.[73] The variety and character of this trade is evident in the cargoes landed at Teignmouth in 1855. Consignments of barley, Portland stone and iron arrived from Dorset; timber, stone and slate were shipped from Torbay, largely on account of the South Devon Railway Company; china clay, bricks and slate were delivered from Charlestown, Penryn and Padstow respectively; while thirty-four vessels, laden mainly with stone, timber and tar, sailed from Plymouth to the Teign, rendering this the most important channel of Teignmouth's intra-regional trade.[74]

Plymouth was similarly the focus of the local trade of many other ports in Devon and Cornwall. This was partly due to the coastwise dissemination of cargoes imported from abroad, an entrepôt role which developed as the West Country's overseas commerce became increasingly concentrated in Plymouth. In South Devon the skewed distribution of foreign trade reflected the long-term decline in activity at Dartmouth and Exeter, as well as the positive advantages accruing from Plymouth's situation. As Table 3.4 indicates, significant changes were apparent in the direction of the region's overseas import trade. In particular, the combined proportion of tonnage entering South Devon from the Iberian peninsula and British North America – areas with which both Dartmouth and Exeter were especially associated in 1789 – fell from 45 to 9.7 per cent during the 1789–1900 period. While Dartmouth's foreign import trade declined precipitously, by 1900 the source of Exeter's incoming traffic – including that of its erstwhile member, Teignmouth – had shifted towards North Europe and France. Plymouth not only extended its linkages with these areas, but also established connections with new sources of imports, a significant volume of shipping entering the port from the Mediterranean, the United States, South America and India.

Such contrasts reflected the broad development of Britain's foreign trade during the nineteenth century. In 1789 Dartmouth and, to a lesser degree, Teignmouth and Exeter, were heavily engaged in the Newfoundland trade. Protected by the Navigation Laws, export-oriented, and dominated by an interest group based in England, this business exhibited the classic hallmarks of the colonial staple of the mercantilist age. For complex historical reasons the trade was centred on the West Country and retained the distinctive migratory pattern which had first developed in the late sixteenth century. Accordingly, vessels departed southwestern ports in the spring, laden with supplies, equipment and labour for the summer fishing season, and returned in the winter months, many with cargoes of wine and fruit which had been exchanged for consignments of dried cod in the markets of southern Europe. However, the migratory basis of the trade

Table 3.4

Origin of vessels entering South Devon Customs Ports from abroad, 1789–1900

(Number of Vessels; tonnage)

		Dh	Ph	Er	Th	% of S Devon Tonnage
North	1789	10–1,068	38–7,882	18–2,487	–	30.9
Europe	1900	12–2,727	165–68,497	33–6,497	32–9,198	33.2
Low	1789	–	2–155	15–823	–	2.6
Countries	1900	–	69–30,375	6–511	4–332	11.9
France	1789	18–1,992	2–222	18–1,485	–	10.0
	1900	3–180	267–20,982	14–1,010	23–1,943	9.2
Channel	1789	3–83	21–975	14–849	–	5.2
Islands	1900	–	56–4,203	1–32	2–116	1.7
Iberia	1789	42–4,550	29–2,872	38–3,204	–	28.7
	1900	1–194	30–13,200	9–1,546	–	5.7
Med'n	1789	3–563	–	1–142	–	1.9
	1900	–	18–17,506	–	–	6.7
USA	1789	2–274	6–712	1–120	–	3.0
	1900	–	18–30,013	–	–	11.5
British	1789	44–3,236	10–1,135	20–1,649	–	16.3
N America	1900	–	14–9,424	10–923	–	4.0
British	1789	–	2–278	2–247	–	1.4
W Indies	1900	–	–	–	–	–
South	1789	–	–	–	–	–
America	1900	–	23–31,565	–	–	12.1
India	1789	–	–	–	–	–
	1900	–	3–7,068	–	–	2.7
Other	1789	–	–	–	–	–
Countries	1900	–	2–3,352	–	–	1.3
Total	1789	122–11,766	110–14,231	127–11,006	–	100.0
	1900	16–3,101	665–236,185	72–10,519	61–11,589	100.0

Key to ports: see Table 3.1.

Sources: 1789 – PRO, CUST 17/11; 1900 – *Annual Statement of Navigation and Shipping.*

collapsed during the 1790s, as the growing resident population of Newfoundland assumed control of the fishery.[75]

Henceforth, South Devon's direct involvement in cod fishing waned. In 1826, for instance, only 28 of the 175 vessels entering British ports from Newfoundland and Labrador landed in Devon and Dorset – 10 at Dartmouth, 7 at Exeter, and 11 at Plymouth – though Poole, with 44 entries, upheld the West Country's interest in the trade.[76] By this stage, few of the craft were actually engaged in catching the cod, the last of South Devon's remaining 'bankers' being withdrawn in the 1830s.[77] The majority were trading vessels, carrying small consignments of Newfoundland produce for sale in the limited West Country market. Typically, in 1855, five vessels – all owned by the firms of Ward and Warren – entered Teignmouth with saltfish, salmon and skins from Labrador,[78] while in 1865 the *Lottery* shipped fish, skins and oil from Labrador to Dartmouth.[79] The trade was by now largely focused on London, Greenock and Liverpool – already, in 1826, thirty-one vessels had entered the Mersey from Newfoundland – with South Devon shipowners supplying some of the carrying tonnage employed.

This gravitation towards the major ports was a significant characteristic of Britain's imports in the nineteenth century. Closely related to this concentration of activity was the increasing deployment of larger, steam-propelled vessels in a widening range of trades as the Victorian age progressed. In a West Country context, Plymouth's development epitomised these trends. Because of its relatively modern, deep-water dock facilities, it was here that large steamships delivered cargoes of food and raw materials from all parts of Europe and, significantly, from primary producing countries in the Americas. In 1900, timber from Scandinavia was chief amongst these imports, with grain from the Black Sea region, Argentina and the United States, refined sugar from the Low Countries, and petroleum from eastern Europe all landed in substantial quantities. Together with fruit, hemp, metals, nitrates, wine and the sundry other goods which passed through Plymouth, these commodities represented 85 per cent of South Devon's foreign imports, by value, in 1900.[80] Although it constituted but a small fraction of total English imports, the nature and source of South Devon's incoming traffic exemplified the way in which British overseas trade had changed over the previous century. Whereas commercial enterprise had been channelled into protected, colonial staples like the Newfoundland cod trade, increasingly it operated in a 'free trade' environment with all parts of the globe. Essentially, a regulated Atlantic system had given way to an unfettered international economy.

Similar conclusions can be drawn from the pattern of South Devon's foreign clearances. In 1789, as Table 3.5 shows, the great majority of vessels clearing the region's ports were bound for British North America, nearly all departing for Newfoundland in the spring and early summer months. Although the migratory fishery had just passed its peak, some 321 British vessels still crossed the Atlantic with supplies and labour for the cod-fishing season.[81] No fewer than 164 of these ships left South Devon, with almost one-third of the entire fleet sailing from Dartmouth alone. Rapid decline was to beset this ancient fishing operation in the 1790s, however, and soon the principal British interest in the fishery lay in the supply of provisions and manufactures to Newfoundland's growing population, and the transportation of cod caught and processed by the islanders. With this structural shift, South Devon's role in the industry altered significantly. Increasingly unable to compete with the industrial districts in the production and delivery of cheap supplies, the region's principal Newfoundland interest centred on the conveyance of saltfish, a carrying trade imperceptible in Tables 3.4 and 3.5. Direct sailings for the 'oldest colony' therefore diminished. In 1826, for instance, only 35 of the 282 vessels clearing the British Isles for Newfoundland and Labrador departed from South Devon – 15 from Dartmouth, 12 from Exeter, and 8 from Plymouth – while 99 now departed Liverpool, compared with only 5 in 1789.[82] By 1900, a trade which had engaged 70.9 per cent of the tonnage leaving South Devon's ports in 1789 accounted for just 3 per cent.

In the long term, this shift affected Dartmouth more than the other South Devon ports. Clearances from the Dart had fallen to nearly one-third of their 1789 level by 1900, though in this period it was Darmouth and its creeks of Brixham and Salcombe which participated most vigorously in the carrying

Table 3.5
Destination of vessels clearing South Devon Customs Ports for foreign parts, 1789–1900

(Number of Vessels; tonnage)

		Dh	Ph	Er	Th	% of S Devon Tonnage
North	1789	–	–	2–178	–	0.8
Europe	1900	5–1,254	101–31,376	4–1,162	20–3,056	24.5
Low	1789	5–271	1–65	11–479	–	3.9
Countries	1900	–	50–10,357	1–79	43–5,890	10.9
France	1789	4–209	1–67	2–197	–	2.2
	1900	6–767	194–15,092	9–436	12–828	11.4
Channel	1789	1–28	18–637	6–264	–	4.4
Islands	1900	6–743	163–17,299	25–2,952	4–231	14.1
Iberia	1789	7–621	1–115	12–812	–	7.3
	1900	26–15,636	30–9,063	–	10–1,738	17.6
Med'n	1789	1–83	–	6–623	–	3.4
	1900	–	9–2,977	–	5–1,691	3.1
USA	1789	1–150	3–474	1–120	–	3.5
	1900	–	12–20,239	–	1–349	13.7
British	1789	100–9,211	10–973	54–4,781	–	70.9
N America	1900	1–194	11–3,810	5–519	–	3.0
British	1789	–	3–757	–	–	3.6
W Indies	1900	–	–	–	1–229	0.2
Central	1789	–	–	–	–	–
America	1900	–	1–321	–	–	0.2
South	1789	–	–	–	–	–
America	1900	–	1–1,268	–	–	0.9
Other	1789	–	–	–	–	–
Countries	1900	–	2–693	–	–	0.4
Total	1789	119–10,573	37–3,088	94–7,454	–	100.0
	1900	44–18,594	574–112,495	44–5,148	96–14,012	100.0

Key to ports: see Table 3.1.

Sources: 1789 – PRO, CUST 17/11; 1900 – *Annual Statement of Navigation and Shipping*.

trades. Exeter, too, experienced a decline in clearances, though it was less marked than Table 3.5 suggests, for the creek of Teignmouth was counted in the 1789 figure. In contrast, the number of ships outward bound from the Teign undoubtedly increased during the 1789–1900 period, while the volume of traffic departing from Plymouth expanded vastly, with vessels clearing for a growing range of destinations in northwest Europe, the Mediterranean and the Americas, pointing once more to the increasingly widespread character of British overseas trade in the nineteenth century.

Underlying these patterns, of course, was the production of export commodities in South Devon. As Table 3.1(b) indicates, the volume of goods shipped overseas from Dartmouth and Exeter was both marginal and declining in the late nineteenth century, a pattern repeated in Table 3.2 with respect to coastwise clearances. Hence it would appear that the hinterlands of the two ports were relatively unproductive, at least in terms of the cargoes most economically transported by sea. In essence, this implies that the handicraft which filled the holds of Dartmouth's Newfoundlandmen with fishing equipment, clothes and provisions, and Exeter's wool traders with serges and kerseys throughout the eighteenth century, were neither supplanted by more efficient local manufacturers nor succeeded by producers of industrial raw materials. In contrast, as Tables 3.1(b) and 3.2 suggest, the foreign and coastwise export business of both Plymouth and Teignmouth tended to increase during the nineteenth century. While neither served a buoyant manufacturing sector, that other dynamic element of Britain's seaborne commerce in the industrial age, the shipment of bulky, low-value commodities, was the predominant factor in the export trade of both ports.

Indeed, in Teignmouth's case, it was virtually the only factor, for clay extracted from the Bovey Basin and carried by barge down the Stover Canal and the Teign estuary was overwhelmingly the port's staple export commodity. In 1911–13, for instance, clay to the value of £21,159 per annum was shipped overseas from the Teign, whereas the aggregate worth of 'all other articles' exported was just £71 per annum.[83] Most of this clay was carried to Belgium, Holland and Germany, with consignments despatched to Scandinavia, the Iberian peninsula and, occasionally, the United States.[84] However, a much greater volume was shipped coastwise. For example, some 334 shipments were despatched in coasters during 1854, as against 17 in foreign-going vessels, the most common destinations being the Thames Estuary, the Mersey and northeast England. Over the next fifty years the focus of the trade tended to shift away from London and the North East, with the Mersey and West Scotland receiving 173 of Teignmouth's 289 coastal clay shipments in 1910.[85] In contrast, a variety of export cargoes passed through Plymouth. Copper, lead, manganese and other ores extracted from the mines of the Tamar Valley were shipped out in large quantities, chiefly to South Wales, during the mid-nineteenth century; stone from the quarries of Dartmoor and the St German's River district was transported by sea, mainly to nearby, intra-regional destinations; while clay

3.6   View of the entrance to the Teign, with Teignmouth to the right, from an aquatint by Henry Haseler, 1818. (*Ian Cook*)

from Lee Moor, 'arms, ammunition and military stores' (presumably from the Dockyard) and miscellaneous manufactured products formed Plymouth's principal overseas exports in the early twentieth century.[86]

These export trades only partially offset the flow of imports into South Devon. Accordingly, a negative balance in the region's seaborne trade account was apparent throughout the nineteenth century.[87] This was particularly marked with respect to inter-regional commerce as the importation of coal proved to be the most dynamic element in the region's coastal trade. Internationally, South Devon's visible balance of trade was also negative, reflecting, in part, long-term changes in the woollen industry and the Newfoundland trade – the area's principal export-oriented interests until the late eighteenth century. Whereas the former experienced absolute decline, South Devon's commercial relationship with Newfoundland adjusted, with direct participation in the fishery giving way to the conveyance of the island's saltfish. Thus, South Devon's shipping industry generated income from this and related carrying trades, invisible earnings which alleviated the region's adverse trade account.

South Devon's Shipping Industry

The British shipping industry was transformed in scale and character between 1786 and 1914, though the pace of change was uneven. Stimulated by high wartime freight rates and rising demand from the manufacturing sector, the industry expanded during the 1793–1815 wars. It then experienced relative stagnation in the 1820s and 1830s, before entering a period of sustained growth which lasted from the 1840s until the First World War. Iron hulls and steam power, though introduced in the first quarter of the century, were not widely adopted until much later, and it was 1883 before the gross tonnage of steamships exceeded that of sailing craft. Thereafter, the transition to steam was rapid and irreversible. Such change was generally associated with concentration in the industry, both in terms of ownership, with the emergence of the highly capitalised 'big' business unit, and in respect of spatial distribution, with the accelerating increase in tonnage registered at London, Liverpool, Glasgow and other major ports.[88] In areas of less dynamic economic growth, shipowning remained a common feature of the local maritime economy, though here the industry followed a different developmental path to that evident in the major ports, a divergence which became more pronounced as the nineteenth century progressed.

South Devon's shipping industry illustrates this point. As Table 3.6 indicates, the tonnage registered in the region's registry ports increased steadily from 33,600 tons in 1795 to a peak of 115,400 tons in 1865. Over the next 25 years, registrations declined to the extent that only 61,800 tons of shipping were owned in South Devon in 1890, though a reversal of this trend meant that a total of 584 vessels, measuring 109,800 net tons, was registered in the region's six ports in 1913. In relative terms, ship registrations in South Devon tended to keep pace with the expansion of the English shipping industry during the 1790–1860 period, the local fleet representing between 2.6 and 3.8 per cent of the nation's registered tonnage. Thereafter, a clear lag was evident, South Devon's shipping representing just 1 per cent of the total fleet in 1895, a proportion which rose slightly to 1.2 per cent in 1913. At the individual ports, shipowning generally reached its height in the third quarter of the nineteenth century, with peaks in tonnage owned evident at Exeter in 1855, Dartmouth in 1860, Teignmouth in 1865, Salcombe in 1875 and slightly later at Brixham, in 1880. In each case there ensued a precipitous decline in registrations during the half-century or so before the First World War. Plymouth's fleet also followed this pattern, as a ten-fold increase in the tonnage registered between 1790 and 1865 preceded a sharp contraction, with only 32,300 tons owned in the port in 1885. Registrations then resumed an upward course, peaking at 95,700 tons in 1913, when Plymouth accounted for 87.2 per cent of the tonnage registered in South Devon.

These figures require qualification on two counts. In the first place, changes in the designation of registry ports depressed registrations at Exeter and Dartmouth. Nineteen vessels were transferred from Exeter to Teignmouth in 1853–5, the first three years of the 'new' port's existence, while Dartmouth's fleet was likewise depleted by defections to Salcombe from

Table 3.6

Tonnage registered at South Devon Registry Ports, 1790–1913

('000 tons)

	Bm	Dh	Er	Ph	Se	Th	Total South Devon	England & Wales	% South Devon
1790	–	17.2	12.9	5.9	–	–	36.0	1,040.2	3.5
1795	–	13.9	13.2	6.5	–	–	33.6	1,207.9	2.8
1800	–	11.2	12.4	14.8	–	–	38.4	1,466.6	2.6
1805	–	17.3	19.0	19.5	–	–	55.8	1,799.2	3.1
1827	–	24.9	18.0	23.9	–	–	66.8	1,752.4	3.8
1841	–	28.8	17.3	29.1	–	–	75.2	2,223.9	3.4
1845	–	30.0	17.3	31.1	–	–	78.4	2,354.4	3.3
1850	–	33.7	18.4	41.8	–	–	93.9	2,721.3	3.5
1855	–	32.7	23.1	42.0	–	6.2	104.0	3,449.8	3.0
1860	–	43.4	18.6	45.7	–	6.8	114.5	3,709.6	3.1
1865	6.5	29.1	14.5	52.5	4.2	8.6	115.4	4,653.8	2.5
1870	14.2	19.4	11.8	43.6	11.5	5.5	106.0	4,463.2	2.4
1875*	18.6	12.3	10.5 (7.1)	42.4	15.0	5.8	104.6 (101.2)	4,692.2	2.2 (2.2)
1880*	19.4	8.0	8.0 (4.7)	35.3	14.9	4.3	89.9 (86.6)	4,839.1	1.9 (1.8)
1885*	15.0	4.2	7.0 (3.8)	32.3	12.5	2.6	73.6 (70.4)	5,405.1	1.4 (1.3)
1890	13.4	3.0	2.4	35.3	5.4	2.3	61.9	5,796.4	1.1
1895	11.4	1.7	1.7	45.9	2.7	2.3	65.7	6,425.0	1.0
1900	9.8	1.6	1.5	55.4	2.1	2.1	72.5	6,780.3	1.1
1905	9.3	3.0	1.4	75.8	2.1	2.8	94.4	7,979.8	1.2
1910	8.4	2.9	1.0	89.5	1.9	2.6	106.3	8,497.2	1.3
1913**	7.6	3.1	0.8	95.7 (9.3)	1.0	1.6	109.8 (23.4)	8,867.8	1.2 (0.3)

* Steamships belonging to John Holman & Sons omitted from figures in brackets.

** Steamships belonging to the New Zealand Shipping Company omitted from figures in brackets.

Key to ports: see Table 3.1.

Sources: 1790–1805 – PRO, CUST 17/12, 17, 22, 27; 1827 – *Accounts and Papers* (BPP, 1828, XIX, 590–1); 1841 – *Accounts and Papers* (BPP, 1843, LII, 375); 1845 – *Accounts and Papers* (BPP, 1846, XLV, 307); 1850 – *Accounts and Papers* (BPP, 1851, LII, 213); 1855–1870 – *Annual Statements of Trade and Navigation*; 1875–1913 – *Annual Statements of Navigation and Shipping*.

1863, and Brixham from 1864 – thirty-one of the first fifty-four registrations at Brixham, for instance, being transferred in from Dartmouth.[89] Secondly, the registration of a vessel in a port did not necessarily mean that her owners resided or operated in that particular locality. Accordingly, Devonians sometimes registered their vessels out of the county, E H R Moon of Plymouth, for instance, being nominated as the managing owner of the *England's Glory*, a 751-ton vessel entered on the London register in 1869. However, this appears to have been a rare occurrence.[90] On the other hand, the volume of 'foreign-owned' shipping registered in Devon was substantial enough to distort seriously the tonnages presented in Table 3.6. John Holman & Sons of Topsham, for instance, continued to register its fleet at Exeter in the 1870s and 1880s, even though its business was based at London by that time and its steamers were too large to enter its home port.[91] While this nostalgic practice accounted for 53.8 per cent of the tonnage registered at Exeter in 1885, a more notable distortion occurred at Plymouth, where the New Zealand Shipping Company, which embarked passengers at the port, began registering its vessels in 1890. By 1913, 17 of the Company's steamers, measuring 86,379 tons, were registered at Plymouth, exposing the illusory nature of the port's (and the region's) shipowning revival in the 1890s and the 1900s.[92] When these vessels are excluded, a more realistic account of the local shipping industry emerges; with Plymouth's fleet now reduced to 9,300 tons, only 23,400 tons of shipping were owned in South Devon in 1913, 0.3 per cent of the national total.

Between 1790 and 1913, therefore, shipowning in South Devon's ports followed a uniform pattern, expanding broadly in line with the national trend until the 1860s, and then entering a period of steep and sustained contraction. This rise and fall was related to the composition of the region's fleet. Quite clearly, as Table 3.7 indicates, local shipowners tended to invest in relatively small vessels, the average tonnage at each port being consistently lower than the national mean. In 1790 the typical South Devon

Table 3.7

Average tonnage of vessels registered at South Devon Registry Ports, 1790–1913

	Bm	Dh	Er	Ph	Se	Th	South Devon	England & Wales
1790	–	59.9	86.3	53.3	–	–	65.5	112.8
1805	–	58.2	81.1	66.2	–	–	67.5	121.7
1827	–	71.5	88.9	86.7	–	–	80.8	120.9
1845	–	66.9	95.0	79.6	–	–	76.8	131.8
1855	–	84.5	127.0	99.3	–	131.2	100.1	176.0
1865	120.6	90.2	114.2	118.6	167.6	114.3	110.3	209.3
1875*	99.7	81.6	135.8 (97.2)	116.1	202.1	121.6	116.0 (112.7)	237.1
1885*	67.4	56.1	149.0 (75.1)	87.4	173.8	107.1	90.8 (87.3)	293.2
1895	43.4	29.3	59.8	133.3	78.5	111.8	87.8	391.6
1905	36.4	43.0	60.2	251.9	75.8	120.6	134.7	492.5
1913**	34.3	53.4	46.1	387.5 (40.6)	46.6	90.1	188.1 (41.4)	554.2

* Steamships belonging to John Holman & Sons omitted from figures in brackets.

** Steamships belonging to the New Zealand Shipping Company omitted from figures in brackets.

Key to ports: see Table 3.1.

Sources: 1790–1805 – PRO, CUST 17/12, 27; 1827 – *Accounts and Papers* (BPP, 1828, XIX, 590–1); 1845 – *Accounts and Papers* (BPP, 1846, XLV, 307); 1855–1870 – *Annual Statements of Trade and Navigation*; 1875–1913 – *Annual Statements of Navigation and Shipping*.

Table 3.8

Steam tonnage as a percentage of total registrations at South Devon Registry Ports, 1841–1913

	Bm	Dh	Er	Ph	Se	Th	South Devon	England & Wales
1841	–	0.1	0.1	1.0	–	–	0.4	2.7
1845	–	0	0.1	1.7	–	–	0.7	3.3
1850	–	0.1	0	0.8	–	–	0.4	4.0
1855	–	0.1	0	1.0	–	0.3	0.4	7.9
1860	–	0.3	0.2	1.3	–	0.3	0.7	9.1
1865	0	1.0	0.1	0.8	0	0.2	0.6	13.6
1870	0	1.3	0.1	1.4	0	0.4	0.9	19.2
1875*	0	2.5	32.3 (0.3)	1.7	0.2	0.4	4.3 (1.1)	31.5
1880*	0	2.7	28.5 (0.1)	2.3	1.5	0.5	4.0 (1.4)	42.6
1885*	8.8	7.4	54.5 (1.4)	11.9	2.2	0.9	13.0 (8.3)	55.8
1890	7.7	25.2	35.6	38.9	5.4	19.2	27.6	66.0
1895	1.1	26.2	13.3	61.5	8.0	50.3	46.3	71.9
1900	0	32.5	16.6	74.3	6.8	47.7	59.3	80.8
1905	0	69.4	17.9	84.8	6.5	59.1	72.5	86.7
1910	0.2	74.8	24.6	90.1	8.7	80.1	80.2	91.1
1913**	1.0	84.4	33.1	92.6 (24.3)	13.3	68.7	84.5 (27.5)	92.9

* Steamships belonging to John Holman & Sons omitted from figures in brackets.

** Steamships belonging to the New Zealand Shipping Company omitted from figures in brackets.

Key to ports: see Table 3.1.

Sources: 1841 – *Accounts and Papers* (BPP, 1843, LII, 375); 1845 – *Accounts and Papers* (BPP, 1846, XLV, 307); 1850 – *Accounts and Papers* (BPP, 1851, LII, 213); 1855–1870 – *Annual Statements of Trade and Navigation*; 1875–1913 – *Annual Statements of Navigation and Shipping*.

vessel measured 65.5 tons, as against the average of 112.8 tons current in the English mercantile marine, craft registered at Exeter being generally larger than those belonging to Dartmouth and Plymouth. During the next half-century these differentials remained roughly intact, though the gap between average tonnage nationally and in South Devon narrowed slightly, reflecting the growing number and mean size of vessels registered at Plymouth. Thereafter, national and regional trends began to diverge. Between 1845 and 1865 there was a rise in average tonnage at each of the South Devon ports, though the rate of increase was slower than that pertaining in the English merchant fleet as a whole. This was but a prelude to a long period in which the average tonnage of the region's fleet declined sharply, a decline fully apparent if the 'foreign-owned' vessels belonging to John Holman & Sons of London and the New Zealand Shipping Company are omitted from the registration figures. In marked contrast, the typical unit of the English mercantile marine increased from 209.3 to 554.2 tons between 1865 and 1913.

The adoption of the steamship underpinned this divergence. Throughout the 1841–1913 period, as Table 3.8 shows, a relatively small proportion of South Devon's fleet was steam-powered. Significantly, in the 1860s and 1870s, when the region's shipping stock, and the average tonnage of its constituent vessels, began to decline, steamers were introduced into the local fleet at a much slower rate than that apparent in the shipping industry at large, particularly if the Holman fleet (of Exeter in name only) is disregarded. During these critical decades less than 1.5 per cent of the region's shipping was driven by steam, whereas nationally the proportion expanded from 9.1 to 42.6 per cent. South Devon's shipowners remained reluctant to embrace the new technology as their industry continued to contract in the decades before 1914. Accordingly, in 1913 (again, excluding the vessels of the New Zealand Shipping Company) only 139 steamships, measuring 6,461 tons and representing just 0.08 per cent of English steam tonnage, were registered in South Devon.

Such reluctance to invest in steamers was not so much an entrepreneurial failure on the part of the region's shipowners as a realistic appraisal of the comparative advantages pertaining in the late-nineteenth-century shipping industry. Indeed, until the final quarter of the century, South Devon's shipping entrepreneurs had generally responded positively to current trends. In the 1850s and 1860s, when improvements in ship design and the quality of sails, ropes and other materials facilitated a general increase in the size of sailing vessels, there had been no shortage of local investment in larger, more efficient craft. In 1851, for instance, the Dartmouth schooners *Eliza* and *Era* were lengthened to 77.6ft and 92.6ft respectively and fitted

with an innovatory third mast.[93] At the other end of the tonnage market, the great sailing ships and barques currently being deployed in the transoceanic trades were introduced into the region's fleet.[94] George Hennet of Teignmouth, for instance, purchased the *Harriet*, a full-rigged ship of 925 tons; John Holman & Sons, before its move to London, built and operated vessels such as the *Hugh Fortescue*, a 505-ton barque; while at Plymouth large wooden craft were common, with ships of over 1,000 tons such as the *Utinia*, the *Princess Royal* and the *Old England* owned and registered in the port.[95] Such vessels, moreover, were deployed in the expanding sectors of the freight market, the *Hugh Fortescue* carrying passengers from London to Adelaide, the *Zephyrus* of Plymouth taking coal from Shields to Bombay, where rice was loaded,[96] and the *Harriet* entering London from Foo-Choo-Foo with a cargo of tea.[97]

However, steamships were a very different proposition. Generally larger than sailing vessels, they consumed much greater quantities of capital, both in construction and in operation. Manifestly the products of the industrial age, they were therefore built in areas where the coal, iron and engineering industries were located; and they required deep-water ports with extensive cargo- and ship-handling facilities. South Devon's shipowners were largely unable to compete in these respects. Based in relatively small, import-oriented ports and operating in a region which was not only distant from the major shipbuilding centres but also experiencing comparatively slow rates of capital accumulation, the local shipping industry was hardly well sited to experiment with steam propulsion.[98] Accordingly, in the late nineteenth century, as the steamship became ever more efficient and prevalent, the region's shipowners tended to pursue one of three main courses. Some flowed with the tide and, like the Annings, the Holmans and the Reardon Smiths, shifted their shipping interests to more advantageous locations such as Cardiff, Liverpool and London. Others simply retired from the business and ventured their capital in different forms of enterprise. And there were Devonians who continued to invest in the local shipping industry, seeking to exploit the distinct, if limited, comparative advantages they themselves held in particular areas of the tonnage market.

Locational attributes, for example, persuaded owners of various substantial yachts to base their vessels in the region's ports. The *Pelican*, a schooner of 58 tons, and the 23-ton cutter-rigged *Veronica* were just two of the yachts

3.7   Venison Tickle, Labrador. A tickle is a sheltered passage between an island and the mainland which can be used as a harbour. Cod is drying on the flakes. There are several local two-masters, while a big three-master is lying loading. (*Public Archives of Newfoundland*)

which formed a growing proportion of Dartmouth registrations from the late 1870s, both spending the summer months of 1878 'cruising for pleasure'.[99] Though not operated for profit, such craft generated local income and employment. The *Patricia*, a 15-ton cutter, was built in Dartmouth and in 1881 sailed to Genoa, 'and then on a Yachting cruise for five months or more', worked by a four-man crew which included three able seamen from South Devon.[100] A somewhat marginal element of the shipping industry, these leisure craft nevertheless signalled future developments in Devon's maritime economy.

The most important facet of South Devon's fleet, however, was deployed in home waters and in certain of the carrying trades of the North Atlantic. In these areas, the region's shipowners could compete successfully, even in the late nineteenth and early twentieth centuries. This was because of – not despite – the nature of their shipping stock, which not only proved well-suited to the delivery of bulky, low-value cargoes to the minor ports and coastal communities of the South West, but was also adept at the collection and conveyance of small consignments of fish or fruit from the bays and creeks of Newfoundland, Labrador, the West Indies and southern Europe. The vessels at the heart of these trades were fore-and-aft rigged and therefore able to sail close to the wind, which rendered them highly manoeuvrable and relatively swift. Ranging in size from around 40 tons to nearly 200 tons, this 'class' in fact comprised a variety of vessel types, the most common being the two-masted schooner and the ketch. Although these 'merchant schooners' were by no means exclusive to South Devon – many so-called 'Western Ocean Yachts' operated from North Wales, for instance[101] – their association with the region was probably longer and stronger than with any other British maritime district.

South Devon's long-standing Newfoundland interest was central to the diffusion and deployment of the schooner.[102] By the late eighteenth century the fore-and-aft rig was prevalent in the coastal waters of North America. At this time, of course, South Devon's historic involvement in the Newfoundland fishery was reaching its climax, with over 160 vessels departing the region for the 1789 cod-fishing season (see Table 3.5). Links with the island were also reflected in the composition of local fleets. At Exeter, for instance, 9 of the 140 craft registered in 1786–8 had been built

in Newfoundland, including 3 of the 6 schooners belonging to a fleet dominated by small, single-masted sloops and square-rigged brigs and brigantines. By 1810 a further 51 schooners had been registered at the port, 13 of these having been built in Newfoundland and transferred from the registry at St John's.[103] Familiarity with the island and its shipping was perhaps more of an influence on the composition of the mercantile marine at Dartmouth, one of the main foci of the transatlantic fishery. Although the port's early register books have not survived, it is clear that schooners formed a substantial part of the tonnage owned at Dartmouth in the early nineteenth century. When legislation passed in 1823 required the re-registration of all British ships, 141 of the 336 vessels registered at Dartmouth were schooner-rigged, many having operated from the port and its creeks of Brixham and Salcombe since the 1790s and early 1800s.[104] While such craft were less common in Plymouth's fleet, 47 of the 185 craft registered in 1824–5 being schooners,[105] there can be little doubt that the schooner rig permeated South Devon's shipping industry much earlier than in other parts of the country, again giving the lie to any notion that the region's shipowners were inherently conservative.

For the next forty years or so the schooner was the predominant vessel type in South Devon's shipping stock, though sloops and cutters, brigs and brigantines, ships and barques, as well as the occasional steamer, continued to feature in the region's fleet. In 1855–6, when locally-owned tonnage was approaching its peak, there were 41 schooners amongst the 133 additions to South Devon's fleet – 12 at Dartmouth, 8 at Exeter, 15 at Plymouth, and 6 at Teignmouth – while in 1864–5, 34 of the first 54 vessels registered at Brixham were schooner-rigged. New investment in schooners declined during the 1870s, however. In 1878–9, for example, such craft represented only two of thirty-nine registrations at Brixham, one of the five made at Exeter, and six of the forty-one added to Plymouth's fleet, while at Dartmouth and Teignmouth no schooners were registered during these two years. A range of smaller craft was added to the shipping stock instead, with luggers, ketches and smacks measuring between 15 and 80 tons dominating new registrations at Plymouth, ketches of 70 to 80 tons preponderant at Dartmouth, and 30- to 40-ton cutters representing the most common addition to Brixham's fleet.[106]

These wooden sailing vessels found employment in a range of trades. Some were deployed as fishing vessels, exploiting local waters 'off the south coast of Devon', 'off the port of Plymouth', or 'between Start Point and Land's End', or else were despatched to work off southern Ireland and South Wales, or, more frequently, to trawl in the North Sea.[107] Known locally as 'dandies', these trawling craft were cutters or ketches equipped with a lug-rigged mizzen, or sometimes a gaff sail, a large number eventually being transferred to the registers at Grimsby and Hull.[108] Cutters and ketches were also deployed in local, intra-regional trades. At Exeter, 'stone' boats such as the *Friend's Goodwill*, the *Mulberry* and *Stag*, all cutters of 76 tons owned by S B Davy of Countess Wear and engaged in the carriage of limestone from the quarries at Berry Head to the Exe,[109] formed a regular part of the port's nineteenth-century fleet. Similarly, a large number of Plymouth's smaller craft were employed in various short-distance trades. The *Agnes* and the *Elizabeth*, for instance, carried regular shipments of limestone to Salcombe, while the *Flower*, the *Speedwell* and the *Pantaloon* sailed to and from Falmouth, Truro or Looe with miscellaneous cargoes, and the *Friendship* was simply employed in 'coasting and barging between the ports of Exeter, Plymouth and Dartmouth'.[110]

More significantly, perhaps, many of the region's sailing vessels operated in the home and international carrying trades. Coastwise, this generally involved some participation in South Devon's expansive coal import trade. In 1869, for instance, the *Perseverance*, a 76–ton schooner registered in Exeter though owned by John Roeby of Plymouth, made seven coastal voyages, leaving Plymouth for Shields, Newport or Cardiff in ballast and running with coal.[111] Similarly, the *Tavy*, a 69-ton ketch belonging to John Bayley of Plymouth, returned from South Wales with coal on three occasions in 1871, though she secured cargoes of timber for the outward voyages.[112] Limestone was also shipped out of Plymouth in schooners like the 79-ton *Peter and John*, which was 'constantly employed from Plymouth to Britonferry with coals and limestone' in 1878, and subsequently engaged in 'coasting regularly from Plymouth to Neath with stones, and from Neath to Plymouth with culm'.[113] At Teignmouth, of course, clay filled the holds of vessels like the *Carthaginian*, a 146-ton brig which sailed to Glasgow, Swansea and Seaham in 1871, carrying coal back on each occasion.[114]

Such craft sometimes mixed both home- and foreign-trade voyages according to the state of the freight market. In 1869, for instance, the *Promise*, a three-masted schooner registered in Exeter, proceeded from Guernsey to London with a cargo of stone, 'thence to one of the Coal Ports in the North to load for a port in the Channel', and, later in the year, from

3.8   The last British schooner to sail in the Newfoundland trade was the *Lady St Johns*, built at Kingsbridge in 1898. She made her last passage in the trade in 1930. This photograph shows her lying in St John's, Newfoundland, in the 1920s. (*Public Archives of Newfoundland*)

London to the Baltic to pick up a cargo of timber for Plymouth.[115] Likewise, in the early 1870s, the 139-ton schooner *S R & H*, belonging to G P Ward of Teignmouth, spent the early part of the year in the clay and coal trades before sailing from the Tyne for Cadiz and St John's, Newfoundland.[116] A similar employment pattern was pursued by the *Lady Mary* of Salcombe; though the foci of her coastal deployment were Ipswich, London and South Wales, she, too, made regular voyages between Cadiz or Madeira and St John's.[117]

In shuttling back and forth across the North Atlantic, the *S R & H*, the *Lady Mary* and many other South Devon sailing vessels were prosecuting a business which was directly descended from the ancient Newfoundland trade. Over a century before the *Lady Mary* was lost when bound for St John's in 1881, the more astute of Devon's fishing merchants, anticipating the collapse of the migratory fishery, had cultivated the service facets of the business, supplying the island with provisions, equipment, and credit, and transporting to market the saltfish produced by the islanders. In essence,

3.9   The schooner *Brooklands*, ex *Susan Vittery*, built at Dartmouth in 1859 for the soft fruit trade from the Azores and subsequently employed in the Newfoundland trade. Built as a two-masted schooner and re-rigged as a three-master at the turn of the century in order to save on crew costs, the vessel as shown in this photograph has been reduced further in rig in her old age. In her early years as a three-master her gaff sails were longer in the hoist, her topmasts taller and her gaff topsails bigger in area, and she set a third squaresail on the fore topmast. (*H Oliver Hill*)

the carrying part of this relationship survived throughout the nineteenth century and was still conducted, on a much reduced scale, after the First World War.[118] In due course, like other former colonial staples, the trade opened out, with vessels from others ports, as well as from Europe and Newfoundland itself, competing in what had been a West Country preserve.

At the same time, West Country shipowners diversified their interests, deploying their merchant schooners – which owed their origins to the Newfoundland connection – in other, closely-related trades. In particular, from the 1820s and 1830s, South Devon schooners were increasingly deployed in the carriage of fruit from the Azores, the Iberian peninsula and the eastern Mediterranean to the burgeoning urban markets served by London and Liverpool. Originating as the final leg of the 'triangular' voyages undertaken by the archetypal Newfoundland trader, this business developed into a distinctive trade conducted in purpose-built fruit schooners. These vessels were fast sailers, and possessed an optimum cargo-carrying capacity so that the fruit neither spoiled in transit nor glutted the market on arrival. Dartmouth and its creeks of Brixham and Salcombe were the principal bases of this winter luxury trade, which reached its peak in the 1850s.[119] During 1855 and 1856, for instance, South Devon vessels entered the port of London on 419 occasions; though some brought tea from Shanghai, wool from Buenos Aires, sugar from Demerara and glass from Antwerp, the majority of these craft arrived between October and February with oranges and lemons from Seville, Gijon and St Michaels in the Azores, or currants and raisins from Greek islands such as Zante and Cephalonica.[120]

However, steamships began to compete effectively in this trade in the 1860s, especially after the construction of Ponta Delgada harbour in the Azores.[121] Although South Devon's wooden sailing vessels were squeezed out of the business, they found employment in similar carrying trades. Craft such as the *Sophie Holten* and the *Elizabeth* of Plymouth were deployed in the Corunna cattle trade, conveying livestock to Plymouth for sale to military quartermasters.[122] Many of the schooners belonging to Brixham, Dartmouth and Salcombe carried pineapples from the West Indies, and timber from Bahia and Pernambuco in the Brazils. Above all, there remained the Newfoundland trade, which, together with the home trade, formed the bedrock upon which South Devon's shipping industry rested in the decades before the First World War. Though the fleet was shrinking from the 1870s as new building declined, the surviving schooners and ketches continued to exploit these niches in the freight market. Technically obsolescent by this stage, the region's wooden craft were 'run into the ground' by owners faced with a capital stock of limited resale value. Driven ever harder, the merchant schooners still eked out profits in the Edwardian era,[123] generating earnings which helped offset the region's visible trade deficit.

Thus, shipowning was a marginal activity in South Devon by 1914. Other aspects of the region's maritime economy continued to thrive, however. Plymouth had developed into the West Country's leading port, with an extensive range of ship- and cargo-handling facilities; seaborne imports into the region remained at a relatively high level, while exports of raw materials, especially stone and clay, were notable at Plymouth and Teignmouth. Apart from these growth points, trading and shipping activity was much less prevalent than it had been a century earlier. In many of the region's estuaries, leisure activities were already an important feature of the local economy. After the First World War this shift continued and leisure rather than commerce emerged as the dynamic element of South Devon's maritime economy.

3: The Ports, Seaborne Trade and Shipping Industry of South Devon, 1786–1914

1 26 Geo III, c.60. 'An Act for the Further Increase and Encouragement of Shipping and Navigation'.

2 PRO, CUST 17/10.

3 *Annual Statement of Navigation and Shipping.*

4 See M J Freeman and D H Aldcroft, eds, *Transport in Victorian Britain* (Manchester, 1988) chapters 5–7 (hereafter *TVB*).

5 See Chapter 6.

6 See M A Havinden, 'The South West. A Case of De-Industrialization?' in M Palmer, ed., *The Onset of Industrialization* (Nottingham, 1977), 5–11; and E L Jones, *De-Industrialization as Economic Adjustment. The Case of South-west England* (La Trobe University Economics Discussion Paper 13, 1987).

7 See G Finch, 'The Experience of Peripheral Regions in an Age of Industrialisation. The Case of Devon, 1840–1914' (Unpublished D.Phil thesis, University of Oxford, 1984); and S Fisher and M A Havinden, 'The Long-term Evolution of the Economy of South-West England. From Autonomy to Dependence', in M A Havinden, J Quéniart and J Stanyer, eds, *Centre and Periphery. Brittany, Cornwall and Devon compared* (Exeter, 1991), 76–85.

8 See G Jackson, *The History and Archaeology of Ports* (Tadworth, 1983); and R C Jarvis, 'Sources for History of Ports', *JTH*, 3 (1957–8), 76–93.

9 G Jackson, 'The Ports' in D H Aldcroft and M J Freeman, eds, *Transport in the Industrial Revolution* (Manchester, 1983), 177–8. (hereafter *TIR*).

10 H J Trump, 'The Port of Teignmouth and the Teignmouth Harbour Commission, 1836–1932' *MH*, 4 (1974), 50–1.

11 *Accounts and Papers* (BPP, 1847–8, LI, 325; 1851, LIII, 233). 'Returns of all Dues . . . Levied on the Importation of Coal'.

12 *Accounts and Papers* (BPP, 1882, LXII, 409). 'Return of the Names, etc, of the Port and Harbour Authorities of the United Kingdom.'

13 Accounts of dues collected are in DRO, 1508M Devon/SS/Harbours.

14 C Gill, *Sutton Harbour* (Plymouth, 1970), 9; R Freeman, *Dartmouth. A New History of the Port and its People* (Darmouth, 1983), 47–50.

15 BPP, 1882, LXII, 409. 'Return of the Names of Port Authorities.'

16 Gill, *Sutton Harbour*, 4–5, 9.

17 Trump, 'Port of Teignmouth', 50.

18 Freeman, *Dartmouth*, 108–9; see also *Accounts and Papers* (BPP, 1868–9, LIV, 449–57). Correspondence between the Duchy of Cornwall, the Board of Trade, and the Committee Representing the Mercantile Interests of Dartmouth.

19 See M C Ewans, *The Haytor Granite Tramway and Stover Canal* (Dawlish, 1964).

20 Gill, *Sutton Harbour*, 35–6.

21 M Langley and E Small, *Millbay Docks* (Exeter, 1987); Gill, *Sutton Harbour*, 8.

22 E Delderfield, *The Exmouth Docks Company. 100 Years of Progress and History, 1865–1965* (1965), 4.

23 Gill, *Sutton Harbour*, 9, 28–9.

24 R Craig, 'Sources for a History of Devon Merchant Shipping, 1750–1920' in D J Starkey, ed., *Sources for a New Maritime History of Devon* (Exeter, 1986), 105–06.

25 *Accounts and Papers* (BPP, 1846, XVIII, 320–3). Second Report of the Tidal Harbours Commission.

26 *Brixham Harbour, The Official Handbook* (1967).

27 Trump, 'Port of Teignmouth', 49.

28 V C Boyle and D Payne, *Devon Harbours* (1952), 16–7.

29 G Jackson, 'The Ports' in *TVB*, 234–50.

30 Gill, *Sutton Harbour*, 28–9; C B M Sillick, 'The City-Port of Plymouth. An Essay in Geographical Interpretation' (Unpublished PhD Thesis, University of London, 1938), 84–103.

31 *Census of the Population* (HMSO, 1801 and 1901). See Chapter 21.

32 PRO, CUST 17/12; *Annual Statement of the Trade of the United Kingdom with Foreign Countries and British Possessions.*

33 PRO, CUST 17/11; *Annual Statement of Navigation and Shipping.*

34 P S Bagwell and J Armstrong, 'Coastal Shipping' in *TVB*, 171.

35 J Armstrong and P S Bagwell, 'Coastal Shipping' in *TIR*, 146.

36 Bagwell and Armstrong, 'Coastal Shipping' in *TVB*, 172.

37 Jackson, 'The Ports' in *TVB*, 251.

38 *Annual Statements of Navigation and Shipping.*

39 *Accounts and Papers* (BPP, 1831–2, XXIV, 237–8). 'Returns Relating to the Trade and Shipping of Dartmouth, 1821–31.'

40 E A G Clark, *The Ports of the Exe Estuary, 1660–1860* (Exeter, 1960), 220.

41 BPP, 1831–2, XXIV, 237–8. 'Returns Relating to the Trade and Shipping of Dartmouth.'

42 *Annual Statements of Navigation and Shipping.*

43 *Accounts and Papers* (BPP, 1819, XVI, 226–7). 'An Account of the Duties Paid on Coal Carried Coastwise in the Year Ending 5 January 1819'; *Accounts and Papers* (BPP, 1902, CXVI (2), 438–9). 'An Account of the Quantities of Coal Received Coastways in 1900.'

44 Bagwell and Armstrong, 'Coastal Shipping' in *TVB*, 190.

45 *Accounts and Papers* (BPP, 1830, XXVII, 131). 'An Account of the Several Counties in England and Wales into which Coals have been brought Coastwise during 1829.'

46 BPP, 1819, XVI, 226–7. 'An Account of Duties Paid on Coal . . . [in 1818].'

47 *Accounts and Papers* (BPP, 1875, LXXI, 35). 'Account of the Quantities of Coal Received Coastways in 1874.'

48 E A G Clark, 'The Estuarine Ports of the Exe and the Teign, with Special Reference to the Period 1660–1860. A Study in Historical Geography' (unpublished Ph.D thesis, University of London, 1956), III, Appendix 18(xiii); Trump, 'Port of Teignmouth', 62.

49 Clark, *Ports of the Exe Estuary*, 213.

50 Calculated from BPP, 1819, XVI, 226–7. 'An Account of Duties Paid on Coal . . . [in 1818].'

51 Clark, *Ports of the Exe Estuary*, 137–9.

52 DRO, 3258A Add/HA/A1. Teignmouth Harbour Commission Import Book, 1853–63.

53 Finch, 'Experience of Peripheral Regions', 66–7.

54 BPP, 1846, XVIII, 320–3. Second Report of the Tidal Harbours Commission.

55 BPP, 1830, XXVII, 131. 'Account of the Several Counties . . . into which Coals have been brought Coastwise during 1829.'

56 See Chapter 5; DRO, 3258A Add/HA/A1. Teignmouth Harbour Commission Import Book, 1853–63; Clark, *Ports of the Exe Estuary*, 136.

57 *Accounts and Papers* (BPP, 1897, LXIX, 206–7). 'A Return showing the Quantity of Bunker Coal Shipped in Foreign-Going Vessels from Each Port in 1895 and 1896.'

58 Freeman, *Dartmouth*, 123–5.

59 *Annual Statement of Navigation and Shipping.*

60 DRO, 1508M Devon/SS/Harbours. Metage Accounts of the Manor of Kenton.

61 DRO, 3258A Add/HA/A1. Teignmouth Harbour Commission Import Book, 1853–63.

62 *Accounts and Papers* (BPP, 1824, VIII, 319–63). 'An Account of the Number of Vessels . . . which have Cleared Out in the years 1811 and 1823 from the Several Ports of the Western Coast of Britain . . . for the Ports in the Southern and Eastern Coasts.'

63 See Chapter 5.

64 DRO, 3258A Add/HA/A1. Teignmouth Harbour Commission Import Book, 1853–63.

65 *Exeter Flying Post*, 12 Jan. 1815.

66 *Exeter Flying Post*, 29 Dec. 1803.

67 Finch, 'Experience of Peripheral Regions', 48.

68 BPP, 1824, VIII, 319–63. 'Account of the Number of Vessels . . . Cleared Out in the Years 1811 and 1823.'

69 Liverpool Customs Bills of Entry, March, July, Oct. 1853. I am grateful to Dr Valerie Burton for this information.

70 BPP, 1824, VIII, 319–63. 'Account of the Number of Vessels . . . Cleared Out in the Years 1811 and 1823.' Bristol Customs House furnished details of 1808 clearances instead of those in 1811.

71 DRO, 3258A Add/HA/A1. Teignmouth Harbour Commission Import Book, 1853–63.

72 Clark, *Ports of the Exe Estuary*, 221; see Chapter 6.

73 Clark, 'Estuarine Ports', III, Appendix 18 (viii.b).

74 DRO, 3258A Add/HA/A1. Teignmouth Harbour Commission Import Book, 1853–63.

75 See Volume 1, Chapter 22.

76 *Accounts and Papers* (BPP, 1826–7, XVIII, 165). 'An Account of the Number of Vessels . . . Entered from and Cleared to Newfoundland and Labrador in the Years 1824 to 1826.'

77 W G Handcock, *Soe Longe as there Comes Noe Women. Origins of English Settlement in Newfoundland* (St John's, Newfoundland, 1989), 45.

78 DRO, 3258A Add/HA/A1. Teignmouth Harbour Commission Import Book, 1853–63.

79 BPP, 1868–9, LIV, 449–57. Correspondence between the Duchy of Cornwall, the Board of Trade, and the Committee Representing the Mercantile Interests of Dartmouth.

80 *Annual Statement of the Trade of the United Kingdom*; Sillick, 'City-Port of Plymouth', 84–98.

81 PRO, CUST 17/11.

82 BPP, 1826–7, XVIII, 165. 'Account of the Number of Vessels . . . Entered from and Cleared to Newfoundland . . . 1824 to 1826.'

83 *Annual Statement of the Trade of the United Kingdom.*

84 *Accounts and Papers* (BPP, 1902, CXVI(2), 422–3). 'Potter's Clay Exported to Foreign Countries from the Port of Teignmouth, 1899–1900.'

85 Clark, 'Estuarine Ports', III, Appendix 18 (viii.a).

86 *Annual Statement of the Trade of the United Kingdom*; Sillick, 'City-Port of Plymouth', 98–103.

87 For an overall assessment of Devon's balance of payments in the nineteenth century, see Finch, 'Experience of Peripheral Regions', 152–71.

88 G Jackson, 'The Shipping Industry' in *TVB*, 253–83.

89 DRO, 3287 and 3328. Teignmouth and Brixham Ship Registers. I am very grateful to Robin Craig for permitting me to use his transcriptions of the Ship Registers cited here and hereafter. My thanks are also due to Roy Eveleigh, who assisted with the transcription of the Plymouth Ship Registers.

90 Based on a survey of the *Mercantile Navy List*, 1870–89.

91 DRO, 3289. Exeter Ship Registers. See Chapter 8.

92 Robin Craig kindly provided this information.

93 DRO, Ship Registers, Dartmouth 1851/29, 1851/30.

94 G S Graham, 'The Ascendancy of the Sailing Ship, 1850–85' *EcHR*, second series, 9 (1956–7), 74–88; and B Greenhill, *The Ship. The Life and Death of the Merchant Sailing Ship, 1815–1965* (1980), 20–9.

95 DRO, Ship Registers, Teignmouth 1853/1, Exeter 1866/1, Plymouth 1868/7, 1852/10, 1863/6.

96 Maritime History Archive, Memorial University of Newfoundland (hereafter MHA, MUN). Crew Lists 1869/51142, 1874/62146.

97 London Customs Bills of Entry, Aug. 1855. I am grateful to Robin Craig for this information.

98 See Chapter 8.

99 MHA, MUN. Crew Lists 1878/63903, 1878/63908.

100 MHA, MUN. Crew List 1881/73420.

101 A Eames, *The Twilight of Welsh Sail* (University of Wales Press, 1984).

102 See D J Starkey, 'Schooner Development in Britain' in R Gardiner and B Greenhill, eds, *Sail's Last Century. The Merchant Sailing Ship 1830–1930* (1993), 133–47.

103 DRO, 3289. Exeter Ship Registers.

104 DRO, 3303. Dartmouth Ship Registers.

105 WDRO, 894. Plymouth Ship Registers.

106 DRO, WDRO. Ship Registers.

107 For instance, see the Crew Lists of the Dartmouth vessels *Brave, Cloud, Rosabel, Ben Nevis* and *King of Peace*. MHA, MUN. 1871/4437, 1871/19454, 1871/4424, 1881/73423, 1879/73417.

108 B Greenhill, *The Merchant Schooners* (4th edn, 1988), 22. For instance, see DRO, 3308. Dartmouth Ship Registers, 1878.

109 MHA, MUN. Crew Lists 1869/11046, 1869/11038, 1869/11040.

110 MHA, MUN. Crew Lists 1869/5678, 1876/5777, 1876/5659, 1873/44340, 1864/45697, 1876/5707.

111 MHA, MUN. Crew List 1869/11041.

112 MHA, MUN. Crew List 1871/62147.

113 MHA, MUN. Crew List 1878/13164.

114 MHA, MUN. Crew List 1871/7029.

115 MHA, MUN. Crew List 1869/11026.

116 MHA, MUN. Crew List 1874/65753.

117 MHA, MUN. Crew Lists 1879/73408, 1881/73408.

118 See Chapter 2.

119 Greenhill, *Merchant Schooners*, 14–6.

120 London Customs Bills of Entry, 1855–6. I am grateful to Robin Craig for this information.

121 Greenhill, *Merchant Schooners*, 24.

122 MHA, MUN. Crew Lists 1871/62140, 1873/990; Craig, 'Sources for a History of Devon Merchant Shipping', 107–08.

123 For instance, see W J Slade, *Out of Appledore. The Autobiography of a Coasting Shipmaster and Shipowner in the Last Days of Wooden Sailing Ships* (4th edn, 1980).

4 *North Devon Shipping, Trade and Ports, 1786–1939*

BASIL GREENHILL **and** MICHAEL NIX

BEFORE THE TRANSFER OF THE CREEK OF APPLEDORE to Bideford in 1814, every vessel entering or clearing the River Torridge had to pass through the waters of the port of Barnstaple. Fourteen years after the redefinition of the port boundaries, the Bideford Collector of Customs complained that a shared entrance to the two ports was an inconvenience to trade. His solution was to redraw the port boundary to give Bideford a clear access to the sea, reversing the pre-1814 arrangement.[1] The divided entrance, however, remained, and the two ports continued to share the deep water roadstead just inside the Bar and the maintenance base in the shipyards of Appledore, famed throughout the nineteenth and twentieth centuries for the speed, quality and cheapness of their repair work. Although inter-port rivalry could be fiercely competitive, it is not always easy to separate the shipping and shipowning enterprises of Bideford and Barnstaple except by the somewhat artificial devices of the geographical location of activities within the limits of the two ports and the place of registration of the vessels. In 1839 Ilfracombe, having now insufficient business to support a Custom House, was merged with Barnstaple, and in 1882 Bideford lost its port status, which it did not regain until 1928. Fortunately, its ship registrations were not interrupted. Thus for the greater part of the period under review we have two ports in the legal sense only to deal with.

During the eighteenth century the overseas trade of Bideford and Barnstaple suffered severely from the effects of a long series of wars and their attendant calamities of privateering and the press-gang. In 1766 a plea, made in a Land Tax dispute on behalf of the inhabitants of Bideford in the Court of Exchequer, wistfully recalled a 'golden age' of trade. Looking back from the standpoint of a 'decayed town' to the days of 'a once flourishing'

port, it recalled that in 1693 the tobacco trade with Virginia and Maryland, the wool imports from Ireland and the fishery of Newfoundland had engaged sixty-four ships in 'foreign parts'.[2] Almost a century later, in 1792, the cleric John Watkins reported of his home town that, 'at the present time, Bideford enjoys no foreign commercial consequence, at least not any worth mentioning', although he advised that something ' . . . like a revival of the trade to America has taken place within these two to three years. A few occasional cargoes of timber, pine, plank, and tar, having been imported from the Bay of Massachusets [*sic*] and Nova Scotia.'[3]

Barnstaple, on the other hand, conveyed the impression of a port which had emerged from the American Revolutionary War commercially more sound. Its fleet of ships, although not much more numerous than Bideford's, was employed in the carrying trades between Britain and Europe, North America and the West Indies. The port town also preserved more direct contacts with foreign markets than either Bideford or Ilfracombe. All three, however, did send some of their largest brigantines, the 166-ton *Albion* of Bideford, the 120-ton *Diligence* of Ilfracombe and the 160-ton *Apphia* of Appledore, for example, to the Baltic for timber and ships' stores. Similarly, North Devon craft continued very occasionally to be employed in the Newfoundland cod fishery, returning, as part of the triangular trade, from Cadiz and Malaga with fruit and wines. Ireland was also a source of employment, as the volumes of *Lloyd's Register* amply show.

The ports of North Devon thus entered the nineteenth century primarily engaged in the coasting trades whose carrier routes were geared to a predominantly agrarian society (Tables 4.1 & 4.2). By far the greatest demand for shipping was required in the transportation of coal, culm and

4.1 The polacca brigantine *Express* of Fremington (Port of Barnstaple) loading limestone on the beach at Lydstep Haven, near Tenby. The *Express* was a constant trader from South Wales to the Bideford River and the Taw in three centuries. She was built at Appledore in 1797 and broken up in 1901. (*Cardiff Public Library*)

4.2 Thomas Burnard, merchant, of Bideford, 1769–1823, from his memorial in Bideford Church. (*Basil Greenhill*)

limestone from South Wales.[4] Domestic coal, brought mostly from Swansea, was in greatest demand in Barnstaple, whose hinterland for this commodity still possibly extended as far as Exeter. Culm, used by limeburners, maltsters, blacksmiths and potters, was exported mostly through Tenby. By the turn of the century, however, the direction of this trade was altering. In 1794 the Corporation of Barnstaple, realising the potential of the proposed Swansea Canal, was one of many groups which petitioned Parliament for the passage of the necessary legislation.[5] After the completion of the Canal in 1798, Swansea, previously having sent little or no culm to North Devon, usurped the traditional role of Pembrokeshire and Carmarthenshire in just over a decade to become the principal supplier.

Although more limestone traders plied the Taw than the Torridge, Bideford required greater quantities of culm, probably to service its larger shipbuilding and pottery industries. Used in the limeburning process, culm was landed alongside Welsh limestone close to the many limekilns scattered along the river banks and along the North Devon shores of the Bristol Channel. After calcination, the lime was used extensively on the lands of North Devon, a stage in the practice of convertible husbandry. It also had a number of uses in the hands of the stonemason.

Exports of agricultural produce were more significant than imports. Bideford, Ilfracombe and Hartland Quay were noted for their export of corn, especially of oats.[6] In November 1800 the Collector of Barnstaple reported to his superiors in London that the surrounding countryside:

> is supposed in average years scarcely to produce sufficient quantity of wheat for its own consumption . . . but the average crops of barley and oats are more sufficient and generally admit to an exportation to other parts of the Kingdom.[7]

But during the bleak war years of the mid-1790s and early 1800s the exportation of agricultural produce, following poor harvests, excited popular resentment and, at times, physical opposition. At Ilfracombe in 1801, for example, a mob attempted to thwart the shipment of 120 quarters of barley, 'the growth of the neighbourhood'.[8] In Barnstaple 'a tumultuous set of women appeared ready for riot in the Corn Market'.[9] Anonymous and inflammatory letters threatened the life of at least one corn factor. In 1802 Israel Doidge of Bideford had apparently agreed 'with all the farmers within 20 miles to bring by the 12th December 10,000 bushels of wheat to ship from this place to Bristol and elsewhere'. The consequences of effecting the plan, he was warned, would be 'death . . . your house on fire your property destroyed, your family in flames, to dust and ashes'.[10] Imports and exports flowed unopposed in calmer times, when there were occasional shipments of wool and livestock from Ireland, and of Barnstaple beer principally to Dublin. Among many other minor consignments, 'fish' and herrings arrived from Clovelly, Padstow, Newquay, St Ives and Teignmouth for local consumption, oatmeal and wheat-flour went to Liverpool and Padstow, and malt was despatched to South Wales.

Like the food shortages, the scarcity of timber during the French Wars proved troublesome. Although the hinterlands of the three ports supplied large quantities of oak timber vital to each of the local communities, agricultural economists were critical of woodland management. Charles Vancouver observed in 1808 that oak trees were not permitted to attain their full maturity and he complained, in general terms, that for 'any one viewing with an eye to utility, the present state and condition of the oak-timber of this country, cannot without pain observe so general a destruction of this our principal bulwark'.[11]

Vancouver also reported that in 1805 6,000 trees were sold publicly at Barnstaple; each averaged twenty feet per stock and half a ton in weight. Two years later 6,500 were auctioned in the same town with 'a destruction of no less than 5 feet per stock which solely arises from the number of young trees growing improvidently felled and taken to market'.[12] Shortages in North Devon and a large warship building programme which delayed the construction of merchantmen on the Torridge and, to a lesser extent, the Taw, coincided with Napoleon's imposition of the Continental Blockade in 1807 which dramatically reduced the supply of timber from the Baltic. In September of that year a cargo of timber reached Bideford from Riga; it was the last to arrive directly from overseas for three years. Shipbuilding slumped. The next cargo of foreign timber, carried in the *Anne* from St Andrew's in New Brunswick in what was then known as British North America, was not reported at the Bideford Custom House until December 1810. It was to prove a significant re-establishment of old ties.

Gross profiteering in the sale of oak bark, used as an astringent in the leather tanning industry, was a further threat to good woodland management. At times during the French wars the value of the bark exceeded that of the timber. William Marshall, in 1796, feared the abuse 'bids fair to reduce to a state little short of annihilation, the Oak timbers of this island, fit for ship building'.[13] It may be, though, that North Devon shipbuilders derived some advantage in being able to purchase timber locally without the need of an intermediary, and, on selling the bark to Scottish and Irish tanneries, used the profits to offset the original cost of the timber. Ireland absorbed about two-thirds of the shipments cleared from Bideford and Barnstaple but, following the Act of Union in 1801, its tanning industry was unprotected from direct competition. Within a few years Scottish and English ports were receiving from Bideford double the shipments of bark sent to Ireland.

The North Devon pottery industry had declined during the eighteenth century and its export trade was eventually to be confined to the South-west peninsula, Bristol and South Wales. Ireland was no longer of any significance. By the 1790s and early 1800s Carmarthen, a market town, Swansea, at the centre of burgeoning industrialisation, and the rapidly developing coal port of Newport, were leading Welsh importers of Bideford and Barnstaple wares. The exports to Pembrokeshire, though, appear to have been in decline, possibly because of the movement eastwards of the culm trade. In the South West, Bideford wares held sway over Barnstaple's in the important naval base of Plymouth and the 'western metropolis' of Bristol, but both shared in the trade with the Cornish port of Padstow. Although the clay used in the manufacture of earthenware was cheaply extracted at Fremington in the port of Barnstaple, lead ore or galena for the glaze was imported from Carmarthen and, to a lesser extent, from Aberystwyth, Cardigan, Hayle and Milford.

4.3 The brig *Jessie*, built at New Bideford, Prince Edward Island, in 1827 and owned by Moses Chanter and Thomas Burnard. (*H H Parkhouse*)

4.4   Thomas Burnard Chanter, merchant, of Northam, 1797–1874. (*Mrs Peter Cardew*)

4.5   In 1844, Thomas Chanter, enjoying the rights of the Lord of the Manor of Northam, encouraged the householders of Market Street, Appledore, to join up a number of small private quays at the backs of their properties to make Appledore Quay, as it was known for almost a century until it was widened in 1940. This was Appledore Quay in the early 1900s. The smack is the *Rosamond Jane*, built at Padstow in 1834 and owned in Barnstaple. She was the last vessel to trade to Hartland Quay and Mouthmill. (*William Fox*)

Argentiferous lead ore was mined at Combe Martin and 208 tons were exported to Bristol between 1813 and 1817, but the silver extracted was insufficient to make continued mining viable. Earlier, between 1796 and 1802, over 9,000 tons of iron ore were shipped through Combe Martin to the iron works at Llanelli.[14] Barnstaple, and even Bideford, exported some copper ore to Swansea. Culm, mined in or near Bideford and suitable for manufacturing into black paint, was sent to Bristol, Liverpool, London, Plymouth and Swansea, or was processed at the local paint works, dispatched to Devonport and applied to the Navy's warships. Cornwall traded Delabole slate for roofing and flooring, and building stone came from South Wales. Tanned hides were carried from Ireland, and occasional consignments of bricks were sent from Bideford and Barnstaple to South Devon and South Wales.

But however much one wishes to produce a definitive list of a port's trade, there is always the term 'sundry goods' to confound any analysis. Locally-owned vessels for and from Bristol could be seen alongside the quays of either Bideford or Barnstaple at least once or twice a month. London traders were less frequent. The goods they contained were diverse and numerous. In November 1811, for example, a consignment taken 'out of the *Resolution*' at Barnstaple quay included ninety-two plough moulds, three bags of nails, a puncheon of rum, six tons of salt, twenty-three planks, two iron boilers, twenty-seven iron pots, a number of shovels, twelve bags of shot, three boxes of candles and fifty dozen bottles. On other occasions the rarer items included a rocking horse for a G Barber, Esq., of Shirwell, a malt mill, a chaffing machine and a harpsichord.[15] Account also has to be taken of the goods smuggled as contraband, and short measures given on the quay side. In 1804, for instance, the brigantine *Margaretta*, owned by the Hartland Quay merchant Edward Hockin, was seized in the act of 'running' off Woody Bay, along with her cargo of 150 kegs of gin, 219 kegs of brandy, about 25 tons of salt, 8 bales of tobacco, 1 bag of pepper, 1 keg of rum, 9 kegs of wine and 200 cwt of pepper.[16]

Using the quay-master's account book, it is possible to define the sundry trading hinterland of Barnstaple. Excluding the town goods, in 1810 'the

Country' received over 500 individual orders for items of varying sizes, value and quantity.[17] Sixty per cent went to South Molton and between four and five per cent went to each of the towns and villages of Ilfracombe, Chittlehampton, Chulmleigh, North Molton and North Tawton. About four-fifths of all orders went to a region delineated by the Barnstaple to South Molton road, the high ground of Exmoor and the coast between Morte Point and Lynmouth. Bampton was probably served by the port of Minehead. Most of the remaining orders were distributed in an area between the Barnstaple to South Molton and Barnstaple to Great Torrington roads. Although the Exeter turnpike bisected this region and was unhindered by any serious topographical barriers, it entered the natural port hinterland of Exeter which Clark defined as extending as far as a line joining Winkleigh, Lapford and Witheridge.[18] Only ten orders were delivered beyond this imaginary line. Even fewer were carried in the remaining locality to the westward of the Barnstaple to Great Torrington road, reflecting an area of strong competition from Bideford.

Most of the goods carried into and out of Bideford were moved between March and November, with a peak of activity reached in August. Vessel turn-round times in the river varied according to trade. The next tide suited most limestone traders, but those carrying 'sundry goods' remained on average up to thirty-two days. Again on average, the largest bulk carriers, excluding those engaged in the Baltic, were, at about 68 tons, employed to carry timber; the smallest, at 32 tons, were found in the earthenware trade. During the winter, locally-owned craft, perhaps not having visited the port during the year, arrived, sometimes with a cargo of coal, to lay-up for a month or two after Christmas. Of 358 cargoes imported in 1806, less than half were carried in Bideford-owned ships, although they transported most of the coal, culm and 'sundry goods' and about half of the limestone. Only a third of the 176 cargoes cleared were in Bideford ships. Of more than 7,000 tons of shipping registered in Bideford, almost 4,000 tons were not engaged to carry a single cargo to or from the town and its environs. By counting just those vessels which transported four or more cargoes, the figure is increased to over 6,000 tons.[19] Thus, on the evidence of Bideford,

4.6 The barque *Elizabeth Yeo*, 895 tons, launched in May 1856 in Quebec by James Oliver, sailed across the Atlantic and completed in the Richmond Dry Dock, Appledore. She was the first vessel to enter the dry dock, doing so on 17 July 1856. (*Maritime Museum of the Atlantic, Halifax, NS*)

many of more than 200 vessels which exceeded 16,000 registered tons owned in North Devon at this time were extraneous to the import and export needs of the local communities, and were engaged in the general carrying trade at sea, which comprised an important part of the local shipping industry.

The commercial dynamic of the Bristol Channel was changing rapidly, and the shifting centre of gravity of trade from Bristol to the ports of South Wales created new possibilities for the profitable deployment of ships. The two-way trade in Cornish tin and Welsh coal, influential in reducing the number of ballasted voyages made in the Channel, was but one carrier route open to vigorous North Devon shipowners and masters. The pace of trade was quickened by war and industrialisation. Yet unlike Bideford, and to a lesser degree, Ilfracombe, Barnstaple was unable to capitalise on this. During the 1790s its trade stagnated and its registered tonnage fell by twenty per cent. In September 1789 the clergyman John Swete visited the town. In his journal he observed:

> . . . the trade of this place is of late very much reduced . . . On its decay, which may be owing in a great degree to the havens, being more shallow and full of sandbanks than formerly, its neighbour Bideford hath risen. Commerce there spreads her full sail, and her incomparable accompanyments, wealth, bustle, spirit and improvements are met with in every street.[20]

Located at the confluence of the Taw and the Torridge, Appledore also accrued some advantage. In 1814 the transfer of this creek and its vessels to Bideford further compounded Barnstaple's decline.

Bideford shipowners were not immediately able to profit fully from the new opportunities of trade and the initiative surrendered by Barnstaple. During the 1790s the increased pressure in the Bristol Channel and elsewhere on the demand for shipping was not echoed by an equivalent upswing in the shipping and shipbuilding industries. Capital in new investments was not released until encouraged by a boom in British foreign trade following the period of deep political and economic gloom of 1797. Further stimulus was given with the prospects of peace in 1801. Bideford shipbuilders were then to become some of the most active in the Bristol Channel. In 1792 John Watkins had noted that ships built in Bideford were cheaper 'than in any other part of England. The principal reason for this is, the great quantity of timber which is continually cut down in the neighbourhood.'[21] Retaining a tradition of purchasing new craft from local yards, in 1803 Bideford shipowners bought a dozen large vessels, ten brigantines, a schooner and a ship, totalling nearly 1,500 tons. A further six were built for owners elsewhere. The enthusiasm of one buyer, William Wheaton of Brixham, encouraged the introduction, albeit temporarily, of the schooner rig into the conservative shipowning circles of Bideford. Before him, only one such vessel, the *Hibernia*, appeared on the Ship Register. Within a year of her registry in 1792 she was re-registered de novo a brigantine. She may well have been a polacca, in which case her description would have been at the whim of the registering clerk. It was about thirty years before Bideford shipowners caught up with their counterparts in South Devon in the use of the schooner rig.[22]

Nearly all the prime registrations in North Devon in the initial period of measuring and certification following the Registry Act of 1786 consisted of either brigantines or sloops, with a smattering of snows, ketches and brigs. At the end of December 1787 the Bideford fleet consisted of fifty-two vessels totalling 3,549 tons, of which eight belonged to the creek of Clovelly and two to Hartland Quay. They were owned in a proportion of thirty brigantines to twenty-two sloops. Their construction, with massive frames and flat bottoms, gave them sufficient strength to survive the overburdening weight of a bulk cargo when loading or discharging on rocky foreshores or on the mud of an esturial river.

The medial Bideford brigantine was 19½ years old, 91 tons, nearly 60ft long and 19ft in breadth. She was square-sterned and unadorned with a figurehead. The average depth of hold of this single-decked brigantine was about 10ft, but there were slightly more craft fitted with two decks. The average sloop, on the other hand, was about 13 years old, 40 tons, 44ft long by nearly 15ft in breadth and possessed a depth of hold of about 8ft. She, too, was square-sterned.[23] Barnstaple brigantines were similar to their Bideford counterparts, although more numerous and larger, at an average of 110 tons. They were also slightly newer. The medial Barnstaple sloop, at 38 tons, was similar to the Bideford model but was not so old at under ten years.[24] A shipwright's formula for building both types of vessel would have been approximately 1 length to 3 beams and 1 beam to 1.9 for the depth of hold.

The effect of the boom in the early years of the nineteenth century encouraged Bideford shipowners to modernise their fleet. The purchasing of new and larger merchantmen not only decreased the average age of brigantines owned in the port by 7½ years on the 1787 figures, but also increased the overall average tonnage of all vessels by about 14 tons. During the same period Barnstaple's average tonnage fell from 89 to 66 tons. But some of Bideford's shipping was speculative building and buying. Just as the name *Peace* belongs to a Bideford-built ship completed at the beginning of the French Revolutionary War, so the name *Speculator* belongs to the turn of the century.

For small maritime communities the merit of shipowning was that it not only offered an outlet for savings in partnership arrangements or in, to a lesser extent, single ownership, but it also assured for the shareholder some feeling of independence and status. At the end of the American War the apparent longevity of many of Bideford's vessels suggests low investment and a port in recession. At the end of 1787 there were 133 shareholders in 52 vessels of whom 54 resided in Bideford, 14 in Clovelly, 12 in Appledore and 8 in Northam. Most of the remainder lived in parishes bordering the coast and along the Torridge and Taw. Two merchants were to be found in

St John's, Newfoundland, and a few in South Devon, Bristol, and South Wales.

By 1803 new investment expanded considerably both the geographical and occupational structure of shipownership in the port. With a finite number of potential investors living in Bideford, expansion partly depended on finding sufficient people with free capital beyond the confines of the town. Of over 240 investors in 85 vessels in 1803, more were now to be found living in North Devon in general than in Bideford. Bristol, South Devon and South Wales tripled their numbers and Cornwall, which could boast of none in 1787, had 23. Several lived in the copper producing region around the port of St Ives. Possibly to accommodate this greater purchasing power and to spread the cost of constructing larger and more expensive merchantmen, the average four-member shareholder group in 1787 was increased by two by 1803. The greatest proportion of investment almost certainly came from those who profited most from the war; the holders of land and those engaged in shipping. The gentry, including retired successful merchants and businessmen, and farmers, constituted about a quarter of shareholders in 1803 (seven per cent in 1787). Another quarter was composed of mariners, already master-owners or ambitious for the status, and those engaged in shipbuilding and ancillary trades, while merchants, possessing the greatest number of holdings, constituted just under one-fifth. Unfortunately, the actual extent of each holding is unknown. Women also played a significant role in shipowning. They were mostly resident in Bideford and Clovelly, and were recorded in the Ship Registers under the patriarchal heading of widow, spinster, or perhaps 'wife of'.[25] Several widows had indeed inherited their husband's shares on their deaths, but others, such as the potter Mary Carder, the wine merchant Judith Smith and the maltster Elizabeth Smith, were, as an early trade directory shows, running their own businesses.[26]

The recovery of North Devon's shipbuilding industry following Napoleon's Continental Blockade was not entirely dependent on the lumber which arrived from British North America in 1810. Another boom encouraged more local investment, but by 1814 the Bideford shipbuilder Richard Taylor was complaining that,

> there are Ten Shipbuilders yards in the two ports of Bideford and Barnstaple, [of which] two . . . could have performed all the work of the three years Past, as this time there is not work to bespoke one yard.[27]

There were hardships ahead with the running-down of the wartime economy. In April 1816 the Appledore merchant Moses Chanter, lessee of a small quay and limekilns at Weare Giffard, up-river from Bideford, wrote to his landlord Earl Fortescue of Castle Hill near Barnstaple, 'I have been singularly unfortunate in my mercantile pursuits having met with losses to the amount of four thousand pounds by Shipping within the last 5 years'.[28] Yet Bideford, having seized the initiative as the premier port in North Devon, was about to increase its maritime activities to new levels of trade and prosperity.

Although men describing themselves as merchants comprised less than 20 per cent of the shareholders in Bideford vessels at the beginning of the new century,[29] the thirty years from 1790 to 1820 covered the rise of one who was usually described as a 'merchant, dealer and chapman', and who became, perhaps, the greatest of Bideford shipowners.[30] He was Thomas Burnard, born in 1769, son of a small local merchant and brewer who had shares in local vessels.[31] Bideford ship registrations alone show the Burnards, over three generations from 1786 to 1849, as holding at various periods shares in at least 102 vessels and as being the sole owners of another 37. Of these vessels Thomas Burnard himself appears to have held shares in sixty-nine, and in addition to have owned all the shares in thirty-two. Over the period from 1803 to 1852 Moses Chanter, described as a mercer and subsequently as a merchant, originally of Chudleigh then of Great Torrington and Weare Giffard, and, after 1806, of Appledore, and his son, Thomas Burnard Chanter, owned shares between them in twenty-nine Bideford-registered vessels and were the sole owners of thirty-five more. Some of the Chanters' vessel property, like the brig *Jessie*, built at New Bideford, Prince Edward Island, Canada, in 1827, was shared with the

Burnards, and Moses Chanter sold his shares in the polacca brigantine, ex smack *Peter & Sarah*, built by Richard Chapman at Cleave Houses in 1809, to Thomas Burnard, who then became the sole owner in 1816. This close financial relationship is not surprising, since Moses Chanter was married to Thomas Burnard's sister.[32]

The rise of these great ship owning dynasties – great, that is, in the terms of the society in which their members lived – marked the beginning of new developments in North Devon's maritime fortunes. It is interesting to review the changing nature of the vessel property of these two linked families. Moses Chanter's largest vessels were the snow *Lord Wellington*, a prize of war of 145 tons in which he held shares from 1815 to 1819; the brigantine *Torridge*, another prize, 110 tons; the *Endeavour*, of 116 tons, an old vessel built in 1752 in which he held property from 1805 to 1810; and the *Friendship*, his largest vessel, 163 tons, in which he held shares from 1811 to 1817. Thomas Burnard held shares in her over the same years. The rest of Moses Chanter's vessels were all small smacks and small brigantines, many of them, no doubt, polaccas, and their average tonnage was 62.5. A somewhat different picture emerges from a study of the vessel property of Thomas Burnard. Of the 101 vessels on the Bideford register in which he was financially interested, 39 were over 100 tons. But of these, twenty-four were investments made after 1810. His largest vessels were the prize (of the war with the United States in 1812) *Golden Fleece*, 279 tons, a full rigged ship in which he had shares from 1812 until 1818; the brigantine, later barque, *Bellona*, 271 tons, built for him at Cleave Houses in 1813 and owned solely by him until his death in 1823; and the *Mars*, 342 tons, built for his sole ownership at what was in effect his own shipyard at New Bideford, Prince Edward Island, in 1819, and probably the largest vessel which had ever been owned in Bideford at the time of her first registration there in 1820.[33]

In the early years of the century Thomas Burnard's vessels had very varied employment. The *Venus*, 136 tons, was in the London Irish trade. The *Brittania*, *Minerva*, *Mary*, *Hebe*, *Susan* and *Agenoria* were also trading with Ireland. The *Hibernia* and the *Juno* sailed to Spain and Portugal, as did Chanter's *Peter & Sarah* before Burnard bought her. The little *Roebuck* of 37 tons was in the West of England coasting trade. The *Nautilus*, 143 tons, was in the American trade, but not sailing from Bideford, and she was taken up by the government as transport on the outbreak of the war with the United States in 1812, as was also the *Bellona* immediately on her completion. The brig *Golden Fleece* sailed to Archangel and Brazil.[34]

With the coming of these bigger vessels and big shipowning families, a change began to come over North Devon's shipping activities. The area was to benefit greatly with the opening up of the Canadian lumber trade on a large scale, a development which followed the Continental Embargo of 1807 and the placing of prohibitive duties on Baltic timber in order to protect the huge investment which had been made by British merchants in the Canadian lumber trade during the Embargo's short life. For North Devon the crucial year may be taken as 1818. Thomas Burnard had already dabbled in the Gulf of St Lawrence lumber trade with the *Bellona* and other vessels, but in that year, perhaps on the advice of Sir Charles Chalmers, a former resident of Prince Edward Island who had settled in Odun House (now the North Devon Maritime Museum), and employing another islander by adoption, Richard Moys, as agent, he sent his little polacca brigantine *Peter & Sarah*, 59 tons, across the Atlantic to the colony of Prince Edward Island. On board was a small shipbuilding gang in the charge of William Ellis, a master shipwright formerly employed by, and later in some form of partnership with, Richard Chapman at the yard at Cleave Houses, where the *Bellona* and the *Peter & Sarah* herself had been built.

The events which followed were complex and have been told in detail elsewhere.[35] A shipbuilding yard was established at a site still known today as New Bideford, and by the time of Thomas Burnard's sudden death in 1823 a second site a mile or two away had been settled on cleared ground and a farm established which was called Port Hill, after the house in Northam of that name. Several vessels had been built at New Bideford by the time of Thomas Burnard's death, the largest of them the brig *Bacchus*, of 234 tons. Thomas Burnard's death left a complex situation. His heirs were his wife and sons, all of whom dropped out of business in the next fifteen years. The shipyard at New Bideford under William Ellis continued to build cheap, large vessels for them, culminating in 1826 in the *Superb*, a full-rigged ship of 501 tons, a large merchant vessel by the standards of her time, which represented a new dimension in shipping enterprise for North Devon owners. But the managerial responsibilities and financial risks involved in developing a project 3,000 miles away in a poorly administered colony were too much for the Burnards, and through Moses Chanter's son, Thomas Burnard Chanter (1817–1874), the business passed into the hands of William Ellis, the master shipwright. Chanter was already a regular visitor to the Island, and until 1830 he became a transatlantic commuter, spending his summers in the colony and his winters in Britain. During this time Ellis built for him two vessels, the brig *Collina* and the barque *Calypso*, the latter of 266 tons. Chanter's business interest in the island grew rapidly, and with vessels built at New Bideford and elsewhere he began to advertise in the West Country and Canadian press as loading, with room for passengers, at Falmouth, Plymouth, Cardiff and Bideford, for North American ports. The first-class fare was £25 and between-decks fare £3.[36]

Bideford's maritime activity reached a new level when, in December 1827, five locally owned vessels and one from Sunderland all lay together discharging Canadian lumber at Bideford Quay.[37] The Rolle Canal to Great Torrington was opened up in the same year, and not only a brick factory, lime kilns and a timber yard were opened on its banks, but the brig *Louisa* was built on Moses Chanter's old property below Halfpenny Bridge.[38] A number of vessels were to be launched at Weare Giffard in the next forty

years. Some of them sailed far and wide. The brig *Margaret*, built there for Thomas Chanter in 1835, sailed to the Mediterranean, the West Indies and North America.

Indeed, the North American trade from the Torridge was becoming firmly established and trade with Spain, Portugal, the Azores and the Mediterranean began to develop once more. More than 100 vessels of all sizes were owned in and around Bideford and Appledore, employing over 400 seamen and many more men and women ashore.[39] The movements of local coasters can easily be followed in the files of the contemporary press. There was a weekly cluster of limestone and coal traders crossing to and from South Wales. The *Dasher*, the *Experiment*, the *Friends* and the *Bucks* were all locally built polacca brigantines and smacks. Their passages were the subject of much local interest. In September 1828 it was reported that 'two of the vessels built for the service to Lord Rolle's Canal, the brig *Lady Rolle* and the sloop *Stevenstone*, made each four voyages from Bideford to Wales and returned and discharged their cargoes in one week'.[40] In October 1830 there was a report that the brig *Mars*, Captain Guy of Appledore, had carried four cargoes in five days from South Wales to Greencleave limekilns in the parish of Abbotsham.[41]

Of the vessels owned by his family, Thomas Burnard Chanter was sole owner at various times of thirty-two. Year by year in the 1830s he usually held all the property in four or five vessels and had shares in perhaps half a dozen more.[42] In the later 1830s he reduced his shipowning commitments and appears to have developed his lumber importing interests. As he himself

APPLEDORE AND INSTOW.

4.7   Appledore from Instow in 1856. William Yeo's new Richmond House stands proud in the saddle of the hill. Staddon is visible at the right hand end of the hill and Chanter's Tower is in the extreme left of the engraving. The new broad-gauge railway from Barnstaple to Bideford occupies the foreground. There are few trees; lime burning and shipbuilding have ensured the stripping of the timber. (*Engraved by G Townsend, published in Exeter, 2 April 1856*)

put it in a private letter to William Ellis in Prince Edward Island in the early spring of 1835: 'I do not wish to own more than one or two vessels at a time for the Captains get their bread when the owners are going to ruin'.[43]

The development of his timber interests perhaps culminated in 1842, when he obtained a contract for the supply of lumber for the building of the Bristol and Exeter Railway and delivered by far the largest quantity of any merchant involved, for which he was paid £36,000, well over one million pounds in 1990s values.[44] He became Mayor of Bideford for two years in succession in 1843 and 1844.

Chanter's vessels were notably larger than those of the preceding generation and, since he was the first owner of many of them, it follows that they were new and represented a higher capital investment than the older ships in which the Burnards and his own father had invested. The average tonnage of the seventeen new square-rigged vessels of which he was the first and sole owner over the years 1829 to 1841 was 260. The largest vessels, the barques *Alchymist* and *Atalanta*, the barque *Collina* of 1838 (Chanter had favourite names, he owned four new *Collinas* and in 1838 gave the name to two vessels, a brig and a barque) and the *Falcon*, the brig *Lord Ramsay* and the full rigged ships *Emma* and *Augusta* were all over 400 tons register – among the larger ordinary merchantmen of the period – while the barque *Emerald* was 523 tons, of a size to rival the Burnard's *Superb*. Moreover, these vessels were constantly employed in the North Atlantic trade, those in which he retained interest for many years, the barque *Calypso*, the brigs *Sappho* and *Lord Ramsay*, and the Burnard's *Bellona* taking emigrants out from and lumber back to Bristol, Bideford or Plymouth.[45] Thus there was a great sight at Bideford on 12 April 1831, when, according to the *North Devon Journal*:

> This day the *Apollo*, Bragg, for New York with 94 passengers, the *Calypso*, Grossard, for St Andrews with 109 passengers, and the *Bacchus*, Howe, for Montreal, to take in passengers at Ireland, left the port; numerous friends of the emigrants were in attendance to witness their departure . . . on the firing of a signal gun, the ships all got under weigh, and were cheered by not less than 5,000 persons who lined the quay and the bridge.

Chanter's *Calypso* landed her passengers all well at St Andrews after a passage of only twenty-two days.[46]

This was a new kind of shipowning for North Devon, involving more capital and more positive and innovatory management than had been applied before. Chanter brought to shipowning a new kind of business enterprise for the region. He was not only a timber merchant, landowner and shipowner, he was a ship dealer. Many of the vessels he had built in Prince Edward Island he retained for only one or two transatlantic round voyages and then sold on the British tonnage market. He had access through his long-standing connections in Prince Edward Island to a source of cheap but marketable tonnage, and he had the contacts in Britain which wanted this class of vessel. After 1835, when Lloyds' shipping surveyors were first appointed in Bideford,[47] he had the means of presenting his tonnage on the market duly graded and branded. Using his favourable position he made himself one of the greater merchants west of Bristol. Among his many services to North Devon was the promotion of the first steamer to be built on the coast, the paddler *Torridge*. which ran from 1835 between Bideford and Bristol. She was built in Appledore by William Clibbet junior (1803–1886).

Chanter's example was soon followed, albeit on a smaller scale, by others of his townsmen; George Hooper, Richard Heard, John Howe, William Grigg, the Chappel family, James Lowther and others. Bideford prospered, on the whole. In January 1842 no fewer than four barques, a brig and three schooners lay at the quay, all discharging timber from Prince Edward Island without the aid of any crane or other shore equipment.[48] Contemporary reports speak of sixty vessels, usually small coasters, lying in Appledore at the same time. In May 1840 forty-four vessels went out over Appledore bar on the same tide.[49] These little vessels were owned by small shareholding groups drawn from the immediate region, many of them from the town of Appledore and the parish of Northam. They included local tradesmen, the vessel's master, perhaps members of her crew, their relatives and perhaps

one of the local shipbuilders, a sailmaker, sometimes local farmers, and wives and widows of seamen.[50]

But the standard of living of the mass of the population remained that of relative rural poverty, or little better. Though Appledore Quay was built with Chanter's encouragement in 1845 to facilitate shipping, Appledore, especially, was a lawless place and there were frequent reports in the contemporary press of robberies and assaults, brawling and fighting in the streets, especially, apparently, among the women.[51] In 1839 there was a strike of the seamen in the limestone trade which created much hardship,[52] and in 1843 the merchants sought to reduce the wages paid to the 'Limestone porters', the casual labourers, mainly female, who performed the very arduous work of discharging the vessels at the lime kilns. The women struck, and after a week with laden vessels collecting inside the bar, the owners had to give way.[53]

Successful though Thomas Chanter was in his exploitation of the resources of Prince Edward Island, it was obvious that, to develop the potential of the situation to the utmost, it was necessary, as always in business in such situations, to take over the source of supply. To make really big business out of the situation – the ability to build good ships cheaply in the Island and market them profitably to meet a demand for them in Britain – required political and financial control of the small colony itself. Prince Edward Island is only seven-eighths of the size of Devon, but in the mid-nineteenth century it was a colony in its own right with its own governor and government to manage its small population.

Control of this government, and through it of the colony, was in due course achieved by a former labourer and carter, once in the employ of Thomas Burnard. His name was James Yeo, and he came from Kilkhampton in northeast Cornwall, near the Devon border. A man of phenomenal energy and business acumen, completely ruthless in his methods and aided in all he did by a dominating personality, he became known from his place of residence as 'the ledger giant of Port Hill'. He acquired control first of the business established by the Burnards and then progressively of large areas of timber bearing land. He established stores through which many of the colonial settlers in due course became indebted to him, the debts being worked off (but hardly ever completely) by work in his shipyards and wood lots. He entered colonial politics and became extremely influential, eventually holding the balance of power in the Colonial Administration, a position which, with reference to his former occupation as a carter, earned him the further nickname of 'the driver of the Government'. For more than thirty years, from the early 1830s until his death in 1868, James Yeo became steadily more powerful and he used his position to facilitate large-scale shipbuilding and shipowning operations. He sent his eldest son, William Yeo, back to Appledore to act as his British agent, and these two between them in the course of a few years built up a great international business.[54]

In due course William Yeo was able to build the Richmond Dry Dock at Appledore, opened in 1856 when it was entered by the barque *Elizabeth Yeo*. As the *North Devon Journal* reported in March 1857:

> On Friday the *Bacchus* and the *Sussannah* were taken out of dock and were succeeded in their berth on the following morning by the *Atlantic*. The dock since it was opened has been constantly occupied – the shipbuilders and owners now admit the greatest benefit its formation has been to the port. The *Sussannah* has been thoroughly repaired and covered with metal in rather more than a fortnight: on the beach, where, without the dock she must have been placed, the same work would have taken more than two months, a matter of some importance to a four-years vessel. For some time past upwards of 100 men have been employed there at wages averaging £1 each weekly: almost the whole of which is spent in the Parish thus indirectly benefitting all classes.[55]

William Yeo eventually acquired control of most of the local shipbuilding capacity. He built Richmond House, now called The Holt, a large mansion designed to rival in its splendour the homes of the local landed gentry, and he himself acquired considerable land holdings in his turn. The ships built in the Island were sailed over by delivery masters, mostly local men of North Devon, some of whom remained in the employ of the Yeos for many years. Often the ships were sailed to Britain with deck houses and fittings incomplete and perhaps with a limited rig, that is without topgallant masts

4.8 The *Geisha* – technically a standing topgallant-rigged vessel – was one of a series of very handsome schooners launched by Robert Cock at the Bell Inn Yard, Appledore, in the early 1900s. Owned by Claude W S Gould of Barnstaple, she was employed in the Newfoundland trade and was lost off St John's in June 1909 when she was only three years old. Shown under tow in Cumberland Basin, Bristol, she is flying her ensign which indicates that she is arriving from a foreign port. Her light loading – she appears to be well above her loadline – suggests a saltfish cargo, probably from Labrador. (*Bristol Museum*)

and yards. They were fitted out and completed in the Richmond Dry Dock, and, either at once or after a few passages under the Yeo's ownership, were sold when tonnage prices were high. A few vessels were retained for long periods and employed in the world carrying trade. The big ships sailed to India, South America, the cotton ports of the Southern States and to the Persian Gulf, as well as continually back and forth across the North Atlantic.[56] The smaller vessels were equally widely employed. To give one example, the brigantine *Favourite* sailed to Cuba with railway iron – a profitable but very dangerous cargo – and back to London with mahogany and sugar, then from Shields to Venice with coal and from the Adriatic to Donegal with wheat.[57]

But of the 350 or so vessels built by, for, or purchased immediately upon completion by James Yeo and his heirs between 1833 and 1893, at least 250 were sold to British owners soon after their arrival in North Devon. Yeo's contemporary Island merchant of Bideford origin, William Heard, working with his brother in Bideford as his agent in Britain, sold thirty new vessels over the same period. The sales were concentrated in the 1850s and 1860s, when up to nine vessels a year were launched and sailed to Bideford. Many of Yeo's ships were large vessels. The *Louisa* of 1851 was of 800 tons, the *Lady Seymour* of the next year was of 907 tons, the *Princess Royal* of 1853 was of 905 tons. The 1,000-ton mark was passed for the only time in 1856 with the *James Yeo*, a vessel which must have given much the same impression of size as does the *Cutty Sark*, preserved at Greenwich today, but the *William Yeo* and the *Isabella Saunders* of 1862 were both of nearly 800 tons, and the *Palmyra* of 1869 was of 932 tons. But these large vessels were somewhat exceptional. The British market wanted small ships from the Island builders, and of the at least 135 vessels which passed through the Yeo family hands between 1850 and James Yeo's death in 1868, only 40 were of over 300 tons, and the majority of these were launched in the 1860s when the general development of industry and trade demanded larger vessels. The peak year of James and William Yeo's achievement was 1865, when eighteen vessels were built and sold through Appledore for at least £43,000 – very roughly £2 million at 1990s values.[58]

In October 1865 the *North Devon Journal* reported from Appledore that, 'The increase which has taken place in the import timber trade has been so great of late that the number of Custom House officials stationed here has not been adequate to the requirements: the authorities therefore sent a reinforcement or two from Bristol'.[59] Nevertheless, even at this time, when the Canadian timber trade was at its height, the coasting trade was still overwhelmingly predominant in terms of tonnage of cargo handled, as the *North Devon Journal* indicated in January 1866; 'Appledore. Number of vessels that entered this creek for the ports of Bideford and Barnstaple during the year ended 31.12.65 coastwise with cargo 2,276 vessels, tonnage 112,311; foreign 32 vessels, tonnage 7,552; windbound 68 vessels, tonnage 4,091; Total 2376 vessels, tonnage 124,254'.[60] Though James Yeo's younger sons in the Island and his son-in-law were to export at least £50,000 worth of vessel property in 1874, these were the last days of prosperity for the big deep-sea square-rigged wooden sailing ship, and henceforth the decline was rapid.[61]

Barnstaple enjoyed no comparable expansion of its shipping activities in the mid-nineteenth century. Shipbuilding was successfully continued, as was the operation of vessels in the home trade. In 1851 the North Devon Shipping Company was launched in Barnstaple with investment from the town, though more than half the capital came from Liverpool, London and elsewhere. The company endeavoured to compete in the international carrying trade, and especially in the emigrant trade to Australia, but it was badly managed and the vessels were too small and incompetently operated. From 1854 it was effectively managed from Liverpool, and North Devon investment in the company was much reduced. It ceased to trade in 1864. During its short life the great majority of its crews had been Appledore men.[62]

Bideford's deep-sea shipowning involvements were at their highest peak in history in terms of numbers and sizes of vessels, capital and labour involved and the wide ranging nature of their trade in the 1850s and '60s. From the 1870s there was a steady decline in deep water activity, though the shipyards were to remain active and in recent years have operated on a larger scale than ever before.

This was the era in which the development of the compound steam engine and the widespread adoption of iron and later steel for shipbuilding, as these materials became available at prices which made them commercial, brought to an end the centuries-long era of the small wooden sailing vessel in the world's carrying trade. Indeed, William Yeo's last surviving nephew, Collingwood Yeo, told Basil Greenhill at his home in Prince Edward Island in 1963 that in 1870 William Yeo had written to his brothers in Prince Edward Island warning them that the business they had so successfully exploited for some forty years was coming to an end, and that they must seek ways of diversifying their investments. It is interesting, if pointless, to speculate as to what form that diversification might have taken in Britain had not William Yeo died in 1872 at the age of only 59, without male heir.

His death really ended the prosperous years when North Devon was one of the main places of sale of North American tonnage in Britain. He died in modern terms a multimillionaire, but it is as well to put the Yeo family activities in a wider context. The enterprise of James and William Yeo and the latter's younger brothers in Prince Edward Island was principally one of shipbuilding and marketing, rather than of shipowning. It is apparent from the statutory ship registration material available in the Public Archives

4.9 The three-masted schooner *Millom Castle*, formerly a ketch, formerly a two-masted schooner. Built at Ulverston in 1870 and purchased by Appledore owners in 1912, she proved a very successful vessel. (*H Oliver Hill*)

of Canada in Ottawa that, from James Yeo's first ship marketing venture with the schooner *Catherine O'Flannagan* in 1833 to the last vessel, the barque *Hero* sold by the Yeo family through the agency of William Pickard in Appledore after William Yeo's death, at least 53,000 tons of shipping were built in the Island by the Yeos and sold through Appledore. The total value involved must have been of the order of £400,000 – a very respectable family business indeed in the scale of the age, financed, as it was, entirely within the family and accompanied by extensive shipowning operations, landed properties and banking businesses on both sides of the Atlantic, merchandising in Canada and a large business in the export and import of lumber.

On the other hand, some idea of the scale of Devon's shipping activities in 1870 can be gained from the fact that besides a host of schooners, brigantines and brigs, forty-two of which were registered at Bideford, nineteen of them employed in the inter-continental trades, with five registered at Barnstaple, fifty three-masted square rigged sailing vessels appeared in *Lloyd's Register* as registered at ports in Devon, all of them employed in intercontinental trade, including trade with the Far East and with the west coasts of South America. All except one were built of wood, and they totalled 16,419 tons of shipping. Plymouth had twenty vessels, totalling 10,866 tons, and Bideford twelve, totalling 6,029 tons. Other ports had twos and threes and fours and Barnstaple one vessel. While this was a very respectable fleet for a county which had undergone no industrial revolution and contained no large centres of trade, it represented but a tiny fraction of the 4½ million tons of sailing ships registered at ports in the United Kingdom in that year – a tonnage which from that year went into rapid decline.

Henceforth North Devon shipping activities were increasingly in the Home Trade, though some vessels were still employed on deep water. The locally manned barquentine *Sedwell Jane*, for instance, built at Weare Giffard in 1869, in the winter of 1871/72 discharged at Pernambuco, Brazil, loaded sugar on the Brazilian coast, and sailed to Plymouth for orders, finally discharging at Bristol. The South American trade employed a number of North Devon vessels. The schooner *Foam*, owned and commanded by Captain Bate of Appledore, was lost at Pernambuco on 30 March 1869. The crew, all North Devon men, were saved. The West Indies and Mediterranean trades employed local vessels and there was some involvement with the Newfoundland trade until the First World War. At various times, to name only a few vessels, the schooners *Ismene*, the Barnstaple-built barquentine *Fanny*, the Bideford ketch *Florrie*, the Appledore-built schooners *Rosie* and *Maude*, the schooner *Norseman*, and the Appledore-owned brigantine *Elizabeth Mclea* were all involved in the business. Claude W S Gould of

Barnstaple maintained vessels in the Newfoundland trade well into the present century, including the very handsome three-master *Geisha*.

Once North Devon had begun to recover from the depression of the 1870s, reinforced as it was by the decline in the North American trade which followed William Yeo's death and the collapse of the world demand for wooden square-rigged tonnage for deep water trade, the coasting trade provided employment for local capital, shipowning and shiphandling expertise. Generally speaking, the vessels employed in the coasting trade in the 1870s, 1880s and 1890s tended to be elderly, bought from other ports, small smacks which worked the trade to the harbourless beaches of the southwest coast and the small harbours of the Bristol Channel. As the demand for larger vessels developed, even in these trades, many of the old smacks, some of which dated from the 1830s and 1840s, were cut in half and the two halves dragged apart by horses. A new midship section was then built into them and their cargo capacity thus increased. The old mast and boom were kept and a small mizzen added to balance what now became the mainsail. Thus, it has been said, the North Devon men 'reinvented the ketch'. As time went on, vessels purchased from other ports were rerigged as ketches and the rig became almost a standard top hamper for a North Devon vessel. Bigger and bigger mizzen masts were fitted until the rig became very close to that of the two-masted schooners without square topsails which were the most commonly used vessels in the short-range coasting trades of the east coast of North America. One or two of the North Devon ketches such as the *Empire* and the 'American' *Annie* were former New England schooners which had been blown across the North Atlantic while bound from one North American port towards another.[63]

North Devon has been very fortunate in that two men who knew intimately the home trade in local vessels in the early years of the present century have left us with a very comprehensive picture of the life, the ways in which the business was conducted, the social and economic background ashore, and of the ships themselves, and the details of their rigging and fittings. Edmund Eglinton in *The Last of the Sailing Coasters* and *The Mary Fletcher*, and W J Slade in the classic *Out of Appledore* and the very detailed study *Westcountry Coasting Ketches*, and in his substantial contributions to *The Merchant Schooners*, have between them recorded perhaps more comprehensively than for any other part of the coasts of Britain the last days of what had been for centuries essentially a rural shipowning industry.[64]

The traditions of this kind of small merchant shipping activity in North Devon were very strong indeed. In Northam Parish, including Appledore, as the mid-century census of 1851 clearly shows, a large part of the population was employed directly or indirectly by this activity. For instance, in Nos 1–45 Irsha Street there were only nine houses not occupied by people who gained a living from the sea. In the other 36 houses lived 137 mariners, ferrymen, etc. and their dependents, plus 6 limestone porters (5 of them women) with 6 dependents, 3 shipwrights with 4 dependents and 2 'Tidewater Customs' with 7 dependents. The same pattern spread through the rest of Irsha Street, Meeting Street and Market Street (where more shopkeepers and innkeepers appear). Bude Street has more 'master mariners' (including, at this stage in his career, William Yeo and family at No 143), while Marine Parade was evidently the select area of Appledore, lived in by people who employed servants. The New Quay area, as might be expected, housed more shipbuilders, shipwrights and sawyers, though there is still a good sprinkling of mariners' wives with the notation 'Husband at Sea'. The total population of Appledore proper was just over 2,000, of whom nearly 1,700 had been born in Northam Parish. Of these 2,000, a rough casting would suggest that over 75 per cent were dependent on shipping for their living.[65]

Appledore, by the nature of its geographical location and the specialised occupations of its inhabitants, was to a degree cut off socially and economically from the surrounding rural communities. There was no other way of earning a living except through seafaring or one of the associated occupations, and the traditions of investment in vessel property was very strong. The vessels were operated as close-knit family affairs and the tightly-knit shareholding groups almost always included some of those who sailed the vessels. There was no question of detachment of the owners from capital, its application and use. In the later nineteenth century investment in vessel property developed in Braunton, partly at least amongst members of the agricultural community. In the early twentieth century more ketches in the home trade were owned in Braunton than in Bideford/Appledore.[66]

During the First World War considerable amounts of money were made, especially in running coal to the north coast of France. The crews were paid by the voyage, which was a great incentive to getting in as many passages with paying cargo as possible. The presence of the Naval Reserve Battery at Appledore meant that while they did their annual drill the reservists received £1 5s per week. This was an important factor in annual income. The vessels operated on the 'thirds system', under which the Master became a contractor to his fellow shareholders, operating the vessel, sailing and maintaining her and paying the crew. This system provided a great incentive for capital accumulation by the Master, who could, and in many cases did, lay the foundations of further investment in vessel property.[67] Shareholders who were sailmakers, chandlers, brokers, provision merchants and shipbuilders, all benefited in several ways from their investment. Vessels were bought very cheaply from other ports which disposed of them in the later nineteenth century. As long as freight rates covered the out-of-pocket expenses of operation, owners of old vessels did better by operating them than by scrapping them.

This latter course was taken only when the net earnings of continued operation represented less than the anticipated earnings of the alternative investment of funds realised by the sale of the vessel, and old wooden sailing vessels had almost no resale value when this situation was reached. The shipyards of Appledore were well run and one legacy of William Yeo was the capacity to do a good cheap job. It was possible, therefore, to keep the vessels running. Even more important was the early adoption of the auxiliary oil engine. North Devon men were pioneers in Britain in the use of this device, which added greatly both to the earning power and the safety of the vessels. The first ketch to be so equipped was the Braunton-owned *Bessie Clark* in 1910, and she was rapidly followed by the *Democrat*, the *Bessie Gould* and the Appledore-owned ketch (later schooner) *Millom Castle*, a vessel which proved to be a 'money spinner' all her long working life of sixty years.[68]

All of these factors resulted in the survival of rural shipowning and seafaring in North Devon long after it had largely died out elsewhere in Britain. In 1927 there were no fewer than thirty-one ketches with auxiliary motors owned and working from North Devon ports, of which eighteen were owned in Braunton and eleven in Appledore, together with eight three-masted motor schooners.[69] All except three of these vessels were relics of the preceding century. In 1939, at the outbreak of the Second World War, the fleet was actually bigger, and a few relatively modern shallow draught motor ketches bought from Continental owners had replaced some of the older tonnage.

Thus North Devon became one of the last rural areas of Britain to operate small vessels in the home trade on a relatively large scale, and certainly the last to operate wooden vessels using sails. Appledore retained much of its old character as a shipping place employing sailing vessels, with all that that entailed, until the quay was broadened in the 1940s. The last passages ever made by a merchant schooner and a ketch with cargo around the coasts of the British Isles were those of the Appledore-owned three-master *Kathleen & May* and the Appledore-manned ketch *Irene* in 1960. Thus North Devon saw the survival of the wooden merchant sailing vessel into the space age.

Appendix 1

North Devon's Trade and Shipping, 1786–1914. Statistical Profile compiled by David J Starkey

Table 4.1

Tonnage entering and clearing North Devon Customs Ports from and for foreign parts, 1789–1905

('000 tons)

a) with cargoes and in ballast, 1789–1905

		Be	Bd	Ie	England & Wales	% North Devon
1789*	Ent	1.5	0.7	0.6	1,177.8	0.2
	Cl	0.2	0.4	0	1,036.7	0.06
1826	Ent	0.4	2.8	0.9	2,189.0	0.2
	Cl	0	2.3	0.6	2,010.1	0.1
1845	Ent	2.0	3.0	–	5,220.3	0.1
	Cl	0.2	2.8	–	5,272.8	0.05
1855	Ent	0.3	3.5	–	7,994.8	0.05
	Cl	0	1.0	–	8,580.9	0.01
1865	Ent	3.7	4.6	–	12,524.2	0.07
	Cl	0	3.2	–	12,914.2	0.02
1875	Ent	2.3	2.2	–	19,485.0	0.02
	Cl	0.1	2.5	–	20,449.5	0.01
1885	Ent	5.5	–	–	27,609.4	0.02
	Cl	2.8	–	–	28,341.8	0.01
1895	Ent	4.1	–	–	34,388.8	0.01
	Cl	0.5	–	–	34,797.8	0.01
1905	Ent	2.4	–	–	48,376.1	0.01
	Cl	1.8	–	–	48,575.8	0.01

b) with cargoes only, 1875–1905

		Be	Bd	England & Wales	% North Devon
1875	Ent	2.3	1.2	16,126.6	0.02
	Cl	0	0	17,874.8	0
1885	Ent	2.9	–	21,863.8	0.01
	Cl	0.3	–	25,725.8	0.01
1895	Ent	2.4	–	26,862.3	0.01
	Cl	0.2	–	31,393.9	0.01
1905	Ent	1.9	–	34,770.3	0.01
	Cl	1.1	–	42,575.0	0.01

* For compatibility with subsequent years, Irish trade is excluded from the 1789 figures.

Key to ports: Be – Barnstaple; Bd – Bideford; Ie – Ilfracombe

Sources: 1789 – PRO, CUST 17/11; 1826 – *Accounts and Papers* (BPP, 1826–7, XVIII, 202); 1845 – *Accounts and Papers* (BPP, 1846, XLV, 307); 1855–65 – *Annual Statements of Trade and Navigation*; 1875–1905 – *Annual Statements of Navigation and Shipping*.

Table 4.2

Tonnage entering and clearing North Devon Customs Ports coastwise, 1789–1913

(with cargoes only; '000 tons)

		Be	Bd	Ie	England & Wales	% North Devon
1789*	Ent	11.2	7.7	3.0	2,564.3	0.9
	Cl	4.2	5.8	1.1	3,398.3	0.3
1845	Ent	41.7	24.7	–	10,414.3	0.6
	Cl	20.2	8.1	–	11,093.8	0.3
1855	Ent	52.8	39.7	–	10,103.8	0.9
	Cl	18.9	21.5	–	10,818.9	0.4
1865	Ent	67.8	37.7	–	11,894.6	0.9
	Cl	25.8	11.2	–	12,684.4	0.3
1875	Ent	84.8	35.5	–	13,883.3	0.9
	Cl	26.0	8.3	–	13,360.0	0.3
1885	Ent	127.3	–	–	16,552.9	0.8
	Cl	9.8	–	–	16,508.3	0.06
1895	Ent	132.1	–	–	18,605.5	0.7
	Cl	54.5	–	–	19,158.6	0.3
1905	Ent	125.6	–	–	19,360.7	0.6
	Cl	68.4	–	–	20,595.9	0.3
1913	Ent	97.1	–	–	21,238.1	0.5
	Cl	51.7	–	–	22,332.6	0.2

* For compatibility with subsequent years, the 1789 figures include Irish trade originally tabulated with foreign trade.   Key to ports: see Table 4.1

Sources: 1789 – PRO, CUST 17/11; 1845 – *Accounts and Papers* (BPP, 1846, XLV, 307); 1855–65 – *Annual Statements of Trade and Navigation*; 1875–1913 – *Annual Statements of Navigation and Shipping*.

Table 4.3

Origin of vessels entering North Devon Customs Ports from abroad, 1789–1900

(Number of Vessels; tonnage)

		Be	Bd	Ie	% of North Devon Tonnage
North	1789	3–435	1–227	2–200	31.2
Europe	1900	5–1,899	–	–	45.5
Low	1789	–	–	1–76	2.8
Countries	1900	1–389	–	–	9.3
France	1789	5–553	3–291	1–28	31.5
	1900	5–1,637	–	–	39.3
Iberia	1789	2–210	1–84	–	17.6
	1900	–	–	–	–
USA	1789	2–281	–	–	10.2
	1900	–	–	–	–
British	1789	1–26	2–93	1–66	6.7
N.America	1900	–	–	–	–
South	1789	–	–	–	–
America	1900	1–247	–	–	45.9
Total	1789	13–1,505	7–695	7–563	100.0
	1900	12–4,172	–	–	100.0

Key to ports: See Table 4.1

Sources: 1789 – PRO, CUST 17/11; 1900 – *Annual Statement of Navigation and Shipping.*

Table 4.5

Tonnage registered at North Devon Registry Ports, 1790–1913   ('000 tons)

	Be	Bd	Ie	England & Wales	% North Devon
1790	6.9	3.8	2.7	1,040.2	1.3
1795	6.1	4.2	2.9	1,207.9	1.1
1800	5.4	4.7	2.9	1,466.6	0.9
1805	6.2	7.0	3.8	1,799.2	0.9
1827	2.2	8.8	4.1	1,752.4	0.9
1841	4.9	9.8	–	2,223.9	0.7
1845	4.5	12.6	–	2,354.4	0.7
1850	4.9	10.1	–	2,721.3	0.6
1855	4.1	10.8	–	3,449.8	0.4
1860	4.8	10.5	–	3,709.6	0.4
1865	5.0	11.9	–	4,653.8	0.4
1870	3.8	10.4	–	4,463.2	0.3
1875	2.8	6.8	–	4,692.2	0.2
1880	2.1	6.5	–	4,839.1	0.2
1885	2.8	4.2	–	5,405.1	0.1
1890	2.5	4.1	–	5,796.4	0.1
1895	2.1	4.1	–	6,425.0	0.1
1900	1.9	4.6	–	6,780.3	0.1
1905	1.9	4.5	–	7,979.8	0.08
1910	2.0	3.8	–	8,497.2	0.07
1913	1.9	16.5	–	8,867.8	0.2

Key to ports: See Table 4.1

Sources: 1790–1805 – PRO, CUST 17/12, 17, 22, 27; 1827 – *Accounts and Papers* (BPP, 1828, XIX, 590–1); 1841 – *Accounts and Papers* (BPP, 1843, LII, 375); 1845 – *Accounts and Papers* (BPP, 1846, XLV, 307); 1850 – *Accounts and Papers* (BPP, 1851, LII, 213); 1855–1870 – *Annual Statements of Trade and Navigation*; 1875–1913 – *Annual Statements of Navigation and Shipping.*

Table 4.4

Destination of vessels clearing North Devon Customs Ports for foreign parts, 1789–1900

(Number of Vessels; tonnage)

		Be	Bd	Ie	% of North Devon Tonnage
Low	1789	–	–	–	–
Countries	1900	3–279	–	–	28.4
France	1789	–	–	–	–
	1900	1–69	–	–	4.5
Iberia	1789	–	1–67	–	13.7
	1900	1–70	–	–	4.6
USA	1789	1–160	–	–	32.7
	1900	1–557	–	–	36.7
British	1789	1–58	3–205	–	53.6
N.America	1900	–	–	–	–
Central	1789	–	–	–	–
America	1900	1–543	–	–	35.8
Total	1789	2–218	4–272	–	100.0
	1900	7–1,518	–	–	100.0

Key to ports: See Table 4.1

Sources: 1789 – PRO, CUST 17/11; 1900 – *Annual Statement of Navigation and Shipping.*

Table 4.6

Average tonnage of vessels registered at North Devon Registry Ports, 1790–1913

	Be	Bd	Ie	North Devon	England & Wales
1790	87.9	67.3	44.0	68.3	112.8
1805	80.2	87.1	57.3	75.8	121.7
1827	52.3	89.1	64.3	73.9	120.9
1845	52.9	79.3	–	71.8	131.8
1855	60.0	81.6	–	74.2	176.0
1865	54.4	89.0	–	75.1	209.3
1875	42.5	65.8	–	56.6	237.1
1885	55.4	57.8	–	56.8	293.2
1895	43.4	50.2	–	47.7	391.6
1905	45.7	48.8	–	47.9	492.5
1913	48.5	217.3	–	159.1	554.2

Key to ports: See Table 4.1

Sources: 1790–1805 – PRO, CUST 17/12, 27; 1827 – *Accounts and Papers* (BPP, 1828, XIX, 590–1); 1845 – *Accounts and Papers* (BPP, 1846, XLV, 307); 1855–1870 – *Annual Statements of Trade and Navigation*; 1875–1913 – *Annual Statements of Navigation and Shipping.*

Table 4.7

Steam tonnage as a percentage of total registrations at North Devon Registry Ports, 1841–1913   (%)

	Be	Bd	North Devon	England & Wales
1841	0	0	0	2.7
1845	0	0	0	3.3
1850	0	0.7	0.5	4.0
1855	0	0	0	7.9
1860	0	0.7	0.5	9.1
1865	0.3	0	0.09	13.6
1870	1.0	0.7	0.8	19.2
1875	0.5	0	0.2	31.5
1880	1.9	0	0.6	42.6
1885	1.2	0	0.5	55.8
1890	1.5	0	0.5	66.0
1895	1.2	0.7	0.9	71.9
1900	3.2	0.6	1.4	80.8
1905	1.9	2.0	1.8	86.7
1910	5.9	2.0	2.5	91.1
1913	10.2	78.9	71.7	92.9

Key to ports: See Table 4.1

Sources: 1841 – *Accounts and Papers* (BPP, 1843, LII, 375); 1845 – *Accounts and Papers* (BPP, 1846, XLV, 307); 1850 – *Accounts and Papers* (BPP, 1851, LII, 213); 1855–1870 – *Annual Statements of Trade and Navigation*; 1875–1913 – *Annual Statements of Navigation and Shipping.*

4: North Devon Shipping, Trade and Ports, 1786–1939

1 PRO, BT 6/237. 'Answers returned by Collectors of Customs at the Outports of England to Certain Queries respecting Port Charges and other Local Dues imposed upon Shipping exclusive of Public Duties', 1828.

2 DRO, R2379A/(1/1) Z53. Typescript of W Rogers, 'Notes on Bideford', I, 137–9.

3 J Watkins, *An Essay Towards a History of Bideford in the County of Devon* (Exeter, 1792), 74.

4 Based on the Arrivals and Departures lists in *Trewman's Exeter Flying Post*, 1791–3; and DRO, R2379A/Z8. Bideford Port Book, 1805–13.

5 *JHC*, XLIX (1794), 310–1.

6 D and S Lysons, *Magna Britannia* (1822), VI, cclxxvi.

7 PRO, CUST 69/70. Barnstaple Outport Letter Book, Collector to Board, 22 Nov 1800.

8 DRO, 1262M/L51. Fortescue Papers, 7 Oct 1801.

9 L Lamplugh, *Barnstaple. Town on the Taw* (Southampton, 1983), 96.

10 *London Gazette*, 12 Nov 1802.

11 C Vancouver, *General View of the Agriculture of the County of Devon* (1808), 267–8.

12 Vancouver, *General View*, 266–7.

13 W Marshall, *Rural Economy of the West of England* (1796), I, 96.

14 Lysons, *Magna Britannia*, cclxxix.

15 Somerset Record Office (hereafter SRO), DD/HC38. Hancock Papers.

16 PRO, CUST 69/71. Barnstaple Outport Letter Book, Collector to Board, 12 Aug 1804.

17 SRO, Hancock Papers.

18 E A G Clark, *The Ports of the Exe Estuary, 1660–1860. A Study in Historical Geography* (Exeter, 1968), 73–4.

19 DRO, R2379A/Z8. Bideford Port Book, 1805–13.

20 DRO, 564 M/F1. J Swete, *Devon Tours*, I. Sept 1789.

21 Watkins, *History of Bideford*, 76.

22 DRO, 3319 S/1. Bideford Ship Registers.

23 DRO, 3319 S/1. Bideford Ship Registers.

24 Barnstaple Ship Registers, reconstituted by Robin Craig.

25 DRO, 3319 S/1. Bideford Ship Registers.

26 *Universal British Directory of Trade and Commerce* (1792), II.

27 DRO, 1148M/Box 11 (ii) 8. Acland Papers.

28 DRO, 1262/E2/Z1. Fortescue Papers.

29 DRO, 3319 S/1. Bideford Ship Registers.

30 DRO, 3319 S/1. Bideford Ship Registers.

31 DRO, 3319 S/1. Bideford Ship Registers; Memorial Plaque, Bideford Church.

32 DRO, Northam Parish Records. At the time of consultation these papers were still lying, unindexed, in Northam Parish Church.

33 DRO, 3319 S/1. Bideford Ship Registers.

34 DRO, R2379A/Z8. Bideford Port Book; *Lloyd's List*; *Lloyd's Register*.

35 B Greenhill and A Giffard, *Westcountrymen in Prince Edward's Isle* (Toronto, 1974). The facts in this and the preceding paragraph were largely derived from the Port Hill Papers, comprising the private correspondence of T B Chanter with William Ellis and the latter's notes and accounts. At the time of consultation these had recently been discovered in a barn on William Ellis's old property at Port Hill, PEI. They are now in the Public Archives of PEI.

36 Examples of these advertisements are to be found in the *North Devon Journal* (hereafter *NDJ*), 19 March 1829, 1 April 1830, 13 Feb 1834; and in the *Prince Edward Island Register*, 14 Oct. 1828.

37 *NDJ*, 13 and 27 Dec. 1827.

38 *NDJ*, 29 March 1827. This vessel was registered as *The Lady Rolle*.

39 *NDJ*, 19 March 1827.

40 *NDJ*, 3 Sept. 1828.

41 *NDJ*, 21 Oct. 1830.

42 DRO, 3319. Bideford Ship Registers.

43 Port Hill Papers, see n.35.

44 *NDJ*, 13 and 20 Oct 1842; Greenhill and Giffard, *Westcountrymen*, 121.

45 DRO, 3319. Bideford Ship Registers; shipping movements listed in *NDJ* and *Lloyd's List*.

46 *NDJ*, 14 April, 9 June 1831.

47 NMM, Lloyd's Survey Reports.

48 *NDJ*, 27 Jan. 1842.

49 *NDJ*, 28 May 1840.

50 DRO, 3319. Bideford Ship Registers.

51 For instance, see *NDJ*, 18 Oct. 1827, 29 March 1832, 29 Dec. 1842, 12 and 19 Jan. 1843, 2 Feb. 1843, 9 March 1843, 22 Aug. 1844, 1 May 1851.

52 *NDJ*, 25 April 1839.

53 *NDJ*, 1 June 1843.

54 Greenhill and Giffard, *Westcountrymen*; also, see L R Fischer, 'The Port of Prince Edward Island' in K Matthews and G Panting, eds, *Ships and Shipbuilding in the North Atlantic Region* (St John's, 1978); and De Jong and Moore, *Launched from Prince Edward Island* (Charlottetown, 1981).

55 *NDJ*, 5 March 1857.

56 See the *NDJ* and the Charlottetown newspapers, the *Royal Gazette* and *The Islander*, during the 1850s and 1860s.

57 W Wallace, *The Wake of the Windships* (1927), 91.

58 The facts in the foregoing paragraphs are derived from the Public Archives of Canada (hereafter PAC), Ottawa, Record Group 12, A1. Registration of Shipping at Charlottetown Custom House, 1833–93.

59 *NDJ*, 26 Oct. 1865.

60 *NDJ*, 1 Jan. 1866.

61 PAC, Record Group 12, A1. For a brief study of the history of the merchant sailing ship in the nineteenth century see B Greenhill, *The Life and Death of the Merchant Sailing Ship* (1980). For detailed case histories, see E W Sager, L R Fischer and R Ommer, 'Landward and Seaward Opportunities in Canada's Age of Sail' in L R Fischer and E W Sager, eds, *Merchant Shipping and Economic Development in Atlantic Canada* (St John's, 1982); A Eames, *Ventures in Sail* (Caernarfon, 1987); and B Greenhill and J Hackman, *The Grain Races* (1986).

62 See A Grant, 'The North Devon Shipping Company, 1831–64' *MM*, 57 (1971), 3–16.

63 W Slade and B Greenhill, *Westcountry Coasting Ketches* (1974); DRO, Bideford and Barnstaple Ship Registers; NMM, Lloyd's Survey Reports; B Greenhill, *The Merchant Schooners* (4th edn, 1988).

64 E Eglinton, *The Last of the Sailing Coasters* (1982); E Eglinton, *The Mary Fletcher* (Exeter, 1990); W Slade, *Out of Appledore* (1980); Slade and Greenhill, *Westcountry Coasting Ketches*; and Greenhill, *Merchant Schooners*.

65 PRO, HO 107/1895.

66 DRO, Barnstaple Ship Registers. For Braunton shipowning, see M Bouquet, *No Gallant Ship* (1959) 157–60, 179–80.

67 For detailed accounts of the working of 'sailing by thirds' and its implications, see Slade and Greenhill, *Westcountry Coasting Ketches*, 21, 23; Greenhill, *Merchant Schooners*, 127; Bouquet, *No Gallant Ship*, 156–7.

68 Greenhill, *Merchant Schooners*, 251–64.

69 DRO, Bideford and Barnstaple Ship Registers; personal recollections of the vessels concerned.

5 Tamar Traffic in the Nineteenth Century

AMBER PATRICK

RIVERS PLAY AN AMBIGUOUS ROLE in the transportation of goods and people. Comprising broad expanses of moving water, cutting deep valleys and flooding adjacent plains, they frequently hinder land-based communication. At the same time, of course, these barriers often constitute vital arteries linking inland areas with the sea. In this latter guise the rivers of the British Isles have been used extensively over the centuries to transport crops, raw materials and manufactured goods between sites of production and consumption. Embanked, diverted, dredged or otherwise improved, these water highways, appended or supplanted by canals, have facilitated the local and regional specialisation which fosters economic growth, while their proximity and utility has conditioned the character of the communities established on their banks.

The Tamar, more than any other river in the English West Country, exemplifies all of these traits. Rising close to the Bristol Channel coast it pursues a tortuous southerly course, crossing the southwest peninsula to emerge some sixty miles distant in Plymouth Sound. For much of its length, the river serves as the administrative boundary between Devon and Cornwall, though the divide is also decidedly physical in the lower reaches of the Tamar, as first it twists and turns through its narrow, steep-sided valley, before converging with the waters of the Tavy and the St Germans River to form a long and deep estuarine tract. A substantial obstacle to communications between the Duchy and the rest of England, the Tamar nevertheless provides a means of transport which has been exploited by inhabitants of both sides of the valley, as indicated by the numerous quays and ferries, ancient and modern, evident on its banks (Map 5.1). Tidal and navigable over the last twenty miles of its course, from Weirhead, below Gunnislake, to Plymouth, the Tamar has borne all manner of traffic; the Danish longships of the tenth century, the medieval vessels which serviced the stannary town of Tavistock, and the motor-driven pleasure craft of today. It was in the nineteenth century, however, that the river reached its zenith as a commercial waterway. At this juncture the Tamar's traffic assumed three principal forms. Schooners and ketches were engaged in the coastwise shipment of minerals, coal and bricks; barges conveyed limestone, manure and other bulky cargoes to the farms of the valley; and steamers were employed in the excursion business and in the carriage of goods and passengers from inland villages and hamlets to the urban markets of Plymouth and beyond (Fig. 5.1). Diverse and expansive, especially in the second half of the century, this traffic reflected the character of a valley in which a substantial extractive industry coexisted with an important agricultural and market gardening sector and a growing tourist business.

In the analysis which follows, the three elements of the Tamar's traffic are considered separately. Although in each case it is difficult to measure the volume of shipping using the river (largely because riverine traffic was not distinguished from the business of the Port of Plymouth in official returns), sufficient documentary, pictorial and oral evidence exists to provide a good impression of the Tamar's significance in the nineteenth century.[1] From these data, it emerges that the river occupied a unique place in the maritime economy of the South West, serving as an arterial route in the manner of the Severn, the Trent and the rivers of the industrial North. As such, the Tamar provides an important riverine dimension to the region's maritime past, a dimension worthy of special consideration.

Coastal Traffic

A marked upsurge was apparent in the volume of coastal traffic using the Tamar in the nineteenth century. Although the river had long been visited

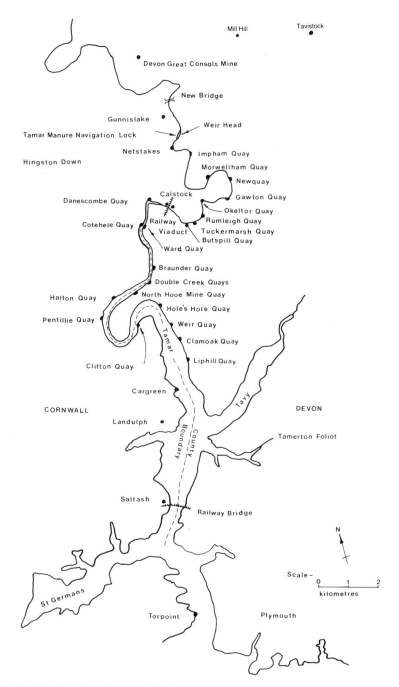

Map 5.1 The River Tamar and its Quays

5.1 The Calstock waterfront photographed from the Danescombe Hotel at the end of the nineteenth century. A brigantine, a schooner and three barges lie upstream, another barge and a schooner lie immediately abaft the steamer alongside in the foreground. She was the *Albion* and she was loading granite for the construction of a breakwater at Dover. She visited Calstock regularly for this purpose for some years. The wind is from the east and the 'inside' barge in the foreground is beating her way upstream with the flowing tide. She has just come round on the port tack and her foresail is still aback. A steam paddle market boat is also going up with the tide. (*Postcard*)

by vessels engaged in the coastwise shipment of goods, it was in the Victorian age, particularly from the 1840s to the 1880s, that Calstock and Morwellham emerged as notable ports in Britain's growing, ubiquitous inter-regional trade. This was a transitory prominence, however, for it was inextricably associated with the mining industry, the most dynamic element in the Tamar Valley's mixed economy. Accordingly, vessels from all parts of the country, and some from overseas, ventured up the river when cargoes of tin, lead, manganese and, most especially, copper awaited shipment to the smelting works and factories of South Wales and elsewhere. When, late in the century, the mineral seams were gradually exhausted, this facet of the Tamar's traffic declined and eventually ceased to exist.

In connecting the extractive industries of an inland area with the sea, the Tamar was similar to many other British waterways. The Tyne and the Wear, for instance, were instrumental in the exploitation of the coalfields of the North East, while the Weaver and the Mersey facilitated the carriage of Cheshire salt to markets throughout the country. In the Tamar Valley copper ore was the principal bulk, low-value commodity rendered accessible by the proximity of relatively cheap riverine transportation. This had been so since the 1770s, when rich deposits of copper were discovered and worked at the Gunnislake Old Mine, on the Cornish side of the river, and exported via Calstock. Stimulated by growing industrial demand, the mine proved highly profitable, encouraging further development of local mineral resources. On the Devon bank, the Tavistock Canal was begun in 1803, to ease the flow of lead and copper ore from Wheal Betsy and Wheal Friendship, near Mary Tavy, to the river at Morwellham. The construction of the canal tunnel revealed more of the mineral potential of the area, and Wheal Crebor was established as a consequence. With mineral output expanding, the trade of Morwellham increased rapidly, and nearly 23,000 tons of copper ore passed through the port between 1805 and 1819, as well as significant quantities of manganese extracted from mines developed to the north of Tavistock in the early years of the century.[2]

Yet the peak of the activity had still to come, for it was the discovery of copper in Blanchdown Woods in 1844, and its exploitation by the Devonshire Great Consolidated Copper Mining Company, which propelled the Tamar Valley into the first rank of mining areas alongside the productive and long-established districts of eastern Cornwall, and heralded the river's apogee as a commercial waterway. For nearly twenty years Devon Great Consols was the world's leading copper-mining enterprise, its output doubling between 1846 and 1856 and remaining high until a marked downturn occurred in the mid-1860s. It brought rich dividends to investors,

provided employment for hundreds of miners and precipitated something approaching a 'rush' in the area as prospectors and speculators eagerly sought to emulate its success.[3] As a consequence, the 1850s and 1860s witnessed a veritable boom in the valley's economy as the output of a growing number of mines increased, the population of towns like Callington, Gunnislake, Calstock and Tavistock almost doubled in size, and a range of industries ancillary to the mining sector were founded.[4]

The development of the mines and their associated industries led to the importation of considerable quantities of coal to fire the steam engines which pumped the mines free of water and powered the smelting works and blacksmitheries which were established in the valley. In addition, a large volume of culm – small, hard coal – was conveyed up the Tamar for the lime kilns which were built at many points on the tidal river system. These manufactured the lime which was used to fertilise the acid soil of the valley's farms, market gardens and orchards, and also in building work. Pig iron for the fabrication of the ironwork for mines and farms was likewise imported, as were wooden pitprops and, later, timber used at Calstock and elsewhere to make punnets, the wooden baskets in which the valley gardens' soft fruit was sent to market.

Although the heyday of the copper ore trade had passed by the 1880s, the Tamar's coastal trade persisted until well into the twentieth century. Photographs show numerous schooners loading and discharging at Calstock in the period immediately before the First World War. The last vessel to bring culm to the Tamar was probably the schooner *Mary Ashburner* of Barrow, which discharged at Halton Quay when the kilns there were temporarily reactivated in 1916. Eleven years later the schooner *M A James* of Plymouth landed the final seaborne cargo of coal at Halton Quay,[5] while timber was imported as late as May 1950, when the Finnish four-masted motor schooner *Svenborg* brought aspen for the Tamar Valley Growers Association's basket factory at Calstock.[6] The stone trade of St German's River – in Cornwall, but part of the Customs Port of Plymouth – was also buoyant in the twentieth century. Between 1933 and 1939, for instance, there were some 1,500 arrivals and departures of vessels in this business, as large a concentration of shipping as the copper ore trade had attracted at its height.[7]

Data relating to the volume and direction of the Tamar's nineteenth-century coastal trade is sparse and imperfect. Nevertheless, a good impression of the character of this traffic, and the main trading linkages, can be gained from a variety of documentary sources. Thus, as Table 5.1 indicates, fuel and mineral ores were the principal commodities conveyed to and from the Tamar. Quite clearly, coal and culm dominated the river's import trade, a preponderance that was evident throughout the West Country.[8] However, unlike importations into the Exe, the Taw and other southwestern rivers, little of this coal was destined for domestic use, as the valley's main fuel consumers were the mines and their ancillary industries. That iron and lead manufactures, engine works, and bricks, tiles and slate were also shipped inwards further attests to the industrial character of the valley's economy in the mid-nineteenth century, though the landing of culm to fire the area's lime kilns reflects the prominence of agriculture locally. In contrast, there was little variety in the goods exported coastwise, with mineral ores accounting for nearly all of the known outward shipments. Despite the bias inherent in the sources utilised, the significance of copper ore to the Tamar's coastal trade is abundantly clear in Table 5.1.

Much of this trade was conducted with South Wales, as Table 5.2 suggests. Though intra-regional linkages were strong, particularly with Cornwall, and vessels carried goods to and from the North West, principally Liverpool and Runcorn, the Clyde and numerous east-coast ports, South Wales was clearly the focus of the Tamar's coastwise traffic (see Map 5.2). At least eleven South Walian ports engaged in this commerce, with Neath clearly the principal destination of vessels clearing the river, Newport the main source of craft entering, and Llanelly and Swansea also featuring notably in the business. If the predominance of this trade flow owes something to the sources upon which Table 5.2 is based, it nevertheless reflects the significance which the Tamar Valley attained in the production of copper ore during the mid-nineteenth century. In 1863, for instance, the valley's mines accounted for 27 per cent of the shipments exported from the South West to the smelting works of Neath, surpassing many noted copper-producing areas in West Cornwall.[9] In return, of course, it was the South

Table 5.1

Coastwise shipments to and from the Tamar, 1840–1899

(Number of Shipments)

Cargo	Inward	Outward
Coal	198	–
Culm	40	–
Bricks/tiles	18	–
Iron & iron works	9	–
Lead pipes/sheet	4	–
Slate	4	–
Salt	2	–
Copper ore	–	820*
Arsenic	–	8
Manganese	–	7
Spare ore	–	4
Oak bark	–	1
Lead ore	5	22
Engine works	1	2
Timber	1	3

* This figure is unduly weighted owing to the utilisation of the Neath Harbour Records, the Rough Stock Book, and the records of Sweetland, Tuttle & Co.

Sources: CRO and DRO, Board of Trade Returns; DRO, Duke of Bedford's Papers, LI258 Canals, Tavistock 27/28, and LI258 Vouchers V6/1 and V13/1; GRO, D/D Xnf 10/1–5, Neath Harbour Records; Richard Pearse's notes on the *Batten Castle*, and the Treffry Papers in CRO; Rough Stock Book, 1877–96, in the possession of Mr G C Penaluna of Wheal Rose Coach Works, Scorrier, near Redruth, Cornwall; *Plymouth, Devonport and Stonehouse Herald; Tavistock Gazette; Western Daily Mercury*; and Sweetland Tuttle and Co records in P H Stanier, 'The Copper Ore Trade of South West England in the Nineteenth Century', *JTH*, V (1979), 18–35.

Table 5.2

Vessels entering and clearing the Tamar coastwise, 1840–1899

	Entrances	Clearances
Inter-Regional (West)		
Severn	13	2
South Wales	518	935
North West	55	30
West Scotland	10	5
Ireland	1	–
Inter-Regional (East)		
South East	2	3
London	3	5
North East	30	1
East Scotland	–	5
Intra-Regional (West)		
Cornwall	74	81
North Devon	1	1
Intra-Regional (East)		
South Devon	12	8

Sources: See Table 5.1

Map 5.2 British Ports trading with the Tamar in the nineteenth century.

Wales coalfield which provided the fuel requirements of the Tamar Valley. Thus a simple exchange – copper out, coal in – underlay the Tamar's linkage with South Wales, the main channel of the river's coastwise trade.

The volume of coastal shipping using the Tamar varied considerably during the nineteenth century. Some indication of the level of this traffic at its peak, in the mid-1850s, can be gained from the *Shipping and Mercantile Gazette*, which for a short time differentiated Calstock's entrances and clearances from those of the Customs Port of Plymouth. As Table 5.3 shows, 646 vessels entered Calstock in 1857, almost one-fifth of the 3,337 entrances recorded at Plymouth during the year. Although, at 457 vessels, the number of clearances from Calstock was typically lower,[10] it represented a slightly

higher proportion, 22.7 per cent, of Plymouth's total clearances.[11] This implies that the Tamar Valley formed one of the more productive, export-oriented parts of Plymouth's hinterland, particularly since the predominant incoming cargo, coal, took up more space per ton than the main outgoing cargo of copper ore. In fact, copper ore was a very concentrated cargo with little bulk, requiring very careful stowage. Accordingly, *Stevens on Stowage*, that classic nineteenth-century guide for mates and masters by a Plymouth author and shipowner, devotes many pages of advice to the loading and stowing of this material.[12]

In terms of seasonality, Table 5.3 suggests that the Tamar's coastal traffic was fairly evenly spread over the year, the busiest period occurring in the summer and autumn, especially in respect of entrances. The daily level of activity varied according to the tide, the wind and the weather in general, with entrances generally more volatile than clearances. In 1857, for example, there were weeks such as 2–5 January in which vessels neither entered nor cleared the Tamar. There were longer periods, like the middle fortnight in February and the last two weeks of the year, when only a handful of shipping movements were recorded at Calstock; yet there were days like 31 March, when the port witnessed sixteen entrances and eight clearances. At such times the river must have been an extremely busy place, and it is perhaps surprising that there were not more accidents such as that which occurred on 28 February 1856, when the *Belle* and the *Excellent* 'came in contact in the river, when the latter had carried away from the bow to the forerigging, her staunchions, bulwarks, etc, but little damage was done to the *Belle*'.[13]

Typically, the ships employed in the Tamar's coastal trade were relatively small wooden sailing vessels. In the early decades of the nineteenth century the brig appears to have been the predominant rig, at least in the copper ore business, though by the 1850s and 1860s the two-masted schooner was more commonly deployed.[14] As Table 5.4 indicates, no less than 90 per cent of the 181 craft of known tonnage which entered the river in the second half of the nineteenth century measured between 49 and 150 tons. In line with the British home trade as a whole (in 1912–13 the average sailing coaster measured 66.9 tons[15]), most of the vessels which carried cargoes to and from the Tamar were less than 100 tons. Some of these craft were built, and many more repaired, in one of the two shipyards established on the Upper Tamar during the nineteenth century. Between 1831 and 1878 Edward Brooming ran a shipbuilding and repair business in the parish of Bere Ferrers, opposite Calstock.[16] Although most of his products were barges, he also constructed the smack *Selina Mary* in 1878, which was later ketch-rigged, while his successor at the yard, James Goss, launched the coasting ketches *C F H* and *Garlandstone* in the early 1900s[17] (Fig. 5.2).

Table 5.3
Coasting vessels entering and clearing Calstock in 1857

	Entrances		Clearances	
	Number	Daily Peak	Number	Daily Peak
Jan	59	12	37	6
Feb	35	11	44	10
Mar	59	16	39	8
Apr	30	9	35	6
May	49	9	39	7
Jun	68	15	43	7
Jul	57	15	30	5
Aug	72	11	33	6
Sep	62	12	44	8
Oct	73	14	46	17
Nov	46	9	39	10
Dec	36	7	28	6
Total	646		457	

Sources: *Shipping and Mercantile Gazette*, 1857.

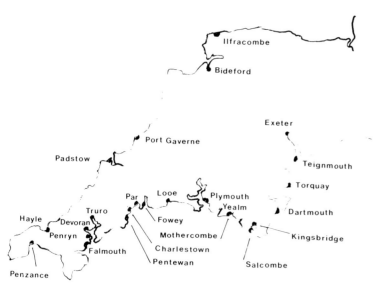

Map 5.2   Insert A – Devon and Cornwall

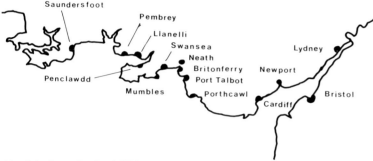

Map 5.2   Insert B – South Wales

Table 5.4
Tamar coasting vessels by registered tonnage, 1840–1899

Tonnage Range	Number of Vessels	% of Vessels
20–49	12	7.2
50–99	110	60.8
100–149	53	29.3
150–199	4	2.2
200+	1	0.5
Total	181	100

Sources: CRO and DRO, Board of Trade Returns; WDRO, 894, Plymouth Ship Registers; GRO, D/D Xnf 10/1–5, Neath Harbour Records; *Lloyd's Register of Shipping*; WSL, Census Returns, 1861, 1871, 1881.

The other Tamar yard was opened by Emanuel Crocker during the boom which accompanied the American Civil War. A local entrepreneur, Crocker located his yard almost at the head of navigation at Netstakes, just below Gunnislake on the Cornish bank of the river. At this site between 1864 and 1868 he built five vessels, the *Tamar Queen*, a schooner of 103 tons, owned in Calstock and employed in the Mediterranean trade, the *Ada*, another schooner of 129 tons built in 1865, Calstock-owned and lost on Rio Grande Bar, the *John Hedley* in 1866, the smallest of Crocker's vessels, a smack of 59 tons, and in the same year the *Thomas Edwin*, a schooner of 74 tons (Fig.

5.2 The shipyard successively occupied by Edward Brooming and James Goss at the Ferry Inn in the parish of Bere Ferrers in Devon, photographed during the construction of the Calstock Viaduct over the Tamar about 1905. The vessel in frame is the ketch *Garlandstone*. The 'inside' barge on the hard is the *William & Fred*, the last barge to be built by James Goss. The barge afloat is the 'inside' barge *Lillie*, built by Goss in 1899. She was still working on the Exe in 1946. (*F Paul, Calstock*)

5.3). Locally owned, she was at once fixed to load dried and salted codfish at Gaspe in Quebec, Canada. Here her crew of five, all Plymouth men, froze to death in mysterious circumstances, and Emmanuel Crocker himself had to go out to rescue her and sail her home.[18] Finally in 1868 the *Merit* was built. A schooner of 162 tons, she was the largest vessel from the yard, almost 100ft long, and was sold to owners in Newfoundland when only eight months old.[19]

A number of the coasters engaged in trade with the Tamar were locally owned. Plymouth Ship Registers indicate that residents of at least twenty-five towns and villages in the vicinity of the Tamar Valley held shares in schooners, the majority hailing from Calstock, Gunnislake and Tavistock.[20] As Table 5.5 shows, only five of the investors identified in the Ship Registers were described as shipowners, the largest occupational groups being mine agents, miners and merchants. This, together with the fact that the peak of local investment in schooners coincided with the mid-century mining boom, suggests, once more, the significance of the extractive industry to the valley's

coastwise trade. Master mariners, grocers and farmers were the next most populous categories, though perhaps the most unorthodox shipowning group associated with the Tamar invested in the *Rhoda Mary*, a relatively large schooner of over 100ft in length. Managed in Gunnislake from 1876 to 1896, she was largely the property of the head warder and various of his colleagues at Dartmoor Gaol[21] (see Fig. 5.4).

Local craft did not necessarily participate in the trade of the Tamar, of course. Indeed, many generated incomes in a range of carrying trades at home and abroad, particularly after the valley's mining industry had passed its zenith in the 1860s. Conversely, vessels owned in numerous ports in the West Country, South Wales and further afield engaged in the river's trade. Surviving evidence infers that few were regular callers at the river's quays. Of 276 vessels identified as trading with the river, 166 visited the river but once, 72 called between two and four times, and only 11 craft made ten or more calls. Amongst the frequent traders were vessels such as *Lord Rolle*, a polacca brigantine, and the iron schooner *Naiad*, both of which were registered in Llanelly and owned by local copper smelters.[22] The *Naiad* entered the Tamar on 171 occasions from January 1877 to the end of November 1895,[23] shuttling back and forth between Calstock and Llanelly with copper ore and coal. If her persistence was rare, the nature of her cargoes and the direction of her voyages epitomised the most significant aspect of the Tamar's nineteenth-century coastal trade.

The Tamar Barge Traffic

Barges were part of the economic and social fabric of the Tamar Valley in the nineteenth and early twentieth centuries. They fell into two distinct groups, locally known as 'inside' and 'outside' barges. The former, operating only in the tidewater of the Tamar, were not required to be registered under the Merchant Shipping Acts and were not subject to regular surveys of their condition and equipment for the granting of a loadline (the so-called 'Plimsoll Mark') which every seagoing vessel had to have on her sides in the later nineteenth century as her licence to sail. In consequence the records of inside barges are scanty, though there were certainly hundreds of them in the nineteenth and early twentieth centuries.[24] Sometimes these craft were refitted for the coasting trade, being equipped with raised bulwarks, improved fittings, larger pumps, better boats and so forth to meet official requirements for registration.

Outside barges were generally bigger vessels, built, equipped and maintained to the standards, such as they were, necessary for them to be

5.3 The schooner *Thomas Edwin*, built by Emanuel Crocker at Netstakes on the Tamar in 1866. Shown here in a painting made in the 1880s by Thomas Chidgey of Watchet in Somerset, she was lost in collision off Falmouth in February 1909. (*Private Collection*)

Table 5.5
Vessel ownership in the Tamar Valley by occupation, 1824–1900

Occupations	Schooners	Barges
Accountant	2	–
Agent	2	–
Assayer	1	–
Baker	1	1
Banker	2	–
Bargeman	1	1
Blacksmith	1	–
Bookseller	1	–
Bootmaker	1	–
Brewer	1	–
Builder	3	1
Butcher	1	1
Carpenter	1	2
Coach builder	1	–
Cooper	1	2
Cordwainer	1	–
Draper	2	1
Engine driver	1	–
Engineer	3	–
Farmer	9	1
Gentleman	4	5
Granite merchant	1	1
Grocer	9	1
Inn keeper	2	–
Labourer	–	1
Land agent	1	–
Machinist	1	–
Manganese merchant	1	–
Mariner	1	22
Master Mariner	9	1
Merchant	11	8
Merchant's clerk	2	–
Mine agent	18	–
Miner	11	–
Painter	–	1
Sadler	1	–
Sampler of copper ore	1	–
Shipbuilder	2	1
Shipowner	5	–
Shipping agent	2	–
Silver refiner	1	–
Solicitor	1	–
Spinster	2	–
Spirit merchant	1	1
Timber merchant	1	–
Widow	5	–
Yeoman	4	3

Sources: WDRO, 894, Plymouth Ship Registers.

5.4 The schooner *Rhoda Mary* at Cotehele Quay. She was owned principally by six warders of Dartmoor Gaol from 1876 to 1896. The photograph was taken between 1896, when the Tamar barge *Myrtle*, visible stern-on lying in the dock, was built, and 1898, when the *Rhoda Mary* was re-rigged as a three-masted schooner. This is the only known photograph of her with two masts. (*Cyril Staal*)

barge, with limestone, manure and coal transported up river, and granite from Gunnislake, Hingston Down and Kit Hill, slate from Mill Hill, and bricks from the various works founded in the valley shipped down the river. Such general carrying work was neatly summarised in the crew list of the *Thomasine*, which, in 1878, was engaged in 'trading between the Weir Head, Calstock, and Plymouth, and in the river Tamar and in no other trade, carrying granite, brick, limestone, and manure'.[26]

Records pertaining to the traffic of the Tavistock Canal suggest the pattern of this trade. Between April 1867 and September 1869 the two main cargoes landed at Morwellham for transfer to the canal were coal and limestone. During this thirty-month period, twenty-seven different barges delivered limestone, though only four could be described as regular traders – the *Tavistock*, which belonged to the lessees of Morwellham Quay and the owners of the canal, making fifty-six calls, the *Edmund and Sarah* calling forty-nine times, the *Thomasine* on forty-two occasions, and the *Albert* discharging twenty-nine consignments at the quay. Although the round voyage from the limestone quarries at Plymouth to Morwellham could be

5.5 Sutton Harbour in the late nineteenth century. The vessel in the left foreground is a small barge for work inside Plymouth Breakwater. The vessel on the right is a larger barge notable for having an open rail in place of bulwarks. Two schooners and a coasting smack lie abreast alongside the quay in the background with another coasting smack ahead of them. (*City of Plymouth Museums & Art Gallery*)

granted a loadline (Fig 5.6). In fact, it is difficult to draw a hard line between the activities of these larger outside barges and those of the coasting schooners and ketches, except that outside barges sometimes spent periods at work of the type done by their inside sisters. The outside barges regularly sailed to Southampton, Lyme Regis, Topsham and Salcombe in the east and to Looe, Fowey, Pentewan, Mevagissey, Charlestown and Falmouth in the west. Some ventured further, the *Mayblossom*, for instance, sailing to the Channel Islands, the *J N B* to London and the *Industry* round to Bridgwater.[25]

The inside barges generally serviced the agricultural sector of the valley's mixed economy. In the early nineteenth century, before the advent of the paddle steamer, the produce of local farms was conveyed to the Plymouth market by barge while limestone, manure and dock dung were carried in the opposite direction to fertilise the acid soil of the valley's upper slopes. Although the marketing function, together with passenger traffic, was lost to the steamers, bulky low-value cargoes remained the preserve of the inside

5.6 A study by H Oliver Hill shows the 'outside' barge *Yealm*, built by David Banks at Plymouth in 1878. She is lying at the Custom House Quay, Falmouth, in the early 1920s. (*H Oliver Hill*)

completed in a few days, on only one occasion, in June 1867, did a barge, the *Tavistock*, make the journey more than three times a month. In terms of load size, the largest limestone cargo conveyed on this route was 48 tons, by the *Tavistock*, while the smallest was the 22 tons carried in both the *Gazelle* and the *Mayflower*. The majority of consignments, however, comprised between 30 and 39 tons of limestone.[27]

In line with the highly localised character of their deployment, many of the barges were built on the Upper Tamar, as well as at Plymouth, Saltash, and Torpoint. Edward Brooming's first vessel, for instance, was the 16-ton *John and Maria*, a barge boasting a counter stern, which set her apart from her square-sterned sisters. Launched in 1831, she was followed down Brooming's slipway by many other barges, including the *Calstock* (1839), *Edward and Sarah* (1844), *Ann* (1850), *Mary Ann* (1856), *Albert* (1863), *Secret* and *Tavy* (1864), *Eleanor* (1865), *Mary* (1866), *Frances* (1868), and *Violet* (1876), all of which were subsequently registered at Plymouth. At the same yard in Bere Ferrers, James Goss continued this business, building

barges such as the *Britannia* (1890), *Lynher* (1896), *Lillie* (1899), *Comet* and *Indus* (1901)[28] (Fig. 5.7). Such vessels were normally owned and operated by inhabitants of the valley. Thus, Calstock, Bere Ferrers and St Dominick were prominent amongst the places of residence cited in barge registration documents, while, as Table 5.5 indicates, the most common occupation given by barge owners was that of 'mariner'. Quite clearly, the inside barges belonged to the communities they served. Moreover, in contrast to locally-owned schooners, the men who sailed the vessels, many of whom also worked market gardens and small farms,[29] often had an interest in the property of the craft.

Although the development of the motor lorry and improved roads meant the end of the inside barges in the 1920s (ironically, the outside barges had carried much of the stone needed to tarmacadam the roads around the West Country rivers), a number of outside barges survived to be amongst the last of Britain's coasting sailing craft. In 1939 there were still fourteen of them at work. The last to survive, *Mayblossom*, *J N R* and *Shamrock*, ceased to work in the early 1950s, though the *Shamrock* has since been restored and, owned principally by the National Trust, regularly sails in the summer from Cotehele Quay.

Steamers on the Tamar

Steamships were utilised on the Tamar from the 1820s, when the paddle steamer *Sir Francis Drake*, built at Hill's yard in Cattedown, Plymouth, ventured up river. Thereafter they were deployed in three main capacities. Some were used as towing vessels, either to transport timber upstream or to assist the sailing coasters in their passage to or from the quays of the valley. Although schooners and ketches could negotiate the Tamar by sail, a tow expedited their progress and therefore reduced costs.

More significantly, perhaps, steamships formed the link between the farms of the valley and the markets of Plymouth. Previously effected by barge, this linkage was critical to the development of market gardening in the valley, for a swift and regular transportation service was required to marry the burgeoning demand of the rapidly-growing town, and its Naval Dockyard, with supplies of fresh produce (see Fig. 5.8). Accordingly, increasing quantities of dairy goods and soft fruit, together with daffodils, anemones and narcissi, were conveyed to Plymouth by steamship, particularly once the metropolitan market could be exploited with the opening of the Plymouth to London railway in 1859. The precise scale and pattern of this trade is difficult to ascertain, though it was probably conditioned by the seasonality of production and the occurrence of market days in Plymouth. However, as these market steamers lacked cold storage facilities, it is clear that they must have sailed regularly. There are references in the local

5.7 H Oliver Hill's classic study of an 'inside' barge below Saltash Bridge. She is the *Indus*, built by James Goss at Calstock in 1901 and she was photographed in 1923. Her working life is described in great detail from her account books, which have survived, by Ian Merry in *Shipping and Trade of the River Tamar*. (*H Oliver Hill*)

newspapers to the steamers making their 'usual trip',[30] while Miss Myrtle Northcott of Boetheric recollects that the market steamer to Plymouth ran from Cotehele Quay three times a week and that the fare was 1s.[31] In the 1880s, moreover, the ss *Telegraph*, which was owned by one of the lesser steamship companies, departed each day, sailing 'to and from Gunnislake, Morwellham, Calstock, Hole's Hole, Saltash, North Corner, and Great Western Docks, and all intermediate quays daily, circumstances permitting, carrying cargoes and passengers'.[32]

Typically, the regular and relatively fast voyages of the steamers soon cornered the passenger market on the Tamar. In one sense this was allied to the marketing role of these vessels, for the vendors of garden produce, and others with business in town, would obviously travel with their goods. However, another type of passenger, the excursionist, formed the third main branch of the steamer's work. These pleasure trips started with the journeys of the *Sir Francis Drake* in the 1820s, but it was not until much later in the century that the business really developed. With rising standards of living and a growing awareness of the healthy attributes of fresh air, the Victorian middle class began to explore the coast and countryside in great numbers. While the natural beauty of the Tamar Valley had already proved attractive to trippers, the visit of Queen Victoria to Morwellham in 1856 gave the Tamar's nascent tourist industry a great fillip.[33] In the following year two new steamers were introduced to the river, the *Wellington* and the *Princess*, the latter a vessel of 40hp able to carry 400 passengers and offering sumptuous accommodation, 'the best cabins having mirrors and satin hair cloth cushions'.[34] Both vessels ran between Devonport and Calstock, and later were bought by the Devon and Cornwall Steam Packet Company, which operated for twenty-seven years on the river, owning a total of nine steamers. Its main rivals were the Tamar and Tavy Steamship Company, established in 1862 with two vessels, and the Saltash and St Germans Steamboat Company, which was founded in 1858 and operated five vessels.[35]

5.8   The paddle steamer *Empress* and passengers. Built in 1880 of iron and fitted with a compound oscillating engine, she served as a 'market boat' on the Tamar from 1880 to 1926, when she became a houseboat on the Yealm. (*Mrs T Hutton*)

These companies ran excursions on the Tamar throughout the summer months of the late nineteenth century, carrying an increasingly working-class clientele from Plymouth to Calstock or Morwellham for cream teas or other, more intoxicating, forms of refreshment. Reflecting the service rather than the productive elements of the valley's economy, it was this facet of the Tamar's nineteenth-century traffic which was to survive most vigorously in the twentieth century.

5: Tamar Traffic in the Nineteenth Century

1 See A Patrick, 'Tamar Traffic, 1836–1900', in S Fisher, ed., *Studies in British Privateering, Trading Enterprise and Seamen's Welfare, 1775–1900* (Exeter, 1987), 43–6.

2 F Booker, *The Industrial Archaeology of the Tamar Valley* (Newton Abbot, 1967), 27–9, 103–18.

3 J C Goodridge, 'Devon Great Consols. A Study of Victorian Mining Enterprise', *DAT*, XCVI (1964), 228–41.

4 Booker, *Industrial Archaeology*, 23–4; Goodridge, 'Devon Great Consols', 240–1.

5 Oral evidence of Mr Rogers of Halton Quay.

6 *Western Morning News*, 26 May 1950.

7 I D Merry, *The Shipping and Trade of the River Tamar* (1980), II, 26–7.

8 See Chapter 3.

9 P H Stanier, 'The Copper Ore Trade of South West England in the Nineteenth Century' *JTH*, V (1979), 21.

10 Entrances generally exceeded clearances at South Devon ports, see Chapter 3. At Calstock, this was true throughout the nineteenth century. See PRO, Customs 66/41, Plymouth Collector to Board, Letter Books, letter number 234, 15 May 1837, and WDRO, Queen's Harbour Master, Plymouth, Letter Book, 641, 18 Jan. 1860.

11 *Shipping and Mercantile Gazette*, 1857; *Annual Statement of Trade and Navigation*, 1857.

12 R W Stevens, *On the Stowage of Ships and their Cargoes* (6th edn., 1869), 400–4.

13 *Liverpool Telegraph and Shipping and Commercial Gazette*, 5 March 1856.

14 Stanier, 'Copper Ore Trade', 26–7.

15 P S Bagwell and J Armstrong, 'Coastal Shipping', in M J Freeman and D H Aldcroft, eds, *Transport in Victorian Britain* (Manchester, 1988), 172.

16 A detailed description of work at the Bere Ferrers yard appears in B Greenhill and S Manning, *The Evolution of the Wooden Ship* (1988).

17 W J Slade and B Greenhill, *Westcountry Coasting Ketches* (1974).

18 B Greenhill, *The Merchant Schooners* (3rd edn, 1988), 234.

19 WDRO, 894, Plymouth Ship Registers. These have been used to provide all the details of Emanuel Crocker's vessels.

20 WDRO, 894, Plymouth Ship Registers, 1824–76.

21 Greenhill, *Merchant Schooners*, 202.

22 I am indebted to Robin Craig and Basil Greenhill for this information.

23 Rough Stock Book, 1877–1896, a document in the possession of Mr G C Penaluna of Wheal Rose Coach Works, Scorrier, near Redruth, Cornwall.

24 See Merry, *Shipping and Trade*.

25 DRO, Crew Lists.

26 DRO, Crew List, *Thomasine*, 1878.

27 DRO, LI258, Canals, Tavistock Nos 27 and 28.

28 WDRO, 894, Plymouth Ship Registers.

29 Merry, *Shipping and Trade*, I.

30 For example, see the *Western Daily Mercury*, 16 July 1863 and 12 Jan. 1866.

31 N Allen, *A Stitch in Time* (1984), 28.

32 *Western Daily Mercury*, 2 June 1883. See A Kittridge, *Passenger Steamers of the River Tamar* (Truro, 1984), 88–91.

33 See Billings' *Directory of Devon*, 1857. For an official account of the visit, see WDRO, Queen's Harbour Master, Plymouth, Transactions, 13 Aug. 1856.

34 *Plymouth and Devonport Weekly Journal*, 21 May 1857.

35 Kittridge, *Passenger Steamers*, 88–99.

6   The Ports of the Exe Estuary, 1701–1972

E A G CLARK

BY LAND, THE MOST ACCESSIBLE VIEW of the port of the Exe estuary is gained from the railway which runs along its western shore. On the train journey southwards from Exeter, a rapidly moving historical panorama is presented, including brief glimpses of the Exe, ponded up at Exeter Quay, itself constructed in 1566, the earliest canal port in England. Then comes the New Basin, opened in 1831, with its gas works, petroleum depots and other industrial premises, until recent years served by canal transport and its own branch railway. Next is the ship canal, winding through the water meadows, with double locks, originally constructed in 1698–1701 when the Elizabethan lighter canal was enlarged to a ship canal. Finally, apparently rising from the fields, comes a view of the linear settlement of Topsham, with its church on a red cliff, perched on the edge of the town. Opposite the church is Topsham lock, near the site of the eighteenth-century entrance to the canal at Lower Sluice. Soon the train passes close to the present canal entrance at Turf Lock, opened after the extension of 1825–27. Then the estuary comes into view, and the long waterfront of the former tide haven of Topsham is exposed, with its medieval quay below the church, its Dutch merchant houses and its quays, and the former shipyards now transformed into gardens. The railway passes the small quay and 'snug boat harbour' of

starcross, the site of abortive port schemes in 1757–71 and 1846. Across the water is Lympstone harbour, spectacularly sited between red cliffs, where vessels for the Newfoundland fishery were fitted out in the eighteenth century, while the tall tower of Exmouth Church, a sea mark for the *British Channel Pilot* (1859), dominates the skyline of the modern resort.

At low tide the estuarine channel winds between mud flats still bearing picturesque names (Figs. 6.1 and 6.2), while at high water the wide lower estuary is crowded with craft below Starcross, where in the 1690s Celia Fiennes saw 'the great ships ride'. Ironically, here in the deep-water anchorage of Exmouth Bight, the multicoloured sails and crowded waters of mid-summer hinder the evocation of a maritime past. Henry Haseler's aquatint, 'View of the Exe' of 1818 (Fig. 6.3), painted from the Exmouth shore, indicates the extent to which the past landscape has been obliterated. The complex sandspit of Dawlish Warren, seen by Leland as a 'great vast plain and barren field', and by the Exeter corporation in the nineteenth century as a vital sea defence for the Bight anchorage, is now eroded at its tip, while on its landward side is an area of recreational blight, where golf course and fun fair sit incongruously side by side, a sad monument to the havoc caused by untrammelled market forces operating on a fragile eco-system. Across

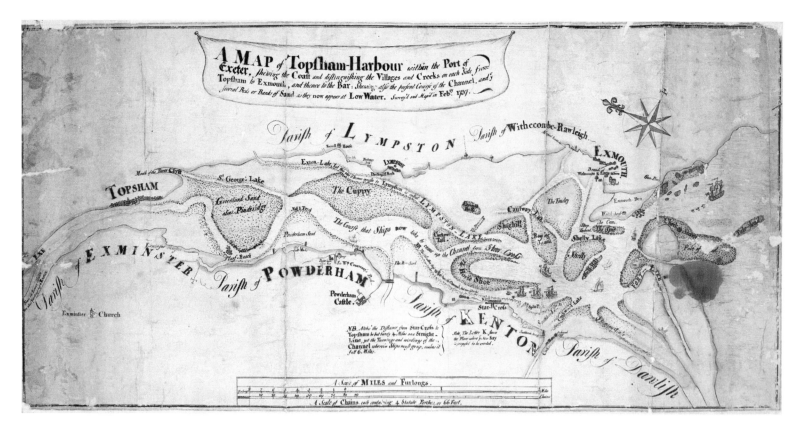

6.1   A map of the River Exe, 1757. (*Devon Record Office*)

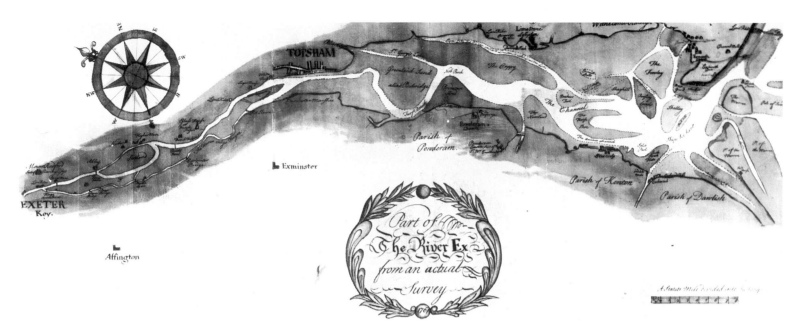

6.2   The River Exe, 1761. (Devon Record Office)

the estuary the twin sandspit of Exmouth Point has been more harmoniously transformed. The terraces and public gardens of the resort face the sea, but on their flank, near where the windmill stood in Haseler's view of 1818, the sturdy dock constructed in 1867 faces the entrance channel of the estuary and was its only remaining commercial port after 1972.

The maritime history of Exeter has received much attention in scholarly studies of the sixteenth-, seventeenth- and eighteenth-century experience by Wallace MacCaffrey, W B Stephens and W G Hoskins respectively. There is a recent history (1984) of Exeter Canal by K R Clew, as well as the 1960 monograph on the Exe ports in the period 1660–1860 by the present author.

The primary sources for a history of the Exe ports are remarkably rich. Apart from the port books, letter books and other records of the Customs Port, there are voluminous local records relating to Exeter Canal and Topsham Quay, both of which were owned and administered by Exeter Corporation. The financial and administrative records of the canal are virtually complete for the period since 1700, while the wharfingers' journals provide a daily record of the canal trade between 1715–25, 1750–1 and 1795–1800. For later years there are the quarterly summaries of trade and shipping in the papers of the city navigation committee. The main series of wharfinger's journals for Topsham (22 volumes) covers the period 1770 to 1840. The journals detail the name of the ship, its master, port of origin or destination and particulars of the cargo, including the names of local merchants importing or exporting the goods. In addition there are bale, cash, freight and arrears books. A later series of day books covers the period 1865–1923 in less detail. The records of the first Exmouth Docks Company have disappeared, but summaries of its and Topsham's trade occur in the reports of the city navigation committee. Law papers relating to the canal, the Exeter Town Customs, and local harbours and railways, also yield rich finds. The Kenton Manor papers provide details of the ships discharging in the lower estuary which were liable for manorial dues. Finally, local newspapers from time to time contain weekly lists of ships entering and clearing from the Exe estuary.

Thus for much of the period since 1700 the day-to-day life of the Exe ports is laid out for the historian in hundreds of manuscript sources. The overwhelming detail they provide increases the danger of emphasising the parochial and ephemeral at the expense of identifying general trends. A chronological account reduces opportunities for analysis, while a general review, port by port or trade by trade, would obscure changes taking place over time. The presentation which follows attempts to avoid these hazards. First, the physical setting of the Exe estuary and the maritime character of its settlements in the eighteenth century are described. Then the era since

1700 is divided into five periods of varying length, each characterised by a particular pattern of trade.

From 1700 to 1827 the trade of the Exe was divided between the 'haven port' of Topsham and the canal port of Exeter. The Customs Port was the most important in Devon and ranked twelth among English ports. Woollen cloth dominated the export trade, and overseas contacts were widespread until the Napoleonic Wars, when the cloth markets closed, never to reopen. The coal, London and Channel coastal trades were the principal coastwise interests. In 1827 the extension of the Exeter Canal to Turf altered the balance of power in the estuary in favour of Exeter, but the broad character of trade remained the same. The advent of the railways in 1844 opened the Exe ports to competition from overland transport and from larger ports, while the increase in the size of ships in the nineteenth century exposed latent weaknesses in the physical endowment of the shallow estuary. The railway initially adversely affected the London, Bristol and Channel coast trades. Exeter began to lose ground among the Devon ports to Plymouth and Dartmouth, and by 1869, in overseas trade it ranked only thirty-seventh among British ports. The opening of Exmouth Dock in 1868 introduced a formidable local rival for Exeter and Topsham, as vessels had the option of discharging in the entrance instead of navigating the shallow estuary to the older ports. Meanwhile, competition from larger ports increased, and several overseas trades ceased. The coasting trade had passed its peak and short hauls were becoming uneconomic. The onset of the First World War was a turning point in the history of the British coasting trade. Hencefor-ward the Exe ports became increasingly restricted to a narrow range of bulky goods such as petroleum, coal, timber and cement. After the Second World War, Exmouth gained an ascendance over Exeter, with first Topsham and then Exeter ceasing as commercial ports.

The Ports and their Setting in the Mid-eighteenth Century

From the viewpoint of maritime trade about 1750, the Exe estuary can be regarded as an arm of the sea, thrust inland ten miles towards Exeter, which was the major route centre of Devon and the commerical capital of the Devon serge industry. At high tide the estuary was and is a lake-like expanse, 1½ miles broad for much of its length, but its shallow, intricate channel, with 6ft on the bar at low tide, contrasts with the more generous physical endowment of its major rivals on the south Devon coast. The hazards it presented to shipping are graphically shown on four extant contemporary maps.[1] These depict the sandbanks and channels in intimate detail, with picturesque names and boldly evocative brushwork. The 1743

6.3   View of the entrance to the River Exe, from an aquatint by Henry Haseler, 1818. (*Ian Cook*)

'View' in particular shows the estuary as a living organism, every facet of which was imbued with significance for those who looked to its vigorous maritime life for their livelihood. Figures 6.1, 6.2 and 6.3 show the narrow entrance channel between Exmouth Point and Dawlish Warren, described in 1698 as 'almost filled with rocks and shoals, continuing above a mile in length'. Although there was only 6ft on the bar, spring tides rose 12–14ft and neaps 6–8ft; ample depths for most contemporary ships.[2] Pilotage was compulsory for all vessels drawing more than 5ft, and was controlled by Exeter Chamber.[3]

In the shelter of Exmouth Point was the fishing village of Exmouth, approached over a jumble of sandbanks. By 1800 Exmouth had become 'one of the most frequented watering places on the Devonshire coast'. Coasters discharged consignments for the resort at Manchester quay on spring tides.[4]

The 1761 chart (Fig. 6.2) provides the earliest mention of the new anchorage, later known as Exmouth Bight. Between Shelly Sandbank and Dawlish Warren, where the main channel swings northward, there was 19ft at low water and a sheltered anchorage with enough room for thirty vessels.[5] Even as early as 1688 'ships . . . that are of great burden usually anchor at Starcross and unlade their goods there because they cannot conveniently go to Topsham'.[6] Transshipment into lighters increased with the growth in the size of ships, as ships over 150 tons burden could not go above Starcross. Between 1782 and 1791 at least 119, and as many as 141 colliers discharged annually near Starcross. By 1795 there were thirty-three registered lighters in the Exe.[7]

Figure 6.1 shows the straggling village of Starcross in an impressive panorama, with large three-masted ships and small lighters lying in the main channel off the port. On Fig. 6.2 however, this is shown as the 'ancient channel', almost closed by the recent extension of the Horse Shoe sands.[8] The main channel now lay in the middle of the estuary. Ironically, in 1757 Sir William Courtenay had constructed a quay at Starcross, and in 1771 he applied for it to be appointed for foreign trade.[9] His port scheme was thwarted by silting. In 1813 the coal meters were removed because 'from the alteration in the channel . . . vessels lay . . . considerably nearer to Exmouth than Starcross'.[10] On the opposite side of the estuary the low red cliffs were broken only at Lympstone. Development as an outport for Exeter was handicapped by the shallowness of the approach through Lympstone Lake, but a customs officer was stationed in the village, which fitted out vessels for the Newfoundland trade. Twenty-five vessels were built here between 1785 and 1813.[11]

At Nob Perch the channel narrowed and wound in a sinuous bend past Turf Reach. Six miles from Exmouth the channel swung close to the eastern shore. Here, built on a low ridge of red sandstone, was the ancient 'haven port' of Topsham, with its quay constructed in 1316. With 4ft at low water and 14ft at high springs, there was more depth than at any other quay in

the estuary. At low tide vessels lay on the mud, which was liquid for about 8ft. The shallowness of the estuarine channel prevented vessels drawing more than 12ft from reaching Topsham even on spring tides.[12] The population of 2,781 in 1801 depended mainly on the sea for a livelihood. There were three shipyards, several private quays and also rope, sail and anchor manufactories. At least 238 ships were built at Topsham between 1785 and 1827, including 27 men-of-war.[13]

Along the river between Topsham and Countess Wear were lime kilns, sugar and glass manufactories, and shipyards where thirteen vessels were built between 1792 and 1812.[14] Half-a-mile above Topsham a tidal channel led to Lower Sluice, the entrance to the ship canal which ran parallel to the river for two miles. Exeter Quay, with a waterfront of 483ft, was described in 1759 as 'one of the finest fresh water keys (quays) perhaps in England'. Here the Exe, ponded up by Trew's Weir, was 120ft wide and 10ft deep. Near the quay were warehouses, the customs house and a coal quay, while fulling mills, dyehouses and the racks of the serge industry spread through the industrial quarter, together with coal yards, timber yards and foundries. All were dependent on water transport.[15]

The first lighter canal, opened in 1566, could accommodate vessels of up to 16 tons on spring tides, and ships discharged into lighters at Topsham. The canal was extended half-a-mile closer to Topsham in 1676. In 1698–1701 Exeter Chamber enlarged the canal to 10ft in depth to accommodate ships. Unfortunately the entrance at Lower Sluice was too far up the estuary to be reached by the largest ships able to use the canal, except on spring tides. Vessels of 80–120 tons, drawing 9ft of water, could enter only four days a fortnight.[16]

1701–1827: Two Ports in Partnership

The opening of the ship canal in 1701 altered the balance of trade between the tide haven of Topsham and the lighter port of Exeter. Coasters could now reach Exeter Quay on spring tides, and the canal captured much of the coasting trade. Canal-bound vessels passed Topsham Quay, however, and many traded with both ports. Topsham was more accessible for larger vessels. In 1717 only 22 out of 123 vessels from overseas came up to Exeter.[17] In 1760 it was claimed, 'no ship exceeding 100 or at most 120 tons can now come up to the city . . . all the coal ships and almost all the ships in foreign trade load and unload at Topsham'.[18] Only three vessels from foreign ports visited Exeter in 1750–1, whereas at Topsham in 1773 seventy-seven cleared for overseas destinations.[19] Because of the expansion in coastwise trade, canal traffic increased from 317 vessels annually in 1716–25 to 878 in 1825–26.[20] Lighters, predominantly coal lighters, outnumbered ships by almost two to one (Table 1). Of the 444 vessels which cleared from Exeter Quay in 1750–1, 135 went down empty and 200 carried woollen

Table 6.1
Traffic passing up the Exeter Canal, 1715–1800

Date	Ships	Coal lighters	Other lighters	Total lighters	Total passes
1715	122	93	32	125	247
1716	158	158	77	235	393
1717	177	73	48	121	298
1718	138	121	49	170	308
1719	156	75	40	115	271
1720	160	99	49	148	308
1721	181	63	63	126	307
1722	126	103	31	134	260
1723	209	127	58	185	294
1724	141	129	29	158	299
1725	216	89	26	115	331
1750–1	181	181	117	298	479
1795–6	158	257	33	290	448
1797–8	162	215	26	241	403
1799–1800	157	274	32	306	463

Sources: DRO, Entry Book of the Town Customs, 1715–25; Book 177, Book of Entries and Waste Book, 1750–1; Books 220–6, Wharfingers' Journals or Collection Books of the Town Duty, 1750–1; Wharfingers' Journals, Exeter, 1795–1800.

goods and/or grain.[21] The canal handled most of the cloth export to London, but less than one-third of the overseas trade.[22]

The overseas trade of the Exe was dominated by the export of serges; in 1783 10,843 bales of cloth were exported from Topsham alone. The serge industry's hinterland extended over the whole of Devon. The trade was handled by some forty Exeter and Tiverton merchants, who were closely associated with cloth finishing processes and had wide-ranging contacts with commission agents on the Continent. In 1764, for example, Samuel Milford sent cloth to merchants in Hamburg, Amsterdam, Bilbao, Berne, Geneva and at least ten Italian towns.[23] In 1771–6 Italy, Spain and Holland were the principal markets for Devon serges (Table 2). Some 19–27 shipments were sent annually to Genoa/Leghorn and Naples/Salerno/Messina. The large vessels used in the Mediterranean trade were London-owned and returned directly to the capital. Three to five vessels cleared annually for Amsterdam and Rotterdam. The Spanish trade expanded to oust the Italian trade from first place in 1783. Contacts were established with several small Biscayan ports such as Ribadeo, but Bilbao and Cadiz were the chief markets, taking seven to twenty-two shipments in most years of peace. Iron, wool, nuts, wine and fruit made up the return cargoes. Less important markets included Hamburg, Ostend and London.[24]

The pivotal overseas woollen trade was destroyed by the effects of war in 1793–1815 (Table 2). Previously, Exeter merchants had used neutral entrepôts such as Ostend, but ties with overseas markets were dissolved through two decades of conflict. The serge industry found a new market in the East India Company, and cloth went coastwise to London. The number of cloth shipments overseas fell from fifty-seven in 1773 to twenty-six in 1794 and two in 1798.[25]

Apart from the cloth export, overseas contacts were on a modest scale (Table 6.3). High duties prevented trade with France. A few shipments of wine, cork and dyestuffs were received from Portugal, and of timber from Scandinavian and Baltic ports. In 1760 Exeter Customs Port accounted for more than a quarter of the British vessels engaged in the Newfoundland fishery, but Teignmouth was more important than Topsham, which contributed fourteen out of the fifty-five vessels which sailed in 1771. The vessels left the Exe early in the year, and sailed from the fishery to Iberian ports with fish and oil, returning to the Exe in winter with salt for the next voyage.[26]

Coastwise transport was much cheaper than carrier waggon. Land carriage rates in the Exeter region in the eighteenth century were one shilling per ton mile, whereas sea freights to London were only ten to fifteen shillings per ton.[27] The configuration of Devon, and the absence of sheltered harbours between Dartmouth and Weymouth, brought an extensive area within Exeter's natural hinterland for coastal trade. Outward coastal shipments from the Customs Port increased from 149 in 1758 to 678 in 1823, and inward shipments from 210 to 1,063.[28] These developments reflect the vigorous expansion of the national economy, and a doubling of the population of Devon. Coal came into increasing use and its importation

Table 6.2
The direction of the Topsham woollen trade, 1754–1820 (in bales)

Destination	1754	1760	1761	1771	1773	1776	1780	1783	1791	1793	1820
Rotterdam				803	476	1,402	811	915	1,352	788	
Amsterdam	3,195	2,248	407	1,902	1,569	1,831	1,561	1,728	1,272	614	
Total – Holland	3,195	2,248	407	2,705	2,045	3,233	2,372	2,643	2,624	1,402	
Ostend	121			413	674	733	3,211	1,302	395	99	
Bruges							846				
Total – Flanders	121			413	674	733	4,057	1,302	395	99	
Hamburg	1,464	842	738	562	239	456		256	204	177	
Bilbao	304	382	516	967	1,581	1,358		3,145	2,014	1,178	
San Lucar	16		71		12						
Corunna					37			124			
Cadiz	99	132	109	830	55	310		741	246	193	
Seville									134	165	
Others	9	42		5	90			52			
Total – Spain	428	514	738	1,797	1,690	1,758		4,062	2,537	1,613	
Oporto	109	39	16	35	97	138	173	187	193	112	
Figueira	30										
Lisbon	192	118	12	36		16			98		35
Total – Portugal	331	157	28	71	97	154	173	187	291	112	35
Genoa/Leghorn	499	188	372	1,843	1,465	2,155	589	1,511	2,013	361	
Naples/Salerno	215	38	48	468	703	816	151	771	1,099	408	
Ancona				70	96	199		111	118	133	
Others		152		35	66						
Total – Italy	714	378	420	2,416	2,330	3,170	740	2,393	3,230	902	
Other Ports	29	16			80	123			36		
Total – Foreign	6,282	4,155	2,331	7,964	7,155	9,627	7,342	10,843	9,317	4,305	35
London	No record			798	223	No record			2,236	437	7,533

Sources: these statistics were compiled by counting in DRO, Wharfingers' Bale Books, Topsham, 1752–84 and Wharfingers' Journals, Topsham, 1770–1840.

quadrupled between 1764 and 1818.[29] Paper, leather, and other industries expanded, and looked to the coasting trade for raw materials and the marketing of products.

Contacts were closest with the ports of the Channel coast (Table 6.4), which was studded with harbours accessible in a few hours or a day or two with fair winds. In 1784 seventy-six vessels cleared for ports west of the Exe, including thirty-nine for Plymouth, twenty-one for Dartmouth, and eight for Falmouth, with timber, flour, hides, paper and naval stores. Return cargoes included paper stuff, fish and train oil.[30] Eight 'constant traders' plied between Exeter and Plymouth in 1828, making five to eight voyages annually.[31] The Exe had at least eleven clusters of lime kilns, to which limestone was brought from Torbay by sloops. Some forty craft were engaged in this long-established local trade, which has been estimated at 15,000 tons annually.[32] In 1784 sixty-nine vessels entered from Channel ports east of Exeter, including Dover and Rye (wool), Chichester, Portsmouth, Southampton and Poole (corn and flour), Lymington (salt), and Weymouth (building stone).[33]

The London trade was a major division. In 1791 there were eleven 'constant traders' bringing a bewildering variety of groceries, raw materials and manufactures, and returning to the capital with cloth, paper, leather, butter, cider, scythe stones (from Blackdown) and manganese (from Upton Pyne). Shipments increased to 132 in 1825, when there were 23 'constant traders', some of them making 5 to 7 voyages annually.[34]

Coal imports took prime place and expanded from 11,957 tons in 1758 to 65,164 tons in 1818. In 1784 66 per cent of the import was from the Northeast coast, especially Newcastle and Sunderland. The Welsh ports of Milford, Tenby and Swansea accounted for most of the balance (Table 6.5). Apart from the London and coal trades, Exeter had few regular coastwise contacts beyond the English Channel (Table 6.4). In 1828 there were five constant traders plying from Bristol, bringing groceries and metal goods,

Table 6.3
Inward shipments at the Exe from foreign ports, 1662–1905

	1662	1666	1701	1717	1754	1791	1793	1804	1810	1820	1830	1835	1872	1875	1890	1905
France	58	21	9	11		2			1				28	106	19	12
Bilbao	4	4		12	10	1	2									
Cadiz			37	1	2	1	2	1								
Others	4	2		7	11	3										
Total – Spain	8	6	37	20	23	5	4	1					10	10	6	3
Oporto	1	1	12	11	6	5	3	2		1						
Lisbon	2	5	4	8	2	2	1									
Others	3	5	3	2												
Total – Portugal	6	10	13	17	21	8	7	4	2		1					
Mediterranean		1			3	1	1				1		16	4		
Flanders/Belgium	1	13	6	3	1	1	2			2	6		1	5	6	14
Amsterdam					3	3	1	3								
Rotterdam	14		20	18		8	3									
Total – Holland	14		20	18	3	11	4	3					1	1	5	
Germany			9	8	3	3	4	1					15	5	6	6
Scandinavia, etc.	4		6	5	3	7	12	14	7	10	4	3	32	18	20	10
Newfoundland	5	2	10	16	25	6	2			1						
Atlantic Islands	3	6														
North America	2	4	10	23	6	3		1	4	8	1	1	14	15	8	4
South America													11	9	2	
Total – Transatlantic	10	12	20	39	31	9	2	1	4	9	1	1	25	24	10	4

Source: PRO, Port Books, 1662–1754; DRO, Wharfingers' Journals, Topsham 1790–1840; *Annual Statement of the Navigation and Shipping of the UK*, 1872 and 1875; DRO, Navigational Committee Minute Books, 1885–1906. Statistics for 1791–1835 are for Topsham only, and for 1890 and 1905 Exeter only.

Table 6.4
The direction of the coastwise trade at Exeter and Topsham, 1674–1830

(upper figures represent outward and lower figures inward shipments)

	1674	1681	1700	1717	1733	1758	1765	1774	1784	1791	1804	1820	1830	
Devon/Cornwall	13	27	15	7	23	53	32	29	76	33	33	39	16	Out
	7	15	13	12	22	19	30	28	91	32	48	65	53	In
South Coast	6	4	1	2	1	38	41	39	34	26	11	18	14	Out
	71	37	31	20	12	28	37	69	67	35	8	31	25	In
Thames Estuary	3	21	39	31	32	39	106	74	47	52	25	86	122	Out
	23	47	52	35	50	46	76	58	61	54	28	92	118	In
East Coast	2					1	3	8	3				2	Out
	7	9	15	1	1		3	1		1	1	1	2	In
NE Coast						1		2	3		2	1		Out
	20	59	35	24	33	26	46	71	83	1	9	17	8	In
Scotland							1	1	1		1		1	Out
														In
NW Ports					1	11	38	15	70		1		2	Out
			4	3	3	5	14	4	13	13	2	4	11	In
Bristol Channel	2	1		4	2	5	4	12	7	4	2	3	1	Out
	114	133	149	88	86	86	96	97	101	14	6	18	36	In
Unidentified	1					1	1			1			4	Out
										1	5	7	35	In
Total	27	53	55	44	59	149	226	181	244	122	78	148	161	Out
	242	300	299	102	207	210	302	329	416	151	107	235	288	In

Source: PRO, Port Books, 1674–1784; DRO, Wharfingers' Journals, Topsham, 1790–1840. The statistics for 1791–1835 are for Topsham only.

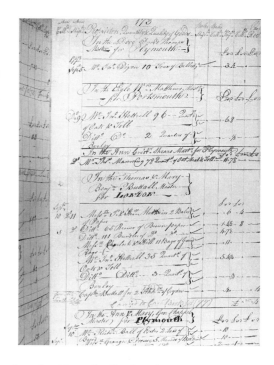

6.4 A page from the Wharfingers' Journal for 1793, showing the ships entering the Port of Exeter, their cargoes, the names of the merchants for whom the goods were intended and the keyage paid. (*Devon Record Office*)

and three from Liverpool, bringing rock salt and coal, and calling at Teignmouth for pipe clay as a return cargo.[35]

The estuarine settlements were intimately involved in the maritime life of the Exe. Exeter had 157 ships registered in 1792, employing 1,049 seamen. To this number must be added the crews of the 33 registered lighters, the 5 pilot boats, the 163 fishing boats and other small craft, the 36 customs officers, clerks in the wharfingers' offices at Topsham and Exeter, the canal staff, and the workers in shipyards, limeburning, coal and timber yards and other port-related industries.[36] Work opportunities ranged from the stone boats which plied between the Exe and the Berry Head quarries to the constant traders to London, Bristol, Rotterdam, Hamburg and Oporto, making up to five round trips in a year,[37] and the Newfoundland fishing vessels which left the Exe after Christmas, picked up provisions at an Irish port and beat across the Atlantic in the path of the westerlies. The Exeter vessels were then laid up for three months while the crew and the 'byeboatmen' passengers fished on the eastern shore of the island, using small boats of 12–15 tons kept at the 'fishing rooms' and 'plantations' owned by Exeter fishermen. In the autumn the Exeter vessels left for Iberian ports with fish and train oil.[38] The life of Richard Bagwell, born at Topsham in 1779, is illustrative. A descendant of Bagwell has collected ship's logs, account books, letters, indentures and testimonials relating to this seaman, but his lengthy career was spent in ships registered in different ports, and there are tantalising gaps in the record. He went to sea as an apprentice at the age of twelve on a Topsham ship. In 1797 he was crewman on the *Oporto Packet* of Exeter, and in 1803 he became mate on the *Start*, a London trader operating from Plymouth. The following year he served as harpooner on a South Atlantic whaler. The *Brothers* sailed from the Thames in September 1804, saw whales on Boxing Day, and killed forty in the next twelve months between the Cape of Good Hope and Timor, where the ship took on supplies. She eventually returned to London in April 1806. Bagwell then took his first command on a naval tender, the *Fanny*, transporting troops between Plymouth and Corunna. There followed service on a Portsmouth vessel, the *Miss Platoff*, trading to Newfoundland. In 1815 Bagwell sought a less adventurous life and became master of the *William* in the coasting trade. Voyages included one from Newport to London with iron in 1816, from Liverpool to Cork, and from Liverpool to Southampton with rock salt. In 1826 he was based in Devon again as master of the *Two Friends* of Sidmouth. In October he made a rare visit to the Exe, shipping paper stuff from London to Topsham. The vessel was chartered to call at twelve British ports. A lawsuit developed concerning a cargo to Belfast. In 1829 a testimonial for Bagwell refers to his 'late losses and unfortunate voyages'. Here the record ceases, apart from the award of a small pension by Trinity House in 1843. He died in 1856.[39]

1827–1844: The Heyday of the New Ship Canal

In 1819 Exeter Chamber engaged the engineer James Green to make suggestions for 'bettering the navigation'. Lower Sluice could be reached by vessels of 80 tons on spring tides only, and the tidal approach was 'full of

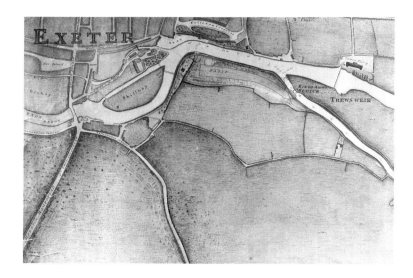

6.5 Part of a plan of the Exeter Canal navigation, showing the improvements proposed by James Green, civil engineer, 1819. The detail of the City Basin is seen here. (*Devon Record Office*)

Table 6.5
The direction of the coal trade of Exeter Customs Port, 1632–1784 (in tons)

	1632	1664	1674	1681	1700	1717	1733	1758	1765	1784
Sunderland		199	142	685	2,033	1,571	2,833	4,266	5,152	17,143
Cullercoats					61					
Newcastle	45	572	1,675	5,544	1,828	1,065	3,002	599	3,275	1,980
Blyth				60						1,341
Total – NE Coast	45	771	1,817	6,289	3,922	2,636	5,835	4,865	8,427	20,464
Milford	1,804	2,790	3,550	3,966	5,554	4,364	4,436	5,392	3,545	3,533
Tenby	72	32			548	174	516	976	939	1,911
Carmarthen									580	683
Barry	264	387	39	45						
Llanelly		319	52	140		312	795	613	774	
Swansea	216	397	524	691	107	947	133	949	603	1,525
Neath		56	35	77	148	56		67	67	120
Total – Wales	2,356	3,981	4,200	4,919	7,357	5,853	5,880	7,997	6,508	7,772
Liverpool								80	449	2,383
Other Ports	39	17	27	40	281			45	476	325
Grand Total	2,440	4,769	6,044	11,248	11,560	8,489	11,715	12,987	15,860	30,944

Source: Compiled from PRO, Exchequer Port Books. For the conversion of chaldrons to tons see Clark, 'Estuarine Ports of the Exe', App. 15 (e.i.).

shoals and very narrow'. Navigational delays caused vessels to miss a vital spring tide. In 1825–7 the canal was extended two miles to Turf Reach, where there was more than 12ft even at neap tide. A modern entrance lock was constructed, the canal was deepened to 15ft throughout, and in 1830 a capacious New Basin opened, providing more depth than at Exeter Quay. Total costs were £113,355. The Chamber had to raise £85,000 by mortgaging the canal dues.[40]

Exeter was now the best equipped port of the Exe, with deep-water facilities in the Basin, whereas at Topsham vessels lay on the mud at low tide. More than two miles of the most shallow part of the estuary were avoided, and the greater depth available in the canal permitted vessels of between 100 and 200 tons to come up to Exeter. The canal experienced its greatest prosperity. The gross income trebled, freight rates were reduced by 20 per cent, and the price of coal halved.[41] The coal trade expanded by 46 per cent in a decade and totalled 33,000 tons in 1843. Exeter's share of the coasting and foreign trade increased. In 1839 there were forty-five shipments from Plymouth, twenty-two from Bristol and eighteen from Liverpool.[42]

Although Topsham was bypassed after the canal extension, it shared in the expansion of the coasting trade. Apart from the vessels which still came up to the quay, goods were sent up from Turf by lighter, or carried through the new side-lock in the canal. In 1833 303 coasters and 40 vessels from

overseas discharged at Topsham, including 165 London traders. Chamberlain's Wharf masters advertised 'they have resolved to clear every week from Topsham . . . whether laden or not'. Topsham enjoyed a monopoly of the early steamer trade, as steaming was not permitted on the canal until 1880. The *Zephyr* was scheduled to visit the Exe weekly, and made thirty-three voyages in 1833. Its speed and regularity had an adverse effect on the sailing 'constant traders', and their number fell from twenty-three to thirteen in a decade.[43]

1844–1868: The Challenge of the Railways – the First Phase

The Bristol and Exeter Railway opened at Exeter in 1844. This was a major turning point in the history of the Exe ports. Not only did they lose trade immediately to the railway, but the development of a national railway network intensified the competition of ports such as Teignmouth, Plymouth, Fremington, Bridgwater, Bristol and Southampton, all of which began to penetrate the hinterland, hitherto protected by the expense of transporting bulky goods overland.[44] The revolution in transport exposed latent weaknesses in the endowment of the Exe ports, the one approached by a canal increasingly ill adapted to the needs of modern shipping, the other a tide haven without docks or rail connections, and both linked to the sea by a shallow estuary. The effects were immediate. By the end of the year the Bristol 'constant traders' had 'ceased to exist',[45] and Topsham's steamer trade with London collapsed. Where four or five ships had discharged weekly, now the incidence was three a month. In contrast to the 100 or more London traders visiting Exeter in 1840, only 37 passed up the canal in 1872.[46] In 1852 220 fewer coasting vessels entered the Customs Port than a decade before.[47] Routes with 'constant traders' were badly affected. By 1872 the Plymouth and Liverpool trades had declined to a twelfth of their value before the railway.[48] Within a decade or so the character of the coasting trade had been transformed to a dependence on a narrow range of bulky goods such as pig iron, building stone, salt, lime, paper stuff for local mills and raw materials for the Ebford Manure Works near Topsham. Railways now handled the paper, leather and other manufactures of the hinterland, and return cargoes became increasingly hard to find. More than half the vessels entering the Exe in 1862 left in ballast. Exports from Topsham included timber and manure.[49]

Not all trades were equally affected by the railways. The coal import increased until the late 1860s, and coal traffic on the canal rose to 39,510 tons in 1850. Colliers from Hartlepool and Middlesbrough dominated.[50] In the case of foreign trade, it was often still economic to send goods to the port nearest the market. Steam was adopted later than in the coasting trade,[51] and hence sailing vessels from foreign ports were unaffected by the prohibition of the use of steam on the canal. Eighty-six vessels entered from overseas in 1841, and 102 in 1868. In 1857–63 annual shipments included thirteen of timber from the Baltic and Canada, seven of hides from South America, ten of valonia from Smyrna, and twenty of grain from France, Germany and Russia.[52]

In 1846 Exeter Council reduced the canal dues in an attempt to counter railway competition.[53] Meanwhile, the canal creditors instituted a lawsuit against the council and a Receiver was appointed. Between 1854 and 1883 the creditors had a virtual stranglehold on the management of the canal, and improvements in the navigation and reductions in rates were often vetoed.[54] Examples of the onerous effect of dues were provided at a conference in 1867. It was cheaper to rail timber to Teignmouth for export than to use the canal. Sea freight rates to Plymouth were 21 pence per ton dearer than rail, and canal and town dues accounted for 45 per cent of the total cost by sea.[55]

In spite of its drawbacks, Exeter was the dominant estuarine port in the Exe estuary in this period. Sixty per cent of the vessels entering the estuary in 1856–70 went up to the canal entrance, 26 per cent discharged into lighters in the Bight and only 14 per cent went up to Topsham. More than half the vessels used the Bight anchorage for a tide or two on the inward or outward run.[56] Facilities were improved at Topsham in 1861, when the London and South Western Railway company extended Topsham Quay and provided railway connections.[57] Meanwhile, Exeter Canal lacked rail

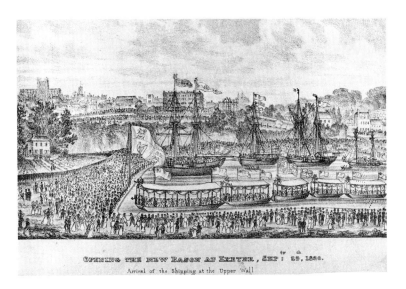

6.6 Print of a drawing of the opening of the new City Basin, 1830. (*West Country Studies Library*)

connections until 1867.[58] An early attempt to develop a railway port in the estuary was the 'snug boat harbour' constructed at Starcross in 1847 by the South Devon Railway Company, whose line to Teignmouth passed through the village. Lighters discharged coal for Exeter gasworks, but the shallowness of the estuarine approach handicapped development. Even in the peak year of 1870 the trade was less than a tenth of that at Exeter, and it virtually ceased in 1877.[59] Another abortive attempt at port development was at Cockwood, on the railway which ran along the western shore of the estuary, where the Exe Bight Oyster Fishery and Pier Company constructed a pier in 1868.[60]

The estuarine settlements continued to be intimately involved with the maritime life of the estuary. More than 100 vessels were registered at Exeter[61] and offered employment. Exmouth and Topsham alone had sixty master mariners resident.[62] Ship ownership was spread widely. In the period 1856–79, sixty-six local residents held part shares in one vessel, and twenty in two vessels. Residents with shares in three to five vessels included an Exmouth surgeon, two ships' masters and two coal merchants. Ownership on a large scale was confined to shipbuilders. Row Brothers of Topsham and John Walters of Exmouth each owned seven ships, while the Redways of Exmouth and the Holmans of Topsham owned eighteen and thirty-two respectively.[63] John Holman, a Topsham master mariner, formed the Exeter Shipping Assurance Company in 1838 and pioneered the principle of mutual assurance to cover marine risks. His three shipyards employed 200 men and 80 apprentices, and built at least 33 vessels between 1847 and 1870, including the *John Fortescue* of 509 tons.[64]

1868–1914: Three Rival Ports in the Estuary

The opening of Exmouth Dock in 1868 transformed the shipping facilities of the Exe and altered the balance of power. Henceforward, vessels had the option of discharging at the entrance instead of navigating the shallow estuary. Meanwhile, the increase in the size of vessels led to more use of the Bight anchorage for transshipment or waiting for a spring tide. The dock was 530 × 300ft, providing a depth of 14ft at spring tide, slightly more than at the other ports. It was the first to have rail facilities. Exeter Council feared the railway would reduce rates 'to attract traffic from the Exeter Canal . . . and then the . . . trade of Exeter would be at the mercy of the dock company'. The exposed position at the mouth of the estuary posed problems for sailing vessels in rough seas. Gales destroyed the west wall in 1871 and the dock gates in 1882. A larger dock which could admit vessels drawing 14ft, about 700 tons, was constructed in 1894.[65]

The coasting trade of the Exe increased to 785 shipments in 1890. Colliers, mainly from Hartlepool and Shields, but also from the Humber and South Wales, made up 43 per cent of the 262 vessels discharging in the estuary below Topsham in 1870. Short-haul contracts had almost ceased, apart from 75 shipments of limestone from Babbacombe. Five vessels were engaged in the stone trade full time, and six others carried stone when they could not find other employment.[66]

The foreign trade fluctuated in volume and direction from year to year, reflecting its 'tramp' character (Table 6.3). Contacts were now closest with France, with a peak, in 1872, of 106 shipments of onions, cereals, wines and other agricultural produce from many ports. Large vessels with timber from the Baltic and Canada, and petroleum from the USA, transshipped in the Bight. From the 1880s trades began to desert the Exe for larger ports, including that in hides (from South America), valonia (from Smyrna), wine, petroleum and potatoes.[67]

Exeter retained its first place in the estuary, though canal traffic declined from 393 vessels in 1870 to 224 in 1905.[68] Table 6.6 indicates the shares of the principal trades. The locks were designed for the narrow sailing vessels of the 1820s. Many vessels, especially steamers, were too long or broad or had to lighten to meet the draught limit, which had deteriorated to 12ft. Schemes to lengthen Turf lock by 30ft, or to build modern locks, were reluctantly ruled out because of cost (up to £75,000).[69] Exeter Council tried to run the canal as a commercial enterprise, reducing rates by one-third in 1883 to attract traffic, offering reductions for guaranteed annual shipments, and negotiating to ameliorate the shortage of exports, which were only one-tenth of imports in 1884–1905 (see Table 6.7 for details of the imports and exports). During this period the deficit of income over expenditure was £9,657.[70] This set a limit to the extent to which dues could be reduced or the channel dredged. In 1908 the Council called for estimates for 'bringing the canal up to date so that it may accommodate the ordinary coasting steamer', but it could not afford to invest £49,000 to achieve this.[71]

Table 6.6

Ship traffic on the Exeter Canal: annual number of visits by vessels engaged in the principal trades, 1872–1900

Date	London	Coal	Other Coasting Trade	Foreign	Total
1872	37	84	134	128	383
1875	27	95	113	175	410
1880	14	64	103	95	276
1885	12	63	91	64	230
1890	21	62	166	52	301
1895	11	84	157	86	338
1900	12	47	189	50	298

Source: Compiled from Quarterly Returns of the Navigational Committee, entered in DRO, Navigational Committee Minute Books, 1861–1906.

Topsham withstood the competition of Exmouth surprisingly well, and its imports were larger in three years out of four in 1868–1908. Imports included coal, manure, building stone and railway materials, each totalling some 6–7,000 tons annually. At first Exmouth handled little more than a tenth of the trade of the Exe, but after the reconstruction of 1894 it began to rival Topsham. Its coal trade was as large as Exeter's.[72]

By this period the voyages of Exeter-owned vessels were usually tramp in character, calling at several ports, with one or more of the British coal ports playing a pivotal part in the charter. Short hauls coastwise were no longer dominant. Between 1863 and 1914 23.6 per cent of the voyages were to Channel ports, including the Babbacombe limestone quarries, and 36.8 per cent to more distant British destinations. Continental ports on the Atlantic seaboard accounted for 16 per cent of the voyages while 23.6 per cent were to more distant areas, including the Baltic, the Mediterranean, West Africa, the Americas and the Indian Ocean. Exeter ships were now less closely linked with the maritime trade of the Exe, and called at their home port on only 43 per cent of the voyages.[73] Fewer Devonians found employment. In 1863 the *Friendship* made five voyages to coal ports and all the crew were recruited from the Exe. In contrast, in 1871 there were only five Devonians on the *City of Exeter* from Hartlepool to Odessa, and none on the *Belle of the Exe* from Cardiff to West Africa.[74]

Table 6.7
Imports and exports on the Exeter Canal, 1883–1905.

Commodity	Measure	1882–3[1]	1891[2]	1892[2]	1893[2]	1901–5[3] (average)
Imports						
Cement	tons	75	772	746	708	2,981
Salt fish	"	911	1,197½	1,236½	1,810	1,516
Window glass	"	137	164½	189	123	138
Grinding stone	"	19½				
Gunpowder	"	1½				
Salted hides	"	807			129	
Horns and hoofs	"	25½			5½	
Pig iron	"	673	360	500	450	721
Iron castings	"	117	172	66½	36	
Scrap iron	"	10	21½	5	5	
Slates	"	706	618	470	450	702
Soda	"	279				292
Soap	"	11½				
Limestone	"	45				
Sugar	"	61	1,287½	1,263½	943	934
Whitelead	"	83½				
Petroleum	"	3,258	5,050½	4,945½	6,071	255
Manure	"	502	441	326	675	219
Benzolene	"	929				
Oil cake	"	495	2,229	3,244	3,063½	2,989
Onions	"	107½	67	70	127	168
Potatoes	"	2,319	1,334½	90		528
Sand	"	1,166	444	350	1,425	958
Salt	"	141	181	310	416	450
Valonia	"	106				
Coals	"	13,179½	16,819	18,572	20,678½	17,854
London "traders" goods	"	579	1,078	470	1,958½	
Stone	"		3,471			3,841
Wax	"		53			
Sundries	"		179			
Culm	"		283			
Currants	"	.	165½			
Oats	"			1,513½	1,417½	
Oats	quarters	1,555				
Rags	tons			38		
Rice	"			30	35	
Barley	"			178		
Flour	"			100		
Hay	"			74		
Granite	"				2,466	
Bricks	"	2,000			3	58
Wood blocks	"					244
Deals	standards	120	221	671	395½	
Timber	tons	581				
Timber	loads		260	34½		
Lathwood	fathoms	11			7	
Wines and spirits	pipes	154½	422½	300	335½	134 tons?
Spirits	cases	518	730	595	439	
Spirits	puncheons	144				
"Grain"	tons					467
Ice	"					156
Exports						
Barytes	tons	87	1,250	1,160	365	255
Scrap iron	"	1,119	377	497	442	
Timber	"	1,267				
Timber	loads		1,987	1,378	1,063½	
London trade	tons		881½	438½	772½	
Pitwood	"		70			
Oxide	"	195	76			83
Bricks	number	25,000				
Bricks	tons			108½	363½	
Tar	"	616				
Lead pipe	"	7				
Callett	"	7				

1 Compiled from imports and exports passing through the Exeter Canal during the
year ending Lady Day 1883, (DRO, NC, 486, 293–4).
2 Compiled from DRO, Quarterly Statements of Imports and Exports through the
Exeter Canal, 1887–97.
3 Average amount of Canal and Town Dues on goods imported and exported (DRO,
Reports of the Earnings of the *Queen of the Exe*, 1905–6). This return does not
distinguish imports from exports, and therefore the 130 tons of bog ore, 58 tons of
coke and 24 tons of zinc are not included in the column.

6.7 The Quay, Fish Market and Custom House (far right) at Exeter, probably in the 1930s.
The vessel is a London River coasting barge. (Exeter Express and Echo)

1914–1972: The Demise of Exeter and Topsham as Commercial Ports

The First World War was a turning point in the history of coastal shipping.
Railway rates were frozen until 1920, whereas shipping costs rose 200 per
cent.[75] Like many other small ports, those of the Exe were badly affected.
Steamers were beginning to outnumber sailing vessels, and were usually too
large for the canal. Transshipment was becoming uneconomic. In 1928 the
steam tug *Queen of the Exe* was sold. Exeter Canal was losing £1,000 per
annum.[76] Relief came providentially in the revival of the petroleum trade.
The National Benzole Company leased land at the Basin in 1923, four other
companies following within a decade. Storage tanks were installed and motor
ships designed for the canal gauge.[77] The *Ben Johnson*, for example, visited
Exeter fortnightly from Southampton. Petroleum imports reached 23,183
tons in 1939. Coal for the gasworks at the Basin ranked second among the
imports, which included bulky goods such as Baltic timber, bricks, tiles and
glass from Antwerp, and Newfoundland fish. Regular importers had
premises at the Basin.[78] Although Exeter handled more ships, Exmouth
emerged as the premier port in cargo tonnage. In 1938 61,215 tons were
discharged at Exmouth, 51,789 tons at Exeter, and 12,441 tons at
Topsham.[79] A new coal quay with mechanised handling equipment was
constructed at Exmouth Dock in 1933.[80]

The Second World War radically affected trade at all the Exe ports. But
by 1953 traffic at Exeter and Exmouth had returned to prewar levels, with
imports totalling 49,026 tons and 53,825 tons respectively. In contrast,
Topsham was almost moribund, receiving two shipments only.[81] Attempts
to revive its trade failed.[82] Traffic on the canal was between 224 and 295
vessels annually in 1954–64, but the range of imports narrowed to a
dangerous dependence on petroleum and timber. Trade in general cargoes
had ceased with the war, and bulk trades such as cement left the canal
because of preferential rail rates.[83] Even the petroleum trade, running at 40–
50,000 tons per annum, was under threat. In 1950 two companies warned
that it would not be economic to replace their small vessels designed for the
canal. Exeter Council could not afford to enlarge the locks.[84] In 1961 the
companies gave notice that their vessels had only two or three years of life,
and then their use of the canal would cease.[85] Traffic fell to 103 ships in
1963–4. The council decided against closure, but commercial use of the
waterway ended with the construction of the low motorway viaduct across
the canal in 1972.[86] With the canal port closed and the ancient 'haven port'
of Topsham moribund, Exmouth Dock became the only port of the Exe.

6.9   An aerial view, taken in 1982, of Topsham, the River Exe, the Exeter Canal and the M5 viaduct (completed 1972), which effectively stopped large vessel navigation of the canal to Exeter. (Exeter Express and Echo)

Conclusion

The search for continuity and the identification of significant changes are major concerns for the historian. The Exe ports reached a peak of national importance in 1714–17 when only London, Liverpool and Bristol had greater overseas connections, as measured by shipping movements.[87] In the 1790s Exeter was a middle ranking port, perhaps twelfth in England and Wales in ships and trade.[88] Its relative decline then accelerated. In the 1860s it ranked thirty-seventh among British ports for overseas trade, and handled only 0.4 per cent of coastwise traffic.[89] By 1953 its share had shrunk to 0.11 per cent of British seaborne commerce.[90] Major factors in this decline were the non-industrial character of the hinterland, the advent of the railways, and the increasing size of ships, which exposed latent weaknesses in the physical endowment of the estuarine ports. To Dummer in 1698, the tides 'were in no wise capable of that force and virtue which the services of great shipping call for'.[91] Nevertheless, as has been shown, for nearly three centuries the opportunities offered for maritime trade were taken in varied and often unpredictable ways. For the fortunes of the individual trades and settlements of the Exe, the picture since 1698 has been almost as kaleidoscopic as the waters and shoals of the estuary which provided their setting.

6.8   An aerial view of the Exe estuary and Exeter Canal in the 1970s. (Exeter Express and Echo)

6: The Ports of the Exe Estuary, 1701–1972

1 DRO, View of the Lakes, Sands . . . on the Exmouth Side of the River Exe, 1743; Plan of the Harbour of Exmouth by William Chapple, 1743; Part of the River Exe, 1761 (shown as figure 6.2); Map of Topsham Harbour, 1757.

2 BL, Sloane MS 3233, Survey of Ports, 1698; G Collins, *Great Britain's Coasting Pilot* (1693), 5; Admiralty, *The Channel Pilot* (1856).

3 DRO, Act Book of the Exeter Chamber (hereafter AB), xiii, 63–5.

4 M Dunsford, *Miscellaneous Observations in the Course of Two Tours through Several Parts of the West of England* (Tiverton, 1800), 84: DRO, Papers Concerning the Exeter Port Dues Bill, 1840; DRO, Papers Concerning the Exmouth Docks Bill, 1870; Exeter Customs House, Letter Book (hereafter ECH, LB), ii, 1813, 201–2.

5 *Chart of Exmouth Harbour* (1830); DRO, Papers relating to Exmouth Docks Bill, 1870.

6 PRO, Exchequer Depositions, E134/4 JAS II East.33.

7 DRO, Petition concerning the Key at Starcross, 1771; List of Boats, Barges etc., Registered at the Clerk of the Peace's Office, 1795; 1508 M 1/30, Kenton Manor Water Bailiff's Accounts, 1820–61; 1508 M 1/28, Water Bailiff's Journal, River Exe, 1838–9.

8 E A G Clark, *The Ports of the Exe Estuary, 1660–1860* (Exeter, 1960), 11–12.

9 DRO, AB xiv, 237; DRO, Papers Concerning Starcross Quay, 1770–1; ECH, LB, vi, 4 May 1771; DRO, 1508 M, Devon, A Map of Starcross with a General Plan of the New Intended Quay, 1756.

10 ECH, LB, xxi, 25 Sep. 1813.

11 ECH, LB, ix, 12 June 1784; Bodleian Library, Oxford, Milles Parochial Collections, x, 90; DRO, Ship Registers, 1785–1879.

12 DRO, Exeter and Exmouth Papers, 1854–5; DRO, Coleman *v* Exeter Papers, 1760; House of Lords MSS (hereafter HL, MSS), Minutes of Evidence (hereafter Min. of Ev.), Exeter, Topsham and Exmouth Railway Bill, 1846; DRO, Hardyk *v* Mayor Papers, 1871–3.

13 Clark, *Ports of the Exe*, 53–5; see C N Ponsford, ed., *Shipbuilding on the Exe. The Memoranda Book of Daniel Bishop Davy, 1799–1874, of Topsham, Devon.* (Exeter, 1988).

14 Clark, *Ports of the Exe*, 69–70.

15 E A G Clark, 'The Estuarine Ports of the Exe and the Teign with special reference to the period 1660–1860' (unpublished PhD thesis, University of London, 1957) 148, 226–31, 240–2.

16 Clark, *Ports of the Exe*, 27–40.

17 DRO, Book 176, Entry Book of the Town Custom, 1715–25; PRO, CO 390/8, Account of the Number of Vessels that have Cleared from England, 1714–17.

18 DRO, Mayor *v* Coleman Papers, 1760.

19 DRO, Book 177, Book of Entries and Waste Book, 1750–1; DRO, Books 220–226, Wharfingers' Journals (hereafter WJ), Exeter, 1750–1; DRO, WJ, Topsham, 1770–5.

20 DRO, Book 176: DRO King *v* Exeter Papers, 1828.

21 DRO, Book 177.

22 Clark, *Ports of the Exe*, 196.

23 Clark, *Ports of the Exe*, 79–80, 97–101; DRO, 71/8, Journal of Samuel Milford, 1760–74.

24 Clark, *Ports of the Exe*, 96–123.

25 Clark, *Ports of the Exe*, 118–23.

26 DRO, WJ, Topsham, 1770–1840; Clark, *Ports of the Exe*, 163–7.

27 DRO, Rates for the Carriage of Goods brought to Exeter from London, 1732; HL, MSS, Min. of Ev., Bristol and Exeter Railway Bill, 1836, 14 March, 17.

28 PRO, Port Books, E190/1005/6, 9; ECH, LB, xxxi, 262.

29 DRO, Town Customs, Collector's Accounts, 1762–91; *Accounts and Papers* (BPP, 1819, XVI, 226–7). An Account of Duties Paid on Coal and Culm Carried Coastwise.

30 PRO, Port Books, E190/1008/6, 7.

31 *Exeter Itinerary and General Directory* (Exeter, 1828), 116.

32 PRO, Exchequer Depositions, E134/9 and 10 Anne, Hil. 20; Clark, 'Estuarine Ports', 418–21; DRO, Z10/43, Accounts of Stone Boats Belonging to the Port of Exeter, 10 07.

33 PRO, Port Books, E190/1008/6,7.

34 DRO, WJ, Topsham, 1790–1840; DRO, WJ, Exeter, 1795–1800; The *Universal British Directory of Trade* (1791), II, 691.

35 PRO, Port Books, E190/1005/6, 9; DRO, WJ, Topsham, 1790–1840; DRO, WJ, Exeter; 1795–1800; *Exeter Itinerary* (1828).

36 *Annual Register* (1792), 106; DRO, List of Boats, Barges, 1795; ECH, Fishing Boats Registered in the Port of Exeter, 1869; ECH, Pilotage Letter Book, 1865–95, 4 June 1872 (refers to fifty years before); BL Add. MS 33,043, Officers of HM Customs, 1971.

37 See, for example, the *John and Elizabeth* to Hamburg, DRO, Wharfingers' Bale Book, Topsham 1752–84; the *Post van Topsham* to Rotterdam, the *Oporto Packet*, the *Unity* to Bristol and the *Expedition* to London, DRO, WJ, Topsham, 1790–3.

38 Clark, *Ports of the Exe*, 163–7.

39 DRO, Wilson Holman Bequest, G12, MS 46, Wharfingers' Journals, Topsham, 1790–1840. H J Trump, 'Adventure under Sail'. *Western Morning News*, 5 March 1973.

40 Clark, *Ports of the Exe*, 38–43.

41 DRO, Transcript of Shorthand Notes taken by Thomas Latimer at the Guildhall, Exeter, 1833. For the canal income 1741–1835, see Clark, *Ports of the Exe*, 225.

42 DRO, Income of the Canal, 1833–43; DRO, Papers Concerning the Exeter Port Dues Bill, 1840.

43 DRO, WJ, Topsham, 1791–1840; *Exeter Flying Post* (hereafter *EFP*), 14 July 1831; *Exeter Itinerary* (1828), 116; *Robson's Directory*, Devon Section (1838), 53.

44 British Transport Commission, Historical Records, Min. of Ev., Teign Valley Railway Bill, 1864, Q.1984 etc; DRO, Miscellaneous Reports Connected with the Canal, 1864–80; DRO, Canal Receiver's Letters, 1860–4, 4 June 1869; DRO, Navigational Committee Minute Book (hereafter NC MB) 486, 13, 242.

45 HL, MSS, Min. of Ev., London and SW Railway Bill, 1846, 22 July, 116.

46 Clark, *Ports of the Exe*, 228.

47 Clark, *Ports of the Exe*, 220.

48 Clark, 'Estuarine Ports', 1072.

49 DRO, Transires In, Topsham, 1864–5, 1868; Transires Out, Topsham, 1862, 1866–8; 3759 A, Ballast Book.

50 Clark, *Ports of the Exe*, 214: *EFP*, 27 July 1854, ff.; DRO, Transires In Topsham, 1864–6, 1868.

51 H C Brookfield, 'Three Sussex Ports, 1850–1950' *JTH*, II (1955), 39. At Exeter Customs Port, few steamers entered in the coasting trade until 1880, and none in the foreign trade until 1888 (Clark, 'Estuarine Ports', App. 15 (1)).

52 Clark, *Ports of the Exe*, 216: CHE, LB, xiix, G.O.1/1859, G.O.4/1860, LB 1, G.O.18/1862, G.O.11/1864.

53 DRO, AB, xxxiii, 361, 376–88.

54 DRO, NC MB, 483, 419–21: DRO, AB, xxxv, 144, 473–9; AB, xxxiii, 29, 321–2; AB xxxviii, 575; Book 522, MB of the Canal Creditors; *Exeter Canal Act* (1883).

55 DRO, Miscellaneous Reports, 1864–80.

56 Clark, 'Estuarine Ports', App. 4 (based on Annual Pilotage Returns, *Accounts and Papers*, BPP, 1854–70); DRO, Papers Relating to the Exmouth Docks Bill, 1870.

57 DRO, NC MB, 1844–61, 444; DRO, AB, xxxv, 482; AB, xxxvi, 122.

58 DRO, South Devon Railway Act and Related Papers, 1865; DRO, AB, xxxvi, 329, 371, 459.

59 DRO, MB of the General Purposes Committee, 1836–50, 333; Peacock, 'Estuary of the Exe', *Nautical Magazine*, (1847), 132; C H Thompson, *The Exeter Canal. How to Restore its Trade* (Exeter, 1876), 7; Clark, 'Estuarine Ports', App. 8.

60 DRO, Report Concerning Exe Bight Pier Suit, 1870; DRO, Mayor *v* Earl of Devon and Exe Bright Oyster Fishery, 1870; DRO, Book 522, 27 Nov 1867, 7 Jan 1868; DRO, 3822 A1, Register of Ships Landed at Exmouth etc. 1870.

61 181 vessels in 1845 and 105 in 1869, *Accounts and Papers* (BPP, 1846, XLV, 308; 1870, XL).

62 *Billings Directory of Devon* (Birmingham, 1857).

63 DRO, Shipping Registers, 1855–79.

64 L E Braddick, 'The Port of Topsham. Its Ships and Shipbuilding' *DAT*, LXXXV (1953), 18–34; Clark, 'Estuarine Ports', 212–5, 433–40; information from the late Mr F R Holman. See chapters 7 and 9.

65 *Exmouth Docks Act* (1865); DRO, Papers Concerning the Exmouth Docks Bill, 1870; E R Delderfield, *Exmouth Milestones* (Exmouth, 1948), 89; A Hurd, *Ports of the World* (1948), 113.

66 DRO, 3822 A1, Register of Ships; ECH, Misc. LB, 1860–80, 332.

67 PRO, Cust 23, Abstracts of Imports; DRO, NV 185, Exeter Canal Imports and Exports, 1884–1905; DRO, NC, MB 1881–1907, *passim* (lists ships from foreign ports); DRO, 3759, MB of Topsham River Commissioners, 1841–1974, 'Port of Exeter', 29 Oct. 1866.

68 DRO, NV 185.

69 DRO, NC MB 1861–73, 44, 51, 55, 144, 188; NC MB, 1873–80, 147–8; NC MB, 1880–84, 82, 96, 209–14; NC MB, 1885–95, 284; 1896–1906, 317, 348, 414; NC MB, 1908, 1910; Miscellaneous Reports Connected with the canal, 1864–80; K R Clew, *The Exeter Canal* (Chichester, 1984) 70–1.

70 DRO, NC Report, 13 Feb. 1911; NV 68, NV 79; NV 103, 21 Feb. 1911; NV 185, 22 Nov. 4 Dec. 1906; NV 185, Exeter Canal imports and exports, 1884–1905.

71 DRO, NC Reports, 1908–10; Clew, *Exeter Canal*, 70–1.

72 Clark, 'Estuarine Ports', App. 8: DRO, 71/7/13, Daybook of Topsham Wharfinger, 1861–1902; Register of Goods Entering Port of Topsham, 1908–23; Quarterly Statements of Imports and Exports through Exeter Canal, 1887–97 (includes Exmouth 1891–4).

73 DRO, Crew Lists (all the voyages of Exeter ships listed in DRO, Handlist No.3 [1987] were examined in the card index for details of ports visited).

74 DRO, Crew Lists, Log Books and Running Agreements, 11919 (*Friendship*), 60301 (*City of Exeter*), 69570 (*Belle of the Exe*).

75 D H Aldcroft, 'The Eclipse of British Coastal Shipping, 1913–21', *JTH*, VI (1963), 24–38.

76 DRO, NC MB, 1907–22, 19 Oct. 1920; NC MB, 1923–38, 477; NC MB, 1938–49, 808; Clew, *Exeter Canal*, 72–3

77 DRO, NC MB, 1923–38, 461, 500a, 508–17, 578a, 584a, 623–4; NV 538, NV 450; *Express and Echo*, 24 Oct. 1935.

78 DRO, J Brierley, Report on Proposed Lengthening of Turf Lock, 1950; NV 126, Papers re Basin, 1905–10; NV 493 and NV 324; NC MB, 1923–38, 517a.

79 DRO, NC MB, 1923–38, 1938–49, passim for statistics of shipping at Exeter, Exmouth and Topsham.

80 Exmouth Docks Company, *The Centenary Year, 1965* (Exmouth, 1965), 11; DRO, NC MB, 1923–38, 617.

81 DRO, NC MB, 1938–1949; NC MB, 1950–1960.

82 DRO, NV 642; NC MB, 1960–67, 111.

83 DRO, Investigation into the Future of the Canal, 1964, App. 1.

84 DRO, Brierley Report.

85 DRO, NC MB, 28 Nov. 1961, 30 Jan. 1962; NV 257, 28 Oct. 1961.

86 DRO, Investigation into the Future of the Canal, 1964; Clew, *Exeter Canal*, 79–83.

87 PRO, CO 380/8, Account of the Number of Ships that have Cleared from England, 1714–17.

88 R Davis, *The Rise of the English Shipping Industry in the Seventeenth and Eighteenth Centuries* (1962), 35; *Annual Register* (1792), 106.

89 *Accounts and Papers* (BPP, 1870, LXIII). Annual Statement of the Trade and Navigation of the United Kingdom.

90 DRO, NC MB, 1950–60.

91 BL Sloane MS 3233.

7 Devon's Shipbuilding Industry, 1786–1970

DAVID J STARKEY

THE SHIPBUILDING INDUSTRY has always been an important facet of Britain's maritime economy. Over the centuries it has produced the bulk of the new tonnage required by the British shipping industry, as well as undertaking much of the repair, maintenance and conversion work which forms such a vital part of ship operation. Shipbuilders have likewise serviced the state sector, private yards having long since supplemented or rivalled the Royal Dockyards in the building and renovation of naval vessels. The shipbuilding industry has also been significant in a spatial sense, in that nearly all of Britain's ports have witnessed the construction and repair of vessels at some stage over the last 200 years.

Such close ties with the port and shipping industries, and with the Navy, have rendered the shipbuilding industry dependent upon the vagaries of world trade, government military expenditure, and foreign competition. Short-term fluctuations in output and employment have therefore been a prominent feature of the industry's development. Underlying these vicissitudes, however, a number of long-term trends are discernible. Production tended to rise during the nineteenth century, especially after the 1850s, with British shipbuilders accounting for a growing proportion of world output – a share which exceeded 80 per cent in the early 1890s.[1] Since 1914, however, the industry has experienced relative – and, from the mid-1960s, absolute – decline, as foreign competitors have penetrated home and overseas markets once served by British yards.[2] In the long run, moreover, technological developments have profoundly changed the character of the vessels built and repaired, wind-driven wooden vessels giving way to mechanically-powered, metal-hulled ships. This transformation occurred chiefly in the last thirty years of the nineteenth century, and was associated with a marked locational shift in the industry. As shipbuilding became increasingly concentrated in northeast England, the Clyde and other northern districts, the majority of yards in the south of the country ceased production.[3]

Devon's shipbuilding industry has both conformed and run counter to these trends. Throughout the nineteenth century the county's shipbuilders were predominantly concerned with the construction and repair of wooden sailing vessels, generally exhibiting a reluctance, in common with many other southern firms, to adopt the technology of the metal-hulled steamship. If this led to a relative decline in Devon's output from the 1870s, other, essentially local, factors contributed to the absolute contraction in production which occurred concurrently. Moreover, in contrast to many nineteenth-century shipbuilding centres, the building and maintenance of ocean-going vessels has continued at various locations in Devon since the First World War. Atypically, a sizeable proportion of this activity has involved wooden craft, though steel ships have formed an increasing part of the workload, particularly since 1945.

This chapter examines Devon's shipbuilding industry from 1786 to 1970, from the Act of General Registry to the opening of the 'ship factory' at Bidna, Appledore.[4] It is hoped that, in assessing the output, products, shipyards and markets of the business during this long period, the development and character of this important branch of Devon's maritime enterprise is both revealed and explained.

Output

The calculation of the output of the British shipbuilding industry is beset with difficulties. While the annual number and tonnage of vessels launched can be ascertained from the 1780s, such figures generally neglect the quality of the ships enumerated and entirely ignore the construction of small, non-registered craft and the volume of repair and conversion work undertaken. Tonnage measurement presents a further problem. Changes in the method utilised to establish a vessel's tonnage, notably in 1824, 1836 and 1854, add to the complexities of long-term comparisons, while even in the short run the coexistence of various yardsticks – net, gross, deadweight and displacement tons – means that a single period might yield at least four different production totals.[5] Treatments of the shipbuilding output of particular ports or regions are hindered by a number of factors. Gaps and

7.1 The brigantine *Clio*, built by R Cock and Sons on the New Quay slip at Appledore in 1894. She is shown here at the moment of launching, the lady concerned holding the bottle in her hand. The *Clio*, built for C T Bennett of Bristol and employed in the Newfoundland trade, was probably the last merchant brigantine ever to be built in Britain. (*Gordon Harris*)

7.2   The launch of ss *Hubbastone* (873 tons) in 1921. She was one of three steam screw vessels built by Hansen Shipbuilding and Repair Co at Barnstaple shortly after the First World War. (*Basil Greenhill*)

inconsistencies occur in the series of port-by-port production statistics compiled by the Customs authorities. Devon's ports, for instance, lack comprehensive data for the 1827–65 and post-1918 periods, shortcomings which necessitate a recourse to alternative sources which are not entirely compatible with the national series. Further problems arise from the classification of shipbuilding figures by Registry Port. This practice tends to obscure local building patterns, for vessels constructed at significant creeks such as Brixham and Salcombe are misleadingly attributed to their respective head port – in this case, the port of Dartmouth. Similarly, changes in port boundaries affect production figures in an area such as Devon, which has witnessed the absorption of Ilfracombe by Barnstaple in 1839, the separation of Teignmouth from Exeter in 1853, and the creation of Salcombe and Brixham Registry Ports in 1863 and 1864 respectively. Moreover, unofficial demarcations, notably Appledore's continuing allegiance to Bideford, rather than Barnstaple, in the 1786–1814 period, also require consideration.[6]

Taking these general and particular qualifications into account, a reasonably accurate assessment of Devon's contribution to Britain's shipbuilding output can be offered. Analysis of the 1776 *Lloyd's Register* reveals that the county's shipbuilders had constructed 9,575 tons of the shipping listed by Lloyd's, just 1.7 per cent of the British-built total.[7] In 1787, when the first port-by-port breakdown of new-built vessels was compiled, Devon's shipyards were responsible for 5,116 of the 94,355 tons launched in the British Isles during the year, 5.4 per cent of the national aggregate. This total was not surpassed until 1799, when fifty-five vessels, measuring 5,275 tons, were completed in Devon.[8] Over the next five years, as Table 7.1 indicates, local shipbuilders launched some 35,527 tons of shipping, as well as numerous naval vessels, a total which represented 6.7 per cent of the 528,400 tons produced nationally. This was almost certainly the highest quinquennial share ever achieved by Devon's shipyards. During the prolonged, if uneven, decline in national output – the 1800–4 aggregate tonnage was not eclipsed until 1835–9 – shipbuilding in the county tended to contract at a faster than average rate; accordingly, only 4.5 per cent of the British tonnage completed in 1820–24 was launched in Devon.

Despite the absence of port-by-port returns for the next forty years, the number and tonnage of vessels built and initially registered in Devon can be gauged from the county's Ship Registers, as shown in Table 7.1. Such an analysis, of course, neglects locally-built vessels registered out of the county. This 'export' market appears to have accounted for approximately 40 per cent of Devon's production during much of the 1825–1864 period. For instance, comparison with Farr's comprehensive production data (see Table 7.3) suggests that vessels built for local owners comprised between 57 and 62 per cent of new building between 1825 and 1850. Likewise, analysis of *Lloyd's Registers* of the early 1860s, which list the ports of build and first registry of newly-constructed vessels classified by the society, suggests that 43 per cent of Devon-built vessels were sold beyond the county's borders.[9] There seem to have been local variations around this norm, however, especially during the 1850s. In North Devon, Farr's data indicate that 63 per cent of the new vessels launched between 1850 and 1864 were 'exported', a tendency supported by newspaper reports of the launch of vessels, usually the larger products, for owners in other parts of the country. For instance, in the early 1850s John Westacott of Barnstaple built the *Springbok* for Messrs Stewart & Co of Liverpool, and laid down the keel of a large barque for Mr Norman of the same port, while in 1861 Cox & Son of Bideford launched the *Unas*, a 500-ton barque 'purchased by the Messrs Bath of

Table 7.1

Vessels built in Devon, 1790–1913

(Quinquennial Totals)

| | Devon | | United Kingdom* | | % Built in Devon | |
	No	Net Tons	No	Net Tons	No	Net Tons
1790–4	227	14,294	3,063	304,100	7.4	4.7
1795–9	240	18,586	3,189	390,000	7.5	4.8
1800–4	376	35,527	4,639	528,400	8.1	6.7
1805–8**	158	15,164	2,318	229,500	6.8	6.6
1815–9	320	27,606	4,051	444,700	7.9	6.2
1820–4	196	14,940	3,161	330,000	6.2	4.5
1825–9***	245	18,190	4,544	499,300	5.4	3.6
1830–4	178	12,030	3,696	439,200	4.8	2.7
1835–9	161	11,983	4,781	672,900	3.4	1.8
1840–4	194	18,474	4,782	678,900	4.1	2.7
1845–9	155	13,437	4,172	635,000	3.7	2.1
1850–4	139	13,859	3,673	850,900	3.8	1.6
1855–9	192	20,948	5,465	1,212,400	3.5	1.7
1860–4	200	19,535	5,440	1,447,100	3.7	1.3
1866–9**	209	28,320	4,471	1,280,800	4.7	2.2
1870–4	258	29,666	4,622	1,982,000	5.6	1.5
1875–9	347	27,147	4,913	1,999,700	7.1	1.4
1880–4	224	12,822	4,814	2,838,300	4.7	0.5
1885–9	237	13,182	3,696	2,159,700	6.4	0.6
1890–4	199	8,270	4,299	3,085,300	4.6	0.3
1895–9	199	6,835	5,460	2,967,300	3.6	0.2
1900–4	177	7,121	5,876	3,677,500	3.0	0.2
1905–9	160	5,293	5,136	3,438,400	3.1	0.2
1910–3**	104	3,660	3,997	3,391,200	2.6	0.1

* 1790–1808 – ships built in Britain. Tonnages rounded. Vessels built for British owners only.

** Four years only.

*** 1825–1864 – Devon vessels built and first registered in the county only.

Sources: 1790–1808 – PRO, CUST 17/12–30; 1815–1824 – *Accounts and Papers* (BPP, 1826–7, XVIII, 286–7); 1825–1864 – DRO, Customs House Ship Registers; 1866–1913 – *Annual Statements of Navigation and Shipping*; United Kingdom figures – PRO, CUST 17/25, 28–30 and B R Mitchell and P Deane, *Abstract of British Historical Statistics* (Cambridge, 1971), 220–2.

Swansea, for the copper ore trade'.[10] In contrast, relatively few vessels constructed in South Devon appear to have been sold out of the county during mid-century. Thus, in the 1850s, only two vessels built in the Exe estuary were registered elsewhere,[11] while just four of the craft launched at Salcombe during the decade were 'exported'.[12]

Imperfect though the 1824–65 data may be, it concurs with other information to suggest that Devon's shipbuilding output was generally depressed in the 1830s and 1840s, before increasing substantially over the next twenty years. Such a pattern is revealed in Farr's analysis, though North Devon production appears to have slumped in the 1860s as new building in South Devon increased. It also tends to fit the trend apparent in the port-by-port returns from 1866. Contemporaries, moreover, perceived that,

> a great increase has of late years taken place in the number and size of vessels built at the various ports in the county of Devon. Ships of large tonnage are being frequently launched, and the demand for them at present seems to be almost brisker than ever.[13]

In spite of this mid-century burst of activity, Devon's output continued to decline in relation to national production levels, even if vessels sold outside the county are taken into account. For instance, the addition of an 'export' factor of 43 per cent to the calculation of the county's 1860–4 output indicates that in this comparatively prolific quinquennium Devon's shipbuilders accounted for just 1.9 per cent of the tonnage launched in the United Kingdom.

In the last quarter of the nineteenth century, new building in Devon diminished in both absolute and relative terms. Between 1875 and 1884 the tonnage launched from the county's yards halved (though the number of vessels completed fell at a much slower rate) as production in the country at large experienced a marked upsurge. This trend continued down to the First World War. By 1913 Devon's output, which had constituted 2.2 per cent of the tonnage launched in the United Kingdom in 1866, represented a mere 0.1 per cent of the national total. In terms of the vessels constructed, however, Devon's yards still accounted for 2.6 per cent of all launchings.

Between the two world wars the county's shipbuilding output fluctuated widely. In the early 1920s, as Table 7.2(a) indicates, production levels were relatively high, with ten vessels of 100 gross tons or over, measuring an aggregate of 5,836grt, launched from Devon shipyards in 1921. Thereafter, in line with national trends, the county's output declined, with clear troughs being reached in 1926 and 1934 when local yards did not complete a single vessel of over 100grt. The Second World War undoubtedly caused an upturn in vessel production in Devon, and to some degree this buoyancy continued in the post-1945 era, particularly from the mid 1950s. In 1960–4, for instance, seventy-three vessels measuring 10,454 tons were completed at Appledore and Bideford, while unprecedented totals of eighty-two vessels and 20,231 tons were reached in the 1965–9 quinquennium.[14]

Vessels were constructed at innumerable sites along both of the county's coastlines during the 1786–1970 period. As Tables 7.3 and 7.4 indicate, South Devon shipbuilders accounted for approximately threequarters of the tonnage launched in the county during the 1790–1913 period. This was true of expansive phases and of times of contraction alike; thus, in the peak quinquennium of 1800–4, 74.5 per cent of the tonnage built in Devon was produced in the south of the county, while in 1870–74, when North Devon's output peaked, and in 1910–13, the equivalent proportions stood at 69.3 and 73.8 per cent respectively. South Devon continued to dominate the county's

Table 7.2
Vessels of over 99 grt built in Devon, 1920–1938

(a) Annual production by port

	Bd		Be		Dh		Ph		Devon	
	No	grt	No	grt	No	grt	No	grt	No	grt
1920	–	–	–	–	5	778	–	–	5	778
1921	3	2,619	4	2,264	2	588	1	365	10	5,836
1922	2	1,354	–	–	2	646	–	–	4	2,000
1923	4	2,266	1	449	11	1,231	1	137	17	4,083
1924	2	1,046	–	–	2	724	1	250	5	2,020
1925	–	–	–	–	4	1,912	–	–	4	1,912
1926	–	–	–	–	–	–	–	–	–	–
1927	–	–	–	–	3	973	–	–	3	973
1928	–	–	–	–	3	1,045	–	–	3	1,045
1929	–	–	–	–	5	922	–	–	5	922
1930	–	–	–	–	1	128	–	–	1	128
1931	–	–	–	–	2	603	–	–	2	603
1932	–	–	–	–	2	271	–	–	2	271
1933	–	–	–	–	1	130	–	–	1	130
1934	–	–	–	–	–	–	–	–	–	–
1935	1	498	–	–	–	–	–	–	1	498
1936	–	–	–	–	3	550	–	–	3	550
1937	–	–	–	–	3	975	–	–	3	975
1938	–	–	–	–	3	896	–	–	3	896
Totals	12	7,783	5	2,713	52	12,372	3	752	72	23,620

(b) Types of vessel constructed

	Bd		Be		Dh		Ph		Devon	
	No	grt	No	grt	No	grt	No	grt	No	grt
Coasters	12	7,783	5	2,713	4	1,099	1	365	22	11,960
Tugs	–	–	–	–	14	2,891	–	–	14	2,891
Lightships	–	–	–	–	7	2,035	–	–	7	2,035
Ferries	–	–	–	–	6	1,985	–	–	6	1,985
Barges	–	–	–	–	11	1,140	2	387	13	1,527
Tankers	–	–	–	–	1	1,083	–	–	1	1,083
Yachts	–	–	–	–	5	705	–	–	5	705
Camel	–	–	–	–	1	459	–	–	1	459
Tenders	–	–	–	–	1	448	–	–	1	448
Survey Ships	–	–	–	–	1	337	–	–	1	337
Pontoons	–	–	–	–	1	190	–	–	1	190
Totals	12	7,783	5	2,713	52	12,372	3	752	72	23,620
Steam:										
Coal	11	7,285	5	2,713	22	5,779	1	365	39	16,142
Oil	–	–	–	–	6	2,523	–	–	6	2,523
Diesel	1	498	–	–	5	705	–	–	6	1,203
Dumb	–	–	–	–	19	3,365	2	387	21	3,752
Totals	12	7,783	5	2,713	52	12,372	3	752	72	23,620

Key to ports: Bd – Bideford (Robert Cock & Sons Ltd, Hansen Shipbuilding and Ship Repairing Co Ltd); Be – Barnstaple (Taw Shipyards Ltd); Dh – Dartmouth (Philip & Son Ltd); Ph – Plymouth (Willoughby [Plymouth] Ltd).

Sources: NMM, Shipbuilding Conference, 'Merchant Shipbuilding in Great Britain and Ireland, 1920–38', I. This information was kindly supplied by Anthony Slaven and Philip Taylor of Glasgow University.

production during much of the interwar period (see Table 7.2), though after 1945 the balance between the two coasts shifted as the south generally shed its shipbuilding interests, while various concerns continued to operate on the banks of the Torridge.

Ships have been built at each of Devon's Registry Ports, though the level of activity has varied considerably, both between the different centres and over time. In North Devon, as Table 7.3 shows, Barnstaple was the most productive port during the 1790–4 period, when an average of four vessels per annum was launched into the Taw. Bideford's output was slightly less extensive at this juncture, but in subsequent years the Torridge emerged as the principal focus of the area's shipbuilding industry, consistently eclipsing the output of Barnstaple and its neighbour (and sub-port from 1839) Ilfracombe. With the cessation of vessel construction on the Taw in the 1880s, Bideford remained the sole producer of ships along Devon's northern coast, a distinction which the port has held, with minor interruptions, ever since.

7.3 The Anglo-Saxon Petroleum vessel *Landak*, built by Philip & Son at Dartmouth in 1951 (*Torquay Library*)

Table 7.3
Vessels built at North Devon Registry Ports, 1790–1913

(Quinquennial totals; number – net tons)

	Be	Bd	Ie	North Devon	Farr*
1790–4	20–1,273	17– 961	9–728	46–2,962	(52– 3,430)
1795–9	21–1,777	20–2,021	10–570	51–4,368	(56– 5,137)
1800–4	18–2,139	49–6,343	8–591	75–9,073	(89–11,113)
1805–8**	13– 929	32–2,637	5–336	50–3,902	(73– 8,899)
1815–9	20–1,477	53–5,068	5–366	78–6,911	(83– 8,268)
1820–4	11– 655	31–2,651	5–317	47–3,623	(50– 4,007)
1825–9	5– 307	40–3,118	8–840	53–4,265	(77– 6,868)
1830–4	6– 476	25–1,601	3– 77	34–2,154	(55– 3,771)
1835–9	8– 523	16–1,338	5–199	29–2,060	(74– 6,206)
1840–4	19–1,661	23–2,429	–	42–4,090	(73– 7,160)
1845–9	8–1,333	25–2,455	–	33–3,788	(54– 6,574)
1850–4	8–1,733	25–2,719	–	33–4,452	(64–11,774)
1855–9	4– 633	30–3,432	–	34–4,065	(71–12,526)
1860–4	8– 799	22–1,624	–	30–2,423	(61– 8,909)
1866–9**	9–1,671	34–5,808	–	43–7,479	(41– 7,292)
1870–4	23–2,358	40–6,756	–	63–9,114	(62– 9,152)
1875–9	19–2,596	38–3,921	–	57–6,517	(58– 6,983)
1880–4	10– 780	11– 884	–	21–1,664	(21– 1,641)
1885–9	0	13– 752	–	13– 752	(19– 873)
1890–4	0	5– 430	–	5– 430	(10– 555)
1895–9	0	26–1,112	–	26–1,112	(17– 624)
1900–4	0	15–1,545	–	15–1,545	(22– 2,136)
1905–9	0	11– 654	–	11– 654	(21– 1,739)
1910–3**	0	15– 959	–	15– 959	(11– 556)

* Figures derived from G Farr, *Shipbuilding in North Devon* (1976).
** Four years only.
Key to Ports: Be – Barnstaple; Bd – Bideford; Ie – Ilfracombe.

Sources: 1790–1808 – PRO, CUST 17/12–30; 1815–24 – *Accounts and Papers* (BPP, 1826–7, XVIII, 286–7); 1825–64 – DRO, Custom House Ship Registers; 1866–1913 – *Annual Statements of Navigation and Shipping*.

Table 7.4
Vessels built at South Devon Registry Ports, 1790–1913

(Quinquennial totals; number – net tons)

	Bm	Dh	Er	Ph	Se	Th	South Devon
1790–4	–	67–3,155	45– 3,586	69–4,591	–	–	181–11,332
1795–9	–	81–5,271	43– 4,016	65–4,931	–	–	189–14,218
1800–4	–	128–9,109	84–10,899	89–6,446	–	–	301–26,454
1805–8*	–	70–5,317	43– 3,283	45–2,662	–	–	158–11,262
1815–9	–	86–7,334	64– 6,819	92–6,542	–	–	242–20,695
1820–4	–	52–4,249	38– 3,040	59–4,028	–	–	149–11,317
1825–9	–	67–4,073	49– 4,639	76–5,213	–	–	192–13,925
1830–4	–	56–4,092	15– 1,136	73–4,648	–	–	144– 9,876
1835–9	–	59–3,935	17– 2,137	56–3,851	–	–	132– 9,923
1840–4	–	72–8,471	13– 2,161	67–3,752	–	–	152–14,384
1845–9	–	63–5,688	13– 895	46–3,066	–	–	122– 9,649
1850–4	–	44–3,841	10– 1,147	48–3,968	–	4– 451	106– 9,407
1855–9	–	99–9,853	14– 1,668	35–3,535	–	10–1,827	158–16,883
1860–4	9–1,157	88–8,125	12– 1,806	55–5,398	–	6– 626	170–17,112
1866–9*	50–4,982	40–4,496	12– 3,006	45–5,018	13–2,638	6– 701	166–20,841
1870–4	75–6,032	43–3,611	4– 627	48–5,818	19–3,665	6– 799	195–20,552
1875–9	93–5,819	100–5,904	7– 824	60–4,329	21–3,433	9– 321	290–20,630
1880–4	62–3,850	63–3,522	0	67–3,523	10– 460	1– 3	203–11,158
1885–9	105–5,601	78–3,914	0	33–2,199	8– 716	0	224–12,430
1890–4	84–3,608	72–2,341	0	31–1,405	6– 471	1– 15	194– 7,840
1895–9	69–2,808	61–1,681	1– 38	32– 676	7– 488	3– 32	173– 5,723
1900–4	64–2,627	74–2,305	1– 5	19– 482	3– 154	1– 3	162– 5,576
1905–9	60–1,944	72–2,172	0	6– 291	8– 214	3– 18	149– 4,639
1910–3*	30–1,083	46–1,231	0	7– 275	4– 93	2– 19	89– 2,701

* Four years only.
Key to Ports: Bm – Brixham; Dh – Dartmouth; Er – Exeter; Ph – Plymouth; Se – Salcombe; Th – Teignmouth

Sources: See Table 7.3

Bideford's output was generally inferior to that recorded at Dartmouth, Exeter and Plymouth during the 1790–1840 period. Here, production levels fluctuated considerably, with each of the ports ascendant at some stage, before Dartmouth began to dominate new building in the south of the county from the 1840s onwards. By the early twentieth century, with Exeter's yards having long since closed and a decline in production apparent at Plymouth, Salcombe and Teignmouth, South Devon's shipbuilding output emanated almost entirely from Dartmouth and its erstwhile creek, Brixham. This remained the case in the interwar years, though the end of vessel construction at Brixham in the late 1940s meant that the Dart was left as the only producer of new tonnage along Devon's English Channel coast for much of the post-1945 era.

At a local level, the distribution of shipbuilding output according to Registry Port provides an inaccurate guide as to where vessel construction and repair actually took place. In the Ports of Bideford and Barnstaple, for example, shipyards were located at Clovelly, Combe Martin and, most importantly, at Appledore, where a large proportion of Bideford's tonnage was built from the early nineteenth century and where shipbuilding continues still. Within the boundaries of these head ports, moreover, there were numerous shipbuilding sites. Thus, in Bideford, vessels were built at one time or another at Cleave Houses and Potter's Pill, near the centre of the town, at Sea Locks, over one and half miles upstream, and across the Torridge at East-the-Water and Cross Park, while Barnstaple's shipbuilding concerns were variously established at Pottington and Pilton, as well as both above and below the town bridge.

Similarly, in the south of the county, shipyards were located at a multiplicity of sites in and around the head ports. Exeter's shipbuilding return included a number of small vessels launched at Beer, Seaton and Sidmouth. It included a great many more – upwards of 50 per cent of new-built vessels registered in the port in the 1820s and 1830s – completed at Teignmouth, Ringmore and Shaldon on the Teign estuary,[15] as well as a sizeable proportion built at Starcross, Lympstone, Exmouth and, most importantly, Topsham, on the Exe. Yet it contained hardly any vessels constructed in the city itself. Indeed, when the *New Exeter*, a modest sloop of 90 tons, was launched opposite Exeter Quay in 1764, 'a very great number of people, many of whom were persons of the first rank' assembled to witness an event which had occurred only twice in the previous forty years,[16] and was to be repeated only a handful of times in the next four decades.

Vessels were built at various places within the Port of Plymouth during the nineteenth century. To the east of the Sound, a considerable number of craft were launched at Turnchapel, while shipbuilding concerns were located at Cattedown, Mutton Cove, Cremyll and, most especially, Stonehouse. Beyond the city itself, shipyards were established upriver at Bere Ferrers (see Fig. 5.2) and across the Tamar at Torpoint, Millbrook, Saltash and Calstock. Production at the Port of Dartmouth was even more widely dispersed, especially before the establishment of registries at Brixham and Salcombe in the 1860s. Although the head port was substantially more prolific than neighbouring Exeter, only 25 per cent of the 41,596 tons built and initially registered at Dartmouth between 1824 and 1862 was produced in the town's yards. Over 36 per cent (226 vessels, measuring 15,133 tons) of the port's home-produced fleet was constructed at Brixham during these years, with a further 23.8 per cent (112 vessels, measuring 9,900 tons) produced at Salcombe. In addition, 8.9 per cent of Dartmouth's output was built at Kingsbridge, where, in 1837, the schooner *Feronia* was the first vessel ever completed,[17] while vessels were also launched at Galmpton, Churston Ferrers and Torquay.[18]

Such refinements of the statistical data indicate that Devon's shipbuilding output was widely spread in the mid-nineteenth century. However, as the volume of new building in the county declined from the 1870s, so production ceased at Barnstaple and Exeter, and diminished to negligible proportions at Plymouth, Salcombe and Teignmouth. In the late nineteenth century, therefore, Devon's shipbuilding industry was chiefly located at Bideford, Brixham and Dartmouth. This concentration was closely linked with the changing character of the industry's products.

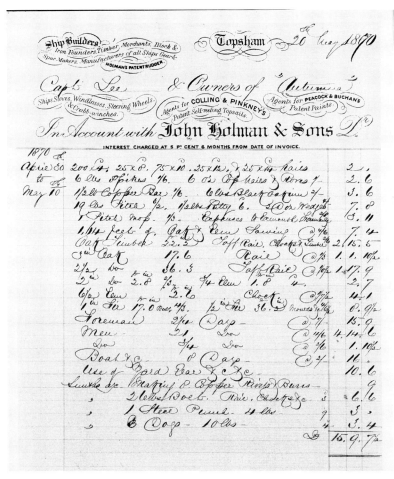

7.4   An invoice from the yard ledger of John Holman & Sons, Topsham, detailing the repairs of the *Autumn*, 1870. The range of the firm's maritime activities is clearly apparent in the letter heading. (*Devon Record Office*)

Products

Although the range of the shipbuilding industry's products is, and always has been, immense, it is convenient to divide its output into three parts – the construction of merchant vessels, ship repair, and warshipbuilding.

Merchant Shipbuilding

The greatest part of Devon's shipbuilding effort has been expended on the production and repair of merchant ships. With regard to new building, it is evident that the county's shipyards have generally concentrated on the construction of relatively small vessels. This tendency is reflected in Table 7.1. In 1790–94, the average Devon-built vessel measured 63 tons, compared with the national mean of 99.3 tons, while in 1820–24 equivalent figures of 76.2 and 104.4 tons pertained, and in 1866–69, when the typical product of Devon's shipyards measured 135.5 tons – a nineteenth-century peak – the national average stood at 286.5 tons. Local and national means diverged considerably thereafter, the average vessel launched in Devon measuring just 35.2 tons in 1910–13, as against a figure of 848.4 tons for the United Kingdom as a whole. After the First World War this pattern was sustained, with local shipbuilders specialising in the construction of craft at the lower end of the tonnage scale.

This preoccupation with small-scale building was reflected in the rigs deployed in Devon's sailing ships. As Table 7.5 shows, the large, three-masted ships and barques constituted but a small part, less than 5 per cent, of the vessels built and initially registered in the county during the 1825–74 period. This probably understates the number of fully-rigged craft produced in Devon, for this was the class of vessel most likely to be sold away from the county. Quite simply, there was little local demand for ships of over 500 tons such as the *Caroline*, the *Glory* and the *Retreat*, which were all built at

Topsham for the East India Company in 1801–2,[19] or for the numerous burthensome vessels constructed in North Devon for South Walian copper ore traders or Liverpool merchants engaged in South American commerce.[20] Nevertheless, it remains clear that the vast majority of Devon's wooden vessels were fitted with one or two masts. A broad range of craft comprised the former category. There were Exe lighters, Tamar barges, and other vessels primarily employed in the 'inland navigation'. There were fishing vessels, measuring between 15 and 40 tons, rigged variously as smacks, luggers, skiffs, hoys and yawls. Above all, there were the sloops, ranging from 30 to 60 tons and operating chiefly in the home and short-sea trades.

Two-masted vessels, however, were the most common products of Devon's shipyards in the 1786–1874 period. The most notable feature of this broad class was the eclipse of the square-rigged brigs, brigantines and snows by the swifter, more manoeuvrable fore-and-aft rigged schooner from the late eighteenth century. This last-named rig had long been popular in North America, and it was perhaps through the county's strong connections with Newfoundland that Devon shipowners and shipbuilders encountered the schooner.[21] Between 1786 and 1810, 17 were built and registered in Bideford and Exeter, against a total of 168 square-rigged two-masters produced in the ports during the same period. In the next decade or so this balance shifted, and by the late 1820s the schooner was the most common type of vessel constructed in South Devon. This remained the case for over forty years. Between 1825 and 1849, 323 of the 742 vessels built and locally registered in the south of the county were described as schooner rigged, with 148 constructed in Dartmouth and its creeks, 128 at Plymouth and 47 in the Port of Exeter. In North Devon the schooner was adopted more slowly, particularly at Bideford where a local variety of brig, the polacca, was constructed in some numbers.[22] Even so, the schooner was still the single most important product of North Devon's shipyards in the second quarter of the nineteenth century.

Table 7.5
Vessels built and first registered in Devon, by rig, 1786–1874

a) 1786–1810

| | Three Masts | | Two Masts | | | One Mast | | | | Total |
	S	Bq	Bg	Sw	Sr	Sp	Lr	Bge	Other	
Bd	6	–	58	6	5	41	–	–	2	118
Er	9	–	74	30	12	74	12	1	–	212
Totals	15	–	132	36	17	115	12	1	2	330

b) 1825–49

| | Three Masts | | Two Masts | | | One Mast | | | | Total |
	S	Bq	Bg	Sw	Sr	Sp	Lr	Bge	Other	
Be*	–	1	3	4	31	23	–	–	–	62
Bd	–	3	31	3	44	46	–	–	1	128
Dh	–	2	9	–	148	158	–	–	–	317
Er	–	7	6	9	47	34	3	1	–	107
Ph	–	3	13	–	128	143	–	30	1	318
Totals	–	16	62	16	398	404	3	31	2	932

* includes Ilfracombe

c) 1850–74

| | Three Masts | | | Two Masts | | | One Mast | | | | Total |
	S	Bq	Sr	Bg	Sr	K	Sp	Lr	Bge	Other	
Be	2	4	–	3	12	–	9	–	–	1	31
Bd	–	6	1	18	55	2	20	–	1	1	104
Dh*	–	4	5	27	151	18	184	–	–	4	393
Er**	2	11	1	15	28	3	18	2	–	–	80
Ph	4	23	–	18	35	7	100	–	30	2	219
Totals	8	48	7	81	281	30	331	2	31	8	827

* includes Brixham and Salcombe
** includes Teignmouth

Key to Ports – See Tables 7.3 and 7.4.
Key to Rigs – S – Ship; Bq – Barque, Barquentine; Bg – Brig, Brigantine; Sw – Snow; Sr – Schooner; K – Ketch; Sp – Sloop, Cutter, Yawl, Hoy, Skiff, Lugger, Smack; Lr – Lighter; Bge – Barge.

Sources: DRO, Custom House Ship Registers.

and Peter Blackburn of Turnchapel Dock, Plymouth, who charged £56,889 for the hull of the *Armada* and £58,329 for that of the *Clarence*.[46] (Fig. 7.6)

At the other end of the scale, Devon's shipbuilders contributed 19 of the 45 sixth-rates, 22 of the 192 sloops-of-war, and four of the seven bomb vessels completed in British private yards before May 1814.[47] Building contracts for these warships were awarded by competitive tender. Accordingly, in September 1811, when William Taylor of Bideford offered to build a 382-ton brig in oak for £15 10s per ton, the Admiralty accepted his bid rather than the more expensive tenders presented by Messrs Brown & Olier of Plymouth (£17 10s per ton) and Robert Davy of Topsham (£15 15s per ton).[48] Penalties for late delivery or substandard work were also written into these building contracts. Thus, Benjamin Tanner of Dartmouth, who claimed to have launched more ships for the Government than any other private shipbuilder, was fined £2,200 in 1807 for failing to meet his completion schedule. Subsequently he was rendered 'thunderstruck at [the] sudden, unexpected, and unmerited display of disapprobation' which saw the Admiralty return the poorly constructed *Thais* with a demand for the repayment of all monies advanced.[49]

Though building for the Navy was restricted to ships' boats and other small craft during the First World War, Devon's private shipyards were kept busy with military contracts during the 1939–45 conflict, much of the work being undertaken by female labour. At Dartmouth, for instance, Philip & Son built 230 vessels for the Admiralty and the RAF, a contribution acknowledged by the enemy when the firm's Noss Works was bombed in 1942 with the loss of 20 lives. Further up the Dart, S B Hall of Galmpton built sixteen vessels on the Fairmile design, while Uphams of Brixham constructed thirteen, Mashford Brothers of Cremyll, Plymouth, launched six, and a further eighteen were completed by P K Harris of Appledore. Blackmores of Bideford and Morgan Giles of Teignmouth produced harbour defence launches during the war, and a number of motor fishing vessels were built at Plymouth (Fig. 7.7) and at Topsham, where long-derelict sites were reactivated for wartime production.[50]

At Appledore, the yards of M W Blackmore and P K Harris were fully occupied with Admiralty work from 1940 until the end of the war. Here, as in South Devon, the ability to build and repair wooden vessels proved of great utility, as the deployment of magnetic mines created a new demand for non-metallic hulls. Various types of craft were produced, 72ft Motor Launches, 120ft Motor Torpedo Boats (MTBs) and Motor Gun Boats (MGBs), 105ft Motor Mine Sweepers (MMSs) and 75ft Motor Fishing Vessels (MFVs) being the most significant. Harris's of Appledore, though heavily engaged in this business, continued to service local coasting vessels in the early stages of the war, attending to naval and commercial craft in the Richmond Dry Dock on an unofficial 'take it in turn' basis. In 1944, with the area playing host to thousands of American troops and the Torridge estuary used for D-Day training exercises, the number of British and American landing craft requiring attention escalated, impelling the Port Admiral to halt mercantile repairs. A new rota then governed the yard's work – 'one British, one American'.[51]

Blackmore's and Harris's gained further naval orders after the war, completing a number of composite-built (wooden planking on aluminium frames) inshore minesweepers in the early 1950s, while in 1961, and again in 1966–69, the Appledore Yard produced series of motor tugs for Dockyard use. In Dartmouth, meanwhile, Philip & Son built a number of service vessels for the Royal Navy, as well as various naval craft for foreign governments.[52]

Shipyards and Shipbuilders

A large number of firms contributed to Devon's shipbuilding output during the 1786–1970 period. In 1804, as Table 7.7 indicates, there were thirty-nine private yards in the county according to Admiralty returns, though this was undoubtedly an understatement, as no reference was made to yards in the Port of Plymouth. Fifteen of these shipyards were located in North Devon, the majority on the Torridge, while fourteen were based in the Port of Dartmouth and a further ten were dispersed between the Axe and the Teign, in the Port of Exeter. Over time, the number of shipbuilding concerns tended to decline, with thirty operational in 1878 (six in North Devon and twenty-four in the south of the county) and just nine in 1923. By 1969 a further reduction had occurred, and shipbuilding (as opposed to yacht and boat building, which experienced substantial growth) was undertaken by just three firms on the Torridge, the industry having effectively died in South Devon in 1965 with the sale of Philip & Son to a firm which concentrated on the maintenance of yachts and leisure craft.[53]

Numerous firms entered and left Devon's shipbuilding industry during this period. This was especially so in the first threequarters of the nineteenth century, when new building in Devon was generally buoyant. At Plymouth, for instance, no fewer than forty-three different builders launched vessels which were subsequently registered at the port between 1824 and 1854, while Dartmouth's registers indicate that at least twenty-four separate firms operated in the sub-port of Brixham during the same period. Such fluidity was due partly to the cyclical nature of the business, with new ventures established in expansionary phases and closures occurring during the ensuing slumps. It also reflected the ready availability in Devon of the requisite factors of production for wooden shipbuilding. The county's many estuaries provided innumerable sites which might be utilised for the construction and launching of the comparatively small sailing vessels in which local shipbuilders specialised. Labour, too, was apparently plentiful, the 1831 census indicating that 1,370 'boat builders and shipwrights' resided in Devon, a total exceeded only by Kent, though both counties, of course, accommodated major Royal Dockyards.[54] Moreover, comparatively long apprenticeships were served by Devon shipwrights, who gained a reputation for producing high-quality vessels.[55] As to industrial relations, the evidence is both limited and ambivalent. For instance, in 1849 John B Mansfield established a shipyard at Teignmouth partly because of the 'existence of a steady and orderly working class',[56] while, in the following year, one shipowner remarked that 'he had never seen so much good feeling prevailing between the employer and employed' as he had observed at John Westacott's yard in Barnstaple.[57] By 1856, however, this harmony had evaporated as Westacott's shipwrights 'struck for wages', alarming respectable Barumites by marching through the town in a procession headed by a fiddler.[58]

If land and labour presented few obstacles to prospective shipbuilders in

7.6   The launch of the *Clarence*, 74, on 11 April 1812. Built at Turnchapel by Isaac Blackburn, she was one of numerous men-of-war constructed in Devon shipyards during the Napoleonic War. (*City of Plymouth Museums & Art Gallery*)

Table 7.7
Shipbuilding firms in Devon, 1804–1923

a) 1804

North Devon	Sw	Ap	South Devon	Sw	Ap
Barnstaple			**Dartmouth**		
Rd Thorn	6	12	Mr Tanner	68	13
Rt Westacott	4	7	Mr Avery	10	14
Bideford			Mr Bennett	11	11
Geo Crocker	6	17	Mr Gibbs	8	13
Jm Evans	4	6	Mr Nichols	5	4
Hy Tucker	0	12	Mr Newman	5	1
Wm Taylor	5	9	**Brixham**		
R Chapman	5	14	Mr Wheaton	3	7
Ed Jenkins	1	5	Avery & Pillar	0	5
Appledore			Lane & Tuckerman	0	4
Wm Record	1	15	Thos Wood	2	1
Wm Clibbet	1	8	Sl Matthews	0	6
Cochrane & Saunders	2	7	Sn Richardson	0	6
Jn Tucker	0	10	Messrs Furneaux	1	2
Wm Barrow	0	10	**Kingswear**		
Clovelly			Mr Paige	2	5
Mr Barrow	3	4	**Beer**		
Ilfracombe			Geo Hook	3	2
Messrs Lock & Co	10	10	**Seaton**		
			Mr Akerman	6*	3
			Sidmouth		
Total	48	146	Thos Bishop	3	0
			Lympstone		
			Mr Bass	4	4
			Topsham		
			Thos Owen	9	13
			Obh Ayles	14	9
			Wear		
			Rt Davy	6	4
			Teignmouth		
			Wm Curtis	7	4
			Heath & Son	5	4
			Wm Randle	10	5
			Total	182	140

	Sw	Ap	Total
Devon	230	286	516
Great Britain	4,926	3,695	8,621

* includes four caulkers

Key – Sw – shipwrights; Ap – apprentices

b) 1878

North Devon	South Devon
Barnstaple	**Brixham**
Westacott & Sons	John Barter
	John Dewdney
	Samuel Dewdney & Sons
Bideford	William Gibbs
John Cox	Thomas Mathews
John Johnson	Upham Bros
Appledore	**Dartmouth**
Robert Cock	Robert Moore
Alfred Cook	Henry Nicholls
William Pickard	Philip & Son
	Redway & Son
	Dodbrooke
	William Date
	Salcombe
	Henry Harnden
	Thomas Sanders, jr
	Exmouth
	Thomas Redway
	Topsham
	John Holman & Sons
	Plymouth
	David Banks & Co
	Charles Gent
	William Hawke
	Richard Hill & Son
	Benjamin Johns
	William S Kelly
	Edred Marshall
	William H Shilston
	Teignmouth
	John B Mansfield

c) 1923

North Devon	South Devon
Appledore	**Brixham**
Robert Cock & Sons	Sanders & Co
The Hansen Shipbuilding & Ship Repairing Co Ltd	John, William & Andrew Upham
Philip K Harris & Sons	
	Dartmouth
	Philip & Son Ltd
Barnstaple	**Plymouth**
Taw Shipyards Ltd	Frederick Hawke
	Willoughby (Plymouth) Ltd

Sources: 1804 – *Accounts and Papers* (BPP, 1805, VIII, 467–86); 1878 – *White's Directory of Devon* (1878–9); 1923 – *Kelly's Directory of Devonshire* (1923).

Devon, the capital requirements of the typical shipyard in the age of the wooden sailing vessel were comparatively modest. A couple of narrow, open-ended sheds, a saw pit and a 'steam-box', 'steaming house' or 'shreeve kiln', in which planks were heated and shaped, comprised the fixed capital of a yard capable of building an average schooner[59] (Fig. 7.8). Many establishments, of course, had more than this basic equipment. For instance, Edward Sibrell's yard at Friery Quay, Plymouth, had a 'pitch house and a mould loft erected thereon', the stock of Bass & Bishop, of Topsham, included a large copper furnace and two pair of smith's bellows, while John Cocks' yard at Sandquay, Dartmouth, was equipped with 'two steam kilns . . . four pan bellows, two anvils, and other smiths' tools'.[60] In all wooden shipbuilding yards, however, the tools of the shipwright belonged to the craftsman himself, and not to his employer. This entailed a considerable saving on capital expenditure for the shipyard owner. As late as 1878, after a 'destructive fire' which caused damage estimated at £7,000 to the uninsured property of Redway & Son of Dartmouth, it was reported that 'many of the workmen are great sufferers through losing their tools – one, it is said, to the extent of nearly £100'.[61]

The working capital of the typical firm was largely embodied in the iron fastenings, nails, pitch, tar, resin and, above all, the timber needed to construct a wooden vessel. Some of the timber lay unused inland, the stock-in-trade of William Record of Appledore, for instance, including 'above 200 oak trees, felled, and now lying in the estates of Ellicott and Langworthy, situate in the parish of Bratton Clovelly' as well as pieces of oak at Little Torrington, Weare Giffard and Sheepwash.[62] Most was stored at the shipyard, however, the untreated trees floating in the adjacent water and the planks, deck deals and spars either seasoning or ready for use in the sheds. Wages were the shipbuilder's other principal variable cost. Although evidence is sparse, it seems that labour accounted for less than 15 per cent of total building costs. In 1819, for instance, the materials used by Davy's of Topsham in the construction of the *Edinburgh Castle* amounted to 86.3 per cent of the total cost of £2,324 14s, with wages accounting for the residual 13.7 per cent.[63] Likewise, at John Holman & Sons' yard in Topsham during the early 1860s, labour costs represented some 12.8 per cent of the £9,000 expended on the construction of the 377-ton barque *John*

Holman, 14.5 per cent of the £4,196 5s 1d charged for the building of the *Semper Fidelis*, a brig of 211 tons, and 14.6 per cent of the ketch *Faith*'s first cost of £1,663 3s 3d.[64]

A number of Devon's wooden shipbuilding enterprises were substantially larger than the typical firm. As Table 7.7 shows, Benjamin Tanner of Dartmouth employed sixty-eight shipwrights and thirteen apprentices in 1804, over three times as many men as George Crocker of Bideford, the next largest concern in Devon. Indeed, by this measure, no other shipbuilder in southwest England approached the scale of Tanner's establishment. Size was not always a sign or a guarantee of success, however, for in 1807 Tanner went bankrupt with debts of £12,066 10s. This was a result, he argued, of his misfortune in contracting to build 'six sloops-of-war at a peace price' only to find his labour and material costs escalating with the unexpected resumption of war in 1803.[65] It was probably not until the mid-nineteenth century that firms of this scale were evident again in Devon. In 1850, for example, John Westacott of Barnstaple employed ninety workmen, all of whom, on the launch of the *Banshee*, were 'regaled with an excellent supper of good old English fare of roast beef and plum pudding'.[66] At Topsham, moreover, Holman & Sons owned two shipyards, a business which, at its peak in the late 1850s and 1860s, employed up to 200 men.[67]

These, and other Devon firms such as Evans & Cox of Bideford, Kelly of Dartmouth, John B Mansfield of Teignmouth and Joseph Banks of Plymouth, were capable of building the relatively large barques of over 400 tons or so which were such a prominent feature of Britain's shipbuilding output in the third quarter of the nineteenth century. Clearly, construction on this scale required substantial capital investment. In 1851, for instance, Westacott's were erecting 'a new shed which is to be covered with zinc' at the same time as two substantial barques were building under cover.[68] Holman & Sons of Topsham, having already installed a 400ft patent slip 'capable of raising ships of 600 tons burthen with perfect ease' at the Upper (Passage) Yard,[69] began an ambitious expansion programme with the purchase of the Lower (Strand) Yard in 1856. A stone-lined dry dock, 200ft long and able to take vessels of up to 1,000 tons, was opened in 1858 (see Fig. 7.9). Alongside, a building shed 170ft long by 50ft wide and 54ft high was constructed, together with a 120ft-long spar shed. Steam-powered machinery was introduced to saw timber, punch, sheer, and hammer metal, pump the dock and manufacture treenails, while a sail loft, blockshop, joiner's loft and sundry sheds and offices completed the extensive site.[70] Development continued in the 1860s, with almost £4,000 spent on new sheds, dock buildings and a Boulton & Watt steam engine between 1862 and 1867.[71]

A similar range of facilities was available at Queen Anne's Shipyard on the Cattewater at Plymouth. With a frontage of 1,200ft, the establishment comprised,

> a first-class stone-built dry dock, 260ft by 52ft, in perfect working condition, with steam engine, circular saw gear, smiths shop, timber sheds, offices and buildings, with slips, quays and other necessary appliances, all in good repair.

Significantly, in 1865, the Plymouth Ship-Building, Dock and Iron Works Company was formed to take over and extend this yard with the intention of constructing and repairing iron as well as wooden ships, and manufacturing 'marine and other engines, armour and other plate, angle iron, and every description of iron work'. With a nominal capital of £250,000, the company proposed to lengthen the existing dry dock by 50ft, and to construct two further dry docks and one large floating dock. Prospective subscribers were assured that the project, which was to be managed by Joseph Banks, would be profitable because,

> at present there are no iron ship building works at Plymouth, and much inconvenience and expense often results to ship owners in consequence of vessels outward bound having to put back to London for repair.[72]

Such confidence was apparently misplaced, as Queen Anne's Shipyard was again offered for sale in 1870. Evidently, few improvements had taken place in the interim, for the property included just the original dry dock, along with a range of slips, stores and buildings. Moreover, interested parties were

7.7   The launch of MFV 1547 at Sutton Harbour, Plymouth. Large numbers of these wooden vessels were built in Devon for the Admiralty during the Second World War. (*City of Plymouth Museums & Art Gallery*)

once more reminded by the vendor, Joseph Banks, that the site held great potential for those willing to invest in new technology, 'there being no iron shipbuilding yard in the West of England'.[73]

It was almost thirty years, in fact, before any of Devon's shipyards were equipped to produce and repair metal-hulled vessels. In the meantime, Holmans had shifted out of both shipbuilding and Topsham, while Westacott's business had moved from Barnstaple to the Torridge, with plans to establish an iron ship-repairing facility at the New Quay Yard. Here, a 270ft by 44ft dry dock had existed since 1860, to which Westacott added a large gridiron and various steam-powered machines. Despite employing up to 150 men during peak periods in the 1880s, the transition to iron shipwork failed to materialise and the firm went bankrupt in 1891.[74]

Within a decade, however, both Simpson Strickland and Philip & Son of Dartmouth, and Robert Cock & Son of the Richmond Yard, Appledore, had acquired the capacity to build and repair relatively small steel vessels. The value of the plant necessary to enter this market ensured that some continuity was achieved at these sites. Thus, the shipbuilding complex constructed at Simpson Strickland's Noss Works in the 1890s, which employed about 230 men, did not remain idle when the firm ceased to exist in 1918. Rather, it was taken over by Philip & Son and added to the capacity which the firm had developed at its Sandquay yard. Such capital accumulation enabled Philip & Son to go on and celebrate its centenary in 1958.[75] In North Devon extensive investment was undertaken at Bideford by the Hansen Ship Building and Ship Repair Company immediately after the First World War, while the British Construction Company spent £30,000 on adapting the old Westacott yard at Barnstaple for the production of ferro-concrete barges, a venture which initially employed 357 men. Although both concerns were shortlived, their assets were sold cheaply, the Barnstaple site passing to Taw Shipyards Ltd for £5,000 and Hansen's stock being acquired by Harris's at a nominal price.[76] Harris's further consolidated their position on the Torridge, purchasing the Richmond Yard and its stock in 1932, as the firm of Robert Cock & Sons was wound up with liabilities of £50,572 7s against assets estimated at £1,166 11s 7d – net debts of over £1.1m at 1993 prices.[77]

While the interwar years witnessed the concentration of North Devon's shipbuilding capital, the post-1945 era was marked by the growing significance of capital investment from outside the region. In the 1950s James Burness & Sons acquired an interest in P K Harris (Shipbuilders) Ltd, and subsequently the Appledore Yard became part of various consortia – Seawork Ltd in 1961, Court Line in 1963, Court Shipbuilders Ltd in 1965 – before becoming the first nationalised shipyard in July 1974.[78] If such

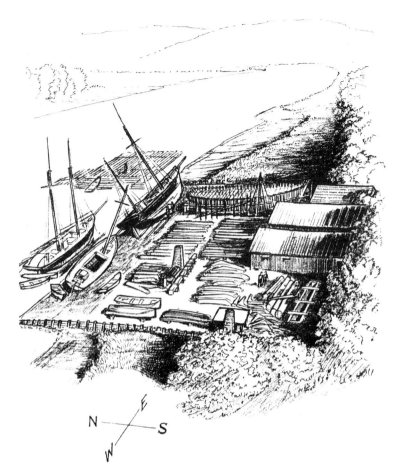

7.8   A drawing of a typical Westcountry wooden shipbuilding yard in the nineteenth century. Note the steam box in the centre of the yard, the saw pit in the southwest corner, and the vessels in frame on the eastern side. (*Sam Manning*)

frequent changes suggest the volatility of the shipbuilding industry, they also attest to the intrinsic and enduring value (much enhanced by the establishment of a 'ship factory' at Bidna in 1970) of Appledore's shipbuilding capital.

Wider Developments and Local Demand

Devon's shipbuilding industry passed through various phases between 1786 and 1970. During the first 100 or so years of this period, output remained at a relatively high level as a large number of small-scale producers, widely dispersed along the county's coasts, built and repaired a range of wooden sailing vessels. From the 1880s until 1939, contraction occurred in the number of yards operational and the volume of work completed. This trend was reversed during the Second World War and was much less pervasive in the 1950s and 1960s. Two central questions arise from this long-term growth pattern. Why did Devon's interest in shipbuilding decline in the final quarter of the nineteenth century? And why, having entered a seemingly terminal spiral of contraction, did the industry survive the interwar years to prosper, in a limited way, during the post-1939 era?

Various explanations might be advanced in response to the first of these questions. Clearly, the evident downturn in Devon's output from the 1880s was related to the locational shift which characterised the British shipbuilding industry in the second half of the nineteenth century. In turn, the gravitation of activity towards the North East, the Clyde, Belfast and Barrow was a function of the technological developments which saw the metal-hulled, steam-powered ship eclipse the wooden sailing vessel. Quite simply, these districts possessed a range of advantages – a cheap labour force, ready supplies of iron, steel and engineering products, and extensive local shipping industries – which made the northward migration of steamship building

both logical and cumulative.[79] Conversely, it follows that the output of areas such as Devon, lacking many of the factor endowments of the dynamic regions, should experience some decline.[80]

Yet such an analysis, however persuasive in general terms, is incomplete from the local perspective. It might account for the decline in Devon's shipbuilding production relative to other regions, but it fails to explain the absolute contraction of the county's output. It disregards the existence of extensive and technologically advanced shipbuilding and repair facilities at Devonport Dockyard and elsewhere in the South West, notably at Hayle in Cornwall, which suggest that factor shortages might have been overcome. Moreover, the analysis does not address the issue of the survival and revival of the county's shipbuilding interest in the twentieth century, the second of the questions posed by Devon's long-term experience. Causalities intrinsic to the county's industry therefore need to be considered, as well as the strong 'pull' associated with the advantages of the northern shipbuilding districts.

Incidental evidence suggests that relatively expensive, high-quality vessels were produced in Devon's shipyards during the mid-nineteenth century. In 1844, for instance, William Bennett Cuming, a Plymouth shipowner, testified that only the 'very best' vessels were built in his home port,[81] while a comparison of the Plymouth-built *Magnolia* with the *Lumley* of Sunderland revealed that the former had cost almost twice as much to construct and fit out, £4,716 19s 6d, as the Weir-built vessel, though both measured 240 tons. That the *Magnolia* was listed as A.1 for twelve years by Lloyd's, while the *Lumley* was A.1 for only eight years, may explain the price differential, yet it was considered irrelevant by prospective freighters who were held to be interested in the letter, not the term, of the classification.[82] In 1851 a local correspondent opined that Barnstaple's 'shipbuilding trade still maintains the high character it has so long had in this neighbourhood', citing the proposed construction of the vessels under cover to be classed A.1 for fifteen years at Lloyd's. Appledore, too, had 'long been celebrated for the superior quality of her vessels'.[83]

These high standards were perhaps due to the skill of the local labour force. Money Wigram, a London shipbuilder, observed that, 'in the North Country the men do not serve such an apprenticeship as would entitle them to Admission into the Dockyard. The Men from the West Country do, and they are better shipwrights.'[84] Whether, having served their apprenticeships many Devon shipwrights actually took up employment in the Dockyard, thereby depleting the resources of local private shipyards, is a moot point.[85] However, in an age when shipyard workers were engaged on a casual, daily basis, with men laid off and wages reduced when business was 'flat and dull', as at Bideford in 1843,[86] the prospect of secure employment in the state sector must have been tempting to many. Certainly, in the 1880s William Westacott tackled a labour shortage at Bideford by recruiting men from Plymouth,[87] while in the 1930s a large number of Appledore's shipyard workers migrated across the county to work at Devonport.[88]

If the high cost of the products and the lure of Dockyard employment disadvantaged Devon's shipbuilding industry, it is highly unlikely that either of these local influences, in itself, precipitated the sharp decline in output during the closing decades of the nineteenth century. Much more significant was the changing pattern of local demand. Between 1800 and 1865, when shipbuilding in the county was generally buoyant, the stock of shipping registered in Devon's ports increased from 51,283 to 132,184 tons. An important part of this incremental tonnage was launched from indigenous shipyards. In the first decade of the nineteenth century, 178 of the 247 vessels added to the registers of Bideford and Exeter, excluding transfers from within the county, were newly-built in the two ports, with 67 of the remainder bought in from other ports, the majority by Exeter shipowners, and just 2 constructed outside the county. Similarly, during the 1845–9 quinquennium, Devon's fleet was augmented by 360 registrations, 150 of which constituted vessels produced by local shipbuilders, with 189 purchased from owners outside the county and a further 21 newly-built elsewhere.

Certain traits can be discerned in this acquisition process. Many of the larger craft registered in Devon were constructed in other regions; thus, the 348-ton *Penelope* of Plymouth was built by John Watson at Sunderland,[89] while the Bideford-owned barque *Hartland*, of 487 tons, was one of

7.10   Noss Works, Dartmouth, between the world wars.

7.9   The brig *Courtney* in the dry dock at Holman & Sons' Lower Yard, Topsham, in the 1860s. The Holman patent rudder, which could be replaced at sea, is well illustrated. (*West Country Studies Library*)

numerous craft imported from Prince Edward's Isle.[90] Likewise, nearly all of the locally-owned steamers were purchased from builders or vendors beyond the county, usually in London or the North East. The majority of Devon's one- and two-masted vessels, on the other hand, were constructed locally. Many of these products were built for particular local employments. The lighters deployed on the Exe and the barges which plied the Tamar were purpose-built in their respective rivers,[91] and 'stone' boats were constructed specifically to carry limestone from Torbay to the Exe estuary.[92] However, the most common product of Devon's shipyards from the 1820s to the 1860s was the two-masted schooner, a swift and manoeuvrable vessel ideally suited to the carrying trades – Newfoundland fish, South European fruit, the general home trade – in which the county's shipowners were heavily engaged. Significantly, the vast majority of the new-built schooners registered in the county between 1824 and 1874 were supplied by Devon shipbuilders.

In the late 1860s Devon's shipping industry began to contract. The tonnage registered in the county declined from its 1865 peak of over 130,000 tons to 121,000 tons in 1870, and still further to 80,000 tons in 1885. This decline was due largely to the penetration of the steamship into the coastal trade and into the Atlantic carrying trades; particularly, as far as Devon shipowners were concerned, into the fruit trade. Critically, however, the local shipping industry did not collapse altogether. Trading vessels still operated from the county, two-masted wooden sailing ketches, employed chiefly in the home and Newfoundland trades, increasingly forming the bedrock of Devon's shipping interest.[93]

This transition was reflected in Devon's shipbuilding output. As the production of schooners and other two- and three-masted vessels contracted, so the tonnage launched in the county declined, with many local shipyards going out of business. Of course, this shrinkage coincided with, and cannot be divorced from, the rapid growth of steamship production, centred so emphatically in regions to the north. Yet, as further proof of the local market's influence, the Devon firms which continued their operations into the twentieth century were those which not only supplied the needs of the county's declining shipping industry but also successfully entered wider markets. Various Brixham yards, notably those of Gibbs, Sanders & Co and Uphams, produced a large number of wooden smacks and ketch-rigged

vessels, measuring between 35 and 90 tons, for deployment as trawlers by the port's substantial fishing industry, a line of supply which extended to Ramsgate, Lowestoft and other fishing ports to which the Brixham men migrated.[94] Likewise, at Appledore, Robert Cock & Sons built and, more importantly, repaired small wooden craft for local owners, while at the same time gaining orders for construction and renovation of steel ships registered elsewhere. The Dartmouth firms of Simpson Strickland and Philip & Son also pursued this bifocal strategy, launching a growing number of steel vessels (over thirty between 1900 and 1913) for foreign purchasers, as well as a range of steam and sail craft for local harbour work, and coastal trade and the marine leisure industry.[95]

Essentially, it was such market opportunism which ensured the survival of Devon's shipbuilding industry in the half-century following the First World War. Philip & Son, for instance, built only a handful of craft, mainly ferries, for Devon buyers in the interwar years. Yet the firm fulfilled orders from British customers as diverse as the Air Ministry, the Mersey Docks and Harbour Board, the Vacuum Oil Co. Ltd and the Corporation of Trinity House, and from foreign purchasers such as the Aden Port Trust, the governments of Ceylon, Sarawak, and Sudan and His Highness the Maharao of Kutch.[96] Harris's of Appledore continued to exploit an unusual, local niche in the market, servicing the far-from-inconsiderable remnants of the wooden sailing fleet during the interwar years, as well as the steel-hulled vessels which now dominated coastwise commerce. Using secondhand materials, accumulating the capital stock of bankrupt rivals and employing a flexible, non-unionised workforce, Harris's was able to provide the cheap, swift repairs which shipowners sought at all times, but especially in times of depression.[97] This permitted the business to continue until demand picked up with the onset of the Second World War and the generally buoyant market which prevailed thereafter. Harris's was then in a position to respond to these favourable demand conditions, redeploying and extending its capital stock to build a growing range of vessels. Further expansion entailed organisational restructuring and an infusion of capital into the firm of Appledore Shipbuilders which eventually emerged. That funds were forthcoming from various sources, culminating in the construction of the covered yard at Bidna in 1970, attests to the confidence with which investors viewed the last remaining unit of Devon's shipbuilding industry.

7: Devon's Shipbuilding Industry, 1786–1970

The author is particularly grateful to Robin Craig for his valuable assistance in the preparation of this chapter. Information was also kindly supplied by Anthony Slaven and Philip Taylor of Glasgow University, and by Martin Benn, Michael Guegan and Michael Nix.

1 S Pollard and P Robertson, *The British Shipbuilding Industry, 1870–1914* (1979), 45.

2 See E Lorenz, *Economic Decline in Britain. The Shipbuilding Industry 1890–1970* (Oxford, 1991).

3 See S Pollard, 'The Decline of Shipbuilding on the Thames' *EcHR*, second series, III (1950–1), 72–89; A Slaven, 'The Shipbuilding Industry', in R A Church, ed., *The Dynamics of Victorian Business. Problems and Perspectives to the 1870s* (1980), 107–25; S Ville, ed., *Shipbuilding in the United Kingdom in the Nineteenth Century. A Regional Approach* (St John's, Newfoundland, 1993).

4 See Chapter 26.

5 Pollard and Robertson, *British Shipbuilding*, 237–8.

6 M Nix, 'The Maritime History of Bideford and Barnstaple, 1786–1841' (Unpublished Ph.D thesis, University of Leicester, 1991), Chapter 11.

7 J A Goldenberg, 'An Analysis of Shipbuilding Sites in *Lloyd's Register* of 1776' *MM*, 59 (1973), 419–35.

8 PRO, CUST 17/12, 21.

9 *Lloyd's Register of Shipping*, 1861–1865; see D J Starkey, 'The Shipbuilding Industry of Southwest England, 1790–1913' in Ville, ed., *Shipbuilding in the United Kingdom*, 76–8.

10 *Exeter Flying Post*, (hereafter *EFP*) 10 Nov. 1853, 8 May 1851; *EFP*, 25 Sep. 1861.

11 I am grateful to Martin Benn for this information.

12 D F Murch, 'Trading Vessels of Salcombe Haven, 1820–1890' in H E S Fisher, ed., *Ports and Shipping in the South West* (Exeter, 1971), 107.

13 *EFP*, 17 Nov. 1853.

14 G Farr, *Shipbuilding in North Devon* (1976), 72.

15 DRO, Exeter Ship Registers.

16 *EFP*, 14 Sep. 1764.

17 *EFP*, 2 Feb. 1837.

18 DRO, Dartmouth Ship Registers.

19 C N Ponsford, ed., *Shipbuilding on the Exe. The Memoranda Book of Daniel Bishop Davy, 1799–1874, of Topsham, Devon* (Exeter, 1988), xxiv.

20 R Craig, 'The Ports and Shipping, c1750–1914' in A H John and G Williams, eds, *Glamorgan County History*, V, *Industrial Glamorgan, 1700–1970* (Cardiff, 1980) 498; *EFP*, 8 May 1851, 11 March 1852.

21 See D J Starkey, 'Schooner Development in Britain' in R Gardiner and B Greenhill, eds, *Sail's Last Century. The Merchant Sailing Ship 1830–1930* (1993), 133–47.

22 M Bouquet, 'The North Devon Polaccas' *MM*, 49 (1963), 120–7.

23 B Greenhill, *The Merchant Schooners* (4th edn, 1989), 22–3.

24 DRO, Exeter Ship Registers, 1866/1. See C N Ponsford, *Topsham and the Exe Estuary* (Exeter, 1979), 35.

25 NDRO, Bideford Ship Registers, 1853/10.

26 DRO, Brixham Ship Registers, 1867/18, 1868/5.

27 DRO, Dartmouth Ship Registers, 1825/30. Remarkably, the *Ceres* remained in service until 1936.

28 See Ponsford, *Shipbuilding on the Exe*, xviii–xx.

29 *EFP*, 20 Jan. 1853.

30 *EFP*, 24 July 1834.

31 WDRO and DRO, Ship Registers. Plymouth 1846/7, Dartmouth 1857/7, Plymouth 1857/29, 1862/23.

32 *Annual Statements of Navigation and Shipping*.

33 DRO, Z 19/65/29.

34 *Philip & Son Ltd, Shipbuilders and Engineers, 1858–1958. A Century of Progress* (Dartmouth, 1958) 13; R Freeman, *Dartmouth. A New History of the Port and its People* (Dartmouth, 1983), 122–3; Brixham Museum, A/SS, Correspondence of Simpson Strickland & Co.

35 Farr, *Shipbuilding in North Devon*, 16.

36 Farr, *Shipbuilding in North Devon*, 9, 59.

37 NMM, Shipbuilding Conference, 'Merchant Shipbuilding in Great Britain and Ireland, 1920–38', I. I am grateful to Anthony Slaven and Philip Taylor of Glasgow University for this information.

38 Farr, *Shipbuilding in North Devon*, 16.

39 *Philip & Son*, 18. The *Edmund Gardner* is now an exhibit at the Merseyside Maritime Museum.

40 See B Greenhill, *The Evolution of the Wooden Ship* (1988), 88.

41 Farr, *Shipbuilding in North Devon*, 16.

42 DRO, Z 19/65/29.

43 NMM, Shipbuilding Conference, 'Merchant Shipbuilding, 1920–38', I.

44 L Harris, *A Two Hundred Year History of Appledore Shipyards* (Combe Martin, 1992), 38–42.

45 Ponsford, *Shipbuilding on Exe*, xxiii; D J Starkey, 'Shipbuilding in the South West during the Napoleonic War' *Maritime South West*, VI (1993), 5–15.

46 *Accounts and Papers* (BPP, 1813–4, XI, 357). Accounts Relating to Ships and Shipbuilders.

47 *Accounts and Papers* (BPP, 1813–4, VIII, 498). An Account of HM Ships Launched from Private Yards.

48 *Select Committee on East India Shipping* (BPP, 1813–4, VIII, 575).

49 *EFP*, 23 April 1807; Starkey, 'Shipbuilding during the Napoleonic War'.

50 *Philip & Son*, 19; J Lambert and A Ross, *Allied Coastal Forces of World War II. 1, Fairmile Designs and US Submarine Chasers* (1990).

51 Harris, *Appledore Shipyards*, 66.

52 Farr, *Shipbuilding in North Devon*, 60–1; *Philip & Son*, 17.

53 Freeman, *Dartmouth*, 140; see Chapter 26.

54 J Marshall, *A Digest of all the Accounts . . .* (1833).

55 *Select Committee on the Navigation Laws* (BPP, 1847–8, XX(2), 570–1). Evidence of Money Wigram.

56 H J Trump, *Teignmouth. A Maritime History* (1985), 50.

57 *EFP*, 24 Oct. 1850.

58 *EFP*, 3 Jan. 1856.

59 Greenhill, *Evolution of the Wooden Ship*, 88–90.

60 *EFP*, 14 June 1792, 6 Nov. 1806, 23 Sep. 1813.

61 *EFP*, 18 Sep. 1878.

62 *EFP*, 8 Jan. 1807.

63 Ponsford, *Shipbuilding on the Exe*, xix.

64 DRO, Z 19/65/29.

65 *EFP*, 23 April 1807; Starkey, 'Shipbuilding during the Napoleonic War'.

66 *EFP*, 24 Oct. 1850.

67 C N Ponsford, *Topsham and the Exe Estuary* (Exeter, 1979), 28.

68 *EFP*, 8 May 1851.

69 *EFP*, 6 July 1848.

70 *Western Times*, cited by Ponsford, *Topsham and the Exe*, 35–6.

71 DRO, Z 19/65/29.

72 *EFP*, 26 April 1865.

73 *Shipping and Mercantile Gazette*, 24 Nov. 1870. I am grateful to Robin Craig for this reference.

74 *Strong's Industries of North Devon* (Newton Abbot, 1971), 103–9.

75 *Philip & Son*, 12; Freeman, *Dartmouth*, 122, 132.

76 Farr, *Shipbuilding in North Devon*, 13, 59.

77 Harris, *Appledore Shipyards*, 22–3.

78 Farr, *Shipbuilding in North Devon*, 17.

79 Pollard and Robertson, *British Shipbuilding Industry*, 49–58; Ville, ed., *Shipbuilding in the United Kingdom*.

80 See S Jones, 'Merchant Shipbuilding in the North East and South West of England, 1870–1913' in S Fisher, ed., *British Shipping and Seamen, 1630–1960. Some Essays* (Exeter 1984) 68–85; Starkey, 'Shipbuilding Industry of Southwest England'.

81 *Select Committee on British Shipping* (BPP, 1844, VIII, 174).

82 *S C on Navigation Laws* (BPP, 1847–8, XX(2), 798). Evidence of Joshua Wilson. See S Ville, 'Rise to Pre-Eminence. The Development and Growth of the Sunderland Shipbuilding Industry, 1800–50' *International Journal of Maritime History*, 1 (1989), 65–86.

83 *EFP*, 8 May, 20 Nov. 1851.

84 *S C on Navigation Laws* (BPP, 1847–8, XX(2), 570–1).

85 See Chapter 21.

86 *EFP*, 29 June 1843.

87 *Strong's Industries*, 105–6.

88 Harris, *Appledore Shipyards*, 58.

89 WDRO, Plymouth Ship Registers, 1849/3.

90 NDRO, Bideford Ship Registers, 1844/9. See B Greenhill and A Giffard, *West Countrymen in Prince Edward's Isle. A Fragment of the Great Migration* (Toronto, 1967). Also, see Chapter 4.

91 See Chapter 5.

92 See Ponsford, *Shipbuilding in the Exe*, xxv–xxvii.

93 See Chapter 3.

94 See Chapters 12 and 24.

95 *Annual Statements of Navigation and Shipping; Philip & Son*; Freeman, *Dartmouth*, 122; Starkey, 'Shipbuilding Industry of Southwest England'.

96 NMM, Shipbuilding Conference, 'Merchant Shipbuilding, 1920–38', I.

97 Harris, *Appledore Shipyards*, 30–3; see W J Slade, *Out of Appledore. The Autobiography of a Coasting Shipmaster and Shipowner in the Last Days of Wooden Sailing Ships* (4th edn, 1980), 90–1.

8 Steamship Enterprise in Devon, 1852–1920

Robin Craig

The application of steam power to ocean-going vessels was among the most significant transport developments of the nineteenth century. Able to move independently of winds and currents, the steamship possessed many obvious advantages over the sailing vessel. Yet diffusion of the new technology proceeded only slowly, largely because the steamer's need to carry its own supply of fuel rendered it relatively uneconomic in all but the low-bulk, short-sea trades. This remained so until such time as her consumption of coal could be reduced. It was not until the mid-1860s, over fifty years after the feasibility of steam navigation had been demonstrated, that the compound engine significantly cut fuel costs, enabling the steamship to compete on numerous transoceanic routes. With the introduction of the triple expansion marine engine in the 1880s, the cost advantages of the sailing vessel were largely eradicated, and before the turn of the century the steamer was ascendant in nearly every branch of seaborne trade.[1]

Associated with this process of technological change and its diffusion was the spatial concentration of activity in the British port and shipping industries. Steam power, together with metal hulls, facilitated the construction of comparatively large ships. These vessels not only consumed great quantities of capital, but also required deeper docks and better cargo-handling facilities, demands which accentuated the growth of the large-scale shipping companies and the major ports in which they congregated. However, coastal and deep-sea steamers were also owned in many of the lesser ports. In Devon, for instance, such steamship enterprise was a feature of the county's shipping industry from the mid-nineteenth century until the 1920s. As Tables 8.1 and 8.2 indicate, local investment in steamers was negligible before the 1870s. A steady accretion of tonnage then began, peaking at just under 30,000 tons in 1892. The fleet declined gradually thereafter, and at the close of the First World War only a handful of steamers remained registered in Devon.

This represented a somewhat marginal interest in steamship operation, for even in 1892 steamers accounted for less than 40 per cent of Devon's total tonnage. At the same time, these craft constituted a mere 0.7 per cent of the steam tonnage registered in England.[2] Yet something of the character of nineteenth-century steamship enterprise can be gleaned from Devon's experience. To this end, the present chapter focuses on the financial structure and managerial performance of the county's coastal and deep-sea steamship companies, and considers the factors which circumscribed Devon's interest in this sector of the shipping industry.

Steam Coasters and Colliers

Paddle steamers, operating more or less regular services, linked the principal South Devon harbours with London and other home ports from the late 1820s. These coastal liners were operated by shipowners based elsewhere, however, and it was not until the 1850s that a Devonian tentatively entered this market. This was George Hennet, a Teignmouth man who has been described as 'perhaps the first West Country example of an entrepreneur on the grand scale'.[3] A keen supporter of economic development in the port of Teignmouth, Hennet had national and international interests as a railway contractor, an engineer, and a timber and coal merchant. He was also the owner of twelve vessels. In 1852 he purchased the wooden screw steamer *Lady Seale* of 264grt, intent on inaugurating a coastwise freight service

between Teignmouth and London. This vessel was something of a curiosity, having been built as a sailing vessel by Samuel and Henry Follett in Dartmouth in 1846. She was converted in the same year to a screw steamer, with 40hp engines installed by T D Marshall of Shields.[4] Her time as a Devon steamship was extremely brief. Registered in Exeter in 1852, her owner was declared bankrupt in the following year with liabilities assessed at some £350,000,[5] *Lady Seale* being sold to Hull owners.

Table 8.1

Devon's cargo-carrying steamship fleet, 1850–1918

(No of vessels & gross tonnage, average tonnage & freight index)

Date	No Tons	Av Tons	Frt Index	Date	No Tons	Av Tons	Frt index (100 = 1869)
1850	–			1884	8–13,792	1,254	64
1851	–			1885	11–13,839	1,258	63
1852	1– 264			1886	12–15,928	1,327	59
1853	–			1887	12–15,928	1,327	65
1854	–			1888	14–18,324	1,309	76
1855	–			1889	15–20,181	1,345	75
1856	–			1890	14–18,378	1,313	64
1857	–			1891	14–20,127	1,444	63
1858	–			1892	17–29,483	1,734	55
1859	1– 280			1893	13–22,167	1,705	60
1860	1– 280			1894	13–21,547	1,657	58
1861	–			1895	12–20,133	1,678	56
1862	–			1896	11–19,007	1,728	56
1863	–			1897	11–19,007	1,728	56
1864	–			1898	11–19,007	1,728	68
1865	–			1899	14–23,802	1,700	65
1866	–			1900	11–18,679	1,698	76
1867	–			1901	12–21,929	1,827	57
1868	–			1902	12–19,440	1,620	49
1869	–			1903	15–22,608	1,507	49
1870	3–1,420	473	103	1904	16–21,286	1,330	49
1871	4–2,688	672	102	1905	16–24,295	1,518	51
1872	5–4,451	890	103	1906	15–21,276	1,418	52
1873	8–6,289	786	117	1907	11–15,742	1,431	54
1874	9–8,310	923	108	1908	9– 8,527	947	45
1875	8–7,042	880	99	1909	10– 9,553	955	46
1876	8–7,042	880	98	1910	9– 6,838	759	50
1877	7–6,885	984	99	1911	10– 8,855	886	58
1878	8–7,916	990	91	1912	8– 6,918	865	78
1879	8–7,015	877	85	1913	7– 6,169	881	68
1880	8–7,015	877	87	1914	8– 7,039	880	67
1881	8–6,599	825	87	1915	8– 7,163	895	199
1882	7–6,425	918	81	1916	6– 4,403	817	365
1883	8–9,537	1,192	75	1917	5– 4,017	803	695
				1918	3– 2,038	679	751

Includes all Devon-owned cargo-carrying steamers whether registered in Devon ports or elsewhere. It excludes vessels registered in Devon but owned elsewhere, notably the vessels of New Zealand Shipping Company, registered at Plymouth.

Freight Index by L Isserlis, 'Tramp Shipping Cargoes, and Freights' *Journal of the Royal Statistical Society*, 131 (1938), 53–146.

Table 8.2
Chronological list of Devonshire cargo steamships, 1852–1918

Year Acquired	Name	Tonnage		Year built	Managing owners	Years owned
		Gross	Nett			
1852	Lady Seale	264	184	1846	George Hennet, Teignmouth	1852–1853
1859	City of Exeter	280	190	1859	James Forster, Newcastle	1859–1860
1870	Seine (ex Caroline)	209	132	1869	T J Stevens, Plymouth	1870–1881
	City of Exeter	1,054	788	1870	John Holman, Exeter	1870–1888
	Collier	157	116	1848	T J Stevens, Plymouth	1870–1876
1871	Kathleen Mary	1,268	806	1871	John Holman, Exeter	1871–1874
1872	Enmore	1,763	1,122	1872	John Holman, Exeter & London	1872–1880
1873	Gertrude	220	137	1873	John Holman, London	1873–1881
	Marne (ex Perthshire Lassie)	248	168	1864	T J Stevens, Plymouth	1873–1882
	Calliope (regd Hull)	1,370	1,124	1871	John Holman, Topsham & London	1873–1888
1874	Blenheim	2,021	1,308	1874	John Holman, London	1874–1878
1878	Northcote	1,031	659	1878	John Holman, London	1878–1889
1879	Coleridge	1,120	714	1879	John Holman, London	1879–1888
1881	Devonia	225	138	1882	R D Renwick, Torquay (London & South West Coast Steamers Co Ltd)	1882–1883
1883	Plymouthian	1,626	1,052	1883	J A Bellamy, Plymouth	1883–1892
	Mount Edgcumbe	1,667	1,074	1883	J A Bellamy, Plymouth	1883–1891
	Torbay	1,414	921	1883	P Varwell Jnr, Brixham	1883–1894
1884	Fortescue	1,184	754	1884	John Holman & Sons, London	1884–1895
	Smeaton Tower	1,406	903	1884	R B Triplett, Plymouth	1884–1893
	Brixham	579	363	1884	F W Baddeley Jnr, Brixham	1884–1884
	Raleigh*	1,341	857	1884	Richard Holman, London	1884–1892
1885	Brixham	626	396	1885	F W Baddeley, Brixham	1885–1889
1886	Saltram (ex Sultana)	2,089	1,354	1881	J A Bellamy, Plymouth	1886–1899
1888	Sir Francis Drake	1,741	1,119	1888	R B Triplett & E D Pearse, Plymouth**	1888–1892
	Dartmeet	655	327	1888	William Ball, Torquay	1888–1889
1889	St Anns	668	448	1889	Whiteway & Ball, Torquay	1889–1893
	Maristow	1,679	1,074	1889	J A Bellamy, Plymouth	1889–1893
	Sir Walter Raleigh	1,934	1,262	1889	R B Triplett & E D Pearse, Plymouth	1889–1906
1890	Bruges	617	397	1886	J A Bellamy, Plymouth	1890–1890
	Torbay	700	426	1890	William Ball Jnr, Torquay	1890–1904
	Beaver	312	188	1889	Carter Bros, Exmouth	1890–1895
1891	Endsleigh	2,366	1,530	1891	J A Bellamy, Plymouth	1891–1903
1892	Sir John Hawkins	2,608	1,670	1892	R B Triplett & E D Pearse, Plymouth	1892–1893
	Sir Richard Grenville	2,715	1,745	1892	R B Triplett & E D Pearse, Plymouth	1892–1909
	Cotehele	2,681	1,715	1892	J A Bellamy, Plymouth	1892–1901
	Powderham	3,019	1,950	1892	J A Bellamy, Plymouth	1892–1905
1894	Devonia	99	29	1894	Henry Dawe, Bideford	1894–1938
	Torbryan	649	363	1894	Whiteway & Ball, Torquay	1894–1898
	Maristow	2,385	1,511	1894	J A Bellamy, Plymouth	1894–1899
	Rook	370	186	1890	John Carter, Exmouth	1896–1915
1899	Player	540	161	1899	G Player, Teignmouth	1899–1903
	Dartmeet	749	413	1899	Whiteway & Ball, Torquay	1899–1912
	Maristow	3,506	2,269	1899	J A Bellamy, Plymouth	1899–1907
1901	Lustleigh	3,250	2,093	1901	J A Bellamy, Plymouth	1901–1906
1902	Velocity	192	102	1879	William Emerson, Plymouth	1902–1906
1903	Mazeppa	1,231	922	1872	Thomas Wilton, Dartmouth	1903–1908
	Vanessa	1,166	709	1872	Thomas Wilton, Dartmouth	1903–1911
	Belliver	755	397	1903	Whiteway & Ball, Torquay	1903–1911
1904	G Player	667	242	1904	G Player, Teignmouth	1904–1914
	Cherrybrook	759	404	1904	Whiteway & Ball, Torquay	1904–1915
	Torridge	158	42	1904	James Cock, Appledore	1904–1906
1905	Endsleigh	3,709	2,391	1905	J A Bellamy, Plymouth	1905–1907
1909	Kingswear	1,457	828	1909	Thomas Wilton, Dartmouth	1904–1920
	Webburn	800	417	1909	Whiteway & Ball, Torquay	1909–1917
1911	Paignton	2,017	1,167	1911	Thomas Wilton, Dartmouth	1911–1915
1914	Torquay	870	435	1914	Thomas Wilton, Dartmouth	1914–1918
1915	Levenwood (Renamed Charles Goodanew)	791	371	1911	E E Wonnacott, Plymouth	1915–1917
1916	Dartmeet	886	446	1916	W Ball, Torquay	1916–1916
1918	Orchis	482	204	1918	R Cock, Appledore	1918–

* *Raleigh* was the last Holman steamer to be registered at Exeter: later vessels owned by the firm were registered in the port of London.

** Triplett and Pearse vessels were later managed by Pearse & Haswell.

Several years were to elapse before another steam cargo-carrying vessel was registered at a Devon port. This was the *City of Exeter*, an iron screw steamer of 280grt, built in 1859 by Palmer Brothers of Jarrow. Significantly, perhaps, she was not owned by a Devon man but by James Forster of Newcastle.[6] Like the *Lady Seale*, the new vessel was to be employed in a regular shuttle service between Teignmouth and London, but like her predecessor she had but a brief spell in that service. Withdrawn from her original employment in 1860, she was re-registered in Newcastle and soon afterwards sold abroad.

These first attempts to adopt the technology of steam and screw, embodied initially in a wooden, then later in an iron, hull, may well have failed because of the competition of pre-existing liner services operated by outsiders to ports such as Topsham, Torquay and Plymouth with evident continuity and success. Moreover, the establishment of railway communication between London and the South Devon coast in the 1840s no doubt diminished the quantity of valuable freight conveyed by sea. Such factors must have had the effect of discouraging local shipowners from investing in this business, for it was over twenty years before a Devonian next attempted to introduce a regular steam coastal cargo service. In November 1882 a new company was launched with the resounding title of the London and South West Coast Steam Ship Company Ltd, of which a Torquay coal merchant, Robert Douglas Renwick, became managing owner. Of the ambitious nominal capital of £19,980, just £6,590 was raised by March 1883, mainly from shopkeepers and local traders, who might have expected benefits from the projected company.[7] The newly built *Devonia*, of 255grt, was acquired, intended for the coastwise general cargo trade. However, this venture proved a disastrous failure and the company was voluntarily wound up in June 1883, a year of depressed freights, the *Devonia* being sold to Turkish owners. Rather more successful was another *Devonia*, a diminutive steamship of 99grt launched in 1894 for the Bideford and Bristol Steamship Company Ltd, of which Henry Dawe of Bideford was manager. This little vessel, as the name of the company implies, was intended for the general cargo trade between Bideford and Bristol. Under different ownership she enjoyed a long life in Bristol Channel trading, surviving until she hit a mine in 1940.[8]

Although their efforts to found coastal steam liner services generally failed, Devon shipowners were more successful in their attempts to exploit the demand for steam tonnage generated by the ubiquitous, ever-expanding coal trade. Thus, from the early 1870s, a time when no locally-owned coastal steam liners were in operation, a growing number of steam colliers were registered in Devon. The first local enterprise in this business was one of the most notable family firms in nineteenth-century Plymouth. In 1869 Thomas Jones Stevens and Sanders Stevens took over the family shipbroking, agency and wholesale coal business at Plymouth on the death of their father, under the new style of T J & S Stevens.[9] A year later they purchased the nearly new iron screw steamship *Caroline* of 209grt, built at Grimsby. Registered at Plymouth in September 1870, she was renamed *Seine*. In the same year the smaller screw vessel *Collier* was acquired. This long-lived steamship was already a familiar sight in Devon ports, having been employed in a regular service between Teignmouth and London whilst under registry at a Scottish port. In fact, *Collier* had led a varied life, steaming regularly between Brighton and the Channel Islands, and, despite her modest size, as far afield as Melbourne, Australia.[10] In 1873 the Stevens partnership bought their final steamship, the *Perthshire Lassie*, renaming her *Marne*. These vessels were engaged mainly in the French trade, with coal the preponderant cargo, often loaded in South Wales. In 1870, for example, *Collier* made several voyages from Plymouth to St Malo and Dunkirk, and carried coal cargoes from Cardiff and Neath to North French harbours. Neath also featured prominently as the departure port of the *Seine* and *Marne*, both of which made frequent calls at Plymouth. The River Seine was the main destination of all three steamships whilst under Stevens management.

Similar enterprises were established at other South Devon ports. For instance, between 1888 and 1909 Messrs Whiteway & Ball, proprietors of Torquay's principal coal concern, acquired the eight steamers listed in Table 8.3. Uncharacteristically for short-sea steam shipowners of the period, Whiteway & Ball rarely kept their ships for very long. The first *Dartmeet* was sold to Mexican owners within a year of being built, and *St Anns* was sold to Spaniards within four years of her launch. All of the tonnage acquired by the firm was new-built and mainly engaged in the coal trade, not necessarily to Devon ports. Some vessels ventured into more distant waters, notably *Belliver*, which made several trips to Morocco. Disaster struck this vessel whilst on a passage from Finland to Plymouth with a cargo of timber. She went missing in the Baltic in September 1911, and it was a remarkable coincidence that the *Webburn*, also owned by Whiteway & Ball, reported sighting deals and battens floating in the water whilst she was likewise engaged in a voyage from the Baltic to Lowestoft. Whiteway & Ball kept one of their vessels until the advent of the First World War, but she was sold during its course, and no further vessels were ordered by the firm.

Table 8.3
Steamships owned by Messrs Whiteway & Ball, 1888–1909

Name	Year built	Builder	Gross Tons
Dartmeet (I)	1888	Harvey & Co, Hayle	655
St Anns	1889	R Craggs, Stockton	668
Torquay	1890	R Thompson, Sunderland	700
Torbryan	1894	R Craggs, Middlesbrough	649
Dartmeet (II)	1899	R Craggs, Middlesbrough	749
Belliver	1903	W Harkess, Middlesbrough	755
Cherrybrook	1909	W Harkess, Middlesbrough	759
Webburn	1909	W Harkess, Middlesbrough	800

Carter Brothers, shipmasters of Exmouth,[11] ventured into steam in 1890, registering their enterprise as the Carter Steam Ship Company Ltd in 1893, with a capital of £7,500. Their first steamer, *Beaver*, of 312grt, traded under the command of H S Carter. In 1895 she had the misfortune to be wrecked at Staithes in dense fog whilst on a coal voyage from Newcastle to Exmouth, though Captain Carter and his crew of ten were saved. The steamship *Rook* was also acquired in 1890. John Henry Carter was sometime master of this vessel, which was identical with her sistership *Robin*, the coaster formerly preserved by The Maritime Trust. The Carter enterprise, so far as steamship owning was concerned, drew to a close during the Great War, like that of Whiteway & Ball.

The development of bunkering facilities in South Devon during the 1880s, notably at Plymouth, Dartmouth and Brixham, stimulated local investment in steamships.[12] Accordingly, entrepreneurs such as George Player of Teignmouth, who was already engaged in the home trade, purchased steam

8.1   ss *Webburn* (1909, 800 tons gross). Owned by Whiteway & Ball of Torquay, she is seen loading coal at Goole. (*Goole Museum & Art Gallery*)

coasters to convey coal from the North East and South Wales to replenish the bunker stores. Under the style of the Player Steam Ship Company Ltd, formed in 1899 with a nominal capital of £10,000, Player's interest in this business extended to two vessels. Thus, the *Player*, of 540grt, was acquired in 1899 and sold in 1902, to be succeeded by the *G Player* of 667grt, built in 1904 and sold ten years later to John Kelly of Belfast.[13] Of greater significance in the bunker trade was the firm established by George Renwick and Thomas Wilton at Dartmouth in 1903. Initially investing in two secondhand colliers, the *Vanessa* and *Mazeppa*, purchased from John Fenwick & Co of London, the Dartmouth enterprise ordered their first new vessel, *Kingswear*, in 1904, and acquired *Torbay* in 1914. *Kingswear* was to serve under an Admiralty charter in the First World War, but was sold in 1920. The firm was known as the Wilton Steam Shipping Company in 1919 when a newly built steamer, the *Paignton*, of 1,514grt, was acquired. This vessel served as a collier during a short time under Devon ownership; in 1920 she was sold to the London & Edinburgh Shipping Company of Leith.

Deep-sea Tramp Steamships

As world trade expanded in the last quarter of the nineteenth century, British vessels carried a great and growing proportion of the goods shipped across the oceans. It has been estimated that 92 per cent of the cargoes transported between Britain and her Empire, 55 per cent of those conveyed between Britain's colonies and foreign countries, and 30 per cent of the traffic between foreign countries sailed under the British flag in 1912.[14] The bulk of this trade was conducted in tramp steamships, vessels which did not operate according to a schedule, but picked up and delivered cargoes as the opportunity offered.[15] Devon shipowners were hardly prominent in this vast business, though local initiative was responsible for the establishment of various concerns which amply illustrate the nature of this branch of steamship enterprise.

John Holman & Sons[16]

In 1870, the year which saw T J and S Stevens engage in coastal steamship operation, John Holman & Sons decided to invest in deep-sea screw steamships, purchasing *City of Exeter*, of 1,054 tons, from her builders, M Pearse & Company of Stockton-on-Tees. Although the firm had transferred its administrative headquarters from Topsham to London in the early 1860s, it continued to register vessels at Exeter until 1884. This was more a token of origins than a reflection of commercial reality (although it is true that some Devon investors continued to hold shares in Holman operated tonnage), for none of the Company's ten 'Exeter' steamers ever entered their

8.2   Steel steamship *G. Player* (1904, 667 tons gross), owned by Player Steam Ship Co of Teignmouth. (*E N Taylor*)

home port. These vessels, together with the Hull-registered *Calliope*, were acquired by Holmans between 1870 and 1884, as Table 8.4 indicates. All of these steamers, again with the exception of the *Calliope*, were newly built. If an average cost of £16 per gross ton is applied to this fleet,[17] it would appear that Holmans invested over £220,000 in steamships before 1884. Such funding was generally raised by the traditional means of dividing the property of each vessel into sixty-four shares. The registration details indicate that the Holman family furnished much of the capital, though Eugene Collins MP was joint owner, with John Holman, of the first *Raleigh*. Collins also held shares in other Holman vessels, along with prominent Lloyds' underwriters such as B H D'Ambrumenil and C E Lamplough, presumably reflecting Holman's intimate connections with the London insurance market.

Exceptionally, Holmans formed a joint-stock limited liability company in respect of *Fortescue*, the Fortescue Steam Ship Company Ltd being registered in July 1884 with a capital of £20,000 divided into 100 shares of £200 each. Among the shareholders in this company were individuals resident in Constantinople (reflecting Holmans' involvement in the Black Sea grain trade), Alexandria (an important bunkering station) and the Irish port of Kinsale, with which Holmans appear to have had a long-standing link through Benjamin Popham, a Kinsale bank manager.[18] Subsequently, most of the shares in the Company were consolidated in the hands of the Holman family until 1895, when the vessel was sold. Two years later the firm went into voluntary liquidation, with Richard Holman as liquidator.

Holmans' steamers were mainly deployed in three bulk cargo trades – the Baltic timber trade, the carriage of iron ore and pyrites from Iberia and North Africa, and, in common with a large part of the British tramp fleet,

Table 8.4

Steamships owned by John Holman & Sons, 1870–1884

Name	Year built	Builder	Gross Tons
City of Exeter	1870	Pearse & Co, Stockton	1,054
Kathleen Mary	1871	Pearse & Co, Stockton	1,268
Enmore	1872	Pearse & Co, Stockton	1,763
Gertrude	1873	Pearse & Co, Stockton	220
Calliope* (acquired 1873)	1871	Humphreys & Co, Hull	1,370
Blenheim	1874	Pearse & Co, Stockton	2,021
Northcote	1878	Turnbull, Whitby	1,031
Coleridge	1879	Pearse & Co, Stockton	1,120
Raleigh (I)	1881	Caird & Purdie, Barrow	1,347
Fortescue	1884	Murdoch, Port Glasgow	1,341
Raleigh (II)	1884	Caird & Purdie, Barrow	1,341

* Registered in Hull.

the Black Sea grain trade. This latter return freight was almost always combined with outward cargoes of coal destined for Mediterranean railway companies, or to the important bunkering depots in the region. It was typical for Holmans' vessels to load coal outwards in South Wales, destined for Italy or Egypt, from where the ships would proceed in ballast to load Black Sea wheat, maize or rye cargoes which were discharged at a range of ports, mainly in North Europe. Such routine activities were supplemented by more unusual voyages. *Enmore*, for instance, not only engaged in the fruit trade,[19] but was also the first steamship to find employment in the indentured labour trade between Calcutta and Demerara (British Guiana), completing the voyage, with 517 'passengers', in an unprecedented forty-nine days in 1872.[20] Holmans' opportunism was likewise evident in the deployment of its smallest steamer, *Gertrude*, chartered as a transport from London to the Volta, West Africa, during the Ashanti War in 1873,[21] and the participation of *Blenheim* in the India to Jeddah 'pilgrim' trade in 1876–7.

Considerable physical risks attended the operation of deep-sea tramp steamers. Although the Holman fleet was exceptionally well managed, it could not escape the vicissitudes visited upon all nineteenth-century steamships, suffering the accidents and tragedies which were a melancholy but inevitable feature of seafaring at this time. *Kathleen Mary* had the misfortune to go missing at sea between Gibraltar and Limerick in 1874, whilst *Blenheim* was stranded and totally lost in the St Lawrence River in August 1878. *Enmore* foundered in the North Atlantic in 1880, and the second *Raleigh* stranded and was totally lost outside Methil Harbour in January 1892, whilst in ballast from Honfleur. The fate of *City of Exeter* was especially poignant. In March 1892, with hurricane winds raging and what were justly described by eyewitnesses as 'dangerous' seas, she was sighted by the steamship *Sarah Ann* off Trevose Head and observed to be flying distress signals, requesting to be taken in tow. The horrified crew of *Sarah Ann* then saw *City of Exeter* roll over and disappear from view. Just one seaman from her seventeen-strong crew succeeded in struggling ashore.

In the early 1880s the firm of John Holman & Sons began registering its vessels at London, thereby severing its formal ties with Devon. At this juncture, however, various other deep-sea steamship enterprises were founded in the county. It is convenient to consider these ventures in three groups, two arranged according to their prime movers, J A Bellamy and R B Triplett, and the third by the base of its operations, Brixham.

J A Bellamy

Joseph Arthur Bellamy rose through the clerical ranks of the Plymouth shipbroking firm of Luscombe, Sons & Company, to become its managing clerk before being made a partner in the restyled firm of Bellamy, Luscombe & Company in August 1872. On Luscombe's retirement, in 1882, Bellamy ventured for the first time into the field of ship management with the acquisition of his first deep-sea steamship. He took his son into partnership in 1893 and later became Mayor of Plymouth, his many public services being recognised by a knighthood in 1904.

By 1907 Bellamy had served as managing owner of the twelve steamships listed in Table 8.5. In contrast with Holman & Sons, which divided its vessel property into sixty-fourths, Bellamy's steamships were owned by joint-stock companies. Most were 'single ship' companies, with shares distributed among a large number of investors, none of whom possessed a large individual holding. Much of the capital raised came from local sources, predominantly from Devon, but with a minority of subscribers hailing from Cornwall. Moreover, Bellamy's own financial stake was usually modest. For instance, he subscribed only five of the £100 shares into which the Port of Plymouth Steam Ship Company was divided. Registered in June 1882 with a nominal capital of £26,500, this company operated the *Plymouthian*, of 1,026 gross tons, until 1892 when she was sold to Messrs Westcott & Laurence.[22] By this time Bellamy had acquired a further fifty-nine shares from other shareholders, an accretion of stock repeated in the case of the Mount Edgcumbe Steam Ship Company, in which his holding of five £100 shares in 1883 had grown to seventy-three by 1898,[23] and in the Maristow Steam Ship Company in the 1890s.

Local banks invested in Bellamy's steamers. Typifying the part that many country banks played in the promotion of maritime enterprise, Thomas

Table 8.5

Steamships managed by J A Bellamy, 1883–1906

Name	Year built	Builder	Gross Tons
Plymouthian	1883	Swan & Hunter, Newcastle	1,626
Mount Edgcumbe	1883	Barrow Shipbuilding, Barrow	1,667
Saltram (acquired 1886)	1881	R Thompson, Sunderland	2,089
Maristow (I)	1889	Ramage & Fergurson, Leith	1,679
Bruges (acquired 1890)	1886	R Thompson, Sunderland	617
Endsleigh (I)	1891	R Dixon, Middlesbrough	2,366
Cotehele	1892	R Dixon, Middlesbrough	2,681
Powderham	1892	R Dixon, Middlesbrough	3,019
Maristow (II)	1894	R Dixon, Middlesbrough	2,385
Maristow (III)	1899	J Blumer, Sunderland	3,506
Lustleigh	1901	R Craggs, Middlesbrough	3,250
Endsleigh (II)	1905	J L Thompson, Sunderland	3,709

8.3 ss *Kingswear* (1909, 1,457 tons gross), owned by Renwick, Wilton & Co of Dartmouth. (*E N Taylor*)

Bulteel of the Naval Bank, Plymouth, offered significant financial support to the Port of Plymouth Company and was nominated one of the three directors of the firm, while J C Daubuz and John James of the Cornish Bank, Truro, invested in the *Maristow*. Notable figures in Plymouth's maritime community, such as the shipowner and shipbuilder William Hole Shilston, and William Evans, harbourmaster of the port, were among the many local figures who held a stake in Bellamy-managed steamers. Occasionally, capital was attracted from further afield. The Saltram Steam Ship Company, for example, was registered with a nominal capital of £17,000 divided into 340 shares of £50 each. Of the 335 shares taken up by May 1886, 75 were subscribed by Bradford investors, the majority described as woollen manufacturers, while other Northern districts furnished 80 shareholders and further contributions came from investors in Bristol, Newport and Cardiff. London was also represented, with G E Bromage of Tatham, Bromage & Company,[24] that constant supporter of Devon maritime enterprise, and E H Watts of Messrs Watts, Watts & Company, an important owner of ships, interested in the venture.[25] Bromage was also an investor in the *Maristow*, the Articles of Association providing that he be entrusted with the homeward chartering and insurance of the vessel, a service for which he was to receive the 'usual' brokerage.[26] With the London based British Steamship Investment Trust also investing heavily in this company, which successively owned three different vessels named *Maristow*, it is clear that Bellamy's enterprises had won the confidence of shrewd investors in the Metropolis.

Bellamy retired from shipowning in September 1906, when the *Endsleigh*, at 3,709grt the largest vessel ever owned in Devon, was sold to Adolf Deppe of Antwerp for £34,750.[27] This decision was possibly reached as a consequence of the loss of the *Powderham* in the same year. Steaming from Barry to Vladivostock with coal for the Russian Navy during the Russo–Japanese War, she was captured by the Japanese and, after a long enquiry, both ship and cargo were confiscated.[28]

R B Triplett

An experienced shipmaster who became a shipping agent in Plymouth, Captain Richard Barrett Triplett entered the tramp steamer business in 1884 with the formation of the Western Counties Steam Ship Company. Triplett subsequently established various other 'single ship' companies in partnership with Edmund Down Pearse, erstwhile secretary of the Western Counties Company. In all, the firm, restyled Pearse & Haswell in 1898, managed five steamers, as shown in Table 8.6.

Much of the capital invested in the Triplett companies came from Devon, with smaller contributions from Cornwall and London. The share capital of the Western Counties Company, amounting to £24,500 in £100 shares, was largely owned by Devonians, though Cornish subscribers possessed a minority interest and G E Bromage held a stake as well as acting as the firm's London agent. As managing owner of the Company, Triplett was entitled to 1.75 per cent of the gross and 1 per cent of the net profits generated by

its vessel, the *Smeaton Tower*.[29] In the case of Sir Walter Raleigh Steam Ship Company, established in 1888, roughly half of the nominal capital of £25,000 was raised in Devon. Among the London investors were three of the Bucknall brothers, for whose Bucknall Steam Ship Company Pearse & Haswell acted as Plymouth agents.[30]

Triplett's steamers generally worked in the Black Sea grain trade. In this prosaic employment a remarkably high casualty rate afflicted the firm's vessels during 1892–3. *Sir Francis Drake* was wrecked during a heavy gale in the Cervi Channel whilst steaming in ballast from Marseilles to Constantinople in November 1892. Four months later the *Smeaton Tower* was wrecked shortly after leaving Novorossisk with a cargo of wheat for Trapani and Palermo. Then, in November 1893, *Sir John Hawkins*, having recently been purchased for £28,750, went missing on her passage from Marianople to Liverpool, a result, perhaps, of the constructional defects apparent before the disaster.[31] In contrast, her sistership, *Sir Richard Grenville*, exhibited none of these structural problems. Indeed, in 1901 she profited from a casualty, earning £4,000 for saving the Cardiff steamship *Mary Thomas* in the North Atlantic. Having served Tripletts satisfactorily for seventeen years, she was sold to Glasgow owners for about £7,000 in 1909.

Brixham's Deep-sea Steamships

Although renowned for its fishing fleet and its fruit schooners, Brixham was also the home of two steamship companies during the 1880s and 1890s. In February 1882 the Torbay Steam Ship Company was registered, its nominal capital of £25,000, in share denominations of £50,[32] being largely consumed by the purchase of the iron steamship *Torbay* of 1,414grt. The other firm, the Brixham Steam Ship Company, was established with a share issue of £11,500 in December 1883.[33] During its six-year existence, two steamers, both named *Brixham*, were successively managed by the Company.

Brixham's shipping community was heavily involved in both ventures. Amongst the leading investors in the Torbay Steam Ship Company were prominent local sailing shipowners such as William Green, Frederick William Baddeley Jr, Jasper Bartlett, John Wheaton Pring, William Robert

Table 8.6

Steamships managed by Triplett & Pearse, 1884–1909*

Name	Year built	Builder	Gross Tons
Smeaton Tower	1884	Murray & Co, Dumbarton	1,406
Sir Francis Drake	1888	Grangemouth Dockyard	1,741
Sir Walter Raleigh	1889	Craig, Taylor, Stockton	1,934
Sir John Hawkins	1892	J Priestman, Sunderland	2,608
Sir Richard Grenville	1892	J Priestman, Sunderland	2,715

* From 1898 vessels were managed by Pearse & Haswell

8.4 ss *City of Exeter* (1870, 1,054 tons gross), the first steamship acquired by John Holman & Sons. (*Topsham Museum*)

Pearse and Peter Varwell Jr, who was appointed ship's husband. Likewise, the Brixham Steam Ship Company attracted local capital, with F W Baddeley Sr and Jr playing leading roles, the son serving as managing owner for a commission of 2.5 per cent of the vessel's gross earnings. Investors from other ports invested in both companies. Thus, the Torbay Steam Ship Company, like contemporary Plymouth ventures, was supported by G E Bromage and his London partner Charles Rudd Tatham, to whose agency many Brixham sailing vessels had been consigned during the great days of the fruit trade. Another metropolitan investor was Manley Hopkins, the best known Average Adjuster of his day, while provincial subscribers included Richard Holman and William Benjamin Gibbs of Cardiff, Foster & Hain, the St Ives shipowners, George Holden of Whitstable (more noted as an owner of sailing vessels) and, representing the fishing interest, Henry Summers, the Ramsgate smack owner. Investors in the Brixham Steam Ship Company were even more widely spread, ranging from Kish, Boolds & Company of Sunderland, builders of the first *Brixham*, to A J Bensusan of Cadiz and the British Consul in Trapani, Sicily.[34]

The three vessels operated by these Brixham-based concerns were variously deployed. Until her sale in 1894, *Torbay* traded to the Mediterranean, taking her place in the Black Sea grain fleet as well as participating in the Patras dried fruit business, no doubt to the consternation of many West Country sailing ship owners who relied upon wind rather than steam

to secure homeward cargoes of currants for the London market. *Brixham*, of 579grt, was designed for the fish, fruit and general cargo trades, but had especially large hatchways so that she could carry locomotives and other heavy machinery. After her trials in mid-June 1884 she was despatched to Grangemouth to load a machinery cargo, but by November of the same year was wrecked on rocks in Corcubion Bay, Finisterre, bound from Lisbon to Cardiff with a cargo of manganese. A Board of Trade Court of Enquiry found that the Master was to blame for the casualty. His Certificate of Competency as a Master was suspended for six months with the proviso that he be permitted to serve as a mate in the meantime. The Court expressed some criticism of the ship's managers as well, declaring that, at the time of the casualty, in a dense fog, the vessel was undermanned.[35]

The second *Brixham*, somewhat larger than her namesake at 626grt, traded to the Mediterranean and Iberian ports in 1885–6. She then crossed the Atlantic to the West Indies and ran a regular series of voyages between Jamaica and Philadelphia, presumably in the fruit trade, which had attracted a number of handy British and Norwegian steamers. The crew signed off at Philadelphia in November 1888, the vessel being sold and put under the American flag.

Managerial Performance

Freight rates, as Table 6.1 indicates, fluctuated widely around a downward trend during the 1870–1914 period, reflecting both intense competition between shippers and the vagaries of demand for cargo-carrying tonnage. A high degree of business acumen was therefore required of ship managers if the shipping market was to be exploited profitably. Such ability was apparent in the steamship sector of Devon's shipping industry. For example, nearly all of the steamers owned in the county, if not technologically advanced, were newly built – notably the large units managed by Holman & Sons, Bellamy and Triplett – with only T J & S Stevens and Wiltons of Dartmouth concentrating on the operation of secondhand tonnage. While the purchase of new vessels naturally increased capital costs, it meant that modern labour and fuel-saving devices were fitted, reducing running expenses so that the vessel could trade at modest levels of profit (or at least cover costs) even in a slack or depressed market. Moreover, Devon's deep-sea firms acquired vessels of steadily increasing deadweight capacity, suggesting an appreciation of the need to achieve economies of scale as competition, from British firms rather than foreigners, intensified in the late nineteenth century. As well as offering more substantial payloads, larger vessels could also justify their capital costs as rapid improvements in port facilities during these years permitted faster turn-round times and reduced costs.

On the negative side, most of Devon's steamship owners seem to have followed, rather than anticipated, market trends and technological innovations. Only Holmans had the depth of resources and the perception to order

8.5 ss *Plymouthian* (1883, 1,626 tons gross). Seen here under Westcott & Laurence ownership, she was stranded in the Dardenelles in 1906. (*E N Taylor*)

ships counter-cyclically, to venture capital in new tonnage when freights were depressed. This policy permitted shipowners to acquire vessels at reduced prices or on extended terms of payment as shipbuilders competed for orders to keep their yards and men employed. Shipbuilders might also promise early delivery, which meant that the time gap between raising capital for a new venture and the realisation of dividends was measurably reduced. Furthermore, the purchase of new, technically-advanced steamers during a depression placed the owner in a position to take advantage of rising freights as soon as the upswing started. The converse was true, of course, for orders placed with shipbuilders in boom years resulted in delays in delivery which meant that the market was already showing symptoms of excess tonnage just as the new vessels were being delivered. A number of Devon enterprises suffered as a result of ill-timed investments. For instance, both of Brixham's steamship companies obtained delivery of vessels in 1883–4 as freight levels were falling, while the slump of 1890 had a similarly adverse effect on the steamship ventures of Bellamy and Triplett. Likewise, the boom of 1898–1900 had evaporated by the time *Maristow* (III) and *Lustleigh* were operational. In the prolonged freight rate depression which ensued, Devon's interest in deep-sea steamers virtually ended, a demise reinforced, perhaps, by the advancing age of the principals of the firms involved and the absence of recruits willing to assume the responsibilities and burdens of ownership.

Initiative was also lacking with regard to the quality of vessels ordered. In the last three decades of the nineteenth century the process of incremental innovation proceeded apace, facilitating reductions in crew size relative to cargo-carrying capacity. The substitution of the compound engine by the triple-expansion unit and the advent of the steel-hulled vessel allowed great strides to be made in efficiency. Moreover, in the design of tonnage other factors enhanced efficiency. For example, larger hatches, holds free of obstruction, better ballasting arrangements and the shift towards easy- and self-trimming cargo carrying helped towards the rapid loading and discharge that was vital in attaining profitability. Although Devon's steamship operators generally purchased new vessels, they were disinclined to speculate in ships and engines of the latest design. For instance, the first steel steamer owned in the county was the diminutive *Devonia*, of 255grt, delivered in 1882, while the second, the *Dartmeet*, of 655grt, was not launched until 1888. It was not until the following year, long after the superiority of steel construction had been acknowledged, that a local shipowner, J A Bellamy, purchased a substantial steel-hulled vessel, the *Maristow* (I), of 1,679grt. Devonians were similarly slow to embrace advances in ship propulsion. All of the vessels acquired before 1888 were powered by relatively inefficient compound engines, the *Dartmeet* being the first local vessel equipped with triple-expansion engines.

Such instances suggest that Devon shipowners were unable to evince the entrepreneurial skill that was to be found in Cornwall, where Edward Hain of St Ives and R B Chellew of Truro built up impressive fleets of up-to-date steamships superior in nearly every respect to their Devon counterparts.[36]

Constraints

No matter how efficiently Devon's steamship enterprises were managed, there were wider factors which inhibited the county's interest in this dynamic sector of the nineteenth-century shipping industry. At base, there was the question of investment. Steamers consumed much greater quantities of fixed and variable capital than sailing vessels of comparable carrying capacity. Not only were the costs of building and fitting out a steamship more substantial, but running costs were also much higher, because larger crews were required to man engine rooms and stokeholds, a considerable quantity of coal was needed to fuel the engines, and aggregate harbour dues increased as the steamer's enhanced work rate entailed more calls at port. Although Devon's maritime economy was not starved of capital, there was a marked reluctance to deploy available funds in steamships during the 1830s and 1840s, when such investments were being made elsewhere. Thus, when the steamer was introduced into more and more trades from the 1860s, Devonians not only lacked experience of this form of ship operation, but had yet to initiate the dynamic process of capital accumulation and

8.6   Iron screw steamer *Saltram*, ex *Sultana*, (1881, 2,089 tons gross). Built by R Thompson & Sons, Sunderland, she was acquired by J A Bellamy in 1886 and assumed Plymouth registry in the same year. She went missing on a voyage from Philadelphia to Havana in 1899. (*E N Taylor*)

reinvestment. Significantly, when it came, belatedly and in small quantities in the 1870s and 1880s, local investment in steamships was undertaken by entrepreneurs with interests in the service sectors of the shipping industry – by ship agents, shipbrokers and marine insurers such as Bellamy, Triplett, and Holman, who would draw upon expertise acquired in servicing other owners' ships, and who could use their contacts locally and elsewhere, especially London, to generate capital.

This reluctance to speculate in the new technology stemmed from various interrelated sources. In the middle decades of the nineteenth century, Devon's shipping capital was concentrated in large numbers of relatively small wooden sailing vessels deployed in various occupations, but especially in the fruit trades of southern Europe and certain of the transatlantic carrying trades. Even though their schooners, brigs and ketches were becoming increasingly obsolete, Devonians continued to invest in and operate these craft (albeit in a diminishing range of trades) down to the First World War.[37] Accordingly, it was only in two firms, the Torbay and the Brixham Steam Ship Companies, that local sailing ship owners transferred their resources to steam-driven vessels. Even then, the investment was comparatively little, late, and in a market – the fruit trades – well known to the operators.

Such tardiness might be explained either as an entrepreneurial failure born of a blinkered conservatism, or as a rational attempt to exploit niches in the tonnage market, notably the home and Newfoundland trades, with a seemingly redundant capital stock. However, any entrepreneurial explanation must take account of the many Devonians who successfully established steamship enterprises in other ports. This migratory process, which took capital as well as talent away from the county, can be traced back to the first half of the nineteenth century. John Glynn had departed to Liverpool, there to establish a major shipowning enterprise based upon the Mediterranean liner trade.[38] G E Bromage of the London firm Tatham, Bromage & Company was trained in Bellamy's Plymouth office; as well as investing in local steamers, his firm held the agency for the fleet of fruit schooners owned in Devon which could often astonish London fruit merchants with their fast passages front the Mediterranean, the Western Islands and the West Indies. No account of Devon-port shipowners would be complete without mentioning the great contribution the sons of Devon made to shipping in Newport, Cardiff and Swansea. Consider just Cardiff, whither many of the rising steamship owners moved. Robert Hooper, William Cory (late of Hartland), W J Tatem and William Reardon Smith (both from Appledore), W H Seager (from Ilfracombe), Richard Holman and J H Anning (from the Exe Estuary) and the Boveys (from Plymouth) – all of these distinguished names in British shipowning testify to the maritime traditions of Devon. Elsewhere there were notable figures such as David James Jenkins, a Welshman resident in Exeter, who left for London to found the celebrated Shire Line to the Far East, the members of the Mansfield family who were to set up an important commercial and shipping enterprise in Singapore,[39] and Marshall Stevens, the son of Sanders Stevens, who moved from Plymouth to Garston on the Mersey, where he inaugurated his own steamship services, later achieving national distinction in connection with the promotion and management of the Manchester Ship Canal and the establishment of the Trafford Park Estate, Manchester.[40]

Topographic and economic considerations persuaded these and other Devon-born shipowners to seek their fortunes elsewhere. With the exceptions of Plymouth and Dartmouth, Devon ports lacked the deep-water facilities to accommodate the typical cargo-carrying steamships of the late nineteenth century. The Exe ports, for instance, were inaccessible to most deep-sea steamers, while the arrival of George Player's moderate coasters caused consternation among port officials and users at Teignmouth.[41] More

importantly, the hinterland served by Devon's ports experienced a relatively sluggish rate of population and economic growth during the nineteenth century, producing and consuming only modest quantities of the staple goods – coal, ores, grain and timber – which underlay the rapid expansion of seaborne traffic in other regions. It was inevitable, therefore, that enterprising Devonians should pursue their shipowning ambitions in a more advantageous context. Thus, by the first decade of the twentieth century, Devon's direct interest in deep-sea steamers had virtually ceased. In contrast, short-sea steamships were owned in the county until just after the First World War, with local investments concentrated in colliers rather than coastal liners. Significantly, the coastwise import of coal, mainly for the bunkering business and the growing urban demand for household and gas coal, was one of the main growth points in Devon's seaborne trade during the late nineteenth and early twentieth centuries.

8: Steamship Enterprise in Devon, 1852–1920

The author would like to thank the late Grahame Farr; Margery Rowe, Devon Record Office; Elisabeth Stuart, formerly of the West Devon Record Office; Crispin Gill, Plymouth; John Horsley, Brixham; Roger Smaldon of Bellamy & Company (Plymouth) Ltd; and David Holman, London, for their generous assistance in the preparation of this chapter.

1 See R Craig, *Steam Tramps and Cargo Liners* (1980); and G S Graham, 'The Ascendancy of the Sailing Ship, 1850–1885' *EcHR*, second series, 9 (1956–7), 74–88.

2 *Annual Statement of Shipping and Navigation for 1892.*

3 H J Trump, *Westcountry Harbour. The Port of Teignmouth, 1690–1975* (Teignmouth, 1976), 83.

4 It is not certain whether *Lady Seale* was originally intended as a sailing vessel or whether she was sent under sail to the Tyne to have engines installed there.

5 Trump, *Westcountry Harbour*, 94.

6 *Ward's North of England Directory for 1857–58* (Newcastle, 1856) lists Forster as a shipbroker with offices at Three Indian Kings, Newcastle.

7 PRO, BT 31/3076/17560.

8 On *Cambria* and her consorts, see G Farr (communicated by V C Boyle) '*Torridge, Devonia* and other Bideford-Bristol Steamers' *DAT*, LXXXI (1949), 347–55.

9 See Chapter 9.

10 According to her London registration, 1854/74, a new master was appointed at Melbourne on 24 Jan. 1854.

11 E R Delderfield, *Exmouth Milestones* (Exmouth, 1948), 68.

12 *Shipping Gazette Weekly Summary*, 9 Sep. 1910, 572. A communication from 'A E M' of Torquay pointed out that Dartmouth's potential as a bunkering port had been demonstrated by the ease with which the *Palgrave*, of 3,078grt, had entered the harbour in the 1880s. Denaby and Cadeby Main Colliery Co established their own bunkering depot at Brixham, purchasing the *Persia*, an old Anchor Line vessel, to serve as bunkering store. *Shipping Gazette Weekly Summary*, 16 Sep. 1910, 592; 11 Nov. 1910, 714. See Chapter 3.

13 Trump, *Westcountry Harbour*, 134–5, 139, 147–9.

14 H J Dyos and D H Aldcroft, *British Transport. An Economic Survey from the Seventeenth Century to the Twentieth* (Leicester, 1969), 234.

15 See Craig, *Tramp Ships.*

16 See Chapter 9.

17 Estimated from the price of steamers built by William Gray. See R Craig, 'William Gray & Company. A West Hartlepool Shipbuilding Enterprise, 1864–1913' in P L Cottrell and D H Aldcroft, eds, *Shipping, Trade and Commerce. Essays in Memory*

of *Ralph Davis* (Leicester, 1981), 185. From the mortgages on shares in *City of Exeter*, the initial cost was about £17,300, roughly £16 8s per ton.

18 PRO, BT 31/3361/20037.

19 See Chapter 9.

20 H Tinker, *New System of Slavery* (Oxford, 1974), 146.

21 The Admiralty was seeking a vessel at this time. See E A V Angier, *Fifty Years' Freights* (1920), 17.

22 PRO, BT 31/3001/16910.

23 PRO, BT 31/3131/18049.

24 G R Newman, *Tatham's Log, 1858–1958* (n.d.).

25 PRO, BT 31/3642/22490.

26 PRO, BT 31/4198/27155.

27 NMM, Kellock MSS, Charter-Party Book 6, f.238; Contract Book, 20 Feb. 1907.

28 *Shipping Gazette Weekly Summary*, 21 Oct. 1904, 679; 27 Jan. 1905, 55; 24 Feb. 1905, 119.

29 PRO, BT 31/3114/17890.

30 PRO, BT 31/4545/29764.

31 *Shipping Gazette Weekly Summary*, 20 April 1894, 26; 1 June 1894, 342–3.

32 PRO, BT 31/2933/16375.

33 PRO, BT 31/3255/19127.

34 I am grateful to John Horsley for information relating to Brixham steamship owners.

35 *Shipping Gazette Weekly Summary*, 17 Dec. 1884.

36 In 1914 the Hain fleet aggregated 35 steamers of 122,549 gross tons, and the Chellow fleet 18 steamers of 56,026 tons. See K J O'Donoghue and H S Appleyard, *Hain of St Ives* (Kendal, 1986); and *Syren and Shipping*, 23 Nov. 1904.

37 See Chapter 3.

38 C Jones, *Pioneer Shipowners* (Liverpool 1938), II, 35–49.

39 On J B Mansfield's shipbuilding in Teignmouth, see Trump, *Westcountry Harbour*. Mansfield was registered owner of the screw steamer *Batara Bayon Sree*, built and registered at Hayle in 1871; see G E Farr, *Ship Registers of the Port of Hayle* (1975) 62. She was intended for Singapore owners, no doubt clients or associates of Mansfield's establishment there; see E Jennings, *Transport and Distribution in South-East Asia* (Singapore, n.d.).

40 D A Farnie, 'Marshall Stevens' in D J Jeremy, ed., *Dictionary of Business Biography*, V (1986), 312–25.

41 See E A G Clark, *The Ports of the Exe Estuary, 1660–1860* (Exeter, 1960) 139; H J Trump, *Teignmouth. A Maritime History* (Chichester, 1986), 89–90.

9 Some Aspects of the Business of Devon Shipping in the Nineteenth Century

ROBIN CRAIG, BASIL GREENHILL, J H PORTER and W J SLADE

IT IS A COMMON ERROR TO ASSUME that large-scale shipping enterprise died out in Devon with the industrial revolution. In fact the industrial revolution did not go to sea until, in the 1860s and 1870s, cheap iron plates of shipbuilding quality made possible the iron ship, and improved boilermaking techniques made practical the compound engined steamer with its relatively high-pressure boilers. Until then the wooden sailing vessel of sizes within the capacity of Devon shipyards to build and Devon shipowners to finance remained the standard vehicle of ocean transport in the world's carrying trade. It is not surprising, therefore, that Devon in the first threequarters of the nineteenth century not only remained an important fount of shipping activity, but also produced its own relatively large-scale maritime entrepreneurs whose interests and commercial empires ran across the whole spectrum of maritime business enterprise, and in at least one case were international in scope.

This chapter examines various aspects of this activity. It opens with the voyage accounts of a typical Devon-owned merchant sailing vessel of the mid-nineteenth century (by Robin Craig). There follow studies of elements of three of the most notable maritime enterprises which developed in Devon – Holmans of Topsham (by Robin Craig, with additional material by Basil Greenhill and W J Slade), Stevens of Plymouth (by Robin Craig) and Yeos of Appledore (by Basil Greenhill). The chapter concludes with an account of labour relations in Plymouth docks during the 1890s, which focuses on the handling of Devon's most significant import cargo, coal (by J H Porter). In presenting these case studies, it is hoped that this contribution illustrates a few of the multifarious facets of shipping and trade in nineteenth-century Devon.

A Schooner's Accounts

Some voyage accounts and master's logs have survived for the Plymouth-registered wooden two-masted schooner *Bess*, covering three-and-a-half years of trading in the early 1840s. During this time the vessel made voyages typical of her class and very characteristic of the deployment of small-scale South Devon shipping for much of the nineteenth century.

Built in 1835 at Franks Quarry, Plymouth, by David Banks, *Bess* was registered at Plymouth in 1853 (No 19). She measured 92 tons (OM) and was rigged as a schooner; from the log it is clear that she set studding sails. Remeasured at Plymouth under the 1836 Tonnage Law in 1838 (No 37), her tonnage was cut to 73 tons. In 1840 she was lengthened by 10.5ft at a cost of £552, after deduction for the sale of old stores and copper, suggesting a cost of about £53 per additional foot of length. As a result her tonnage was increased by 18 tons, which is equal to about £31 per ton of increased tonnage. These data are of interest in that a large number of Devon vessels were lengthened, some, mostly later in the century, being converted to three-masted schooner rig. The figures quoted are at least a yardstick which may be adopted in calculating what was a common process of technological refinement.

Accounts exist for the following voyages made between October 1840 and April 1844. After lengthening she left Plymouth for Mevagissey, where she loaded pilchards for Venice, coming home to London from Greece with currants. A short ballast trip took her to Newcastle, where she loaded 143 tons of coal for Barcelona, returning from Salou to Liverpool with 107 tons

of nuts. There ensued a round trip from Liverpool to Beirut and back, which was followed, in June 1842, by a trip out to Labrador with a nominal freight of £60 (probably salt) returning to Ancona, Italy, with 2,000 quintals of stockfish. Captain Martyn, the master of *Bess*, makes illuminating remarks on his passage to Labrador, and describes America Tickle in unflattering terms: '. . . it is impossible to describe a more desolate looking spot than those islands, the few houses or huts look from outside miserable indeed, being to all appearance a mud house'.[1]

After discharging at Ancona, *Bess* again picked up a currant cargo in Greece, and made her way to Rotterdam for discharge. Then it was but a short hop to Sunderland to load 52 chaldrons of coal for her home port, where she underwent repairs and renewals. A further voyage to Labrador earned another nominal freight of £60, after which fish was again her cargo, this time for Leghorn. She then sailed back to England to discharge a cargo at Liverpool. All of these passages were conducted on separate voyage charters, but in January 1844 *Bess* went on a round trip from Liverpool to Lisbon and back on hire at £87 10s. per month. Here the series of voyage accounts ends.

The profitability of Devon sailing vessels is often difficult to determine because of the lack of records, but in respect of *Bess* we are afforded a glimpse of what was perhaps typical trading experience. Between October 1840 and April 1844 she returned to her shareholders £720, or about £205

9.1   John Bagwell Holman (1800–63). (*Topsham Museum*)

per annum. If we estimate the original cost of *Bess* in 1835 as about £15 per ton (OM), ready for sea, this gives us a prime cost of £1,380. If we then adopt a reasonable depreciation rate on the vessel of 5 per cent (straight line), she would have been worth around £700 at the time she was lengthened. We know the cost of lengthening her, so that her presumed value when ready again for sea would be about £1,300, close to the estimated prime cost. These calculations suggest that her earnings thereafter until April 1844 work out at about 16 per cent on the capital employed. However, this is without depreciation, not allowed for in the available accounts, although wear and tear is included. Perhaps, then, her earnings were about 10 per cent per annum, net of depreciation, which may be regarded as a better than average return for that class of vessel. It is worthy of note that her voyage costs may be apportioned as follows:

	Per Cent
Disbursement at ports	55
Wages and victuals	29
Insurance	14
Commission to Master	2

A LIST OF SHIPS
ENTERED IN THE
Exeter Shipping Insurance Association.

ESTABLISHED JUNE 15th, 1836.—CORRECTED TO APRIL 1st, 1844.

BANKERS, NATIONAL PROVINCIAL BANK OF ENGLAND, EXETER.

COMMITTEE.

WILLIAM MAER, Exeter.
JOSEPH PERRIAM, Exeter.
EDWARD HAWKINS, Exeter.
PETER PALMER, Exeter.
THOMAS POPHAM, Topsham.

GILBERT PERIAM, Topsham.
JAMES SALSBURY, Topsham.
J. S. HARRISON, Topsham.
FREDERICK BARTLETT, Topsham.
EDWARD HURDLE, Topsham.

GEORGE CALLAND, Exmouth.
ARTHUR PARKER, Exmouth.
ROBERT ELWIN, Exmouth.
JOHN PARKER, Exmouth.
HORATIO REEVES, Exmouth.

WILLIAM ANNING, Starcross.
ARTHUR OWEN, Teignmouth.
EPHRAIM MATTHEWS, Bridport.
JOHN HOARE, Bridport.
THOMAS WALKER, Lyme.

JOHN RANDALL, Lyme.

JOHN HOLMAN, Secretary,
TOPSHAM.

FORD, PRINTER, TOPSHAM.

9.2 Ships covered by Exeter Shipping Insurance Association. The list is corrected to April 1844. (Topsham Museum)

Captain Martyn, her master, held 26/64ths in *Bess*, as did David Banks, her builder. Other shares were held by a Charlestown cooper, spinsters from Charlestown and Plymouth, and a widow from Devonport. *Bess* was sold away from Plymouth in 1854, being re-registered at Wexford, Ireland, from whence she was still trading in 1857.

Holmans of Topsham

The Holmans of Topsham played a conspicuous part in the British shipping industry during the nineteenth century.[2] Two brothers, Thomas (1771–1822) and Richard (1776–1824), were master mariners and shipowners, the latter being drowned at sea whilst in command of a vessel. Thomas's son, John Bagwell Holman (1800–1863), also a master mariner and a substantial shipowner, came ashore and established a shipbuilding yard at Topsham. Subsequently he added to the business by purchasing the nearby shipbuilding premises of Daniel Davy, a shipbuilder of more than local importance who, aside from the construction of merchant vessels, completed as many as sixteen vessels of between twelve and twenty-eight guns for the Royal Navy between 1804 and 1814.[3] To his activities, Holman added sailmaking and the manufacture of iron bolts for ship construction purposes. In 1858 John Holman opened a substantial graving dock at Topsham, and employed over 200 men in his shipyard. He also invented a novel kind of rudder which was fitted to many vessels from the 1850s[4] (see Fig. 7.9).

For a time in the 1840s, John Holman was non-exclusive Lloyd's Surveyor at Exmouth, but much of his attention as a surveyor of shipping was devoted to the activity for which the firm of Holman is still known throughout the world – marine insurance. Mutual marine insurance societies and clubs were a familiar feature of many, indeed perhaps most, British ports in the nineteenth century. They flourished in the first decade of the century on the northeast coast of England, and quickly spread to other parts of Britain. They were formed as a means by which shipowners could obtain insurance cover on hulls at lower premiums than those prevailing on the London market, dominated as it was by Lloyd's and the incorporated insurance companies. John Holman was not the first West Countryman to form an insurance association, but his were by far the most successful and commanded the most universal support. The West of England Insurance Association was formed by him in 1832, with its offices at Topsham, and he followed this with the Exeter Shipping Insurance Association in 1836.

Thanks to Holman's judicious assessment of seaworthiness and the quality of ship design and construction, and his shrewd evaluation of risk, his insurance business flourished, and the 'Western Clubs' as they were to be called, could cover risks on a mutual basis at a relatively low premium compared with the London rates. However, it has to be remembered that the amount of cover was limited to £1,000 or £1,500 on each vessel, sums which were not exceeded by many vessels constituting Devon's fleet. Holman did not just cover the risks on local shipping; his reputation soon resulted in his accepting risks on vessels owned elsewhere in Britain.

Before 1855 Holman had extended the range of risks covered to include cargo and freight. In that year his Ocean Cargo and Freight Club had a capital of £30,000, whilst the insured sums in the hull clubs amounted to more than £400,000 – a measure of his vigilant management, and no less a tribute to the confidence reposed in him by large numbers of shipowners in all parts of Britain.[5] After many years managing hull and cargo clubs, John Holman ended his involvement in this activity and applied his accumulated experience to the establishment of Protection and Indemnity Insurance, a business that still carries the name Holman to the present day. Other Mutual Insurance Clubs were to provide insurance cover for shipowners in the West Country, but none was on the scale of the Holman enterprise. As late as 1907 Braunton Shipowners Mutual Insurance Association was organised, and there were similar institutions covering the risks of fishing vessels at ports such as Brixham. The working of these Mutuals has been described as follows:

> The shipowners of a small port formed the Association. There was often a paid, part-time secretary, but the other officials, Chairman, President, and Treasurer and the Governing Committee, usually called the 'board of directors', were not paid. Each member of the

Association registered each of his ships as to be insured for a given sum, often compulsorily much less than her market value, in order to dissuade him from throwing her away. At Appledore and Braunton, for instance, it was stipulated that no ship was to insure for total loss above one half her purchase price. For each ship, he paid an entrance fee of 2 or 3 per cent of her value. If the ship was lost the Association called a levy, each member contributing in proportion to the total value of the ships he himself had covered by the Mutual. In some associations, in the event of a total loss claim being paid, the wreck became the property of the Association and the price obtained for her became part of the Association's funds; in others, the proceeds were divided equally between owner and club. At Braunton the Association's profits were used to build up members' deposits until they were roughly 12 per cent of the insured value of members' ships, then the surplus was returned to members each year. Sometimes, if a ship was salved and sold these returns were considerable. Salved vessels were not always disposed of. At Gloucester, it seems probable that the Association itself operated vessels which it had acquired in this way for the benefit of members.

It was a very simple insurance system and a very economical one, since there was no capital, no profits, and the very small overheads were covered by occasional small levies. To work economically, the Association had to be of a certain size, so the levies on each member were small. The members were saved the annual drain on profits of ordinary insurance, and sometimes years would elapse during which they were required to pay only very small sums. At the same time they were covered, if barely, against all risks . . .

The Association had their own rules about standards to which ships were to be maintained and the qualifications of their masters, over and above the requirements of the classification societies and the Board of Trade. Masters were examined by senior members of the Association, some of whom held no certificates. Uncertificated mates were sometimes allowed to pass, while Board of Trade-passed masters might be rejected as far as ships belonging to members of the Mutual were concerned.[6]

The Braunton 'club' provides an interesting example of how the Mutuals worked in practice. Captain W J Slade wrote about his schooner *Haldon*, damaged in collision with a steamer, thus,

It now became plain that, being so badly damaged, we should have to throw the ship on the Braunton Insurance Club for survey, but as no-one could decide, it was agreed that a surveyor from the Sailing Ship Mutual Insurance of London should survey without prejudice. Two qualified men attended and a figure was agreed between them of £760. Now I had always acted for my father in his dealing with the Club as a member of its committee and in consequence I had acquired a thorough knowledge of its functions and, in fact, there was little anyone could tell me about it. I got a statement in writing from the surveyors and on the strength of this claimed my insurance.

To have a proper outlook on this matter, it is, perhaps, necessary to explain how our insurances worked. The Braunton Club was only for Total Loss and/or Constructive Total Loss and Salvage. The Club enrolled in the Sailing Ship Mutual Insurance Association, and they undertook to fight law cases, pay for damage done to others, and give protection in various ways, such as recovery of freight, compensation, etc. The Total Loss and Constructive Total Loss were entirely on the Braunton Club. If the ship damaged herself the owner paid for it. Now in the case of our collision it was evident that, despite what the crew said, the *Haldon* was entirely to blame and, therefore, the owner paid for his own repairs but a clause in the policy stated, if the damage exceeded 50 per cent of the total value as agreed by the Club, she became a Constructive Total Loss and, therefore, entitled to claim insurance. A clause limiting this amount barred the owner from being fully insured, i.e. if the ship was valued by the Club at £1,000, the amount of insurance allowed from all sources could not exceed £500 or half value. The owner was compelled to accept the risk in Total Loss or Constructive Total Loss or half the ship's value. For this, each ship paid £3 per cent per annum on the half value insured. Similarly in case of salvage the owner paid one half and the Braunton Club the other half.

The *Haldon* was valued for insurance purposes at £1,200 and insured for £600. As the estimate of damage was £760, which was more than 50 per cent of the total value, I was entitled to £600 insurance less £7.10s. owing in premiums. In the course of time I therefore received £592.10s. from the Braunton Shipowners Mutual Insurance Association Limited.

The ship now theoretically became the property of the Club. When I asked what they intended to do with her, I was told to take her up on the mud and let her rot. To this I objected pointing out that according to her policy the ship should be sold by auction to the

9.3   Document of call on the members of a Devon mutual insurance association for payment of contributions to cover other members' losses. (*Devon Record Office*)

highest bidder and the proceeds, less expenses, shared equally between the owner and the Club. A meeting of the committee was held and it was considered by them she was not worth putting up for auction as it would all be swallowed up by expenses. I offered £80 as she stood and the Club asked for £100. We compromised and I agreed to £90, sending a cheque for £45 and retaining my half, £45, to which I was entitled.

I had to try to buy another ship but failed to get a suitable one. I therefore determined to repair the *Haldon* as the cheapest way out. We were fortunate to be able to get a large quantity of splendid secondhand wood, African mahogany, for repairs and also a second-hand bowsprit. This was a great help towards the cost of repairs but even with this help and all the work we ourselves did the cost of repairs was considerably in excess of the amount I received in insurance. When the *Haldon* came out of dock she was a much better ship than before. Her old knightheads were found to have been broken years before and now she was practically rebuilt forward.[7]

John Bagwell Holman died in 1863, leaving four sons who continued their family interests in shipowning and shipbroking. One brother set up a broker's office in Cardiff with a Mr Fry, the firm being styled Fry, Holman and Fry. The move to Cardiff was, of course, a common feature among late nineteenth-century Devon shipowners, but it should be noted that members of the Holman family had investments in shipping registered at a number of British ports outside the principality.[8] The later shipowning activities of the Holman family are illustrated by two of the Stott charter-parties preserved in the Merseyside Maritime Museum, both of which relate to the *Enmore*, a steamer belonging to John Holman.[9]

Although the fruit trade was the speciality of fast schooners from South Devon, the first of these charter parties shows that Devon-owned steamships were also engaged in the business during the 1870s. Signed on 18 May 1877, this printed charter-party is headed 'Mediterranean Line to New York' – presumably the principal interest of the Mediterranean and New York Steamship Co Ltd of Liverpool – for whom W H Stott & Co were brokers. At the time, *Enmore* was on a voyage from Cardiff to Port Said in ballast. Under the terms of the charter she was required to call at any four ports in Sicily, and/or ports in Mediterranean and Atlantic Spain and load a cargo of green or dried fruit for New York. For this the freight was to be £1,700 lump sum, with an extra £100 payable for loading in Spain and £50 extra for each additional port of loading. Consigned to the agency of Phelps Brothers & Company in New York, she was to discharge at a specified covered wharf, the ship paying £7 per day wharfage, with a commission to the Agents of 2.5 per cent on the gross freight. Twenty-three days (Sundays excepted) were allowed for loading and discharge, with demurrage payable at the rate of £30 per day up to a maximum of ten days.

According to the second of the Stott charter-parties, signed on 5 February 1878, the *Enmore* was chartered by the well-known firm of Ross T Smyth & Company of Liverpool for a voyage from Odessa to a safe United Kingdom port, calling at Queenstown or Falmouth at master's option for orders, the master undertaking to notify the charterers within 24hr of arrival. The cargo specified was tallow, wheat, maize or other grain, freight being agreed at 40s per ton of 20cwt, with proportionate rates for the different commodities in accordance with the printed London and Baltic agreement. Fifteen running days were allowed for loading, awaiting orders and discharge, with demurrage agreed at £35 per day. Ross D Smyth & Co were closely associated with Rathbone's of Liverpool in the major commodity staple trades,[10] and this charter in 1878 occurs near the end of what has been described as 'the golden days of the corn trade in the nineteenth century'.[11]

These two charter-parties indicate John Holman's commercial dexterity. The fruit charter is representative of countless others in which British vessels were deployed in cross trades outside the Empire, thus making a significant contribution to Britain's considerable invisible earnings in the nineteenth century. That Holman fixed his vessel for an Atlantic voyage in May 1877 was due to the closure of the Black Sea and the Danubian ports consequent upon war between Turkey and Russia. The second charter-party demonstrates Holman's enterprise in taking advantage of the commercial opportunities arising from the end of the blockade early in 1878. The freight rate obtained also testifies to the accuracy of Angier's Freight Reports, upon which so much reliance has been placed by historians.[12]

Stevens of Plymouth

The Stevens family made a major contribution to the prosperity of the port of Plymouth in the nineteenth century.[13] John Stevens (1762–1831) had been a shipmaster and shipowner from the later eighteenth century, and seafaring and shipowning were to occupy the attentions of several of his offspring. His eldest son, John Lee Stevens (1795–1863), combined proprietorship and editorship of the *Shipping Gazette* with the writing of poetry and the invention of two types of paddles for steamers, obtaining patents in 1827 and 1851.[14] John Stevens' third son, Thomas (1799–1869), became, like his father before him, a master mariner and shipowner. Mayor of Plymouth in 1854, he consolidated the position of the Stevens family as one of the most important shipping firms in Plymouth. Among other activities in which he engaged was acting as agent for the loading of china clay at the Cornish ports of Pentewan and Charlestown, and he possessed important coal vending interests which included the supply of gas coal to Plymouth gasworks. His waterfront property included Granary Wharf,

Plymouth, which, together with his retail coal sales, he sold to the Phoenix Coal Company in 1858. It was at this time that he offered for sale by auction eight of his wooden sailing vessels at Plymouth.[15]

The fourth son of John Stevens was Robert White Stevens (1806–1870), who, among other things, began a printing business in Plymouth which still exists today and publishes a widely used tide table. He is, perhaps, best remembered for his valuable compendium *Stevens on Stowage*, once known throughout the shipping world, and in its day the essential reference book for shipbrokers, shipowners and shipmasters alike, warmly praised by, among others, no less a figure than Joseph Conrad.[16] The accumulated knowledge and expertise embodied in this book, which ran through several editions, bears testimony to the acumen and experience of this remarkable man.

The Stevens family also illustrated one of the outstanding characteristics of Devon-born shipowners and entrepreneurs in the late nineteenth century. This was the frequency with which they deserted the county that nurtured them for pastures new. A remarkable case of this tendency was manifested in the son of Sanders Stevens, Marshall Stevens (1852–1936), who moved from Plymouth to Garston on the River Mersey, there to inaugurate his own steamship services. He was later to achieve national distinction in connection with the promotion and management of the Manchester Ship Canal, and he was also notable for having been the founder of the Trafford Park Estate in Manchester.[17]

The activities of the Stevens family also illustrate another aspect of the business of shipping in Devon in the nineteenth century. For hundreds of years Plymouth has been a most important port of call for shipping, irrespective of whether vessels actually loaded or discharged cargoes there. The embarkation and disembarkation of passengers, the handling of baggage and mail and the bunkering of steamers were all aspects of this activity. Vessels took in fresh water and fresh stores of meat and vegetables. The business generated for shipping agents and brokers was considerable, and it is significant that all the Plymouth shipowners who deployed capital in steamships in the later nineteenth century enjoyed the cash flow and profits generated from acting as agents to the many vessels which made use of the facilities of the port.

In June 1889 a group of Plymouth shipping agents came together to sign an agreement, with a penalty originally of £10 for non-compliance, to levy standardised agency charges for certain classes of vessels using the port. This agreement specified those types of vessel to be covered as follows:

Minimum rates of charges for ships' agency on steamers and sailing vessels discharging cargoes in the Port of Plymouth.

Grain Steamers and General Cargo Steamers:

For steamers of 800 tons register and under	£ 3 3s 0d
For steamers over 800 tons, not exceeding 1,000 tons	£ 4 4s 0d
For steamers over 1,000 tons, n/exc. 1,200 tons	£ 5 5s 0d
For steamers over 1,200 tons, n/exc. 1,400 tons	£ 6 6s 0d
For steamers over 1,400 tons, n/exc. 1,700 tons	£ 8 8s 0d
For steamers over 1,700 tons	£10 10s 0d

Phosphate and Manure Steamers:	£ 5 5s 0d

Sailing Vessels:

For vessels of 500 tons register and under	£ 3 3s 0d
For vessels over 500 tons, and n/exc. 1,000 tons	£ 5 5s 0d
For vessels over 1,000 tons, and n/exc. 1,500 tons	£ 7 7s 0d
For vessels over 1,500 tons	£10 10s 0d

The original signatories to this arrangement were: Bellamy & Co, Collier Brothers, Fox, Sons & Co, Sanders Stevens & Co, William Henry Sarah & Co, Smith, Sundius & Co, Stevens (Barbican), R B Triplett, Henry J Waring & Co, Weekes, Phillips & Co, and Wright & Co. The agreement excluded '. . . steamers of the regular mail lines calling to land passengers and mails or steamers landing part cargoes . . . vessels under 300 tons register trading with the Baltic . . . vessels trading to the North Sea ports between the Elbe and Brest . . . (vessels in the) coasting trade'. The exclusion of regular liners and passenger ships was probably due to there being individual contracts between the owners of such vessels and their customary agents in Plymouth.[18]

9.4   The three-masted motor schooner *Haldon*, built at Plymouth in 1892–3 and owned in the 1920s and 1930s by Captain W J Slade of Appledore, motor sailing out of the Torridge. (*W J Slade*)

It is not known how common such arrangements were at other British ports, but the signatories of this particular document were generally referred to as 'The Combine'. In due course the agency rates levied on shipping at Plymouth must have been in accordance with the scale recommended by the Institute of Chartered Shipbrokers, once that organisation had been established.

We have already suggested that agency business was important in Plymouth shipping circles, but it could also affect the wider community. When in 1935, *Compagnie Generale Transatlantique* proposed transferring its call from Plymouth to Southampton, it was calculated that the loss of income to the local community would be as much as £8,000 per annum. The impact of such transfers away from Plymouth was to be postponed, however, because on 20 May 1937, in less than six hours, seven liners of over 130,000 aggregate tons arrived at Plymouth, constituting a record for the Port.[19]

A list of liner companies in 1928, together with the names of their Plymouth agents (Table 9.1) attests to the volume of seaborne traffic attracted to Devon's premier port. The progressive loss of such maritime connections during and after the Second World War, and the diminution of regular calls by cargo liners, played its part in reducing the number and income of shipping agents in the City. In times past that income might have been invested in shipping.

Yeos of Appledore

The third of the entrepreneurs, aspects of whose activities are described in this chapter, is William Yeo of Appledore, son of James Yeo of Port Hill, Prince Edward Island, Canada, whose career is described in Chapter 4. William Yeo's function was to turn the shallow triangular shaped bay around which Appledore had developed into the European headquarters of James Yeo's international lumbering, shipbuilding, mercantile and banking business. There was some difficulty because the land and the buildings on it belonged to several different people and the foreshore rights belonged to the public. It took six years before the land was bought and filched and some buildings torn down, including almshouses which had been given to the poor of the parish of Northam more than a century and a half before. But it was done, and the Richmond Dry Dock was built, big enough to take four of Yeo's smaller Island-built ships together for fitting out for sale.

There was always opposition. The case of Tatem *v* Yeo was heard before Chief Justice Bovill and a Special Jury at the Devon Lent Assizes in Exeter in mid-March 1868. The proceedings revealed a great deal about the way in which William Yeo and his associates ran the British end of the Yeo's international business and in so doing sought to run also the community of Appledore as a 'company town'. They also revealed the degree of opposition the Yeos encountered, and especially they revealed the depth of local feeling which existed over the way in which Appledore's triangular-shaped sheltered bay, the lower part of which was known as the 'Parlour' and which had provided the best lying-ground for small ships in all North Devon, had been appropriated by the Yeos.

Although this dock greatly improved the prosperity of the area, its building meant the loss of common mooring rights in this sheltered, safe place with its firm sand, on which ships could lie at low tide and be repaired, and in which ships had been built for several centuries. It also meant the division of the community into those who were Yeo's people, who gained from their enterprise, and those who were not Yeo's people. William Yeo may have lacked legitimate male offspring, but he was in a position often to take what he wanted, and the nickname the town gave him, 'the black ram' was more than just a play on the old Appledore pronunciation of the word 'ewe', which approximated to 'Yeo'. Those who crossed him, if they were working men, found employment denied them: they were the 'black Leicesters'. If they were shipowners or merchants, they found difficulties placed in the way of their use of the facilities of Appledore, and their efforts impeded in all sorts of ways.

9.5   An illustration from *Stevens on Stowage* showing coal being loaded at Sunderland.

Table 9.1
Plymouth's liner services and shipping agents, 1928
Cargo services

Port	Sailing	Name of Line	Plymouth Agents
Amsterdam	fortnightly	Holland Steamship Co	G Haswell & Co
Antwerp	irregular	Bristol Steam Navigation Co	Fox Sons & Co
Belfast	weekly	Clyde Shipping Co	Clyde Shipping Co
Glasgow	weekly	Clyde Shipping Co	Clyde Shipping Co
Gothenburg	3-weekly	Adolf Bratt Line	Orlando Davis & Co
Greenock	weekly	Clyde Shipping Co	Clyde Shipping Co
Guernsey	weekly	Plymouth, Channel Islands, & Brittany SS Co	Plymouth, Channel Islands, & Brittany S.S. Co
Hamburg	weekly	Hutchison Line	T Nicholson & Co
Hamburg	irregular	Bugsier Line	T Nicholson & Co
Jersey	weekly	Plymouth, Channel Islands, & Brittany SS Co	Plymouth, Channel Islands, Brittany SS Co
Oslo and East Norwegian Ports	monthly	Stang Line	Orlando Davis & Co
Rotterdam	irregular	Bristol Steam Navigation Co	Fox, Sons & Co
St Brieux	fortnightly	Plymouth, Channel Islands, & Brittany SS Co	Plymouth, Channel Islands, & Brittany SS Co
Waterford	weekly	Clyde Shipping Co	Clyde Shipping Co

Passenger and mail services
Arriving from:

Port	Sailing	Name of Line	Plymouth Agents
Africa, East	fortnightly	British India Steam Navigation Co	Weekes, Philips & Co Ltd
Africa, East & South	monthly	Union Castle Line	Coast Lines, Ltd
Africa, South	irregular	Ellerman & Bucknall Steamship Co Ltd	G Haswell & Co
America, South & Central	fortnightly (March to Sept)	Pacific Steam Navigation Co	Coast Lines, Ltd
Australia	weekly	P & O Steam Navigation Co	Fox, Sons & Co
Australia	fortnightly	Orient Line	Orient-Cunard, Joint Office
Australia	monthly	Australian Commonwealth	Weekes, Phillips & Co Ltd
Bombay	weekly	British India Steam Navigation Co	Weekes, Phillips & Co Ltd
Bombay	weekly	P & O Steam Navigation Co	Fox, Sons & Co
Brazil	fortnightly	Blue Star Line	Weekes, Phillips & Co Ltd
Calabar	monthly	Elder Dempster & Co Ltd	Coast Lines Ltd
Calcutta	weekly	British India Steamship Co	Weekes, Phillips & Co Ltd
Canary Islands	monthly	Union Castle	Coast Lines Ltd
China	weekly	P & O Steam Navigation Co	Fox, Sons & Co
Colombo	fortnightly	Orient Line	Orient-Cunard, Joint Office
Colombo	fortnightly	P & O Steam Navigation Co	Fox, Sons & Co
Colombo	fortnightly	Bibby Line	Weekes, Phillips & Co Ltd
Colon	monthly	French Line	G Haswell & Co
Cuba	monthly	Hamburg-American Line	W H Muller & Co (London) Ltd
Egypt	fortnightly	Bibby Line	Weekes, Phillips & Co Ltd
Galveston	monthly	Ozean Line	Wainwright Bros & Co
Guernsey	weekly	Plymouth, Channel Islands, & Brittany SS Co	Plymouth, Channel Islands, & Brittany SS Co
Halifax	fortnightly	Cunard Steamship Co	Orient-Cunard, Joint Office
Havana (Cuba)	monthly	Ozean Line	Wainwright Bros & Co
India	irregular	Ellermans City Line	Weekes, Phillips & Co Ltd and Fox, Sons & Co
Japan	weekly	P & O Steam Navigation Co	Fox, Sons & Co
Lagos	fortnightly	Elder Dempster & Co Ltd	Coast Lines Ltd
Madeira	fortnightly	Blue Star Line	Weekes, Phillips & Co Ltd
Marseilles	fortnightly	Bibby Line	Weekes, Phillips & Co Ltd
Mexico	monthly	Hamburg-American Line	W H Muller & Co (London) Ltd
Mexico	monthly	Ozean Line	Wainwright Bros & Co

Passenger and mail services, continued
Arriving from:

Port	Sailing	Name of Line	Plymouth Agents
Montreal	fortnightly	Cunard Steamship Co	Orient-Cunard, Joint Office
New York	weekly	American Merchant Line	Orlando Davis & Co Ltd
New York	weekly	Cunard Steamship Co	Orient-Cunard, Joint Office
New York	weekly	French Line	G Haswell & Co
New York	weekly	Holland-American Line	Bellamy & Co
New York	weekly	North German Lloyd	Orlando Davis & Co Ltd
New York	weekly	Red Star Line	Weekes, Phillips & Co Ltd
New York	weekly	United States Line	Orlando Davis & Co Ltd
New York	monthly	Atlantic Transport Co	Weekes, Phillips & Co Ltd
Quebec	weekly	Cunard Steamship Co	Orient-Cunard, Joint Office
Rangoon	fortnightly	Henderson Line	Weekes, Phillips & Co Ltd
Rangoon	fortnightly	Bibby Line	Weekes, Phillips & Co Ltd
River Plate	fortnightly	Blue Star Line	Weekes, Phillips & Co Ltd
Spain	monthly	Hamburg-American Line	W H Muller & Co (London) Ltd
Trinidad	monthly	French Line	G Haswell & Co
Vancouver (via Panama Canal)	irregular	Johnston Line Ltd	Orlando Davis & Co Ltd
West Indies	fortnightly	Hamburg-American Line	W H Muller & Co (London) Ltd
West Indies	fortnightly	Royal Nederlands	Bellamy & Co
West Indies	monthly	French Line	G Haswell & Co

Sailing to:

Port	Sailing	Name of Line	Plymouth Agents
Africa, South & East	monthly	Union Castle Line	Coast Lines, Ltd
America, Central	monthly	Hamburg-American Line	W H Muller & Co (London) Ltd
Amsterdam	fortnightly	Royal Nederlands	Bellamy & Co
Amsterdam	monthly	Hamburg-American Line	W H Muller & Co (London) Ltd
Antwerp	weekly	Red Star Line	Weekes, Phillips & Co Ltd
Bordeaux	monthly	French Line	G Haswell & Co
Bremen	weekly	North German Lloyd	Orlando Davis & Co Ltd
Bremen	monthly	Ozean Line	Wainwright Bros & Co
Canary Islands	monthly	Union Castle Line	Coast Lines, Ltd
Bremen	weekly	United States Line	Orlando Davis & Co Ltd
Cherbourg	weekly	North German Lloyd	Orlando Davis & Co Ltd
Cherbourg	weekly	United States Line	Orlando Davis & Co Ltd
Colon	monthly	French Line	G Haswell & Co
Cuba	monthly	Hamburg-American Line	W H Muller & Co (London) Ltd
Hamburg	monthly	Hamburg-American Line	W H Muller & Co (London) Ltd
Havre	weekly	French Line	G Haswell & Co
Jersey	weekly	Plymouth, Channel Islands, & Brittany SS Co	Plymouth, Channel Islands, & Brittany SS Co
London	weekly	American Merchant Line	Orlando Davis & Co Ltd
Mexico	monthly	Hamburg-American Line	W H Muller & Co (London) Ltd
New York	weekly	French Line	G Haswell & Co
Rotterdam	weekly	Holland-American Line	Bellamy & Co
St Brieux	weekly	Plymouth, Channel Islands, & Brittany SS Co	Plymouth, Channel Islands, & Brittany SS Co
Trinidad	monthly	French Line	G Haswell & Co
West Indies	monthly	French Line	G Haswell & Co
West Indies	monthly	Hamburg-American Line	W H Muller & Co (London) Ltd

Source: H. N. Appleby, *Great Western Ports* (1928), 175–7.

The issue under trial at Exeter can be summed up in the opening submission of the plaintiff's leading counsel.[20] Mr Coleridge, QC, stated:

In this action the jury would have to investigate the question of damage which had been sustained by Mr Tatem to his ship *Georgina* by reason of the conduct of Mr Yeo in imprisoning it for a considerable length of time on the beach at Appledore, and preventing her being repaired, thus rendering it impossible for her to proceed on her voyage to the Mediterranean. The plaintiff, Mr Tatem, was a shipowner, who had been for many years an inhabitant of Appledore, and his vessels had for considerable period plied to and from that port. He was the owner of 52/64ths of the brigantine *Georgina*, 230-tons register, in respect of which this action arose, and he had been so for a considerable period. Mr Yeo was also a shipowner, and the owner of a dry dock which he had made at Appledore, and he claimed the foreshore on which the *Georgina* was under a grant from the Crown in 1857. On the 20th March, 1867, the *Georgina* went on a voyage to the Mediterranean with a cargo of iron, tin, and cocoa, and she wanted to get there if possible in time for the fruit season, so as to return from Sicily with a fruit cargo. She sailed from Liverpool, but on her passage down the St George's Channel, she encountered very bad weather, and in consequence of the injuries she received she was obliged to run down the Bristol Channel and make for the port of Appledore. She approached the port and a pilot was sent out to bring her in. She came across the bar and was a good deal damaged by so doing; a survey was in consequence held on her, and it was decided that it would be very unsafe for her to proceed further without going to some place near for her to be repaired. A shipbuilder at Appledore, named Cock, was applied to by Mr Tatem to do the necessary repairs and he entered into an agreement. Application was then made to Mr Yeo to allow her to be placed in his dry dock for the purpose of repair, in answer to which Mr Cock received a letter from Mr Yeo to the effect that his dry dock was engaged and would be so for two months, and expressing his regret that he could not accommodate him. This being so it was necessary to obtain another place for the purpose. There was a spot on the beach just close to the dock called the 'Parlour', he supposed from the fact of its being protected from the wind and the current, and the *Georgina* was there beached, and brought up to the side of the Quay. This happened on Saturday and they had a witness who would prove what Mr Yeo thereupon did. Seeing the vessel on the beach he told this gentleman that he thought it was put there for the purpose of doing him some bodily harm. He went to his church on Sunday and having there deliberated on the matter, he determined on the Monday morning to pay her out – or rather pay her in. Early in the morning a ship called the *Orient* left her moorings and was brought alongside the *Georgina*, and fastened up so 'taut' that she was forced against the side of the quay. She was so tightly wedged that she knocked down a portion of the quay, and of course she could not do this without doing herself considerable injury. Fenders were put down by Mr Tatem to protect the *Georgina*, but notwithstanding this a great deal of damage was done. This state of things continued and it was utterly impossible for the repairs to be done. Everything that was put up was immediately knocked down; and, for fear that the *Georgina* was not wedged in tight enough, Mr Yeo drove an iron stanchion into the rock underneath, got some tremendously heavy chains, and tied up the *Orient* not only to the quay at each end but also to the iron post in the rocks. They were not content with this even, for as the *Orient* rose with the tide the chains must fall, and the *Georgina* would get out over the chains. This was not according to Mr Yeo's notion, so he went to Mr Beer's and bought three large padlocks, with which he locked up the chains, and thus kept them out perfectly 'taut', so that whatever was the state of the tide the *Georgina* could not get over these adamantine chains, which formed complete lines of circumvallation. This continued from April 1st to July 12th. There were pleasant little interludes of proceedings before the magistrates, binding over to keep the peace, etc., but he would not trouble the jury with these matters.

The 'pleasant little interludes' included an occasion when Mr Tatem was told by one of Yeo's men: 'if you presume to touch the chains, here is a sledgehammer, and, although I may miss you the first time, you may depend I shan't the second; you'll be dead as a doornail if you do'. There was also an episode when Mr Tatem, no doubt suitably supported, boarded the *Orient* and attacked Mr Yeo's men with a cutlass.

There is no doubt that Mr Tatem deliberately sought to challenge William Yeo's claims to the foreshore rights and that the two sections of the Appledore community, Yeo's men and the rest, were, to use the words of one of the witnesses of this case, 'at daggers drawn', and that both were prepared to fight it out regardless of the law. Yeo lost the case, the judge ruled that the foreshore mooring rights lay with Thomas Chanter, who exercised the privileges of the Lord of the Manor of Northam and who claimed 'postage' from those who moored in the 'Parlour'.

Labour Relations

The Stevens family fortune was derived in part originally from a coal importing business. Although the Stevens themselves ceased this activity in

9.6   The offices of Luscombe, Bellamy & Co, on the Barbican, Plymouth. This firm was one of the port's leading ship brokers in the late nineteenth century. (*City of Plymouth Museums and Art Gallery*)

9.7   William Yeo (1813–72). (*Collingwood Yeo*)

the 1850s, Plymouth remained a port of import for coal on a large scale as long as coal was consumed as industrial and domestic fuel. The business continues today on a reduced scale. The Report of the Royal Commission on Labour of 1892 reveals a good deal about the way the business of discharging the coal cargoes on which Plymouth depended was handled in the late nineteenth century.[21] Some of the questions, and the answers given to the Royal Commission when it considered Plymouth, are as follows:

Mr Alexander Henry Varnier called and examined
Question

12,469 You represent the Plymouth and District Free Labour Association do you not? – I do.

12,471 What class of labourers for the most part compose that Association? – Those connected with the coal trade.

12,477 (I Employ) . . . a large number of casual labourers.

12,479 What are the general hours of labour in the district? – From 6am to 5pm with time for meals.

12,481 And what is the ordinary rate of wage for men regularly employed? – About £1 a week, but in addition there are various ways, particularly in the house coal trade by which trade is increased 2s 5d a week.

12,483 In reference to the men employed in discharging cargoes what are they paid? – They are paid at the rate of 2d per ton per man which averages for sailing ships about 6s a day, and for steamers 8s to 10s or 12s a day in accordance with the quantity discharged.

12,494 Now in the Free Labour Association what special conditions have you? With reference to engagement of the men? It is perfectly free: any man is perfectly free to join the Free Labour Association.

12,498 And has the effect of your Association being formed been to diminish the amount of support given to the Unions? – Yes, most materially.

12,500 You do not take in everyone who wishes to be admitted? – Not everyone, not indiscriminately.

12,542 So that the way it stands at present in Plymouth is that employment is given to men only who hold the free-labour ticket? – The free-labour ticket.

Mr George Frederick Treleaven called and examined

12,549 You are a coal merchant of Plymouth? – Yes.

12,550 And how many hands do you employ? Nineteen regular hands, but mostly casual.

12,551 Besides men who are paid by the job? – Yes, they are the more numerous by far.

12,560 Have you had any trouble with the unions? – Yes a great deal.

12,561 Did they object to your employing non-unionists? – Yes very strongly.

12,564 What followed? – In plain English I was threatened with ruin if I did not . . . [discharge non unionists]. I took the consequences. It ended in a very long law suit.

12,573 As a matter of fact you carried your point? – I did.

12,574 And now you have no further trouble? – They are working better than I have known for several years now.

12,576 Will you explain what is meant by paying 2d per ton per man? – Yes, in this way. We will suppose a steamer is in, or a ship. It is the custom of the port to recognise it as necessary to discharge that there shall be a certain number of men in each gang – whether there are one, two, three or four. This is to say there must be five men to work the coal in the hold and to lift it – three in the hold and two on the deck, or vice versa, according to whether it is at the bottom or the top. Then there must be three men to carry, that makes eight. There must be a weigher; that is nine and a unhooker who stands on the plank and unhooks it after it gets on the men's back. The unhooker is generally a youth or an old man who is past-work and gets half pay. Then 1s 7d a ton is the amount paid on that steamer for discharging into carts or trucks alongside.

12,577 Does that apply to sailing ships too? – Sailing ships are a bit different. Sailing ships discharge less rapidly and they have a rate per day running from 30 to 50 tons on their charter party . . . The crew in that case work the cargo in the hold – that is if there are men enough – if not men are put on to do it at the captain's expense . . . Then I or any other merchant has to provide three men to work and one weigher, for which the captain pays half . . . the weigher.

12,578 . . . One I was discharging yesterday, I was by contract obliged to work not less than 45 tons a day. Therefore every porter engaged on that ship was given 45 twopences a day which was 7s 6d a day.

Mr James Hill called and examined

13,949 You are a steamship owner and coal merchant of Plymouth? – Yes.

13,951 You merely come to speak for yourself? – . . . I only represent my own firm. Of course, we are really opposed to the coal merchants of Plymouth. We are supporters of union labour . . .

13,952 You have contracts for the carrying of coal for use at Devonport, Portsmouth and Chatham Dockyards, for a period extending over 20 years, I understand? – Yes.

13,971 The coal merchants of Plymouth must have made very large profits before you went there? – They seemed to do very well before we went there. They are not making very large profits now . . of course we have special advantages which they have not, as we have our own steamships . . . There is no doubt the Coal Merchants' Association was nothing more than a coal ring, formed for regulating the price of coal, and they had things so much to their own way that they thought they would also regulate the wages of the coal porters and grind them down as much as they possibly could.

Varnier and Treleaven, the former the secretary of the Plymouth Coal Merchants Association and both prominent coal merchants, had been two of the principal opponents of trade unionism in the commercial docks of the town. In 1889 the foundation of the Dock, Wharf and Riverside and General Labourers Union by Ben Tillett, Tom Mann and Tom McCarthy had led to an upsurge in trade unionism in London and provincial ports. This was countered in 1890 by the foundation of the employers' fiercely anti-union Shipping Federation and the formation of 'Free Labour Associations', first in Liverpool and then in other ports.[22] The three unions which were involved in recruiting in Plymouth were the Dockers, the Gasworkers and the Bristol and West of England and South Wales General Labourers Union. The unskilled unions adopted a policy of excluding non-unionists from employment. The hostility of the employers' organisations and the nature of casual employment illustrated in the extracts from the *Royal Commission* made this difficult. In Plymouth success was even more problematical, as there was rapid immigration from Devon's rural areas where there was little tradition of trade unionism and where wages were equally low.

The unskilled dockworkers in the strikes of 1890 relied on mass picketing in disputes. The first occurred in Plymouth in a brief dispute lasting three days at the end of March. At that time the union claimed 800 members, probably an exaggeration. On 20 October Treleaven secured the conviction of Peter Curran before the Plymouth bench for intimidation (this was confirmed by the Recorder of Plymouth, Henry Bompas, but overturned in the High Court by Coleridge LCJ). This raised the temper of feelings and on 29 October a strike began against the employment of non-unionists. The Three Towns Coal Merchants Association decided to support Varnier and Treleaven and announced a payment of 3d per ton, 1d above the customary rate, for the unloading of the *Crystaline, Tullochgorum* and *Harriet Williams*[23] at Polkingsthorne's stores at Sutton Wharf, and decided to form a free labour association. A major confrontation came on 3 November, between 200 strikers and 30 police and an inspector protecting those unloading the vessels. The close organisations of the coal merchants and their recruitment of 'free' labour defeated the strikers, and henceforth known trade unionists were excluded from work. As George Creech, a former union man who became Chairman of the Stevedores of Plymouth and District Free Labour Association, said: 'there was no getting work, and you could not starve or see your wives and children starve'.[24]

James Hill was clearly an exceptional employer in the Plymouth story. However, although he might undermine the monopolistic coal merchants' profits, that was of no help in securing economic justice for their labourers.

Conclusion

In this chapter we have given some examples of the multi-faceted business of shipping in Devon in the nineteenth century. It would easily be possible to give many more. For instance, the working of the system by which vessel property was divided, under the Merchant Shipping Act of 1824, into 64

9.8   This is the scene of the events which led to the case of Tatem *v* Yeo. The entrance to the Richmond Dry Dock is between the crane on the left hand side of this photograph and the white house behind it. The *Georgina* was tied up to the wall under the house with the cupola in the centre of the photograph, astern of the barquentine under repair. This area of mud and sand, now partly filled in, was all that was left of the sheltered bay round which Appledore had grown up. It was here in the 'Parlour' that most of Appledore's shipbuilding and ship repairing activity took place until much of it was taken over, not all of it after due legal process, by the Yeos to build the great dry dock. (*Basil Greenhill*)

shares which were often spread among diverse elements in the population from the master of the vessel through landowners, local professional people, labourers, merchants, farmers, wives and widows, even quarrymen and labourers, could lead to social mobility among the inhabitants of shipping places to a degree impossible in a comparable agricultural or fishing community. Its workings were very complex, since shareholders in a position to do business with the vessel – brokers, bankers, mine-owners, coalfactors, sailmakers, foundrymen, shipbuilders – benefited doubly from their interest. In this and in many other ways the effects of the business of shipping in its broadest sense penetrated deep into the life of Devon and influenced events far beyond the coastal fringe.

This was especially so in the first threequarters of the nineteenth century. Almost inevitably, however, shipping enterprise in Devon tended to wane with the demise of the wooden merchant sailing vessel from the 1870s. Some of those engaged in this many-sided business simply shifted into other industries, while others, like the British branch of the Yeo family, 'daughtered out', as Canadians say, the premature death of William Yeo in 1872 leading to the dissipation of the fortune among numerous descendants. On the other hand, many of the leading shipping families, whose entrepreneurial drive had sustained Devon's maritime enterprise, moved, like the Holmans and the Stevens, to London, Liverpool and other of the major ports. Moreover, those Devonians destined to prosper from industrialisation at sea grasped their opportunity beyond the county of their upbringing. William Reardon Smith, for instance, who once worked as a boy on Yeo's polacca brigantine *Joe Abraham*, migrated to South Wales to found a great steamship line, registering his vessels as of the Port of Bideford even though they were far too large to cross the bar. Likewise, members of the Lamey family of Appledore moved to Liverpool to establish a famous towage company.

Nevertheless, shipping enterprise in Devon did not cease in the 1870s. Of the countless small-scale entrepreneurs, shipowners, shipbuilders, merchants, bankers and agents whose business was in many ways more typical than the substantial enterprises of Holman, Stevens and Yeo, some continued to profit from the ownership and operation of merchant vessels (see Chapters 3 and 4). Indeed, from these ranks of small investors there emerged businesses like those of the Westcotts of Plymouth and the Slades of Appledore, which prospered over two or three generations to become locally significant and influential.[25]

9: *Some Aspects of the Business of Devon Shipping in the Nineteenth Century*

1 Captain Martyn's notebook was made available to Robin Craig by Captain Hugh Ferguson, late Trinity House pilot, St Margaret's Bay.
2 Robin Craig is grateful for help from Mr David M Holman of Holman & Sons Ltd, London; see also D M Bradbeer, *Story of the Manor and Town of Topsham in Devon* (Bracknell, 1968), 42–5.
3 See C N Ponsford, ed., *Shipbuilding on the Exe. The Memoranda Book of Daniel Bishop Davy (1799–1874) of Topsham, Devon* (Exeter, 1988).
4 *Shipping Gazette*, 28 Sep. 1859, gives a list of vessels so fitted.
5 *Shipping Gazette*, 10 Apr. 1855.
6 B Greenhill, *The Merchant Schooners* (4th edn, 1988), 126–7.
7 W J Slade, *Out of Appledore. The Autobiography of a Coasting Shipmaster and Shipowner in the Last Days of Wooden Sailing Ships* (4th edn. 1980), 94–5.
8 For example, *Lady Clive* (1869); *Richmond* (1871); *Mary Anning* (1888); *Eastgate* (1889); *Tynehead* (1890); *Kestor* (1890).
9 Robin Craig is grateful to Mr Michael Stammers and Dr Valerie Burton for making the Stott charter-party books available.
10 See Sheila Marriner, *Rathbones of Liverpool, 1845–73* (Liverpool, 1961).
11 G J S Broomhall & John H Hubback, *Corn Trade Memories* (Liverpool, 1930), 176.
12 E A V Angier, *Fifty Years' Freights, 1869–1919* (1920), 33.
13 G Hamilton Edwards, *Twelve Men of Plymouth* (Plymouth, 1951), 70–5.
14 B Woodcroft, *Alphabetical Index of Patentees of Inventions* (1854, reprinted 1969), 543.
15 *Shipping Gazette*, 19 June 1858.
16 R Craig, 'Printed Guides for Master Mariners as a Source of Productivity Change in Shipping, 1750–1914', *JTH*, third series, III (1982), 32–3.
17 D A Farnie, 'Marshall Stevens', in D J Jeremy, ed., *Dictionary of Business Biography*, V (1986), 312–25.
18 Robin Craig is grateful to Mr Roger Smalldon of Bellamy & Co (Plymouth) Ltd, for making available a copy of the 'Combines' agreement.
19 *Journal of Commerce*, 16 Feb. 1935.
20 *North Devon Journal*, 19 March 1868.
21 *Royal Commission on Labour* (BPP, 1892, XXXVI (2)).
22 J Lovell, *Stevedores and Dockers* (1969), 92–146; J Scheer, *Ben Tillett* (1982), 32–9; J Saville, 'Trade Unions and Free Labour', in A Briggs and J Saville, eds, *Essays in Labour History* (1960), 317–50.
23 Evidently the barque *Crystaline*, built at Chester in 1856, 250 reg. tons, owned in Liverpool in 1890; the brigantine *Tullochgorum*, of Plymouth, built at Kingstone, Moray, in 1867, 157 reg. tons, owned in Port Isaac in 1890; and the schooner *Harriet Williams* of Fowey, built at Burton Stather in 1866, 144 reg. tons, owned in Fowey in 1890.
24 J H Porter, 'The Incidence of Industrial Conflict in Devon, 1869–1900', *DAT*, 116 (1964), 63–75; J H Porter, 'Economic Justice and Freedom of Contract', *Journal of Interdisciplinary Economics* (1986), 155–62.
25 For a detailed account of the history of this Plymouth shipowning and merchant family see I Merry, *The Westcotts and their Times* (1977); for an account of the Slades, see Slade, *Out of Appledore*.

10   *The Emigration Trade in Nineteenth-Century Devon*

MARK BRAYSHAY

Emigration via the Ports of Devon in the Nineteenth Century

BRITAIN'S LONG WAR WITH FRANCE, finally concluded in 1815, broke the continuity of a British emigration movement which had begun to accelerate rapidly in the later eighteenth century. By the 1820s, however, there were already signs that the resumed outflow was about to become a flood which continued, virtually unchecked, for the rest of the century. Although they almost certainly under-record the true scale of the movement, official statistics suggest that more than 15.4 million emigrants left the British Isles between 1815-1901, and that while at least 75 per cent travelled to the United States, significant numbers made their way to destinations in every continent of the world.[1]

The role of the Devon ports in this unprecedented exodus has been somewhat neglected in the literature, being overshadowed by the attention focused on Liverpool, which came to dominate the emigrant trade by the mid-Victorian period.[2] But ships carrying emigrants departed from almost every sizeable British port during the nineteenth century,[3] and the key ports located in both north and south Devon actively shared in the movement to countries throughout the world. Unlike that from Liverpool, however, emigration from Devon's ports was much more heavily weighted towards colonial, rather than foreign destinations. Surviving evidence of departures, though not fully comprehensive (in the Victorian era record-keeping at British ports was notoriously casual), indicates that 434,806 people left Britain via a port in Devon in the period between 1840-1900 (See Table 10.1).[4] Of these, only 1.1 per cent headed for the United States (4,864 people), a further 6.8 per cent travelled to British North America (29,775), and 4.8 per cent (20,962) went to South Africa. However, an overwhelming 86.1 per cent (374,503 people) made their way to the Australian and New Zealand colonies. This pattern of destinations stands in marked contrast to those for both Liverpool and Britain as a whole, where the United States route was supreme, and may in part reflect the geographical location of Devon, which meant that while North West England could best serve the North Atlantic trade, ports in the South West were better placed to meet the demand for passages to the southern hemisphere, especially the Antipodes. In addition, the designation in 1842 of Plymouth as one of the official emigration ports from which those selected for a free or assisted passage to the colonies were directed to depart, inevitably exerted a further influence on the balance of destinations of the emigrants who left via Devon.[5] Moreover, the facilities and arrangements provided in Plymouth to cater for 'government' emigrants undoubtedly helped to stimulate the expansion of privately-funded emigration. Plymouth thereby came to dominate passenger traffic departing from Devon (see Figure 10.1). Indeed, by the mid-1840s the port handled the third largest volume of emigration in the United Kingdom, after Liverpool and London.[6]

Compared with other ports in Devon, Plymouth therefore belonged to the first division in terms of the volume of its passenger traffic and the scope of its emigrant trade. The concentration of emigration agents, passage brokers and passenger ship owners was far larger in Plymouth than in any other port in the county. And the impact within the county of assisted-passage emigration schemes of various kinds was largely confined to Plymouth, but it should nonetheless be emphasised that, for much of the century, and particularly in the mid-Victorian period, privately-financed emigration was

an important feature of the lesser ports in Devon. Although the numbers involved were comparatively insignificant in national terms, the outflow from Devon's small ports represents a special kind of emigration. In marked contrast to those departing via the large United Kingdom ports, the passengers were almost entirely local in origin.[7] Moreover, they were rarely drawn from the truly impoverished classes. On the contrary, they were able to afford the higher fares and thereby benefit from the better standard of accommodation provided on the less-crowded, locally-owned vessels. There was thus a very sharp contrast between the emigration trade of Plymouth and that of other ports in Devon. While Plymouth shared in the large-scale national pattern of emigration, other ports were involved in a more intensely local, and much less regular, participation in the emigrant trade.

Emigration via Plymouth

Information concerning the flow of emigration via Plymouth was collected in a systematic and comprehensive manner only from about 1840 (see Table 10.2). These detailed records begin at a time of marked increase in the volume of movement. British North America remained an important destination (as it was in the eighteenth century), but much larger numbers began to travel to Australia and New Zealand. In addition, the first large groups of emigrants left for Cape Colony, thereby establishing a link which was taken up more emphatically later in the century. Besides these more important destinations, the records for Plymouth also show that between 1840 and 1900 small numbes of emigrants travelled to a strikingly diverse range of places including India, Argentina, the Falkland Islands, Hong Kong and the West Indies. Some 4,000 made their way to the United States, and in both 1849 and 1850, following the gold discoveries in California, a small number even sailed direct from Plymouth to San Francisco via the treacherous seas off Cape Horn.[8]

Table 10.1
Officially recorded emigration from Devon ports, 1840–1900[1]

	Plymouth	Bideford[2]	Dartmouth	Teignmouth	Exeter	Total
United States of America	4,445	284	135	–	–	4,864
British North America	26,660	2,467	342	128	178	29,775
Australian Colonies & New Zealand	374,335	–	168	–	–	374,503
South Africa	20,862	–	100	–	–	20,962
All Other Destinations[3]	4,699	3	–	–	–	4,702
Totals	431,001	2,754	745	128	178	434,806

1 Official emigration totals for individual ports were not published for 1874 and 1875, between the disbandment of the Colonial Land & Emigration Commission and the resumption of publication of full reports by the Board of Trade.
2 The figures for Bideford refer to 1840–56. Thereafter official statistics record no further emigration.
3 Includes the West Indies, India, Hong Kong, Central and South America, and the Falkland Islands.
Note: Until 1853 Torquay came within the port of Dartmouth, thereafter it came under Teignmouth. Barnstaple came within the port of Bideford.
Sources: These figures are drawn from 58 different Parliamentary Papers, including 32 Annual Reports of the Colonial Land & Emigration Commission and 26 Board of Trade Reports on 'immigration and emigration'.

Table 10.2
Officially recorded emigration from Plymouth, 1840–1900

Year	United States of America	British North America	Cape Colony West Africa & Natal	Australian Colonies & New Zealand	Others[1]	Totals
1840	–	176	5	5,128	–	5,309
1841	–	211	–	5,546	9	5,766
1842	–	1,114	–	924	–	2,038
1843	–	769	–	235	–	1,004
1844	19	402	–	92	5	518
1845	–	661	38	79	17	795
1846	–	612	273	1,636	–	2,521
1847	353	1,141	292	3,258	–	5,044
1848	–	996	195	7,314	–	8,505
1849	163	1,171	433	14,106	10	15,883
1850	316	1,033	641	6,218	–	8,208
1851	170	1,761	10	9,206	–	11,147
1852	194	1,512	–	8,117	–	9,823
1853	210	1,495	–	7,659	23	9,387
1854	262	2,701	–	13,454	–	16,417
1855	–	2,026	–	9,012	21	11,059
1856	–	1,673	–	7,207	18	8,898
1857	–	2,805	276	8,779	–	11,860
1858	–	538	156	4,236	–	4,930
1859	–	166	547	2,400	1,011	4,124
1860	–	110	–	3,552	653	4,315
1861	–	129	–	2,477	–	2,606
1862	–	193	3	5,541	–	5,737
1863	–	150	–	7,650	–	7,800
1864	–	139	144	7,019	181	7,483
1865	–	53	99	7,921	7	8,080
1866	–	55	81	4,631	8	4,775
1867	–	43	42	3,981	15	4,081
1868	–	18	88	2,865	–	2,971
1869	13	30	61	4,647	–	4,751
1870	–	–	43	4,835	36	4,914
1871	–	399	22	3,040	142	3,603
1872	–	1,199	–	2,137	121	3,457
1873	–	866	–	4,135	40	5,041
1874 } 1875 }	No Data[2]					
1876	–	37	1,107	11,062	–	12,206
1877	624	–	633	14,596	2	15,855
1878	14	–	371	14,997	7	15,389
1879	–	–	687	15,112	55	15,854
1880	–	–	630	9,676	40	10,346
1881	–	54	1,727	9,351	81	11,213
1882	3	–	1,795	17,658	103	19,559
1883	–	–	710	38,106	95	38,911
1884	823	–	608	16,828	54	18,313
1885	110	93	678	9,894	114	10,889
1886	–	73	819	10,347	106	11,345
1887	–	56	1,159	5,602	191	7,008
1888	–	–	1,164	3,832	228	5,224
1889	–	–	1,483	3,283	175	4,941
1890	–	–	1,374	2,188	229	3,791
1891	–	–	627	1,770	194	2,591
1892	–	–	31	1,793	118	1,942
1893	–	–	60	1,121	90	1,271
1894	–	–	87	1,120	85	1,292
1895	–	–	510	1,179	140	1,829
1896	–	–	426	1,186	73	1,685
1897	–	–	180	1,338	62	1,580
1898	–	–	212	1,003	48	1,263
1899	57	–	139	1,052	48	1,296
1900	1,114	–	196	1,204	44	2,558
Totals	4,445	26,660	20,862	374,335	4,699	431,001

1 Includes Central and South America, the Falkland Islands, Hong Kong, the West Indies and the East Indies.
2 Official emigration totals for individual ports are not available for 1874 and 1875 between the disbandment of the Colonial Land & Emigration Commission and the resumption of publication of full reports by the Board of Trade.

Sources: BPP, *General Reports of the Colonial Land & Emigration Commission*, Appendices, 1842, XXV; 1843, XXIX; 1844, XXXI; 1845, XXVII; 1846, XXIV; 1847, XXXIII; 1847–8, XXVI; 1849, XXII; 1850, XXIII; 1851, XXII; 1852, XVIII; 1852–3, XL; 1854, XXVIII; 1854–5, XVII; 1856, XXIV; 1857, XVI; 1857–8, XXIV; 1859, XIV; 1860, XXIX; 1861, XXII; 1862, XXII; 1863, XV; 1864, XVI; 1865, XVIII; 1866, XVII; 1867, XIX; 1867–8, XVII; 1868–9, XVII; 1870, XVII; 1871, XX, 1872, XVI; 1873, XVIII. BPP, *Reports to the Secretary of the Board of Trade: Accounts & Papers, Emigration and Immigration*, 1874, LXXVI; 1877, LXXXV; 1878 LXXVII; 1878–9, LXXV; 1880, LXXVI; 1881, XCIV; 1882, LXXIV; 1883, LXXVI; 1884, LXXXV; 1884–5, LXXXV; 1886, LXXI; 1887, LXXXIX; 1888, CVII; 1889, LXXXIV; 1890, LXXIX; 1890–1, XCII; 1892, LXXXVIII; 1893–4, CII; 1894, XCIV; 1895, CVII; 1896, XCIII; 1897, XCIX; 1898, CIII; 1899, CVII; 1900, CII; 1901, LXXXVIII.

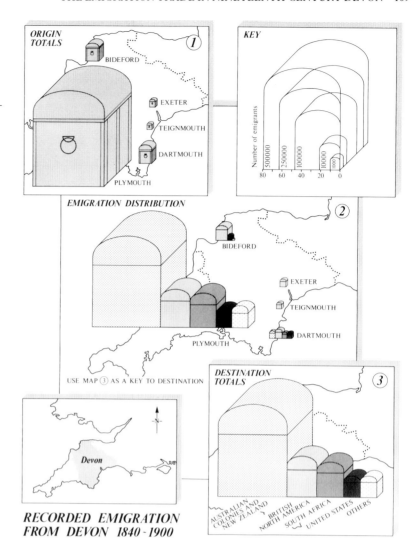

RECORDED EMIGRATION FROM DEVON 1840-1900

10.1 Recorded Emigration from Devon, 1840–1900. (Source: see Table 10.1)

Table 10.2 clearly indicates, however, that the number of people emigrating via Plymouth was subject to considerable fluctuation. These variations may in part be explained by the changing opportunities available in overseas destinations for would-be emigrants. Thus in the 1850s the gold discoveries in New South Wales and Victoria attracted exceptionally large numbers of people to emigrate. In 1861 gold was discovered in New Zealand, and this proved a further attraction. By the early and mid-1870s the Australian governments were actively promoting immigration from Britain because labour was in short supply. In Britain the beginning of the agricultural depression, the collapse of mining in Cornwall and the years of depression in the economy meant that candidates for emigration readily came forward. The outflow peaked in the early 1880s, when Plymouth handled more than half of all passengers going to the Antipodes. By the early 1890s, however, Australia's economic boom collapsed. Assisted emigration was suspended for a time, and the numbers travelling via Plymouth fell sharply. Heavy emigration to British North America occurred in the late 1840s and 1850s. This may similarly be explained in terms of the demands of the colonies. The emigration agents of New Brunswick and Upper Canada both reported that the demand for labour from Britain was acute in that period. Wages were generally higher than at home, and there was a shortage of skilled workers including blacksmiths, wheelwrights, tailors, carpenters and agricultural labourers.

Although, during the nineteenth century as a whole, emigration via Plymouth accounts for only around four per cent of the total United Kingdom outflow, the port's share of the traffic to Australia amounted to almost a quarter. At certain times it was even higher. Equally, though only two per cent of the emigrants bound for British North America departed from Plymouth, in the five-year period between 1853 and 1858, when labour shortages in the Canadian colonies were exceptionally acute, this share temporarily leapt to more than 10 per cent. Emigration flows from Plymouth thus represent a complex of responses to conditions both at home and abroad, as well as to the official policies of assistance or encouragement which were pursued at any particular time.

Emigration via Other Ports in Devon

Emigration from five other departure points in Devon was also separately recorded in the official statistics published from 1840 onwards. These comprise Bideford, Dartmouth, Teignmouth, Exeter and Torquay. But departures from Barnstaple were subsumed in those recorded for Bideford, while emigrants leaving directly from Torquay are hidden in the figures for Dartmouth until 1853, and in those for Teignmouth thereafter.[9] Despite such complications it is still reasonable to assume that, after Plymouth, Bideford ranked as the county's second most active emigration port (see Table 10.3). Thus, in the period of its peak activity, between 1840–56, at least 2,754 people left Britain via Bideford, the majority heading for a destination in the British North American colonies.

Table 10.3
Officially recorded emigration from Bideford, 1840–56

Year	United States of America	Canada[1]	Prince Edward Island	Destination New Brunswick	Nova Scotia	Central & South America	Totals
1841⎱ 1842⎰	216	384	–	–	–	–	600
1843	53	468	–	–	–	–	521
1844	15	72	48	–	–	–	135
1845	–	109	75	–	–	–	184
1846	–	119	75	7	–	–	201
1847	–	24	16	–	–	–	40
1848	–	7	5	–	8	–	20
1849	–	176	15	–	–	–	191
1850	–	94	17	9	–	3	123
1851	–	222	24	–	–	–	246
1852	–	221	19	–	–	–	240
1853	–	161	29	–	–	–	190
1854	–	–	1	–	–	–	1
1855	–	23	23	–	–	–	46
1856	–	–	16	–	–	–	16
Totals	284	2,080	363	16	8	3	2,754

[1] This column includes all destinations in British North America before 1844.

Sources: BPP, *General Reports of the Colonial Land & Emigration Commission*, Appendices, 1842, XXV; 1843, XXIX; 1844, XXXI; 1845, XXVII; 1846, XXIV; 1847, XXXIII; 1847–8, XXVI; 1849, XXII; 1850, XXIII; 1851, XXII; 1852, XVIII; 1852–3, XL; 1854, XXVIII; 1854–5, XVII; 1856, XXIV; 1857, XVI.

Vessels leaving from Dartmouth, Teignmouth, Torquay and Exeter also tended to be bound for Canada, particularly those sailing during the first half of the century, but the numbers involved were comparatively small and, in any case, these ports do not feature regularly in the annual returns made by the emigration officers and the officers of customs stationed in Devon. Emigration to South Africa via Dartmouth appears to have become significant during the last quarter of the century, but unfortunately from 1877 the Board of Trade emigration statistics combine the returns for Dartmouth with those of Plymouth.[10]

There were, of course, some vessels originating in London which called at ports in South Devon to embark additional emigrants. While those who joined government-chartered vessels first despatched from London do seem to have been carefully recorded, it is not safe to assume that every 'pick-up' passenger embarking on a private emigrant ship was properly noted by the authorities, and the true volume of emigration from Devon's lesser ports in the nineteenth century cannot be accurately established without more local studies of the kind carried out by Bouquet and by Greenhill. By the 1860s, however, the volume of emigration they handled had dramatically declined.

Large steam-driven vessels were by this time increasingly taking a share of the emigrant trade and, in Devon, only Plymouth offered facilities sufficient to cater for this new breed of passenger shipping.

Access to Emigrant Ports in Devon

While most emigrants departing from the smaller ports of Devon were drawn from the immediate locality, those who embarked in Plymouth, and to a lesser extent in Bideford and Dartmouth, often came from much further afield. They would doubtless have recognised the distinct geographical advantage to be gained by departing from a location in Devon rather than from a port located further east. This fact was certainly stressed both by the compilers of local directories and by emigration brokers based in the county: 'The loss of time consequent upon embarking in the River Thames, or any other port higher up the Channel is avoided as well as the dangers, discomfort and annoyances of a Channel passage – often the worst part of the entire journey'.[11]

Plymouth, it seems, was regarded as particularly well placed: 'It frequently happens that ships sailing from the Thames exceed a fortnight (oftentimes much more) in their passage to Plymouth; a serious delay is also occasioned to ships sailing from Southampton or other ports less favourably situated than Plymouth'.[12] But Bideford also claimed an advantage: 'Passengers find this a very desirable port to start from the western shores, and it is remarkable that no accident has happened to any of the ships which have left Bideford with emigrants during the last twenty years'.[13]

By the late 1840s intending emigrants could travel to South Devon by railway. The Plymouth terminus at Millbay opened in April 1849. Passengers belonging to the 'lower orders' (travelling third class) were permitted on only three of the ten trains running daily on the South Devon Railway, and emigrants in particular were accorded only the most grudging welcome by the company.[14] As late as 1936 the rule book of the Great Western still stipulated:

> . . .it is imperative that all carriages used for the conveyance of foreign emigrants should be thoroughly disinfected after the journey is completed and before the vehicles are utilised for other traffic . . .this applies not only to foreign emigrants travelling in large numbers, but also to small parties for whom one or more compartments are reserved. In the latter case it is essential that any small number should not be allowed to mix with ordinary passengers.[15]

Notwithstanding these somewhat discriminatory attitudes, certain categories of emigrant could obtain free rail travel to their port of departure. Paupers sent out to the colonies at parochial or union expense travelled free to Plymouth and, in particularly needy cases, ordinary families sometimes received a pre-paid railway warrant made available by one of several emigration charities.[16]

It was, of course, possible to reach all the emigration ports of Devon by means of road transport, and also by the regular packet boats which plied coastal waters. Bideford, for example, had a twice-weekly service to Bristol, while Plymouth had equally frequent links with London, Falmouth, Southampton, Cork and Dublin. By the mid-1850s there were additional weekly sailings to Liverpool and services to Portsmouth, Bristol, the Channel Islands and some French ports.[17] Irish emigrants travelling to the colonies on assisted or free passages via Plymouth were provided with a free steamboat passage from either Dublin or Cork on the first leg of their journey.[18]

Passage Brokers and Devon-based Shipping Lines

Devon's large shipping community inevitably encouraged the establishment of numerous emigration agents, or brokers, and many of these were listed in the local trade directories and newspapers. One of the most respected and enduring of these agencies was that of James B Wilcocks, who had offices in Plymouth's Barbican[19](see Fig. 10.2).

White's Directory of 1850 lists seven established emigration agencies in Plymouth alone, including not only Wilcocks, but also Collier & Son (Southside Street), William Henry Foulds (Marine Place), Fox & Sons

(Hoegate Street), S C Johnson (Parade), Luscombe Driscoll & Co (Vauxhall Street), and J Walker (Parade Wharf).[20] Inland towns also often had a local emigration agent, such as Edmund Turner of Tavistock, or William Tepper of South Molton.[21] These agents sold 'contract' tickets to privately-funded emigrants. It was usual for the agent to collect a brokerage fee of 12.5 per cent on the passages he sold on behalf of the shipowner or emigration line.[22] Agents not only advertised the availability of passages, but also provided an advice service to intending emigrants on matters such as the length of the voyage, the clothing and other items that a traveller might require and the conditions to be expected in the country of destination.[23]

Local agents in Devon sold passages on vessels of all kinds, including not only those operated as packets by the large emigration companies such as the Eagle Line or the Black Ball Line, which had interests in the larger United Kingdom ports, but also the less-regular sailings of ships which belonged to Devon owners.[24] With James Wilcocks and William Henry Foulds also acting as agents for government-assisted emigration, there was therefore a very considerable body of locally-based expertise and experience in the emigration trade. Even so, the majority of ships carrying emigrants from the ports of Devon, whether temporarily chartered and fitted for the conveyance of emigrants or regularly engaged in passenger transport, tended to be based elsewhere in Britain and not in the South West. Thus a return made to the

House of Commons in 1852 makes it clear that ships departing from Plymouth were predominantly vessels en route from London (see Table 10.4)[25] This concentration of ownership of emigrant vessels in London was explained by the Colonial Office in a letter in 1853: 'Ships carrying emigrants carry also a considerable quantity of cargo and they are therefore obtainable most cheaply at the great ports where the trade with the colonies to which they are proceeding is normally carried on'.[26] Moreover, as steamships came to dominate the emigrant trade during the latter half of the nineteenth century, the share of total shipping despatched from Devon which was locally-owned further declined.

The Plymouth-based shipowners identified in Table 10.4 were typically small-scale businessmen owning perhaps three or four vessels which were, from time to time, taken up and temporarily fitted for the purpose of carrying emigrants. Refits of cargo vessels carried out elsewhere were often criticised as inadequate and crude, but the Plymouth owners seem to have maintained relatively high standards and to have enjoyed a favourable local reputation. Much the same may be said of other Devon shipowners engaged in the emigrant trade. Richard Heard of Bideford, for example, operated 'four first-class emigrant ships . . . sailing to America'.[27] John Crossman of Torquay used his empty cargo vessels, the *Margaret* and the *Sarah Fleming*, to convey emigrants to Quebec in the 1840s and 1850s in relative comfort.[28] Equally, Ambrose and Isaac Nichols of Plymouth could boast more than a decade in the emigrant trade by 1848, during which period they had conveyed '3,323 souls to Quebec . . . out of whom not ten . . . had died on

Table 10.4
Emigrant vessels departing from Plymouth, 1 Jan–15 June, 1852

Name of Ship	Owner	Registered tonnage	Total crew	Number of emigrants
Plymouth-based owners				
John	Rawle	464	17	194
Spermaceti	Nichols	412	16	157
Queen Victoria	Pope	634	18	50
Oriental	Rawle	713	21	216
Rose	Nichols	643	22	273
Dahlia	Pope	650	19	82
Lady Peel	Nichols	567	21	235
Carshalton Park	Hocking	441	17	107
Totals		4,524	151	1,314
Owners based elsewhere				
Success	Phillips & Co	621	27	11 (220)
Anglia	Prowse	570	26	2 (311)
Duke of Cornwall	Eyles	580	22	49 (113)
Euphrates	Tindall	557	32	15 (119)
Surge	Phillips & Co	543	22	118 (101)
Phoebe Dunbar	Dunbar	704	32	229 (52)
Maria Somes	Messrs Somes	785	31	194 (88)
London	Teighe & Co	611	34	182 (105)
Fortitude	Tindall	608	31	28 (106)
Mary Harrison	Harrison	780	31	6 (207)
Raleigh	Booth & Co	491	23	71 (93)
Chowringhee	Hay	893	39	252 (84)
Mount Stewart	Chapmans	611	30	87 (87)
Asiatic	Middlesex Dock Co	954	40	13 (146)
Chatham	Messrs Somes	470	25	119 (116)
Emma Eugenia	Wade Campbell	383	20	86 (115)
Sir Robert Sale	Gladstones & Co	741	37	125 (191)
Argyle	De Wolf	584	29	173 (83)
Bengal Merchant	Haviside & Co	503	27	34 (127)
Lady McDonald	Elder	678	39	133 (159)
Gipsy Queen	Kilt & Co	839	38	18 (88)
Dalhousie	Allan	754	34	17 (243)
Saladin	R & J Henderson	856	37	18 (63)
Totals		15,116	706	1,980

Notes: Figures in brackets refer to emigrants embarked already at Deptford. The *Nestor*, the *Caroline Agnes* and the *Standard* also departed from Plymouth in the six-month period (having first cleared out of London). Together they carried a further 336 Plymouth passengers, but details of ownership, tonnage and crew were omitted from the return presented to the House of Commons.

The Plymouth-based owners were J Pope of 14 Gibbon Street (he also owned the *Geelong*, which sailed from Liverpool in this period with 136 emigrants), Philip Rawle of 8 Portland Villas, R Hocking & Son of Newport Street (Stonehouse), and Isaac Nichols of Coxside.

Source: *Accounts and Papers* (BPP, 1852, XLIX, c.542). *Emigrant Ships*, A Return Made to the House of Commons.

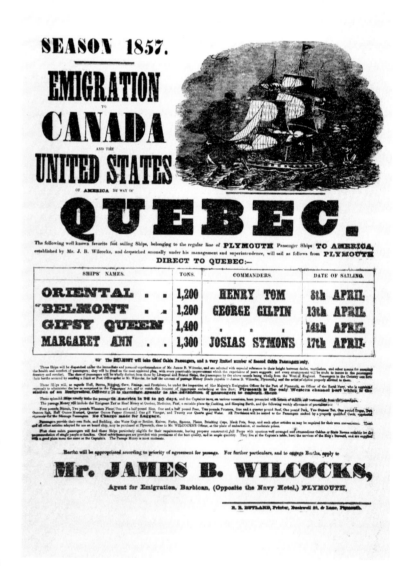

10.2 An emigration poster, 1857.

the passage'.[29] The Nichols' line comprised just 'three very fine ships . . . as well appointed and equipped as can possibly be for the conveyance of emigrants'. The fact that such assurances were given at all indicates that not all emigrant vessels offered similarly good standards of accommodation. High levels of demand encouraged unscrupulous owners to make hasty and inadequate conversions of the cargo decks of their ships, thereby offering 'steerage' passages in overcrowded, insanitary and ill-ventilated conditions.[30] To guard against the worst abuses, a series of increasingly restrictive Passengers Acts were added to the statute book between 1828-55, and emigration officers were appointed to serve in the busiest ports, with responsibility to inspect departing vessels and to ensure compliance with the Acts.[31] But while conditions for cabin passengers may always have been tolerable, for most of the nineteenth century those who travelled in steerage endured cramped and disagreeable berthing arrangements. There was no privacy, scarcely any furniture and only rudimentary sanitation. But emigrants drawn from the working class population of Victorian towns and villages were well-used to living conditions comparable with those they encountered on board the usual sailing vessel taken up for the conveyance of emigrants. Were it not for their background, surely few could have so cheerfully endured months at sea, cooped up in such inferior accommodation.

Competition on the Liverpool-New York route had caused a very marked reduction in the cost of a steerage passage by the mid-nineteenth century, when a contract ticket could be obtained for as little as £3 10s.[32] In sharp contrast, however, the passage from Plymouth to Cape Colony was likely to cost more than £30 and, in 1852, *Cassell's Emigrants Handbook* indicates that £15 was needed to secure the least-expensive berth on the steerage deck of a ship travelling to Australia. Cabin passengers could expect to pay as much as £90.[33] Children under fourteen were generally permitted to travel for half the adult fare, and infants were carried free, but even so the cost of family emigration to the colonies was often beyond the pockets of ordinary working-class people in Britain. For this reason the prospect of emigration to the United States was always more attractive. The journey time, at less than a month, was considerably shorter than that to the Antipodes, which usually involved a trip lasting three or four months, and the opportunities were, in any case, widely considered to be superior in America.[34] But in the nineteenth century successive colonial secretaries considered it desirable to divert some of the emigrants away from the United States (which was, after all, a *foreign* destination) and to encourage them to settle instead in Imperial territory. However, it was recognised that, in order to attract sufficient numbers of emigrants to the colonies, some form of assisted passage would be required.

The Development of Government Assisted Emigration to the Colonies

The development of Britain's vast Empire in a way which mutually benefited the individual colonies as well as Britain herself clearly depended heavily upon its settlement by hardworking, reliable emigrants. There was also a widespread belief that emigration could alleviate some of the pressure of a rapidly growing population and the threat of unemployment and unrest at home. Moreover, the colonies were a huge potential market for British manufactured goods, and they offered the eventual prospect of cheap agricultural imports to the mother country. The problem, therefore, was one of inducing more potential emigrants to opt for the colonies, rather than the United States.

For years British governments, however, drew back from any official initiatives in the emigration field. It could, after all, prove an expensive burden on the home taxpayer and there was always the risk of failure which could seriously discourage the flow of further would-be emigrants. The real obstacle was that no one had yet devised a self-financing scheme of emigration.[35] In the 1820s a limited attempt was made to arrange for the emigration of paupers financed by borrowing on the security of the parochial poor rates, but it was not until clauses enabling parishes to fund the emigration of workhouse inmates were included in the Poor Law Amendment Act of 1834 that any significant pauper emigration began.[36] The numbers involved were never large, though such emigration did then continue for much of the rest of the century.[37]

In the 1830s a new solution to the problem of assisting emigration to the colonies was proposed by Edward Gibbon Wakefield, who argued that the existing system of granting away colonial lands to almost anyone prepared to organise their settlement militated against their successful development. Instead, he suggested a policy whereby British overseas crown territories should be *sold* and the revenues raised should be used to finance large-scale assisted emigration from Britain.[38] Wakefield's proposals, attractive because of their simplicity and cheapness, speedily changed official minds, and in 1831 the British Government ruled in favour of selling land in the Empire rather than granting it away free. In fact it was already too late to do much to rectify the situation in Canada, where the reckless alienation of land had left little to sell, and in 1841 the remaining Crown Lands were placed in the hands of the new Canadian government. So it was to other parts of her Empire that Britain began to assist emigrants on the proceeds of the sale of land. In 1837 T F Elliot was appointed as the first Agent General for emigration.[39] Although Elliot's primary role was the collection and distribution of information and the administration of the terms of the Passenger Acts, he also organised the first large-scale programme of assisted emigration to New South Wales. Arrangements were formalised still further in 1840 with the appointment of the Colonial Land & Emigration Commission.[40] Significantly, Plymouth-born Frederic Rogers was selected

10.3 Thomas Chanter's brig *Lord Ramsey*, built in Quebec in 1832. She carried hundreds of emigrants across the North Atlantic in the 1830s and 1840s and her master, Richard England, received many presentations of silver from grateful passengers. Seen here in a painting by Nicholas S Cammillieri of Malta, she was the last vessel in which Thomas Chanter held shares. (*Private Collection*)

in 1847 to serve on the three-man Commission, and his appointment may in part help to explain the importance later accorded to Plymouth as a key government emigration port.[41]

Until 1872, when the Merchant Shipping Act transferred most of the Commissioners' powers to the Board of Trade and the Crown Agents, this group of rather anonymous civil servants, operating from their cramped office in Park Street, Westminster, on a shoestring budget, acted as the executive link between the various colonial administrations and Her Majesty's government in all matters relating to the sale of Imperial territory to British subjects and its settlement by expatriate countrymen.[42]

Plymouth's Emigration Depot on Baltic Wharf

The port of Plymouth had been involved in privately-organised schemes of assisted emigration for at least five years before the Colonial Land & Emigration Commissioners were appointed. The shipowner John Marshall, for example, had devised his so-called 'bounty-order' emigration project in 1835 to assist colonists in New Zealand, Australia and South Africa to obtain the labour they needed from Britain. Under the scheme it was possible to nominate specific types of worker and to purchase bounty orders to assist their emigration. Marshall then undertook to select and ship suitable emigrants. Bounty emigration was well established in Plymouth and Southampton by the later 1830s.[43] After 1835 Plymouth also became engaged in emigration to the newly-formed State of South Australia, sponsored by the 'Wakefield' group which had set up the South Australia Company.[44] Travel costs were met by reselling, at a set price of 12s per acre, those lands already purchased *en bloc* by the Company. Four years later the New Zealand Company was formed along very similar lines, and the first party of settlers sailed from Plymouth to Auckland that same year. In January 1840 a group of local merchants then formed the Plymouth Company of New Zealand, with the object of purchasing land specifically for the settlement of emigrants from Devon and Cornwall. Several sailings conveyed more than 800 West Country settlers to land located around New Plymouth on New Zealand's North Island.[45]

Thus, in 1842, when the Government began to consider the acceleration of their official programme of assisted emigration, Plymouth already possessed both the experience and facilities to deal with a large outflow of passengers. Indeed, when in 1835 the old Lambhay Victualling Yard was vacated by the Ordnance Board,[46] the buildings at the southern end of the complex were acquired by John Marshall and converted for use as an emigrants' hostel or depot and thereafter used to accommodate both privately-funded and assisted emigrants awaiting embarkation.[47] The census of 1841 affords us one brief glimpse of Marshall's Baltic Wharf depot in use for this purpose, when some 267 emigrants (all from Ireland) were enumerated there just before sailing.[48]

Within two years of their appointment, the Colonial Land & Emigration Commissioners had hired a depot located in Deptford to accommodate assisted emigrants directed to embark in the Thames. At the same time, tenders were sought for a similar establishment in Plymouth. John Marshall immediately offered his Baltic Wharf premises at the rate of 1s 6d per day for each emigrant over fourteen and 1s 0d for all those below that age.[49] On 22 February 1842 Stephen Walcott, Secretary to the Commissioners, wrote to accept Marshall's terms, and in March the first group of government emigrants lodged in the depot before boarding the *Orleana*, which was chartered to sail to Van Dieman's Land (Tasmania).[50] By the end of the year Marshall's receipts totalled £118 11s 0d, but his contract with the commissioners was not renewed until 1846.[51] Thereafter, however, apart from a brief period in the early 1860s when premises in Stonehouse were temporarily hired during a measles epidemic, the Baltic Wharf depot was in continuous use until the Emigration Commission was dissolved in 1876.[52] Even then, colonial agents continued to lodge emigrants in the building until it was finally closed in 1890.[53]

In giving evidence to the Parliamentary Select Committee on the Passenger Acts in 1851, Frederick Marshall (who had become owner of the depot four years earlier) reported that his premises were licensed to accommodate 650 emigrants and that there were separate sleeping quarters for married couples with young children (under fourteen), for single women and for single men. The depot was hired on an annual contract running from 1 July - 30 June and was, by then, exclusively employed for government emigrants.[54] In 1851 Marshall's charges had increased to 2s 0d per head for the first three days in the depot and 1s 6d for each subsequent day.[55] In return, the Commissioners stipulated that the waiting emigrants were to receive three good meals a day according to a prescribed dietary scale. Notwithstanding the fact that his premises had not been hired between 1843-5, in a little over a decade Marshall received £18,737 7s 2d from the Emigration Commissioners for the board and lodging of government emigrants in his Plymouth depot.[56]

There were no fixed baths in the depot, although there was a large washroom and a sick bay. In 1848, when the risk of cholera loomed large in Britain and outbreaks of typhus had claimed many lives on board private emigrant ships travelling to New York, the Government Emigration Officer in Plymouth was asked to report on the hygiene arrangements in the Baltic Wharf depot. His reply was emphatic:

> I beg to inform you that I consider the Government Depot at this port to possess every facility for washing the emigrants and for purifying their clothes . . . On the arrival of emigrants before any are permitted to enter the eating or sleeping apartments, [they] are first obliged to strip off their clothing and to undergo a thorough cleansing with soap and water.

All of the emigrant's boxes were then carefully examined and their clothes were well washed and dried, while those thought to be infested with fleas and lice received special attention: 'should there be the slightest reason for suspicion there are ovens where a thorough purification would be effected by baking'.[57]

In fact the health record of the depot remained good throughout the period of heavy emigration in the wake of the Irish potato famine, and in 1852 Lt Carew told a health inquiry that during his five years as Emigration Officer in Plymouth there had been only 25 deaths in the depot. At a rough estimate this amounts to a mortality rate of only 0.6 per thousand – a remarkably low figure in the circumstances.[58] Billing's *Directory of Plymouth* (1857) described the depot as 'a spacious building with 700 places, commanding a fine view of the Sound'.[59] By the 1880s the available accommodation had been increased to 900 places as the result of extensions and improvements. In 1883, in response to the massive expansion of the emigrant trade, Arthur Hill of Reading, who then owned the premises, carried out still further extensions when adjacent buildings were acquired and adapted.[60] However, just seven years later, when the flow of emigrants was greatly diminished, the depot was closed, although the buildings were not finally demolished until the 1930s, when the Madeira road was extended[61] (Fig. 10.4).

Rivalry with Bristol, Southampton and Birkenhead

There can be little doubt that official government emigration brought significant economic benefits to Plymouth. Apart from the sums paid by the commissioners for the accommodation of emigrants in the depot, those waiting to depart could be expected to buy for themselves a range of personal items of clothing and food from local traders.[62] Indeed, the commissioners recommended that emigrants purchase an 'outfit' for their long voyage which included, for males, 'two complete sets of exterior clothing, six shirts, six pairs of stockings and two pairs of shoes'. Women were advised to take 'six shifts, two flannel petticoats, six pairs of stockings, two pairs of shoes and two gowns'. In addition, government emigrants were told that they would need three sheets for each berth on board ship as well as four towels and 2lb of marine soap for each person.[63] Not all assisted emigrants possessed funds sufficient to procure such a list of items, but in Plymouth there were several charitable organisations which made available small grants to needy families about to travel to the colonies.[64] The Kelsall Fund, for example, allocated £3,000 per year for this purpose divided equally between Plymouth, Liverpool and Southampton.[65] The British Ladies Female Emigration Society also made small allowances, although its chief contribution was in supplying items of haberdashery to occupy female

10.4   The Plymouth Emigration Depot on Baltic Wharf. This photograph was taken in the 1930s prior to the demolition of the quayside buildings to accommodate Madeira Road. The group of buildings in the centre foreground comprised the depot. (*Pat Lay, Queanbayan, New South Wales*)

emigrants on their long overseas voyage.[66] Thus waiting emigrants could clearly be expected to generate considerable local business in addition to the contracts for victualling the ships themselves. Indeed, the trade as a whole brought valuable profits and employment to the town which rival ports became increasingly anxious to share.

As early as 1848 the Colonial Secretary was approached about establishing another government depot, in Liverpool, to accommodate assisted emigrants en route for Canada.[67] Premises were eventually found in Birkenhead, and a depot was opened there in June 1851.[68] Meanwhile both Bristol and Southampton tried hard to persuade the Emigration Commissioners of the advantages to be gained by transferring the trade to their ports and away from Plymouth.[69] Bristol's case was weaker. Private emigration from the port was by now greatly diminished, with the inevitable result that the chartering of vessels was relatively expensive. There was, moreover, no real advantage for ships 'cleared out' either in London or Liverpool embarking additional emigrants in Bristol. Its application in 1854 was emphatically rejected.[70]

By contrast, the bid made in 1850 on behalf of Southampton was much more of a threat to Plymouth. The London & South Western Railway Company announced its willingness not only to transport emigrants from London to Southampton on very favourable terms, but also to make available the disused terminal buildings at Nine Elms as a collecting depot where emigrants could be assembled before going down to the port to embark.[71] Although initially rejected, the Southampton bid was submitted a second time in 1851, when all the contracts for government depots were up for renewal.[72] For a time there was a real chance that all operations in Plymouth would be transferred to Southampton. In the event, however, it was the Deptford depot which lost its contract to Southampton in 1852.

Plymouth therefore retained its government contract in spite of these challenges, and by early 1853 ships chartered in London embarked their first consignment of passengers in Southampton before making their way to the Sound to collect the remainder. One reason for retaining this two-centre operation was to allow time to cope with the unpredictable problem of 'defaulters'. Approved emigrants notified that a place was reserved for them on board an emigrant ship sometimes failed to turn up at the depot, and occasionally the number 'defaulting' in this way could climb as high as 35

per cent of the available places.[73] By embarking some emigrants in Southampton and requiring the rest to assemble in Plymouth to await the ship's arrival from the Solent, it was possible to ascertain the precise number of spare places. Any shortfall could then be remedied by the Commissioners' recruiting agents, who were called upon to make urgent searches for further eligible candidates prepared to go at very short notice. Frequently this task rested upon James Wilcocks of Plymouth, who scoured the West Country for last-minute emigrants in order to fill the Commissioners' ships.[74] He employed almost 50 sub-agents who shared his commission, and there can be little doubt that his activities in part account for the disproportionately heavy levels of emigration from Devon and Cornwall compared with other English counties in the mid-Victorian period.[75] Wilcocks was probably the busiest and most well-known emigration agent in Britain. He corresponded directly with colonial governments, with the emigration commissioners and with the Colonial Secretary himself. His offices on Plymouth's Barbican were at the centre of a business spread throughout Devon and Cornwall, and as early as 1847 Wilcocks' agency swallowed up more than half of the sum paid that year to all the selecting agents on the Commissioners' payroll in Britain (see Fig. 10.5).

The Plymouth Operations of the Colonial Land & Emigration Commission

Ultimate local responsibility for the Plymouth operations of the Colonial Land & Emigration Commission rested, as in other key ports in Britain, with the Emigration Officer.[76] The first officer appointed in Plymouth was Lt S H Hemmans, who transferred from Greenock in 1843[77] (see Table 10.5). He received an annual salary of £208 5s 0d plus half his navy pay. No emigration officer was appointed to any other port in Devon. The officer was provided with facilities in the Customs House in the Parade, and his main duties included the issue of certificates of clearance to emigrant vessels after an inspection to ascertain their standard of general seaworthiness, passenger accommodation, victualling (up to the minimum scale required by the Passenger Acts), crew and the stowing of any cargo. He was also required to muster and inspect the emigrants themselves to ensure that the ship was not overcrowded and that there was no sickness on board.[78]

Table 10.5
Government emigration agents in Plymouth

Appointed

1843	Lt S H Hemmans, RN
	Transferred from Greenock, Dismissed 1847
1847	Lt Timothy Carew, RN
	Resigned 1855
1855	Capt C E Patey, RN
	Retired 1858
1858	Cdr J L R Stoll, RN
	Retired 1875, promoted to Rear Admiral
1875	Civilian agent appointed

Sources: PRO, *Emigration, Original Correspondence*, CO 384/80, ff. 98–101; *Land & Emigration Commission Papers*, CO 386/118, f. 228; CO 386/2, f. 108; *Western Daily Mercury*, 25 Jan. 1877.

A Despatching Agent to deal expressly with government-chartered ships was not engaged in Plymouth until 1848. Until then, a member of the Commission's staff was sent down to Devon to deal with each departure. This system worked quite well while the amount of government emigration remained small, but when the scale of activity began to increase sharply in 1846–47 a permanent local appointment was needed, and the following year James Wilcocks was engaged. There is later evidence to show, however, that William Foulds subsequently took over. The salary was set at £200 per year, plus an allowance for clerical assistance at the rate of £1 per ship. The despatching agent was responsible for procuring supplies for the emigrants and for overseeing their accommodation in Plymouth and on board ship. He arranged for the payment of harbour dues and for the hire of rowing boats to take emigrants out to the vessels anchored in the Sound or the Cattewater (see Fig. 10.6), and once on board he was required to muster and check the embarkation orders of all the passengers about to sail.[79]

Likely candidates for assisted or free passages were brought to the attention of the Commissioners by a nationwide network of Selecting Agents, who received a remuneration consisting of 2.5 per cent on all land sales transacted, a fee of £1 for each married couple, and seven shillings for each single adult selected for a free passage. Each agent was assigned a strictly-defined area and his fees were meant to cover all of his costs including advertisements (the wording having been approved by the Commission).[80] More prominent agents such as James Wilcocks, who sold private contract tickets as well as acting as a 'selector' on behalf of the Commissioners, were kept abreast of the needs of the colonies by receiving local newspapers direct from the colonies as well as copies of the various 'employment gazettes'.[81] By 1865 agents could expect ten shillings for single women and might get fifteen for certain categories of servant recruited for New South Wales, Victoria and Western Australia.[82]

On arrival at the depot, the emigrants would be irretrievably caught up in a tide of bureaucracy which would end only after their disembarkation in the colony several months later. Their feeling of bewilderment and apprehension as they waited in Plymouth for their ship to arrive can only be guessed. Many families had left their native village or town for the first time, and most would have realised that they were unlikely ever to return. If their ship was due to sail first from London or Southampton, they could face a wait of as much as two weeks in the Baltic Wharf depot. By February 1853 the commissioners had arranged for the appointment of a chaplain in each of their embarkation ports, and doubtless he afforded some comfort and reassurance to the waiting emigrants.[83] In May of the same year the services of a local medical practitioner were secured to attend at the depot, and representatives of various local emigration charities also called in to offer help and advice.[84] James Wilcocks would undoubtedly have visited the emigrants. He had personally arranged the passages of many of them. Once the ship arrived in the Sound, the Emigration Officer would embark the passengers after carrying out his inspection to ensure full compliance with the terms of the charter party. Fig. 10.7 shows part of the charter party of the *Agincourt* which sailed from Plymouth to Adelaide at 5 o'clock on 18 October 1849.

Who Were the Emigrants?

Although the lesser ports of Devon undoubtedly drew the majority of their emigrants from a relatively confined, local hinterland, those leaving via Plymouth were always more cosmopolitan in origin. Tables published in the *General Reports of the Colonial Land & Emigration Commission* categorise all United Kingdom emigrants according to nationality (English, Scottish, Irish or Foreign), but separate listings by port of departure are only provided for the period between 1855–72. For Devon, only the departures from Plymouth are tabulated. Nevertheless, these statistics do indicate that only 56.6 per cent of Plymouth's emigrants were from England & Wales, 5.6 per cent were from Scotland and 33.8 per cent were Irish. The remaining 4 per cent include both foreigners and British emigrants whose origin was not reported (see Table 10.6). The importance of Irish emigrants leaving via Plymouth is noteworthy. Indeed, in the eight-year period 1846–53 – a period of great distress in Ireland following the famine – some 26,166 assisted-passage Irish emigrants passed through the Baltic Wharf depot, accounting for 50.6 per cent of all assisted emigrants despatched by the commissioners in that period.[85]

It may be confidently assumed that the group classed in the table as from England and Wales was dominated by emigrants from Cornwall, Devon, Somerset and Dorset. This assumption is based on a study of 14,415 emigrants arriving in South Australia between 1857–67.[86] Of these, some 902 (6.3%) were from Devon, 5,577 (38.7%) from Cornwall, 1,006 (7.0%) from Somerset and 198 (1.4%) from Dorset. The combined total accounted for by these four West Country counties therefore amounted to 7,683 people, or 53.3 per cent. Moreover, since the figures include some shiploads sailing directly from London or Liverpool, it may be supposed that were it possible to focus attention only on those vessels which had sailed from a port in Devon, the dominance of West Country emigrants would be even more pronounced.

The Emigration of Special Groups

While the great mass of emigrants departing from Britain via a port in Devon during the nineteenth century were ordinary working-class people travelling steerage, there were in addition several categories of passenger who were accorded special assistance and facilities.[87] Foremost amongst these, of course, were the 'cabin passengers' who could afford the limited supply of better accommodation on board ship, and who were often drawn from the ranks of professionals and businessmen. At the opposite end of the social

No. 5.

AMOUNT paid to SELECTING AGENTS.

1847.

	£.	s.	d.		£.	s.	d.
Brickman, Mr. C.	3	10	–	Morris, Mr. Charles	6	15	–
Bromley, Mr.	1	10	–	Newman, Mr. James	17	–	–
Brown, Mr. John	3	–	–	Reynolds, Mr. C. B.	3	–	–
Bull, Mr. Humphrey	114	–	–	Roberts, Mr. William	7	5	–
Chew, Mr. Thomas	1	10	–	Ross, Mr. Edward	–	10	–
Denniston, Mr. John	3	–	–	Sergeant, Mr. Joseph	1	10	–
Duckham, Mr. A. B.	11	15	–	Smedley, Mr. Joseph	1	10	–
Ellis, Mr. Samuel	363	5	–	Smith, Mr. J. E.	2	–	–
Ennals, Mr. William	15	10	–	Strange, Mr. John	16	5	–
Geake, Mr.	39	15	–	Wilcocks, Mr. J. B.	797	15	–
Holt, Mr.	17	–	–	Winchcombe, Mr. John	–	15	–
Horsfall, Mr. I. T.	6	–	–	Withers, Mr. Frederic	21	10	–
Ibbs, Mr. C. W.	55	15	–	Wood, Mr. Thomas	2	15	–
Johnson, Mr. Josias	6	15	–				
Kelly, Mr.	56	–	–	£.	1,592	–	–
Moore, Mr. Charles	15	5	–				

10.5 Commission paid to selecting agents employed by the Colonial Land & Emigration Commission in 1847. James Wilcocks, the Plymouth agent, already earned the largest fee. (BPP, 1849, XXXVIII, 'Returns of expenses at each of the depots . . . for the reception of emigrants')

10.6 Emigrant ships leaving the Cattewater, Plymouth, *c*1855, from a watercolour by John Callow (1822–78). (*City of Plymouth Museums and Art Gallery*)

Table 10.6
Nationality of emigrants departing via Plymouth, 1855–72

Year	English & Welsh	Scottish	Irish	Other	Not distinguished	Total
1855	5,391	198	4,929	–	541	11,059
1856	6,390	144	2,003	4	357	8,898
1857	7,862	315	3,370	2	311	11,860
1858	3,169	125	1,432	–	204	4,930
1859	2,010	253	1,532	3	326	4,124
1860	1,746	479	1,462	–	628	4,315
1861	1,081	300	699	5	521	2,606
1862	2,262	350	2,540	–	585	5,737
1863	3,406	410	3,508	4	472	7,800
1864	3,568	492	3,375	48	–	7,483
1865	5,588	795	1,677	20	–	8,080
1866	2,392	637	1,736	10	–	4,775
1867	2,169	305	1,585	22	–	4,081
1868	1,543	180	1,233	15	–	2,971
1869	2,814	250	1,630	57	–	4,751
1870	3,088	274	1,518	34	–	4,914
1871	2,492	262	822	27	–	3,603
1872	2,706	153	563	35	–	3,457
Totals	59,677 (56.6%)	5,922 (5.6%)	35,614 (33.8%)	286 (0.3%)	3,945 (3.7%)	105,444

Sources: BPP, *General Reports of the Colonial Land & Emigration Commission*, Appendices, 1856, XXIV; 1857, XVI; 1857–8, XXIV; 1859, XIV; 1860, XXIX; 1861, XXII; 1862, XXII; 1863, XV; 1864, XVI; 1865, XVIII; 1866, XVII; 1867, XIX; 1867–8, XVII; 1868–9, XVII; 1870, XVII; 1871, XX; 1872, XVI; 1873, XVIII.

Table 10.7
Poor-Law assisted emigrants arriving in Quebec from a port in Devon, 1844

Vessel	Port of departure	Date	Number of paupers
Rainbow	Plymouth	26 May 1844	40
St Anne	Plymouth	13 June 1844	64
Marion	Bideford	11 July 1844	8
St George	Plymouth	17 July 1844	118
Cairo	Plymouth	8 Aug 1844	183
Total			405

Source: PRO, *Poor Law Emigration, Correspondence*, MH 19/22, f.1871a, Stuart Walcott to Edwin Chadwick, 14 Feb. 1845.

scale were the inmates of union workhouses or the families of transported convicts, who were berthed in the usual 'tween decks bunks.

Of all the special groups of assisted emigrants, those drawn from the nation's workhouses were undoubtedly the most significant. In the early 1840s small numbers were despatched to Quebec in government-chartered ships on passages pre-paid out of the poor rates. Thus in 1841 some 1,058 were reported to have arrived in Canada, including many who had sailed either from Plymouth or Bideford.[88] By 1844 even larger schemes of pauper emigration both to Quebec and to New South Wales were in operation (see Table 10.7). Then, in the wake of the Irish famine, the British Destitution Relief Fund Committee was formed to raise money to assist the emigration of female orphans to South Australia, where there was a great demand for female domestic servants.[89] Candidates travelled to Plymouth by steam packet and then embarked on emigrant ships bound for Adelaide. The first group of 221 girls arrived in October 1848. Newton Abbot Union was one of many which actively urged the promotion of workhouse emigration at this

time, and many South Devon girls travelled by the *Eliza* and the *Diana* from Plymouth in 1850.[90]

The use of the Australian colonies of New South Wales and Tasmania as penal settlements since the end of the eighteenth century posed special difficulties for those who later wished to promote the development of a prosperous and well-balanced Antipodean community. Transported convicts, frequently guilty of only relatively minor misdemeanours, were predominantly young adult males who had been brutally torn from their families.[91] Few would have been really hardened criminals, but their enforced single status, and the lack of any prospect of finding a marriage partner in a population where males outnumbered females by seven to one, made ex-convicts footloose and disaffected. Recognising these problems, the British government developed a programme to assist the families of ex-convicts to emigrate to Australia at public expense. The cost was met, not from the Crown Land fund, but directly by the British government through the annual Treasury 'Transportation Vote'.[92] Large numbers of 'convict families' sailed on government-chartered ships departing from Plymouth. Among them were Devon families who made an application for a passage. Thus in 1849 the family of Richard Wakeham applied from Modbury for a passage to join him in Van Dieman's land, where he had been transported five years before on board the *Equestrian*. Wakeham's relatives were sent out by the *Success* in June that year. By the 1860s well over half of the Treasury Vote for convict transportation was being employed to send out 'convict families', rather than felons.

A rather different group of citizens was offered the opportunity to emigrate at public expense in a scheme devised in the late 1860s. These were 'discharged' artisans and mechanics who had been employed in the Royal Dockyards of Chatham, Portsmouth and Devonport, as well as in the Woolwich Arsenal.[93] In exchange for surrendering their pension entitlement, such ex-employees were offered a free passage to the colonies with their families.[94] Working through the British and Colonial Emigration Society, the Admiralty financed the scheme and despatched volunteer

10.7   The charter party of the *Agincourt*, 1849.

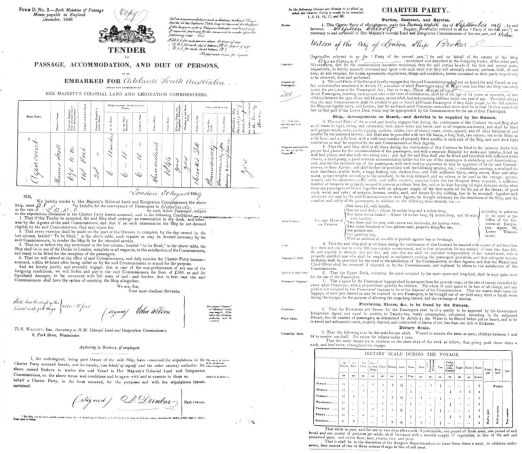

candidates on board troop ships. The first of these sailed from Portsmouth in 1868 with 390 dockyard pensioners and their families. In May a second group left on board the *Serapis*, which embarked additional passengers in Plymouth. Thereafter the same offer was made to 'ex-day-pay' labourers, and Devonport families of both categories were then despatched to Canada in the *Simoon*, the *Tamar* and the *Crocodile* in 1871 and 1872.

Conclusion

This paper has sought to indicate that the role of Devon, and particularly of Plymouth, in overseas emigration during the nineteenth century deserves rather more attention than it has previously received. Quite apart from the very large numbers of people who travelled privately via Devon, the activities of the Colonial Land & Emigration Commission in Plymouth undoubtedly made it one of Britain's premier passenger ports. But the pattern of destinations of those travelling via a port in Devon differs markedly from that of Britain as a whole. The colonial emphasis was much stronger, and only a minority travelled to the United States or other foreign destinations. Plymouth was a major port of departure for Irish emigrants travelling to Australia and paupers assisted to go to both Canada and the Antipodes. Moreover, as the last major port of call for government-chartered vessels, Plymouth's agents were often called upon to fill places left empty in the commissioners' ships by last-minute defaulters who failed to embark in London or Southampton, by recruiting extra emigrants from the local area, thereby ensuring that Devon and Cornwall people were always well-represented in the outflow to the colonies. Because of its dominance in the emigration trade of the county, the characteristics of the outflow from Plymouth do tend to distort our general picture of the county's overall nineteenth-century passenger movement. Emigration from the lesser ports was not only much smaller in its scale of operation, but also tended to cater only for a very restricted catchment area. In Plymouth, by contrast, a large and sophisticated infrastructure was gradually developed for handling the emigration trade which brought substantial economic benefits to the local community. Links with Australia and Canada were forged which have remained remarkably strong ever since, and although virtually all visible trace of emigration activities have now been removed, in Victorian times it represented a busy and flourishing aspect of maritime activity in Devon.

10: *The Emigration Trade in Nineteenth-Century Devon*

Research for this contribution undertaken in London and South Australia was aided by a personal grant from the British Academy, for which I am grateful. Thanks are also due to Mr Brian Rogers, who drew the figures.

1 W A Carrothers, *Emigration from the British Isles* (2nd edn, 1965), 1–3, 23–31, 61–89. N M Carrier and J R Jeffery, *External Migration: A Study of Available Statistics* (1953), ch.3.

2 T A Coleman, *Passage to America* (1972). M L Hansen, *The Atlantic Migration 1607–1860: A History of the Continuing Settlement of the United States* (Cambridge, Mass., 1940; reprinted 1951). M A Jones, *Destination America* (1976).

3 See, for example: *General Report of the Colonial Land and Emigration Commissioners* (BPP, 1852, XVIII (2), Appendix 1, 74–6).

4 This total is derived from data presented in 58 Parliamentary Reports presented by the Emigration Commissioners (1842–73) and the Board of Trade (1876–1901). See also D V Glass and P A M Taylor, *Population and Emigration* (Dublin, 1976), 89.

5 PRO, Land and Emigration Commission Papers, CO 386/29, f.98 and f.168.

6 See for example, *Sixth General Report of the Colonial Land and Emigration Commissioners* (BPP, 1846, XXIV, Appendix 1, 68).

7 See, M Bouquet, 'Passengers from Torquay: Emigration to North Amerrrica, 1849–59', in H E S Fisher, ed., *Ports and Shipping in the South-West* (Exeter, 1971) 131–48. A Grant, *Sailing Ships & Emigrants in Victorian Times* (1972).

8 W White, *History, Gazetteer and Directory of Devonshire* (Sheffield, 1850), 649.

9 See Bouquet 'Passengers from Torquay', 144.

10 *Accounts and Papers* (BPP, 1878, LXXVII, 10).

11 M Billing, *Billing's Directory and Gazetteer of Plymouth, Stonehouse and Devonport*, (Birmingham, 1857), 9.

12 Billing, *Directory and Gazetteer*, 10.

13 White, *History, Gazetteer and Directory*, 757–8.

14 D St John Thomas, *A Regional History of the Railways*, I, *The West Country* (Newton Abbot, 4th edn, 1973), 62.

15 *Great Western Railway: General Appendix to the Rule Book* (1936), 'Coaches Requiring to be Disinfected', 309. The Great Western acquired the South Devon's line in 1876.

16 Public Record Office of South Australia, Adelaide (hereafter, PROSA) GRG/55 Series 4, Newlands to Walters, 8 Aug. 1862.

17 G Flintoff, *Flintoff's Directory and Guidebook to Plymouth, Devonport and Stonehouse* (Plymouth, 1844), 25. See also, White, *History, Gazetteer and Directory*,

766; J W Elvins, *Directory of Plymouth, Stonehouse, Devonport, Stoke and Morice Town* (Plymouth, 1862), 243.

18 *Emigrant Ships Select Committee: First Report* (BPP, 1854, XIII) *Minutes of Evidence* QQ. 1530, 1577, 4906, 4930. See also, PRO, CO 386/118, ff.72–3, Murdoch & Wood to Merivale, 29 April 1854.

19 J Thomas, *Thomas's Directory* (Plymouth, 1836), 107. This lists James B Wilcocks as a solicitor residing in Princess Square, Plymouth; F Brendon, *A Directory of Plymouth, Stonehouse, Devonport, Stoke and Morice Town* (Plymouth, 1852), 95 and 240, lists James Wilcocks as a 'Government Emigration Agent' with offices at 15 Barbican, and resident at 82 Navy Row, Stoke.

20 White, *History, Gazetteer and Directory*, 672.

21 *Tavistock Gazette*, 18 Nov. 1859. See also, *Post Office Directory of Devonshire* (1856), 197 and 289.

22 See, for example, Advertisements in *Salisbury & Wiltshire Herald*, 12 Aug. 1842. Also, *Immigration Correspondence, Papers Ordered to be Printed*, South Australian Parliamentary Papers (hereafter SAPP), 1865, I, 34.

23 PROSA, Emigration Agent Correspondence, EA/367, 10 Feb. 1865, Walters to Hon. Commissioner for Crown Lands and Immigration.

24 For example, Edmund Turner of Tavistock was agent for the Black Ball line and for the Eagle line sailing out of Liverpool.

25 The majority of locally-owned ships were relatively small. See, R S Craig, 'Ship-owning in the South West in its National Context, 1800–1914', in H E S Fisher and W E Minchinton, eds, *Transport and Shipowning in the West Country* (Exeter, 1973), 39.

26 PRO, CO 386/71, Murdoch & Rogers to Merivale, 23 July 1853.

27 White, *History, Gazetteer and Directory*, 757.

28 Bouquet, 'Passengers from Torquay', 135.

29 PRO, CO 386/81, 437–8. A & I Nichols to Earl Grey, 27 March 1848.

30 *Emigrant Ships Select Committee: First Report* (BPP, 1854, XIII), *Minutes of Evidence*, *QQ*. 493–4, 618, 3728. See also, B Greenhill and A Giffard, *Travelling by Sea in the Nineteenth Century* (1972), 11–24.

31 PRO, Register of Private Letters from Sir Frederic Rogers, 1852–60. CO 386/120, Rogers to Capt Patey, RN, 30 Aug. 1855.

32 Coleman, *Passage to America*, 22–3.

33 T Tegg, *Tegg's Handbook for Emigrants* (Glasgow, 1839) 82; J Cassell, *Cassell's Emigrant's Handbook* (1852), 17.

34 P Taylor, *The Distant Magnet: European Emigration to the United States* (1971). See also, M A Jones, *American Immigration* (Chicago, 1960).

35 H I Cowan, *British Emigration to British North America* (Toronto, 1961), 68–80, describes some of the early schemes to assist destitute Irish and Scottish crofters to emigrate to Canada.

36 Carrothers, *Emigration from the British Isles*, 52–7.

37 Glass and Taylor, *Population and Emigration*, 78–9. See also, PRO, Poor Law Emigration, MH 19/22, 1836–76.

38 E Gibbon Wakefield, *Art of Colonisation* (1849); see also, G Sutherland, *The South Australia Company* (1898).

39 *Report from the Agent-General for Emigration to the Secretary of State for the Colonies* (BPP, 1837–8, XL, 388).

40 *Commission Appointing Several Colonial Land and Emigration Commissioners* (BPP, 1840, XXXIII, 3), 24 Jan. 1840; See also, F H Hitchins, *The Colonial Land and Emigration Commission* (Philadelphia, 1931), ch.3.

41 PRO, Emigration, Original Correspondence, CO 384/80, f.137, Feb. 1847.

42 See *Seventeenth General Report of the Colonial Land and Emigration Commissioners* (BPP, 1857, XVI, 49). Between 1850–6 the Commissioners received 500,790 letters and despatched another 503,558. In 1849 the total Treasury vote funding their operations amounted to £13,554 5s 0d. PRO, CO 386/56, ff. 128–41, Murdoch, Wood and Rogers to Merivale, 12 Feb. 1849.

43 Carrothers, *Emigration from the British Isles*, 105. See also, *Correspondence between the Colonial Office and the Authorities in the Colonies relating to Emigration* (BPP, 1842, XXXI).

44 Sutherland, *South Australia Company*, 18. See also, R M Gibbs, *A History of South Australia* (Kent Town, SA, 2nd edn, 1984), 21–30.

45 See, J S Marais, *The Colonisation of New Zealand* (1927).

46 *Report of the Select Committee on the Passengers' Act* (BPP, 1851, XIX), *Minutes of Evidence*, Q. 3936.

47 See, M Brayshay, 'Government Assisted Emigration from Plymouth in the Nineteenth Century' *DAT*, 112(1980), 185–213; also M Brayshay, 'Manpower for Britain's Empire', *History Today*, 32 (1982), 41–5.

48 PRO, Census Enumerators Books, HO 107/270 2/12, Emigrant Depot, Commercial Wharf. Sometimes the name Commercial Wharf is applied to the three wharves: Baltic, Phoenix and Commercial.

49 PRO, CO 386/29, f.99, Walcott to Alger, 16 Feb. 1842.

50 PRO, CO 386/29, f.168, Walcott to Marshall, 21 Feb. 1842.

51 PRO, CO 386/118, f. 73. 'Depots employed . . . for the reception of emigrants sent out by Colonial funds'.

52 PRO, CO 386/119, f. 520, Murdoch to Herbert, 3 April 1876.

53 Eyre Bros, *Port Office Directory of Plymouth, Devonport and Stonehouse* (1890), 73, 222.

54 *Report of the Select Committee on the Passengers' Act* (BPP, 1851, XIX), *Minutes of Evidence*, Q. 4007.

55 *Returns relative to tenders for board and lodging emigrants and emigrant depots* (BPP, 1851, XL, 20–1).

56 PRO, CO 386/118, f.73.

57 PRO, CO 384/81, ff. 76–7, Carew to Walcott, 1 April 1848.

58 See, R Rawlinson, *Report to the General Board of Health on a Preliminary Enquiry into the Sewerage, Drainage and Supply of Water, and the Sanitary Condition of the Inhabitants of the Borough of Plymouth* (Plymouth, 1852).

59 Billing, *Directory of Plymouth*, 9.

60 'Plymouth Emigration Depot', *Western Daily Mercury*, 10 March 1883.

61 C Gill, *Sutton Harbour* (Plymouth, 2nd edn, 1976), 45.

62 Suggestions were made, for example, in the advice sections of *The Emigrants Penny Magazine* 1(4, 1850), 93; Cassell, *Emigrants Handbook* 65. See also, PRO, Colonisation Circular, CO 384/79, 456.

63 PRO, MH 19/22 f.7674. See also, *Regulations for the Selection of Emigrants and Conditions on which Passages are Granted* (South Australia Council Papers, hereafter SACP, 1854, 21), 5–9.

64 See, *Papers ordered to be printed* (SACP, 1, 1852), Atchison to Sir John Packington re: Family Colonization Loan Society, 10 Nov. 1851; also (SAPP, 1854, 21, 8). The South Australian British Destitution Relief Fund was set up in 1847.

65 PROSA, GRG 55, Series 4, Newlands to Walters, 8 Aug. 1862.

66 PRO, CO 386/118, f.233.

67 PRO, CO 384/81, f. 150, Earl Grey to Emigration Commissioners, 9 Sept. 1848.

68 *Report of the Select Committee on the Passengers' Act* (BPP, 1851, XIX), *Minutes of Evidence*, Q. 3936.

69 Brayshay, 'Assisted Emigration from Plymouth', 204.

70 *Application from the Authorities at Bristol that Bristol should be made a Government Emigration Port* (BPP, 1854–5, XVII, 523).

71 PRO, CO 384/86, f.16. 'Memorial from the Town Council of Southampton', 20 Dec. 1850.

72 *Returns relative to tenders for board and lodging emigrants and emigrant depots* (BPP, 1851, XL, 25–31).

73 See, *Return showing the number of emigrants summoned, the percentage of defaulters, and the detention consequent thereon for the last four ships despatched by the Commissioners* (SAPP, 1859, II, 52), Moorhouse to Dutton, 16 Aug. 1858.

74 *Immigration Correspondence* (SAPP, 1859, II, 59), Dutton to Dashwood, 8 Nov. 1858.

75 *Papers ordered to be printed: Immigration* (SAPP, 1858, I, 8–9), Walcott to the Hon. Commissioner for Crown Lands and Immigration, 9 Feb. 1858. See also, *Correspondence on Emigration* (SAPP, 1865, XXXIV), Walcott to Walters, 15 Feb. 1865; *Immigration Correspondence* (SAPP, 1858, I, 18), 'List of Selecting Agents'.

76 *Reports, Accounts and Papers Relating to Emigration* (BPP, 1854, XLVI, 255).

77 PRO, CO 384/80, f.90, Emigration Commissioners to Colonial Secretary, 27 Feb. 1847.

78 PRO, CO 384/80, f.101, Hemmans to Walcott, 9 Feb. 1847.

79 PRO, CO 384/84, Commissioners to Merivale, 5 Jan. 1849.

80 PROSA, Correspondence on Emigration, EA 367, Walters to H M Hon. Commissioner for Crown Lands and Immigration, 10 Feb. 1865. *Immigration Correspondence* (SAPP, 1865, 34), Newlands to Walters, 25 Feb. 1865.

81 *Monthly Labour Market Reports* (SAPP, 1862, II, 26).

82 PROSA, EA 367, Walcott to Walters, 15 Feb. 1865.

83 PRO, CO 386/118, f.233.

84 PRO, CO 386/117, f.215.

85 PRO, CO 386/118, f.73.

86 These statistics were gathered during a recent study visit to South Australia.

87 Greenhill and Giffard, *Travelling by Sea*, 14–15.

88 PRO, MH 19/22, f.270, Walcott to Chadwick, 17 March 1842.

89 PRO, MH 19/22, 1 Sept. 1848.

90 PRO, Register of Ships Chartered by the Colonial Land and Emigration Commissioners, 1847–75, CO 386/179, 4–6.

91 G Sherrington, *Australia's Immigrants* (Sydney, 1980), 23–9.

92 PRO, CO 386/72, f.144, Murdoch to Rogers, 27 Nov. 1860.

93 *Twenty-ninth General Report of the Colonial Land and Emigration Commissioners* (BPP, 1868–9, XVII, 40), 'Emigration of discharged artizans and mechanics from HM Dockyards'.

94 *Thirty-first General Report of the Colonial Land and Emigration Commissioners* (BPP, 1871, XX, 4), 'Emigration of commuted pensioners from HM Dockyards'.

11 Emigration – The Human Dimension

Ann Giffard

The terrible travelling conditions which faced Irish emigrants from Liverpool to North America in the mid-nineteenth century, particularly during the famine years of the 1840s, were not encountered by westcountrymen sailing from the ports of Bideford and Barnstaple. Here the crews often contained members of the same local families and the vessels themselves were well known, locally owned and regarded with affection. Psychologically emigration was probably not such a desperate problem as it was to those Irish who were forcibly shipped out by their landlords. As the *North Devon Journal* put it in 1831: 'Many of those persons who had thus expatriated themselves are respectable farmers and their families carry with them very considerable property'.[1]

Westcountrymen had fished in North American coastal waters since the late sixteenth century. They were therefore already familiar with North Atlantic waters and now in the nineteenth century vessels arrived year after year laden with timber from Canada, bringing with them news of relatives who had settled in the New World. James Ellis, writing from Monkleigh in 1845 to his uncle in Prince Edward Island, describes the situation of many:

I am thinking of trying America as there is nothing here to look to for a living for the inhabitants is so thick and Labour is so dead there is nothing going on . . . an if ever I come to America I think it will be next Summer for I am thinking then to take a wife an after people get settled it is a great Difficulty of removing again . . . the young woman I intend to make my wife has got a brother on the Island an he is Doing very well.[2]

Even people from inland villages who came to Bideford and Barnstaple on market days were familiar with the sailing vessels at the quays, whose comings and goings were always noted in the local papers. The barques *Devonia*, *Secret* and *Civility*, owned by Richard Heard of Bideford, were described as:

very substantial and fast sailing Ships, [they] carry experienced Commanders, are very roomy in the twixt decks, and can afford accommodation (in each Vessel) for about Ten Cabin Passengers. A more desirable opportunity for individuals and families about to emigrate cannot be offered, as only a limited number of passengers will be taken in each Vessel, which will very much increase the comfort of the passengers.[3]

11.1 These coasters alongside Bideford Quay, c1860, and other deepwater vessels were familiar to the people from the inland villages who visited the town on market day. (*Postcard*)

11.2 One fact alone made possible the cheap passages of vast numbers of emigrants. This was the arrival in England of vessels laden with timber from Canada. This photograph shows the 'tween decks of a timber ship with a partially stowed cargo of squared timber. There are no known photographs of accommodation in an emigrant vessel, but this one shows the space in which their bunks and benches would be built. On the return voyage to England it would once again be filled with timber. (*Nottman Collection*)

These timber vessels would have returned to North America almost empty, and berths were therefore available at a very reasonable price.

Because two contemporary accounts of Atlantic crossings by emigrants from North Devon are extant, it is possible to form a very vivid idea of the communal life and routine of these little vessels during the mid-nineteenth century. William Fulford of Southwood House, Buckland Brewer, boarded *Civility*, barque, 247 tons, together with his brother Bat, Bat's wife Prudence and their children, Edward, known as Ned, and 'little Alice'. The now fading pages of 'Uncle Billie's' Journal, closely-written in a small red-bound notebook, are to be found in the Barnstaple Athenaeum. The family

> left Bideford Quay at 7 o'clock in the morning and sail'd down the River to Appledore opposite Graysand Hills and cast anchor for the night where I had to bid farewell to all my dear Relatives and to give vent to my natural and painful feelings and to uncomfortable an inconveniences of domestic life, attending on Board a Vessel. At 8 o'ck at night me and brother Bat and wife and children retired to our berths to rest, all in good health. Thank God for it, but I did not sleep all the night.

The *Civility* might make two crossings of the Atlantic in each direction (as indeed she did in this year of 1848, when she left Plymouth for the second round trip on 8 August). It was of great advantage to the emigrant to take

the earliest voyage so that he allowed himself the maximum time to settle in before the beginning of the North American winter of ice and snow. *Civility* was built in 1842 at Vernon river, PEI, by Thomas Richards for George Heard of Charlottetown, PEI, but in May 1843 she was transferred to Bideford, England, to Richard Heard, who owned her until 1852, when he sold her for use as a collier in Hartlepool. Her register was closed in 1857 and there is no indication of her eventual fate.

William Gliddon, a young man from Barnstaple, whose log was published in *The Mercantile Gazette* for August and September 1855 by F Searle, Barnstaple, left home seven years later at the same season of the year as Uncle Billie. If the two journals are read in parallel, the day-to-day incidents seem as routine as a crossing from London Heathrow to Montreal is today. He was travelling in the full-rigged ship *Ocean Queen*, 630 tons. She also was built in Prince Edward Island, but in 1845 at New Bideford by William Ellis for James Yeo, a weekly carrier from Kilkhampton who had emigrated in 1819 and later became a merchant, landowner, banker and powerful politician. Yeo's story is told in Chapter 9, and more fully in *Westcountrymen in Prince Edward's Isle*.[4] *Ocean Queen* continued to trade until she was found abandoned on 19 May 1865, having sprung a leak on a passage from Newport with coal for Halifax, Nova Scotia. In 1855 almost her entire crew were North Devon men from Appledore, Braunton, Northam and Clovelly,

11.3 Buckland Brewer. William Fulford lived at 'Southwood', midway up the street on the lefthand side. (*M F Snetzler*)

11.4 'Today we have been visited by about 500 people who have came on board to see the ship that is intended to carry us across the wide Atlantic . . .'. This harvest jug commemorates the *Ocean Queen* and is witness to the pride and interest taken in the locally-owned vessel. (*Bideford Museum*)

many of them closely related and none over forty years of age.

William Gliddon described his feelings as he set out:

We boarded the ship on Saturday March 31st 1855, between 4 and 5pm. Our first attention was to get the boxes arranged and lashed, and our beds made. There is something novel in making preparations for a home on board ship to those who have always been accustomed to land. It was a lovely evening, the moon shining brightly on the water, and in the distance was a large fire, caused by the burning of the gorse on Sandown End, forming a beautiful scene, such as could not be seen on shore. About 11 o'clock we turned in, with the idea of trying to sleep on the water for the first time in our new bedrooms, but we were all in too good humour to sleep, and jokes passed freely round amid shouts of laughter till near daylight.

Sunday, April 1st: Today we have been visited by about 500 people who came on board to see the ship that is intended to carry us across the wide Atlantic, and to take their last farewell, previous to our leaving our native land.

It was customary for the owner to see to the safe departure of his vessel:

Thursday the 6th: At 7 o'clock Mr Heard came on board and gave orders to the Captain to go over the Bar, also the Custom House Officers and Pilotmen came on Board, and while they were performing their offices and hauling the anchors we had breakfast on our temporary table, viz on our chest and box, and to despatch it as quickly as possible.

(W F, *Civility*)

Monday, 2nd: About half past four we got under way with a good breeze, having on board a fine crew of twenty, Mr Yeo (the owner) [this was James Yeo's son, William, who lived in Appledore and was his English agent], the pilot, 22 passengers, a pig, a cat, and a dog. Half past five, the pilot has taken us safe over the Bar, and he and the owner took leave amid the cheers of all on board.

(W G, *Ocean Queen*)

But William Gliddon's euphoria was quickly over:

The weather is beginning to look dirty: the wind is freshening and the sea is rising. Passengers are beginning to look queer and to 'shoot the cat'. We are just abreast of Lundy, and I am compelled to go below myself. There is a great difference between the first night on board ship and the first night at sea,

Tuesday, 3rd: Strong breeze. I am confined to my bed and doing all in my power to turn my inside out.

Wednesday, 4th: Strong breezes, still very sick, but I have managed to creep on deck for about an hour. We are now on the broad Atlantic with nothing but water and birds to look at. It is a grand sight to see the sea rolling so high and the ship riding it so gracefully.

Thursday, 5th: Weather a little more moderate. I am able today to keep a little biscuit and coffee inside me. We sick folk have experienced great kindness from the steward, who has tended us with coffee, etc., during our sickness.

Uncle Billie and his fellow passengers in the *Civility* also retired to their berths, 'to throw up the contents of the stomach' as soon as they were over the Bar. But by next day he was 'quite freed from seasickness and not in the least giddy in my head. I believe that my remedy was by drinking a little best brandy yesterday.' However, the experience made such an impression on him that on Sunday, when 'the Captain gave orders to all the passengers that possibly could to come on Deck and assemble themselves together in front of the Cabin to unite in the service of Almighty God,' he read them the 107th Psalm, which begins 'They that go down to the sea in ships'. It contains a vivid description of seasickness: 'They mount up to heaven, they go down again to the depths: their soul is melted because of trouble. They reel to and fro, and stagger like a drunken man, and are at their wit's end.'

The Fulfords of Buckland Brewer were keen Wesleyans, and Uncle Billie throughout the voyage encouraged the Captain to conduct Divine Service on Sundays, got 'a blessing while changing the tracts and talking to those that read them', made friends with a Miss Crealock of Littleham, a Wesleyan member and cabin passenger, with whom he read and conversed on religious subjects on Sunday afternoons, and held prayer meetings every evening at

11.5 'Our water is delivered every morning and this morning it was taken from a treacle cask and it stinked aloud and we were obliged to use it with pepermint for tea and with vinegar to drink . . .'. Emigrants collecting boiled drinking water. (Illustrated London News)

7. On one of these occasions one feels he enjoyed 'the painful necessity of reproving the disorderly conduct of some persons, and their sinful conversation was hushed into silence and attention'.

Uncle Billie's amusements were on the solemn side but at least one prayer meeting turned into 'a general Consort' at which he 'pitched and led the tunes' whilst Bat and children and all followed. 'So many of the sailors as can conveniently assemble and unite with us'. Young William Gliddon was more light-hearted, and, as soon as he got his sea-legs, he recorded:

We have plenty of amusement on deck today in the shape of chess etc., and plenty of singing every day from the sailors; they sing every two hours, when they pump the ship out. It makes one laugh to hear some of their songs:
   And now my boys we're outward bound,
    Young girls go a-weeping;
   We're outward bound to Quebec Town,
    Across the Western Ocean.
We have had a complete merrymaking below tonight, a sort of return of our first night's spree.

(*Ocean Queen* – 5 April)

The Fulford family and William Gliddon were all travelling steerage, and the space in which they were to live for six weeks would be filled with timber on the return passage to England. Uncle Billie with fifty-five fellow passengers in the smaller vessel would have been very cramped for space. Their living quarters were damp and unheated; the creaking of a wooden vessel, the rattling of the rigging, the flapping of the sails, the sound of the sailors' feet as they worked the vessel, even in the small hours, meant that there was almost constant noise. After two weeks at sea, Uncle Billie remembered:

11.6 'This fore noon whilst myself and several passengers were in the cabin the Capt. kindly took out and pricked off every day's work, that we might see the course we have made.' (Illustrated London News)

He states later that:

> . . . on Monday and Thursday Mornings Our Provision is Delivered to us from the store-room by the steward and our water every morning and this morning it was taken from a treacle cask and it stinked aloud and we were obliged to use it with pepermint for Tea and with Vinegar to drink and boil dry peas in it for Dinner with onions and peper and Sallery together and do the best.
>
> (*Civility* – 1 May)

Sometimes the bad water was augmented by 'soft rainey water from the clouds'. Fresh food was abundant on the Banks of Newfoundland:

> One of our sailors with a hook and line caught a large codfish, 17¾lbs and cut it in pieces and divided it among the Passengers.
>
> (*Civility* – 6 May).

Other methods of obtaining it were not so legitimate:

> . . . passed by a French Vessel laying at anchor as they were A Fishing; and their mode of fishing is this they have a long line perhaps 3 miles long in length with hooks tied on every fathom, and A weight to each and to sink it. Also a line at one end to come to the surface of the water, with A Buoy so that they may find it again and their Buoy pole standing Upright with a little Flag on top . . . so just as we were past the Vessel we saw the little flag; then the Sailors for Mischief and fun would go and take up the line, so they let down the Boat from our vessel and got along side of their lines and took what they could but they could not take one Quarter of them as our Vessel would be out of sight, as the Mist was so ful. The Frenchmen could not see our sailors at their wickedness so what they left of the lines was no use to the poor Frenchmen for they destroyed the Buoy . . .
>
> (*Civility* – 8 May)

Relationships between the passengers and crews of the *Civility* and the *Ocean Queen* were excellent. It was like life in a commune, and all were busy. William Gliddon learned about ships' signals and the meaning of different flags. He played draughts with Captain Dart and:

> This fore noon whilst myself and several passengers were in the cabin the Capt. kindly took out the chart and pricked off every day's work, that we might see the course we have made, from the evening we sailed up to this morning. It is one of the prettiest courses imaginable: East, West, North, and South; backwards and forwards so that we have sailed more miles than would have fetched America, instead of which we are only 1,200 from Lundy and 1,750 from Quebec.
>
> (*Ocean Queen* – 27 April)

Distinctions were blurred and, although they were travelling steerage:

> Myself, Bat, Prudence and the children thus far on the voyage have been accommodated in the Day time in the Cabin, and little Alice is become the pet with the Cabin Passengers and many times taken dinner with them. She has become the pet of her Uncle John, the Captain, and Richard the Capt's Mate and Edward Bale the Cook and Steward and most of the sailors . . . She can walk on the top Deck, from the Steerage to the bough sprit, and the leeward to the windward side of the vessel equal to any on board and climb Ladders up and down the hatchways.
>
> (*Civility* – 14 April)

Goodwill was reciprocated:

> . . . as there are 56 passengers, ten of them under the age of 14 years and four infants, the Captain desired of me to collect all the children that were fit for tuition and teach them to read and spell in the cabin for two or three hours a day. I readily consented to do so.
>
> (*Civility* – 18 April)

the value of good bread and the Western Wells water at Buckland Brewer . . . To every person that would prove and Estimate the Excellency an Value of the priveliges and Comforts of Domestic Life in Sleeping or Wakeing in Wearing eating or drinking must first engage encounter Suffer and endure the Privations attendin on A Sea Voyage and Surely they will in most Respects prove the Sea Voyage to be Not Desirable, for myself Bat Prudence the Children and all the Passengers on Board I believe have proved it.

> (*Civility* – 20 April)

He describes the passengers' efforts to:

> prepare for the Sabath so we set to cleaning and shaving and we find it verry difficult to perform. We are obliged to kneel at our Chest and hold the looking Glass in one hand and shave with the other and in the time of shaving away we slide with the Razor and Glass brush and all and abliged to exercise much patience in the performing of it in consequence of the Rowlling of the Vessel.
>
> (*Civility* – 22 April)

But in spite of the discomforts, life was well-ordered:

> Continued fine weather . . . Cap. ordered a general clean-up of clothes and bedding to be brought on deck, the hold to be opened, berths to be cleaned to prevent disorder, so we were busy as bees in preparing for a rainy day.
>
> (*Civility* – 28 April)

Food, as for all travellers, was a constant preoccupation. Provisioning was regulated by the current Passenger Act. In 1851 Richard Heard advertised in the *North Devon Journal*:

> Provisions supplied weekly to each passenger – 2½lbs of bread or biscuit, 1lb wheaten flour, 5lbs oatmeal, 2lbs rice, ½lb sugar, ½lb treacle or molasses, 2oz Tea, 21 quarts of good water.[5]

Uncle Billie writes:

> I here state the Provisions we have found to be most useful and profitable on our voyage such as flour and substitute for barn [bran] to bake household bread every three days if we like for 1d a loaf; also a pie or puddin at ½d each. There is an excellent cast iron oven and Boiler in the Galley on Board and it belongs solely to the Cook (Ed Bale) who is an excellent Cook. also flesh viz, baken or Ham dry or in pickel Salt Herrings or large fish Rice dry peas potatoes good sweed turnips and Sallery lump sugar treacle currants . . . Bat and Wm. Shute might have sold their cider at a High price, 2½ per pint if they would have disposed of it. Also Some eggs is useful.
>
> (*Civility* – 10 April)

11.7 'The Captain desired me to collect all the children that were fit for tuition and teach them to read and spell . . . two or three hours a day.' A group of emigrant children having a reading class. Other emigrants are sunning themselves and airing their bedding, whilst others with buckets are drawing their water ration. (Illustrated London News)

Although he was suffering from a bad cold, for which he took gruel consisting of groats, best brandy, currants, carraway seeds, lump sugar and water boil'd well, Uncle Billie continued to keep himself busy:

> I have attended to the children in the cabin, also done a job of sewing for the Mate, so you will perceive that my time is improved through the course of the day and in conducting the prayer meeting in the evening.
>
> (*Civility* – 20 April)

Every little incident was recorded by these country people and they noted natural phenomena with interest and delight. In these small vessels they were on much closer terms with the sea than were passengers on latter-day liners. On Good Friday, Uncle Billie saw:

> for the first time in our lives, a live Whale, about two-thirds the length of our vessel, skipping along at the rate of twenty miles an hour, spouting the water high up into the air.

On the Banks he saw:

> abundance of fish floating around the vessel and as it was moonlight they were beautiful to behold. They shone like silver in the water.
>
> (*Civility* – 7 May).

On Easter Sunday, William Gliddon noted:

> Weather beautiful. This morning we have passed a bale of cotton, evidently washed off the deck of some ship. We have seen a whale and a grampus; it is a great sight to see such huge monsters playing about in the water. We have also seen three ships today. There are no bells to be heard chiming, nor anything to point out Sunday from the other days of the week, except there is no work doing aboard.
>
> (*Ocean Queen* – 8 April)

At times the North Atlantic seemed full of ships of all nations:

> This afternoon we have overtaken another vessel. We hoisted our ensign to see what countryman she was: up went in answer a French ensign. It is customary when answered to dip your ensign, that is, lower it half way, and raise it again: but the French are always more polite than we are: consequently they dipped to us three times.
>
> (*Ocean Queen* – 29 April)

William Gliddon was always ready to learn and to impart knowledge:

> Seen two ships, one passed almost close under our stern and we signalled with each other; they can talk by means of these signals just as if they were speaking to one another with their tongues. The first thing most commonly spoken is the longitude, then the ship's name, etc . . . the Capt has a book in which all the vessel's names are with their numbers . . . The number of the *Ocean Queen* is 9085 . . . There is a feeling on seeing another ship so close which cannot be described; you feel overjoyed to see other faces than those on board.
>
> (*Ocean Queen* – 10 April)

Uncle Billie also records a close encounter:

> We have been in company with a Brig today. She came near and this day in the forenoon the Captains spoke with their Trumpets, enquiring where from and where bound for, also their Latitude, which proved to be alike. She was from Waterford bound to Quebec.
>
> (*Civility* – 18 April)

But the following day:

> Another ship passed us this evening towards England. They came near and our Captain hoisted the Ensign or British flag and Hailed them with his Trumpet, but as soon as they saw our British flag they sheered off again and would have nothing to say. They were sulky Yankeys. She was called the *Columbia* of Bath Me. from the United States.
>
> (*Civility* – 19 April)

The comments on navigation are revealing, since it would appear that Captain Bale of *Civility* was navigating by sailing down his latitudes in a Westerly direction and obtaining his longitude – perhaps more likely his distance sailed – by dead reckoning. Captain Dart in *Ocean Queen*, seven years later and in a larger vessel managed by an altogether more sophisticated owner, was evidently keeping check of his longitude either by chronometer or by lunar observations.

Both *Civility* and *Ocean Queen* encountered severe weather and the passengers wrote up their stories for their relatives at home. Uncle Billie's account of Monday 1 May is his most purple passage:

> In the beginning of this night when we were Retired to our births to rest the wind waves and sea were tremendious Rough with torrents of Rain pouring in Over the Bulwarks on the Deck and down the Hatchway, in the Hold and the Vessel Rowlling from side to side like A Rocking Horse to that Degree that the Females were Screeching and Men and all Exclaining, O what can we do we cannot lye here; we cannot sleep we shall be thrown out of our Births; and I said to Bat's boy Ned for we sleep together; Well Ned we must get a rope and lash or tie ourselves to our Birth; or out over we must go; but, however we set to and Hold fast with our hands with all our might to the side of our Births and lay fast til Ned fel Asleep and Slept well all the Night and I almost believe that he could sleep on the top Deck for he is an astonishing lad to sleep that I ever witnessed in my life. But I could not Sleep all the Night and Heard one continual Confusion the waves Roaring and the winds Blowing in the Riging of the Vessel like Thunder and our Household Furniture in the Hold Making a Constant Racket But in the midst of Danger we were all preserved Thro' the power of God by whom the Hairs of our Head are all numbered and we are Alive and all in Health.
>
> (*Civility* – 1 May)

William Gliddon's storm was almost more alarming:

> Thunder is no more than a dog's bark compared with the tremendous roar of the wind and sea. Ten o'clock all but three passengers went below, to turn in and try to sleep, and I being the hindmost left the scuttle open, thinking the other three would follow. We had scarcely turned in when a sea struck her, making her reel most awfully. It came down the scuttle like a millstream, washing some of us nearly out of our beds. Two of our boxes broke from their lashings and rolled about from side to side, strewing their contents as they went.
>
> It was an anxious time: females shrieking, the water almost floating our things and the pails, cans, etc., knocking about. It is impossible to convey an idea of such an awful sight. We had very little sleep this night.

11.8 'We finished up this week with a good dance'. (Illustrated London News)

On entering the Gulf of St Lawrence, Cape Breton, 'to the joy of every heart' was the first landfall. 'It is covered with snow and looks very pretty', noted William Gliddon. After forty days at sea a pilot was put on board the *Civility*, his first duty being to see, 'if we were in good health and had kept clean, and if our hold was whitewashed'. Three days later 'he took charge of the vessel so that for a hundred miles he will have the sailing of the vessel, and the sailors under his charge.' (*Civility* – 19 May). William Gliddon also notes after forty days at sea: 'We have plenty of ships in company now. This evening about 7 o'clock the pilot-schooner came alongside, and left us a pilot. We finished up this week with a good dance.' (*Ocean Queen* – 12 May).

Gliddon writes:

About 4 o'clock am Friday there was a dead calm which lasted until about 7am when the storm recommenced with all its fury. The sailors on deck were obliged to be lashed, as they could not stand. We could cook nothing today, but the steward brought us some coffee, etc., and the Capt. comes down now and then to see us.

I went to the top of the steps this morning just to see the sea. I never witnessed such a sight before; it was one mass of foam, rolling as high as our topmast, threatening every moment to swallow us up. About 2am another sea struck the ship, smashing in the cabin skylight and some of the bulwarks. This completed the disaster of last night. We were now fairly washed clean out. This appeared to be the height of the storm, for it began to abate, and, thank God, by His aid we were carried safely through it.

(*Ocean Queen* – 12–13 April)

After a month at sea the Grand Banks were reached and the weather became piercing cold:

At noon we met an iceberg which made it still colder; it was about (as near as could be guessed) sixty feet above the sea, seventy feet wide, and two hundred in length. This was indeed a splendid sight as the sun was shining on it brilliantly which added greatly to its grandeur. Took soundings in thirty fathom of water.

(*Ocean Queen* – 3 May)

There were fogs and sudden changes, so on the *Civility* 'the men passengers attend to their watch . . . at intervals they walk the deck and blow the horn if they see anything'. This was only one of the tasks they might be called upon to do. After the storm:

As there is a joiner, Carpenter and wheelwright and a ship's carpenter on board they all set busily to work making a ladder for the hatchway, and many of the sailors and tradesmen passengers are helping to place the new jibboom in the vessel.

(*Civility* – 17 & 22 April)

It was traditional to have a crossing the Banks ceremony, similar to crossing the Line. William Fulford and William Gliddon both describe the elaborate entertainment given by the sailors. 'The money collection [in *Civility*] will be divided on arrival at Quebec, so that they may get themselves grog and have a spree.' Eight shillings were subscribed in the *Ocean Queen* on 3 May, but sadly five days later a sailor sent to loose the jib fell overboard and, despite efforts to save him, was instantly drowned in the frigid Labrador current, the only casualty in either vessel.

The money which we subscribed for the crew to spend in Quebec they handed over to the Capt for his mother. It was very singular that it was the same man who had acted as Neptune; little did he think, nor did any of us, when he said 'I must now return to the deep', that he would so soon be there in reality!

The River St Lawrence is one of the most dangerous in the world to navigate being so full of islands and rocks . . . Scenery all along the shore magnificent, studded with houses all painted white, with here and there a spire rising above the rest. Between this and Quebec there is a church every seven miles . . . About 6pm we reached the River de Loup. Here there is a telegraphic station; our name (signal) was hoisted and will be telegraphed to Quebec this evening, so that tomorrow the report will be forwarded to England. [In the next vessel bound for England, there being as yet no transatlantic cable].

(*Ocean Queen* – 16–17 May)

William Fulford describes the journey up the river:

At five o'ck we could see an extensive range of woodland and lumber land, not so high, with enclosed fields, a great many settlements with farms and dwelling houses. The land looks very fertile. We have seen uncultivated land enough to accommodate millions of the labouring class and population of England . . . The men passengers are busy in washing and cleaning their berths, the females are washing linen and performing laundry work, so that the inspection can be satisfactory to the doctors on the Quarantine Grounds when we arrive.

(*Civility* – 18 and 19 May)

A quarantine station had been established on Grosse Île in 1832. Here a battery of three guns, which are still in position, was set up to command the passage between the island and the southern shore of the river. All vessels proceeding up the St Lawrence were obliged to stop:

At half past seven this morning we arrived at Quebec Quaranteen Ground, which is thirty miles from Quebec. We cast anchor, which is on the North side of the river. There is an English settlement and hospital under our Government, and doctors for the reception of sick passengers; but through the mercy of God it was fortunate for us: we were the most decent and healthy passengers the doctor has ever seen or examined. So we were detained only two hours.

(*Civility* – 21 May)

The summer before Uncle Billie passed through there had been queues of vessels, performing their quarantine but unable to land their sick as the hospital facilities were inadequate. In a small valley, the only place on the island where the soil was deep enough to bury the dead, there is still today a long row of plain wooden crosses. Under the trees a stone monument bears the famous inscription:

In this secluded spot lie the mortal remains of 5,294 persons, who, flying from pestilence and famine in Ireland in the year 1847, found in America but a grave.

The *Ocean Queen's* visit on 19 May, 1855, was also brief. They were:

11.9   The Battery of three guns set up to control the deepwater channel between Grosse Île and the southern shore of the St Lawrence River. (*Basil Greenhill*)

'summoned on deck and ranged before him [the doctor] like a lot of soldiers about to be drilled. He gave us a clean bill, and we are allowed to proceed.

But William Gliddon observed:

> There are two ships lieing close in to the island: their passengers are fetched ashore to undergo a cleansing process. There are about 300 of them ashore, and by means of the Capt's glass we can see a big fellow with a rake and a pair of tongs turning over the clothes and making the people clean them. They are scattering about the island, washing and scrubbing like fun: it is a very pretty island.

Both William Fulford and William Gliddon disembarked at Quebec and continued up the St Lawrence by steamboat to Montreal, where we lose trace of them. Uncle Billie found it:

> as great a trial to part from our fellow passengers and acquaintances as it was to leave friends in England, as the Captain and sailors were very kind and good to us all. I do not regret leaving England, as I feel I am still in the way of the Lord.

He received a parting gift from his friend Miss Crealock – a copy of *The Cottager's Friend* giving 'an account of the introduction of Wesleyan Methodism in Bideford and Buckland Brewer'. To Captain Richard Dart, in *Ocean Queen*, the following letter, dated Quebec, May 22, 1855, was addressed:

> Dear Sir,
>
> We, the undersigned passengers on board the ship 'Ocean Queen', which has been so ably commanded by you during the voyage from the port of Bideford to Quebec, cannot take our leave of you without expressing our deep feelings of gratitude for the extreme kindness you have shewn us, and for your unremitting attention to render us all the ship could afford. We would also, through you, convey to the chief mate, Mr J Dart, the steward, Mr D Nicholls, and the ship's crew in general, our best thanks for the extreme kindness we have experienced from them.
>
> (Signed) G GRIBBLE,
> W GLIDDON,
> W KERSWELL,
> F GILBERT,
> G FLEMING,
> R MOORE, and others.

11: Emigration – the Human Dimension

1 *North Devon Journal*, 14 April 1831.
2 The Port Hill papers in the Public Archives of Prince Edward Island, quoted in Basil Greenhill and Ann Giffard, *Westcountrymen in Prince Edward's Isle. A Fragment of the Great Migration* (Toronto, 1967).
3 *North Devon Journal*, 22 Feb. 1849.
4 Greenhill and Giffard, *Westcountrymen*, chap. 10.
5 *North Devon Journal*, 13 Feb. 1851.

12 The Devon Fishing Industry in the Eighteenth and Nineteenth Centuries

Anthony Northway

The Eighteenth Century

THERE WERE FISHERMEN ALL AROUND the coasts of Britain in the eighteenth century, and the more than twenty species of fish found in large numbers in British waters were caught by them using a multitude of different methods. Much of this fishing was purely for subsistence, and was often a part-time or seasonal occupation that could usefully be combined with agriculture or other employments. For this reason there are few records of this widespread occupation, even when the surplus catch was sold to local populations. Devon shared many of the features of this national picture. The fisherman and his small craft was found at almost every beach, quay and harbour on the Devon coasts in the eighteenth century. Abundant supplies of many kinds of fish in the coastal waters and in many bays and estuaries ensured that those who lived near the sea needed little encouragement to add to their food supplies by some form of fishing. Their ingenuity resulted in a wide range of fishing techniques using hooks and lines, nets and traps. As with much of the activity found on other coasts, a lot of the fishing in Devon was undertaken to provide the fisherman and his family with an additional source of food. And, as in the other areas, it was a mainly small-scale, seasonal occupation.

Even in eighteenth-century Britain, however, there were a number of examples of large-scale fish production for the market that together formed what may fairly be described as an industry. This industry was organised into a number of fairly distinct branches, with a marked emphasis on the pursuit of those types of fish that could be preserved. The chief of these was the herring fishery.

The herring fishery was particularly suitable for commercial development. Surface shoaling herrings could, in favourable years, be caught in immense quantities by existing techniques of seine and drift netting. They were also capable of being preserved for future consumption by traditional methods of salting and smoking which enabled them to be transported over a wide area or exported. Herring fishing was also the subject of intense government interest and encouragement, so that substantial records of its incidence survive.[1] Records of the preserved herrings that were taken for home consumption and export in the eighteenth century originated in the regulations surrounding the salt duties, as well as records of the bounties paid on herring vessels and their catch, which stemmed from governmental attempts to encourage the growth of this fishery. The often detailed records of this branch of the industry, while indicating considerable annual fluctuations, also show an overall long-term increase in the larger vessels engaged in the trade. The bulk of these larger vessels originated in Scotland, but they fished extensively along the coasts of Britain following the seasonal migration of the fish. There was also a large commercial herring fleet at Yarmouth.[2] The available records also show an increase in the catch of these larger vessels from 20,000 barrels to 58,000 barrels.[3] The smaller vessels also increased their catch until it reached 23,000 barrels in England and 65,000 barrels in Scotland by the 1790s[4] with an increasing surplus for export. So although herrings formed part of the diet of local subsistence fishermen, the bulk of the catch was sold commercially.

Another important commercial fishery was for pilchards. Like herrings they were a surface shoaling, seasonal fish caught by nets. They were caught in large numbers and preserved by traditional methods of barrel salting which produced both fish and oil. They were also the subject of government attention in an attempt to encourage the industry. Pilchard fishing, however, was virtually restricted to the coasts of Devon and Cornwall, and although it was a substantial regional industry, with 180 Cornish drift boats in 1785 and 110–140 seine boats,[5] its national contribution was less significant.

So in Devon as elsewhere there was a marked concentration on the pursuit of fish that could be preserved, such as herrings and pilchards. The available records suggest that the fishermen of the North Devon coast were the most active in the pursuit of herrings. In South Devon the pilchard fishery was probably more important, and there were a number of places which had long been noted for this fishery, such as Hope Quay, Dartmouth, Teignmouth and Dawlish, although Plymouth was the main centre in Devon. However, some herrings were caught in the region, and the large yawls equipped with drift nets which operated along the south coasts of Devon and Cornwall, many of which were stationed at Plymouth, caught both types of fish. There are, moreover, many records of herring fishing on the South Devon coast and there is evidence that Teignmouth kept a large fleet for this purpose by the 1780s.[6]

Salted herrings or pilchards could be used to supply many inland areas of the county, in spite of the slow and expensive transport of the period,

12.1 Brixham in the early nineteenth century.

and a number of places, such as South Molton and Tiverton, were found to have supplies of these fish by the end of the eighteenth century.[7] They could also be sold outside the county, and some of the herrings caught on the north coast were doubtless shipped to Bristol, as there was a well-established coastal trade between this area and the city. Both Exeter and Plymouth were active in the export of fish, and it was in the latter city that many of the pilchards were prepared for export or used to victual ships. Not surprisingly the fish imported into Devon, whether they were herrings from Liverpool or Scotland, pilchards from Cornwall, or cod from Newfoundland, were also of this preserved type.[8]

A further case of English commercial exploitation of fish supplies was in the cod fishing industry. In contrast to herring and pilchards, fish such as cod and hake were caught by rather less efficient methods using hooks and lines. Nonetheless, large numbers of these fish were caught and they also were sold in a preserved form, either salted or dried. They were not only caught off the coasts of Britain, but also off Iceland and Newfoundland. By the second half of the eighteenth century, however, it was no longer common for fishing vessels to sail each season to the Newfoundland Banks. Trading vessels bought the processed fish from resident fishermen or from those who had gone out for the season. There is also some evidence that the Iceland cod fishery from the East Coast had declined by the late eighteenth century; a decline probably associated with the Salt Laws.[9]

Although cod was caught by hook and line off the Devon coasts, and some was preserved, it was not a large-scale commercial fishery. Furthermore, by the second half of the eighteenth century fishing vessels no longer sailed from Dartmouth and Bideford to the Newfoundland fishing grounds, although some fishermen were still recruited in the county to fish the season on the Banks. For some time a quantity of cod and similar types of fish had been sold fresh in the London market. The fish were kept alive and conveyed there in specially adapted vessels, many of which originated in Harwich.[10] In the eighteenth century there was a significant increase in the number of Harwich vessels engaged in this trade and a growth in the supply of fresh fish to the London market, although Harwich was later displaced by the ports of the inner Thames estuary such as Gravesend, Barking and Greenwich.[11]

Devon fishermen were unable to participate in the sale of fresh cod to the London market. The Devon fishing grounds were too remote for this enterprise. But a surprising amount of fresh fish of all types was sold in the county, mainly to people living on the coast who, because of the limited extent of the market for this perishable commodity, were normally supplied with a wide range of fish at low prices.[12] Devon was fortunate in that few parts of the county were far from the sea and a high proportion of the large population was concentrated near the south coast, where the cities of Exeter and Plymouth were both open to waterborne supplies and had flourishing fish markets by the eighteenth century.[13] Fish markets had also been established at many other small Devon towns, whether on the coast, as at Bideford and Brixham, or inland at Totnes and Honiton.[14] But even where markets had been established, some fish was still hawked around the local population by the fishermen's wives and families.

The final branch of the British fishing industry in this century worthy of mention was that of trawling. This method of fishing was capable of catching all those fish which lie on or near the sea bed, such as cod, plaice, sole and turbot. Although some of the fish caught in this way could be preserved, the principal aim was the capture of fish for fresh consumption. This old-established practice, which had long been used in shallow waters, was successfully adapted in the eighteenth century so that it could be used in comparatively deep waters often far out to sea.[15] This achievement was probably related to improvements in vessel design, particularly the introduction of better fore and aft rigs for small craft, which gave them the speed and power to overcome the resistance of a trawl net whose mouth was kept open by a heavy wooden beam mounted on iron shoes.[16]

Both Barking and Brixham claimed to have introduced this method of fishing into the British industry. Certainly by the second half of the eighteenth century the practice was well-established at Brixham. Initially the vessels used for trawling were quite small, although larger than the majority of Devon fishing boats at the time, and the seven vessels recorded at

12.2   The Fish Market, by Nicholas Condy. (*City of Plymouth Museums and Art Gallery*)

Brixham in 1756 were only about 15 tons each.[17] But by the 1780s and 1790s trawling was carried out in sloops of 20 to 30 tons and, moreover, the port had, by 1786, seventy-six vessels of this type,[18] and by 1791, ninety.[19] By the latter date, at least, Plymouth had also been able to establish a small trawling fleet.[20]

The herring and pilchard fisheries, the cod fishery and trawling were the most significant branches of the British fishing industry in the eighteenth century. Together they produced substantial quantities of fish that, preserved and fresh, could be consumed at home or exported. And in spite of the limitations that poor transport imposed on the industry, there is every indication that these interests underwent considerable, if irregular, expansion in the second half of the century.

As will be seen in Table 12.1, by 1772 there were at least 1,378 large fishing vessels in England and Wales, amounting to some 22,760 tons. By 1786 the number had grown to 1,584 and their total tonnage was recorded at 38,679. To this number of vessels on the English and Welsh coasts may be added a further 250, which was the approximate number recorded for Scotland at both the earlier and later dates. There are a number of difficulties in the use of these figures,[21] but they can safely be taken as at least the minimum numbers of ships that were present, a minimum that increased by just over 200 vessels in those years. The tonnage increase was much greater, but although the tonnage figures also present difficulties because of changes in the methods of ship tonnage measurements after 1773, the increase of 16,000 tons must indicate a substantial growth in the average size of vessels used in fishing at this time.

The Devon industry also grew significantly in the second half of the eighteenth century, as indicated in Table 12.2 by the number and tonnage of vessels recorded in the county.

Table 12.1
English fishing vessels, 1772–1786

Year	Ships	Tons	Men	Number of ports making returns
1772	1,378	22,762	6,118	46
1773	1,404	23,646	6,396	42
1774	1,356	23,890	6,225	41
1775	1,382	25,348	6,515	45
1776	1,474	25,582	6,608	41
1777	1,455	26,379	6,484	44
1778	1,385	24,521	6,325	41
1779	1,341	22,846	6,100	40
1780	1,285	23,014	5,366	38
1781	1,229	21,108	4,984	39
1782	1,297	22,274	5,442	39
1783	1,272	22,010	5,483	40
1784	1,316	24,476	5,809	40
1785	1,420	30,540	6,737	43
1786	1,584	38,679	7,823	46

Source: PRO, Customs 17/1–10.

This indicates an increase of approximately 2,000 tons by 1786, with the number of vessels recorded reaching over 400 by this date. This implies that at this time Devon contained over 25 per cent of the fishing boats recorded in England and Wales and some 13 per cent of the total tonnage.

These figures, when taken in their original form as returns from Devon customs ports or coastal regions, can also be used to reveal other aspects of the fishing industry. First, they show something of the distribution of fishing vessels around the Devon coasts. Although there may be omissions in the

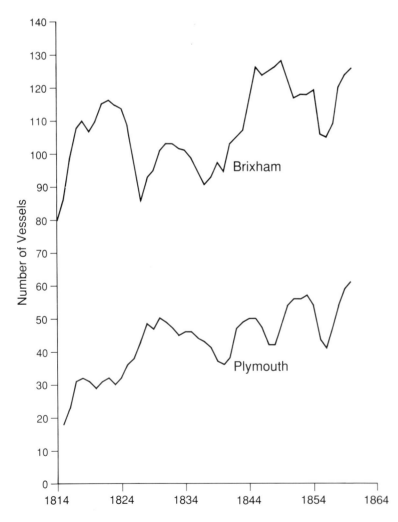

12.3   Fishing vessels belonging to Brixham and Plymouth, 1814–64.

Table 12.2
Devon fishing vessels, 1755–1786

Year	Ships	Tons	Men
1755	–	3,134	–
1760	–	2,151	–
1765	–	2,691	–
1770	–	3,027	–
1772	271	3,593	891
1776	317	4,240	1,078
1781	336	4,541	1,168
1786	403	5,096	1,497

Source: BL, Add. MS 11255; PRO, Customs 17/1–10.

returns from the north of the county, there was clearly a much larger tonnage engaged in fishing on the south coast. This is perhaps predictable given the greater marketing opportunities of the south and the long ria coastline. On this southern shore one of the main concentrations was at Brixham, which came under the Dartmouth Customs jurisdiction (Table 12.3).

Table 12.3
Fishing vessels belonging to Dartmouth Customs Port, 1772–1786

Year	Ships	Tons	Average size
1772	35	639	18
1773	40	720	18
1774	43	804	18½
1775	44	804	18
1776	40	768	19
1777	42	800	19
1778	39	740	19
1779	41	780	19
1780	38	674	17
1781	45	870	19
1782	46	850	18½
1783	60	1,080	18
1784	47	1,050	22
1785	58	1,380	24
1786	94	2,068	22

Source: PRO, Customs 17/1–10.

Table 12.4
Fishing vessels belonging to Exeter Customs Port, 1772–1786

Year	Ships	Tons	Average size
1772	172	1,617	9½
1773	187	1,631	9
1774	200	1,912	9½
1775	197	1,840	9
1776	205	2,082	10
1777	224	2,452	11
1778	235	2,353	10
1779	235	2,571	11
1780	230	2,406	10½
1781	235	2,493	10½
1782	232	2,183	9
1783	224	1,935	8½
1784	238	1,935	8
1785	253	2,112	8
1786	231	2,008	8½

Source: PRO, Customs 17/1–10.

Another important concentration was the long stretch of the Devon coast centring on the Exe estuary, which comprised the Exeter Customs Port.

Secondly, these records suggest that, in many areas, Devon fishing boats were smaller, often much smaller, than the county averages suggest. Those in the Bideford area, for example, rarely averaged more than three tons, as Table 12.5 shows.

12.4   A busy scene at the Barbican, Plymouth, in the 1880s. (*City of Plymouth Museums and Art Gallery*)

Moreover, the large number of boats in the Exeter Customs Port – more than 200 for much of the latter part of the century – averaged only ten or eleven tons or smaller. It follows from this, of course, that there were some areas, such as Dartmouth, where the vessels were correspondingly bigger, but other records of the eighteenth century support this impression of large numbers of small craft. For example, at Beer all the fishing boats seem to have been three or four tons or less, and those recorded at Clovelly in the 1780s were only about five or six tons.[22] They were probably clinker-built open boats, propelled by oars alone or by simple lug or sprit sails.

Taken together, the details of fish consumption and of the vessels that were employed give a view (if somewhat impressionistic) of the types of fishing mainly practised in Devon in the eighteenth century. They show a still fairly small industry, one that was still very largely for subsistence or the supply of local markets, and one, too, in which there was much emphasis on the seasonal production of those fish most easily preserved. In many respects, including the tendency towards slow if irregular expansion, Devon reflected many of the features of the national industry during this period.

The Development of Trawling

Of more importance for the future was the development within the county of the practice of trawling. For although the main catch of the trawlers was unsuitable for preserving, it was largely composed of those sea-fish which were regarded as luxuries in the eighteenth century and was, therefore, capable of commanding high prices in many city markets. This meant that in spite of the expense involved in conveying fresh fish at the necessary speed, the more expensive types of fish were marketed over surprisingly long distances, even though the cost of the journey equalled the price paid to the fishermen and doubled or trebled the final market price. As early as

Table 12.5
Fishing vessels belonging to Bideford Customs Port, 1772–1786

Year	Ships	Tons	Average size
1772	15	57	4
1773	17	90	5
1774	19	38	2
1775	20	50	2½
1776	20	60	3
1777	18	54	3
1778	18	54	3
1779	12	36	3
1780	3	24	8
1781	13	38	3
1782	9	27	3
1783	15	48	3
1784	21	49	2
1785	28	72	2½
1786	48	112	2

Source: PRO, Customs 17/1–10.

12.5 Sutton Pool, looking north, from an original lantern slide. (*City of Plymouth Museums and Art Gallery*)

the 1760s there were at least two firms engaged in the transport of fish from Brixham to London in carriages which took from 36 to 48hrs on the journey. One of these firms claimed to have carried 71 tons of soles on this route in one year in the early 1760s,[23] while another stated that it had conveyed 87 tons of soles and turbot in the 2½ years between June 1765 and December 1767, for which it paid £2,626 at Brixham, the carriage to London being at least £2,162, with the fish finally sold for £6,165.[24]

The growth of this branch of the Devon fishing industry was undoubtedly related to the possibility of supplying distant as well as local markets, and this traffic grew with the expansion of the trawling fleet. In the 1780s it was estimated that 500 carriages of fish, worth £6,500 at Brixham, were sent to London, Bath and Bristol.[25] Plymouth was also supplying these markets in the late eighteenth century,[26] and by 1791 an anonymous writer estimated that at Brixham:

> The average weekly exports of the sloop fishery throughout the year are to
>
> | | |
> |---|---|
> | London | 180 |
> | Bath and Bristol | 80 |
> | Exeter | 50 |
> | Other markets | 50 |
>
> 360 or £18,770 per annum as above stated.

. . . which when brought to market is expected to make double the sum to pay the carriage and other expenses.[27]

The Nineteenth Century

The most important development of the English fishing industry in the nineteenth century was the growth of deep-sea trawling, and it was this which largely determined the major locational changes that also occurred. Trawling was a highly efficient method of capturing a wide range of fish. It could be followed in any season, and it produced large quantities of fresh fish for which there was a growing demand. It is not surprising, therefore, that it soon spread from South Devon and the Thames, which were the first areas to adopt it, to many new parts of the coast. The main obstacle to this expansion was the difficulty experienced in conveying the trawler's highly perishable cargo to market while it was still fresh. Similar considerations also made it necessary to discover and exploit new fishing grounds near to the increasing number of ports used by these vessels. The problem of overland transport was largely solved by the building of the railways, and

the rise of Hull and Grimsby to a pre-eminent position owed a great deal to their easy rail communication with the principal urban markets of the country. The increasing concentration of the industry on the East Coast ports, however, was also determined by their location near to the North Sea fishing grounds, which were the most important of the many trawling areas discovered in the nineteenth century.

The Devon fishing industry played an important part in the development of trawling, and the fleets of Brixham and Plymouth, already well established by the end of the eighteenth century, soon came to dominate the local industry. In the nineteenth century, in terms of both production and investment, they were the major sector of the county's fisheries, so attention may justifiably be concentrated on their expansion. The number of trawlers at the two ports continued to increase, and the total of 151 in 1830 had grown to 190 by 1860,[28] which represented a more than 25 per cent growth over the thirty-year period. Furthermore, the degree of expansion and the amount of capital invested would be seriously underestimated if seen solely in terms of the growing numbers, since both the size and the cost of trawlers was increasing. Not only were a number of the older trawlers lengthened, but new ones, which had been about 40 tons in the 1830s, had increased to 50 tons new measurement by the 1860s, and their cost, when fitted out ready for sea, had grown from about £400 to as much as £800 over this period.[29] It can therefore be claimed that capital investment had grown by at least 50 per cent, especially when allowance is made for those new vessels that had moved to other areas before 1860. The course of this increase is illustrated in Fig. 12.3, which shows the periods of most rapid growth in numbers. These increases were largely achieved by the addition of many newly-built trawlers, the transfer of vessels from other port areas playing only a marginal role in the expansion. The new Brixham trawlers were constructed either in the town or on the River Dart, while those of Plymouth were built within the port at such districts as Teats Hill, Stonehouse, Saltash or Franks Quarry.[30] The trawler fishing fleets of South Devon, then, were very much the creation of the local shipbuilding industry and contributed towards its prosperity.

The growing number of trawlers at Brixham and Plymouth, and the manner by which this was achieved – by new building and increasing investment – suggest that this branch of the industry was able to obtain good profits during the first half of the nineteenth century; profits high enough to encourage new shipbuilding. It is also possible to point to a number of reasons for high profits during those years. The early adoption by Devon fishermen of the practice of deep-sea trawling was itself an important reason, since this was such a productive method of fishing. Profits would also arise from the expanding market for fish and through the flexible response of the fishermen to this growing demand within the changing conditions of the nineteenth century. The local, but more particularly the national, population was growing rapidly in these years, especially in the industry's distant markets such as Bristol and London. Together with the transport improvements of the early nineteenth century this expanding market enabled these Devon fishermen to sell larger quantities of their fish. When faced with low fish prices in London in the 1830s they were still able to supply the market profitably by increasing their catches through the use of larger and more efficient vessels and by making greater use of water transport, in this case by shipping their fish to Portsmouth, from whence they were forwarded the remaining 72 miles to London by road.[31] Some fishermen also began to extend the area of their fishing operations into regions where they could obtain easier access to markets, the earliest recorded example being their visits to South Wales.[32] One of the results of this was the discovery of new and prolific fishing grounds, and this, too, was a source of increased profits because of the larger catches that were then obtained.

Although it may be possible to ascribe reasons for good profits in these years, it is much more difficult, in the absence of reliable accounts, to determine the actual level of profits. From the few indications that are available it seems that, in the 1860s, the annual catch of a trawler was between 70 and 80 tons, some of which was prime fish that brought high prices, some being offal which sold more cheaply, but that the two types together made on average about £6 a ton.[33] This suggests an average gross income of about £500 a year. From this figure, however, a number of expenses had to be met, such as the repair and maintenance of the vessel and her gear, as well as contributions to the fishermen's mutual insurance fund, so that perhaps only £300 would be left to be divided between the owner, the master and a crew of two or three.[34] Unfortunately average estimates such as these are not very reliable, and in any case serve to disguise the considerable variations between vessels. The quantity of fish caught each year depended partly on weather conditions, partly on the skill and industry of the master, and to a certain extent simply on luck. The amount realised for the catch was equally variable, as the price of fish in the market was noted for its volatility. The best indication of profitability in the mid-nineteenth century, therefore, remains the indirect evidence that the level of returns was sufficient to encourage the building of new ships and that much of the capital for this construction came from the reinvestment of profits earned through fishing.

The method by which some men acquired new vessels certainly suggests that this was a profitable industry. For instance, at Brixham in 1863 it was said that

> A man may have £150 to £200, and he has a new vessel built. He can find people who are ready to put the remainder of the money into that, and thus assist him. Tradesmen are ready to put their goods on board, if he is an industrious man, and they will give him credit for everything he requires.[35]

The most common method of raising the remainder of the money would have been by a loan or mortgage secured on the ship. It appears that at least fifty-eight Brixham vessels were so mortgaged in 1861, and eleven of the Plymouth boats.[36] Almost all of these mortgages were raised locally from friends, relations or from local tradesmen, and although the influence of the larger capitalists can be seen at this stage, those who in 1861 had lent large sums, such as Jasper Bartlett or Robert Hellyer, were men whose families had reputedly made their fortunes from fishing or had been smack owners themselves.[37] It was claimed that in this way many men who began as fishermen ended their days as owners of one or two trawlers. It is likely that this was not just an expression of the prevailing sentiments of self-help and social advancement, since so many examples of 'going in at the hawse hole and coming out at the taffrail' were quoted.[38] There was, of course, a good deal of inherited wealth, fishing being very much a family tradition, but a number of the men who were subscribed as masters in the earlier registers reappear as owners by the 1860s, and the pattern of ownership itself lends credence to claims for the increasing wealth of trawler fishermen and their ability to buy new vessels.

There was a marked lack of concentration in the ownership of the larger Devon fishing boats, and, in spite of the increase in their number and cost, relatively few examples of men owning or having an interest in more than two smacks can be found even by the 1860s. Where amalgamation had occurred it was usually along family lines, with the sons or other relations of established fishermen gaining control of their own vessels.[39] Most of the owners therefore were, or had been, fishermen, and although a wider range of occupations was introduced among the owners in latter years, the majority of boats remained the property of fishermen or mariners, many of whom still went to sea themselves. Thus at Plymouth in 1861, out of fifty-two vessels where this information can be traced, it was found that seventeen of the masters were also the managing owners. The same was true at Brixham, where master and owner were identical in 36 out of the 100 vessels for which such information was recorded.[40]

This pattern endured because of the low cost of entry into the industry. It was only necessary for a fisherman to save or borrow a fraction of the total cost of a new trawler, as the rest could be obtained through a mortgage and the credit provided by local tradesmen. He need not, of course, begin with a new vessel. Two- or three-year-old trawlers of 40 to 50 tons were being offered for sale in the 1860s for about £500.[41] But although the initial investment was small when compared with the total cost of a trawler, the level of profits and local capital availability could not have been the sole explanation for the pattern of ownership. This is clear from a comparison with Barking vessels in the 1850s, where profits were by all accounts equally high but ownership was largely concentrated in the hands of one or two families.[42] It seems likely that even the small amount of capital needed for

12.6   Fishermen at Brixham in the late nineteenth century. (*Torquay Natural History Museum*)

the purchase of a trawler would have been beyond the means of most fishermen if it had not been for the Devon industry's unusual payments system.

The Fishermen

Within the trawl fishery at both Brixham and Plymouth it was not the practice to pay wages either to the captains or to the full crew members. The usual method was for all parties, owners, masters and crew members, to share in the proceeds of the voyage after expenses had been deducted. Normally seven shares were made, the owner receiving three and a half of these, the master one and a half and the two crew members one share each.[43] Those who shared in the catch supplied their own provisions, but the owner was responsible for the welfare of the apprentices and boys on his vessels, who were sometimes paid a small wage. This system meant that crewmen were able to share in the industry's profits and were sometimes able to amass enough money to buy their own vessels. It also meant that an owner who was also a trawler's master could claim five of the seven shares, while his wage costs were proportionately fixed and only grew with increases in productivity and income. Furthermore, although the normal complement of a trawler when fishing off the South Devon coast was four, including the captain, they did not all carry two full crew members. Many – 72 vessels out of 150 at Brixham and Plymouth in 1861 – carried a boy, sometimes as young as ten but normally between 14 and 15 years old. After this age, and usually until they were 21, the boys became apprentices, and these two together, boys and apprentices, made up a large proportion of the crew on many vessels. Of the 50 large trawlers at Plymouth in 1861 that have left records of their crew, 28 had apprentices aboard and 14 of these had two per vessel: while at Brixham in 1861 a similar picture can be seen, with 61 out of 100 vessels carrying apprentices, 36 of the vessels having two apprentices aboard, and there were even two examples where three apprentices made up part of the crew.[44]

The place of origin of the boys, the apprentices and the other crew members may perhaps be taken as evidence not only that the industry was profitable, but also that those who worked in it were able, or expected to be able, to share in this prosperity. For instance, of the 101 apprentices on Brixham vessels in 1861, the place of birth of 24 was given simply as Devon, 48 were reputedly born in Brixham, while most of the others came from nearby towns, with the exception of five from Beer, and with only a very small number coming from outside the county. The forty-two apprentices at Plymouth in 1861 were even more overwhelmingly local in origin, no fewer than thirty-nine having been born in Plymouth itself, with only two coming from Beer and one from Torquay.[45] The industry and the demand for crew was growing, yet there seems to have been little difficulty in

the smaller second- and third-class vessels whose numbers also tended to increase in this period as a result of railway development.[50]

The railway was one of the main factors which determined the degree of timing of the expansion in the Devon fishing industry in the mid nineteenth century. But reference to total registrations of first-class trawlers over 15 tons indicates that the period between 1825 and 1860 was not one of sustained and continuous growth (see Fig. 12.3). There were also times when numbers declined. Vessels were lost to the registers by such hazards as collision or wreck, by vessels being broken up as a result of age or seizure for smuggling, or because they were transferred to other ports away from South Devon. These were the factors which could cause the loss of one or two vessels each year. But a comparison of the incidence of new building with the fluctuations in the totals shows that the birth rate, i.e. the addition of new vessels, was the main determinant of the total numbers of trawlers. Nevertheless, there were periods, most notably in the 1820s and again in the 1850s, when a dramatic loss of vessels occurred through the transfer of trawlers to other ports.[51] Such times of transfer should not, however, be seen as periods of decline which interrupted the long-term growth of the industry. The emigration of vessels, at first seasonally and later by permanent transfer, was a response by Devon fishermen to changing marketing and other conditions, and provided an important stimulus for new capital investment. It appears that times of extensive transfer of ships from Brixham and Plymouth coincided with, and were closely followed by, periods of renewed growth in the South Devon fleets by new building.[52]

The Migration of Devon Fishermen

The migration of vessels and fishermen had been a feature of the Devon industry in the eighteenth century,[53] so it was only the scale of this nineteenth-century movement that was new. In 1863 witnesses before a Royal Commission recalled that the range of the county's fishing vessels in the early years of the nineteenth century had been from Land's End to Portland, and that about ten years later it was said that they had begun to go to Liverpool and Dover.[54] There is also evidence that by the 1820s some of the Devon fishing vessels were stationed at Dublin and others were operating in the bays along the Cornish coast.[55] By the 1830s they were moving further up the English Channel, about seventy being stationed at Ramsgate, which they had been visiting 'for the last eight or ten years'.[56] This gradual movement along the coast was at first seasonal, with a return to Brixham in the summer, while the practice of fishing in the Bristol Channel, while stationed at Tenby, was a summer fishery. In the 1830s about twelve boats were involved in this, and there were a further five or six which visited Liverpool.[57] However, some of this migration soon became permanent. Before 1847 the principal transfers from Devon were to Dover, Ramsgate, Dublin and the ports of South Wales. There were only a small number of transfers to South Wales, and the migration to Ramsgate was spread over a long period, so that neither of these movements had as great an impact on the totals of the remaining vessels as did the early transfers to Dublin and Dover in the 1820s or the migration to Hull after 1847.[58]

The principal reason for this migration was the Devon fishermen's desire to supply their markets more effectively, especially before the railways were constructed. But it was necessarily accompanied by the discovery and exploitation of new fishing grounds, and this was an additional factor in the later movement of many vessels to the East Coast ports. In the 1830s the principal grounds 'up Channel' were still off Dover and Margate, but Torbay boats were already getting into the North Sea,[59] and tradition has it

obtaining recruits from among the local population, in spite of the certainty that work on a small sailing trawler in the nineteenth century was hard, difficult and sometimes dangerous. Perhaps more significantly, the boys and young men recruited into the trawl fishery were in many cases related either to the owner, the master or the other crew members. For example, the *Kent*, owned and captained by a 43-year-old Brixham man, J Stockman, in 1861, had three apprentices as crew, two of these being 18-year-old J Stockman and 15-year-old W Stockman. The *Diligent*, with its crew of three, had 52-year-old second hand G Warren and 14-year-old cook S Warren, while the *Diligence* was owned, captained and completely crewed by members of the Sparks family, and had 15-year-old S Sparks as the cook.[46] No evidence has been found that it was necessary to obtain new entrants from young boys in Poor Law Unions, as occurred in other areas such as London and the East Coast ports,[47] and this must to some extent be explained by the inducements of high earnings and good opportunities. It must be conceded, however, that it also owed something to the traditional nature of an industry in which the family survived as the basis of ownership and as the unit of production and employment.

The Impact of the Railways

Any discussion of the growth of the Devon fishing industry in the first half of the nineteenth century would be incomplete without reference to the considerable impact wrought by the coming of the railways. They provided a great stimulus to the trawl fishery, and the generally upward trend seen in vessel ownership during the 1840s and early 1850s is clearly related to their influence (see Fig. 12.3). The South Devon Railway did not reach Brixham itself until 1868, but it was at Teignmouth and Newton Abbot by 1846, approaching Torbay by 1848, and arrived at Plymouth in the following year.[48] The building of the railways meant that the trawl fishermen could now supply their traditional markets, such as London, Bath, Bristol and Exeter, more easily and cheaply, and many other parts of the country as well. The reduction in transport costs also meant that they were able to send both the luxury fish, which made up about a quarter of their catch, and the less expensive component to distant inland markets. In 1854 the South Devon Railway carried 940 tons of fish, but by 1864 this had risen to more than 3,000 tons a year from a growing number of stations along the southern coast of the county.[49] Not all of this was the product of the trawlers, however, as it should not be forgotten that the vigorous growth of trawling, concentrated at just two ports, was grafted on to a well-established tradition of fishing from small boats that existed along the whole length of the Devon coasts. Fishing remained a ubiquitous feature of the coastal regions, and the railways enabled many types of fishermen to engage in the long-distance sale of sprats, mackerel, herrings and shellfish which were the main products of

that in this period the prolific fishing grounds of the Great Silver Pits were first discovered by some Brixham fishermen engaged in an abortive attempt to establish themselves at the port of Scarborough.[60] However, the importance of this area of the North Sea fishing grounds was not fully realised until after 1850, by which time the fishermen of Barking had also laid claim to the discovery and Hull was becoming an important fishing port. After 1847 many Devon vessels were transferred to Hull,[61] and at this time the Devon men frequently joined the trawler fleets that had come from Barking and, like them, sent their fish to the London market by fast sailing cutters.[62] They could also use the railways from Hull and from Grimsby after 1852. At Brixham in 1863 the President of the Fishing Club stated that there were 152 vessels insured by the Society, the main condition being that they belonged to Brixham men, but, of these, 41 were permanently settled at Hull and 16 in Ireland, and there were also three at Liverpool, one at Plymouth and another at Ramsgate.

This meant that:

> The number of vessels employed at Brixham at this time is 90. In addition to which there are five extra, making 95 that fish here the greatest part of the year. I find by referring to the list, that there are about nine or ten that go to Tenby from May to September, and about a dozen that go to Hull and Ramsgate to fish from November to May; that makes an average of from 80 to 85 here throughout the year.[63]

This piece of evidence illustrates the scale of the movement away from Devon by the 1860s, and provides further confirmation of the growing area of trawl fishing.

The extended range of operations, especially the working of the North Sea grounds, provided one incentive for the continued growth in the size of Devon trawlers and modifications in their design. It was found that the mainsail of a large sloop or cutter was too big for a small crew to handle easily, so after 1870 the ketch rig became the standard sail pattern for all the largest smacks. At the same time there evolved a smaller class of boat for working close inshore and on the home grounds, which were between 10 and 20 tons, sloop rigged, and known locally as Mumble Bees.

Not only did the size of trawlers increase, but the Devon industry remained profitable and continued to expand for much of the second half of the nineteenth century in spite of the permanent departure of so many vessels. This was partly because many of the Devon boats were able to fish in other areas in some seasons of the year. For those who remained, the trawling grounds off the South Devon coast were limited in extent, and rail costs were high, but smacks from Brixham and Plymouth, fishing near the port, stayed only a short time at sea so that their catch was fresher than that landed at Hull or Grimsby and, until late in the nineteenth century, usually commanded a premium in the market. Such considerations meant that the time of fastest growth in the number of large trawlers in Devon, many of which worked for at least part of the year in home waters, occurred after 1870. In addition, the further development of the railway network, and the rise of a smaller class of trawler, ensured that this prosperity was not confined to the first-class vessels, the smaller second-class boats maintaining their aggregate tonnage into the twentieth century, as shown in Table 12.6.

As will be seen, the continued and, at times, rapid growth in the Devon

12.8   Sutton Harbour in the 1880s, the days when so many trawlers and drifters were crammed into the creek that it was possible to walk from side to side by stepping from boat to boat. (*Basil Greenhill*)

Table 12.6
Devon fishing vessels, 1869–1913

| Year | 1st class* | | 2nd class* | |
	Number	Tons	Number	Tons
1869	171	6,040	865	2,095½
1871	212	7,898	1,018	2,334
1876	232	9,076	1,064	3,262
1881	336	14,094	604	2,586
1886	397	12,614	457	2,590
1891	343	13,731	396	2,417
1896	333	13,276	346	2,195
1901	276	10,176	321	2,016
1906	301	10,780	406	2,002
1911	274	9,567	397	2,100
1913	279	9,404	394	2,109

* First-class vessels are those of more than 15 tons. The second class includes all fishing boats of less than 15 tons 'navigated otherwise than by oars only'. After 1876 the smaller vessels of this type, with keels of less than 18ft or undecked craft, were omitted and are unrecorded, but they have been included in the above table after 1902.

Source: BPP, Trade and Navigation Returns, Appendix of Shipping.

Table 12.7
English fish landings, 1886–1901

| Years | Fish landings in tons | | |
	England and Wales	East Coast (Hull and Grimsby in brackets)	South Coast (Brixham and Plymouth in brackets)
1886	320,623	266,082 (88,219)	43,552 (9,499)
1891	298,303	233,532 (92,499)	29,685 (12,040)
1896	377,533	306,158 (139,664)	34,572 (11,510)
1901	432,390	351,224 (167,144)	35,662 (12,521)

Source: BPP, Reports to the Board of Trade.

fishing industry lasted until at least the 1880s. However, it must be recognised that the national industry was growing even more quickly. The East Coast ports, with their locational advantages, had outstripped all other areas by 1860 at the latest, and it is from this time that the Devon industry's long relative decline began. The increasingly lesser role played by Devon within the national industry was already apparent when the absolute fall in

the number and tonnage of Devon fishing vessels first occurred. When, in 1886, the first national statistics of fish landings were collected, they showed the overwhelming importance of the East Coast ports and the growing dominance of Hull and Grimsby.

On this evidence, the Devon ports no longer produced a significant proportion of the country's fish supply. But the declining importance of Devon in this respect, as in the number and tonnage of her fishing vessels,[64] should not obscure the important contribution that the Devon fishermen had made towards the development of the English fishing industry. By their migration they spread the practice of deep-sea trawling to many new parts of the coast: they were also instrumental in the discovery of new fishing grounds. It is true that on the East Coast and in the North Sea they shared this achievement with the fishing vessels that originated in the Thames, but the Devon fishermen also took the practice to many other areas such as South Wales, Liverpool and Ireland. It is for this that they should be particularly remembered.

12.9   The smack-rigged Brixham trawlers of the 1870s and 1880s were fine, powerful vessels, but as always with this rig, their size was limited by the difficulty of handling the huge main boom. From the 1880s onwards, more and more bigger ketch-rigged vessels were built. Some of them were among the biggest and finest of all British sailing trawlers. (*Postcard*)

12: The Devon Fishing Industry in the Eighteenth and Nineteenth Centuries

1 BPP, 1785, X, 52–6. Third Report from the Select Committee on the State of the British Fisheries, Further Report on the State of the British Herring Fishery, 1798, 286–300.

2 C L Cutting, *Fish Saving* (1955), 79.

3 BPP, 1798, X, Account Nos. 12 and 13, 292–5.

4 BPP, 1798, X, Account Nos. 16 and 17, 297–9.

5 J Rowe, *Cornwall in the Age of the Industrial Revolution* (1953), 299.

6 W G Hoskins, *Devon* (1954), 212–3.

7 DRO, Miscellaneous Papers, Box 10.

8 DRO, Misc Papers, Box 10; PRO, E 190/1008.

9 Cutting, *Fish Saving*, 158.

10 BPP, 1785, BPP, X, 21–2, Third Report; BPP, 1833, XIV, Report of the Select Committee on the British Channel Fisheries, Mins. of Evid., QQ, 1617, 1783–5.

11 BPP, 1833, XIV, 16.

12 D Defoe, *A Tour through England and Wales* (1928), 226, 259; Charles Vancouver, *General View of the Agriculture of the County of Devon* (1808), 414; DRO, Misc. Papers, Box 10.

13 W G Hoskins, *Industry, Trade and People in Exeter, 1688–1800* (1935), 23; WDRO, Q/591 and Q/593.

14 J Watkins, *An Essay towards a History of Bideford* (1792), 10; A Brixey, *The Story of Torbay* (1905), 125.

15 M Graham, ed., *Sea Fisheries. Their Investigation in the United Kingdom* (1956), 12–14; G L Alward, *The Sea Fisheries of Great Britain and Ireland* (1932), 11; Cutting, *Fish Saving*, 217; E W H Holdsworth, *Deep Sea Fishing and Fishing Boats* (1874), 54, 200–1.

16 P Russell, 'Some Historical Notes on the Brixham Fisheries' *DAT*, 83 (1951), 285.

17 PRO, ADM 7/381–4.

18 BPP, 1786, X, App. 192, First Report.

19 DRO, 1579 A.

20 W Marshall, *The Rural Economy of the West of England* (1796), quoted in R P Chope, ed., *Early Tours in Devon and Cornwall* (1918), 281; WDRO, T 668 (1803).

21 R C Jarvis, 'British Ship Registry: The Quantification of Source Material', in H E S Fisher, ed., *Ports and Shipping in the South West* (Exeter 1971), 164–5; R Davis, *The Rise of the English Shipping Industry in the Seventeenth and Eighteenth Centuries* (1962), 395–6.

22 PRO, ADM 7/381–4.

23 Blake, *A Brief Detail of the Home Fishery, from Early Time etc.* (1763), 70.

24 Grant & Co, *An Account of the Land-carriage Fish-Undertaking Continued by Grant and Co* (1768), 6.

25 BPP, 1786, X, App. 192, First Report, quoted in T C Barker, J C McKenzie and John Yudkin, eds, *Our Changing Fare* (1966), 101.

26 W Marshall, *Rural Economy*, 281; WDRO, T. 668 (1803).

27 DRO, 1579 A.

28 DRO, Ship Registers, Plymouth and Dartmouth.

29 DRO, Ship Registers, Plymouth and Dartmouth; BPP, 1866, XVIII, Report of the Royal Commission on the Sea Fisheries of the United Kingdom, Minutes of Evidence, QQ, 8051–2, 18698–702.

30 DRO, Ship Registers, Plymouth and Dartmouth.

31 BPP, 1833, XIV, Report of the Select Committee on the British Channel Fisheries. Mins. of Evid., QQ. 1325, 1517, 1520, 1556; E and S Lysons, *Magna Britannia*, VI (1822), 71.

32 R J H Lloyd, 'The Swansea Fishery (1775)' *MM*, 45 (1959).

33 *United States Fish Commission Bulletin*, VII (1887), 367; Alward, *Sea Fisheries*, 203–5; E J March, *Sailing Trawlers* (1953), 54–5; J G Bertram, *The Harvest of the Sea* (1869), 316; J C Inglis, 'Harbour Accommodation in the West of England' *Transactions of the Plymouth Institution*, IX (1884), 168–9.

34 For a discussion of the size and category of crew, see below.

35 BPP, 1866. XVIII. Mins. of Evid., Q. 9253.

36 DRO, Ship Registers, Dartmouth and Plymouth.

37 DRO, Ship Registers, Dartmouth and Plymouth; BPP, 1866, XVIII, Mins. of Evid., Q. 9246.

38 BPP, 1866, XVIII, Mins. of Evid., Q. 7792.

39 DRO, Ship Registers, Dartmouth and Plymouth.

40 Registrar of Seamen and Shipping, Crew Lists, 1861.

41 *Dartmouth Chronicle*, Dec. 1869.

42 Alward, *Sea Fisheries*, 147.

43 BPP, 1866, XVIII, Mins. of Evid., QQ. 18839–41.

44 Registrar of Seamen and Shipping, Crew Lists, 1861.

45 Registrar of Seamen and Shipping, Crew Lists, 1861.

46 Registrar of Seamen and Shipping, Crew Lists, 1861, Nos. 4505–6, 4511.

47 J Tunstall, *The Fishermen* (1962), 21.

48 Hoskins, *Devon*, 160–2.

49 BPP, 1866, XVIII, App. 18, 16.

50 BPP, 1866, XVIII, Mins. of Evid., QQ. 8662, 18146–7.

51 DRO, Ship Registers, Plymouth and Dartmouth.

52 DRO, Ship Registers, Plymouth and Dartmouth.

53 BPP, 1833, XIV, Mins. of Evid., Q. 2305; Lloyd, 'Swansea Fishery'.

54 BPP, 1866, XVIII, Mins. of Evid., QQ. 8978, 8980–1.

55 DRO, Ship Registers, Dartmouth; Russell, 'Brixham Fisheries', 288; Rowe, *Cornwall in the Industrial Revolution*, 28.

56 BPP, 1833, XIV, Mins. of Evid., Q. 2101.

57 BPP, 1833, XIV, Mins. of Evid., QQ. 2185, 2230.

58 DRO, Ship Registers, Plymouth and Dartmouth.

59 BPP, 1833, XIV, Mins. of Evid., Q. 2064.

60 J M Bellamy, 'Pioneers of the Hull Trawl Fishing Industry', *MM*, 51 (1965), 185.

61 BPP, 1866, XVIII, Mins. of Evid., Q. 6865; DRO, Ship Registers, Plymouth and Dartmouth.

62 BPP, 1866, XVIII, Mins. of Evid., Q. 12969.

63 BPP, 1866, XVIII, Mins. of Evid., QQ. 9356–7, 9360–1.

64 For national statistics of fishing boat tonnage see D J Oddy, 'The Changing Techniques and Structure of the Fishing Industry', in T C Barker and John Yudkin, eds., *Fish in Britain* (1971), 20.

13 *The Rise of the Devon Seaside Resorts, 1750–1900*[1]

John Travis

Seaside tourism is of particular significance in the general context of a maritime history of Devon. At a time when some of the traditional maritime activities were experiencing a relative decline, the rise of the holiday industry provided new business opportunities and alternative forms of employment. Tourism breathed new life into the flagging economies of many Devon coastal communities, enabling them to prosper and expand significantly.

This chapter examines the rise of the Devon seaside resorts from the mid-eighteenth century to 1900. It identifies four distinct phases in their emergence, and analyses the nature and pace of development in each period. It shows that while each of the Devon resorts was unique, a similar range of economic and social factors influenced them all.

1750–1788

The cult of sea bathing developed in the eighteenth century as a natural consequence of the popularity of the spas. For many years the medical profession had been recommending the therapeutic qualities of certain mineral springs, and rich gentlefolk had been congregating there to 'take the waters'. In the mid-eighteenth century physicians realised that sea water contained a much wider range of mineral salts, and they began recommending it as a sovereign remedy for many ailments. Invalids were advised not only to bathe in the sea, but also to drink sea water.[2] Scarborough, Margate and Brighton all began to develop summer sea-bathing seasons in the 1730s, and by the middle of the century they were becoming established as England's first seaside resorts.[3]

Small resorts emerged at an early date on the South Devon coast. In 1750 Exmouth was described as 'a place to which the people of Exeter much resort for diversion and bathing in the sea'.[4] By 1759 a second resort was developing at Teignmouth, with many 'handsome and delightful buildings' being built there to accommodate visitors arriving 'both for health and recreation'.[5] In the 1770s Dawlish began to build a reputation as a small watering place catering especially for invalids.[6] Sidmouth also began to develop a holiday function. By 1776 it was entertaining 'company resorting hither for the benefit of bathing and drinking the waters'.[7]

Many of the early visitors to the South Devon coast were attracted there by the claims being made for the healing properties of sea water. In 1762 the *Royal Magazine* advised its readers that at Teignmouth:

> For the sake of drinking that fashionable purging draught, sea water, and bathing, for which purpose two machines were lately constructed, numbers of people from all parts resort here in the summer season, and cripples frequently recover the use of their limbs, hysterical ladies their spirits and even the lepers are cleansed.[8]

Sea bathing was regarded as a necessary evil rather than a pleasure. Bathers were carried out into deep water in bathing machines and were dipped under the waves by attendants (Fig. 13.1). Fanny Burney found this an unpleasant experience when she visited Teignmouth in 1773. She wrote, 'The women . . . wheeled the bathing machine into the sea themselves . . . I was terribly frightened and really thought I should never have recovered from the plunge'.[9] Invalids seeking the health-giving properties of sea water must have found this daily ritual a dreadful ordeal.

A strong local demand stimulated early resort development on the South Devon coast. The woollen industry had brought prosperity to many Devon towns. Exeter's commercial prosperity was at its peak; it was one of the richest cities in England. As the merchants, manufacturers and professional men of the inland Devon towns increased in numbers and wealth, so they generated a growing demand for the health and recreational facilities becoming available on the nearby coast. The county also had an unusually large number of landed families, and they were equally keen to enjoy the new leisure opportunities.[10] The first visitors to the South Devon resorts nearly all came from the immediate hinterland.

Tourism was slower to develop on the North Devon coast because of the paucity of demand from the sparsely-populated interior. Ilfracombe was the only coastal settlement in North Devon to attract early visitors. By 1771 a few people were frequenting the town 'for the benefit of the . . . salt water'.[11] These early arrivals originated almost entirely from Devon.

Initially, then, the Devon seaside resorts were only of local importance. Their early growth was severely limited by their distance from England's major centres of population, and by the atrocious state of the roads connecting them with the outside world. In 1760 it still took four days to complete the 170-mile coach journey from London to Exeter, and that was a powerful deterrent to all but the most intrepid tourists.[12] Members of fashionable London society preferred to visit resorts on the Kent and Sussex coast, which were much closer to the capital.

A few 'strangers' began to arrive at the South Devon resorts in the 1770s, having made the comparatively short journey from Bath. The road from Bath to Exeter had been improved following the formation of turnpike trusts in the 1750s. Coaches had taken three days to complete the 75-mile journey in 1727, but the travel time was reduced to 1½ days in 1768 and to only 15hrs in 1778.[13] These transport improvements persuaded a few members of the select society frequenting Bath to join the small company at the South Devon resorts for the summer sea-bathing season.[14]

In this early period the Devon seaside resorts entertained only small numbers of visitors, and tourism provided only a relatively small part of their incomes. They all evolved from old-established fishing communities.

13.1 Bathing machines at Torquay, c1845. (*Devon and Exeter Institution*)

The holiday industry was grafted on to their established economies and, although it was beginning to flourish, it had not reached maturity. Investment in tourism was cautious and small in scale. Some new houses were built, but most of the visitors had to stay in unsophisticated accommodation, often renting fishermens' cottages. The Devon resorts were still only small and were providing only limited facilities to a restricted provincial market, whereas some watering places on the Kent and Sussex coast were already becoming large, specialised resorts offering a wide range of social amenities to wealthy visitors from London.

1789–1815

A number of favourable factors enabled the South Devon resorts to gain national recognition in the period between 1789 and 1815. The Continent was closed to English tourists during the long wars which followed the French Revolution, and this meant that some wealthy Englishmen began to seek alternative holiday destinations in their own country. At the same time there was a change in medical thinking, with attention beginning to focus on the merits of sea air, rather than sea water, in the treatment of disease. The pure air and mild winters of the South Devon resorts became the subject of considerable publicity, and many eminent doctors began to recommend this coast once their wealthy patients were prevented from wintering in Mediterranean France.[15] Sidmouth, for example, by 1793 was 'being very commonly recommended to invalids, particularly those affected by consumption, as many of the faculty think this situation equal to the south of France'.[16] Soon all the South Devon resorts were being compared favourably with those of Mediterranean France. In 1803 one guidebook claimed that 'the mild and genial softness of the air on the south coast of Devon is generally esteemed equally salutary with that of Montpellier or Nice'.[17]

The closure of the Continent also encouraged a new interest in the scenery on the Devon coast. English tourists had long admired the scenery of the Alps and the Rhine, but they could no longer visit those regions. William Gilpin, a Hampshire clergyman, published a series of books pointing out that in England there were landscapes which, while less spectacular, could be admired for a different quality; for their picturesque beauty. His books inspired a new vogue for picturesque scenery.[18] Travel writers soon began to call attention to the superb landscapes to be found on the Devon coast. Teignmouth was described as being 'remarkably picturesque',[19] while Torbay was likened to 'the scenery on that part of the coast of the Mediterranean on which Monaco and other picturesque places are situated'.[20]

The patronage of army and naval officers was also a stimulus to trade at the South Devon resorts in the war years. Exeter was a garrison town throughout this period, and army regiments were also camped near the coast.[21] Many of the army officers and their families frequented the coastal resorts. The Channel Fleet was often stationed in Torbay. Naval officers spent time ashore and some of their wives and families took up residence in the emerging resort of Torquay.[22]

Royal visits to the South West also helped to publicise the attractions of the region. Between 1789 and 1805 George III holidayed regularly at Weymouth, on the Dorset coast.[23] This royal patronage brought in its wake an influx of visitors, many of whom extended their tour to include the South Devon resorts. Then, in 1806, Teignmouth, Exmouth, Dawlish and Sidmouth were favoured by visits from the Princess of Wales and benefited considerably from this cachet of royal approval.[24]

Yet another factor encouraging the growth of the tourist trade was that coach travel to Devon had been greatly accelerated in the 1780s. The journey time from London to Exeter had been cut to 32hrs in 1784 and then, on the new mail coach, to only 24hrs in 1785.[25] These transport improvements at last placed the Devon resorts within reach for those who could afford the high coach fares.

It is clear that in the period between 1789 and 1815 there was a substantial increase in the number of visitors arriving at the South Devon resorts for the summer sea-bathing season. At Teignmouth, for example, it was reported in September 1792, 'the arrivals this season have greatly exceeded any other season; and at this time there is not a single lodging vacant'.[26] Other resorts were equally busy. Dawlish in July 1795 was said to be 'full of lodgers'.[27] Exmouth in August of the same year was reported to be 'full of the most respectable and fashionable families'.[28]

The South Devon seaside resorts also became the first in England to gain the added benefits of a winter season. In December 1794 it was reported that Exmouth was enjoying 'all the gaiety of the summer season', being 'extremely full of company, notwithstanding which genteel families arrive continually'.[29] At Teignmouth in the same month there were so many visitors that the *Exeter Flying Post* described it as the 'Montpellier of England'.[30] Dr Maton visited Sidmouth in the same year, and was astonished at the number of wealthy families taking up winter residence there.[31] Some of these winter visitors to the South Devon coast were consumptives, who went there in a desperate attempt to recover their health.

The new arrivals included many members of the nobility and gentry. Contemporary reports suggest that the South Devon resorts were astonished to find themselves playing host to the 'cream of society'. In October 1789 the *Exeter Flying Post* reported in awed terms that in the courtyard of the Globe Inn at Teignmouth had been seen the unprecedented sight of 'seven carriages with coronets'.[32] Genteel visitors arrived in increasing numbers, and local newspapers frequently referred to resorts 'overflowing with fashionables'.[33]

There was a rush of building activity to provide accommodation for this influx of new visitors. These new developments were nearly all close to the sea, reflecting the importance being attached to the therapeutic influences of the maritime air, and also the new interest in coastal scenery. At Teignmouth, for example, it was reported in 1790: 'A regular and genteel row of houses has been started . . . especially for the invalid, being within a few yards of the beach'.[34] Building operations steadily increased there to meet the growing demand, and by October 1799 Robert Jordan, a local banker, could write: 'Teignmouth is still full of company and enquiries are daily made for purchasing building plots . . . people are absolutely building mad'.[35] At Sidmouth and Dawlish many new houses were erected along the shore (Fig. 13.2).[36] Development also went on apace at Exmouth, work starting on the prestigious Beacon Terrace in 1791.[37]

Many of the fashionable new arrivals were accustomed to the stylised pleasures of the spas, and they expected to find similar amenities on the South Devon coast. The increase in visitor numbers soon justified investment in a range of social institutions closely modelled on those long in vogue at the inland watering places. Elegant assembly rooms were erected to provide the fashionable company with a range of diversions designed to dissipate some of their endless free time. Facilities at the assembly rooms opened on the sea front at Teignmouth in 1796 included not only a spacious room for card parties and splendid balls, but also a billiard room and a reading room.[38] Circulating libraries were also opened at the principal resorts. The books and newspapers available to readers usually were relatively few in number, despite the substantial subscriptions that the users had to pay. Jane Austen described the Dawlish library of 1802 as 'pitiful . . . and not likely to have anybody's publication'.[39] But many subscribers regarded them principally as social centres where they could relax and enjoy good company. So when the Royal Marine Library opened at Sidmouth in 1809, it prided itself on being a 'lounging place' providing opportunities for 'saunterers at a watering place to chat and gossip together'.[40]

13.2 Sidmouth sea front, 1820. (*Devon and Exeter Institution*)

regarded them principally as social centres where they could relax and enjoy good company. So when the Royal Marine Library opened at Sidmouth in 1809, it prided itself on being a 'lounging place' providing opportunities for 'saunterers at a watering place to chat and gossip together'.[40]

Baths were another amenity sought by fashionable visitors accustomed to the regimen of the spa. In 1791 Sidmouth became the first Devon seaside resort to provide this 'convenience', when a local surgeon opened hot and cold sea-water baths there.[41] By 1801 Exmouth had two heated sea-water baths, both managed by local doctors.[42] Other Devon resorts soon offered similar facilities (Fig. 13.3). These baths catered particularly for those who sought a sea-water cure but were unable to face the rigours of a dip in the open sea.

The Devon seaside resorts also emulated the spas by providing promenades. In 1789 Sidmouth opened a 'pretty new gravel walk by the seaside for the company to walk on'.[43] Invalids were pushed in bath chairs along these esplanades, for they were ideal situations in which to inhale the therapeutic sea air. Promenades also provided splendid opportunities to parade and impress, and equally to evaluate the quality of the company frequenting a resort. In 1792 Teignmouth's new promenade was reported to be 'lined with a grand assemblage of genteel and fashionable company' on every fine evening (Fig. 13.4).[44]

The growing demand also led to the emergence of new resorts on the South Devon coast. In 1793 John Swete found Seaton 'beginning to have its share of company'. But in this period Seaton was only a minor resort catering for a handful of visitors who were seeking 'cheapness and retirement'.[45] At Budleigh Salterton, two years later, Swete noticed 'improvements in equipping a few cottages for invalids'.[46] By 1810 this coastal village had many new lodging houses and was 'increasing in reputation as a watering place'.[47] Torquay also began its rise to importance. Swete visited the small fishing village in 1792, and saw there a few new houses erected for the accommodation of visitors. He was shown plans to create a new resort drawn up under the auspices of the principal landowner, Sir Robert Palk, and wrote, 'If the plans which I have seen be carried into execution, Torquay will be one day raised into importance'.[48] These were prophetic words, for Torquay embarked almost at once on a period of rapid expansion.

Difficulties of access prevented a similar boom in tourism on the North Devon coast. The roads there were in an appalling condition. Coach services to North Devon were only established in the later part of the eighteenth century. A coach service was operating between Exeter and Barnstaple by 1778, but in 1787 it was still taking over 12hrs to complete the 39-mile journey.[49] By 1796 another coach was running on the alternative approach to North Devon via Taunton, but it took 24hrs to complete a distance of only just over 50 miles.[50]

Another serious impediment to the development of a tourist industry in North Devon was that the region had serious drawbacks when climate became a principal criterion in selecting a holiday resort. By the end of the eighteenth century the medical faculty were emphasising the advantages of warm winters and shelter from cold winds, and in both of these respects the North Devon resorts were thought to compare unfavourably with their South Devon rivals.

The small tourist industry that did develop on the North Devon coast was in part induced by the cult of the picturesque. Just as some tourists travelled to South Devon in search of picturesque scenery, so others made the much more difficult journey to North Devon in their quest for perfect vistas. The remote Bristol Channel coast had been avoided by early travellers, but now it began to gain recognition as an area of exceptional beauty.[51]

The decline of traditional maritime activities on the North Devon coast provided a spur for diversification into the holiday industry. For many years herring fishing had been the mainstay of the economy at both Ilfracombe and Lynmouth, but in the second half of the eighteenth century the shoals disappeared, leaving the fishing communities in an impoverished condition.[52] Likewise, on the South Devon coast a recession in some branches of the fishing industry had helped to prompt a move into tourism. But on the North Devon seaboard the need to develop a holiday industry was rendered even more urgent by the 'wretched' state of farming in the immediate interior.[53]

By the start of the nineteenth century Ilfracombe was beginning to attract a few more visitors. In 1800 one tourist commented favourably on its superior bathing machines and on the provision of 'a number of good houses, chiefly for the accommodation of strangers in the summer season'.[54] In 1803 its status as a coastal resort was confirmed by its inclusion in the national *Guide to All the Watering and Sea-Bathing Places*, which noted that it was becoming a 'fashionable place of resort in the summer months'. But this same publication devoted much more attention to the 'mild and genial softness of the air on the south coast of Devon', which had enabled the southern resorts to develop a second season in winter.[55]

The fishing village of Appledore, on the Torridge estuary, for a time acquired local recognition as a small sea bathing resort. By 1815 it had become 'the resort of the neighbouring gentry' and provided 'the usual accommodations of lodgings and bathing machines'.[56] But Appledore is an example of a resort which failed to fulfil its early promise. Its trade waned rapidly in the 1830s when it was faced with competition from the rising resort of Instow on the opposite side of the estuary.

In the remote northeast corner of the county another resort was emerging at Lynton and Lynmouth. In the 1790s reports of their spectacular scenery persuaded a few adventurous tourists to make the difficult journey over the moor. The principal focus of attention was the Valley of Rocks, a gigantic cleft overhanging the sea. Robert Southey described it in 1799 as 'a spot which, as one of the greatest wonders in the west of England, would attract many more visitors if the roads were passable by carriages'.[57] Improvements to the ancient moorland tracks soon enabled a few more tourists to visit the twin villages. By 1807 two new inns and several lodging houses had been

13.3   The Baths at Dawlish, 1831. (*Devon and Exeter Institution*)

13.4   The Promenade at Teignmouth, *c*1845. (*Devon and Exeter Institution*)

opened.[58] They were beginning to cater for a wealthy clientele who alone could afford to make the long journey there.

Table 13.1 shows that in 1801 the principal Devon resorts still had relatively small populations. At a time when Margate's population was approaching 5,000 and Brighton had over 7,000 inhabitants, Exmouth, the largest Devon resort, had a population of only 2,601, while nascent Torquay had only 838 inhabitants. Table 13.2 shows that the principal South Devon resorts experienced high growth rates in the next two decades. This expansion was part of a wider pattern. The temporary inaccessibility of the Continent helped most of the resorts on the fashionable south coast of England to expand substantially in this period.[59] On the North Devon coast Ilfracombe, and Lynton and Lynmouth were also beginning to grow, but at a slower rate than most of their South Devon rivals.

Table 13.1

Populations of the principal Devon resorts, 1801–1841

Resort	1801	1811	1821	1831	1841	Increase 1801–1841
Exmouth*	2,601	3,160	3,895	4,252	5,119	2,518
Teignmouth**	2,012	2,893	3,980	4,688	4,459	2,447
Dawlish	1,424	1,882	2,700	3,151	3,132	1,708
Sidmouth	1,252	1,688	2,747	3,126	3,309	2,057
Budleigh Salterton	1,014	1,190	1,706	2,044	2,319	1,305
Torquay	838	1,350	1,925	3,582	5,982	5,144
Ilfracombe	1,838	1,934	2,622	3,201	3,679	1,841
Lynton and Lynmouth	481	571	632	792	1,027	546

Table 13.2

Percentage growth rates of the populations of the principal Devon resorts, 1801–1841

Resort	1801 –1811	1811 –1821	1821 –1831	1831 –1841	1801 –1841
Exmouth*	21.5	23.3	9.2	20.4	96.8
Teignmouth**	43.8	37.6	17.8	-4.9	121.6
Dawlish	32.2	43.5	16.7	-0.6	119.9
Sidmouth	34.8	62.7	13.8	5.9	164.3
Budleigh Salterton	17.4	43.4	19.8	13.5	128.7
Torquay	61.1	42.6	86.1	67.0	613.8
Ilfracombe	5.2	35.6	22.1	14.9	100.2
Lynton and Lynmouth	18.7	10.7	25.3	29.7	113.5

Sources: Decennial Census.

* Exmouth figures are for Littleham and Withycombe Raleigh parishes.

** Teignmouth figures are for East and West Teignmouth parishes.

1816–1843

The pace of development slackened at most of the South Devon resorts in the period between 1816 and 1843. After the Napoleonic Wars ended, in 1815, some fashionable members of society deserted the South Devon coast and began holidaying on the Continent again, but there was no significant increase in local demand to compensate for this loss. The strongest growth in this period was experienced at resorts such as Blackpool, Southport and Scarborough, where increasing numbers of middle-class holidaymakers were arriving from nearby areas of industrial expansion. But in Devon the woollen trade had suffered depression during the French wars and no other major industries were developing to take its place.[60] This meant that the South Devon resorts could not expect a substantial increase in the number of middle-class visitors from the immediate hinterland to compensate for the loss of part of the upper-class trade.

Tables 13.1 and 13.2 show that most South Devon resorts grew at a more gradual rate between 1821 and 1841 than in the two previous decades. At

Teignmouth and Dawlish the population actually fell slightly between 1831 and 1841. Torquay was a notable exception to the general trend, for its population increased dramatically. By 1841 it had developed from a tiny seaside village into the largest Devon resort and had a population of 5,982 (Fig. 13.5).

Torquay's expansion resulted mainly from the rapid development of its winter season. In 1821 it was reported that Torquay was being 'much resorted to by winter visitants on account of its warm and sheltered position'.[61] By 1841 Torquay was firmly established as England's principal winter health resort, catering especially for people with lung complaints. In that year Dr Granville, a leading authority on health resorts, commented that 'it is the very nature of the place to have, as it were, a permanent residentiary set of invalids, who hurry thither on the coming on of winter'.[62] Torquay's growing specialisation as a winter retreat also enabled it to attract many genteel visitors seeking good company rather than renewed health.

The winter season at the other South Devon resorts slowly declined in importance until it was a mere adjunct to the main summer season. In 1825 a national guide to watering places could still report that Sidmouth was 'very commonly recommended to invalids, particularly those who are affected by consumption', while Exmouth was still in winter 'a salutary retreat to invalids and particularly to the consumptive'.[63] But Torquay gradually captured most of the winter trade formerly enjoyed by its older South Devon neighbours. Exmouth, for example, had been one of the first seaside resorts in England to develop a winter season, but when Dr Granville visited it in 1840 he found that it was declining in favour because medical opinion had begun to regard it as too exposed to cold winds. He reported, 'The influx of strangers is much smaller than it was wont to be in former times, and invalids have gone in search of a more sheltered and more genial situation'.[64]

The popularity of Torquay led to the development of a new resort at nearby Paignton. In 1810 Paignton had consisted only of some miserable habitations where the peasantry were 'wretchedly lodged',[65] but by the 1830s a few visitors to Torquay had begun moving along the coast to this seaside village, which could boast one of the best beaches in South Devon. In 1832 it was reported, 'Paignton has much improved within a few years; many new houses have been erected and much attention has been paid to the accommodation for invalids'.[66] Torquay had already achieved importance as a winter watering place, but Paignton was to build a reputation as a summer sea-bathing resort.

In the 1820s improvements in land access to the remote North Devon coast at last made it somewhat easier for tourists to reach. New turnpikes were constructed from both Exeter and Taunton, and coach services were accelerated. By 1827 the 'North Devon' coach was running from London via Taunton to Barnstaple in only 28¼hrs.[67] This was a greatly improved time, but still significantly slower than the coaches from London to Exeter, which were completing their journey in only 19hrs.[68]

The advent of steamer services on the Bristol Channel in 1822 heralded the start of an important new means of travel to the North Devon coast.[69] Steamships provided a much easier way of reaching North Devon from important centres of demand in South Wales and at Bristol. Ilfracombe had the best harbour and benefited most from this revolution in water transport. By 1828 it was reported that 'many families of distinction' were holidaying there, brought by the 'different steamboats which have been plying to and from Bristol and Swansea'.[70] Lynmouth never enjoyed the advantage of a packet service from South Wales, but by 1830 packet steamers from Bristol were calling regularly.[71] Seaborne tourist traffic from Bristol to Ilfracombe and Lynmouth was encouraged still more in 1841 by the opening of the railway from London to Bristol. The combined rail and steamer journey for a short time provided the quickest possible travel from the capital to Devon.[72]

These transport improvements enabled Ilfracombe, and Lynton and Lynmouth to expand significantly. Tables 13.1 and 13.2 show that between 1821 and 1841 they registered substantial increases of population, at a time when the pace of growth was slackening at many of the South Devon resorts.

A new resort also began to emerge on the North Devon coast. Instow had attracted a few sea bathers as early as the 1790s, but it was only after the construction of the new turnpike from Barnstaple via Instow to Bideford in 1832 that it really began to develop as a resort.[73] In 1838 the opening of hot

13.5 Torquay, *c*1845. (*Devon and Exeter Institution*)

and cold sea-water baths and adjacent furnished lodgings was proudly announced.[74] Instow for a time enjoyed moderate success, with the local press quite often reporting a small influx of holidaymakers. But it was never more than a minor resort catering largely for a local demand.

1844–1900

The fortunes of many of the South Devon resorts revived after they gained the benefits of a rail link. In May 1844 the formal opening of the last section of the Bristol and Exeter Railway to Exeter initiated a new era in fast travel to South Devon. By May 1845 express trains were completing the journey from Paddington to Exeter in only 4½hrs. Extra coach services were soon established to carry passengers from the new railhead to the coast.[75]

The South Devon Railway soon connected several South Devon resorts to the growing national rail network. Passenger trains began running to Dawlish and Teignmouth in May 1846 (Fig. 13.6). A branch line reached Torquay in December 1848, and was extended to Paignton in 1859.[76] The South Devon Railway channelled demand into the resorts west of Exe estuary, but those resorts east of the Exe languished in the absence of a railway.

The opening of the final section of the line from Waterloo to Exeter in 1860 provided a lifeline for the sinking economies of the resorts east of the Exe estuary. But, whereas the South Devon Railway had been deliberately taken close to the coast, the London and South Western Railway (LSWR) was intent only on reaching Exeter and followed an inland route. So small, locally-sponsored companies had to take the initiative in constructing branch lines to the coast. Exmouth obtained a rail link in 1861, and was followed by Seaton in 1868, Sidmouth in 1874 and Budleigh Salterton in 1897.[77] However, these watering places never derived as much benefit from their rail links as had their rivals west of the Exe, for, while the LSWR provided a good service from London, it had only very poor cross-country links with the Midlands and North.

Railway politics delayed the construction of railways to the North Devon coast, and the resorts suffered badly because tourists were being diverted away to South Devon. Trains only began running between Exeter and Barnstaple in 1854. In 1855 the Bideford Extension Railway was opened and the little resort of Instow became the first in North Devon to be reached by the railway. It was 1874 before Ilfracombe was connected to the national network by a line from Barnstaple. Lynton and Lynmouth by this time were further from the railway than almost any other coastal resort in England. It was only in 1898 that they finally obtained a rail link with Barnstaple.[78]

Railways opened the Devon coast to visitors drawn from wider social and geographical backgrounds. Rising real incomes created an increasing demand for seaside holidays, and the railway made it possible for growing numbers of the middle class to make the long journey from London and other far-off cities. But the time and cost of the journey still insulated the Devon resorts from major incursions by the working class, and thus helped to preserve their high social tone.

The delay in the arrival of the railway at the North Devon resorts meant that for many years they had to depend on steamboats to bring in a substantial proportion of their visitors. The regular steamer services from Bristol and South Wales provided a quick and cheap form of transport, but they only operated from May to September, and this hampered attempts to extend the season. By 1863 there were no fewer than nine steamers calling regularly at Ilfracombe,[79] but services rapidly declined after the arrival of the railway in 1874. The steamer service from Portishead, however, remained an important means of access to both Ilfracombe and Lynmouth. Cheap fares encouraged many people from the Midlands and London to travel to North Devon by this route.[80] The closure of this service at the end of the 1886 season was greeted with dismay in Ilfracombe, but for Lynton and Lynmouth it was a much more serious blow.[81] In the absence of a railway this little resort had relied heavily on the Portishead steamer to bring in visitors, and the tourist trade suffered badly until a rail link was finally obtained.[82] But sea travel to Ilfracombe and Lynmouth did not come to an end with the passing away of the regular steamer services, for they were replaced by a growing number of pleasure steamers which brought with them excursionists rather than long-stay visitors.

Tables 13.3 and 13.4 show that those resorts that were fortunate enough to obtain an early rail link expanded significantly, while other resorts without the advantage of a railway grew very little. The railway arrived first at Dawlish and Teignmouth in 1846, and for a time revived their fading fortunes. Later in the century, when the advantages of rail links were more evenly spread, their growth rates slowed and for a time they even experienced slight falls in population. Torquay's population grew rapidly after it obtained a rail link in 1848. By 1881 it ranked eighth in size among the nation's seaside resorts. The tables also highlight the rise to importance of Paignton after it obtained a rail link in 1859. On the other hand, Exmouth grew very little in the 1850s, but it began to flourish again after it obtained a branch line in 1861.

The growth of Sidmouth, Seaton and Budleigh Salterton was restricted by the late arrival of the railway. The tables indicate that they stagnated for

13.6   A train approaching Teignmouth, *c*1850. (*Devon and Exeter Institution*)

much of the period before they obtained rail links, with slight falls in population being experienced at Sidmouth between 1851 and 1861, and at Budleigh Salterton between 1871 and 1891. After the railway reached them there was some revival in their fortunes, but their lack of good sandy beaches prevented any really substantial growth. It is clear that the railway's role in influencing demand flows lessened once it had reached most of the principal resorts, and that other factors, such as the natural advantages of individual watering places, became more important in determining where the bulk of the demand would go.

Tables 13.3 and 13.4 also show that North Devon development was hindered by the late arrival of the railway. The slight fall in population at Ilfracombe between 1841 and 1851, and at Lynton and Lynmouth in the following decade, can be explained by the fact that the railway had reached some of their competitors on the South Devon coast and was drawing away some of their visitors. Ilfracombe began to grow again in the 1860s, at a time when substantial investment was being made in the confident expectation that it was about to obtain a rail link.[83] The belated arrival of the railway there in 1874 was followed by a period of sustained growth. Lynton and Lynmouth's slow growth was due largely to the delay in obtaining a railway. Only in the 1880s did the population of the twin villages at last begin to increase significantly, at a time when proposals for a railway and a deep-water pier encouraged new investment in the resort.[84]

Swings of the pendulum of fashion also affected the fortunes of individual watering places on the Devon coast. Initially the emphasis had been on sea bathing, so Exmouth and Teignmouth, which had sandy beaches and the advantage of being close to Exeter, had been the first resorts to emerge. In the period after 1789 attention had swung towards pure sea air and mild winters, and the resorts of Torquay, Sidmouth, Seaton and Budleigh Salterton had begun to develop, largely because they were thought to have salubrious climates. In the second half of the nineteenth century the importance attached to climate gradually diminished, while the beach took on a new importance as the focal point for a family holiday. Watering places with sandy beaches, such as Paignton and Exmouth, benefited from this shift of public interest. But Sidmouth, Seaton and Budleigh Salterton lost trade because they had shingle beaches and were unable to attract many of the middle-class families who were forming a growing section of the holiday market.

Torquay was easily the most important resort in Devon in the second half of the nineteenth century. Its resort trade had many facets. It catered especially for invalids and was the leading English health resort for the

Table 13.3
Populations of the principal Devon resorts, 1841–1901

Resort	1841	1851	1861	1871	1881	1891	1901	Increase 1841–1901
Torquay	5,982	11,474	16,419	21,657	24,767	25,534	33,625**	27,643*
Exmouth†	5,119	5,961	6,049	6,524	7,224	9,297*	10,485	5,366*
Teignmouth‡	4,459	5,149	6,022	6,751	7,120	7,006	7,366	2,907
Sidmouth	3,309	3,441	3,354	3,360	3,475	3,758	4,201	892
Dawlish	3,132	3,546	4,014	4,241	4,519	4,925*	4,681	1,549*
Paignton	2,501	2,746	3,090	3,590	4,613	6,783	8,385	5,884
Budleigh Salterton	2,319	2,447	2,496	2,897	2,856	2,636	2,660	341
Seaton	765	766	809	1,013	1,221	1,293	1,325	560
Ilfracombe	3,679	3,677	3,851	4,721	6,255	7,692	8,557	4,878
Lynton and Lynmouth	1,027	1,059	1,043	1,170	1,213	1,547	1,641	614

Table 13.4
Percentage growth rates of the populations of the principal Devon resorts, 1841–1901

Resort	1841 –1851	1851 –1861	1861 –1871	1871 –1881	1881 –1891	1891 –1901	1841 –1901
Torquay	91.8	43.1	31.9	14.4	3.1	31.7**	462.1*
Exmouth†	16.4	1.5	7.9	10.7	28.7*	12.8	104.8*
Teignmouth‡	15.5	17.0	12.1	5.5	−1.6	5.1	65.2
Sidmouth	4.0	−2.5	0.2	3.4	8.1	11.8	27.0
Dawlish	13.2	13.2	5.7	6.6	9.0*	−5.0	49.5*
Paignton	9.8	12.5	16.2	28.5	47.0	23.6	235.3
Budleigh Salterton	5.5	2.0	16.1	−1.4	−7.7	0.9	14.7
Seaton	0.1	5.6	25.2	20.5	5.9	2.5	73.2
Ilfracombe	−0.1	4.7	22.6	32.5	23.0	11.2	132.6
Lynton and Lynmouth	3.1	−1.5	12.2	3.7	27.5	6.1	59.8

Sources: Decennial Census.

* Boundary changes affect precise comparability of figures.

** In 1900 parts of St Marychurch and Cockington were added to Torquay, thus increasing substantially the 1901 figure for Torquay.

† Exmouth figures are for Littleham and Withycombe Raleigh parishes.

‡ Teignmouth figures are for East and West Teignmouth parishes.

treatment of lung diseases. So many consumptives went to live in Torquay that in 1872 the local Member of Parliament was referred to as 'the representative of the pulmonary interest'.[85] It had the added advantage of being recognised as a desirable place of residence for retired people. Torquay was also an extremely fashionable resort attracting the cream of society. It was first and foremost a winter resort, but it also attracted some summer visitors who arrived seeking the simple delights of the seashore. The secret of Torquay's success was that it appealed to so many groups: it was at once a health and pleasure resort, a retreat for the elderly and a playground for the young.

None of the other Devon resorts catered either for invalids or for fashionable society on anything approaching the scale of Torquay. All were quiet, decorous resorts entertaining comparatively small numbers of holidaymakers and providing retirement homes for some affluent residents. They all maintained their sedate, select character right up until the end of the nineteenth century. Teignmouth, for example, was described in 1899 as a 'highly respectable resort rather than a popular one', attracting 'many Anglo-Indians and other elements of good society', while Exmouth was also considered to have 'social advantages which would be an advantage to retired officers, Anglo-Indians and the like'.[86] Dawlish in the same year was reported to have 'all the attractions of a small seaside holiday resort without any of the disturbing influences or jarring noises that often mar the enjoyment of those who frequent the larger seaside towns'.[87]

It is true that at Ilfracombe in the 1890s there were a few complaints that the 'masses predominated over the classes',[88] but, while this resort was undoubtedly exposed to influxes of working-class excursionists from South Wales, it was still essentially a middle-class resort with a substantial number of military officers, clergymen and doctors among its clientele. In 1892 one travel writer pointed out that, while Ilfracombe lacked 'the sad dignity of Torquay and the subdued gentility of Teignmouth', it could still 'turn up its nose at the high jinks' of Weston-super-Mare and many other popular resorts elsewhere on the English coast.[89]

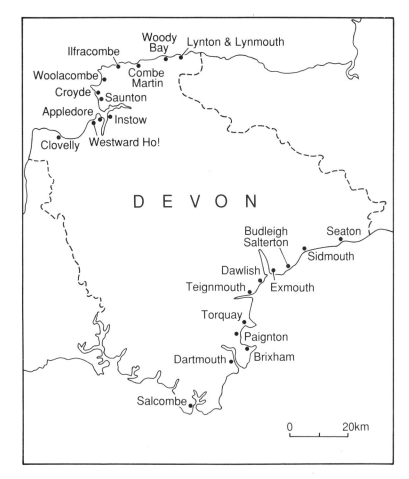

Map 13.1 Devon's Seaside Resorts.

Working-class excursionists generally intruded far less at the Devon watering places than at the majority of English resorts. The high cost of the train fare placed the Devon coast well out of reach for most of the poorer inhabitants of London and other distant centres of inland population. Early rail excursions originated mainly from towns in the immediate hinterland and brought relatively small numbers of trippers who did little to disrupt the genteel resorts. Excursion trains from distant parts of the country began arriving more frequently in the final decade of the nineteenth century, but distance and the high cost of travel still filtered out most of the working class.

The excursion steamers operating on the Bristol Channel posed more of a threat, for they placed the North Devon resorts within easy reach of the labouring class of South Wales. Steamers and even tugs had begun carrying day trippers from South Wales to Ilfracombe and Lynmouth in the 1840s, but the early excursions were comparatively few in number and, while there were occasional complaints of drunken and disorderly behaviour, in general they did little to upset the established resort users. In the 1880s, however, a new breed of fast, purpose-built pleasure steamers appeared on the Bristol Channel. Some operated from the ports of South Wales, often in conjunction with local railway companies. Others began running from Bristol, for these powerful new steamers could now reach Lynmouth and Ilfracombe from there in as little as four hours, which at last made a day trip to North Devon a practical proposition.[90]

The resident gentry and wealthy visitors viewed with horror the drunken trippers occasionally landed, especially from Wales. Measures were taken to preserve the resorts' high social tone. At Ilfracombe by-laws were passed banning excursion steamers on Sundays, and this largely confined working-class visits to bank holidays and other special days.[91] At Lynton and Lynmouth the opposition of the wealthy residents defeated five different schemes for a pier, which, if constructed, would have allowed large numbers of trippers to disembark.[92] Steamer trips steadily increased, but even at the end of the century the trippers arriving at Ilfracombe harbour were numbered usually in hundreds rather than thousands, while at Lynmouth the lack of proper landing facilities meant that only limited numbers could be brought ashore in small boats.

The Devon resorts were careful not to introduce vulgar commercial amusements which might have attracted excursionists. The holiday industry depended on the patronage of the leisured class, and it was not prepared to seek the 'pence and impudence' of transitory trippers if it risked losing the sovereigns and support of long-stay visitors. In this period recreations at the Devon resorts tended to be of a serious nature, with an unusually marked emphasis on improvement. Activities designed to stimulate the mind included marine biology and fern collecting, both of which first became fashionable on the Devon coast. Recreations promoting physical improvement included golf, tennis, archery and yachting, all of which were socially exclusive sports. The Devon resorts were sometimes criticised for being dull, but 'respectable' middle-class visitors felt secure there because there were no fairgrounds or catch-penny amusements to encourage mass influxes of the working class.[93]

The tripper incursions at the Devon resorts certainly caused much less disruption than they did at many other English seaside resorts. Even on a fine bank holiday in the 1890s, Dawlish and Teignmouth rarely entertained more than 2,000 excursionists, Torquay might have up to 4,000 present, while Exmouth and Ilfracombe might play host to up to 6,000.[94] These figures were very small in comparison with the huge numbers of excursionists arriving at many seaside resorts within easy reach of major centres of inland working-class demand. At Margate in 1879 16–24,000 trippers arrived by train every Sunday during the summer season, while Blackpool in 1884 was entertaining up to 40,000 excursionists at a time.[95]

The growing demand from those seeking to distance themselves even further from the working class encouraged the development of a number of minor resorts on the remoter stretches of the South Devon coast. Brixham began to be frequented by artists and other discriminating visitors who could appreciate the scenery of Berry Head and find fascination in the activity of the fishing harbour. One travel writer was less sold on its charms, and described it as 'a sort of Devonshire Wapping with a Billingsgate smell'.[96] Dartmouth was also late in developing a tourist trade. It was difficult to reach by land and suffered the drawback of having a rocky coastline offering few facilities for bathers. It catered for a small, select clientele who were attracted there by the opportunities for boating and fishing. Salcombe was an attractive coastal village blessed with exceptionally mild winters, but, like Dartmouth, was handicapped by the difficulty of land access. It similarly attracted a small band of discerning visitors who could appreciate fine scenery and the facilities for yachting.

The principal Devon seaside resorts evolved from pre-existing settlements, but Westward Ho! is an example of a minor resort which was created on a previously uninhabited stretch of coast. A business syndicate was formed in 1863 to establish this new watering place at Northam Burrows on the North Devon coast. 'The recent publication of Mr Kingsley's charming work *Westward Ho!*', had, claimed the prospectus, 'awakened public interest in the romantic and beautiful coast of North Devon'.[97] The Westward Ho! Hotel began trading in 1865, and expensive villas soon proliferated around it.[98] Hot and cold sea-water baths were opened in 1866, and bathing machines soon appeared on the beach as the new watering place made a belated bid for recognition as a national health resort.[99] But only a few invalids arrived to seek a marine cure and, despite the provision of a golf course and a swimming pool for more active holidaymakers, Westward Ho! enjoyed only modest popularity.[100] It was a small but exclusive resort. In 1899 one guidebook reported that it was frequented only by 'the families of captains, colonels and "knights at arms", Anglo-Indians and other persons who find here congenial company'.[101]

Clovelly, on the other hand, is an example of a coastal settlement where the landed proprietors deliberately prevented the growth of a large resort. This quaint fishing village had begun to attract a few wealthy tourists in the 1840s,[102] and might have been expected to grow substantially. Clovelly's continuing remoteness from the rail network was certainly an obstacle to development, but it was easily reached by sea and, having such a strong visual appeal, it could have fallen victim to uncontrolled expansion. It was the lords of the manor who imposed strict controls on building and ensured that Clovelly remained a picturesque but somewhat primitive place for a day visit, instead of becoming an over-built but well-appointed resort in which to stay.[103]

In the late nineteenth century a minor resort began to emerge at Combe Martin on the Exmoor coast. This seaside village appealed to some who sought peace and seclusion, for it was far removed from the railway. In 1884 one guidebook had condemned the village as being 'devoid of interest and . . . at times none too sweetly odorous',[104] but by 1889 it had a few lodging houses and was attracting a limited number of visitors who used it as a centre from which to tour Exmoor.[105]

Woody Bay, a few miles to the east, was the setting for another attempt to establish a new resort on a virgin site. Colonel Lake, a wealthy solicitor, purchased the wooded cliffs in 1885 and at once made plans to develop an exclusive new resort. New roads were made to improve land access and a pier was built to enable steamers to call.[106] By 1895 he had opened two hotels and several lodging houses,[107] but in 1900 he was arrested and charged with embezzling his clients' funds to finance his scheme. He was sentenced to twelve years in prison and the estate had to be sold to pay off his debts.[108] It was purchased by a neighbouring landowner who at once put a stop to all further development. Thus ended an ambitious attempt to create an entirely new resort, which for a time had been perceived as a very real threat by nearby Lynton.

Efforts to create small resorts on previously undeveloped stretches of the Atlantic coast, northwest of Barnstaple, proved more successful. This region was exposed to westerly gales and had not been considered suitable for resort development earlier in the century, when the medical faculty had been stressing the importance of sheltered locations. But in the later nineteenth century a new generation of the visiting public began to seek relaxing family holidays rather than renewed health, and for them the extensive sandy beaches on this coast held considerable appeal. By 1888 a large estate at Woolacombe had been laid out for development, and already several lodging houses and an hotel had been completed and were taking visitors.[109] By 1896 building work had begun in earnest at both Croyde and Saunton Sands, and a number of newly-constructed boarding houses had been opened for business.[110]

Devon thus ended the nineteenth century with Torquay as its only major seaside resort, but with no fewer than nine medium-sized watering places and with a growing number of minor ones. It was difficulty of access from the major centres of inland population that had set the Devon watering places apart from the more popular seaside resorts in other parts of England, for this was the principal factor that had limited their growth and safeguarded their select character.

13: *The Rise of the Devon Seaside Resorts, 1750–1900*

1 This chapter is based on J F Travis, 'The Rise of Holidaymaking on the Devon Coast, 1750 to 1900, With Particular Reference to Health and Entertainment' (unpublished PhD thesis, University of Exeter, 1989). A revised version of this thesis has been published; John Travis, *The Rise of the Devon Seaside Resorts, 1750–1900* (Exeter, 1993).

2 J A R Pimlott, *The Englishman's Holiday, A Social History* (Hassocks, 2nd edn, 1976), 21–54.

3 J K Walton, *The English Seaside Resort. A Social History, 1750–1900* (Leicester, 1983), 11.

4 J J Cartwright, *The Travels through England of Dr Richard Pococke during 1750, 1751 and Later Years* (1888), I, 102.

5 A Brice, *The Grand Gazetteer* (Exeter, 1759), 1284.

6 DRO, John Swete, Picturesque Sketches of Devon, 564/M, (hereafter Swete, Picturesque Sketches), (1795), X, 159–60.

7 A Oliver, ed., *The Journal of Samuel Curwen, Loyalist* (Cambridge, Mass., 1972), I, 204.

8 'Teignmouth', *Royal Magazine*, VI (1762), 128. A reference by J A Bulley led me to this quotation; J A Bulley, 'Teignmouth as a Seaside Resort before the Coming of the Railway' *DAT*, LXXXVIII (1956), 145–6.

9 A R Ellis, ed., *The Early Diary of Frances Burney, 1768–1778* (1907), I, 254.

10 W G Hoskins, *Industry, Trade and People in Exeter, 1688–1800* (Exeter, 2nd edn, 1968), 28–58; W G Hoskins, *Devon* (1954), 60, 74, 124–8.

11 *Exeter Flying Post* (hereafter *EFP*), 2 Aug. 1771.

12 G Sheldon, *From Trackway to Turnpike. An Illustration from East Devon* (1928), 92, 99.

13 *EFP*, 8 April 1768, 26 Dec. 1777; Sheldon, *Trackway*, 83, 100.

14 Ellis, *Early Diary*, 229, 231.

15 R Fraser, *General View of the County of Devon, with Observations on the Means of its Improvement* (1794), 9.

16 R Polwhele, *The History of Devonshire* (1793), II, 233.

17 *A Guide to All the Watering and Sea-Bathing Places* (1803 edn), 197.

18 C Hussey, *The Picturesque. Studies in a Point of View* (1927), 110–24.

19 'Description of East Teignmouth and its Environs', *Gentleman's Magazine*, LXIII (1793), Part 2, 785–6.

20 J Greig, ed., *The Farington Diary. By Joseph Farington* (1925), 264.

21 R Newton, *Eighteenth Century Exeter* (Exeter, 1984), 103.

22 O Blewitt, *Panorama of Torquay* (2nd edn, 1832), 36; A B Granville, *The Spas of England and Principal Sea-Bathing Places* (1841), III, 476.

23 S Ayling, *George III* (1972), 351, 378.

24 *EFP*, 24 April, 1 May, 8 May, 23 May 1806.

25 Sheldon, *Trackway*, 100, 145.
26 *EFP*, 6 Sept. 1792.
27 G D and E G C Griffiths, *History of Teignmouth* (Teignmouth, 1965), 38.
28 *EFP*, 20 Aug. 1795.
29 *EFP*, 18 Dec. 1794.
30 *EFP*, 25 Dec. 1794.
31 W G Maton, *Observations Relative Chiefly to the Natural History, Picturesque Scenery and Antiquities of the Western Counties of England* (Salisbury, 1797), II, 84.
32 *EFP*, 8 Oct. 1789.
33 *EFP*, 25 Aug., 15 Sept. 1796.
34 *EFP*, 24 June 1790.
35 Griffiths, *History of Teignmouth*, 42.
36 Edmund Butcher, *An Excursion from Sidmouth to Chester in the Summer of 1803* (1805), 452; S Woolmer, *A Concise Account of Exeter, its Neighbourhood and Adjacent Watering Places* (Exeter, 2nd edn, 1811), 88.
37 *EFP*, 14 April 1791.
38 *EFP*, 15 Sept. 1796.
39 R W Chapman, *Jane Austen's Letters to Her Sister Cassandra and Others* (1952), 98.
40 *The Beauties of Sidmouth Displayed* (Sidmouth, 1810), 51–2.
41 *EFP*, 9 June 1791.
42 Robin Bush, *The Book of Exmouth* (Buckingham, 1978), 45.
43 Suffolk Record Office, Ipswich Branch, Tour in Devonshire by Revd Sir Thomas Gery Cullum in 1789, E2/44/6, 9 Aug. 1789.
44 *EFP*, 6 Sept. 1792.
45 Swete, Picturesque Sketches, IX, 149.
46 Swete, Picturesque Sketches, X, 38.
47 *Beauties of Sidmouth*, 136.
48 Swete, Picturesque Sketches, II, 98, 112.
49 *EFP*, 27 Nov. 1778, 4 Jan. 1787.
50 J R Chanter, 'Devon Lanes' *DAT*, VI (1873), Part 1, 191.
51 T H Williams, *Picturesque Excursions in Devonshire and Cornwall* (1804), 27–41, 54–5.
52 T H Cooper, *A Guide containing a Short Historical Sketch of Lynton and Lynmouth* (1853), 8–9; A M Northway, 'The Devon Fishing Industry, 1760–1860' (unpublished MA thesis, University of Exeter, 1969), 58–9.
53 C Vancouver, *General View of the County of Devon* (1808), 440.
54 Richard Warner, *A Walk through Some of the Western Counties of England* (Bath, 1800), 119.
55 *A Guide* (1803 edn), 197, 227.
56 *A Guide* (1815 edn), 17.
57 C C Southey, *Life and Correspondence of Robert Southey* (1849), II, 23.
58 Cooper, *Historical Sketch of Lynton*, 11.
59 Walton, *English Seaside Resort*, 58.
60 Hoskins, *Industry*, 81–6.
61 Woolmer, *A Concise Account* (1821, 3rd edn), 98.
62 Granville, *Spas of England*, III, 486.
63 *A Guide* (1825 edn), 374, 387.
64 Granville, *Spas of England*, III, 466.
65 D Webb, *Observations and Remarks during Four Excursions made to Various Parts of Great Britain in the Years 1810 and 1811* (1811), 71.
66 Blewitt, *Panorama*, 102.
67 *North Devon Journal* (hereafter *NDJ*), 27 April, 4 May 1827.
68 *EFP*, 11 June 1827.
69 Grahame Farr, *West Country Passenger Steamers* (Prescot, 2nd edn, 1967), 6–7.
70 T H Cornish, *Sketch of the Rise and Progress of the Principal Towns of the North of Devon* (Bristol, 1828), 28–9.

71 *NDJ*, 12 Aug. 1830.
72 Farr, *Passenger Steamers*, 117.
73 *A Guide* (1803 edn), 227; *EFP*, 8 March 1832.
74 *North Devon Advertiser*, 20 July 1838.
75 *Western Times*, 4 May 1844; E T MacDermot, *History of the Great Western Railway* (2nd edn, 1972), I, 92, 340; II, 68–75.
76 *EFP*, 4 June 1846; *Western Times*, 23 Dec. 1848; J R Pike, *Paignton* (Torbay, 1974), 16.
77 D S J Thomas, *A Regional History of the Railways of Great Britain. The West Country* (1960), 29–35, 39–40; R A Williams, *The London and South Western Railway* (Newton Abbot, 1968), II, 214, 217.
78 *NDJ*, 13 July 1854; *EFP*, 1 Nov. 1855; *Ilfracombe Chronicle* (hereafter *IC*), 22 July 1874; *North Devon Herald*, 12 May 1898.
79 *NDJ*, 27 Aug. 1863.
80 *IC*, 17 June, 7 Oct. 1882.
81 *IC*, 22 Oct. 1887.
82 *Lynton and Lynmouth Recorder*, 25 Oct. 1887.
83 F B May, 'The Development of Ilfracombe as a Resort in the Nineteenth Century' (unpublished MA thesis, University of Wales, 1978), 66–76.
84 Travis, *Rise of Devon Seaside Resorts*, 133–6.
85 *EFP*, 17 Jan. 1872.
86 A R H Moncrieff, *Where Shall We Go?* (1899 edn), 78, 188.
87 *A New Pictorial and Descriptive Guide to Dawlish* (1899), 2.
88 *Ilfracombe Gazette*, 30 Dec. 1893.
89 Moncrieff, *Where?* (1892 edn), 115.
90 Farr, *Passenger Steamers*, 214, 222–37.
91 *IC*, 21 Oct. 1899.
92 Four of these pier schemes are discussed in J Travis, 'Lynton in the Nineteenth Century. An Isolated and Exclusive Resort', in E M Sigsworth, ed., *Ports and Resorts in the Regions* (Hull, 1980), 159–61.
93 This section is based on Travis, *Rise of Devon Seaside Resorts*, Chapter X, where full documentation can be found.
94 *Western Times*, 4 Aug. 1891, 2 Aug. 1892; *IC*, 12 Aug. 1893; *Exmouth Journal*, 7 Aug. 1897.
95 F M Stafford, 'Holidaymaking in Victorian Margate, 1870–1900' (unpublished M Phil thesis, University of Kent, 1979), 103; Walton, *English Seaside Resort*, 71.
96 Moncrieff, *Where?* (1899 edn), 192.
97 *Bideford Gazette*, 2 June 1863.
98 *EFP*, 1 March 1865.
99 *EFP*, 22 Aug. 1866; R Mayo, *The Story of Westward Ho!* (Yelland, 1973), 12.
100 *Bideford Gazette*, 15 Feb., 24 May, 9 Aug. 1870, 3 Oct. 1871; *EFP*, 10 Aug. 1870, 17 July 1875.
101 Moncrieff, *Where?* (1899 edn), 219.
102 *NDJ*, 25 Aug. 1842.
103 Moncrieff, *Where?* (1899 edn), 202.
104 M J B Baddaley and I S Ward, eds., *North Devon and Cornwall* (1884), 44.
105 *Black's Guide to Devonshire* (13th edn, 1889), 179.
106 *Lynton and Lynmouth Recorder*, 13 March 1894; *NDJ*, 19 Sept. 1895, 30 Dec. 1897.
107 *NDJ*, 19 Sept. 1895.
108 *North Devon Herald*, 24 Jan. 1901.
109 W Walters, *Guide to Ilfracombe and North Devon* (Ilfracombe, 1888), 150.
110 *Seaside Watering Places. Being a Guide to Strangers in Search of a Suitable Place in which to spend their Holidays* (1896 edn), 292–3.

14 Education and Welfare of Merchant Seafarers

ALSTON KENNERLEY

SEAFARING, BY VIRTUE OF THE NATURE OF SHIPPING, has always been a national, and usually an international activity. Yet all seafarers must originate from a particular locality. Devon has been known, in the past at least, as a source of seafarers who served both in ships belonging to local ports (fishing, coastal and naval vessels, as well as vessels trading overseas), and in vessels owned elsewhere. Seafarers of the last category, having left the county, might only return to take leave, or might never return, having relocated their homes (if they had them) in a port more convenient to their sea life. Another group of seafarers were brought to Devon's ports by the trading voyage patterns of the ships in which they found themselves, or through serving in the Royal Navy (a very numerous category), and some of these would have found it convenient to base themselves in the county. Whether seafarers were native Devonians or settlers, whether they served in merchant vessels or naval warships, it is pertinent to ask about the kind of education and training for their calling which was offered in the county, and to investigate how the county responded to the social needs of seafarers.

Although this chapter will focus on education and welfare provision in Devon for the merchant seafarer (Dr Payton has a chapter in this volume on naval education), the line between the two has not always been clear cut. From the mid-nineteenth century, however, separate patterns of mercantile and naval education and training became firmly established. In contrast, voluntary organisations offering spiritual and social welfare to seafarers have never made any distinction, though local circumstances have often made it for them, as naval ports have evolved in a distinctly different way from commercial ones.

Much of the following discussion will concern developments in the nineteenth century, when initiatives in social matters were increasingly taken on a national scale, perhaps superseding earlier local efforts. There will also be some consideration of provisions made before 1800, and of those in the twentieth century. Evidence for the existence of nautical education or of charitable welfare provision before 1800 is not easily found, but comparison with other ports of the country suggests that both were available, at least in the more important Devon ports, and at least as early as the seventeenth century.

The term 'seafarer' embraces all those who found their employment in ships, whatever the capacity in which they served or had served. Other commonly used terms, such as sailor or seaman, have overtones or precise definitions which tend to exclude certain categories of seafarer, such as officers and apprentices.

Education and Training[1]

The traditional social structure on board ships – master, mates, seamen and apprentices – demonstrates roots in the craft guild system of the late medieval period, a system related to practical occupations in which essential skills were passed on to trainees through work experience.[2] Until the second half of the nineteenth century, training in the practical elements of seafaring – seamanship – required no assistance from shore establishments, though certain kinds of seagoing were recognised as of particular value in generating a pool of trained seafarers which could be tapped to strengthen others, the Royal Navy, for example. Two areas of seafaring so valued were the collier trade, particularly between the coal fields of the North East and London,

and the fishing fleets, Devon being especially significant in the latter because of its interest in the cod fishery off Newfoundland. The changing nautical environment after 1850, with its concern about the standard of skills amongst able seamen, the attempt of charitable organisations to supply ratings and officers to the mercantile marine (and the Navy) using static training ships, and the introduction of statutory certification of masters, mates, and (later) engineers, made seamanship a subject of formal teaching.

A more limited training may have been all that was needed for coastal shipping, but with the opening up of oceanic commerce it became essential that each convoy of ships, if not each ship, had someone on board with a knowledge of what was involved in oceanic navigation and some understanding of maritime commerce. These were subjects calling for a secondary education as a foundation. Although the personal interest of some masters might have provided instruction in these subjects at sea (certainly the large chartered trading companies made provision for educating their apprentices), such training was mostly found ashore, in the hands of private mathematical teachers (mathematics being almost synonymous with navigation between the sixteenth and nineteenth centuries) or at charitable navigation schools such as Christ's Hospital, London, or Trinity House School, Hull.[3]

Because of its long-time status as the country's leading port, London became something of a centre for nautical education, and no doubt some Devon seafarers, including youngsters 'intended for the sea', completed their education there. A late example is H B G Keys, who was sent to Christ's Hospital in 1835 from Stoke Damerel under the Samuel Travers Charity. He took the navigation course from 1842, and in 1844 was apprenticed in the barque *Kezia* for seven years.[4]

In seafaring areas, in Devon and elsewhere, it seems likely that many schools offered the chance of completing secondary education with studies in navigation and perhaps aspects of commercial practice. It is not unreasonable to suppose that navigational instruction was to be found in Devon from the start of the seventeenth century. Bideford Grammar School (established in 1625), for example, had six free places for the sons of seafarers lost at sea, and probably offered navigation as a subject. In 1761 a mathematical school was opened in the same town, the master receiving £10 per annum for the free education of ten poor boys in navigation to qualify them for the sea service; and in about 1775 the funeral took place there of Mr Alvan Dunn, a teacher of arithmetic, astronomy and navigation.[5] Nearby at Braunton, the supporters of Chaloners Foundation Free School (established in 1667) considered navigation a more useful subject for the youths of the parish to study than Latin.[6] In 1727 a teacher sued the Trustees of this School for wrongful dismissal. The depositions in the case indicate that all the deponents were keen to demonstrate that navigation had been taught in the past, and that several former pupils had become masters and mates of ships. One stated,

> . . . this [deponent] doth not know nor did know or doth believe that any youth of the said parish or other persons was ever sent from the free school of Braunton as scholar to any university to be a student there & this deponent doth not apprehend or believe the teaching of [Latin] grammar to be of any use in the said school & doth believe that reading writing & arithmetic & navigation are the most & only useful learning to be taught in the said school.[7]

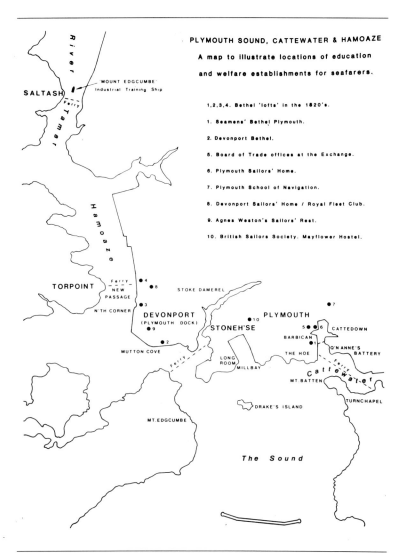

PLYMOUTH SOUND, CATTEWATER & HAMOAZE

A map to illustrate locations of education

and welfare establishments for seafarers.

'MOUNT EDGCUMBE'
Industrial Training Ship

1,2,3,4. Bethel 'lofts' in the 1820's.

1. Seamens' Bethel Plymouth.

2. Devonport Bethel.

5. Board of Trade offices at the Exchange.

6. Plymouth Sailors' Home.

7. Plymouth School of Navigation.

8. Devonport Sailors' Home / Royal Fleet Club.

9. Agnes Weston's Sailors' Rest.

10. British Sailors Society. Mayflower Hostel.

Map 14.1 Plymouth Sound, Cattewater and Hamoaze, illustrating the locations of education and welfare establishments for seafarers.

That navigation must have had a fairly high profile in Devon, at least in the eighteenth century, is evident from it being a subject at schools inland as well as on the coast. This was the case at the charity school at Gittisham, near Honiton, where Thomas Drake was licensed on 4 February 1754 to teach reading, writing, arithmetic and navigation.[8]

Such provision continued to the middle of the nineteenth century. Navigation teachers are recorded at various dates at Teignmouth, Bideford, Dartmouth and Exeter, while in the three towns of Plymouth, Stonehouse and Devonport at least four schools or teachers existed in 1852.[9] These appear to have died out, as only references to the Plymouth School of Navigation have been found after 1883. Paradoxically, this apparent decline in provision, at a time when the British merchant fleet was expanding rapidly to dominate world shipping, might be attributed to the growing national concern about the quality of seafarers and the measures which resulted from it.

However, concern for the inadequate educational level of most navigators was being expressed, and solutions to the problem were being debated in the press by merchants, clergy, navigation teachers and others, and in other publications and in speeches, at least as early as 1815 when, for instance, a group of merchants promoting the Marine Free School at Liverpool wrote to the authorities of all the main British ports, including the mayor of Plymouth, advocating the establishment of similar institutions.[10] This concern was given formal expression by the Select Committee on Shipwrecks in 1836, whose report recommend,

the establishment of cheap nautical schools, either in ships afloat adapted to the purpose, or appropriate buildings ashore, in which the practical duties of seamanship and the elements of navigation should be taught . . .[11]

The Committee also recommended the formation of a board to regulate the affairs of the mercantile marine and

the formation of certain standards of qualification in seamanship and navigation to be attained by officers before they should receive licences . . .[12]

As the debate continued, it focused on the nature of this education and licencing, who was to promote and enforce it, and how it was to be financed. The Select Committee no doubt envisaged action by the state. But in a period which was soon to see the repeal of the Navigation Laws, and in which the state had only just made its first reluctant, small grant in aid of elementary education, when self sufficiency was a creed, and when technical education was to be found only through self-help societies such as the mechanics' institutes, and, furthermore when the powerful shipowning lobby was resisting state interference, such changes would not come quickly.

That the British government was reluctant to take positive action is borne out by the type of licencing system which was first tried. In 1845 an Order in Council of 19 August introduced a system of voluntary examination and certification for masters and mates of merchant vessels, in which the administration was delegated to the various Trinity Houses or pilotage authorities in the main British ports.[13] An examination syllabus was agreed and boards of examiners were established. One was to be at Plymouth, its pilotage being under the control of Trinity House at Deptford. It was the only one in Devon. No attention was given to the problem of how examinees were to prepare themselves. While the arrangements had little practical effect, as there was little advantage to be gained from holding a certificate, the scheme did provide a testing ground for a compulsory system which was to be introduced from 1 January 1851, as a result of the Mercantile Marine Act, 1850. This remained substantially unchanged until 1987.[14]

This Act provided for a central administration through the creation of a Marine Department within the Board of Trade. But, owing to the pressure of the shipping interests, it preserved one of the weakest points of the previous system; namely local examining, with its variable standards and even irregularities. Local marine boards were established to run both the oral and written parts of the examinations, the members being mainly local shipowners. The board for the far South West was established at Plymouth, which meant that all Devon candidates for certificates were to be examined there, unless they chose to travel to other ports where examinations were held, such as Bristol or London. The standards were set 'as low as possible', the form of the written questions being known in advance and the local examiner supplying only the details. Across the British Isles the rigour of the examination varied considerably. Cork, for example, became well known as a port where it was easy to pass. Between 1857 and 1866 its average failure rate was 16 per cent, compared with 48 per cent in London and 36 per cent in Plymouth.[15] Masters and mates who could demonstrate previous employment in those capacities were granted certificates of service, but all other seafarers who had sufficient sea time, and wished to progress beyond the rating of able seaman or had completed apprenticeships, had to sit the examinations, and most of these would wish to take a short course in preparation. Serving this requirement became the main source of income of navigation teachers, probably to the detriment of teaching pre-sea students, which seems to have been the focus of navigation teaching previously.

Thus the provision of nautical education was not left entirely to market forces, and it can be argued that the recommendation of the Select Committee on Shipwrecks of 1836, calling for a network of cheap nautical schools, was achieved. The new Marine Department acted quickly, and funded the establishment of navigation schools in the Sailors' Homes at Liverpool (1853) and London (1854). In 1856 these were placed under the supervision of the Department of Science and Art (formed 1853) as the first of its 'science' schools, and, having assessed the need, it extended the network of navigation schools which would receive its support, but subject to its conditions.[16] The School of Navigation at Plymouth, established in

1862, was the last of seventeen similar establishments in British and Irish ports.[17]

The Plymouth School of Navigation

The conditions under which the Plymouth School was formed seem to have been typical of the formation of the navigation schools set up with the support of the Science and Art Department. No local records have survived, but it is certain that, in order to qualify for Science and Art support, a local committee of management was formed, probably comprising the same persons who were members of the Plymouth Local Marine Board. This committee had to provide the premises and furnishings, and find a trained teacher, subject to the approval of the Department, which would then provide a grant for the purchase of 'apparatus' and guarantee a minimum salary for the teacher. Half of the fees collected from students would be used to maintain the school, and it was intended that the remainder should comprise the teacher's salary. The *Western Daily Mercury* reported that the charges would vary from 6d per week for boys to 6s per week for officers.[18] At this time the Torpoint Naval School was charging all students one guinea per month. The fees at the Navigation School, which assisted seamen at the start of their studies while established officers paid full fees, are almost identical with those at Newcastle Trinity House School when it became part of the Science and Art network.[19]

It is not possible to assess the size or success of the Plymouth School of Navigation, as few enrolment statistics have survived and there is no information on pass rates. However, the return for the first year of operation, 1863, seems to list all enrolments and indicates the range of students:

> . . . the total number of students receiving instruction in or through the agency of the School during 1863 has been 240 [and] the entire number of adults and boys who have at any time paid fees during the year are: masters 39, chief mates 26, only mates 70, second mates 39, master home trade 1, mate home trade 1, second engineer 1, seamen 10, apprentices 6, boys 22. The number of boys who have gone to sea during the year is 18 . . . most of the students attend both day and evening classes.[20]

Possibly the pre-sea boys were taught in formal classes on a programme of fixed duration, but the majority of students attended whilst on leave between voyages, when they would have been without income. Attendance would have been perhaps for only two to four weeks, with a steady turnover of those attending, ensuring that most teaching would have been of a tutorial nature.

The requirement that teachers in Science and Art Schools should be qualified emulated that for elementary school teachers. But it ensured that the navigation schools were perhaps the first technical schools to have qualified teachers. It also meant that young men with mathematical ability were selected, rather than seafarers holding Masters' or Extra Masters' certificates. Most of the teachers at the other navigation schools were put through a special training course. After a period as pupil teachers under Edward Riddle at the Royal Naval School at Greenwich, they were sent to the London Navigation School for a period of teaching practice with seafaring students before being sent to take charge of the new navigation schools in the provinces.[21] By 1862, however, the Science and Art Department had its own system of examinations, and certification both for students and teachers, in a wide variety of science subjects including those of maritime interest. John Merrifield, first head of the Plymouth School of Navigation, took this route after a two-year training course at Exeter Diocesan Training College in 1854–6, whilst in charge of Mary Tavy National School.[22]

The Plymouth School was still in its infancy when a change in funding policy – payment by results – was applied to all Science and Art classes. This was the same approach which had such a narrowing effect on the curricula of elementary schools. For most of the navigation schools it was disastrous, and effectively forced them out of the Science and Art umbrella. From 1 January 1864 payments were only to be made for navigation, nautical astronomy, mathematics, physical geography and steam if the teacher held the appropriate certificates, if the students were successful in the Department's examinations, if they had attended classes for a minimum period since the last results payment, and if they subsequently went to sea.[23] Few of the seafaring students could have been interested in those examinations, and it was impossible to guarantee attendance. Plymouth was one of only three schools to continue to receive Science and Art payments to the end of the century, though at a reduced level. Like the other schools it became dependent on fee income, and its main clientele were students for the masters' and mates' certificates.

In 1908, following the demise of the Science and Art Department and of local marine boards, control of the Plymouth School of Navigation passed to the local education authority. But it remained independent until 1932, when it was absorbed by the Mathematics and Physics Department of Plymouth and Devonport Technical College, though retaining a separate identity. Annual enrolments fell in the 1930s to twenty-eight, though it seems to have remained the only navigation school west of Bristol. Despite the efforts of its first three heads, John Merrifield, Charles Morris and W J Liddicoat, none of whom had been seafarers though they were all authors of navigation textbooks, the Plymouth School remained, in the national context, a minor establishment compared with the provision, for instance, in Liverpool or London.

The Training Ship Mount Edgcumbe

As well as requiring officers capable of navigating safely, ships, particularly sailing vessels, needed seamen with the experience to handle the propulsion unit in the worst of conditions, when trainees would be a liability. Engaging sufficient able seamen was always a major concern of masters before sailing, and in times of national stress or of rapid expansion in shipping the supply of seamen was of national concern. One partial solution was seen in providing youngsters with some pre-sea training. Although the Marine Society of 1756 was originally established to supply boy seamen to the Royal Navy, and pioneered the use of static ships in 1786 with its training ship *Marine Society* (later *Warspite*), this approach was not taken up in a significant way until the 1850s. In 1859 the *Royal Commission on Manning the Navy* recommended that,

> school ships should be established in the principal commercial ports capable of accommodating 100 to 200 boarders in each ship, of whom 100 should be supported by the state.[24]

The availability of numbers of redundant 'wooden walls', and the recognition of the need for training in the increasingly specialist Royal Navy, led to the Navy taking up the general idea, and thus to the appearance of naval training ships on the rivers Tamar and Dart in Devon. While there was no such central initiative for the development of training for the mercantile marine, something of a training ship movement developed. The shipping

14.1 John Merrifield. (Western Figaro, *8 January 1880*)

industry had a hand in the founding of the two ships for officer cadets, *Conway* on the River Mersey (1859) and *Worcester* on the River Thames (1862), but the other eighteen training ships founded between 1856 and 1883 were promoted by voluntary societies concerned as much with social welfare as with training seamen. Of these, eleven, including *Mount Edgcumbe* (1877), were industrial training ships (for boys at risk who were sent under court orders but had not been convicted), and three were reformatory training ships (which accommodated boys who had been convicted of crimes) receiving the bulk of their income from the state.[25] The remainder, together with the *Warspite*, were for destitute or voluntary boys and relied entirely on donations.

One purpose of the Devon and Cornwall Industrial Training Ship Association, formed in Plymouth on 5 November 1874, was to supply trained boy seamen to the mercantile marine.[26] But this objective was associated with a need to provide care for, and to reform, the large numbers of 'street arabs', or waifs and strays, and with an attitude which prevailed amongst contemporary philanthropists and magistrates that being sent to sea was a suitable alternative to imprisonment. The Association's records have not survived, but the objects of the *Formidable* (1869) (Portishead), demonstrate this:

> The object of this institution shall be the reception and training of boys, who through poverty, parental neglect, or being orphans, are left destitute and homeless, and in danger of being contaminated by association with crime and vice.[27]

In fact *Mount Edgcumbe* was part of a sub-group of a much larger number of British industrial schools having similar objects, amongst which was that of providing training in a skill useful in future employment. The training ships offered seamanship as their skill. The Exeter Boys Industrial School, in comparison, offered agriculture, as well as tailoring, shoemaking, wire working and firewood cutting.[28]

By 1877 the Association had accumulated sufficient funds to acquire and refit the second *Conway*, whose Committee had obtained a larger ship.[29] Renamed *Mount Edgcumbe*, after the President of the Association, she was inaugurated for her new role in June 1877, having been moored on the River Tamar off Saltash. Refitting cost £2,100, and she was registered to accommodate 250 boys under the Industrial Schools Act. This bill was met from accumulated donations of £3,408. Members of the Association had promised subscriptions of £525 annually, well below the estimated needs of £580 for salaries and £260 for other running costs. By February 1878 150 boys had been admitted and the staff comprised the Captain-Superintendent, Chief Officer, schoolmaster, three seamen instructors, a carpenter and a cook.[30] It is probable that, as the number of boys increased, the number of staff increased to between twelve and eighteen, though it is likely that they were paid at the lowest rates prevailing on training ships. The lower staffing figure seems more likely as, to judge from various newspaper reports, *Mount Edgcumbe* probably operated below her full complement for most of her time.

Except for the schoolmasters, the staff had usually served in the Navy, and the routine on board emulated the adult world of naval vessels. The full daily routine occupied a boy's waking hours from 5.30am until 8pm. Of this time about one and a half hours was spent at meals, about three hours each at

14.2 Industrial Training Ship *Mount Edgcumbe*. (*City of Plymouth Museums and Art Gallery*)

'household duties', 'school' and 'seamanship', and the remainder at recreation and miscellaneous duties. The boys were divided into port and starboard watches; while one was at seamanship the other was at school. Smaller units – messes – functioned at meal times. In school the classes and curriculum were on elementary school lines, concentrating on reading, writing and arithmetic, many boys being illiterate when admitted.

Seamanship included all the rope and sail handling skills required on ships, and through the fleet of small boats boys became expert at rowing and sailing. In 1898 *Mount Edgcumbe* acquired a seagoing tender, *Goshawk*, a brig of 150 tons with accommodation for 30 boys, which provided sea experience during cruises in the Channel in the summer months. The ship's band was an important element in the routine on board, performing at morning divisions and as a recreational activity, and was in demand ashore at events such as local fêtes, providing rare opportunities for the boys to get ashore.

Whether Devon and Cornwall really needed a training ship is questionable. From the start, most of the boys she received came from other parts of the country, particularly London. In 1896, out of sixty-eight boys admitted, fifty-one came from London, two each from Plymouth, Stonehouse, Devonport and Exeter, and one each from Barnstaple and Cullompton, all in Devon. The rest came from Truro, Fowey, Cawsand and St Germains, in Cornwall, as well as Jersey, Yarmouth and Hereford.[31] For the ship to qualify for maintenance payments of about 6s per head per week, boys had to be sent under a court order, even though no offence had been committed. Originally they could be sent between the ages of eleven and fifteen, but this was later raised to twelve to sixteen. Voluntary boys, paid for by parents, comprised a small proportion of boys on board, and were sometimes admitted as young as ten years of age. Towards the end of the period of committal, the ship tried to obtain a berth at sea for those who wanted it. A significant proportion did not. Of the boys discharged from *Mount Edgcumbe* in 1896, thirteen went into the merchant service, four to the army, thirty-two to friends, three to naval service, one to Canada and three had died.

The cramped conditions on board training ships, coupled with the often poor physical condition of the boys when received, meant that there was a higher rate of illness and mortality than in shore establishments and amongst the population as a whole. In 1875 there were 15 deaths per thousand inmates on British training ships, 11.6 in all industrial schools, and 3.8 in the population at large (10–14 age group). In 1898 the figures were 5.4, 3.7, and 2.2 respectively.[32] The First World War left *Mount Edgcumbe* very short of staff, and no doubt maintenance of the now elderly ship suffered. In the winter of 1916–17 there was much illness amongst the boys and five deaths occurred. The government health inspector reported that conditions on board were 'horrid'.[33] At the end of the war the Society was unable to raise the large sum needed to renovate the ship to the standard required by the Home Office, and she closed in 1920, the ship being broken up at Queen Anne's Battery on the Cattewater in 1921.

Spiritual and Social Welfare

With the exception of very localised seafaring such as inshore fishing, ordered communities on land always found it difficult to understand seafarers, particularly seamen, who chanced to be amongst them for short periods of time. They had no place in local society, their dress, language and behaviour might be alien and, unless they had families locally, they had no abode, except possibly their ships. Thus they tended to congregate in the inns close to the quayside, perhaps the only buildings open to them. Seafarers, for their part, soon became socialised to the total environment of the ship, with its ordered lifestyle providing for their basic physical needs. Is it to be wondered that when they were released or ejected from this environment, their behaviour ashore was at times uninhibited, a pattern not dissimilar from that of some package holidaymakers today, released also from confining environments? Is it surprising that, especially in larger ports, there evolved a port district or 'sailortown' to cater for seafarers ashore, as was the case in Plymouth and Devonport? Seamen easily became destitute, perhaps because employers delayed their pay, or through their own naivety, or because of the activities of the 'land sharks' or 'crimps' who preyed on

14.3   Divisions on TS *Mount Edgcumbe*, c1917. (*Mrs F Parcelle*)

them. Being outside ordered society, seamen might not qualify for such local welfare provision as existed, and like many working people they were unlikely to participate in local religious activity, the focus of middle class life which administered welfare.

The needs of seafarers were, of course, recognised before the nineteenth century, when they came to be addressed on a national scale. In Britain the various seamen's guilds and the trinity houses had welfare provisions, and local charities were endowed for the benefit of seafarers and their dependents, such as the almshouses built in Bideford in 1663 for the widows of six seamen.[34] From time to time individual clergymen addressed themselves to the spiritual state of seafarers. One such was the Rev John Flavel, who ministered in Dartmouth from 1656. A puritan, he was ejected from his Church position in 1662, but continued to preach and write privately. His devotional work, *Navigation Spiritualised . . .* (1671), was addressed to all seafarers, especially those belonging to Dartmouth.[35] In Bideford, in 1719–20, John Copplestone, a dissenting minister from Chulmleigh, preached a sermon there on 'God's works and the wonders of the deep, and the seafaring man's duty'. Possibly this was part of a tradition of preaching an annual sermon to mariners.[36]

But it was the nineteenth century which was to see a systematic and widespread voluntary effort on behalf of the 'seamen's cause'. To understand this movement it is necessary to draw attention to two characteristics of the middle classes in that period, a preference for evangelical religion and the support of the principle of voluntary organisation, which underpinned the concern for the spiritual, moral and physical well-being of the less fortunate sections of the population. The many societies directed towards seafarers were but a small section of a vast number of similar bodies, local and national, of a similar nature. Their spiritual objective, in general, derived from evangelism and its doctrine of personal salvation through Grace, reinforced with the Victorian sense of sin and fear of death. The temporal objective was connected with the gospel of work, 'seriousness' of character, respectability and self help, virtues which the poor were seen as lacking. In particular, a lack of respectability was identified with a lack of cleanliness, sobriety, forethought and thrift. There was nothing unusual in the connection between spiritual and social welfare; the Christian religion had always recognised the need to address physical wellbeing in order to achieve progress in religious belief.

The voluntary societies for seafarers may be loosely categorised as seamen's missions, which had as their prime concern spiritual welfare, though in time they became significant providers of social facilities, and those societies primarily concerned with social welfare, such as sailors' homes. Even these were likely to have strong religious overtones. Although the prime focus was on the serving seafarer, the missions also concerned themselves with seamen's families and elderly seamen. Here again specialist social welfare societies were formed, such as those for seamen's orphans. Thus the ports of Devon came to be provided with many local, independent societies as well as with the branches, in due course, of those surviving today which developed as national organisations in the nineteenth century. These include the British Sailors' Society (1833), the Missions to Seamen (1856) and the Royal National Mission to Deep Sea Fishermen (1881). Between them, and the Seamen's Christian Friend Society (1846), all ports in Devon have been provided with a seamen's missionary and usually an institute for significant periods since 1820.

Seamen's Missions

The genesis of the seamen's missionary movement in the nineteenth century has been identified in the 'Thames revival' amongst merchant seafarers following the end of the wars with France.[37] In turn, its roots lay in the evangelical upsurge of the late eighteenth century and the impact of the Bible societies in the Royal Navy. The 'Thames revival', which was under way by 1816, had started with services on board ships moored in the Pool of London run by seafarers for seafarers. Many of these were in the coastal trades, and such was the fervour that it seems likely that this 'spontaneous' practice would have occurred when some of the ships berthed at ports in Devon. Notification of services was achieved by hoisting a flag bearing the word 'Bethel' (God's House), a word that rapidly achieved great significance in the movement. Many of the societies formed in the wake of this revival included it in their titles, and the buildings ashore, which usually incorporated a chapel, were often known as 'Seamen's Bethels'. Local examples include the Plymouth, Plymouth Dock, and Stonehouse Soldiers' and Seamen's Friend Society and Bethel Union (1820), which was soon referring to itself as the Bethel Union Society (Fig. 14.4), and the Bideford and Appledore Seamen's Friend Society and Bethel Union (1822).[38]

The common elements in the titles of these early seamen's missions reveal their links with the London scene, and in particular their emulation of a society there which was conceived with a national and international role in mind. This was the British and Foreign Seamen's Friend Society and Bethel Union (1819), which was one of the ancestors of the British Sailors' Society. The founder of this Society, and a prime mover in the spread of the movement in the early period, though by no means its only activist, was the Rev George Charles Smith. Formerly a seafarer in the Royal Navy, he had trained for the Baptist ministry between 1804 and 1807 at the Baptist Chapel, Morice Square, Devonport, and then became pastor of a chapel in Penzance. His involvement with seafarers, and particularly with the movement in London, led to lengthy absences from his charge, and eventually, in 1826, to him working full time in London as a seamen's minister. A key element in the spread of the movement was Smith's publishing activities, which included numerous religious tracts and, in particular, the *Sailor's Magazine* (1820), which he edited (and largely wrote), originally under the auspices of the British and Foreign Seamen's Friend Society. It is the main surviving source for the origins and early years of the movement.

Smith did not confine himself to London, but, together with associates, engaged in preaching tours. These took him to many British ports, where he advocated the 'seamen's cause' and urged the formation of societies. His method involved both direct missionary work amongst seamen through *ad hoc* conversations and preaching in local nonconformist chapels, and appeals to the more prominent lay and religious persons of the locality. One example is Smith's own record, entitled 'A Bethel Tour', of a short travelling ministry in the spring of 1820, which must have been influential in the formation of the Plymouth Society later in that year, of which the following is a summary:[39]

Wednesday, 15 March	9pm departed Penzance; overnight at Falmouth.
Thursday, 16 March	5pm arrived Plymouth Dock. Visited 'several respectable persons' with printed papers on the Bethel Union.
Friday, 17 March	To Newton Bushel; preached there.
Saturday, 18 March	Boat to Teignmouth; obtained use of a ship for a service; hoisted Bethel flag; 7pm preached on deck to a large crowd.
Sunday, 19 March	11am preached to sailors at Baptist meeting; 3pm preached to sailors at Methodist meeting; 6pm preached to sailors at Baptist meeting at Shaldon.
Monday, 20 March	Morning – distribution of tracts to seamen; evening preached at Independent Chapel.
Tuesday, 21 March	Departed Teignmouth for Plymouth Dock.
Wednesday, 22 March	Visited ministers and gentlemen; talked to seamen; evening preached at Mr Wilcox's chapel.
Thursday, 23 March	10am hoisted Bethel flag at Mutton Cove and met seamen; pm hoisted flag at North Corner; 7pm preached on board ship at Mutton Cove to a large congregation.
Friday, 24 March	Departed for Penzance.
Saturday, 25 March	Arrived in Penzance.

Considerable effort went in to the preparation of ships' holds for these shipboard services. In the case of that at Mutton Cove there was

> . . . a stage from the shore, a long ladder down the mizzen hatchway for the men, and the captain's ladder by the cabin for the females, of whom there were far more than 100, many of whom were respectable. The owners . . . providing every accommodation . . . The hold was hung round with flags and deal boards, laid athwart for seats; the middle deck over the forehold being open, formed a sort of gallery. The beams had flags rolled over them, and three candlesticks on each. The cover of the main hatchway was raised as a platform from the larboard side of the ship to the pump-well amidships. This and the beam above it formed the pulpit . . . with an immensely crowded congregation we forgot we were in the hold of a ship . . .

The early volumes of the *Sailor's Magazine* contain numerous reports of ship prayer meetings and tours, and of the formation of societies and reports

PLYMOUTH PLACARD.

To Sailors, Watermen, and others.

The Committee for the

Bethel Union Society,

Anxious to promote the present and eternal Welfare of their Fellow Subjects employed in the Seafaring Line, beg to acquaint them that, for their better Accommodation,

ROOMS ARE OPENED

For the Performance of Divine Worship

At the following places and times, which may be known by a

Flag, having the word "Bethel" in it,

Flying at a Staff on shore, or at the Mast-head when the Services are performed on board of a Ship.

Mutton-Cove, and North-Corner Dock,

SABBATH DAYS, half-past Two and half-past Six, P. M.
TUESDAYS and FRIDAYS, half-past Six, P. M.

Stonehouse, New Slip, near the Point,

SABBATH DAYS, Nine, A. M. and Six, P. M.
TUESDAYS and FRIDAYS, Six, P. M.

Plymouth, Fishermen's Steps, near the Barbican,

SABBATH DAYS, half-past Two, and Six, P. M.
WEDNESDAYS and SATURDAYS, Seven, P. M.

Attendance will be given from Nine to a quarter-past Ten every Sabbath Morning, to instruct those who may wish to learn to read.
Bibles and Testaments sold to Seamen and Soldiers at a Reduced Price.
January 31st, 1822.

——o——

14.4   Poster advertising meetings held by the Plymouth, Plymouth Dock and Stonehouse Seamen's Friend Society and Bethel Union. (Sailor's Magazine, *3 [1822], 130*)

of their activities, from British and overseas ports. There was activity in every port in Devon, though that in Plymouth and Dock was extensively recorded, possibly because Smith seems to have made several return visits. It is probable that few of the societies survived beyond the initial flush of dedicated activity. This seems to have been the case with the first society at Bideford and Appledore, where the report of the formation of a new one in 1828 reads as though the previous one had never existed. In South Devon, with the exception of Plymouth, this early work does not seem to have taken root. However, in Ilfracombe a Bethel society founded 'about 1840' led an uneasy existence until the 1970s, and a room in the building on the quay which housed the original Bethel meeting room is still called the Seamen's Bethel, and is used as a rest room by local fishermen (Fig. 14.5).[40]

National seamen's mission societies working through a branch network did not operate in Devon until some 35 years after the Bethel movement. The British (and Foreign) Sailors' Society, as it emerged in 1833 following a period of inter-society strife in London, was not yet equipped to undertake a role beyond its limited activities in London, while the Anglican Missions to Seamen was not formed until 1856. Individual Anglican clergy did, however, undertake self-appointed, personal ministries to seafarers, the most well known example being that of the Rev John Ashley to the shipping in the Bristol Channel between 1835 and 1850. In Plymouth, the Vicar of St Andrew's, the Rev John Hatchard, established a fund in 1826 for the building of a mariners' church close to the Barbican.[41] Although nothing came of this then, a temporary Mariners' Church was opened as a base for an Anglican ministry in 1857.[42] This was probably the first base of the Missions to Seamen's station there. A later example in Appledore was the attention given to seafarers by the Rev H C Muller between 1901 and 1904.[43] He returned as vicar in the 1920s, and was listed as an Honorary Chaplain at that port in both periods.

Once the Anglican society had been established, it was in a much better position than the Bethel societies for establishing its sources of funds and developing a network of 'stations'. The Bethels had to 'tout' for subscribers and persuade people to serve on management committees; support from local chapels was a patchy, uncertain source of funds. The Missions to Seamen was able to 'tap' the diocesan and parish system of the Church, inland as well as on the coasts. In coastal regions it could enlist local clergy who took an interest in seafarers as honorary chaplains. They would be supported with literature for distribution, would encourage the formation of local committees for the collection of funds, devote some of their time to work amongst seafarers and perhaps oversee the work of lay readers paid by the Mission.

The first annual report of the Missions to Seamen, in 1856–7, stated,

> The station established . . . at Plymouth is intended to be worked through the aid and co-operation of local clergy . . . We desire to plant a Mission for Torbay, by which the shipping frequenting Exmouth, Teignmouth, and Dartmouth shall also be visited . . . It is our wish to strengthen, without delay, our stations at Plymouth . . .

Plymouth soon had a full-time chaplain and later a paid lay helper. Much of the work was afloat, ships being reached by the Mission yacht and later by its steam launch. A mission room near the Mercantile Marine Office in the Exchange was superseded by an Institute and Mariners' Church in Vauxhall Street by 1907. Torbay had to wait twenty years for the appointment of a lay reader. In 1877 a reader was based in Teignmouth, with the River Exe as part of his territory. Mission rooms were established on the quays at Teignmouth and Exeter. A reader was appointed for Dartmouth in 1883 and an Institute was opened. When the Dartmouth reader departed, Mr J F Dunning, appointed to Teignmouth in 1881, added Dartmouth to his area, where he remained in post until the mid 1930s. By 1920 the Mission to Seamen institute in Plymouth had closed, but the long-serving chaplain, the Rev H J Holderness, continued his work visiting ships in port and in the Sound. It appears from the annual reports of the Missions to Seamen that the level of activity of its field workers gradually declined and that it decided not to replace them. No stations in Devon are listed in 1941. The Mission continued to receive financial support from Devon parishes and honorary chaplains continued their part-time ministries.

14.5 Ilfracombe Sailor's Institute and Bethel occupied the top floor of this quayside building until 1972. (*Alston Kennerley*)

The British Sailors' Society does not seem to have become involved in Devon until 1869, when the Plymouth and Stonehouse Soldiers' and Seamen's Friend Society and Bethel Union affiliated with it.[44] The Plymouth Society thought it had merged with the national Society to become a branch; this does not seem to have been the case legally. The real effect was that a new missionary was appointed to the approval of the national Society, which also provided a grant for his salary, the existing missionary being dismissed by the local Society. The new missionary sent reports to the national Society, and extracts from these began to appear in its annual reports. However, he worked out of the Bethel buildings in Castle Street which continued under the control of the local Society, and he appears to have remained subject to the control of the local committee (Fig. 14.6). It is likely that the British Sailors' Society grant was intended to be discontinued when local funds allowed. When and if this happened is unclear, as few accounts have survived. In 1920 the British Sailors' Society took over the Plymouth Sailors' Home, which it used as an annexe to its new hostel at the Octagon.[45] The Sailors' Home building in Vauxhall Street was soon closed, but the Society continued its work from the other building into the 1950s. The British Sailors' Society was also associated with the Sailors' Rests at Exmouth and Torquay.

The first national society to operate in North Devon seems to have been the Seamen's Christian Friend Society. This had been founded in 1846 by associates of George Charles Smith, when his labours in London were brought to a close. In the latter part of the nineteenth century it extended its work beyond London, establishing stations in Sussex, the North West, Scotland, Ireland, South Cornwall and North Devon. The Appledore Sailors' Rest and Seamen's Mission was opened in 1888, established in co-operation with a local committee led by W D Hanson. There was a Bethel chapel adjacent to the Rest, and a full-time missionary was appointed. Presumably the earlier Bethel Society had ceased to exist. The Society maintained its operation in Appledore until 1972, but the Bethel continues in use as a place of worship for local people.[46]

The reasons why many of the early local seamen's Bethel societies in Devon, as in other areas, seem not to have survived for very long, are as yet unclear. Perhaps in an era receptive to revivalist preaching, when the memory of the debt owed to seamen for their service in the wars with France was still fresh, societies were formed too easily and some lacked the proper structures for permanence. But many did survive, particularly, as with that at Plymouth, those in the larger ports such as the Liverpool Seamen's Friend Society and Bethel Union (1821), or the Glasgow Seamen's Friend Society (1822), which existed well into the twentieth century.

Sailors' Homes

Although the seamen's missions were gradually drawn in to provide social facilities for seafarers in port, eventually becoming major providers of accommodation in some ports, it is clear that, where possible, they left this aspect to other agencies, in particular sailors' homes. The mission rooms referred to above were of the nature of day centres, used (as well as for services) as reading rooms and for providing light refreshments. They might, in an emergency, be used for temporary overnight accommodation. It is probable that the local societies in Devon never had the resources to extend their provision further. Indeed, it is unlikely that in the smaller ports in Devon the need for such accommodation was ever large enough to warrant special provision. But in the larger ports there were always many seafarers in a sense 'tied' to the port whilst waiting to be paid off from their last voyages or seeking berths in ships outward bound. In both circumstances seafarers were short of money and easy prey to those in port districts prepared to provide accommodation (and other services) in anticipation of payment later. Thus cheap boarding houses flourished, often providing easy access to drink, entertainment and female company, and in the process undermining any progress the missionaries might make on the spiritual side.

Plymouth was probably the only port in Devon where the problem was anything like that in ports such as London or Liverpool, and it was there that sailors' homes (or rests) first appeared in the county, though small ones were later established in Teignmouth, Torbay and Exmouth. Once again the example was a child of George Charles Smith's concern for the needs of the 'whole' seafarer: the Sailors' Home, in London (opened 1835). The idea was endorsed by the Select Committee on Shipwrecks of 1836, and by the 1850 Mercantile Marine Act. The development of a network of homes may well be attributed to Captain W H Hall, who toured the country promoting the idea, though the ground had already been prepared by the seamen's missionary movement and the propensity of middle class Victorians, not least naval officers, to participate in voluntary welfare activity. By 1861 there were thirty-one establishments in the larger British and Irish ports.[47]

Each sailors' home was formed as a separate society, with a management committee, officers, and members paying annual subscriptions. In additon they usually sought donations. These funds were intended to be used in the acquisition and fitting out of premises and for ongoing maintenance. The homes were not intended to make profits, but seafarers were charged for the cost of accommodation and meals. However, these charges could be set no higher than those of seamen's boarding houses in the vicinity, and this meant that homes were often dependent on subscriptions and donations to balance their outgoings. No records have survived for either the Devonport Sailors' Home or the Plymouth Sailors' Home, but newspaper reports of annual meetings and census returns indicate that they were not untypical.

Devonport seems always to have had a stronger financial base, because of its links with the Royal Navy; Plymouth was usually in financial difficulty. Devonport opened on 31 December 1852 with the approval of the board of Admiralty, the patronage of Queen Victoria (£100), and with a number of naval officers willing to contribute. It occupied a rented building in St Aubyn Street, Devonport, with 24 rooms and cabins for 200 persons. There was a reading room, accommodation for the superintendent and a kitchen capable of serving 150. Plymouth opened on 9 May 1853, after it had had to make a separate appeal for funds, the hopes of running the two establishments under the same management committee having foundered. Its premises in Vauxhall Street had been purchased by a supporter and rented to the Society.[48] The Devonport home moved to 67 Duke Street in 1855. It appears to have had fairly heavy use: 5,215 entries were reported for 1866, and a total of 81,227 since the home opened. It had 52 residents on census night 1881, whereas the Plymouth home reported only 14. In 1861 the Plymouth Home had 815 entries, making a running total of 4,795 since it had been founded.[49] Perhaps this contrast in activity may be attributed to the much lower level of mercantile marine activity compared with naval activity, though additional factors could well have been poor management and the merchant seamen's dislike of the type of accommodation offered.[50]

In the 1870s a new force arrived in Plymouth which seems to have somewhat eclipsed the welfare efforts of the existing homes and of the missions. This was Agnes Weston, who through great force of personality persuaded the naval authorities to allow her to address boy seamen on the training ships on temperance principles, probably with a little evangelical religion. Through a national appeal she gathered sufficient funds (including some of her own money) to open a sailors' home, which she called a Sailors' Rest, in converted buildings on 1 May 1876.[51] The Rest contained a hall for meetings and services, and a restaurant, recreation rooms and cabins. The census return for 1881 showed eighty-eight persons resident on the census night, of whom sixty-nine were aged 25 or under and seventy-four were naval seamen. The hall was used for entertainments each night and for temperance and gospel meetings. The success was such that extensions were added and eventually the original building was pulled down and rebuilt. These developments were financed in part by offering parts of the building, such as a cabin, for endowment.[52] In the 1890s the rate for a cabin was 30 guineas (Fig. 14.7).

The Devonport Royal Sailors' Home also used this latter device to erect its new building in Morice Square, which was opened on 30 April 1902.[53] The cost had been about £9,000, but major donations were received from the Admiralty (£2,000) and Lord St Levan. Such had become the status of Agnes Weston's Rests that the *Western Daily Mercury* asked the new home if 'they were rivals of Miss Weston'. The answer was no, they both had temperance aims. Both establishments catered almost exclusively for naval seafarers, but it seems clear that at that time there was ample scope for each.

Particular aspects of the welfare needs of seafarers also gave rise to specialist provision. These included shipwrecked seamen, seamen's orphans, elderly seafarers and the medical needs of seafarers. The Shipwrecked Fishermen's and Mariners' Royal Benevolent Society (1839)

14.7 Royal Sailor's Rest, Fore Street, Devonport, *c*1911, from the Dockyard. (*City of Plymouth Museums and Art Gallery*)

cared for the survivors of shipwreck, providing clothing, finding temporary accommodation (usually in missions and sailors' homes) and funding travel home. The Plymouth home was part of its network. The homes also provided medical services, usually in the form of the gratuitous services of a local practitioner, as at Plymouth, though the Royal Cornwall Sailors' Home at Falmouth had its own hospital wing. No aged seamen's homes seem to have been founded in Devon, but seamen's orphans have been cared for since 1860 at the British Sailors' Boys Home at Brixham, which could accommodate seventy-five boys in 1888.

Seafarers' Education and Welfare in the Twentieth Century

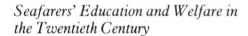

Both themes examined in this chapter need to be related to the general social context in Britain as well as to the maritime context. How did nautical education and the provision of welfare for seafarers fare as society and social thinking evolved? To what extent did the societies and establishments continue to have a role through to the third quarter of the twentieth century, given the growing activity of the state in the provision of education and social welfare?

The 1890s saw the first real boost to British technical education. This was the period when many technical colleges were established in the larger towns and cities, including Plymouth and Devonport. The central examining of masters, mates and engineers remained in the hands of the Board of Trade Marine Department, but the navigation schools and marine engineering schools, some independent, some like that at Plymouth under a form of local control, began their gradual migration towards full local-authority control, some as separate establishments, others within the local technical college. The last of the independent establishments disappeared in the 1950s.

The transformation of the Plymouth School began in 1949, with the formation of a pre-sea cadet course. In the 1950s and 1960s full advantage was taken of the general expansion of further and higher education to develop courses, initially for cadets, which would provide qualifications, national diplomas and certificates, recognisable throughout the country in addition to the long-established government certificates which were not understood outside the shipping industry. The advent of the Council for National Academic Awards (1964) permitted the development of the first degrees in nautical and fisheries subjects (1966 and 1973), post graduate studies and research in all sea-related subjects. In 1954 the School of Navigation achieved full departmental status, and in 1970, as the School of Maritime Studies, it became one of five departments in the newly created Plymouth Polytechnic. As that institution matured, the School became a Faculty in 1980 and, in 1987, in recognition of its interdisciplinary interests, the Institute of Marine Studies. In 1989 the Polytechnic, now a significant force in higher education in Devon, was renamed Polytechnic South West, and in 1992 it was designated the University of Plymouth. Meanwhile, British shipping was in rapid decline, leading to a dramatic reduction in the numbers of seafarers requiring professional courses. Classes were becoming too small to be sustained. In 1991 the Institute of Marine Studies became a department in the Faculty of Science, and in 1992 the Institute took the unwelcome decision to close its courses for practising seafarers, some 130 years after the work had been started under John Merrifield. However, the Institute's academic work concerned with all dimensions of the seas and

their uses had become very strongly established, serviced by over forty teaching staff and an equal number of researchers, addressing all the subject areas of concern a century ago as well as many new ones.

The closure of the *Mount Edgcumbe* in 1920 marked the end of the provision of training of ratings for the merchant service in Devon. Had it been possible to raise funds to develop a shore establishment, she might have evolved as an agent of the state system, as the *Formidable* did at Portishead near Bristol. She 'came ashore' in 1906, and was progressively an approved school and community home continuing to offer a general education and nautical training until 1982. Some of the other training ships also managed these changes, though most have now closed, training for ratings now being concentrated at the National Sea Training College at Gravesend in Kent.

The withdrawal of the national seamen's missions from Devon has already been noted. Operating on a national and international scale, they have always kept their operations under review, moving their resources, financial and human, to where the need was felt to be greatest. The only one that maintains a presence in the county is the Royal National Mission to Deep Sea Fishermen, which operates an institute and supports a missionary at Brixham. The Bethel at Appledore continues to exist, serving a local congregation, and the Plymouth Bethel survived until 1980. There was always a tendency for the Bethels to become dissenting churches with their own congregations, because of their attention to local residents as well as seafarers' relatives through visiting, and the running of Sunday and day schools and bible classes, particularly once they had their own chapel and ancillary accommodation.

The social welfare work of the missions and the sailors' homes was subject to the changes affecting the shipping industry and to the increasing provision of welfare services by the state. The homes continued to have a role to the 1950s. They had been particularly valuable during the two world wars, when so much activity was focused on the ports, and there was sufficient demand to warrant rebuilding, as took place at the London home. The Royal Sailors' Rests at Plymouth and Portsmouth had been bombed, and were rebuilt in this period. The decline in the size of the Navy and the development of its own welfare service has meant the closure of the Rests' residential accommodation, though they continue to provide recreational facilities. Those sailors' homes that survive have evolved. The Bristol Sailors' Home has continued a trend apparent in the 1920s and is now a residential home for retired seafarers. The Devonport home, still in Morice Square, has become the Royal Fleet Club, essentially a modern hotel for naval personnel.

Conclusion

In neither of the themes examined in this chapter has it proved possible to identify any aspects peculiar to Devon. Rather, local developments were typical of the national scene. Indeed, those of the nineteenth century might be considered imports promoted initially by outsiders. Excepting provision in London, seamen's missions and sailors' homes were established in Devon as early as anywhere else, and seem to have had similar patterns of existence culminating for the most part in final decline and closure by the 1970s. Perhaps the period of most widespread activity, after that of the 1820s, was in the latter part of the nineteenth century when evangelical religious influence was still strong and before secular welfare provision began to render provision under religious auspices unnnecessary. The network of state-aided navigation schools was created well ahead of post-school educational provision for most other subjects, though the Plymouth School was the last to be founded. *Mount Edgcumbe*, representative of another national development, also amongst the last of its kind to open, was being overtaken by more modern ideas on youth care when it closed after 1918. The navigation schools, perhaps at the forefront of post-school teaching in the 1860s, became locked into a central examining system run by a government department which kept them outside progress in further and higher education until the 1960s. Plymouth, with only a handful of students in the 1930s, ought to have closed. Even its growth in the 1960s was part of a national pattern for nautical education, the one local factor being the decision of the local authority to support its development.

14: Education and Welfare of Merchant Seafarers

1 For a full discussion see Alston Kennerley, 'The Education of the Merchant Seaman in the Nineteenth Century,' (unpublished MA thesis, University of Exeter, 1978).

2 H Dorothy Burwash, *English Merchant Shipping, 1460–1540* (Toronto, 1947, Newton Abbot, 1969), 40.

3 See David W Waters, *The Art of Navigation in England in Elizabethan and Early Stuart Times* (1958); and Eva G R Taylor, *The Mathematical Practitioners of Hanoverian England, 1714–1840* (Cambridge, 1966).

4 Scholars' Registers of Christ's Hospital, Guildhall Library, MS 12, 818/15, f. 189.

5 B F Cresswell, *Bideford and its Surroundings* (Homeland Assoc./F Warne, 1909), 5; M Goaman, *Old Bideford and District* (Bristol, 1968), 29; Roger Granville, *The History of Bideford* (Bideford, 1883), 103.

6 I am indebted to John Gammon, of Braunton, for drawing my attention to, and clarifying, this source.

7 DRO, Penrose II v. the Trustees of Chaloners School: depositions of witnesses taken at Barnstaple on 4 Sept. 1727.

8 DRO, Exeter Diocesan Registers of Licences and Perpetual Cures.

9 Devon and Plymouth Directories.

10 WDRO, report and letter, W668T.

11 BPP, 1836, XVII, IX (section 35).

12 BPP, 1836, XVII, VIII (section 31).

13 BPP, 1847, LX, 526, 2–5.

14 Mercantile Marine Act, 1850, 13 & 14 Vict., c. 93.

15 Kennerley, 'Education of the Merchant Seaman', 51, 57–9; PRO, MT9/37/M9729/67/8223, Report of E H Coleman to the Marine Department.

16 First Report of the Science and Art Department (BPP, 1854, XXVIII, 269).

17 Alston Kennerley, 'Navigation School and Training Ship. Educational Provision for the Mercantile Marine in Plymouth in the Nineteenth Century' in Stephen Fisher, ed., *West Country Maritime and Social History. Some Essays* (Exeter, 1980), 56.

18 *Western Daily Mercury*, 3 Jan. 1863.

19 *Western Morning News*, 17 Jan. 1863; Journal of the Corporation of Trinity House of Newcastle upon Tyne, 1857.

20 10th Report of Department of Science and Art (BPP, 1863, XVI, 21).

21 Second Report of the Science and Art Department (BPP, 1854/5, XVII, 215), report of Edward Hughes, Master of the lower school, Royal Naval School, Greenwich, on the London Navigation School.

22 Merrifield's teaching certificate is held at Plymouth Central Library.

23 Science and Art Department minute R 87, 15 May 1863.

24 BPP, 1859, VI, xv.

25 Reformatory and Industrial Schools Acts, 29 & 30 Vict., c117 and c118. These acts consolidated earlier measures and were themselves subsequently amended.

26 *Western Daily Mercury*, 5 Nov. 1874.

27 PRO, HO45/9898/8159, *Rules and Regulations for the Management of the Bristol Training Ship 'Formidable' for Homeless and Destitute Boys*, approved by the Inspector of Industrial Schools, 29 November 1869.

28 *Western Daily Mercury*, 10 Oct. 1875.

29 Formerly HMS *Winchester*, built at Woolwich, 1816–22, 487 tons, 60-gun frigate.

30 *Western Daily Mercury*, 14 June, 27 July 1877, 5 Feb. 1878.

31 *Western Morning News*, 31 Aug. 1897.

32 Kennerley, 'Education of the Merchant Seaman', 228, Appendix 13.

33 PRO, HO 45/11051/155236.

34 Inkerman Rogers, *A Concise History of Bideford* (Bideford, 1938).

35 Edward Windeatt, 'John Flavel. A Notable Dartmouth Puritan and his Bibliography' *DAT*, XLIII (1911), 172–89.

36 John Watkins, *An Essay Towards a History of Bideford in the County of Devon* (1792, reprinted 1883), 71–2.

37 See, Roald Kverndal, *Seamen's Missions. Their Origin and Early Growth* (Pasadena, 1986).

38 *Sailor's Magazine*, III (1822), 130, 169; II (1821), 22. Other societies noted in this journal include: Saltash Seamen's Friend Society and Bethel Union (1821), Catdown, Oreston, and Turnchapel Seamen's Friend Society and Bethel Union (1821), Torpoint Seamen's Friend Society and Bethel Union (1821), Dartmouth Bethel Union (1821), Ilfracombe Bethel Union (182?), Appledore and Bideford Bethel Union; and Seamen's and Fishermen's Friend Society (1828).

39 *Sailor's Magazine*, I (1820), 186–9. Newton Bushel was probably Newton Abbot.

40 Reports of annual meetings: *Ilfracombe Gazette & Observer*, 10 April 1897; *Ilfracombe Chronicle*, 27 June 1914, 10 April 1920, 12 Feb. 1921.

41 *Sailor's Magazine*, VII (1826), 473.

42 WDRO 1170/1–2, Diary of Thomas Brooks, Missionary to the Plymouth Bethel, 22 Oct. 1857.

43 *Bideford Weekly Gazette*, 26 April 1904.

44 Minutes of the Management Committee of the Plymouth Society, 1 Dec. 1868 to 7 Oct. 1869, held by Mr R Meathrell of Plympton.

45 British Sailors' Society, Annual Reports.

46 Seamen's Christian Friend Society, Annual Reports.

47 BPP, 1860, LX, 387, 1–3; 1861, XXXVIII, 485–6.

48 *Plymouth, Devonport and Stonehouse Herald*, 1 Jan., 14 May 1853.

49 *Western Daily Mercury*, 3 May 1867; 31 Jan. 1861.

50 Alston Kennerley, 'Seamen's Missions and Sailors' Homes. Spiritual and Social Welfare Provision for Seafarers in British Ports in the Nineteenth Century, with some Reference to the South West', in Stephen Fisher, ed., *Studies in British Privateering, Trading Enterprise and Seamen's Welfare, 1775–1900* (Exeter, 1987), 146.

51 Doris Gulliver, *Dame Agnes Weston* (1971) 39.

52 Portsmouth City Record Office, 205A/3/1, Royal Sailors' Rests records.

53 *Western Daily Mercury*, 30 April 1902; 15 Dec. 1900.

15   *Devon and Naval Strategy since 1815*

Peter Hilditch

The Nineteenth Century

THROUGHOUT THE NINETEENTH CENTURY British naval strategy continued to be dominated by the perception of France, either by itself or in partnership with another major power, as the principal threat. Concern increased as France recovered strength after the Napoleonic Wars, becoming acute in the three invasion 'panics' of the mid-1840s, early 1850s and 1859–61. France's defeat in the Franco–Prussian War (1870–1) proved only a temporary lull, since its subsequent recovery precipitated the scares of 1884 and 1888, led to the Naval Defence Act of 1889 which began the end-of-century naval arms race, and was followed by a further Anglo–French crisis over Fashoda in 1898. It was only after 1902 that France ceased to be seen as Britain's main naval rival, a strategic shift emphasised by the signing of the Anglo–French Entente in 1904.[1]

Besides this principal strategic determinant, there were three lesser factors. First was the pressure for economy resulting from the long periods of relative peace after the immensely expensive wars of the eighteenth century. Bartlett characterises British naval policy between 1815 and 1853 as:

Frequently reduced to a level of hand to mouth improvisation, with the sole reservation that Britain should be in a position, at the beginning of a war, to command the English Channel, and perhaps the more vital of her trade routes, and that from this essential base she could gradually mobilise her vast resources to carry the war to the enemy.[2]

For fifty years or so after 1815, defence expenditure consumed only about 2–3 per cent of Britain's Gross National Product, a remarkably low figure for the world's leading power, and a much lower proportion than in the eighteenth or twentieth centuries.[3] Secondly, there was a steady growth of naval strength in foreign waters relative to home waters which only started to be reversed towards the end of the century. Finally, there was the impact of technological change, with development of steampower, gunnery, and torpedoes.

The basic strategy of the Royal Navy throughout the nineteenth century remained similar to that pursued during the Napoleonic and Revolutionary wars: a close blockade of the principal French naval ports. Most of the strategic development in home waters therefore concentrated on improving the facilities for conducting such a blockade. This strategy required

15.1   Plymouth Sound as a safe anchorage in the 1840s after the completion of the Breakwater. From a lithograph by Mitchell. (*City of Plymouth Museums and Art Gallery*)

conveniently situated and secure base facilities, including reliable victualling arrangements. The experience of the French wars demonstrated that neither Plymouth nor Torbay could be considered safe anchorages in all conditions. The lack of confidence of the principal naval commanders in the two anchorages prompted the Admiralty in 1806 to adopt a basic plan to construct a large breakwater to protect Plymouth Sound, and work on this began in 1812. The Admiralty's high priority for the project is reflected in the decision, subsequently supported by the Select Committee on Finance, to triple the planned expenditure in 1817 despite great pressure to economise in peacetime. In 1834 the Admiralty also took the unusual step of taking over control of the entire construction project, including the employment of all labour. The breakwater was officially completed in 1841, although work on further modifications and extensions continued for some time thereafter. It proved totally successful, with no significant losses of vessels in Plymouth Sound once it had been completed (Fig. 15.1). Torbay's subsequent naval use was consequently restricted to the occasional exercise, Royal Fleet Reviews (in 1910, 1922 and 1979) (Fig. 15.2), and as a wartime base for minor vessels. The Plymouth breakwater allowed the concentration of the fleet anchorage, dockyard and supply facilities in the same area. The Admiralty also greatly improved the victualling facilities at Plymouth with the completion of the Royal William Victualling Yard between 1823 and 1834.[4]

During the Revolutionary and Napoleonic wars the Admiralty had instituted a substantial degree of specialisation in the use of dockyard resources. Plymouth and Portsmouth provided immediate support to the fleet blockading the French coast, whilst the less accessible Thames yards, Chatham, Deptford and Woolwich, tended to undertake a higher proportion of new construction and longer-term refit and repair work. Sheerness refitted and repaired smaller vessels such as frigates, and generally acted as an adjunct to Chatham.[5] Peacetime developments after 1815 served to consolidate this division of work. In 1869–70, for example, ship construction (including work carried out on fitting out hulls built in private yards), accounted for 97.2 per cent of wage costs at Chatham, 47.8 per cent at Sheerness, 29.7 per cent at Portsmouth and only 11.6 per cent at Devonport.[6] The last two remained the principal operational dockyard-bases of the Navy, carrying out repairs and refits and fitting out ships being sent out on the manifold tasks throughout the world to which the nineteenth-century Royal Navy was committed in the enforcement of the *Pax Britannica* (Fig. 15.3).

The Victorian era saw the closure in 1869 of the old yards at Woolwich and Deptford, outmoded by the rapidly increasing size and complexity of warships. On the other hand, new yards and anchorages were brought into being, intended to complement the functions of Portsmouth and of Plymouth in particular.

Pembroke dockyard, formally established in 1816, concentrated almost exclusively on ship construction, its maximum nineteenth-century employment of 3,118 placing it well behind Portsmouth, Devonport, and Chatham. As Andrew Lambert describes, Pembroke's activities were closely linked and integrated with those of Devonport (see chapter 16). The conversion into a dockyard of the supply base on Hawlbowline island, near Queenstown in southern Ireland, was to enable it to fulfil a very different role. Work began in the 1860s and was completed in 1894. The dockyard could handle the then largest warships, but was designated an emergency dockyard for repairs and maintenance with a planned peacetime workforce of about 100. Hawlbowline never constructed any warships. The Admiralty specifically designed the dockyard to support fleet operations in the Eastern Atlantic. Hawlbowline therefore represented a western extension of current dockyard facilities at Devonport.[7]

The Victorian period also saw a substantial increase in the ability of the Navy to operate safely in the English Channel, with the development of the Harbours of Refuge. These were designed to provide sheltered anchorages for merchant ships in peacetime and naval vessels in war. The relatively limited endurance and mechanical unreliability of early steamships further reinforced the need for more strategically-placed naval anchorages. Following earlier abortive proposals, Peel's 1844 Commission recommended the establishment of four such harbours, protected by massive breakwaters, at

Dover, Seaford, Portland and Harwich. Seaford was deleted in the 1845 estimates, but three harbours in the Channel Islands at Alderney, Jersey and Guernsey were added, at an estimated cost of £2 million.[8] The Portland and Channel Islands proposals reflected anxiety over the development by the French of Cherbourg to provide her Navy with a first-class naval base in the Channel. Patrick Barry described Cherbourg with its nine dry docks in 1864 as 'the best existing specimen of what a dockyard ought to be'.[9]

Of the Channel Islands proposals, only Alderney's harbour was partially completed and it never saw any significant naval use.[10] However, the Admiralty did complete the harbours at Dover, Portland and Harwich. Construction of the breakwater at Portland started in 1847 and by 1875 had cost over £1 million. Portland's role was closely linked with Plymouth, which provided dockyard support. Portland provided a much larger, more sheltered harbour and was much easier to defend than the proposed works in the Channel Islands, and it was better placed than Plymouth or Portsmouth to support a close blockade of Cherbourg. Although the government attempted with some success to represent the harbours of refuge as primarily works for civilian peacetime use, their location, and the failure of other proposals for harbours on the west and north east coasts and in Scotland, reveal their true purpose.

Plymouth's function, however, was not simply confined to supporting the blockade of France, nor to securing trade in the Western Approaches. The deployment of so large a part of the Navy overseas in the nineteenth century gave it added importance as the closest major home dockyard for those far-flung vessels. Although a network of overseas bases and dockyards was developed to sustain the fleet, overseas dry-dock capacity did not really develop until the latter part of the century, before which even the largest designated overseas dockyards provided facilities only for routine maintenance and emergency repair. The extent of Devonport's repair role in comparison to overseas yards can be seen in the 1869–70 breakdown of dockyard work, which shows Devonport Dockyard working during the year on 37 ironclads and 132 other vessels in commission, for a wide variety of repairs and maintenance. The 11 overseas yards handled, in total, 33 ironclads and 192 other vessels. Malta, the first to open a dry dock, in 1847, received the largest number of ironclads (8) and Hong Kong the largest number of other vessels (38). The relative scale of repairs, and types of ships received, is reflected by the £1,488 average value of material per ship used at Devonport, against £376 overseas.[11]

Consequently, when the French concentrated their most modern battle-ships at Toulon in the 1880s and obliged Britain to build up its own Mediterranean fleet, Devonport became the lynch-pin of the strategic shift. In the new naval war plan, Devonport's first priority was to get the Channel Fleet away to Gibraltar as quickly as possible to link up with the Mediterranean Fleet. It would then play its part in mobilising the reserve fleet to blockade Brest and Cherbourg and thereafter fulfil a triple role: sustaining the blockade of Brest, co-operating with cruiser squadrons at Queenstown and Berehaven in Southern Ireland in guarding commerce in the Western Approaches, and acting as back-up for the combined fleet in the Mediterranean. The two dry docks at Malta and another opened at Gibraltar in 1893 were inadequate to deal with the possible consequences of a major fleet action, and even the major expansion of dry-dock capacity at Gibraltar between 1894 and 1902-3 could not provide total cover. Warships requiring major repairs would have to be brought to Devonport, whose expanded importance led to the authorisation of the doubling of the dockyard's size by the Keyham extension in the Naval Works Act of 1895. Before its official opening in 1907, however, the strategic focus switched eastward.

The Naval Challenge from Germany

British concern at a potential threat from Germany became significant with the passing of the German naval laws of 1898 and 1900, and by 1902–3 began to be more a dominant influence on British naval policy than any possible challenge from France. Anglo-German naval rivalry prompted a redeployment of the majority of British front-line units to home waters, and by 1914 largely to the North Sea. The possibility of an invasion of the South West,

15.2 The Fleet Review in Torbay, July 1910.
(*Postcard*)

which had so exercised the minds of the Admiralty and politicians at various points in the nineteenth century and led to the vast fortification programme of the 1860s, receded. The naval war plans of 1909–14 for the defence of the South West emphasised the threat of small raids, sabotage and espionage rather than that of a major invasion.[12]

The concentration of the fleet in the North Sea highlighted the lack of suitable dock and naval base facilities in that region. Existing facilities developed in response to threats from the French, Spanish or Dutch were all too far south and/or west to provide immediate support to a battle fleet based in the northern North Sea facing the main German bases. As a consequence, the Admiralty announced in 1903 its intention to construct a first-class naval base at Rosyth on the Firth of Forth with the capacity to repair the largest classes of warship. By 1912 the Admiralty also decided to develop the Cromarty Firth in northeast Scotland as a second-class naval base and Scapa Flow in the Orkneys as a war anchorage, although the exact status and functions of each remained in the balance up to the outbreak of the war.[13]

Both the strategic shift in naval deployment away from the Channel, and the policy of allocating an increasing proportion of new construction work to private yards, might suggest that Devon would have lost much of its traditional importance to the Navy in the years leading up to the First World War. However, this did not occur. The scale of the recent investment in the Keyham extension was too great not to be exploited, and Devonport specifically benefited from both the scale of the total demand for warships, especially battleships, and a redistribution of work between the dockyards. Its share of new construction allocated to the royal dockyards increased by about threequarters in terms of labour values between the 1889 Naval Defence Act programme and the First World War, and new construction now accounted for well over half of the labour resources employed. This change is clearly linked to the relative demise of Chatham as a front-line building yard owing to limitations of space. Chatham could be regarded as an essentially Victorian yard, ill-equipped to participate in the Edwardian naval race. The Medway yard's workforce, larger than Devonport's at its high tide of construction efforts in the middle of the nineteenth century, was actually reduced in 1907.[14]

For the Navy, the expansion of shipbuilding at Devonport served three specific purposes. Firstly, it made a vital contribution to the expansion of the Navy. Between 1907 and 1914 Devonport completed six and Portsmouth seven out of a total of twenty-six battleships built. The proportion of Dread-

noughts constructed in these two dockyards was much higher than for any other class of vessel. In August 1914 the Grand Fleet could claim a superiority over the German High Sea Fleet of twelve capital ships, thus highlighting these dockyards' contribution. Secondly, dockyard shipbuilding provided a check on prices and afforded some protection against strikes, which tended to be more frequent in private yards.[15] Thirdly, and probably most importantly, dockyard shipbuilding allowed the Admiralty to maintain a sufficiently large labour force with the relevant and increasingly complex skills needed to maintain the fleet in wartime. The Admiralty had a clear view of the primary role of the dockyards, expressed in the naval estimates for 1904:

> The first business of the Royal Dockyards is to keep the fleet in repair, accordingly the amount of new construction allocated to those dockyards should be subsidiary to this main consideration.[16]

The royal dockyards maintained a virtual monopoly of naval repair work. The only prewar exception came in 1904, when 44.5 per cent by value of repair work was allocated to private yards in order to relieve congestion in the dockyards. However, this experience appeared to support the conclusion of Lord Ravensworth's 1884 Committee on Warship Construction and Repair that repair in private yards normally proved to be more costly. The repair of warships requires specialist plant and labour, whilst the actual final cost is difficult to predict until the vessel is opened up. None of these features makes naval repair work especially attractive to private yards.[17] The dockyards' monopoly of repair was not seriously challenged until the 1980s.

The years leading up to the First World War saw an almost unbroken expansion in virtually all areas of naval activity. Work patterns in the operational yards changed as the active fleets were kept in a permanent state of readiness by sending in only limited numbers at a time for repair and refit, rather than all going in at once. Naval personnel built up at the main

15.3 The Channel Fleet in Plymouth Sound in the late 1860s/early 1870s, from a print in the Whinran-Bluer Collection. (*City of Plymouth Museums and Art Gallery*)

bases, particularly following the 1905 decision to keep the reserve fleet manned up to two-fifths complement at Plymouth, Portsmouth and Sheerness so as to expedite war mobilisation. The Census, whilst a very imperfect indicator of naval importance, shows that 21,581 naval and Royal Marine personnel were ashore or in port in Devon on Census night, 1911 (25.3 per cent of the total for England and Wales). This figure compares with the 8,298 in 1881 (29.2 per cent of the England and Wales total). The 1911 Devon total included 7,566 men aboard 131 ships in Plymouth and Devonport harbours, 2,097 men on board 8 ships in Torbay, 91 men on 2 ships on the Dart and 78 men on 1 vessel off Sidmouth.[18] As other contributors to this volume describe in more detail, this period saw major investment in physical facilities including the Dockyard extensions, barracks, hospitals and training facilities in Devon. For example, the 1905 Naval Works Act authorised expenditure of £4.5 million on the Keyham Extension to the Dockyard, £0.28 million on Keyham Barracks, £0.02 million on Keyham Engineering College, and £0.43 million on the Britannia Naval College at Dartmouth. Authorised expenditure in Devon totalled £5.23 million, 21.1 per cent of the national total of £24.79 million which can be allocated to specific areas.[19] At Devonport Dockyard the civilian labour force expanded from 5,206 in 1890 to 12,290 by April 1914. This level of expenditure, reflecting developments in shipbuilding and in the professionalisation of the Navy, also suggests that Devon and the South West remained strategically important.

This continued importance derived partly from the position of Plymouth in relation to the vital Atlantic sea lanes. Britain was not only reliant on seaborne commerce, but in a conflict would expect to receive substantial supplies and manpower from her overseas empire (in October 1914 thirty-three liners brought 25,000 troops from Canada to Plymouth Sound.[20] (Fig. 15.4) The investment in upgrading the dockyard's facilities for repair and fleet support was also necessary because of the slow progress in developing the new dockyard at Rosyth and the other east coast bases. The Admiralty did not sign the main contract for the physical development of the latter facilities until 1909. In 1912 Winston Churchill announced that the new yard would not be complete until 1920, although many of the facilities could be usable before then. At the outbreak of war that dockyard was far from being fully operational, and the first vessel did not enter dry dock until March 1916. Until well into the war, Rosyth suffered from a chronic shortage of accommodation and lacked any provision for shore training. The bases at Scapa Flow and Cromarty Firth were also far from complete in 1914.[21]

The South West therefore actually benefited in terms of extra resources from the German naval challenge. If this challenge had developed less rapidly, then a real shift of resources may well have occurred, though equally, if the rapid pace had continued, a different scenario might be envisaged, stressing the difficulty of the British economy in sustaining the historically high levels of naval expenditure which took place just before the First World War. Here again the South West could have suffered cutbacks in investment and employment, with the Dockyard particularly badly hit. From this very narrow perspective the First World War probably broke out at the right time for the South West.

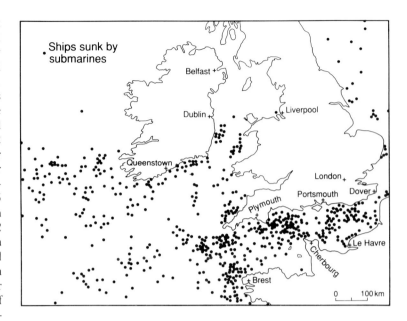

Map 15.1   The U-Boat offensive off the British coasts, 1916–17. (*H Newbolt, 'Naval Operations' in* The Official History of the War)
a   September 1916–April 1917

The First World War

The pattern of surface ship actions during the First World War broadly conformed to that forecast in the Admiralty's prewar plans. Significant battles were concentrated in the North Sea and against commerce raiders in the South Atlantic and Pacific. However, neither the sporadic character of surface naval battles nor their location far from the South West served to reduce the naval importance of the region, while the development of unrestricted submarine warfare again placed the South West in the front line of naval operations by 1917. Even before then, Devonport Dockyard and Plymouth naval base played a vital role in supporting the fleet and continued to do so throughout the war. The slow progress in developing Rosyth placed the major burden of repairing and refitting the Grand Fleet, especially up to 1916, upon Portsmouth and Devonport, the only dockyards able to accommodate the largest warships. Partly as a consequence, the workforce in Devonport Dockyard increased from 12,290 to 15,803 men between 1914 and 1918. Fears that the Germans might take advantage of any temporary weakness in the Grand Fleet led to the establishment of a planned and continuous programme of short refits for each battleship and battlecruiser lasting five or six days, with only one Dreadnought permitted to be absent from the fleet at any one time. Jellicoe, the Commander in Chief in 1915, expressed 'great satisfaction' with the work of Devonport in a signal to the

15.4   The arrival in Plymouth Sound of thirty-two liners with the Canadian Expeditionary Force, October 1914. (*Crispin Gill*)

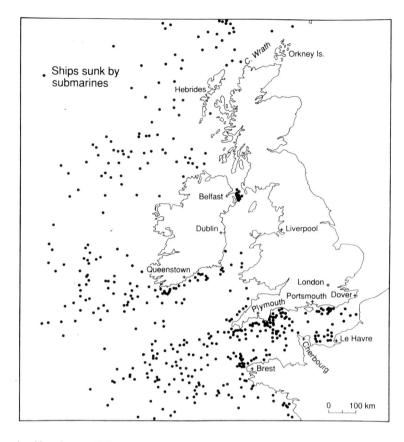

b   May–August 1917

c   September–December 1917

Commander in Chief, praising the 'willing and energetic manner in which the men of the Dockyard have worked'.[22]

Devonport's world role as the major western yard was emphasised by the hurried preparation of the battlecruisers *Invincible* and *Inflexible* for their cruise to the South Atlantic in order to avenge the crushing defeat at Coronel. The first telegram warning that the vessels were due to arrive was received on 5 November 1914, followed five days later by orders that, 'if necessary dockyard men should be sent South in the ships'. The Admiralty made it clear that the Commander in Chief Devonport was to be 'held responsible for the speedy dispatch of these ships in a thoroughly efficient condition'. The battlecruisers did leave on schedule on 11 November 1914, and destroyed Von Spee's squadron at the Falkland Islands on 8 December.[23]

One new feature in the First World War was the sustenance given not just to the British, but also to a wide variety of Allied warships. French warships, mainly based at Brest, were fairly frequent visitors: perhaps the most closely guarded visit occurred in May 1915, when seven destroyers discharged bullion for onward transport to London.[24] Italian, Portuguese and Russian warships also called and, following the United States' entry into the war in 1917, American warships became regular visitors, including in 1918 the battleships *Nevada*, *Oklahoma* and *Utah* based in Berehaven, Southern Ireland. The American battleships released Royal Navy ships for the North Sea and provided cover for the all-important American troop convoys. In June 1918 the advanced party of a force of thirty-six submarine chasers (110ft craft) arrived and established a base at the Victoria Wharf, Plymouth.[25]

The work of maintaining and manning the fleet makes it misleading to describe the South West as a naval backwater at any point during the war. However, it was the development of submarine warfare which restored it to prominence. The sinking by U 24 off Start Point of the pre-dreadnought battleship *Formidable*, with the loss of 547 of its 780 complement on 1 January 1915, during an exercise by the 5th Battle Squadron, alerted the Admiralty to the vulnerability of the Grand Fleet and heralded the start of a new era of maritime warfare.[26] The German acquisition of new bases at

Zeebrugge and Ostend, combined with the introduction of longer-range submarines, soon shifted the focus of the U-boat campaigns to the crucial sea lanes of the Western Approaches (Fig. 15.5).

The main burden of anti-submarine warfare off the southwestern coasts fell upon the Auxiliary Patrol, comprised of a wide variety of lightly-armed trawlers, drifters, yachts, paddle-steamers and other small craft. This organisation was developed following prewar experiments in minesweeping using steam trawlers, which resulted in the establishment of the Royal Naval Reserve (RNR) Trawler Section in late 1911. The initial wartime emphasis was on minesweeping, but it rapidly expanded to a multitude of other tasks including minelaying, shipping examination, and especially anti-submarine patrol work. The number of vessels under the command of the new post of Admiral of Patrols expanded rapidly from fewer than 100 in August 1914 to 827 in January 1915, reaching 3,301 by January 1918. Patrol areas with numerical designations covering the coasts of the British Isles were first listed in December 1914 and were largely established by the summer of 1915.

Three areas held responsibility for the coasts of Devon and Cornwall: Area XV, commanded from Milford Haven; XIV, commanded from Falmouth; and a smaller Bristol local area command. The Devonport Extended Defence Area originally lay outside this network, presumably reflecting its role as a dockyard-port for major warships. From 1 April 1917 a new area XIIIa (Devonport), was created out of parts of Areas XIV and XIII (Portland). The number of vessels allocated to the South West coast patrol areas increased from 37 in January 1915 (4.5 per cent of the total in British home waters) to 295 (11.5 per cent of the total in British home waters). Each patrol area contained several sub-bases. In Area XIV, for example, these included the Scilly Isles, Penzance (covering Newquay to the Lizard), Falmouth (Lizard–Looe) and Dartmouth (Looe–Dartmouth).

The Auxiliary Patrol struggled manfully to combat the new menace with craft unsuited to the hunter-killer role now imposed on them. As the senior Naval Officer at Falmouth reported to the Commander in Chief, Devonport, in May 1915, amidst the first U-boat offensive into the Channel and Western Approaches:

Speed is the greatest thing really required for Patrol Boats – drifters are good for 9kt at best in smooth weather and trawlers for possibly 12kt, but a submarine going at 18kt on the surface can laugh at them, especially in any sea.[27]

The need for better and faster vessels formed a common theme in the reports of local commanders. For example, on 13 September 1916 the Senior Naval Officer, Falmouth, requested that the Admiralty furnish additional destroyers which provided much greater speed and endurance than existing vessels.[28]

Before 1917 the Admiralty tried a great range of measures to counter the U-boat threat, including the avoidance of danger areas, the employment of defensive minefields, booms and nets, and the introduction of protected sea lanes on the main approach routes to the UK. The four main protected sea lanes had at their apex Falmouth, Berehaven, Inistrahill, and Kirkwall. South-Western-based naval vessels (it is impossible and meaningless to isolate a specific Devon contribution) patrolled the Falmouth lane, for shipping from the South Atlantic and Mediterranean heading for the English Channel, and the Berehaven lane, designated for vessels from the North Atlantic towards the English Channel, and from the South Atlantic for the Bristol Channel and Mersey.

The protected lanes proved unsuccessful because it was impossible to patrol effectively a sea area of 10,000 square miles. In his 10 May 1915 report, the Senior Naval Officer at Falmouth declared,

It is hopeless work looking for submarines and only pure luck when one bobs alongside a patrol boat . . . We must provide the right bait for the fish so that they will come after the patrol and the patrol will not have to look for them like a needle in a bundle of hay.[29]

The Captain went on to stress the need for some form of decoy ship, and by late 1915 this type of expedient was developed in the shape of the Q-ship, an armed vessel disguised as an unarmed merchantman. Many of these were converted and fitted out at Devonport, including all three of those commanded by the most successful Q-ship captain, Commander Gordon Campbell. Q-ships were a limited success up to March 1917, with seven U-boat 'kills' against four losses, although thereafter, with the Germans adopting a sink-on-sight policy, only four more kills were achieved against 27 losses.[30]

In July 1915 the Admiralty responded to the German submarine blockade by appointing Admiral Sir Lewis Bayley Admiral Commanding the Western Approaches, with his headquarters in Southern Ireland. By the end of the year four Devonport-based destroyers were assigned to anti-submarine operations under his command; the start of a mounting Devonport commitment to keeping clear the Western Approaches. By April 1917 there were forty-four destroyers based at Devonport (the largest concentration after those attached to the Grand Fleet at Scapa Flow), escorting particularly valuable military cargoes such as troopships and munition ships or engaged in anti-submarine work.[31]

The German introduction of unrestricted submarine warfare in February 1917, followed by the entry of the United States into the war in April and the ensuing American dispatch of troops and munitions to Europe, reinforced the strategic role of the South West by virtue of its geographic position in the battle to protect transoceanic shipping. From a 1915 August peak of 148,464 tons lost, and a 1916 December peak of 182,292 tons, British merchant shipping losses rapidly peaked in April 1917 at 545,282 tons. In that month 135 vessels were sunk in the Western Approaches, representing 24 per cent of the total, and a further 127 vessels off the South and West coasts (26 per cent), compared with 12 per cent off the East coast (Map 15.1). The particular pressure placed on the Navy in the South West can be seen from one day's signals to Devonport: 1 May 1917, when five merchant vessels and a French fishing boat were sunk and nine other submarine sighting reports made. Many of these sightings may have been false alarms or duplications, but this did not help hard-pressed local naval commanders deploy scarce resources. Only two attacks were carried out on submarines, both unsuccessful, one by an armed trawler and one by a French seaplane.[32] The sheer volume of shipping and the convergence of important shipping lanes through the area made a policy of dispersal as a

counter to U-Boats impossible to follow and necessitated more vigorous measures.

The crisis led to a steady build-up of resources in the South West. Between January and April the vessels allocated to the important Penzance Auxiliary Patrol sub-base increased from sixteen to twenty-seven. Most significant for the future, the Admiralty threw its most recently formed arm, the Royal Naval Air Service (RNAS), into the battle. The first significant use of aircraft for antisubmarine work in the South West began in early 1917, with the commissioning of RNAS *Cattewater* in Plymouth (Fig. 15.6). This seaplane base became the forerunner of RAF Mount Batten, which remained in use until the mid-1980s. Other bases for anti-submarine work were established at Torquay (landplanes), Prawle Point near Salcombe (seaplanes and landplanes), Westward Ho! in North Devon (landplanes), Newlyn near Penzance (seaplanes), Padstow (landplanes), Port Mellion on St Mary's in the Scilly Isles (seaplanes), Tresco in the Scilly Isles (flying boats) and Mullion on the Lizard (seaplanes). Falmouth harbour was also used as a resting place for aircraft from Plymouth and the Scilly Isles, but lacked base facilities.[33]

A major disadvantage of aeroplanes for anti-submarine work was their limited endurance and their inability to hover over a stationary target or track a slow-moving target. These factors contributed to the widespread use of airships for anti-submarine work. The RNAS established six new airship stations in 1917 specifically concerned with anti-submarine operations: Pembroke (January), Howden on the Humber (March), Longside near Peterhead in northwest Scotland (March), Caldale (later renamed Kirkwall) in the Orkneys (May: closed January 1918), Mullion (June), and East Fortune on the Firth of Forth (August). Table 15.1 shows both the vast increase in hours flown by the whole Service following the introduction of the long-range (500 miles) C-type airships in 1916 (Fig. 15.7) and the increased importance of the South West. Mullion and Pembroke (including sub-stations), the two airship stations chiefly concerned with anti-submarine operations in the South Western Approaches, increased their hours flown from only 10.1 per cent of the British Isles total in 1916 to 23.7 per cent in 1918.

Table 15.1

Flights from principal operational airship stations, 1915–1918

Station (including sub-stations)	1915	1916	1917	1918
Anglesey	58	1,217	1,559	3,982
Caldale	–	70	346	–
East Fortune	–	308	2,212	3,966
Folkestone	587	1,144	1,912	6,370
Howden	–	521	2,132	3,966
Longside	–	477	1,310	4,207
Luce Bay	90	411	1,757	4,432
Mullion	–	363	2,889	7,936
Pembroke	–	401	2,349	4,767
Polegate	462	1,503	2,985	7,921
Totals	1,197	6,415	19,451	47,547

Note: 1918 statistics are for 1 Jan.– 31 Oct. inclusive.

Source: PRO, ADM 116/1335.

Mullion (and sub-stations) flew more hours in the first ten months of 1918 than any other station, and more hours than the entire Service in 1915. These statistics represent a considerable achievement given the loss of the first Mullion airship, C.8, off Prawle Point in Devon following a navigational error when being delivered, and the ditching off the Lizard of the second, which had become deflated after rifle fire from 'friendly' forces in Jersey.[34]

The operational range and value of Mullion-based airships was greatly extended in 1917–18 with the development of several mooring stations, including Laira at Plymouth, Bude in North Cornwall, and Toller near Bridport in Dorset. A further planned sub-station at Tresco in the Isles of Scilly did not become operational owing to the end of the war.

The success of the airship and aeroplane antisubmarine patrols is difficult to assess. Only one submarine was actually sunk by an aircraft, and none by an airship. During 1917, at the peak of the U-Boat campaign, airships from

15.5 The new face of war in the Western Approaches. The German submarine U29 photographed from ss *Headlands* shortly before the steamer was torpedoed off the Scilly Isles in March 1915. A week after sinking four steamers in this area, U29 was rammed and sunk by HMS *Dreadnought* while attempting to attack the Grand Fleet off the Pentland Firth.

Mullion achieved seventeen sightings and carried out only eleven bombings. Mullion's record still remained incomparably better than that of any other station. However, only five vessels were sunk whilst under air escort and, in the final analysis, the numbers of ships sunk must be the most important criterion of success.

It was not air surveillance of the sea which most effectively contained the submarine menace, however. Rather it was the introduction of an extensive convoy system. High-value targets such as troopships and ammunition vessels were escorted from the outbreak of the war, whilst the Grand Fleet itself represented a form of convoy since it never put to sea without a strong escort of destroyers. The success of these special convoys failed to persuade the Admiralty to redeploy its precious ships, but mounting losses did force a gradual change of policy.

Crisis came first in the vital Anglo-French coal trade. With so much of France's coal-producing capacity lost on the Western Front, it needed at least 1½ million tons of coal each month, brought across in some 500 colliers from Britain, to fuel its war effort. By December 1916 less than that target was getting through. Hence, on 7 February 1917 the first French coal trade convoys began. The convoys were assembled at Mount's Bay, Penzance, for Brest, at Weymouth for Cherbourg and Le Havre, and at Dover and Folkestone for Boulogne and Calais. The Mount's Bay convoys were supported by eleven armed trawlers, and those from Weymouth by fifteen. This successful experiment encouraged the convoying of traffic between Britain and Scandinavia from 29 April 1917, but much more significantly helped produce the decision to run a trial convoy from Gibraltar to Britain which departed on 10 May. The convoy of sixteen merchantmen received an escort of two Q-ships and three armed yachts before meeting eight Devonport-based destroyers off the Scilly Isles. The experiment was followed with the introduction of regular homeward Atlantic convoys in July and outward Atlantic convoys in September. Devonport and Falmouth acted as two of the four main assembly points.[35]

The expansion of the Auxiliary Patrol and increasing air patrol, combined with the development of convoys, never totally overcame the submarine problem but did substantially reduce losses. Only 0.6 per cent of ocean-going convoyed vessels were sunk between February 1917 and October 1918, compared with 5.93 per cent of those sailing independently during the same period. In April 1917, before the introduction of regular ocean-going convoys, approximately one in five of the ships in this category failed to make port.

Devon and Naval Strategy Between the Wars

The First World War had introduced two new factors in naval strategy, the submarine and the aircraft, and during the 1920s and 1930s critics of the Navy suggested that the latter weapon made effective naval operations in the English Channel impossible and southern Dockyards inoperable. Inter-Service competition for scarce resources intensified the debate.

An Air Staff report of 1922 on the potential vulnerability of Plymouth and Portsmouth to air attack forecast that, in a future war, the dockyards and port facilities would suffer crippling damage. Work would be further disrupted by delayed-action bombs and false alarms. Both dockyards lay within a range of 80–110 miles from airfields in Northern France, well within the estimated 180-mile operating radius of contemporary French bombers. Without any effective means of detection, the RAF considered that it could only intercept bombers with fighters 35 miles or more inland.

The Air Staff considered Portsmouth to be the more vulnerable, both because of its shorter range from France and also because the port's position on the bomber route from France to the industrial Midlands would lead to a continual stream of false alarms causing constant disruption. It therefore concluded that Portsmouth should be completely abandoned and Plymouth reduced to the role of a minor naval port. Chatham and Sheerness, even closer to the Continent, should definitely close.

However, during the 1920s the Navy distributed its dockyard and base resources in exactly the opposite way to that suggested by the RAF. The RAF based its assumptions on the perceived threat from France, the only significant Continental air power of the 1920s.[36] The Navy did not totally neglect planning for a war against France, and initially paid lip-service to the threat of air attack, but it placed a greater emphasis throughout the 1920s and into the 1930s on its other traditional role of imperial defence, and especially on meeting the Japanese threat in the Far East. The development

15.6 Short seaplanes parked on the pier at RNAS *Cattewater*, c1917. They were taken into and out of the water by the ex-Dockyard mobile crane to the left of the photograph. (*Crispin Gill*)

of Singapore into a major naval base and dockyard formed the cornerstone of this strategy. In contrast to the RAF, the Navy progressively downgraded any threat from France. In 1925 an Admiralty plan to defend the Thames estuary carried the unusual assumption that 'France would not be at war with this country unless allied by Japan'.[37]

The Navy had no intention of virtually abandoning the English Channel and southern North Sea at the behest of the RAF. Such a policy would effectively concede that the air force constituted Britain's front line of defence, with the Navy reduced to a peripheral and subordinate role. In the event of war with France, the Navy planned to station capital ships at Portland plus a host of smaller vessels in the English Channel and Western Approaches.[38]

The Admiralty's commitment to imperial defence had great importance to the size and distribution of fleet support facilities in two ways. Firstly, it encouraged the Admiralty to discount the possibility of air attack on the southern dockyards in planning; and secondly, given the severe financial restrictions of the time as exemplified by the Geddes Committee cuts, finance for the development of Singapore and matching the Japanese fleet had to be found at the expense of the home dockyards.

The drive for economy resulted in the announcement in 1925 that Rosyth and Pembroke would be put on a 'Care and Maintenance' basis, with the discharge or transfer of almost their entire workforce.[39] Rosyth was selected owing to the elimination of German seapower and because of the reduced number of capital ships in service, and Pembroke because no need now existed for a building yard. Since Rosyth and Pembroke were the two dockyards theoretically least vulnerable to air attack, the Admiralty sought to justify its choice. It argued that, within Western Europe, France was the only conceivable enemy, but that a war was highly unlikely. If such an unlikely conflict did take place, the southern dockyards might suffer severe damage. However, the attacks would not be so overwhelming because of the French Air Force's other commitments; to the fleet in the Mediterranean and in attacking London, for example. Having covered the possible scenario of an unlikely war with France, the Admiralty went on to discuss what the Navy considered to be a much more likely prospect, war with Japan. In such a conflict, the home dockyards, having set the main fleet off eastward, would then be devoted to shipbuilding, since attack from Japan was an obvious impossibility.[40] The possibility that dockyard resources might be redistributed outside the effective range of air attack from the Continent was rejected.

This viewpoint predictably met strong opposition from the RAF and its influential supporters when debated within the Committee for Imperial Defence. Their preferred option was to retain in full commission Rosyth and Pembroke and transfer the resources at Chatham and Sheerness, the yards most vulnerable to air attack, to Plymouth and Portsmouth.

The Admiralty received unexpected support from the Chancellor of the Exchequer, Churchill, who disagreed with the strategic concepts upon which their policy had been based. Churchill's support was largely on

grounds of economy. He suggested that Pembroke possessed inadequate facilities with 'no apparent part in the fundamental arrangements of the Navy'. Rosyth had far more modern and extensive facilities but the southern yards remained vital. Churchill argued that the cost of shifting the machinery and workforce from, for example, Chatham to Scotland, would be prohibitive. Churchill also opposed the upsetting of the domestic economy of the Navy by which ships were paid off at certain southern ports where men had their homes and attachments and which had developed on lines peculiar to and necessary for good dockyard purposes. This consideration did not apply to Rosyth.

After prolonged debate, the Committee of Imperial Defence recommended the retention of the general principle that dockyards and other establishments should be situated in areas less vulnerable to air attack, but accepted that it was a 'policy of perfection to depend more on Rosyth and Pembroke than on the southern yards' given the great cost of any shift. These recommendations were framed in the belief that there was 'no immediate or prospective prospect of war and air attack on this country'.[41]

The opponents of the Admiralty policy did not give up the battle. The RAF worked on influential politicians and civil servants, among them the Secretary of the Committee for Imperial Defence (and of the Cabinet), Maurice Hankey, who expressed the view that,

> Our naval position is being placed so much at the mercy of any combination of nations especially of France with whom we have so often been at loggerheads in the past . . . sometimes quite soon after periods of close ententes.[42]

Nevertheless, despite the efforts of the air lobby, the Cabinet approved the Admiralty decision. The short White Paper outlining the reasons for the closure of Rosyth and Pembroke Dock forecast that further cutbacks in the remaining dockyards would also be required. In the event these cutbacks were severe; Devonport, for example, suffered a reduction in its workforce from 15,803 men in 1918 to 13,950 in 1925 and 11,670 by 1930. However it is worth noting that the latter figure had only been surpassed since 1912–13. Devonport Dockyard benefited from three factors. Firstly it retained a role in the construction of smaller warships, helped by the elimination of Pembroke Dockyard as a rival. Secondly, the limitations imposed by the Washington Naval Treaty on building further battleships placed greater emphasis on dockyard refitting and upgrading of First World War veterans during the 1930s. Thirdly, the mothballing of Pembroke Dock and the closure of the Hawlbowline Dockyard at Queenstown (largely owing to the formation of the Irish Free State) by 1925 left Devonport as the only operational home western yard and, moreover, one whose repairing as well as building role might extend to the Far East until the dry dock being constructed at Singapore could be completed.

Between 1920 and 1938 Devonport launched nine cruisers, twenty-two sloops and a fleet oiler. However, with rearmament, formally announced in 1935, the dockyards' primary wartime role of repair and maintenance came to be more strongly emphasised. Following the first Czechoslovakian crisis of early 1938, which led to a partial naval mobilisation, the Navy was asked to report any deficiencies which had been revealed. According to the Admiralty: 'The Emergency made plain that the A/A defences of the fleet bases at home and abroad are totally inadequate'. Vital oil fuel installations suffered from a complete lack of protection, whilst passive defence measures (air raid shelters, blackouts, etc.) appeared to be lamentably inadequate, the lack of which it was forecast might well have disastrous results. The Admiralty further questioned its ability to escort merchant shipping because of 'grave' shortages of escorts and minesweepers.

The crisis also revealed the shortage of dockyard facilities. Rosyth, considered in the mid 1920s to be of lesser importance, was now of vital importance in a future conflict with a reviving German sea power. The Admiralty therefore required an urgent cabinet decision to make the yard fully operational. The Admiralty concluded,

> We are at present quite unable to undertake hostilities simultaneously against Germany, Italy, and Japan. It may be said indeed that our forces will remain insufficient to conduct a war satisfactorily against Germany and Italy at the same time until they are greatly strengthened, that is during the second half of 1940.[43]

15.7   A C-type airship patrolling over a convoy. (*Imperial War Museum*)

15.8   The capital surface fleet at the Keyham Extension, *c*1960. In the foreground is the cruiser *Belfast*, moored on the south side of No.4 Basin, with the frigates *Tenby* and *Salisbury* at her bows. The aircraft carrier *Ark Royal* is in No.10 Dock, and ranged up the Hamoaze are *Eagle*, *Hermes* and *Bulwark*, with the cruiser *Tiger* at the top right of the photograph. (*Devonport Dockyard Museum*)

The Admiralty's analysis of naval deficiencies in 1938, subsequently confirmed in the war itself, might be taken as a condemnation of its own set of priorities established in the 1920s. The Admiralty had mothballed the two dockyards least vulnerable to air attack and given a low priority to the air defence of naval bases. In the process it had thrown the entire burden of dockyard support for the defence of the Western Approaches on to Devonport, at least until Pembroke could be brought into service. Policy developments in the 1920s clearly reflected a dilemma facing the Navy. If the Service had stressed the importance of trade protection, then the pattern of dockyard and base resources should have shifted to the south and west, making the closure of Pembroke very questionable. Such a shift would also have sharpened the debate over the vulnerability of naval bases to an air attack, which became reality in 1940. By placing the emphasis on meeting the Japanese threat, the Navy could evade this issue, but only at the cost of unpreparedness in the late 1930s for war against Germany. The failure to develop an effective policy towards the distribution of support facilities is a reflection of the general confusion surrounding British foreign and defence policy of the period, not helped by bitter inter-Service rivalry. How Devonport and the South-West coped with the consequences, not of war with France, which the Admiralty had evaded contemplating, but with a German-occupied France, which it had never envisaged, is described by Ian Skinner in Chapter 20.

Postwar Strategy

The lesson of the prewar mistakes had undoubtedly been learnt by 1945. As early as 1941–2 the Admiralty was seeking more space in order to disperse facilities at Devonport as protection against bombing attacks, and a paper of May 1945 established certain broad principles for the future strategic location of dockyards and other naval facilities, stressing dispersal and the location of vital installations in north and west Britain and away from other likely targets such as London.

The Admiralty still retained its interwar belief that a 'wholesale transfer of dockyard facilities' was impracticable, but it was now prepared to suggest a redistribution of resources. Thus the southern dockyards were to be modernised and rehabilitated with some dispersal of facilities within the yards, but their redevelopment would take place only to the limits of the prewar capacity. In this context in 1945 the Admiralty intended to enlarge Devonport by 252 acres to disperse facilities. By contrast, Rosyth 'must have first consideration over the Southern yards'. As part of the same policy the Admiralty proposed to relocate as many as possible of its training and research installations away from the south coast.

The concern to redistribute naval establishments away from air attack, however, was largely overtaken by the development of long-range missiles and aircraft which meant that no part of the United Kingdom could now be

15.9   The modern Naval Base in operation, *c*1988, with the aircraft carrier HMS *Invincible* undergoing major refit in No.9 Dock and two submarines in the entrance lock.
A Type 22 frigate is moored in No.4 Basin, with three more outside it, and a *Leander* class frigate is at the bottom of the picture with two more outside the Typed Frigare Complex
towards the top. (*Devonport Management Ltd*)

considered remote from attack. Atomic weapons also made the planned dispersal of facilities within dockyards irrelevant. As a consequence, the proposed extensions to Devonport Dockyard proceeded at a very leisurely pace, occupied rather less land than originally intended, and were not finally completed until the early 1960s.

Between 1950 and 1980 the workforce at the four largest home dockyards, Devonport, Portsmouth, Chatham and Rosyth, fell from 40,500 to 32,000.[44] The decline in the workforce was much less dramatic than the fall in the numbers of major warships (frigate-sized and above and submarines) and including reserves, from 390 to 104 between 1950 and 1979–80.[45] Four factors have contributed to maintaining the workload. Firstly, the great complexity of modern ships: nuclear submarines, for example, require a similar number of man-hours when undergoing a major refit as the old *Ark Royal*, the large fleet aircraft carrier which entered service in the 1950s.

Secondly, the much reduced complement of modern warships, because of shipboard automation and the replacement of labour-intensive large naval guns, has removed the pool of spare manpower which used to be available for maintenance. Thirdly, the closure of the smaller home dockyards, Pembroke Dock in 1947 and Sheerness in 1960. Lastly, the virtual disappearance of overseas bases and dockyards has thrown a much greater burden on the surviving home dockyards when overseas deployments are made (Fig. 15.8).

The first postwar decades saw a major shift in the distribution of resources between the leading dockyards. By 1980 Portsmouth's workforce had declined by 47 per cent to 7,400, Chatham's by 32 per cent to 6,000, Devonports' by 9 per cent to 12,700, whilst Rosyth experienced an increase of 37 per cent to 5,900.[46] Three factors helped influence this distribution of resources. Firstly, the replacement of the battleship by the nuclear submarine as the Royal Navy's main Capital Ships. Problems of access for the large nuclear submarines and the proximity of housing meant that Portsmouth did not develop facilities for these vessels. Major nuclear submarine operating bases were developed at Devonport and Faslane on the Clyde, whilst refitting facilities were provided at Rosyth, Devonport and Chatham. Devonport was therefore unique in provided the full range of facilities to both operate and refit these vessels. Secondly, the recruitment and retention of skilled workers became an increasingly severe problem at Chatham and, especially, Portsmouth, relative to the more isolated Devonport and Rosyth dockyards. Thirdly, the extension of fishing limits and the discovery of North Sea oil and gas made the retention of some kind of North East coast base important, and therefore contributed towards the expansion of Rosyth.[47] The overall result for Devonport was that the size of its workforce tended to fluctuate moderately rather than go through any dramatic changes, and remained well above what it had been for most of the interwar period.

The mid 1980s saw a much sharper reduction in the total workforce, resulting from the changes in policy outlined in the 1981 Defence White Paper, *The Way Forward*, which led to the closure of Chatham and Gibraltar dockyards in 1984 and the reduction of Portsmouth to a Fleet Maintenance and Repair Base with a much reduced workforce, leaving Devonport and Rosyth as the only two remaining Royal Dockyards. The cutback in capacity resulted from the reduction in the surface fleet by approximately one-third, combined with an end to the normal mid-life major refits for surface warships. The Falklands conflict of 1982 only served to delay and modify these cuts, though yet again it emphasised Devonport's transoceanic support role, being the third time this century that it has provided the back-up for operations in the South Atlantic (the others being in 1914 and in early 1940, when it repaired the *Ajax* and *Exeter* after the Battle of the River Plate).

The introduction of commercial management in 1987 provided Devonport with an allocation of 60 per cent of dockyard naval refits, compared with 30 per cent for Rosyth and 10 per cent for Portsmouth. Whilst the government has encouraged competition from private ship repairers for naval work, they have continued to concentrate upon auxiliaries and minor warships. Between 1987 and 1992 only one major warship refit new contract, a Type 42 Destroyer awarded to warship builders Swan Hunter, went outside the dockyards.[48]

Commercial management in the dockyards has sharpened the distinction between the civilian-manned dockyard and the adjacent Fleet Maintenance Base run by uniformed personnel, which is now organisationally and financially completely separate. Fleet Maintenance Bases have developed since the 1950s to provide maintenance and repair beyond the scope of ship crews in isolation but below the level provided by the dockyards. The six UK Fleet Maintenance Bases for 1989–90, with service personnel and running costs, were Devonport (1,115/£3.2 million), Faslane (661/£31.7 million), Portsmouth (370/£12 million), Rosyth (358/£28.2 million), Gosport (240) and Portland (139/£3.2 million). In addition, small units were located in Hong Kong and Gibraltar.[49] At Devonport, the Fleet Maintenance Base is housed in a purpose-built complex opened in 1978 following the transfer of personnel from improvised provision in ships berthed in the dockyard.[50] Although labour costs are estimated to be up to 20 per cent higher in the Fleet Maintenance Bases than in the dockyards, the Navy has justified their function in a way reminiscent of past justifications for the retention of the dockyards. The Fleet Maintenance Bases have already provided personnel for sophisticated forward maintenance and repair vessels operating in the South Atlantic and Gulf.[51]

Whilst Devonport emerged from the early 1980s shake-up of the dockyard system in a relatively favourable position, during the later part of the decade its long-term future again appeared in doubt. Employment in the dockyard fell from 11,460 in 1987 to about 5,500 in mid-1993. Two important factors contributed towards this contraction. Firstly, the accelerated rundown in the fleet which has followed the end of the Cold War, with frigate/destroyer numbers now set to fall to about thirty-five ships in the late 1990s; and, secondly, the reduced maintenance requirements of modern warships. Gas turbine units and electronic equipment are now replaced, in the former case if necessary by ships' crews at sea, rather than repaired. The rapid

retirement of older steam turbine powered vessels such as the *Leander* class frigates from the mid-1980s, and their replacement by newer classes specifically designed for low maintenance, has accelerated the fall in dockyard workload. Rosyth, where, despite the transfer of some surface ship work from Portsmouth, the main priority in the 1980s has remained the maintenance of the aged Polaris submarine fleet, suffered a much smaller reduction in workload than Devonport during the 1980s, with employment remaining above 4,000 workers.[52]

The year 1992–93 saw a reassertion of Devonport's traditional strength of gaining relative importance in periods of overall naval contraction at the expense of other ports. The Naval Operational and Sea Training Base is to be transferred to Devonport with the closure of Portland by April 1996. About 550 service and 475 civilian personnel will be affected, some being transferred to Devonport.[53] The prime rationale for Portland's demise was clearly financial, but also the separation of training from operations makes less sense with a smaller fleet. During the late 1990s Plymouth is likely to see a wider variety of visiting vessels: in 1991–2 Portland provided training facilities for forty-two Royal Navy and twelve NATO warships.[54] Also in late 1992 came the decision to cease major refit work at Portsmouth, now employing about 2,000 civilians. Britain's former leading dockyard will now be restricted to the routine maintenance and repair of Portsmouth-based ships.[55]

Even more significantly, in 1993 Devonport Dockyard won the bitter and protracted battle to refit Trident submarines, against competition from Rosyth. Devonport's victory was based upon refurbishment of docks once used by battleships, reflecting the yard's versatility. From the late 1990s Devonport will refit all of the Navy's submarines. Rosyth is to receive a compensatory package of surface-ship work amounting to about 50 per cent of the total and including some refits transferred from Devonport. As a consequence employment at Devonport is set to fall by a further 350, against 450 for Rosyth.[56] However, with further cuts in the fleet announced days after Devonport's victory, it remains to be seen whether the government's commitment to two dockyards can be honoured. Devonport must be in a stronger position, Trident submarines having a lifespan of possibly thirty years whilst Rosyth's core programme is only guaranteed for twelve years.

Of the three first-class home dockyards in 1815, only Devonport has survived with its status undiminished. Since none of the newer dockyards has grown as large, it stands alone in the early 1990s as Britain's biggest naval dockyard and base. While the introduction of commercial management heralded a further period of uncertainty for the dockyard and marked the start of more drastic labour force cuts, the strategic role of the naval base has remained clear. The decision to retain some control of the dockyards' physical assets when introducing commercial management in 1987, plus retention of full control of the now separated naval base facilities, rather than going for an outright sale, as in the case of the Royal Ordnance factories, is a further reflection of the continued strategic importance of Plymouth and the dockyard in support of the Navy.

Fundamental to Devonport's survival to become Britain's biggest dockyard and naval base has been its strategic location. As long as Britain still possesses overseas dependencies and responsibilities, it requires a major western naval base to support them. The Falklands conflict was a reminder of this. Even more importantly, so long as Britain remains dependent on transoceanic trade and supply, a major western naval base is essential for the protection of ships in passage. Such was the lesson of the French wars and war-scares, and such has been the lesson of two world wars against a rival from the opposite direction, Germany, which still held true for a rival still further east – Russia. Although a northeastern naval base and air power can shut off the surface menace, they cannot stop submarines getting to westward, and Plymouth retains a key role as a naval base supporting the Navy's major non-nuclear deterrent task: anti-submarine warfare in the Eastern Atlantic and English Channel within NATO. By the late 1980s the Royal Navy provided approximately 70 per cent of NATO's readily available naval forces in the Channel and Eastern Atlantic.[57] The Flag Officer, Plymouth (Port Admiral, Devonport), holds the NATO post of Commander Plymouth Sea Area, which stretches from the Irish Sea to Mauritania. Ship allocations can change, but in the late 1980s, and largely in support of this role, Plymouth acted as a base for four of the Royal Navy's nine frigate and destroyer flotillas, two out of four submarine squadrons and the surveying flotilla (Fig. 15.9).

The end of the Cold War has shifted the emphasis towards operations outside the NATO area, possibly in support of the United Nations. As the Gulf, and especially the Falklands conflict, demonstrated, non-NATO deployments require a high level of support and improvisation. Devon, with its combination of dockyard, operational and training roles, is likely to play a key role in any future British naval operations to an even greater extent than in the past.[58]

15: Devon and Naval Strategy since 1815

1   C J Bartlett, *Great Britain and Seapower 1815–1853* (Oxford, 1963); C I Hamilton, *Anglo-French Naval Rivalry 1840–1870* (Oxford, 1993); A J Marder, *The Anatomy of British Sea Power, 1880–1905* (London, 1964).

2   Bartlett, *Britain and Seapower*, 333.

3   P Kennedy, *The Rise and Fall of the Great Powers* (1988), 196.

4   See chapter 16.

5   R Morriss, *The Royal Dockyards during the Revolutionary and Napoleonic Wars* (Leicester, 1983), 14.

6   *Shipbuilding and Dockyard Transactions 1869–70* (BPP, 1871, LXIV, 1).

7   *Report to the Lord Commissioners of the Admiralty on the completion of the Haulbowline Dockyard*, (BPP, 1896, LXV, 499).

8   M S Partridge, 'A Supplement to the Naval Defences of Great Britain: Harbours of Refuge 1814–1870' *MM*, 72 (1986), 17–24; *Report of the Commission Into Harbours of Refuge* (BPP, 1845, XVI, 1–13).

9   P Barry, *The Dockyards, Shipyards and Marine of France* (London, 1864), 43.

10   A G Jamieson, *A People of the Sea. The Maritime History of the Channel Islands* (1986), 227–40.

11   *Shipbuilding and Dockyard Transactions 1869–70* (BPP, 1871, XLI, 1).

12   PRO, ADM 116/3096, Admiralty War Plans 1911–14.

13   A J Marder, *From Dreadnought to Scapa Flow, The Royal Navy in the Fisher Era 1904–1919* (Oxford, 1961–70), I, 424–6; Marder, *The Anatomy of British Seapower*, 466–7; P MacDougal, *The Royal Dockyards*, (Newton Abbot, 1982), 169–73.

14   *Dockyard Expense Accounts* (BPP, 1889–1914, passim).

15   *HCD*, 19 July 1910, col. 1167.

16   *Statement Explanatory of Naval Estimates* (BPP, 1905, XLVII, 9).

17   PRO, ADM 116/239, Committee to enquire into the Conditions under which Contracts are Invited for the Building and Repair of Ships (1884, chairman Lord Ravensworth).

18   Census of the Population, 1911.

19   *Naval Works Act*. (BPP, 1905, XLVII, 493).

20   G Dicker, *A Short History of Devonport Dockyard* (Devonport, n.d.), 21.

21   Marder, *From Dreadnought to Scapa Flow*, I, 421–6.

22   PRO, ADM 131/78.

23   PRO, ADM 131/79, Plymouth War Pack.

24   PRO, ADM 131/65, Plymouth War Pack.

25   PRO, ADM 131/65, Visits of Allied and Neutral Vessels 1914–16.

26   Marder, *From Dreadnought to Scapa Flow*, II, 98–100.

27   PRO, ADM 131/71, Auxiliary Patrol Reports, Plymouth Station, 10 May 1915.

28   PRO, ADM 131/71, Auxiliary Patrol Weekly reports.

29   PRO, ADM 131/71, Auxiliary Patrol Reports, 10 May 1915.

30   K V Burns, *The Devonport Dockyard Story* (Liskeard, 1984) 81–2; Marder, *From Dreadnought to Scapa Flow*, II, 356.

31   Marder, *From Dreadnought to Scapa Flow*, II, 359, 362; IV, 123.

32   PRO, ADM 131/65, Submarine Attack reports Plymouth Station.

33   PRO, ADM 131/71, Plymouth Station Records: Aircraft, Airships, and Balloons and Kites: Organisation and Operation.

34   PRO, ADM 131/64.

35   Marder, *From Dreadnought to Scapa Flow*, IV, 138, 186, 268.

36   M Dean, *The Royal Air Force in the Two World Wars* (1979), 38–40.

37   PRO, ADM 116/3103, The Defence of the Home Ports 1925–35.

38   PRO, ADM 116/3103, Admiralty Staff Meeting, 22 Feb. 1923.

39   *Rosyth and Pembroke: Savings to be effected by a Reduction to a Care and Maintenance Basis* (BPP, 1924, XVIII, 873).

40   PRO, CAB 21, Letter Admiralty to Secretary Committee of Imperial Defence, Oct. 1925.

41   PRO, CAB 21, Committee of Imperial Defence, 15 Oct. 1925.

42   PRO, CAB 21, Letter Hankey-Lord Trenchard, 6 Sept. 1925.

43   PRO, ADM 116 3637, Memo on Naval deficiencies for Sub Committee Meeting CID, 6 Oct. 1938.

44   *The Royal Dockyards: A Framework for the Future* (HMSO, 1980) Appendix F-I.

45   D Wettern, *The Decline of British Seapower* (1980), 394, 433.

46   *The Royal Dockyards* (1980), Appdx F–I.

47   P Beaver, *Encyclopedia of the Modern Royal Navy* (1985), 50–62: *The Royal Dockyards* (1980), I, 15–52.

48   National Audit Office (hereafter NAO), *Ministry of Defence: Operation of the Royal Dockyards under Commercial Management* (1992) HC 23 1991–92, 26.

49   NAO, *Ministry of Defence: Fleet Maintenance* (1990) HC 249, 20.

50   Burns, *Devonport Dockyard Story*, 113–4.

51   NAO, *Ministry of Defence: Fleet Maintenance*, 24.

52   NAO, *Ministry of Defence: Operation of the Royal Dockyards under Commercial Management*, 9.

53   *HCD*, 12 November 1992, col 883–884.

54   *HCD*, 29 October 1992, cols 779–800.

55   *HCD*, 12 November 1992, col 883–884.

56   *The Times*, 24 June 1993.

57   *Statement on the Defence Estimates 1988* (1988) Cmd 344 – I, 19.

58   The author gratefully acknowledges the assistance of Michael Duffy and Todd Gray in the preparation of this chapter.

16 *Architecture and Development of Devonport Naval Base, 1815–1982*

Jonathan Coad

At the end of the Napoleonic Wars over 15,600 people were employed in the seven home dockyards, nearly half working in the great bases of Portsmouth and Plymouth.[1] These figures exclude all those employed by the Ordnance and Victualling establishments and in the naval hospitals at Stonehouse, Haslar and Great Yarmouth. They do, however, clearly indicate the tremendous industrial strength that was then sustaining the Royal Navy.

Although the ending of the Napoleonic Wars inevitably led to a reduction in the armed services, a notable feature of British political life for most of the nineteenth century was a general agreement among politicians that Britain must retain its naval supremacy.[2] The annual naval estimates reflect this continuing concern. Indeed, the dockyard vote for 1821 was almost as large as that for 1813, at the height of the war years.[3] At Plymouth, the work of extending and modernising the dockyard, following the plans largely laid down in the 1760s, continued after 1815 and was finally completed in 1822.[4] Thereafter, except for extending or modernising individual workshops and making minor additions to the estate, little was done to the dockyard facilities until the 1840s. Instead, money was concentrated on two major engineering projects: the construction of the breakwater in Plymouth Sound and the centralising of all the local victualling facilities in a monumental new victualling yard at Stonehouse (Map 16.1).

The Plymouth Breakwater

It had long been recognised that a major drawback to Plymouth's use as a fleet base was the absence of an easily accessible sheltered anchorage. As the Admiralty had noted during their 1771 inspection of the dockyard,

> '. . . the crookedness and intricacy of the entrance of the harbour render the getting ships in and out more precarious [than at Portsmouth], and for the want of a spacious safe roadstead it can never be a principal rendezvous for great fleets in times of war, the Sound not being a safe place for ships to lie in except in Summer, and then only for an inconsiderable number, because of the small space of clear ground . . .'[5]

Tor Bay, well protected from the westerly gales, was the inconvenient but only alternative.

Proposals to make Plymouth Sound a sheltered anchorage by means of a pier or a breakwater had been seriously mooted towards the end of the eighteenth century, and a survey had been undertaken in 1788.[6] In 1806 John Rennie, assisted by Joseph Whidbey and the Master-

Attendant at the dockyard, James Hemmans, drew up plans for a detached breakwater across the centre of the Sound. It was to have a central section 3,000ft long and two arms, each 1,050ft long, inclined inwards at an angle of 160°. It was to be formed of huge blocks of rubble, weighing up to five tons apiece, tipped and by the action of the sea allowed to find their own angle of repose. Above low-water level the top was to be secured using granite and limestone masonry carefully dovetailed and jointed.

After five years of debate between the Admiralty and the Navy Board, an Order-in-Council was issued for the work on 22 June 1811 and the first stones were tipped on 12 August 1812.[7] By the spring of 1814 part of the breakwater was visible and was already proving its worth during southwesterly gales. In 1821 construction of a lighthouse on the breakwater was authorised, although it was to be 1836 before work on the latter was sufficiently far advanced for a start to be made on the former.[8] Construction of the major part of the breakwater was spread over thirty-seven years, and was one of the engineering wonders of the early nineteenth century (Fig. 16.1). Work could only proceed in calm weather, and supplies of the huge quantities of stone required were not always easy to obtain.[9] The Admiralty purchased twenty-five acres of the Duke of Bedford's estate at Oreston (and four more in 1829), conveniently close, a mile and a quarter up the Plym estuary, to quarry blocks for the main body of the wall, which was then faced with granite. Ten large ships fitted with rails, windlasses and tilting platforms carried the larger blocks, another forty-five carrying smaller stones. By the end of 1848 3,670,444 tons of rubble and 22,149 cubic yards of masonry – 'an amount of material at least equal to that contained in the Great Pyramid' – had been put in place at a total cost of about one and half million pounds.[10] Work on construction, as distinct from the ceaseless

16.1 Plymouth Breakwater under construction. One of the special stone-carrying craft, purpose-designed by Joseph Whidbey, can be seen to the left. An engraving by H Wallis from a drawing by Thomas Allom, published in 1832. (*City of Plymouth Museums and Art Gallery*)

maintenance, continued into the 1860s. By 1862 the only work outstanding was the completion of 817ft of buttressing.[11] Writing the same year, Samuel Smiles noted with satisfaction:

> As forming a convenient and secure haven of refuge for merchant ships passing up and down Channel, along the great highway between England, America and India – as a capacious harbour for vessels of war, wherein fifty ship of the line, besides frigates and smaller vessels, can at all times find safe anchorage – Plymouth Breakwater may in all respects be regarded as a magnificent work, worthy of a great maritime nation.[12]

The Royal William Victualling Yard

In 1821 the Victualling Board took the decision to centralise all of its victualling operations, then scattered in freehold and rented premises around Plymouth and alongside Millbrook Creek. By September 1823 the Board had approved a site on the Stonehouse Peninsula and their solicitor was instructed to make the necessary purchases.[13] Acquiring land occupied the next twelve months. The new yard was extremely well sited: the Victualling Board obtained a short rocky promontory jutting into the Hamoaze at its confluence with Plymouth Sound. From here victualling craft were within easy reach of warships at the dockyard or riding at anchor in the Sound, while incoming grain and cattle ships could berth alongside the victualling wharves. The only serious drawback, and one not apparent until the advent of the juggernaut lorries of the late twentieth century, lay in the restricted and tortuous road access through Stonehouse itself.

To make the best use of the site, considerable engineering work was required. The southern part of the promontory was left largely undisturbed to provide shelter and to allow the construction of a high-level reservoir, but most of the eight acres was dug and blasted away to form a level site and to produce both stone for the buildings and rubble to reclaim a further six acres from the shore of the Hamoaze at its juncture with the entrance to Stonehouse Pool. This preliminary work took the contractor, Hugh McIntosh, three years, and not until November 1827 did the Victualling Board authorise construction of the first building, the present Clarence Store, at the western end of the yard.[14]

It was probably the magnitude of engineering works here which prompted the Navy Board, responsible since July 1823 for all construction works in the Victualling yards, to employ John Rennie (Jr) rather than to use their own architect, as was to be done later when Royal Clarence Yard was built at Gosport.[15] In many ways, Rennie was an obvious candidate. Although aged only 29 in 1823, he was already involved with the construction of the great Sound breakwater, having assumed this responsibility on his father's death two years earlier. He was to prove himself equal to this new challenge, and today the Royal William Victualling Yard is one of the finest monuments to this age of the engineer/architect, as well as one of the grandest groups of early nineteenth-century buildings in the west of England (Fig. 16.2).

Land reclamation and quarrying had given Rennie an irregular L-shaped site on which to group his buildings. Much of the short stroke of the L he planned for occasional open storage for such items as casks, while on the eastern side he located two houses for the senior victualling officers. The rest of the buildings were to be sited on the main axis of the yard and centred around the tidal basin to be used by victualling craft.

Plymouth victualling facilities, in common with the other large establishments at Portsmouth and Deptford, were not just holding depots, but manufactured many of the comestibles and brewed most if not all of the beer supplied to the Navy. The two main manufacturing buildings and their equipment which Rennie had to design were a large brewery, sited to the west of the basin, and a combined granary, flour-mill and bakery which he located to the east of the basin. Both of these buildings had central bays projecting to the edge of the adjacent wharves so that supply vessels could be offloaded directly by wall cranes.

The southern side of the basin, beyond the broad main road which forms the main axis of the yard, was closed by a huge quadrangular storehouse. This was of three storeys and fronted the basin; its storage capacity was probably not exceeded by any other storehouse possessed by the Victualling Board. It was named the Melville Square storehouse after the second Lord Melville, First Lord of the Admiralty from 1812 to 1827. West of Melville Square, Rennie sited a substantial cooperage. This consisted of four irregular ranges of two storeys facing inwards to a central courtyard. These ranges seem to have provided stables for victualling yard horse teams as well as workshops and stores for the coopers. In later years the centre of the courtyard was to be partly occupied by an additional coopers' workshop. The overall size of this cooperage reflected the vital storage role of barrels in the Navy. Everything from gunpowder (kept in special copper-hooped barrels made by the Board of Ordnance) to salt beef, beer and butter went to sea in a variety of different sizes of barrels, the great majority made and repaired in naval cooperages.

All of Rennie's buildings here were constructed of Devonian limestone, some from the site and the rest bought from local quarries. Details such as pilasters, archways and the heavy cornices were in granite and everything was on a monumental scale. Cast iron columns were used extensively inside, but only in part of the bakery were these used in conjunction with iron beams and stone flags for a fireproof construction.

The landward approach to the victualling yard was dominated by the huge entrance archway. Built almost entirely of rusticated granite, the main archway is flanked by pilasters surmounted by carved ox heads, symbols of the Victualling Board, below an elaborate entablature. In the centre of this a series of stepped plinths are crowned by an heroic statue of William IV, after whom the yard was named.

Clarence Wharf Storehouse was begun in November 1827. The following year work was begun on the brewery, boundary walls and the excavation of the basin. This was followed in 1829 by the start of the Melville Square Storehouse, and in late 1830 by a group of buildings around the main gateway. Apart from the gateway itself, these included the porter's lodge, guard house, colonnades, slaughterhouse, cattle yard and beef and vegetable stores.[16] The same autumn, at a time when the scale and cost of the whole project were causing anxiety to both Treasury and Admiralty, Rennie was ordered to draw up plans and specifications for the mill and bakery and for officers' houses.[17]

The brewery was completed by January 1833, and it seems that the bulk of the victualling yard was operational by the end of that year.[18] There have been few additions since then. A new cooperage was built to the east of Melville Square storehouses late in the nineteenth century, its simple design complementing Rennie's earlier work, but externally the victualling yard remains large as completed in the mid years of William IV's reign. The brewery and bakery have long ceased to be used for their original purposes

16.3 Devonport and the Dockyard, showing the covered slips. An engraving by T Jeavons after an oil painting by J M W Turner. For an interior view, see Vol I, Fig 31.3. (*City of Plymouth Museums and Art Gallery*)

and their machinery has gone, but in other buildings there have been surprisingly few alterations. Royal William Yard ceased to be used by the Royal Navy in 1993, and its future must be a matter of concern to all who value naval history and fine architecture.

Dockyard Developments 1815–1845

By the end of the Napoleonic Wars the huge expansion and reconstruction of the dockyard begun over half a century earlier had been largely completed. Although it was spread over fifty years, there had been surprisingly few deviations from the plans drawn up in the first years of George III's reign. This was a reflection not only of the basic soundness of the 1760's replanning, but also of the largely unchanging technology of sailing warships, which enabled such long-term reconstructions of the dockyards to be undertaken without serious risk of shore facilities being obsolete almost as soon as they were completed. No subsequent generation of dockyard planners has had similar good fortune.

Shortly before the end of the war, plans were drawn up to begin construction of timber roofs over slips and such docks as were not intended to take masted vessels. The huge scale of such timber roofs had deterred earlier generations of Navy Board officials, and the impetus can be traced to Brigadier General Sir Samuel Bentham, Inspector General of Naval Works from 1795–1812. Concern about the problems of dry and wet rots in warships was long standing. In the 1770s large numbers of timber-seasoning sheds had been constructed in all the dockyards in an effort to ensure that only seasoned timber was used for warship building.[19] The next stage was to cover over the building slips, which served a double purpose in protecting both the warships under construction and the shipwrights working on them. Both the French and Swedish dockyards had had some slips covered since the latter part of the eighteenth century, and serious planning in Great Britain seems to have begun with Bentham's visit to Karlskrona in 1807.[20] The 1814 estimates for Plymouth include a sum of £6,000 to roof over one of the dry docks, and between then and 1821 monies were allocated each year for dock and slip housings (Fig. 16.3).[21] With the advent of metal warships in the 1860s, the need for building hulls under cover diminished, and today only three timber slip-housings survive: two at Devonport and a later one at Chatham.

In 1814 work began on a long-overdue replacement of the original and by now cramped dockyard chapel. It was designed by Edward Holl, the Navy Board architect, and by 1816 work was sufficiently far advanced for Portsmouth Dockyard to be requested to supply mahogany for constructing the pulpit. The chapel probably came into use the following year.[22] It was a handsome rectangular building of stone with a tower over the west entrance; the use of shallow arcading to define the window bays clearly derived from Holl's earlier chapel at Chatham. Inside, again following a Chatham precedent, the three-sided timber gallery was carried on cast-iron columns. The chapel was destroyed in the Second World War.[23]

Although minor works continued for a number of years, the architectural history of Georgian Plymouth Dockyard can conveniently be terminated in 1822 with the construction of the delightful little gazebo overlooking the south part of the yard and across to Hamoaze. An inscription just below the conical metal roof reads 'To perpetuate the recollection of the visit of His Majesty George III of blessed and glorious memory, and of His Majesty's admiration of the rock on which it stands, and the scene around. This building was erected in the year 1822'. Although the gazebo commemorates

the king's visit, the rock itself is of note, for its top is an indication of the general height of the upper parts of the dockyard before the huge quarrying operations associated with the Georgian expansion.

The Keyham Steam Yard

Over the next quarter of a century, developments were under way in ship technology which were to have a profound effect on all of the royal dockyards. These changes came gradually – very gradually as far as the Navy was concerned, for there was no desire to make the existing fleet obsolete without very good reason. The Navy had built its first steam vessel, *Congo*, in 1816. In 1835, in response to the gradual increase in the numbers of steam-powered naval vessels, the Admiralty appointed the first Chief Engineer and Inspector of Machinery. By 1842, if Navy-operated steam packets are included, approximately one-fifth of the ships in commission were steamers. In 1840 the Navy acquired its first iron-hulled vessel, the cross-Channel postal packet *Dover*.[24] By then it was becoming apparent that the days of sailing fleets might be numbered, although it was to take another twenty years before iron technology was sufficiently advanced to make an all-metal armour-plated warship a reality, an event hastened by the introduction of heavy rifled ordnance firing explosive shells. These technological developments were paralleled by advances in the design and construction of the traditional sailing ship-of-the-line. Partly in response to warship development by the French and American navies, and partly through the work of Seppings and Symonds, successively Surveyors of the Navy, the size of individual warships grew. Thirty years after the end of the Napoleonic Wars it was apparent that the dockyards again needed to be modernised, not just to accommodate larger warships, but to provide the facilities needed to service steam machinery and to supply the increasing amount of metal used in warship construction. In 1842 work began at Portsmouth to provide a new basin and associated engineering workshops north of the Georgian dockyard.[25] The western yard followed suit two years later, the beginning of its modernisation coinciding with an Admiralty decision to change its name from Plymouth to Devonport Dockyard.[26]

At Devonport the existing dockyard was incapable of any further expansion, as it was hemmed in on its landward sides by the town. North of it a thin strip of urban development separated the dockyard from Morice Ordnance Yard, but beyond that lay open land on which stood the Board of Ordnance's Keyham powder magazine. Thirty-eight acres of this land, together with a further forty-three acres of foreshore, were purchased by the Admiralty in 1844. In 1845 further land was purchased up-river at Bull Point to enable the relocation of the powder magazine.[27]

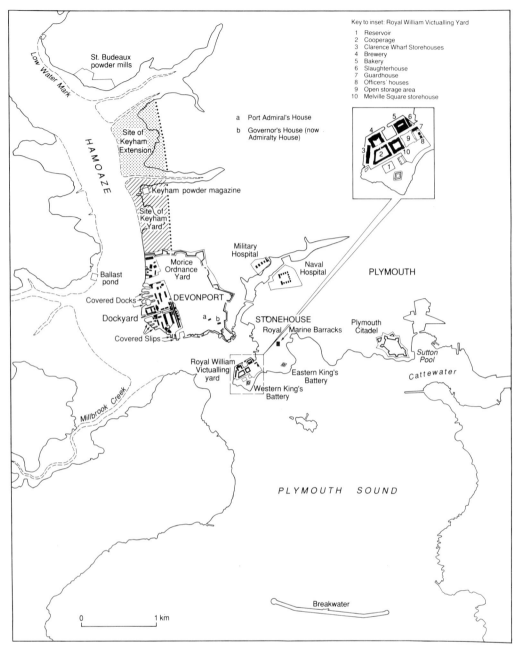

Key to inset: Royal William Victualling Yard
1 Reservoir
2 Cooperage
3 Clarence Wharf Storehouses
4 Brewery
5 Bakery
6 Slaughterhouse
7 Guardhouse
8 Officers' houses
9 Open storage area
10 Melville Square storehouse

a Port Admiral's House
b Governor's House (now Admiralty House)

Map 16.1 Devonport Dockyard and Plymouth naval and military installations in the 1840s

Select Committee, was urging a slowing of construction work in order to save money – a thoroughly specious argument not unknown today. This prompted a rejoinder from Greene, one of two Royal Engineers supervising the project for the Admiralty, that 'postponing the works to a more distant period . . . [would be] a culpable mistake'.[33] Clearly, Greene was not alone in this view, for the only delay in the completion of the whole project appears to have been due to problems relocating the ordnance facilities to Bull Point. Until this was done the North Basin could not be finished.[34]

In 1848 the architect Charles Barry was commissioned to draw up plans for the complex of foundry, machine shops and stores, known as the Quadrangle, to be built along the eastern side of the North Basin.[35] The Quadrangle remains the largest and most ambitious group of such buildings ever erected by the Navy, proof enough that by the late 1840s the Admiralty was fully alert to the needs of the steam fleet.

The original layout, which is still remarkably intact, provided for a central set of dockyard offices in the west range flanked by two large storehouses. Coppersmiths and blacksmiths were located in the south range, with erecting shops and fitting shops to the rear. The north range contained the boiler shop and platers' shop, while the eastern side had iron and brass foundries and millwrights' and pattern shops. The open central area, a space approximately 800ft by 350ft, was soon roofed and devoted to various other engineering- and metal-related trades. In all, the Quadrangle occupies some six acres, much of which had to be laboriously levelled from the rocky hillside.

Barry's design for the iron foundry was not built. Instead, a far larger one was erected to a design by G T Greene. This remained in use until the early 1980s, its twin Italianate chimneys forming notable local landmarks.[36] The wisdom of increasing the scale of the foundry was soon demonstrated when the construction of HMS *Warrior* in 1859 inaugurated the era of the all-metal armour-plated warship, with concomitant effects on dockyard metalworking facilities. In 1862 it was little problem making provision for handling armour plate within the Quadrangle, where space was allocated adjacent to the foundry.[37]

Number 2 Ship Shop at Portsmouth, completed in 1848, had set a scale for the new engineering workshops for the early Victorian Navy,[38] but even this building could not match the Devonport Quadrangle for the range of facilities grouped within a unified design. Indeed, the Quadrangle perhaps best epitomises the thrusting confidence of the Admiralty engineers as they oversaw a revolution in the construction, propulsion and fighting capacity of the Navy's warships. This confidence is apparent in the bold detailing of the main elevations of the building, with its pilasters and pediments, its little turrets, mostly containing spiral stars, and its monumental corbelled granite cornices. The recessed window bays run the full height of the two-storey ranges, their bold detailing in part reflecting the use of cast iron for the frames, mullions and transoms. Within the Quadrangle, out of public sight, walls were of stock brick rather than expensive stone. The acres of roofs were from the first supported on metal frames. The scale of the building,

The prime requirements for the new yard were that it should be capable of maintaining the largest warships in the Navy, together with all steam machinery, and that large vessels should be capable of docking at any state of the tide – something which large warships were unable to do in the existing dockyard.[28] Initially, proposals were for a single basin and two dry docks opening off it, together with associated engineering facilities, and the 1844 estimates allowed £400,000 for this project.[29] The following year the Admiralty added a second or North Basin, raising the estimate to £675,000. By 1849 further improvements to the plans, including a very large set of machine shops, a foundry and stores alongside the east wharf of the North Basin, had increased the estimate to £1,225,000. The following year a further £97,627 had to be allocated for building the new and larger powder magazines and associated facilities at Bull Point.[30] Construction, which began in 1846, was concentrated on the massive engineering works involved in creating the two basins, three docks and entrance lock (Map 16.2). The site had to be protected by a coffer dam 1,600ft long, and the main contractor was Messrs George Baker and Sons.[31] Rapidly rising estimates and the scale of the work attracted the attention of Parliament, and by late 1848 a Select Committee was urging economies.[32] Four years later, with the main engineering works nearing completion, the Treasury, quoting the

with its monumental entrances, high ceilings and, in the central area, roofs largely supported on iron columns, has meant that it has been among the most adaptable of naval buildings, still performing a vital role in modern Devonport naval base. Its cost was such that it was not repeated at any other dockyard (Chatham had to adapt some of the Woolwich metal slip roofs as engineering workshops a few years later), and only at Malta and Gibraltar, where stone was plentiful and skilled labour cheap, was stone used extensively as a building material for engineering workshops.[39]

The Steam Yard, as North Yard was originally called, was formally opened on 7 October 1853 (Figs 16.4, 5, 6), although work on new buildings continued into the 1860s.[40] Not only was it quite separate from the existing dockyard, now known as South Yard, but its dockyard workmen had different rates of pay, conditions and hours of work compared with the established workforce. Not until 1876 was the Steam Yard fully integrated with the older yard, although by then it had been long been physically linked by a railway tunnel under the the Morice Ordnance Yard which had been proposed in 1854[41]

The Late-Victorian Dockyard

Although facilities provided by the new yard were on a generous scale compared with those of the older dockyards, advances in warship size meant that, within ten years of the official opening, the Navy was experiencing problems docking its largest vessels. Although the basins held 34ft of water, the largest warships could enter and leave only on spring tides. In 1864 a Select Committee charged with investigating the Navy's basin and dock accommodation commented unfavourably on Devonport facilities and recommended not just two more first-class dry-docks, but also a third basin.[42] This project was too expensive at the time; instead, the north basin was dredged to a depth of 40ft and extended a further 382ft, making it some 450ft wide and 882ft long. This was to be the last significant addition to the dockyard until after the Naval Works of 1895.[43]

In 1880 the new Royal Naval Engineering College was built outside the dockyard wall, immediately to the east of the Steam Yard Factory. Designed by EM Barry, it was sited to allow the young Constructor Officers easy access to the Factory's machine shops and foundry which played central parts in their technical training.[44] The college remained here until new buildings were completed at Manadon in the 1950s; the old buildings were demolished in 1986.

In the second half of the nineteenth century the change to the all-metal warship freed naval architects from the construction limits imposed by timber shipbuilding technology. The size and shape of ships altered radically, forcing the Admiralty to modernise the launching, berthing and docking facilities at its main naval bases. Further impetus was added by the Naval Defence Act of 1889, with its provisions for ten new battleships and no fewer than sixty cruisers, some of which were to be built in the royal dockyards and all of which were to be based and maintained in them.[45] With France still seen as the principal naval rival, Admiralty attention focussed on further expansion and modernisation of the dockyards and naval establishments best located to meet the presumed French threat. The culmination was the 1895 Naval Works Act, which proposed considerable expenditure on Chatham, Portsmouth, Portland, Devonport, Hawlbowline and Gibraltar.[46]

At Devonport the 1870s and 1880s brought a number of suggestions for further expansion from various dockyard officials. These had come to nothing. By the 1890s the Admiralty was well aware that expansion could not be long delayed. In 1891 it agreed a new coaling jetty at Keyham,

key:

1 Torpedo boat slip
2 Steam reserve
3 Coal store
4 Breaking-up tripod
5 100-tons masting sheers
6 100-tons boiler sheers
7 Boiler shop
8 North Storehouse
9 Office
10 South Storehouse
11 Fitting and erecting shop
12 60-tons boiler sheers
13 Queen's Dock
14 No 2 Dock
15 No 1 Dock
16 Pumping Engine
17 Police
18 Officers' offices
19 Reservoirs
20 Officers' houses
21 Iron foundry
22 Royal Naval Engineering College
23 Works Department Yard
24 Workshop
25 Dock smithery
26 Steam reserve office
27 Engine house
28 Engine smith shop
29 Coppersmith's shop
30 Brass foundry
31 Hydraulic engine and dining room
32 Platers' shop
33 Boilersmiths' shop
34 Millwright and pattern shop
35 Foundry store

0   100   200 yards

Map 16.2   The Keyham Steam Yard in 1868.

provided it was sited so as not to obstruct further expansion, '. . . a work which has for many years been proposed and is now becoming imminent in consequence of the increase in the number and dimension of HM ships . . .'.[47] That year the Director of Works had drawn up plans for major expansion of Devonport Dockyard. A year or so later these plans were referred to Sir John Coode, President of the Institute of Civil Engineers. His firm's report in July 1893 suggested various modifications, and it was

16.4   The South Basin of Keyham Steam Yard, with HMS *Queen*, 110 guns, shortly after its opening. (Illustrated *London News, 19 November 1853*)

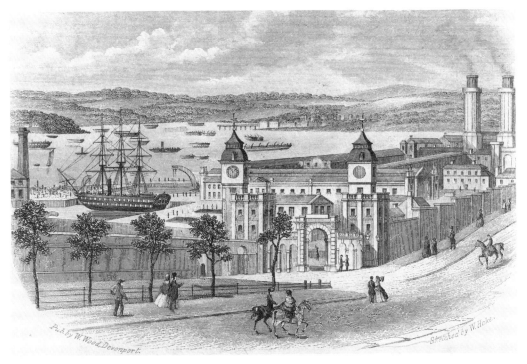

16.5   An early sketch of Keyham Steam Yard by W Hake. (*City of Plymouth Museums and Art Gallery*)

their submission to the Treasury that autumn for extra money:

> The question of the length of Docks has been under consideration during the last two years in connection with the possible increased lengths of certain types of future men-of-war. The cruisers *Powerful* and *Terrible*, now under construction greatly exceed in length any of the vessels in the Navy, and the necessity for additional speed points to a still greater length in vessels which may be designed in the near future. There is also a tendency in the Merchant Marine to increase the length of their fastest and most powerful vessels such as would be used as armed cruisers in case of war, and which might have to be docked in the Royal Dockyards . . . The port of Devonport . . . would probably be the first point reached in time of war by battleships injured in action . . . and as the value of a single battleship approaches a million, it is necessary that every arrangement should be made to provide proper docking for them . . .[49]

on these revised plans that the Keyham extension of the late 1890s was based.[48]

The Keyham Extension

The 1893 plans were reckoned to cost around £2 million, but with Sir William White's naval warship building programme well under way, and with warship sizes steadily increasing, doubts within the Admiralty as to the adequacy of the new extension were not long in forthcoming. Discussions and amendment over the next two years added a further £646,361 to the original estimate, and by November 1895 the total, with contingencies, stood at £3 million. The dilemma facing the Admiralty was clearly expressed in

On 28 December 1895 the Treasury sanctioned the revised estimate and the contract was awarded to the civil engineering firm of Sir John Jackson, which began site works in February 1896.[50]

The Keyham extension scheme, one of the largest and most complex ever undertaken at a royal dockyard, involved expanding the existing Steam Yard northwards up the Hamoaze. The new facilities were partly sited on land reclaimed by rubble dumped from the earlier excavations for the Steam Yard, but the major part of the extension, 78 acres out of around 112 acres, was sited along the muddy tidal foreshore. To secure the works, a huge coffer dam 7,600ft long was constructed along the western or river side of the site. Protected by this, steam cranes, scoops and cable-ways, aided by vast teams of navvies and railway trucks, shifted over 4¼ million cubic yards of mud, which was dumped at sea, and a further 1¼ million cubic yards of rock. Approximately 80 acres of the site was excavated to a depth of 40ft.[51] Only when foundations could be securely based on the underlying rock could construction of the basins, wharves and docks begin (Fig. 16.7).

The Keyham extension was formally opened in February 1907 by the Prince and Princess of Wales.[52] As completed, it provided a 35½-acre closed basin and a tidal one of some 10 acres (Map 16.3). The closed basin could be entered directly from the Hamoaze or by an alternative 730ft-long entrance lock which could also be used as a dry dock. On reclaimed land between the two basins were three dry docks. The smallest of these, No 8, could only be entered from the closed basin; Nos 9 and 10, 715ft and 711ft respectively, had sliding caissons at both ends. The principal stone used in the construction

16.6   The *Duke of Wellington*, 131 guns, in dock at Keyham in March 1854 while preparing for service in the Baltic as flagship of Vice-Admiral Sir Charles Napier in the Crimean War. The new Steam Yard can be seen still under construction beyond her stern. From an original paper callotype by Linnaeus Trife. (*City of Plymouth Museums and Art Gallery*)

work was Cornish granite, but this had to be supplemented by supplies from Norway when it was found that the Cornish quarries had insufficient quarrymen to meet the Admiralty's needs. Admiralty forebodings about the adequacy of the size of dry docks as the Navy entered the Dreadnought era led to No 8 dock being lengthened twice, first in 1906 and again in 1910, by which time it was close to the length of its two neighbours. This and other modifications pushed the final cost of the enterprise to some £4,000,000.[53]

The driving force behind this huge expansion, which effectively doubled the area of Devonport Dockyard, was the pressing need for extra berthing and docking facilities. The construction and maintenance of warships remained the preserve of South Yard and the Steam Yard, now known as North Yard, which were already well-equipped with foundries, workshops and storehouses. The Keyham Extension remained largely devoid of buildings until well after the Second World War. Its most conspicuous elements were the heavy cranes and the loading gantries of the large coal depot established at the northwest corner of the site.[54]

Between 1883 and 1914 Devonport Dockyard built seventeen battleships (including five Dreadnoughts and two battle cruisers) and fourteen cruisers, totals which comfortably exceeded those of any other royal dockyards.[55] Such an output, and the subsequent maintenance work, was only possible as a result of the heavy capital investment in North Yard and, later, the Keyham extension. By 1914 Devonport had become the largest naval base in western Europe, a position which it still retains.

Barrack Accommodation for the New Navy

The mid-nineteenth-century revolution in warship construction which so changed the dockyards had a similar effect on the lives of naval seamen. The new warships required new manning skills, making it no longer practical or economic to recruit seamen for a particular ship and to discharge them after a short commission. In 1853 Long Term Service was introduced for naval ratings. One immediate consequence was the need to provide accommodation for crews awaiting new postings when their ships came out of commission. Hulks provided an instant and cheap solution, and indeed remained conspicuous features of most naval bases into the early years of the twentieth century. They were, however, far from satisfactory; the accommodation they provided was necessarily cramped, proper exercise and training were difficult for their inhabitants, and in the popular mind hulks tended to be associated with prisons.[56] Proper naval barracks with classrooms, drill sheds and recreational facilities had to be the answer.

At Devonport the first suggestion in 1860 had been to construct barracks within the dockyard boundary, but the three suggested sites were either too small or were needed for dockyard expansion. Instead, a virgin ten-acre site at Keyham was favoured.[57] Over the next five years various proposals were made, and in 1864 £5,000 was allocated to start work on the project. However, financial considerations led to the Admiralty shelving any plans for barracks at Devonport and Portsmouth.[58]

In 1876 there was renewed Admiralty interest in providing barracks for 4,000 seamen at Portsmouth and 3,500 seamen at Keyham. This time sufficient finance was forthcoming for a start to be made in 1879 on accommodation for 1,000 seamen at the West Country base.[59] In addition to the accommodation blocks, the contractors were responsible for canteen and recreation rooms, galleys, stores, guard rooms and cells and a large drill shed. A conspicuous feature was the ornate clocktower, which had to be sited so that it would be visible from most parts of the barracks. This caused the Superintending Civil Engineer some problems. In the end he settled for placing it with the guard house, 'although it is not an essential part of such a building . . .'.[60] This exchange of letters gives an indication of the authority wielded by the resident civil engineer, for it is clear that he had considerable latitude in the final disposition of buildings. His task cannot have been an easy one, for as late as April 1884 the Admiralty's Barrack Committee recommended that the barracks be designed for 2,000 seamen 'and that space should be left in this arrangement so that it may be expanded to suit either 3,000 or 4,000 men'.[61] By February 1886 the first phase of barracks was ready for occupation, although some work remained to be done on the stores and main gate.[62] Although there have been subsequent

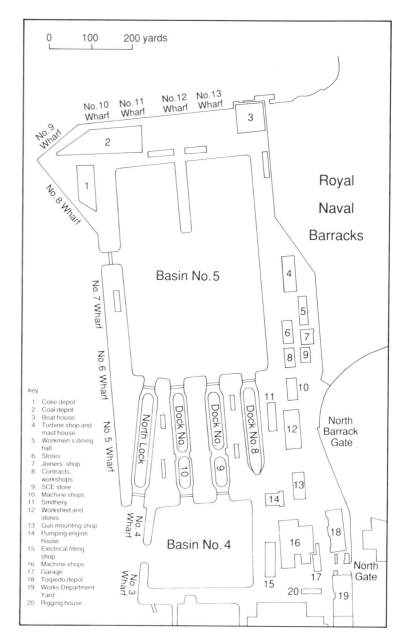

Map 16.3 The Keyham Extension between the world wars.

alterations and additions, many of the early buildings remain, as does much of the original layout centred on the parade ground.

All of the Victorian buildings were designed in a free Italianate style and were richly endowed with rusticated pilasters, elaborate cornices and pediments (Fig. 16.8). They were built of squared local limestone rubble with Portland stone details and slate roofs. Dominating the barracks is the tall clocktower, which rises over the buildings like the elaborate centrepiece of a wedding cake. Its six storeys are enriched with pilasters, pediments and elaborate corbelled balconies, those at the top having intricate cast-iron balustrades.

Although the initial requirement was for seamen's barracks, officers' accommodation was also provided. This was laid out on a far more generous scale, perhaps best epitomised by the handsome wardroom overlooking the parade ground. This is a group of three linked buildings with rusticated ground floors and a projected central entrance tower surmounted by a tall domed cupola. The wardroom itself, like its near-contemporaries at Portsmouth and Chatham, is notable for the unusual wooden relief panels of naval engagements.[63]

With the exception of the Central Offices completed near the North Yard Quadrangle in 1911, the naval barracks were the last major group of buildings to be built at Devonport before the outbreak of the 1914–18 war.

16.7   The construction of No.9 Dock of the Keyham Extension looking north towards the great North basin, c1906. For a view of the completed Dock, see Fig 15.8. (*City of Plymouth Museums and Art Gallery*)

was completed in 1929, when the lock was increased in width from 95 to 125ft.[65]

After the Second World War Devonport Dockyard was to expand yet further, but architecturally the base reached its apogee by 1914. Then, South Yard and the adjacent Morice Yard, together with the naval hospital at Stonehouse, stood intact witnesses to the industrial power which sustained the Georgian Navy. The Royal William Victualling Yard, North and Keyham Yards and the naval barracks, now HMS *Drake*, were impressive architectural statements of nineteenth-century resolve to maintain and expand this great West Country naval base. Much of architectural and naval interest was to be destroyed in air raids in the 1939–45 war – South Yard in particular was badly affected – but further expansion and redevelopment, particularly in the 1970s, has served to reinforce the wisdom of the Admiralty and Navy Boards in choosing to establish a dockyard at Plymouth in the 1690s.

That war saw the number of men employed in the dockyard rise from some 14,000 to over 20,000. After the war, financial stringencies left little money for dockyard improvements, while, in an effort to save jobs, Devonport built a number of merchant ships for private owners.[64] One major engineering undertaking, forced on the Admiralty by the increasing beams of major warships, was the widening of the main lock into the Keyham basin. This

The Modernisation and Transformation of the Yard, 1957–80

The devastation wrought by the bombings of March-April 1941 was a disaster for the old yard, but it did provide planners with the opportunity to modernise on a site now less trammelled with sentimentality and the

16.8   The seamen's barracks at Keyham, with the clock tower and guardhouse to the right. This photograph was taken in the late 1880s before the officers' quarters were built between the clock tower and the building in the foreground. (*City of Plymouth Museums and Art Gallery*)

inertia of fixed plant, which was expensive to clear. It also opened the chance to expand from a cramped shoreline site by incorporating land now made available by the destruction of so many of the surrounding civilian buildings of Devonport and Keyham. Naval technology had advanced considerably in the forty years since the last great modernisation of the yard when the Keyham extension was built, and in the next thirty years it would advance at an even faster rate. Equally, the nation's requirements of its Navy also changed with withdrawal from empire and the rise of the nuclear deterrent. Electronics and guided missiles have replaced the big gun as the dominant factors of naval warfare, and this has resulted in the demise of the battleship and cruiser, the rise and decline of the aircraft carrier, the emergence of the nuclear submarine as the Navy's capital ship and the survival and development of the frigate and destroyer as its predominant surface warship. The type of navy that the dockyard is required to service has altered dramatically, and Devonport Dockyard, which has become the Navy's sole operational western yard, has had to keep pace with these changes to enable Britain to remain a considerable naval power.

Immediate postwar financial difficulties, naval retrenchment and the changing state of naval requirements delayed reconstruction of the yard until the late 1950s and reduced the expansion of its area to 51½ acres. It was nevertheless in the newly acquired area that the first postwar modernisation took place. Advantage was also taken of the acquisition of surviving civilian buildings amidst the bomb sites to convert the former Kelly College Mission of St Chad, formerly in Moon Street, Morice Town, into the new dockyard church to replace the Georgian chapel destroyed in the bombing. A new workshop area was created out of the former Goschen and Hamilton Street areas of Keyham and named Goschen Yard, including a new Main Electrical Factory (1957–63), an Internal Combustion Engine Workshop (opened in 1963), and a new Apprentices Training Centre (1967–70). The opportunity was also taken for rationalisation when departments formerly scattered around the yard were concentrated into new central offices, built in two stages between 1964 and 1970, while a series of large storehouses were opened for the Naval Stores Department on former Devonport-town land between 1963 and 1980. The new buildings were of contemporary functional industrial and office-block design, lacking the monumental and decorative grandeur of their forebears of the imperial era.

The most significant changes, however, came with the defence reviews of 1968–9, which sought to rationalise yard work by concentrating maintenance of specific warship types at specific yards. Devonport was assigned the *Leander* and Type 21 and 22 frigates; it was an operational base for nuclear submarines and would provide for the regular refitting and refuelling of all except ballistic-missile submarines; and it became the Fleet Maintenance Base, providing support for the maintenance of ships overseas. In 1969–70 it was decided that new purpose-designed facilities would be built for each of these functions.

The Typed Frigate Complex was constructed on the site of the old South Basin at Keyham between 1972 and 1977. It is a lasting tribute to Dummer's pioneer 1691 design of a dry dock fronted by a basin in South Yard, that South Basin at Keyham had repeated the concept with a cluster of three dry docks, and the Typed Frigate Complex developed upon that tried arrangement. More efficient pumping systems have enabled the locks at the entrance to the basin to be dispensed with and replaced by a falling leaf-gate and caisson. Closure of the former communication with North Basin made three berths available at the sides of the basin, serviced by 12½-ton tower cranes, with a 50-ton crane at the sea-wall berth to provide for major

16.9   HMS *Galatea* entering the basin in front of the new frigate complex at its formal opening in 1977. See also Fig 15.8. (*HM Naval Base, Plymouth*)

stripping-out (Fig. 16.10). The greatest advance on former designs, however, is seen in the covered docks designed by Sir Alexander Gibbs and Partners. All three dry docks are incorporated into one building, roofed to a height of 160ft above each of the docks (Fig. 17.11), and dominated on its basin front by three vast doors, each of four separate vertically-overlapping sections which can be hauled up on their twin supporting columns to a height of 130ft to provide clearance for all conceivable masthead electronic systems, or which can be lowered to allow ventilation at the upper door level. Subsequent adaptations to enable the level of water in basin and docks to be raised have made it possible to dock Type 42 destroyers if necessary.

The Submarine Refit Complex was built between 1970 and 1980 on the northwestern corner of the Keyham extension. The area inside the northern basin was converted into two separate dry docks, with docking support buildings between them dominated by a massive 80-ton cantilever crane (itself costing £2½ million) capable of lifting 72-tonne nuclear core-packages over a 72m radius between submarines and rail transporters during major refuelling. Designed by architects Howell, Killick, Partridge and Amis and consulting engineers Sir Alexander Gibb and Partners, the support facility provides five storeys above ground and four below, with an eight-storey central management office at its landward end. With its building, Devonport

16.10   The Submarine Refit Complex at Devonport. (*HM Naval Base, Plymouth*)

was confirmed as the Navy's major submarine refitting yard, handling SSN nuclear fleet submarines and SSK hunter-killer submarines but capable of docking SSBN nuclear ballistic-missile submarines in an emergency.

The Fleet Maintenance Base was also built during the 1970s, on the north side of the Submarine Refit Complex on the site of the former coaling depot. It was completed in 1978 as a long quay backed by workshops with electrical and mechanical repair facilities, ships' stores and ships' command offices.

Between 1962 and 1982 £150 million was spent on the reconstruction of Devonport Naval Base, as the dockyard was renamed in 1970.[66] This has been the fifth major redevelopment in its 300-year history. If Britain wishes to continue to possess an up-to-date, fully maintained naval force, then it is unlikely that it will be the last.

16: Architecture and Development of Devonport Naval Base, 1815–1982

1 NMM, ADM/BP/34b. The totals for Portsmouth and Plymouth were 4,133 and 3,914.
2 C J Bartlett, *Great Britain and Sea Power 1815–1853* (Oxford, 1963), 1. This supremacy was to be retained 'over her nearest rival at least, possibly over the next two or even three naval powers'.
3 Bartlett, *Great Britain and Sea Power*, 20. The Admiralty justified this by saying, with perfect logic, that it was better to carry out major improvements, especially the Plymouth Breakwater, during peacetime.
4 J G Coad, 'Historic Architecture of HM Naval Base, Devonport', *MM*, 69 (1983), 360–1.
5 PRO, ADM 7/659, 5 June 1771.
6 PRO, ADM 140/369.
7 S Smiles, *Lives of the Engineers*, II, (1862; reprinted Newton Abbot, 1968), 263.
8 PRO, ADM 1/3432, 6 May 1839; ADM 1/3421, 15 May 1836.
9 The problems of construction are well recorded in PRO, ADM 1/3423–3433.
10 Smiles, *Lives of the Engineers*, 263. For a fuller account see also L H Merrett, 'A Most Important Undertaking: The Building of the Plymouth Breakwater', *MH*, 5 (1977), 136–47, and J Naish, 'Joseph Whidbey and the building of the Plymouth Breakwater', *MM*, 78 (1992), 37–56.
11 PRO, ADM 1/5810, 14 April 1862. Smiles, *Lives of the Engineers*, II, 263, gives 1848 as the completion date, but it is clear from records cited here that works continued for at least another fourteen years.
12 Smiles, *Lives of the Engineers*, II, 263. It is worth noting that, in 1828, the Lord High Admiral, the future William IV, asked Mr Whidbey to prepare plans and estimates for a similar breakwater at Torbay to protect the anchorage from easterly winds. The project was estimated to take twenty-eight years at a cost of £40,000 per annum. PRO, ADM 7/665.
13 PRO, ADM 114/40; ADM 111/257, 14 Nov. 1822; ADM 111/258 20 Sept. 1823. See also Coad, 'Historic Architecture of HM Naval Base, Devonport', 382–92, for a more detailed building account.
14 PRO, ADM 111/259, 23 Sept. 1824; ADM 111/262, 17 Nov. 1827.
15 J G Coad, *The Royal Dockyards 1690–1850: Architecture and Engineering Works of the Sailing Navy* (Aldershot, 1989), 276–90.
16 PRO, ADM 111/262, 17 Nov. 1827; ADM 111/263 20 Aug. 1828, 30 Aug. 1828; ADM 111/265, 27 Jan. 1830, 30 Aug. 1830.
17 PRO, ADM 111/265, 17 Sept. 1830.
18 PRO, ADM 111/267, 19 Jan. 1832. In 1835 plans were prepared for gas lighting for the yard. Forty-five lamps were to be installed at a cost, including pipes, of £360. ADM 1/3419, 23 May 1835.
19 J G Coad, *Historic Architecture of the Royal Navy* (1983), 45–6.
20 Coad, *Royal Dockyards 1690–1850*, 110.
21 *Accounts and Papers* (BPP, 1813–4, XI, 101); (BPP 1814–5, IX, 160); (BPP, 1816, XII, 211–2); (BPP, 1817, XIII, 328–9); (BPP, 1818, XIII, 165–6); (BPP, 1819, XV, 109–11); (BPP, 1820, XI, 94–5). For drawings see PRO, ADM 140/226.
22 NMM, ADM/B/180, 3 Aug. 1767; PRO, ADM 174/300, 5 Oct. 1814, 16 Aug. 1816, 16 Oct. 1816. PRO, ADM 140/234 pts 1–6. K V Burns, *The Devonport Dockyard Story* (Liskeard, 1984), 26.
23 PRO, ADM, 140/234 pt 6.
24 Bartlett, *Great Britain and Sea Power*, 209–11; E H H Archibald, *The Metal Fighting Ship in the Royal Navy 1860–1970* (1971), 4; D K Brown, *A Century of Naval Construction. The History of the Royal Corps of Naval Constructors* (1983), 273.
25 Coad, *Historic Architecture of the Royal Navy*, 81–2.
26 The town of Plymouth Dock had been renamed Devonport on 1 January 1824. Burns, *Devonport Dockyard Story*, 40.
27 Burns, *Devonport Dockyard Story*, 45.
28 For example, in 1837 HMS *Canopus*, by then near the end of a long career, had had to sail uncareened as she was too large to enter any of the dry docks without unloading stores. PRO, ADM 1/3424, 1 April 1837. See also the comments in the 1850–1 estimates (BPP) on the state of dry docks in the old yard: '. . . There is at present but one dock in which First Rates can be docked . . . and then at high water spring tide only, and when the ship has been lightened almost to her lightwater draught . . .'.
29 PRO, ADM 181/55. Estimates 1844/5; PRO, ADM 1/5614, 20 Aug. 1852. For plans see PRO, ADM 140/346–362.
30 PRO, ADM 181/59. Estimates 1848/9; PRO, ADM 181/60. Estimates 1849/50.
31 Burns, *Devonport Dockyard Story*, 43.
32 PRO, ADM 1/5614, 13 Sept. 1852.
33 PRO, ADM 1/5614, 31 Aug. 1852. An attached report details the inconveniences then being suffered by the Navy, which was having to rely on far from perfect arrangements for mounting ships' machinery at Portsmouth and Woolwich.
34 PRO, ADM 1/5614, 13 Sept. 1852 suggests that in 1850 work on the foundry buildings was not to start for reasons of economy. It is possible that the ground in any event was not yet ready at this date. The annual estimates in PRO, ADM 181/54–76 give a good indication of the progress and sequence of work between 1844 and 1865, when the whole project was nearing completion.
35 Original plans are in PRO, ADM 140/363.
36 PRO, ADM 140/363 shows Charles Barry's proposals dated 7 and 24 Jan. 1848. ADM 140/364 shows the foundry as built. Others of G T Greene's drawings are in the PSA Plans Room, PSA, Albert Road, Devonport.
37 PRO, ADM 1/5803, 12 July 1862.
38 Coad, *Historic Architecture of the Royal Navy*, 81–2.
39 Burns, *Devonport Dockyard Story*, 45.
40 PRO, ADM 181/63–75 Navy Estimates.
41 PRO, ADM 1/5632, 4 July 1854, ADM 181/66. 1855–6 Estimates allowed £35,000 for the cost of constructing the tunnel. For construction details see Burns, *Devonport Dockyard Story*, 47. For drawings, see PRO, ADM 1/5660, 1 Nov. 1855.
42 Report quoted in Burns, *Devonport Dockyard Story*, 48.
43 Money for extending the North Basin first appears in the 1860–1 Estimates, when an extra £120,000 was proposed. PRO, ADM 181/71. See Burns, *Devonport Dockyard Story*, 49.
44 Brown, *Century of Naval Construction*, 274, 337.
45 Archibald, *Metal Fighting Ship in the Royal Navy*, 54; Brown, *Century of Naval Construction*, 65–73.
46 BPP, 1895, V, 159.
47 PRO, ADM 116/464, 14 July 1891.
48 PRO, ADM 116/464, Dec. 1895.
49 PRO, ADM 116/464. Draft Memo for the Treasury, Oct. 1895. The full Admiralty Board had approved the revised scheme on 12 March 1895, and this was firmly endorsed by a further meeting on 6 Dec. 1895 in the First Lord's room, attended by a number of officials including the Director of Dockyards and the Director of Works.
50 PRO, ADM 214/39 is a bound set of contract documents and the tenders of seven firms which competed for the job.
51 Burns, *Devonport Dockyard Story*, 70.
52 Burns, *Devonport Dockyard Story*, 72; The 1895 contract documents had specified, in clause 25, that the work had to be completed by 31 March 1903, barring unforeseen alterations or exceptionally bad weather. PRO, ADM 214/39.
53 Burns, *Devonport Dockyard Story*, 71.
54 This replaced the coaling depot proposed in 1895. It is now the site of the Fleet Maintenance Base.
55 Brown, *Century of Naval Construction*, 275.
56 Some ideas of the problems of hulk accommodation can be gleaned from E Davies and E Grove, *The Royal Naval College, Dartmouth* (Portsmouth, 1980).
57 PRO, ADM 1/5752, 10 Oct. 1860.
58 PRO, ADM 1/5775, 4 Nov. 1861; ADM 1/5803, 24 July 1862; ADM 1/5888 27 July 1864; ADM 1/5939, 25 March 1865.
59 PRO, ADM 116/727, 14, 18 Jan. 1876. Keyham barracks just preceded those at Portsmouth, which were not begun until early in 1880; ADM 116/727, 13 Jan. 1880.
60 PRO, ADM 116/727, 19 June 1884.
61 PRO, ADM 116/727, 16 April 1884.
62 PRO, ADM 116/727, 20 Feb. 1886.
63 The history behind the construction of naval barracks has yet to be investigated in any detail, so this is necessarily a tentative history of HMS *Drake*, as the barracks are called. I am grateful to Dr N A M Rodger for drawing my attention to the information in PRO, ADM 116/727.
64 Burns, *Devonport Dockyard Story*, 83, 85.
65 Burns, *Devonport Dockyard Story*, 89.
66 Burns, *Devonport Dockyard Story*, 125. See also 101–2, 107, 109–20.

17 The Impact of Naval Technology on Warship Construction and Repair at Devonport, 1815–1986

ANDREW D LAMBERT

THE ROLE OF DEVONPORT DOCKYARD, supporting British seapower, developed during the last two centuries within the context of national policy. The functions of a first-class base and a construction and repair facility should be seen as mutually supporting. While the great breakwater might appear only to serve the fleet base function, it also made increased demands on the yard repair facilities. Within this framework, dominated in peacetime by demands for economy, the Dockyard moved from the pre-industrial arsenal of 1815 to the nuclear refuelling and frigate complex of the 1980s. The impact of these changes on the yard has been examined in the preceding chapter. In the context of naval policy Devonport was a major national dockyard, and particular developments reflected overall policy, tempered by the advantages of the location. Until the present period the royal yards were always at the forefront of maritime technology, insofar as it was applicable to warship construction and repair, because their function was to construct, repair and maintain warships, which, by definition involved the exploitation of the latest technology.

The individual contribution of Devonport had only a relative importance, something that became more apparent with the advance of technology. The Admiralty did not permit major local experiments without central authorisation, while the regular movement of senior dockyard officers prevented the creation of an identifiable Devonport 'school' of work. At most, individual dockyards could develop their own skills and approaches to work. With iron warships, opportunities for specialisation became more frequent. The education of naval architects was centralised from 1811 to 1832, and then after 1864. The First School of Naval Architecture was based at Portsmouth, the Third at Kensington and then at Greenwich. Education at Devonport was limited to the apprentice system until 1844, when dockyard schools were established to provide practical training. The most promising students would be rewarded with additional instruction in draughtsmanship, and after 1864 might be sent to London. This system was far better than that available in private yards in the nineteenth century, and consequently the private builders were not equipped to design warships to meet Naval standards.[1] The *Captain* disaster of 1870 has been attributed to the weakness of commercial designers.

British warship design has been centralised throughout the period of shipbuilding at Devonport. The Surveyor of the Navy, or after 1875 the Director of Naval Construction, and his staff worked in London, and in Bath after the outbreak of the Second World War. The design parameters were established by the Board of Admiralty, or, after the abolition of that body in 1964, by the Naval Defence Staff, and then translated on to paper by the naval architects. This process reflected the level of scientific knowledge, their professional heritage and the limitations of their materials. After 1860 iron and steel allowed alternative designs, from which the Board would select the most suitable. With the exception of Sir William Symonds, Surveyor 1832–1847, the individual responsible for design was a professional shipbuilder/designer. The belated success of the Third School of Naval Architecture reduced the input of individual dockyards in the design process still further. Private builders have become much better equipped in this respect in the twentieth century; Vickers' work on the *Colossus* class Light Fleet Aircraft Carriers of 1942 being a particular example.[2]

In terms of direct imput, the Torquay ship test tank, which pioneered hydrodynamic development, had more influence on ship design than anything that took place at Devonport (see chapter 18). This was the

17.1 The first rate HMS *St Vincent*, 120 guns, launched at Devonport in 1815. Although built before the structural improvements of the Seppings period, she was a remarkably durable ship and is photographed here ending her days alongside Whale Island in Portsmouth Harbour as a Boy's Training Ship at the turn of the century. The poop deck was removed in the 1840s to improve her sailing qualities, giving her an unusual flush deck profile. She was finally sold for demolition in 1906. (*National Maritime Museum*)

17.2 The fleet 'in ordinary' in the Hamoaze after the Napoleonic Wars. A lithograph by W Walton from a drawing by N C Condy. (*City of Plymouth Museums and Art Gallery*)

function of the ship tank; that of the dockyard was to build and repair warships designed elsewhere using information obtained by specialist facilities.

The British Royal Dockyards have always existed within the contect of national policy, so their roles have varied, according to the contemporary perception of national requirements. Several roles for the dockyards can be established: building new ships, repairing and maintaining those already in service, preparing supplies for bases overseas, and supporting smaller yards or private builders with Government contracts. In wartime the dockyards were dominated by the immediate needs of the fleet at sea. Although Plymouth continued new construction in the period 1793–1815 to a greater extent than the other royal yards, this was overshadowed by the day-to-day running repairs to the Channel Fleet. The pattern was repeated in 1914–1918 and 1939–1945.

While new construction has always been more prestigious, repair and reconstruction filled a large part of workload at Devonport. This was the case from 1815, and after 1968 it became the only work. This reflected several factors, the size of the skilled labour force, the small number of slipways, the growth of a specialist building yard at Pembroke, and later the inability of the yard to handle the largest types and the economic need to keep private firms in business. Throughout its history Plymouth/Devonport has been a naval arsenal, responsible for the maintenance and supply of fleets, as well as their construction. This demanded a labour force adequate to meet emergencies and mobilisation, as the Tamar and Fal were major reserve fleet anchorages. In many ways repair and maintenance were more important than new construction, in which other yards were favoured for reasons which will become apparent.

The work of the Dockyard after 1815 can be divided into six sections, based on the nature of the work in hand.

1 Between 1815 and 1860 the construction, repair and modification of large wooden warships, latterly steam powered.
2 The ironclad revolution bypassed the yard, and between 1860 and 1886 only composite-hulled colonial patrol vessels were built.
3 From 1887 to 1897 the large-scale modernisation of the yard allowed the construction of all-steel cruisers.
4 The period 1898 to 1915 was dominated by large-scale battleship construction.
5 Between 1915 and 1945 the yard was restricted to cruisers, submarines, frigates and a solitary light aircraft carrier.
6 Postwar, only a handful of warships was built before construction ceased in 1969. The yard now emphasised repair and maintenance, and was taken out of government control in 1986.

Only in the period 1888-1915 did new construction take precedence over other aspects of yard work.

The Wooden Navy, 1815–1860

After the Napoleonic wars, British naval policy stood in need of reconsideration. The existing fleet, comprising almost 900 vessels with over 200 battleships, was both too large and in need of considerable maintenance. Referring back to 1792, the last year of peace, and considering the number of men that could be raised in the first year of war (no more than 70,000), the Admiralty accepted a total strength of 100 battleships and 160 frigates, with smaller craft in proportion.[3] With hindsight these figures were approximately one-third larger than required in the existing international situation. France was the only serious rival, the Spanish, Dutch and Danish fleets were all much reduced, while the large Russian navy was a facade. The United States' effort was on a small scale. Even the French had difficulty maintaining a powerful fleet, which never exceeded forty of the line. However, the Admiralty accepted the figures, providing a 'three power' standard.[4] The problems were compounded by the experience of war and the growth of technology; a major change was in prospect for the fabric of seapower.

This encouraged the Navy Board to promote a cautious, long-term policy. In 1815 four designs were selected as combining the necessary sailing qualities and armament for reproduction in the battle fleet, two more were chosen for frigates. First rates would be replicas of the 120-gun *Caledonia*, second rates would copy the ex-French *Canopus* of 84 guns, and 74-gun third rates would be modelled on *Blake* or *Impeteux*.[5] As the majority of existing battleships were 74s, the only new construction undertaken was of

120s and 84s. The wartime problem of premature decay, caused by the use of unseasoned timber, persuaded the Navy Board that future ships should be built slowly, using well-seasoned timber.[6] The slipways of the British yards (only twenty-six in 1815) were soon filled, and the Admiralty expanded the new yard at Pembroke, where ten new slips eased overcrowding in the older yards. Pembroke was an outstation of Devonport; the Dockyard officers were subordinate to Devonport, and received supplies of ironwork from Woolwich via the parent yard along with guidance on shipwright work.[7] Ships built at Pembroke were fitted out and received engines at Devonport.

The wars of 1793 to 1815 depleted the native timber resources, although not as seriously as the leading authority argues.[8] Anticipating a period of peace, the Navy Board recommended the exploitation of foreign resources, to allow the British forests to recover. African iroko, Indian teak and Italian oak were selected, halving the demand for native timber.[9] Ships were built at Devonport using all three; Africa provided straight-grained pieces of large siding, ideal for heavy beams. The teak *Hindostan*, laid down in 1820, was the duplicate frame of the 74 *Malabar*, stretched out to an 80-gun ship. The 46-gun frigate *Tigris*, another duplicate frame, was broken up in 1833 to provide timber for steamers building at Pembroke. Italian oak was used for the 90-gun *Albion* of 1842. Indeed, the frames of almost all oak-built warships of this period were of Italian timber, supplied from mountainous areas of Northern Italy. This included a large percentage of the curved pieces required for frames. English timber, largely straight and forest-grown, was used for plank and thickstuff.[10]

During twenty years of war the Dockyard labour force had grown. Plymouth employed 3,869 in 1814, a quarter of the total for all the Royal Yards, making it second only to Portsmouth, although Chatham was more prestigious.[11] In 1817 Plymouth had more shipwrights than any other yard. In the twenty years after 1793 the labour force had doubled: this expense could not be justified in peacetime. The key workmen, the shipwrights, were reduced from almost 5,000 in all yards to only 2,000.[12] The reduction at Plymouth was in proportion, causing unrest. With the Thames shipwrights at the head of the radical movement, the Comptroller, head of the Navy Board, Admiral Byam Martin, opposed reducing the shipwright establishment, particularly as merchant shipbuilding collapsed after 1820. Believing shipwrights and domestic timber were a vital resource for war, he shifted policy to favour repairs, which used more labour and less timber than new construction.[13]

After 1815 almost the entire fleet required thorough examination in dock. Even defective ships used up manpower, and in 1832 the old 64 *Diadem* cost £400 in labour for a team of 70 shipwrights, three apprentices and convict labourers to dismantle, although she produced £4,000 in serviceable or saleable materials. Devonport carried out relatively little new work in the last years of the sailing Navy. With only

five slipways, and with a reserve fleet in the local anchorages of 106 first to sixth rates to repair, it had more pressing tasks. Opponents of the postwar Tory government took a hostile view of their naval policy. Earl Grey, Whig Prime Minister in 1830–1834, spent three winters in the yard and was appalled by the apparent waste; 'not a stroke of new work was done during all that time'. After leaving office, Grey's First Lord of the Admiralty, Sir James Graham, even called for the end of all new building at Devonport in favour of Pembroke.[14] By this stage he had accepted the economic imperatives supporting repairs against new work. The obsession of Grey's ministry with reducing public expenditure, along with the abolition of the Navy Board in 1832, destroyed the careful policy of the postwar period. In 1830 the Admiralty demanded a total dockyard labour force of no more than 6,000, pensioning off disabled men with more than twenty years service. The Admiralty were not even anxious to keep the establishment up to 6,000. The shift from task and job pay to a day rate, and the withdrawal of convict labour, reduced the amount of work done in the yards.

There was considerable opposition to the reductions at Devonport, culminating in assaults on the Members of the Board during their 1832 inspection.[15] Fifteen years elapsed before any serious effort was made to take stock for the future. In the interval the Navy lived on the accumulated strength of ships ordered before 1830. Just four battleships ordered after 1826 were launched before 1846, and only *Albion* at Devonport. Only the careful construction methods of the Navy Board ensured that there was still a large battlefleet in the 1850s.

At Devonport the first indications of the new policies were the permanent sheds built over the slipways between 1815 and 1821, which improved the durability of the ships under construction by keeping out rainwater.[16] Building large wooden ships in the Royal Dockyards after 1815 became increasingly time consuming. The ship would be halted at various, predetermined, stages to allow the united pieces of the frame to season as a whole before the planking and decks were added. Even then the entire ship would remain high and dry for years. Ships built slowly and carefully in this way lasted many years, *Nile* of 1839 being afloat over 100 years later (Fig. 17.1).

At this stage the natural sciences were far from exact, leading to all manner of projects to prevent dry rot, the most costly threat to the Navy. Up to 1832 the favoured method was long-term immersion in salt water, to remove any sap, followed by thorough drying in covered sheds before conversion. This was demonstrated by the innovative Surveyor of the Navy, Sir Robert

17.3 The first British steam battleship, HMS *Sans Pareil*, 70 guns. She was laid down in 1845 (as a copy of her namesake, captured from the French in 1794) on the orders of Admiral Sir George Cockburn, the First Naval Lord, as part of his attack on the controversial Surveyor, Sir William Symonds. Too small and rather outdated, she was ordered to be lengthened and converted into a steamship in 1849–51. Unlike the majority of steam battleships, she had her funnel between the main and mizzen masts. She proved to be a profound failure, being slow, weakly armed and unreliable. Her engines stopped at a critical moment in the bombardment of Sebastopol on 17 October 1854, and were replaced in early 1855. She is seen here at Devonport on 6 June 1863 on her return from China. The ship under her bowsprit is the *Edgar*, the last wooden flagship of the Channel fleet. (*Imperial War Museum*)

Seppings. The infected sloop *Eden* was scuttled in the Hamoaze for five months, and when she was raised the rot had been cured.[17] After 1832 the new Surveyor, Captain Sir William Symonds, ordered a new report on the *Eden* and abandoned the practice. Supported by the Master Shipwrights, he argued that it damaged the fastenings, promoted splitting and encouraged damp.[18] Symonds substituted felt patches on the joint surfaces between timbers and used non-ferrous bolts. He also abandoned the use of oil and tar injections.[19] For ships afloat, improved circulation of air and the exclusion of rainwater were considered essential, and those in ordinary were roofed over (Fig. 17.2).

Reconstruction was a vital part of battlefleet policy. Ships were docked, stripped down to the frame, examined and reported upon. If the report was favourable they were then rebuilt with new timber where required, introducing structural improvements and the latest fashion in bow and stern. This would occupy at least twelve months. Badly decayed ships were dismantled. Several Devonport-built ships were rebuilt, notably *Caledonia* (120 guns), *Hibernia* (110 guns) (at Portsmouth) and *Foudroyant* (80 guns). All three cost more to rebuild than the construction of new ships of their rate, and such effort was only expended on ships of proven qualities. The cost of lesser rebuilds often equalled that of a new third rate, but the savings in timber and the increase in labour made the process viable. The ex-French *Canopus* was rebuilt between 1814 and 1816 at a cost of £78,709; improved copies ordered on her lines were less expensive. Small 74-gun ships still fit for service were reduced to powerful 50-gun frigates to save manpower and provide a modern armament. *America* and *Dublin*, converted at Devonport, gave several years' service in this new role, but only shortage of timber could justify the spending of £52,839, more than the cost of a new ship.[20]

The early development of the steam warship almost bypassed Devonport. Only two paddle warships were built, *Rhadamanthus* and the ill-fated *Avenger*. The principal reasons for this were the lack of available slipways (*Rhadamanthus* had to be built in the south dock), allied to the distance of the yard from the Thames engine works and the Admiralty steam factory at Woolwich. London became the home of marine engineering at the beginning of the nineteenth century. Proximity to the major merchant shipbuilders and easy water transport maintained the dominance of Thames-side engine builders for fifty years, making the concentration of Admiralty steam expertise at Woolwich inevitable. The Devonport paddle steamers had to be sent to Woolwich under sail to have their machinery installed, but the steam factory opened at Keyham in 1853 altered this position. By the 1840s the Admiralty accepted that steam would play a major role in any future war. Therefore it was vital the two south coast yards should have facilities to repair steam engines. The new factories at Portsmouth and Keyham were designed in the light of experience with the cramped, obsolescent facilities at Woolwich. Keyham proved particularly successful, being well laid out and spacious. Begun before the decision for an all-steam fleet, the work proved to be well over budget. Sir James Graham, First Lord again between 1852 and 1855, believed the whole idea had been a political 'job'. However, after inspecting the works he revised his opinion, supporting government-owned maintenance facilities as the only guarantee of rapid and reliable work.[21] With the opening of Keyham, Devonport and Pembroke entered the steam age, building or converting fourteen of the sixty-seven steam battleships completed in Britain, and fitting out or installing the machinery in another eight. This fleet met the two great challenges faced by the Royal Navy in the nineteenth century; the naval race with Imperial France and the Russian War of 1854–1856.

Throughout the war with Russia, work on the steam battlefleet continued, reflecting the underlying tension between the temporary allies. The Anglo-French naval race of 1851–1865 began with French attempts to use technology to offset the British advantage in sailing ships and seamen. The first thorough attempt came with the perfection of the wooden steam battleship in 1851; the *Napoleon* demonstrated that steam and heavy broadsides could be combined, and after a brief hesitation the Admiralty adopted the type as the basis of all future construction. The first British steam battleship, the *Sans Pareil* of 1851, built at Devonport (Fig. 17.3),

17.4 HMS *Warrior* off Keyham, 1861. (*Devonport Dockyard Museum*)

17.5   The battleship HMS *Anson*, 10,000 tons, 4 × 13.5in, 6 × 6in guns, fitting out off Keyham after her launch at Devonport's feeder yard, Pembroke Dock, 1886. (*Heath*).

was an unsatisfactory conversion of an incomplete ship. More ambitious designs were developed, and in October 1852 the Surveyor of the Navy, Captain Sir Baldwin Walker, advised the Admiralty to meet the French challenge with a large programme of steam battleships. Devonport's second battleship, the *St Jean d'Acre* (101 guns), laid down in June 1851, proved a complete success, making over 11 knots on trials. *Conqueror*, *Donegal* and *Gibraltar* were developed from the original design. Two similar ships, *Robust* and *Ocean*, were not launched as wooden battleships.

French policy was to build as many new vessels as the dockyards could manage, and convert every suitable ship. This forced Britain into a large-scale programme of conversions. At Devonport *Exmouth*, *Algiers*, *Nile*, *Aboukir* and *Albion* (all 90 guns), *Lion* and *Centurion* (80 guns) and the old three-decker 120s *Royal William* and *St George* were cut down into 90-gun two-deckers. These efforts restored a clear British supremacy by 1860. In fact, the French had never posed a serious challenge. Their paper strength was always greater than their actual power, and they were markedly less well prepared in the smaller classes. Walker and other policymakers would have preferred an all-new fleet, but shortage of timber made conversions vital. The French abandoned the wooden battleships for the seagoing ironclad in 1857.[22]

Just as the steam battlefleet was started, the focus of British strategy was abruptly shifted to make war on Russia, in alliance with France. Although it was only a limited maritime conflict, the war made considerable demands on the naval bases. Devonport supported elements of the powerful Baltic and Black Sea fleets, although the direct contribution of the yard was small, construction facilities being concentrated on the challenge from France. Devonport had built, converted or fitted out a large proportion of the steam battleships that ensured allied command of the sea. This work was increased during the war, and other tasks directly relating to wartime requirements were taken on. The old teak 74-gun *Cornwallis* was converted into a coast attack steam blockship in six months during the winter of 1854-5. She went into action at Sweborg in August 1855.[23] Other work included rebuilding the engines of the battleship *James Watt* and replacing those of the *Sans Pareil*. The Prussian Government exchanged the iron gunboats *Weser* and *Recruit* for the small frigate *Thetis*, which gave excellent service in the Sea of Azov. Finally, as the Great Armament of flotilla craft was being prepared to attack Cronstadt in 1856, Devonport built two gunboats, *Ant* and *Angler*. The Armament never left Spithead, but its latent power so impressed the Russians that they accepted the allied terms of peace.

One feature of the period 1815 to 1860 was the increasing use of iron to reinforce the structure of the wooden warships, beginning with iron knees. Seppings used iron diagonals in his postwar frigates, and Symonds extended their use to the battleships. These straps, up to one inch by six inches in section, provided the additional strength for longer ships. Additional length was required to meet the contemporary ideas on hydrodynamic efficiency, which called for long, fine forms. Combined with the weight and vibration of the early steam engines, this forced the architects to add more iron into each succeeding class, particularly around the stern. Keyham provided this ironwork, both for Devonport and to support Pembroke. Hitherto it had all come from Woolwich. This enabled Devonport to continue new construction in the ironclad period, albeit in much reduced circumstances.

The Ironclad Period, 1860–1888

After 1860 Devonport's role as a construction yard was greatly reduced. The steam battleship *Ocean* completed as an ironclad, while her sister, *Robust*, was retained on the stocks for conversion in the event of war. They were followed by wooden- and composite-hulled cruisers and colonial patrol vessels. The reasons for this were simple. For the first time in 300 years the royal dockyards were unable to build the type of warships required by the Navy. They lacked both the experience and engineering facilities for iron construction, and slipways for the longer vessels of the *Warrior* type (Fig. 17.4). To meet the demand the yards would have to be modernised and reorganised, at considerable cost. The Admiralty elected to proceed slowly, as it had with steam, allowing the early ships to be built by the merchant constructors and gradually bringing the royal yards up to date. The first four iron-hulled ironclads were built by private firms. Chatham was first yard to be brought up to date, because it was already in process of expansion and was the only royal yard with a dock long enough for a *Warrior*-type ship. The fifth ironclad, *Achilles*, floated out of this dock in December 1863. Pembroke's first ironclad, *Penelope*, was launched in 1868, and *Devastation* at Portsmouth in 1869. These were the only royal yards to build large iron warships. Many important ships were built by private firms, a practice which had been condemned for wooden ships after 1815. Iron changed the old rules; ships could be built quickly and private yards had the necessary experience.

Walker had intended to begin two more ships of the *Warrior* type, at Pembroke and Devonport, once the docks were lengthened. Admitting this might take some time, he placed *Minotaur* and *Agincourt* with private yards.[24] The requirement to modernise Devonport never arose; Woolwich and Deptford were closed in 1869, being too small and far from the sea; so Portsmouth was the only yard to combine the facilities of a first-class base with those of a major construction yard. Devonport remained a first-class base, but with her construction capacity at Pembroke. Ships built in the Welsh yard in this period have a particular relevance to Devonport. All were fitted out and engined at Devonport, along with many built at private yards on the Mersey and on the Clyde, including the second ironclad, *Black Prince*.

Repairs remained vital at Devonport. An incident of 1884 is typical; the ironclad *Defence* was docked after bending her stem in collision with *Valiant*. The bow plating was removed and a temporary furnace built around the frame, which was heated and then pushed back into shape by hydraulic jacks.[25] One critic of the royal yards in the early years of the ironclad era attacked what he saw as waste and inefficiency, contending they had no real work. This was unjust, reflecting a temporary shortage and the critic's support by the specialist private warship builders, who had to maintain their order books. In 1859 each royal yard had more work in hand than all could display in 1863.[26] In addition, iron forced a revolution in working practices, although after experience at Chatham the shipwrights were allowed to convert to the new trade.

Devonport was not modernised for iron construction, as planned, because the French challenge collapsed after 1865, allowing a sharp reduction in the estimates between 1867 and 1884. Without serious rivals Britain made her early ironclad battle fleet last over twenty years, with only sporadic new construction. Occasional scares, such as that of 1877–8, led to marked

17.6 The launch of Devonport's first Dreadnought, HMS *Temeraire*, 18,600 tons, 10 × 12in guns, in 1907. (*Devonport Dockyard Museum*)

increases in orders for private builders and the purchase of ships they were building for foreign governments. The crisis years of the later nineteenth century, 1868–70, 1876–7, 1886, 1891–2 and 1895–6, were all marked by increased work for the private builders. This fluctuated from 19 per cent in 1870–7 to 50 per cent between 1910 and 1914.[27] Governments used the private trade to smooth out irregularities in demand. Competition among specialist builders ensured that prices remained low, while their political activities did nothing to harm their chances. The new Controller of the Navy, Rear Admiral Robinson, and the Chief Constructor, Sir Edward Reed, were committed liberals.[28] At Devonport there were large reductions in the labour force.[29]

The Steel Era, 1888–1897

When the Naval estimates did rise, they rose dramatically. The impact on Devonport was the direct reverse of the 1860s, involving large-scale investment, a tremendous increase in work and a corresponding need to take on more skilled labour. However, much of the new workforce was made up by hired, rather than established men. In 1870–3 the royal yards employed

6,600 established men and 5,700 hired, but by 1899–1903 there were only 6,000 established against 21,200 hired men. Working conditions in the royal yards were better than those elsewhere, and although basic wages were lower the compensations were numerous. Shorter hours, 51 up to 1894 and 48 thereafter, pensions and continuity of employment given to established men, in combination with better rates for the high percentage of skilled men, made them better places to work. In 1891 the Admiralty attempted to introduce new graded pay scales, but the Shipwrights Constructive Association viewed this as an invitation to nepotism and, after pressure from several yards, particularly Devonport, the Admiralty backed down. Throughout the nineteenth century the Admiralty removed regional differences between hours, conditions and rates of pay in the several yards.[30]

Once the royal yards had recovered the private yards' initial lead in iron construction, they quickly resumed technological primacy. Steel was a notable example. Experiments began in 1873, with the cruiser *Iris* being built at Pembroke in 1875. This was to have particular significance for Devonport. After experimental work with the frames of several small ships, the twin-screw gun vessels *Curlew* and *Lapwing* were laid down in 1885, the first all-metal warships built in the yard. Increased orders under the Naval Defence Act of 1889, the turning point in the reconstruction of the Navy, caused a shortage of shipwrights. More hired men were taken on, and the old yard was modernised in the early 1890s. Significantly a new slipway was built over the mast ponds. However, these developments were not completed in time for Devonport's first steel battleship, a new *Ocean*, laid down in 1897. Delayed by shortages of material, she fell behind her sisters by over a year.

The Naval Defence Act emphasised the two-power standard of naval strategy, calling for a fleet equal to that of France and Russia combined. After twenty years of reductions there was much ground to make up, and expansion was not achieved without growing pains, notably the reform of working practices. Further problems were caused by the block ordering of the 1889 Act. In 1892 the royal yards had 102,000 tons of work in hand, but in the following year only 33,000 tons remained. Private firms were also short of work.[31] This was caused by poor long-term planning at the Admiralty. Fortunately the Spencer Programme of 1894 arrived in time to forestall extensive lay-offs. These controversial increases in expenditure were the direct cause of Gladstone's final retirement, and with him went the Victorian emphasis on economy.[32] The political influence of the major private contractors, notably Armstrong's, had grown during the ironclad period, and by the 1890s they were in a position to pressure government into additional orders to keep their works in profit. Government accepted the need to support private industry as a capacity for expansion in wartime. The late 1890s were a boom period for the warship industry; faced with the expansion of almost every other navy, the Admiralty could not cut back.[33]

The Battleship Yard, 1898–1915

To support the new fleet, work began in 1895 on the Keyham extension under the Naval Works Act. The object was to bring Devonport up to date as a base and a construction facility. This programme effectively recovered all the ground lost after 1860, establishing Devonport and Portsmouth as the leading yards. The new work effectively doubled the size of the existing yard, much of it by reclamation. In terms of construction and repair the doubling of the yard had little impact, the greater part of the work being new

17.7 HMS *Warspite* under repair in No.8 Dock, Keyham, after the Battle of Jutland, 1916. (*Devonport Dockyard Museum*)

17.8   The aircraft carrier HMS *Terrible* (later HMAS *Sydney*) being built on No.3 slip, South Yard, in 1943.

basins, locks and docks to service the latest battleships. When the bulk of the work was completed, in 1907, the cost was already £4 million. In addition an enormous coaling facility was built, to emphasise that Devonport remained a first-class naval base as well as an arsenal.[34] After the panic of the last decade of the nineteenth century, Devonport settled down to a consistent workload of battleships and cruisers, including the only two battlecruisers built in the royal yards, *Indefatigable* and *Lion*. The reforming work of the First Sea Lord, Admiral Sir John Fisher, 1904–10, aimed at greater efficiency and economy, reduced the yard workforce by a small amount after 1904, reflecting the shift from repair and maintenance to construction.

With the complete change to steel construction the yard resumed battleship construction from 1897. It was no coincidence that Pembroke's last battleship, *Hannibal*, was of the *Majestic* class and Devonports' first, *Ocean*, was of the succeeding *Canopus* type. This marked a deliberate reversal of the post-1815 policy of spreading out construction facilities to meet the problems of wooden shipbuilding. Pembroke was run down, while work began at Rosyth in 1903 to provide a fleet base for war with Germany. Clearly this was far more important than Pembroke, which had only ever been a construction facility. Devonport had been modernised at a time when France remained the potential enemy, as she did at least up to the Fashoda Crisis of 1898, making a major base in the Western Approaches essential. After 1900 there were three royal yards building battleships, but the size of *Dreadnought* and the geography of the Medway forced Chatham to turn to cruisers and submarines.

Portsmouth and Devonport were the last royal yards to build first-class warships (Fig. 17.6, Fig. 19.5). Portsmouth retained the dominant position built up after 1870, constructing the lead ship of each *Dreadnought* class, including the name ship in the record time of a year and a day and culminating with *Queen Elizabeth* and *Royal Sovereign*. Devonport built *Warspite* and *Royal Oak* of the same classes. Pembroke continued to build armoured cruisers, ending with *Defence*. The 1904 reforms were intended to close the yard, but political pressures kept it open, building light cruisers, up to 1918. Fisher considered it wasteful to keep so much capacity in the Royal Dockyards when private builders had extensive facilities. He thought the two south coast yards equal to the real needs of the Navy, and believed that by speeding up construction periods less slip capacity would be required to produce the same number of ships. He also delayed work on Rosyth, arguing that new docks at Palmer's on the Tyne would meet the need.[35] *Lion* had to be docked there in 1915 after the battle of the Dogger Bank because Rosyth was not ready. Devonport, controlling the Western Approaches, remained vital. During Fisher's period as First Sea Lord 6,000 hired men were laid off from the royal yards, but few from Devonport.[36]

Fisher also overhauled refitting and reconstruction. The latter policy was all but ended, while the work involved in the former was reduced by keeping nucleus crews aboard ships in dock to carry out routine tasks, cutting the need for dockyard labour.[37] The object, as ever, was economy through efficiency. The results were seen in a considerable downturn in the naval estimates, despite the increased tempo of battleship construction. The large-scale scrapping of obsolete warships and the refusal to modernise those of limited war potential removed a burden from Devonport.

The World Wars, 1914–1945

The declaration of war in 1914 effected a profound change at Devonport. On 26 August all work that could not be completed in six months was cancelled, the projected R class battleship *Resistance* being the principal victim. For the first time in a century the royal yards were called on to support an unlimited war effort, and they could not continue construction at the prewar rate. Maintenance and repair were now the major functions, and new work could be carried out in private yards, as in previous large-scale conflicts. However, as Devonport was well outside the main theatre, the North Sea, its work was more concerned with the Mediterranean and other distant theatres. Most repairs after Jutland, for example, took place at Rosyth and in the northern private yards, although *Warspite* was brought back to Plymouth (Fig. 17.7). *Royal Oak* and *Cleopatra* were completed and, more significantly, five submarines were constructed. Submarines were built in the royal yards during both world wars because they had skill levels which non-specialist private yards could not match. The only other new ship, the cruiser *Frobisher*, became a standby job. The labour force increased from 14,000 to 20,000. The real work of the war lay in refits and work on escort vessels, particularly in the last two years, when the German submarine campaign dominated the war at sea.

In 1919 the dockyards were brought back to an approximate peacetime labour force and put on short-time working. In the harsh postwar economic reality the pressure for reduction was overriding. The Colwyn Committee of 1919 considered building merchant ships as an alternative to large-scale lay-offs. Devonport did very little work under this scheme.[38] Merchant shipbuilding was not an ideal palliative, as it involved too little skilled work. More satisfactory were a series of commercial rebuilds and refits. In addition, several incomplete warships were moved to the yard, including the aircraft carrier *Hermes* and the cruisers *Durban* and *Enterprise*.

When capital ship construction was considered, in 1921, the royal yards were no longer equipped for the task. The size of warships had grown dramatically during the war (see table 17.1). Despite having the longest slip of any yard, Devonport could not handle the new G3 class battlecruisers, and modernisation was not considered. The Geddes Committee, appointed in August 1921 to investigate national expenditure, called for large reductions in the Navy and support facilities. It also criticised dockyard costs in comparison with those of private firms. This was unjust, given the level of specialist skill required in wartime to support a first-class base. How this could be ignored so soon after the war is difficult to explain, particularly as the chairman had been First Lord of the Admiralty in 1917–18. However, the Washington Treaty of 1922 imposed limits on the size and number of large warships the Navy could retain. Rosyth and Pembroke were placed on a care and maintenance basis, with reductions at other yards. Devonport survived this troubled period rather better than the other yards, but the royal yards were never again to be in the forefront of shipbuilding. No more

17.9 The cruiser HMS *Belfast* moored in Plymouth Sound following major reconstruction at Devonport between June 1940 and October 1942 after her back had been broken by a mine on 21 November 1939 in the Firth of Forth. (*Imperial War Museum*)

Admiralty decided to experiment with all-welded construction and, with almost all the private builders unwilling to undertake this form of construction, Devonport was selected for the experiment. The minesweeping sloop *Seagull*, launched in 1937, was the first all-welded warship to be built for the Royal Navy, representing a major change in construction methods. The structure of the ship was completely redesigned to save weight, and *Seagull* was the best ship of the class.[39] Welding was not used for larger vessels until late in the war. Several other nations had attempted to exploit the weight savings in welded construction to improve their designs, which were for the first time limited by international treaty. German cruisers were all welded in the 1920s, but Japanese vessels of the early 1930s were structurally weak, later classes returning to the traditional riveted hull.

In addition to the prewar new building, several large rebuilds were carried out at Devonport in the 1930s, those of the battleships *Royal Oak*, *Malaya* and *Valiant* being the most important. The last was carried out in a floating dock, despite the considerable technical problems of replacing the main machinery, removing and overhauling the 15in gun turrets, and installing a new secondary armament and superstructure. It was only completed after the outbreak of war.

War once again reduced new construction in favour of repair and maintenance. The cruiser *Trinidad*, although launched in late 1939, was delayed by wartime demands until the end of 1941. During the war a mooring vessel, six submarines and the light aircraft carrier *Terrible* were laid down (Fig. 17.8). Two of the submarines were expended incomplete in postwar damage trials, and the carrier was completed in 1949 as HMAS *Sydney*. The cruisers *Exeter* and *Belfast* were the most spectacular repairs (Fig. 17.9), but the main contribution once again lay in supporting escort forces. Toward the end of the war the yard took on a more conventional appearance, with the fleet being prepared for service in the Far East. In 1940 and 1941 the yard was subjected to severe enemy attack for the first time in its history. Although the bombing did considerable damage, the work of the yard was little interrupted. The labour force was not increased to the same degree as in 1914–18, although the 15 per cent increase did include a considerable number of women.

Table 17.1
The increase in the size of capital ships, 1815–1951

1815	*Britannia* wooden 2,616 tons, old measurement, 205ft overall length × 54ft 6in breadth
1842	*Albion* wooden 3,083 tons, old measurement, 204ft × 60ft
1860	*Warrior* iron 9,137 tons displacement (Thames Iron Works), 420ft × 58ft 4in. 14.5 knots.
1900	*Ocean* steel 14,300 tons deep load displacement, 421ft 6in × 74ft. 19 knots.
1915	*Warspite* steel 31,500 tons deep load displacement, 645ft 9in × 90ft 6in. 24.5 knots. The heaviest warship launched by any Royal Dockyard.
1920	*Hood* steel 42,200 tons deep load displacement (John Brown), 860ft × 104ft. 30 knots.
1921	*G3* battlecruiser (never built) steel 53,900 tons deep load displacement, 856ft × 106ft. 31 knots. This class, like *Hood* before them, would have been built in private yards. None of the Royal Yards had the facilities for such ships.
1951	*Eagle* (aircraft carrier) the largest British warship. Steel 53,390 tons full load displacement, 803ft 9in × 112ft 8in breadth at waterline. 30 knots. (Harland & Wolff).

Postwar to Privatisation, 1945–1988

The post 1945 run-down was in many ways more dramatic than that after 1918. By 1947 only 10,000 men remained engaged in warship construction in the royal yards, a 90 per cent reduction from the wartime peak figures. With the economic imperative to export, skilled labour was at a premium throughout the country. Pembroke closed in 1947, and Sheerness in 1960. Devonport received further modernisation, which, with the repair of war damage, reinforced her position as a first-class base with full dockyard support. When postwar rearmament began during the Korean war, shortages of skilled labour, raw materials and design staff hampered the exploitation of the funds made available.[40]

Postwar construction was limited to six frigates and a variety of support craft. The frigate *Salisbury* was the first all-welded prefabricated design built in the yard. She was intended to be a mobilisation prototype, with diesel engines to avoid the wartime shortage of gear cutting facilities for marine turbines, and her main armament, featuring aircraft direction radar, was also new. After the completion of the frigate *Scylla* in 1969 (Fig. 17.10), the

battleships were ordered, and no heavy aircraft carriers. Similarly, the peculiar demands of destroyer construction, light weight and high speed, were met by private builders.

This did not end the work of the yards, but it did modify the nature of what was done. The return to a heavy load of repair and refit reflected the impact of Washington Treaty battleship construction holiday, and the economic imperatives of post-1918 Defence policy. Converting the light battlecruisers *Furious*, *Courageous* and *Glorious* into aircraft carriers during 1922–1930 was one beneficial side-effect of the Washington Treaty. With the defeat of Germany, Devonport was once more in the ideal position to support the Atlantic and the Mediterranean fleets. The basins and docks were widened for the bulged battleships; by 1939 the docks were wide enough to take every ship in the fleet, and only too short for *Hood*.

New construction in the 1920s was restricted to the cruiser/minelayer *Adventure* and the 8in-gun cruisers *Cornwall*, *Devonshire* and *Exeter*, reflecting reduced demand and the need to keep the private builders open. From 1930 the tempo picked up, with fourteen patrol sloops, six minesweeping sloops and the 6in-gun cruisers, *Leander*, *Orion*, *Amphion* (later HMAS *Hobart*), *Birmingham* and *Gloucester* being built. In 1936 the history of the royal yards as constructors of major warships came to an end. The position is now the reverse of that pertaining after 1815, when all work was concentrated in the royal yards. It is a mark of the impact of new economic and political philosophies that in the 1970s the Government nationalised the warship building firms, taking control of all warship building for the first time since 1860. This policy was reversed after 1979.

Devonport's main role after 1945 was repair and reconstruction. Wartime technological advances ensured that ships only just completed were no longer adequate for their intended roles, a problem that had faced the Navy in 1815. The outstanding examples were the War Emergency destroyers and aircraft carriers. The former were gun- and torpedo-armed surface escorts, and as completed they were ill-equipped to deal with heavy air attack and of only limited value against submarines. All-round fleet escorts required far more displacement, as the *Daring* type demonstrated. However, new submarine designs developed in Germany and anticipated in Soviet service doubled underwater speed from 9 to 18 knots, depriving the 18–20-knot wartime escorts of any margin of speed for attack.

To provide that speed the obsolescent destroyers were given a profound reconstruction. Two were taken in hand in 1949, *Rocket* at Devonport, for the full Type 15 anti-submarine warfare frigate conversion which involved stripping out the original armament and superstructure, building up the hull to forecastle level as far aft as the quarterdeck, fitting a new aluminium superstructure, doubling electrical generating capacity, fitting new sonar, adding two new three-barrelled depth charge mortars (Squid or the improved Limbo), and providing a measure of nuclear and chemical protection. Five of the twenty-three ships converted, more than any other yard, were handled by Devonport: *Rocket*, *Roebuck*, *Ulyssess*, *Venus* and *Wizard*, the last completing in 1953. Devonport's pioneering work on aluminium welding was vital for the new lightweight superstructure.[41] Similar experience was also called on for non-naval tasks. Devonport performed all the stainless steel welding for the first British nuclear reactor at Windscale.

Work on aircraft carriers developed from the impact of the jet engine on naval flying. The angled deck, steam catapult and mirror landing sight were essential for safe jet operations at sea. None of the aircraft carriers built or building for the Royal Navy in 1950 had been designed with these developments in mind, but with several available, either afloat or in various stages of completion, it appeared logical to modernise. However, there was a fundamental problem. Increasingly large, heavy and fuel-inefficient jets meant that none of the ships available were large enough to exploit the full potential of the new aircraft. Instead they were always struggling to meet the demands and, unlike the destroyers, they were not sacrificing any function. In additiion, the pace of development between 1950 and 1960, when much money was being spent, was so rapid that ships in hand were redesigned while rebuilding, or were rebuilt more than once.

The first major reconstruction, that of *Victorious* at Portsmouith 1950–1957, proved a salutary experience, running well over budget, and overdue from a combination of unexpected problems and altered design. So much skilled labour was absorbed that a sister ship for *Salisbury* had to be moved to a private builder.[42] In the wider context, new management procedures were adopted before Devonport's first large carrier project, *Centaur*, which was completed on time in 1958 after two years. The follow-on was the modernisation of *Eagle*, at 50,000 tons the largest ship in the Navy. Between 1959 and 1965 the ship was renewed throughout, with uprated electrical equipment, full air conditioning and a full machinery overhaul. This project absorbed the efforts of well over half of the shipwrights and 80 per cent of the design staff at the yard. Despite this, other work continued, notably frigate building and submarine refits. *Ark Royal*'s 1966–9 modernisation was similar, although her main machinery was not given the same attention. As the historian of the Royal Corps of Naval Constructors has written:

> The modernisation of these aircraft carriers of 50,000 tons, with 10 decks below the flight deck and four more in the island (itself the size of a big destroyer) and 2,000 compartments, represented probably the largest single tasks ever undertaken in a UK Dockyard.[43]

Subsequent work, although not on this scale, involved converting *Hermes*

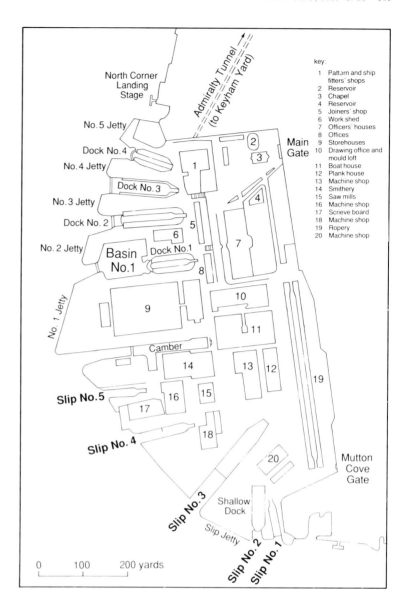

Map 17.1   South Yard with Devonport's building slips in the early twentieth century.

into a commando carrier in 1971 and the cruiser *Blake* into a cruiser/helicopter carrier during 1968–1972.

In 1969 the Admiralty elected to alter the basis of dockyard work by allotting complete warship types to individual dockyards, both for maintenance and refits. This sacrifice of flexibility would secure an improvement in the turn-round time, vital if the shrinking Navy was to keep a satisfactory force at sea. Devonport was allotted *Leander* and all subsequent frigate classes. An existing basin was modernised and enlarged between 1973 and 1977, allowing frigates to be brought into a covered dock all standing. As in the 1820s, the benefits of covered work were considerable, a 10 per cent reduction in refit time and a better quality of finish being achieved (Fig. 17.11).[44] However, it is worth noting that the size of the existing docks has now become a limit on the length of the latest Type 23 frigates, and modifications have been prepared to allow the emergency docking of a short Type 42 destroyer.[45]

Another new complex was established between 1975 and 1980 to refit nuclear-powered fleet submarines. Initially this was seen as a supplement and eventual replacement for the facilities at Chatham, working on the new *Swiftsure* and *Trafalgar* classes. However, the closure of the Kent yard in 1982 added the *Valiant* class to the workload at Devonport. As a result it was not considered viable to give the prototype boat *Dreadnought*, with her unique American reactor plant, a final refit at Devonport.[46] This decision was part of the 1981 Defence review Cmd 8288, which revised the 1980

17.10 The launch of the frigate HMS *Scylla* in 1968. (*Devonport Dockyard Museum*)

17.11 A *Leander* class frigate under refit in the Typed Frigate Complex in the early 1980s.
(*Devonport Dockyard Museum*)

report, supporting the maintenance of all four remaining royal yards. Cmd 8288 closed Chatham and reduced Portsmouth to a base with a small repair capacity.

Devonport and Rosyth, now the only major dockyards, have been under commercial management since 1986. The reduction in capacity was, like that planned by the Geddes Committee, connected with a reduction in the surface fleet. These schemes were developed to meet economic criteria, without reference to the issues of national or NATO strategy. In addition, warship refits, for so long the mainstay of the royal yards, were opened to commercial tender. While the Falklands conflict of 1982 reversed several cuts in the surface fleet, the exceptional performance of the dockyards did nothing to improve the position of the support facilities. Both south coast yards carried out rapid conversions of merchant vessels for war.

This is a peculiarly apposite juncture at which to reflect on the history of Devonport as a Royal Dockyard. Changing perceptions of strategy and the future of the Royal Navy have culminated with Devonport at last pre-eminent, but in a changed environment. Since 1987–8 commercial requirements have led to severe job cuts, and there are no promises for the future. The latest round of Defence Cuts, following the collapse of the Soviet Union, under 'Options for Change' forced Devonport and Rosyth to compete for the contract to refit the new *Trident* class ballistic missile submarines. Devonport's success has left the future for Rosyth bleak, and that would leave one dockyard to maintain the entire Royal Navy. Until the 1980s it was accepted that the Navy should maintain a capacity to mobilise reserves, and Ships Taken Up From Trade (STUFT) in the event of war, along with maintenance and repair facilities to meet anticipated demands. Economic men like Graham and Fisher might have objected to the level of dockyard expenditure, but they did not question the need for Government controlled dockyards at an appropriate level. In wartime the requirements of the Navy for repair and maintenance have generally exceeded both capacity and expectation. The purpose of Royal Dockyards was to maintain a highly skilled labour force as the nucleus for wartime expansion. It would be peculiarly difficult to replace that capacity in an emergency.

The Royal Dockyards have always been at the forefront of shipbuilding technology, but, shorn of new construction, that role became difficult to maintain. In the period after 1915 pioneering work on welding at Devonport demonstrated that skill levels were maintained where funding was provided. However, the economic and political realities of the twentieth century have seen, after a series of violent fluctuations, a changeover to complete reliance on private enterprise. Within the framework of the royal yards Devonport was always one of the two or three most important, and as such shared in the role of the royal yards as pioneers in naval technology. Against this, it must be emphasised that the direct contribution of any yard was controlled from London, and that investment at any one reflected a role in the overall national strategy. Consequently, while Devonport has become the premier yard, replacing Portsmouth, the situation has altered profoundly since 1815. Once it has been stripped down to a refit depot, run on commercial lines, it is difficult to see how the last dockyard can maintain the flexibility of skills so often required in wartime.

17: The Impact of Naval Technology on Warship Construction and Repair at Devonport, 1815–1986

1 S Pollard & P Robertson, *The British Shipbuilding Industry 1870–1914*. (Cambridge, Mass., 1979), 143–6.

2 D K Brown, *A Century of Naval Construction. The History of the Royal Corps of Naval Constructors* (1983), 183.

3 BL, Add. MS 41,394, f1. Memorandum by the Controller of the Navy, Admiral Sir Thomas Byam Martin, April 1816. Andrew D Lambert, *The Last Sailing Battlefleet. Maintaining Naval Mastery 1815–1850* (1991).

4 Stephen S Roberts, 'The Introduction of Steam Technology in The French Navy, 1818–1852' (unpublished Ph.D. thesis, University of Chicago).

5 PRO, ADM 83/1, f218. Admiralty to The Navy Board, 8 Dec. 1815.

6 PRO, ADM 7/593, 102, 135–6, 420 and 685–91. Report of Dockyard Visitations by the Board of Admiralty 1813–14, with particular reference to Plymouth Yard and the ships inspected there; K V Burns, *The Devonport Dockyard Story* (Liskeard, 1984), 35.

7 PRO, ADM 83/2, f142. Admiralty to Navy Board, 10 July 1817; PRO, ADM 83/4, f524. Admiralty to Surveyor 31 Oct. 1832; PRO, ADM 83/8, f3681. Admiralty to Surveyor 16 Dec. 1833.

8 R G Albion, *Forests and Seapower* (Harvard, 1925).

9 BL, Add. MS. 41,394, f66. Memorandum by Byam Martin 7 Dec. 1816.

10 NMM, ELL/268, Minto Papers. Earl Minto (First Lord of the Admiralty 1835–1841) to Lord Duncannon (First Commissioner of Woods and Forests 1835–1841) 15 Oct. 1840.

11 Roger Morriss, *The Royal Dockyards during the Revolutionary and Napoleonic Wars* (Leicester, 1983), 108–9.

12 PRO, ADM 83/2, f55 11. Admiralty to Navy Board 21 Feb. 1817.

13 Iowerth Prothero, *Artisans and Politics in Early Nineteenth Century London, John Gast and his Times* (1979); BL, Add. MS 41,394, f84. Memorandum by Admiral Sir Thomas Byam Martin on Bombay Shipbuilding, 5 July 1821.

14 Cumbria Record Office, Graham Papers, MS.54. Earl Grey (Prime Minister 1830–1834) to Sir James Graham (First Lord of the Admiralty 1830–1834), 4 Feb. 1831; NMM, PAR/150A, Parker MS. Graham to Admiral Sir William Parker (Second Naval Lord) 20 April 1835.

15 PRO, ADM 222/2–4. Surveyor to Admiralty, 1833/4 includes numerous reports on the disabilities of individual workmen and their pensions. The maximum pension for long service and serious disability was £28 per annum. See J Barrow, *An Autobiographical Memoir* (1847), 420, for an account of the assault on the Board Members.

16 Jonathan Coad, *Historic Architecture of the Royal Navy* (1983), 41, 46.

17 PRO, ADM 106/2271, f47. Admiralty to Navy Board, 9 Oct. 1816; PRO, ADM 106/2274. Admiralty to Navy Board, 11 Sept. 1817.

18 PRO, ADM 87/2, f160. Master Shipwrights to Surveyor, Feb.–March 1833. See also ADM 95/11, Surveyor's Report of 1833.

19 PRO, ADM 87/2, f151. Portsmouth Dockyard to Surveyor, 13 July 1835.

20 James A Sharp, *Memoirs of the Life and Services of Rear Admiral Sir William Symonds* (1858), 419.

21 B L, Add. MS. 44,163, f99–100. Sir James Graham (First Lord of the Admiralty 1852–1855) to William Gladstone (Chancellor of the Exchequer 1852–1855) 3 Nov. 1853. R Gardiner, ed., *Steam, Steel and Shellfire. The Steam Warship 1815–1906* (1992).

22 Andrew D Lambert, *Battleships in Transition. The Creation of the Steam Battlefleet 1815–1860* (1984), 44–5, 50; Andrew D Lambert, *The Crimean War. British Grand Strategy 1853–1856* (Manchester, 1989).

23 Lambert, *Battleships*, 97–119.

24 E Corlett, *The Iron Ship* (1978); Andrew D Lambert, *Warrior. Restoring the Worlds' First Ironclad* (1987), 9–38; and PRO, ADM 87/77, S6011, Surveyor to the Admiralty, 28 Sept. 1860.

25 P Hichborn, *Report on the European Dockyards* (Washington, 1885), 13.

26 P Barry, *Dockyard Economy and Naval Power* (1863); and Pollard & Robertson, *British Shipbuilding Industry*, 205–6.

27 Pollard & Robertson, *British Shipbuilding Industry*, 213–6.

28 Vice Admiral P H Colomb, *Memoirs of Sir Astley Cooper-Key* (1898), 379; and PRO, ADM 1/5990. Admiralty to Controller's Department, 16 Aug. 1866, 1/5990 complaining about a political speech made by Edward Reed.

29 Burns, *Devonport Dockyard Story*, 59.

30 Pollard & Robertson, *British Shipbuilding Industry*, 169–72.

31 A J Marder, *The Anatomy of British Seapower* (1940), 35; and Pollard & Robertson, *British Shipbuilding Industry*, 207.

32 Peter Gordon ed., *The Red Earl: The Papers of the Fifth Earl Spencer* (Northamptonshire Record Society, 1987), II.

33 Marder, *Anatomy & British Seapower*, 36–43.

34 Burns, *Devonport Dockyard Story*, 69–71.

35 R Mackay, *Fisher of Kilverstone* (Oxford, 1973), 336–7, 342–3; P Kemp, ed., *The Fisher Papers* (NRS, 1960, 1964), vol. I, xvi–xxi. 23; Pollard & Robertson, *British Shipbuilding Industry*, 204.

36 *Fisher Papers*, vol. II, xii.

37 *Fisher Papers*, vol. II, 22–4, 149.

38 Burns, *Devonport Dockyard Story*, 85.

39 D K Brown, *Century of Naval Construction*, 152.

40 Eric Grove, *From Vanguard to Trident* (1987), 22–3.

41 John Lambert, 'Type 15 Fast Anti-Submarine Frigates' *Warship World*, Spring 1987, 15–8.

42 Grove, *Vanguard to Trident*, 72.

43 Brown, *Century of Naval Construction*, 297–302.

44 Brown, *Century of Naval Construction*, 304–5.

45 Grove, *Vanguard to Trident*, 389.

46 Grove, *Vanguard to Trident*, 351.

18 *William Froude and the Model-testing Tank at Torquay*[1]

L J Taylor

WILLIAM FROUDE (FIG. 18.1) WAS BORN IN 1810 in Dartington rectory and, just at the time when he was enjoying considerable success in his career as a railway construction engineer as one of I K Brunel's assistants, he was obliged to retire and return to live there to care for his father, who had become a permanent invalid. He was then only 35, and his career had lasted less than ten years. While he was with Brunel the iron-hulled, steam-and-propeller driven ss *Great Britain* had been planned and its construction completed, and it is known that Froude undertook special investigations, probably concerned with her design. Shipbuilding had now become the concern of engineers, and no longer that of traditional shipwrights.

Through the first 15 years of retirement Froude continued to interest himself in ships, but only by constructing models and sailing them on the Dart, close to the rectory. Their behaviour was studied by towing them from a boat and by the use of clockwork and propeller drives, all skilfully made by Froude himself. On his father's death, in 1859, he moved to Paignton and continued model experiments, using a tank he built in the garden. He acquired land in Seaway Lane, Torquay, to build a large house, 'Chelston Cross', now the Manor House Hotel. A cistern was built into the basement for use as a test tank (about 1864) and a larger tank added outside the house about 1867.

By 1867, with valuable assistance from his son, Robert Edmund Froude, then aged 20, and Brunel's 24-year-old son Henry, a near neighbour, he had solved to his own satisfaction the problems of how to employ models as aids to design. He himself was 57, and made his first approach to the Admiralty

to consider his theories and provide practical support for the continuation of his work. He received no reply.

By this time he already had one achievement to his credit. Brunel had launched his last and largest ship, *Great Eastern*, in 1858, and found she rolled excessively in a sea. From his investigations, Froude recommended roll dampers, known today as bilge keels, attached to the hull, and these subsequently became standard equipment on many ships, including warships. Froude published papers on this work, and when the British Association for the Advancement of Science set up a committee about 1866 to consider '. . . the stability, propulsion, and the seagoing qualities of ships, . . . and to make recommendations for improvements', he was one of its six members, along with other well-known engineers and academics.

Their findings accepted that Froude had set out the true principles of the motion of a ship rolling among waves (recognised as such today). However, in the matter of how to design accurately for specified performance, and how to achieve the most efficient design, the committee were divided. Each member had his own pet ideas. It was recommended that full-sized ship-models of various dimensions and shapes should be towed at different speeds. Froude had put forward his own solution in committee – conducting tests on models and then scaling the results up to full size, thus saving much time and money, but as he had not completed his research, no mention of this was made in the findings. Instead, he wrote his own letter to the chief constructor of the Admiralty, who, after a visit to Torquay to view Froude's methods, gave the suggestion some support. After Froude received no reply

18.1 William Froude, FRS. (*Superintendent, Admiralty Experiment Works*)

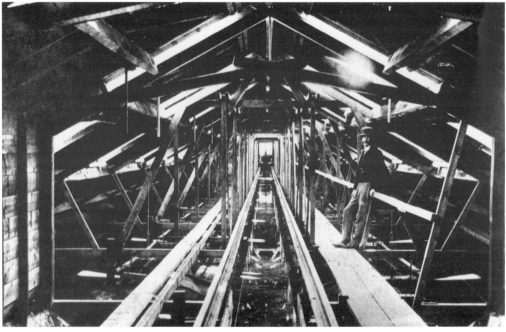

18.2 A general view of the Admiralty Tank at Chelston Cross, Torquay. The man on the right is almost certainly Robert Edmund Froude. (*Superintendent, Admiralty Experiment Works*)

18.3   The carriage with a model under test. (*Superintendent, Admiralty Experiment Works*)

from the Admiralty to his first letter, he had to wait about a year before they replied to a second, in which he set out and costed his proposals in detail. He was nearly 60 – too old to wait much longer – so he even offered to give his services free.

It is clear that the Lords of the Admiralty regarded him as a crank, and were probably influenced by the opinions of the leading authorities of ship design of the day, who could point to the failure of all previous efforts at scaling models. However, their construction programme had suffered a severe check during that period of waiting. Probably, but for that, Froude's offer would never have been considered.

In 1859 France had launched *La Gloire*, intended to be the first armoured warship of a modern steam fleet. An early counter to *La Gloire*, the more powerful HMS *Warrior*, was launched in 1860 but was herself obsolescent within a year, when the Admiralty experimented with a turret ship, HMS *Trusty*, and her American counterpart, *Monitor*, went into action in the American Civil War some months later. The latter was armoured, steam driven, and mounted two 11in guns in a power-driven rotating turret. Ominously, she sank in a storm with the loss of her crew.

An international arms race between the major powers had begun. If naval superiority could be secured, domestic security, trade protection and world wide colonial expansion would be the reward, but the problem ahead was to design ships equal to the task – seaworthy, fast and economical. This could only be ascertained after a ship had been launched and undergone sea trials. Hence the need for the British Association Committee, on which Froude had served.

The Admiralty's latest experiment with an iron-hulled, armoured, turret ship, HMS *Captain*, was launched in 1869. It was soon realised that the

design was faulty. Freeboard was inadequate and she sank with 450 crew in a storm off Finisterre in September 1870. The realisation that the design of *Captain* was flawed, coinciding with pressure from the scientific establishment for effective trials, forced the Admiralty to look to Froude, whose scaled-down-model proposals were considerably cheaper than the full-scale towing trials urged by the British Association. Yet it is clear from the phrasing of their Lordships' letter in February 1870 that it was expected that Froude would fail. To quote from it,

> . . . my lords desire that you should distinctly understand that the total outlay that they can sanction on these experiments is a sum of £2,000, of which £1,000 only will be provided for during the financial year next ensuing, ending March 1871. No claims shall be made to them hereafter for any sums in excess of the abovementioned amounts . . . in addition . . . experiments of rolling are to be carried out on the understanding that their costs will be included in the sum stated above . . .

Also, Froude was to give his service free. He did so, for the few years of his life remaining. The 'rolling experiments' mentioned entailed experiments at sea making measurements of ship's motion in a sea. For these he devised and made accurate instruments.

Froude, assisted by his son and Henry Brunel, had the tank built and began experiments to collect basic data and to assess its potential in 1871. The tank was 278ft long and, with a wave absorbing beach at the end, the total length of its enclosure would have been about 100 yards (Fig. 18.2). The sides, protected and waterproofed with asphalt, sloped to a depth of 10ft and the width at the waterside for most of its length was 34ft, so width and depth were sufficient to avoid interference with tests from reflected waves.

Additionally, there was a brick-built boiler and engine house, a workshop and office. During acceleration of the model undergoing tests, the engine was assisted by a descending weight. Wave making facilities were allowed for in the plans, but were only installed after operations transferred to Haslar, Gosport. Along the length of the building, over the water, there was a 3ft 3in gauge rail track. Its construction was integral with the roof members, which were substantial enough to avoid vibration, and the roof, almost 50ft wide, cut off interference from the weather. On the track ran a carriage, which towed the model under test (Fig. 18.3). Links were used for towing, not cable, so that a steady, straight, course could be assured.

The carriage itself was hauled by an endless cable, running over sheaves, and was driven through gearing by a two-cylinder, 10hp steam engine. The engine and governor were designed and made by Froude. The governor was remarkable for its precision. It could be adjusted to a control at set speeds up to 1,000ft/min and would control the chosen speeds within a tolerance of ½ft/min. A second carriage for tests of propellers was added later. An observation carriage may have been attached behind the dynamometer carriage, enabling the testing to be studied at close range. On the dynamometer carriage towing the model, a rotating chart recorded distance travelled, and timing marks at one-second intervals were made by an electrically actuated pen controlled by a clock mechanism. Thus all readings, being automatically recorded, were free from personal judgement or error.

To have provided timber for the Navy's orders to be tested would have required a forest. Making the models to specification and subsequent modifications would have required hours of skilled labour. Froude's solution was to use paraffin wax, cast on a wooden core. Both sides of the model were cut simultaneously by a pair of spinning cutters. The cutting machine was controlled direct from the drawing of the model, and to a scale that could be selected. Alternatively, it could be copied direct from another model, again to a different scale. A uniform, smooth, surface on the model was produced by incorporating beeswax with the paraffin wax. The same methods are used today with modifications such as the use of glass-reinforced plastic, to take advantage of modern technology.

To obtain data for the formulation of the 'laws of comparison', defining the mathematical relationship between model and full sized ship, the early tests were of models 3ft, 6ft and 12ft long. Energy losses owing to various surface finishes were evaluated by towing long planks. The mathematical laws – Froude's 'laws of simulation and comparison' – confirmed as valid by the earlier tank tests, stated the relationship between the ship and its scale model in terms of 'scale time', 'scale speed' and 'scale force'. These are still recognised as valid today. They have been refined, but the amount of modification has been described as 'astonishingly small'.

Indisputable success came in 1873. A model of a 1,160-ton ship, HMS *Greyhound*, was tested, and from the results the performance of the ship herself was predicted. The ship, stripped to be the equivalent of the model, was then towed by the larger HMS *Active*. To do so, Froude himself had to devise special equipment to measure the large amounts of power involved. Results tallied with predictions to everyone's satisfaction, discrepancies being accounted for by the difference in texture of ship and model and the effect of shallow water. The Admiralty could hope to embark safely on a naval construction programme with the benefit of ship tank experiments. New ideas could be evaluated quickly and pursued, or rejected with confidence. A major problem was the improvement of propeller design and matching of hull and propeller. This work was started by William Froude and continued after his death by his son. For the time being, until 1886, the Admiralty Experiment Works at Seaway Lane, Torquay, was an important naval establishment. Ninety-seven separate reports and memoranda were produced on work carried out. The first, dated 14 August 1872, was an *Interim Report on Surface Friction Experiments* and the last, dated 27 March 1886, was a *Report on the Data for determining the size of Screw Most Favourable to Efficiency for Any Given Ship*. The operation was then transferred to Haslar, Gosport, to use a larger tank. Robert Edmund Froude became its director, and delayed his retirement until 1919, after the end of the First World War. Hotels and houses now occupy the site of the Torquay tank.

The benefits and effects of William Froude's work extend, nationally and internationally, far beyond the narrow limits of his brief connection with the Admiralty. He retired in 1878, when his wife died, and survived her by only about a year. By helping his friend, W Denny, to construct a second tank, almost an exact copy of his own, he helped give British shipbuilding and the merchant navy a long lead over foreign competition. By the end of the century only three such establishments existed outside Britain, and all were copies of the Torquay tank. In some instances the connection was direct. One Torquay trainee, Frank P Purvis, after establishing a copy at Dumbarton, went on to become Professor of Naval Architecture in Japan and built the first Japanese ship tank at Nagasaki. By 1950 there were about fifty establishments worldwide, and their organisations co-operated in 1954 to collect and publish Froude's technical papers and to erect a memorial to him on the site of the tank in Seaway Lane. There are now some 150 such establishments.

18: William Froude and the Model-testing Tank at Torquay

1 The writer is grateful for information supplied by D K Brown and by Geoffrey Tudor, Historical Adviser to the 'Brunel in Devon' Trust, in the preparation of this piece. The main published source of information for Froude and the Torquay tank is A F Duckworth, ed., *The Papers of William Froude . . . 1810–1879* (Institution of Naval Architects, 1954). See also Froude's own publications: *On the Rolling of Ships. Paper read at the Second Session of the Institution of Naval Architects, March 1 1861* (1863); and *The Laws of Fluid Resistance* (South Kensington Museum, Science Lectures, II, 1879).

19   Naval Education and Training in Devon

PHILIP PAYTON (MARINE TRAINING by DEREK OAKLEY)

The Emergence of Technical Training

'BEFORE THE THIRD DECADE OF THE NINETEENTH CENTURY, technical education in its modern meaning was almost non-existent.'[1] This was true for civilian education throughout the United Kingdom, but it was also true for military training within the Royal Navy. By the 1830s, however, it was slowly being realised that Britain's early progress in industrial development could be maintained (and further technological advance facilitated) only through the establishment of a system of technical education. Debate and educational innovation continued thereafter throughout the rest of the century, at precisely the same time that rapid technological change within the Royal Navy – sail giving way to steam, wood being replaced by iron and steel, the introduction of electricity – was provoking reassessment of its training methods for Officers and Ratings. Changes in naval education and training, therefore, reflected generally the pattern of development in civilian technical and scientific education, both moulded by the momentum of societal and economic advance. As Morrish noted,

> During the nineteenth century scientific and technical education gradually evolved and increased in importance, largely as a result of the political and industrial revolutions which had spread throughout Europe . . . Steam and electrical power did more than revolutionize modes of transport: they changed men's minds, the way they thought and believed.[2]

In Britain, scientific and technical education at higher levels received a significant boost when Cambridge introduced its Natural Science Tripos in 1848. Oxford followed with its School of Natural Science in 1853, London with its Faculty of Science in 1859, and in the second half of the century 'civic universities', such as those of Manchester, Leeds and Liverpool, emerged as significant expressions of the Victorian ethos and a reflection of the new professional, expert and technological society. As such, the 'civic universities' were important models for educational institutions that developed later, not least, as we shall see, the Royal Navy's engineering colleges of Keyham and, later, Manadon.[3]

Technical and scientific education at the lower levels ('elementary' and 'secondary') in Britain was developed largely, as Musgrave has written, to overcome the pressure of foreign competition.[4] This was as true for the Royal Navy (which became faced with increasing French, American and German rivalry) as it was for British industry, and here again we see a close parallel between civilian and naval educational development. Between 1836 and 1852 seventeen technical 'schools of design' were opened in Britain, and the Newcastle Commission's Report of 1861 provided the first thorough-going survey of English education, a prelude to the Act of 1870. Thereafter, concern for technical and scientific education continued apace, the Samuelson Commission reporting (1882–4) the superior ' . . . general diffusion of elementary education in Switzerland and Germany . . .' and concluding, 'We find that our most formidable assailants are the best educated peoples'. The Bryce Report argued for greater emphasis upon science and technology in teaching (at the expense of the Classics), and in the wake of the 1902 Education Act the system of Junior Technical Schools was set up in 1905.[5]

In the Royal Navy, education in general and technical education in particular took on a new significance in the middle of the nineteenth century as new technologies arose and were applied. The Instructor Branch of the Navy became correspondingly more important, the old rate of 'naval schoolmaster' giving way to replacement by a new body of graduate Instructor Officers. By 1842 the Naval Instructor was, according to the *Navy List* of that year, ' . . . in all respects a wardroom warrant officer'.[6] By 1856 there were ninety-six such Instructors, of whom thirty were graduates, and in 1861 they were elevated to the status of commissioned officers with (after 1864) the possibility of promotion to the rank of commander.

The Royal Navy's concern to develop general and (most especially) technical education and training was manifested throughout the Service. Devon, however, by virtue of the county's strategic maritime position, had long since emerged as a principal home of the Royal Navy. It comes as no great surprise to discover, therefore, that Devon was to feature so prominently in the saga of naval educational and training development. Devon, indeed, especially in the last century-and-a-half, was often the stage upon which was acted-out the many innovations devised in the corridors of power in London, innovations designed to meet the changing requirements of the Fleet at sea and reflecting new responses demanded by technological change. The advance of technology necessitated an almost continuous process of review, with naval education and training evolving constantly, often with a keen eye upon developments in the world of civilian education and training and, of course, upon changes effected in the other major navies.

Britannia

In all this, Devon acquired – not through any grand design, but rather as a result of this process of evolution and innovation – a particular association with the education and training of Royal Navy (and also many foreign and Commonwealth) officers, focussed upon the Britannia Royal Naval College, Dartmouth, and the Royal Naval Engineering College, Manadon, at Plymouth. That is not to say, however, that the education of Naval ratings (and of Royal Marines and of naval-employed civilians) has not been of importance, for clearly it has, especially if we widen our sphere of interest to include those naval establishments which are in southeast Cornwall but which nonetheless have been considered traditionally as being within the orbit of Plymouth Naval Command.

The story of Devon's place in the evolution of naval education and training is fascinating in itself, but equally enthralling is the social history of this process, of the effect of this education and training, and particularly the manner and environment in which it was conducted, upon Serving men and women. Here, the experience in Devon may be taken as a cross-section or typical example of the broader naval experience in Britain, for it encompasses the entire process from training afloat in often ill-suited and unsatisfactory hulks to education ashore today in purpose-built and highly-specialised establishments.

The practice of training afloat in hulks survived surprisingly late into the twentieth century, this longevity being a measure of the support it enjoyed in naval circles. As well as providing continuing employment for the 'wooden walls of England', to which much sentiment was still attached, training afloat provided an authentic nautical atmosphere and environment, and also afforded the means by which the trainees could be easily controlled and isolated from non-naval influences ashore. Amongst the most celebrated of the Royal Navy's hulks were those which constituted *Britannia*, moored permanently at the mouth of Old Mill Creek in the River Dart, near Dartmouth. *Britannia* exhibited all the qualities of training afloat, but also manifested many of the deleterious and unsavoury aspects of life in the hulks.

Britannia was created as a result of Admiralty policy to improve the effectiveness of officer training. The old Naval Academy at Portsmouth, which had been known as the Royal Naval College since 1806, had proved unequal to the task and had disappeared by 1837, leaving the Navy with an *ad hoc* and highly unsatisfactory method of recruitment and training of officers. Potential cadets were 'nominated' by Serving Senior Officers of influence and, according to the reminiscences of one naval officer writing in the 1890s,

> . . . having obtained a nomination, [the boy] had to appear before a doctor, and if the candidate looked healthy his ordeal was very short. He was made to run across the room, jump over a chair or something of that kind, had to take a long breath, got a slap on the back or a dig in the ribs, and was dismissed with a kindly "You'll do". Then a sum in the first four rules and a scrap of dictation having been more or less successfully accomplished, the small boy, aged perhaps twelve and a half or thirteen years, donned the blue uniform and brass buttons, and was sent off to take his chance in a sea-going man-of-war as a 'volunteer of the first class'.[7]

In the days of sail and simple weaponry, such selection and preparation may have been enough, but in the face of technological advance a more rigorous system was obviously required. The Admiralty, in a manner at odds with its usually supposed resistance to change, recognised this and acted accordingly.

Thus, in 1857, the hulk *Illustrious* was earmarked for officer cadet training at Portsmouth. A nine-month training course was devised, soon extended to fifteen months and later to two years. In 1859 the cadets were moved aboard the three-decked hulk *Britannia* at Portsmouth, which in 1862 was moved to a new mooring at isolated Portland where the cadets would be more insulated from distractions ashore. Portland, however, proved an exposed and unsatisfactory anchorage, and in September 1863 *Britannia* was moved again, to the equally isolated but far more protected reaches of the Dart. In 1864 she was joined by the hulk *Hindustan*, and in 1869 was replaced by *Prince of Wales*, which became the new *Britannia* (Fig. 19.1).

Life aboard the *Britannia* hulks was uncompromisingly naval, and there can be no doubting the success of the 'navalising' process (what today one would term 'Naval General Training') in attuning young thirteen- and fourteen-year-old minds to the traditions and discipline of the Service. The hectic course was divided into nine terms. One former cadet recalls,

> Although there was only a year's difference between News and Niners, there was, in fact, all the difference in status and outlook which pertains in a public school between boys of the fourth form and those of the sixth. This exaggerated superiority of the Niners was probably due to the profoundly different conditions and training in the *Britannia*. Niners were familiar with reefing a topsail, sailing a cutter, making a long splice, taking a sight etc, while the News were finding out the difference between Port and Starboard, a course and a topsail, and what was the time when the sentry struck seven bells.[8]

The *Britannia* course also included academic studies, from French to physics, and the recruitment policy was altered accordingly to try to ensure that new cadets would possess the necessary academic abilities. Although there were still nominations reserved for the prerogative of admirals on first hoisting their flags and captains on first hoisting their pennants in command, along with four cadetships a year for the ' . . . sons of gentlemen in the colonies . . .',[9] the great bulk of nominations were made directly by the Admiralty itself upon the basis of results from competitive examinations in which candidates had been tested in a variety of subjects from algebra to scripture and Latin to arithmetic.

The process by which young schoolboys were turned by degrees into typical officers of Her Majesty's Royal Navy was described lovingly, with great pride and affection, by Capt F G D Bedford RN (' . . . lately in command . . . ' of *Britannia*) in a series of articles in the *Boy's Own Paper* in 1890. He dwelt upon the creation of a Naval atmosphere in the hulks, drawing a picture at once both patriotic and cosy, in which (for example) the cadets' mess-room was said to be ' . . . prettily and well lighted by a number of incandescent lights in round ground glass globes, and warmed by steam heaters'. All 240 cadets, he said, could sit down to dinner without overcrowding, ' . . . it looks comfortable; and there are some fine old engravings of famous naval battles hanging around'. He pictured the cadets at their recreation: 'It is a sight to be remembered to see the boys in their neat uniforms and with happy, healthy faces . . . and to hear them joining in the choruses of the songs, an especial favourite being "Ye Mariners of England" . . . '. Preparation time in the evening was ' . . . more or less voluntary . . . ', lasting little more than an hour, and did not encroach upon the entertainment of the day when ' . . . the band plays . . . ' and ' . . . the boys dance away most vigorously'. But at last the musicians would strike up 'God Save the Queen', and

> At nine or a quarter past, according to the season, all are mustered in the mess-rooms for prayers, and afterwards the bugle sounds 'To bed'. The chief cadet captain on duty reports "all turned in" to the lieutenant of the day who then goes round both sleeping-decks; and quiet reigns throughout the ship.[10]

This benign and reassuring portrait was welcomed enthusiastically by the Navy's supporters, with the tailoring firm of Gieves and Hawkes publishing Bedford's articles as a booklet entitled *Life on Board HMS Britannia* (Portsmouth, 1895). However, Bedford's fulsome praise disguised the less attractive aspects of hulk life. Naval discipline was, by its very nature, often rigid ar.d sometimes harsh, but there were occasions in *Britannia* when it seemed excessively so. In 1867 there was a hint of scandal when a number of cadets accused of bullying were birched severely. Questions were asked in the

19.1 Britannia and *Hindostan* moored in the Dart, c1890. (*Britannia Royal Naval College*)

House of Commons, and an article in *The Times* reported allegations that

> . . . when a cadet was punished his legs and arms were tied to ringbolts so that he could not move, and that he was flogged with a birch broom which had been previously steeped in water to make it more pliant; that fifteen cuts were inflicted with it on the back, and that doctors invariably attended.[11]

The Admiralty denied the allegations, but nonetheless the practice of corporal punishment for cadets was thereafter abandoned. Strict discipline remained, however, especially the greatly-feared punishment of 'Third Class For Conduct' where the miscreant was forced to suffer all manner of indignities and deprivations, from incarceration on alternate days in a cell on bread and water, to having to stand alone on the middle deck for one hour after evening prayers for up to a maximum of six days. Even as late as 1903–4, joining instructions sent to the parents of new cadets emphasised that ' . . . cadets are liable to severe punishment for any breach of the regulations'.[12] Formal discipline was accompanied by an 'unofficial' code of behaviour which sometimes bordered on the eccentric. Osbert Leverson-Gower, a cadet in *Britannia* in 1904, observed:

> There are most queer sort of customs here: all "news" have to double wherever they go, while we are not allowed to wear our cap on the back of our heads, swing our keys, or open our coats, these being Third Term privileges; if we are found doing any of these things, we are made to sing before a large audience of Third Termers . . . .[13]

More serious was the lack of satisfactory sanitary conditions, and the general unhealthiness that prevailed in the hulks. In 1949 one *Britannia* 'old boy' could recall that in 1899 the 'heads' (toilets) on board ' . . . would today be described as barbarous even in the foc'sle of a tramp steamer',[14] and in 1901 came the terrible outbreak of influenza and pneumonia which led to the deaths of two cadets and the temporary evacuation of the hulks ' . . . so that the Establishment may be thoroughly disinfected'.[15] In 1904 Leverson-Gower noted, 'We have had a very sad event last week in the death of pneumonia of a cadet called Boycott in the First Term . . . '.[16]

It was hardly surprising that even as early as 1874 serious attention had been afforded to the possibility of replacing the hulks with a purpose-built establishment ashore. In 1875 the 'Wellesley Committee' considered no fewer than fifty-two potential sites for such an establishment before recommending a site at Mount Boone, Dartmouth, where the *Britannia* playing fields already existed and where easy access to shore and the river's 'smooth waters' met the Committee's approval. Naval expenditure, however, was then seriously constrained, and it was not until 1896 that Admiral Goschen, then First Sea Lord, could announce changes which not only raised the age of entry of cadets to 15½ and reduced training time to sixteen months, but also necessitated the construction of a Naval College. The *Navy and Army Illustrated* noted the decision to build at Mount Boone, ' . . . a remote corner of Devonshire' as it called it, and emphasised that 'The sanitary arrangements are on an ample scale, and nothing will be neglected to ensure their being as perfect as science and money can make them'.[17] The architect chosen was Mr (later Sir) Aston Webb, an Associate of the Royal Academy.

Although it had not been foreseen by Goschen and the earlier planners, the decision to build a new College ashore at Dartmouth was especially fortuitous because the period of construction was accompanied by a thorough-going reappraisal of officer education and training which resulted, on Christmas Day 1902, in the publication of the famous 'Selbourne Memorandum' which outlined what was to become known as the Selbourne-Fisher Scheme. The hulks would have been totally unsuited to the demands of the scheme, and even the new Britannia Royal Naval College (as it was to be known) fell short of the requirement, so that plans had to be made for the erection of an additional College in the grounds of Queen Victoria's Osborne House on the Isle of Wight.

Keyham and the Rise of Naval Engineering

Behind the 'Selbourne Memorandum' lay the great energy, determination and foresight of Admiral Sir John 'Jacky' Fisher, the Second Sea Lord, who

19.2 Sleeping deck on *Britannia*, showing cadets' hammocks and chests, *c*1890. (*Britannia Royal Naval College*)

saw that the education and training of naval officers (and ratings) had to be improved radically and at once if they were to be able to cope with the demands of the new technological age. In particular, Fisher was concerned that naval training should keep abreast of the latest developments in civilian schools, colleges and universities. He was also aware of the superior training that was already emerging in the navies of the United States and, more ominously, Germany. The Selbourne-Fisher Scheme envisaged the homogeneous training of executive, engineer and Royal Marine officers, welding them together as an effective officer corps for the Royal Navy. The plan was that cadets would enter between the ages of 12 and 13, each then receiving identical training until the age of nineteen and twenty when, having passed for the rank of Sub-Lieutenant, individuals would be able to categorise as Executive, Engineer or Royal Marine.

This proposal was, to say the least, revolutionary. Before 1902 the executive (or seamen) officers had been assured and confident of their special status. They alone could aspire to command at sea or ashore, they alone trained in *Britannia*. Royal Marines were dismissed as little more than soldiers afloat, and engineers were deemed hardly worthy of the designation 'naval officer'. Given the rapidly increasing importance of the engineer in

19.3 Officer cadets training at the Royal Naval Engineering College, Keyham, at the end of the nineteenth century. (*RNEC, Manadon*)

19.4   Britannia Royal Naval College, Dartmouth. The college of 1905 and its extensions, 1990. (*Britannia Royal Naval College*)

the Victorian Navy, as sail gave way to steam, as iron replaced wood, as new applications for electricity were found, and as weapon and propulsion systems swiftly became more complex, the degree of prejudice and class distinction levelled against him seems incredible. As the *Windsor Magazine* complained in October 1897,

> . . . for many years, anyone was good enough to look after the engines, and the engineers were treated with little consideration. They were merely granted warrants instead of the Queen's commission, which is conferred on every executive officer from the admiral of the fleet to the sublieutenant, and they ranked with other subordinate officers. They were regarded, in fact, as equal in social status to railway engine-drivers.[18]

The lack of status caused considerable hardship, not to mention resentment, amongst naval engineers and had a serious effect upon recruiting. Too few came forward to train as naval engineers, and many of those who did were of indifferent calibre. In 1875 a committee chaired by Admiral Sir Astley Cooper Key (first President of the Royal Naval College, Greenwich, set up in 1873 to administer the further training of junior officers) addressed the problems of engineer recruiting, training, and status. Cooper Key concluded,

> Students should be in all respects fitted to take their place with officers of corresponding rank in the Wardroom and Gunroom Messes . . .
> Too many engineer students are being taken from the sons of dockyard artificers, of seaman and marines and of others belonging to the same class of society.[19]

To ensure that students would indeed be fitted to take their place alongside other officers, Cooper Key advocated that engineers be given 'Military' titles (something that was not directly implemented until after 1902) and that an Engineer Students' establishment be formed. Within a year of the report's publication, the hulk HMS *Marlborough* at Portsmouth had been set aside as accommodation for the Engineer Students, and in July 1880 a purpose-built Training School for engineer students was opened at Keyham, in Plymouth, at the edge of the newly-constructed Devonport north dockyard, where all the very latest and most sophisticated equipment that the Navy had to offer would be in easy reach.

Keyham College,[20] as it was soon known (later the Royal Naval Engineering College, Keyham), afforded accommodation only. There were no classrooms, and instruction, both academic and practical, took place in the neighbouring dockyard, where all the latest technological innovations were to hand (Fig. 19.3). Although the building's impressive facade suggested a pile erected on the grand scale, early inhabitants of Keyham complained of poor ventilation, cramped recreation spaces and generally spartan conditions. Harry Lister, who had been in *Marlborough* and was later to rise to the rank of Engineer Rear Admiral, was amongst the first to join Keyham in July 1880 and, while admitting that 'The building is really splendid . . .', was forced to add that '. . . my cubical which was No 1 was an awful place like a police cell . . .'.[21] However, students spent only a small part of their time physically within the college. During the working day and in the evening they attended the dockyard workshops and the Royal Dockyard School, and recreation time was spent in such pursuits as swimming from the Bathing Stage or boating up the Tamar to Calstock.[22]

All was not well at Keyham, however, for the standard of instruction offered in the Dockyard School was not high enough to fulfil the requirements of the Engineer Students' course. Accordingly, the Admiralty reacted by establishing classes within the college itself and, significantly, by acquiring the services in 1888 of Professor A M Worthington, who became Head of Keyham. Standards did improve, but the Keyham graduate was still only a ' . . . glorified mechanic . . . '[23] (even after five years of study), only the very brightest few being selected for further training in Greenwich. The *Navy and Army Illustrated* waxed lyrical about 'The studies of the young Naval engineer at Keyham . . . ' where 'Everything that concerns thermo-dynamics, electricity, and hydraulics . . . must be understood by him' so that he could appreciate ' . . . intimately the construction of extraordinarily complex and varied machinery . . .'.[24] But in reality the problems of recruitment, training and status were still such that the Royal Navy could not meet its own requirements. The Navy did not have enough Engineers to cope with the ever-increasing demands of technological change.

An appreciation of the failings of Keyham and engineer training, like that of the failings with executive officers in the *Britannia* hulks, lay behind many of the provisions of the Selbourne-Fisher Scheme of 1902. In March 1903, as a result of these provisions, the existing engineers in the Royal Navy were at last given full 'Military' rank, so that, for example, a Chief Inspector of Machinery became an Engineer Rear Admiral, while newly-recruited Engineer Students were designated 'Engineer Cadets'. With some relief *Page's Magazine* of 1904 explained that,

. . . a great deal has been written concerning class prejudices between the executive and the engineering branch in the senior service, but that is simply a relic of bygone days. For the last ten years, the students who have entered Keyham College have been, for the most part, public school boys, and have often formed friendships at school with those whom they have afterwards met again as midshipmen or sub-lieutenants in the gunroom of a warship.[25]

Selbourne-Fisher and the new Dartmouth

The Selbourne-Fisher Scheme was designed, however, to take the process a stage further by integrating the education and training of Executive and Engineer (and Royal Marine) Officers from entry at 12 and 13 until age 19 or 20, when specialisation would take place. The integrated course thus devised was designed to be broad, a deliberate movement away from the old *Britannia* hulk training where navigation and seamanship had been emphasised at the exclusion of much else, with little time devoted to English and naval history and almost nothing about naval engineering. There was also to be more effort devoted to what it meant to be a naval officer, an attempt to improve upon the woeful situation described by an officer who had joined in 1899 and had written,

I never heard a lieutenant of a Term address his cadets on any subject but games. Never did we have a lecture on how to be an officer, how to treat one, and how to conduct oneself on duty and off.[26]

Naturally, the Selbourne-Fisher Scheme provoked considerable public interest and debate, and not a little controversy. The *Daily Telegraph* exclaimed that the plan was 'revolutionary', but *The Times* counselled that it was not revolutionary but 'evolutionary'.[27] The scheme was generally welcomed in the House of Commons, but in the Lords it received a distinctly rougher ride. Its chief critic was the Earl of Glasgow, who alleged that the Admiralty had succumbed to unwarranted pressure and demands from disgruntled engineers who aspired to higher status. In an age of specialisation, argued Glasgow, the scheme did not make sense because it promoted a principle of interchangeability which could not endure. Selbourne himself retorted that it was essential in the fighting of a modern warship that every officer was a combatant and trained as such.[28] This was a view which won the public support of the distinguished naval commentator Julian S Corbett, who wrote approvingly of 'Lord Selbourne's memorandum' in the *Monthly Review*,[29] and both public and Parliamentary support swung behind Selbourne.

As the new college ashore at Dartmouth would not be really until 1905, and as it had been built to accommodate only four terms, the first batch of new-style Selbourne-Fisher cadets entered Osborne, on the Isle of Wight, in September 1903, where they spent two years, followed by a further two years at Dartmouth and another three at sea as midshipmen. Those who then chose to be engineers spent two terms at Greenwich before going down to Keyham for one year's specialist training. This meant that the first of the new-style entries would not reach Keyham until 1913 and, as the last of the old-style entries had joined in 1905, the college was empty from 1910 and indeed remained closed until 1913.

The Britannia Royal Naval College, Dartmouth (Fig. 19.4), was at last opened on 14 September 1905, and from the beginning the emphasis was upon making as clean a break as possible from the old *Britannia* hulks.[30] To ensure that cadets from the pre-Selbourne-Fisher entries would not unduly influence the development of the new college, following their removal from the decommissioned hulks, they were packed off to sea training early, leaving the college itself in the hands of new-entry and Osborne boys. Although many of the trappings of a naval environment remained – quarterdeck and chest-flats, gunroom and wardroom – there was also a determined attempt to foster the atmosphere of a modern and progressive public school. Professor J A Ewing, appointed Director of Naval

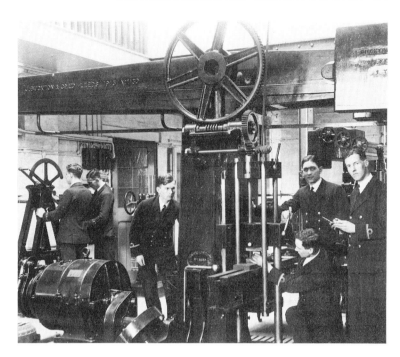

19.5 Engineer officer training in the Metallurgical Testing Laboratory at Keyham after the First World War. (*RNEC, Manadon*)

Education from Cambridge in 1903, was well known as an educational progressive, as was Cyril Ashford, Headmaster of Osborne and later of Dartmouth. By 1907 the new college had settled into its new routine, with 359 cadets under training, the academic courses including mathematics and science, engineering and applied science, and an attempt to develop critical faculties and liberal values through the study of subjects such as English and History (instead of the traditional Classics) – a revolutionary innovation in its day. A report of a Board of Education Inspector commented in May 1912 that,

As a whole the work appears to be singularly successful in teaching the cadets to express themselves in clear and vigorous English, and in inspiring them with a taste for reading . . . In intelligence and in the range of their general education the more capable sets compare very favourably with most boys of similar age who have been educated in Public Schools.[31]

In 1912, as the war clouds began to gather on the horizon, Winston Churchill (then First Sea Lord) recognised that the Royal Navy would be short of officers in the forthcoming conflict (it took 4½ years to produce a midshipman under the Selbourne-Fisher Scheme), and so instituted the 'Special Entry Scheme' in which older boys who had already completed their education could be recruited and prepared quickly for life in the Navy. At first this 'Special Entry' training was at sea in HMS *Highflyer*, but with the outbreak of war in 1914 the cadets were sent to Keyham instead.

On Saturday afternoon, 1 August 1914, Dartmouth received the order to mobilise, and almost at once the cadets were dispersed to Devonport, Chatham and Portsmouth. They went not to the ships of the Grand Fleet (already fully-manned) but to older ships on secondary duties, and thus many found themselves early in the war in actions such as the Narrow Seas, Coronel and Gallipoli. Although shorn so suddenly of its inhabitants, Dartmouth soon regained its strength from cadets moving down from Osborne, and training continued throughout the war years.

In 1919 Keyham reopened for the training of Engineers, but in the immediate aftermath of the war the atmosphere was generally one of uncertainty. The Royal Navy now had far too many officers for its peacetime needs, and in the 'Geddes' Axe' cull of March 1920 a 40 per cent reduction of the four junior terms at Dartmouth (along with 40 per cent of the three terms at Osborne) was sought. Parents were offered a £300 bounty to withdraw their sons, with a warning that if there were not enough voluntary withdrawals then compulsory removals would be made. Part of the attendant economies involved the closure of Osborne, and from 20 May 1921 Dartmouth became the principal training establishment for new-entry naval officers.

The direction of training at Dartmouth came increasingly under attack, however, with much criticism of the engineering components of the course. Until 1921 the Admiralty had decided whether an officer would specialise as either executive or engineer, but by then enough engineers were coming through the 'Special Entry Scheme'. It was assumed, therefore, that a Dartmouth cadet would automatically become an executive officer unless he expressed a strong desire to be an engineer. In this climate, engineering as a subject became less important at Dartmouth. There were those, however, who complained that there was now too much engineering taught at Dartmouth, while still others argued that, to keep apace of modern technological developments, engineering should be taught earlier in the careers of engineer officers. This latter point, of course, was an argument in favour of reducing the integrated nature of officer education and training, and was listened to closely by the Admiralty.

'The Great Betrayal' and the war

As a result, a number of changes in the training and status of engineer officers was instituted. In response to the view that engineers should start their specialist training earlier, midshipmen selected for engineering duties were sent to Keyham about a year after having completed their Dartmouth training (aged around 19) to pursue a four-year course in engineering. This course, launched in 1922, soon dubbed the 'Long Engineering Course', proved so successful that it remained in being with only minor adjustments until Easter 1951. It also lent the Royal Naval Engineering College, Keyham, a great deal of academic credibility and kudos during the 1920s and '30s. York speaks of the College's ' . . . formidable reputation . . .', and Penn adds that the 'Standards of technical education were the equal of those achieved in universities'.[32] Amongst the staff were academics of some standing, including John Case, author of the highly respected standard work *Strength of Materials*, and the eccentric but brilliant instructor Capt D'Arcy Lever.

The emergence of the 'Long Engineering Course' served to emphasise the re-emerging and widening differences between engineer and executive officers. Elsewhere in the Royal Navy differences in function and status between different types of officer (instructor, chaplain, and so on) were increasingly apparent, and in 1925 an Order in Council attempted to remove the anomolies and inconsistencies (and to regularise the system) by creating twelve distinct categories of officer. In addition to the executive officer, there would also be engineer, instructor, accountant, chaplain, medical and dental officers, all of whom would hold the King's Commission, along with five categories of warrant officer: shipwright, ordnance, electrical, schoolmaster and wardmaster. Of these, only the executive officer could aspire to

19.6   Lord High Admiral's divisions in the presence of The Princess Royal, Dartmouth, April 1990. (*Britannia Royal Naval College*)

command, while all officers – except for executive officers – were instructed to wear distinguishing colours between their rank stripes.

The developments of 1925 represented a considerable retreat from the spirit of the Fisher-Selbourne Scheme. It seemed to many to re-establish the 'superiority' of the executive officer, with the engineer officer in particular reduced to his old, inferior position of pre-1902. To the engineers 1925 was 'The Great Betrayal', although it did at least have the beneficial effect of creating a renewed esprit de corps amongst the engineer officers – not least at Keyham, with its highly successful 'Long Engineering Course' and flourishing college life (Fig. 19.5).

At Dartmouth the 1920s and '30s were less glittering than at Keyham. In the aftermath of 'Geddes' Axe' the college slipped into a quiet and generally happy routine, with encouraging reports from the Board of Education inspectors praising the general standard of education received by the cadets. But by 1929 the college was coming increasingly under attack. The number of cadets under training had declined considerably – from 580 after the wielding of 'Geddes' Axe', to 546 in 1926 and 373 in 1934 – and in the face of public disquiet about the apparently excessive 'staff-student' ratio, the number of staff officers was reduced significantly. By 1934 there were only twenty-two Naval Officers and thirty-six schoolmasters on the college staff, and there were some who considered that the college was lucky to have survived at all.

By the late 1930s it was becoming increasingly apparent that war with Germany was looming, and, inevitably, both Keyham and Dartmouth braced themselves for yet further changes in their roles. Recruiting was increased, reversing the decline of the previous decade, and at Keyham it was recognised that the existing facilities were too restricted to cope with increasing numbers and the ever-more-sophisticated course. In 1937 there were 112 officers under instruction; by May 1941 the number had swollen to 322, and in the summer of 1945 it reached an enormous 771.

Accordingly, consideration was given to the possibility of an expansion of the Royal Naval Engineering College, and in June 1938 the 100-acre estate around Manadon House, at Crownhill, to the north of Plymouth, was purchased with a view to constructing a second College. Wartime huts were erected hurriedly at the new site, and on 7 May 1940 Manadon was opened as an extension of the college. By now Keyham and Manadon together were training not only Royal Navy Officers but also many Poles, Norwegians and Dutch, along with Commonwealth officers from India, Australia, New Zealand and Canada. The 'Long Course' was modified to take account of the new specialisms in aeronautical engineering and ordnance engineering, and the college itself became involved in the war, lending a helpful hand where it could amidst the destruction of blitz-torn Plymouth.

At Dartmouth the outbreak of war led not to a sudden exodus (as in 1914) but rather to an increase in the numbers of cadets in residence with – as at Keyham and Manadon – a wide cross-section of foreign and Commonwealth officers also under training. Despite its topographical prominence, the College was at first ignored as a target by enemy aircraft, but on 18 September 1942 it was at last the victim of a bombing raid. The seven junior terms were hastily evacuated to Muller's Orphanage in Bristol (appropriately renamed HMS *Bristol* for the occasion), and in February 1943 the whole College was reunited at Eaton Hall, the Duke of Westminster's Cheshire seat. Dartmouth itself, once vacated, was used by Combined Operations for training, and from December 1943 until February 1945 was occupied by the United States Navy as the US Amphibious Base for Combined Operations, whose activities included the now infamous exercises at Slapton Sands.

Postwar: Dartmouth and Manadon

The cadets did not return to Dartmouth until September 1946, by which time there was already considerable change in the air. A system of scholarships to the college had been introduced in 1941, but in September 1948 the recruiting base was widened still further with the introduction of a new joining age of sixteen and the complete abolition of fees for boarding and tuition. Cadets would now join Dartmouth for a two-year course, after which they would be eligible to categorise as executive, engineer or supply (formerly accountant) officers. The engineers then passed on to fleet training

19.7 Practical engineering problem solving at RNEC Manadon in the 1980s. (*RNEC, Manadon*)

and arrived at Keyham or Manadon at the age of about 22 for a two-year course. The first of these new-style engineers reached the Royal Naval Engineering College in 1958, with the better-qualified ones being sent on to London University to read for a degree.

Dartmouth entry was still as a result of competitive examination, in which candidates had to display broad academic competence in subjects such as physics, mechanics, engineering drawing, mathematics, chemistry and biology, with questions in the humanities asking candidates to consider such issues as 'Peace and prosperity depend upon each other' or to 'Write a concise account of the development of heavy industries in the USSR during the present century'. In English the candidate might be asked to 'Write an appreciation of Milton's English Sonnets'.[33] But despite the rigours of the system there was still unease because it was felt that age 16 entry was inappropriate, age 18 being a more natural break in a boy's education. Accordingly, the 'Committee on Officer Structure and Training', set up in 1954, was given the task of constructing an '18 Entry' scheme. With considerable foresight the committee perceived that its principal task was to alter the nature of Dartmouth training, so that the college would become a true 'Naval Academy' with emphasis upon the professional training of all naval officers. By 1955, with this in mind, changes were already under way at Dartmouth.

The '18 Entry' and move towards more 'professional' training was given further impetus by the report of the Murray Committee in September 1958. The ensuing Murray Scheme dominated Dartmouth education and training during the 1960s, involving a rigorous mix of Naval General Training, training afloat in a Dartmouth training squadron, and a high standard of academic education. With the introduction or the so-called General List of Officers drawn from all specialisations, the Murray Scheme emphasised common aspects of training for all officers – an echo of the spirit of Selbourne-Fisher. The 1960s, however, were dangerous days for Dartmouth, for the college fell under Government scrutiny as the Ministry of

new mechanisms for the educating of naval engineer officers should be sought. Accordingly, the decision was taken to close Manadon by the late 1990s, presenting the Royal Navy with the imminent demise of what Vice-Admiral Sir Louis Le Bailly had as recently as 1990 described as '. . . unarguably . . . the greatest naval engineering college in the world . . .'.[35]

By the postwar era, then, Devon had become set in its role as the principal home of Royal Navy officer education and training, with ultimately all officers undergoing their initial training at Dartmouth and with Manadon, as the Navy's engineering university, offering both undergraduate and postgraduate training well into the 1990s. The processes which had led to this state of affairs were mirrored to some degree in the development of rating training, particularly of artificers, the Navy's technicians. The rate of engine room artificer had emerged as early as 1868, but it was not until the regime of 'Jacky' Fisher that a comprehensive programme of artificer training, capable of matching the already developing German naval technician training, was instituted. Equally, it was not until Fisher's reforms that the artificers emerged as the 'élite' of the rating corps.

Defence looked for ways to cut costs and to rationalise military training. Several assaults were beaten off, but the college entered the 1970s with the awesome task of attempting to accommodate the complexities and often conflicting requirements of an increasingly diverse range of entries. Graduates as well as schoolboys had to be catered for, as did special duties officers (senior ratings who had been promoted), instructor officers, Womens' Royal Naval Service officers, doctors, nursing officers, dentists, chaplains, constructors, Royal Marines, pilots and observers. The accommodation of these disparate groups led to further emphasis upon the professional aspects of naval education and training, so that the Dartmouth of the 1980s and into the 1990s has become first and foremost the place where all officers of the Royal Navy acquire their initial grounding in Naval General Training. To that extent, the spirit of Selbourne-Fisher is still alive (Fig. 19.6).

The changes at Dartmouth in this period were matched by complementary developments at the Royal Naval Engineering College. After the war it continued to operate from both its sites at Keyham and Manadon, but in December 1946 the latter was commissioned as HMS *Thunderer*. Thereafter, Manadon became increasingly the more important of the two sites, the scene of a hectic building programme, with engineer officer training at Keyham finally coming to an end in 1958. The new facilities at Manadon were the envy of the Navy, and indeed of many civilian institutions, the journal *British Machine Tool Engineering* enthusing over '. . . what is virtually a university course . . .' conducted in '. . . modern premises with a better educational environment . . .' (Fig. 19.7).[34] The familiar 'Long Course' was terminated in 1951, and was followed by a period of experimentation which led in 1962 to the introduction of London External BSc degree courses. In 1966 the Council for National Academic Awards (CNAA) granted Manadon the right to design its own BSc (later B Eng.) degree course, and in 1976 it approved the course leading to an MSc, arrangements which obtained until the demise of the CNAA and the subsequent accrediting of degrees by the University at Plymouth.

By the 1980s Manadon seemed set for further expansion, with a BA degree in Maritime Defence, Management and Technology (taught jointly with Greenwich) introduced in 1990, and with plans for the removal of the Nuclear School from Greenwich to Manadon. However, this period of confident growth came to an abrupt halt in 1993, a casualty of the continuing 'Options for Change' *ad hoc* defence review process which had decided that

Artificer Training

In March 1903, in the wake of the 'Selbourne Memorandum', an Admiralty Order in Council sanctioned the plan for the training of boy artificers in establishments at Chatham (HMS *Tenedos*), Portsmouth (HMS *Fisgard*), and Devonport (HMS *Indus*).[36] *Indus* was created in 1904 from a collection of hulks moored at Wilcove, on the Cornish side of the Tamar, known officially as the 'Establishment and Workshop for Supernumerary Engine Room Artificers and Boy Artificers'. A strong sense of identity was fostered in the *Indus* hulks, generating a sense of superiority over the *Tenedos* and *Fisgard* boys but also more particularly over 'inferior' categories of rating. Training was hard and rigorous, a candid account in the *Industrian* magazine in summer 1918 describing both the appearance and routine of the establishment. It considered that 'To the outward eye the establishment is not without a touch of disappointment' for,

> There is a feeling that in the fitting of these four quondam ships, moored in a picturesque cove on the western side of the Hamoaze, an opportunity for beautifying their appearance has been lost by too official love of corrugated iron.

However, the report went on to emphasise that 'The interiors of the ships are a contrast . . .', containing '. . . every type of marine engine and attendendent diverting intricacies . . .' with '. . . old engines, new parts; old parts, new engines. A whirl of and mass of machinery and belting, such a noise and clanking . . .'. In the accommodation hulk there were '. . . decks like driven snow, brass and steel polished to mirror-like perfection, spotless paintwork – indeed, it seemed a sacrilege to tread the very boards'. In the lecture rooms, the report continued, there were displayed '. . . experimental engines, slide valve diagrams, machine drawings in profusion, electrical and chemical apparatus, in toto everything connected with the theoretical part of engineering.'[37]

But, despite the obvious high standards, *Indus* suffered the usual shortcomings of training afloat, as evidenced in the following entry in the *Industrian*:

It is with deep and sincere regret that we chronicle the death of one of our shipmates, Trevor Williams, who died of influenza in Stonehouse Hospital on 12 February 1918.
We take this opportunity of conveying the fervent sympathy of the whole ship to his sorrowing relatives.
Williams was a good, clean sportsman as well as a cheery companion, and in him we have lost one of the best of comrades.[38]

In the end it was 'Geddes' Axe' which killed off artificer training in HMS *Indus*, the hulks after 1921 being devoted to the training of mechanician ratings. *Tenedos* having been closed some years before, artificer training was then concentrated in the *Fisgard* hulks at Portsmouth.

In the usual manner, the *Fisgard* hulks proved themselves at length to be unequal to their task, leading to a transfer of artificer training to Chatham in 1932. Its sojourn there was relatively brief, however, for in 1937 part of the task was moved to HMS *Caledonia* at Rosyth, while in 1939 the Admiralty decided to cease artificer training at Chatham altogether. In attempting to identify a suitable new location for artificer training, the Admiralty considered a site at Westward Ho! in North Devon, but in the end decided in favour of Torpoint in Cornwall, an attractive and obvious choice given the town's close proximity to Devonport Dockyard.

With the outbreak of war in September 1939, the artificer apprentices (as they were now known, the term 'boy artificer' having been abandoned in 1920) were evacuated from their vulnerable accommodation in Chatham, certain classes moving to Portsmouth but others travelling down to a temporary home in the Ebenezer and St Mark's Church Halls in Devonport. Certain classes were accommodated aboard *Marshall Ney*, an old monitor in Devonport Dockyard, and in February 1940 the rest of the apprentices were moved from the draughty and cramped Church Halls to more acceptable accommodation at the local Stoke Damerel High School for Girls. By then work on the new establishment at Torpoint had already started, and as early as July 1940 the first apprentices were arriving at what was termed the 'Royal Naval Artificer Training Establishment'.

Although erected hurriedly, the workshop and classroom facilities at Torpoint were extensive, artificer apprentices by now falling into the diverse categories of engine room, electrical, ordnance, and air. Artificers at sea had emerged as vital components in the teams which kept ships steaming and fighting, and their aircraft servicable, and the skill and training of these naval technicians were recognised widely. The motivation, therefore, to ensure that the new establishment was fully operational at the earliest date was overwhelming. Curiously, although not yet commissioned, the establishment had already acquired the unofficial sobriquet 'Fisgard' – a name by now inextricably associated with artificer training.

The Plymouth Blitz impinged upon the life of the new Fisgard, part of the workshops being demolished in an air raid in January 1941, but the establishment and apprentices survived the trials of war so that in December 1946 the Royal Naval Artificer Training Establishment was formally commissioned as HMS *Fisgard*. In the postwar era the training at *Fisgard* developed rapidly, in many respects reflecting the innovation that was occurring at Manadon, the most noticeable change being the move from craft to technician apprenticeships. Although the craft element remained an important component in the artificer's range of skills, greater emphasis was placed upon academic and technical training, mirroring the technical changes that were happening in the Fleet at sea. The 1960s saw the emergence of a process in which technological advance accelerated rapidly, leading to the intro-

duction of nuclear technology at sea, and to rapid advances in radar, sonar and communications. Guided missiles replaced big guns as principal weapon systems, and computer technology was increasingly applied to ships' systems.

By the 1970s *Fisgard* had settled into its role as the new entry artificer apprentice training establishment, the new recruits joining between the ages of 16 and 21 and spending three terms at *Fisgard* before moving on to their specialist training establishments elsewhere. In 1981, however, the Government's Defence Review led to the 'Slimtrain' process which, amongst other things, recommended the streamlining of artificer training and the closure of *Fisgard* (whose wartime buildings were now in any case beginning to deteriorate). Accordingly the task of new entry artificer training was moved to a 'Fisgard Squadron' in HMS *Raleigh*, the Royal Navy's modern and vast training establishment situated, ironically enough, in Torpoint, directly opposite the old *Fisgard*.

The Lower Deck

The rise of HMS *Raleigh* has been one of the great success stories of Royal Navy education and training in the postwar era. Opened at the end of 1939 as one of three new, large basic training establishments, its role was to train some 4,500 'hostilities only' seamen. Erected hurriedly, it consisted of '. . . long narrow single story wooden huts with dining halls, drill sheds, canteens, sick bays, offices and parade ground and wardroom and one boat'. One early inhabitant recalled that there was '. . . an air of unreality . . . cut off, in our small peninsula, by the River Tamar and the sea from Devonport and Plymouth . . .',[39] but the realities of war were soon brought home by an air raid in April 1941, which killed forty-one Naval Ratings and twenty-five Royal Engineers, and by the later arrival of the Americans, who used the establishment as a base in the D-Day preparations.

After the war, *Raleigh* moved swiftly to the point where, by the 1970s, she had become the sole new entry (non-artificer) rating training establishment, a massive rebuilding programme replacing the old wooden building with modern units. Subsequently, in the early 1980s, *Raleigh* acquired a 'Dauntless Squadron' for the training of new entry Women's Royal Naval Service ratings (following the closure of HMS *Dauntless* near Reading), along with the Fisgard Squadron and the Royal Navy Supply School. This concentration of facilities at *Raleigh* was consistent with the Navy's desire to rationalise, consolidate and centralise education and training – a far cry from earlier days, when there had been a bewildering plethora of training hulks afloat at Plymouth and elsewhere.

Like the *Britannia* hulks for officer training, the training of ratings in

19.9 Training at the Naval Gunnery School, March 1941. (*Imperial War Museum*)

ancient hulks had a long and venerable (if not always hygenic and suitable) tradition, but it was not until the middle of the last century that the Admiralty began to take its lower-deck education and training seriously. In 1857 Dr Wooley, one of Her Majesty's Inspectors of Schools, was invited to report upon the training hulks *Impregnable* and *Cambridge* at Plymouth (Fig. 19.8). He found that there were no general regulations controlling the nature of education and training, and that the formation of the syllabus was more or less at the discretion of the Commanding Officer. Moreover, he found that many of the newly-recruited boys in *Impregnable* had arrived with no competent knowledge of reading and writing, and made little progress in those subjects thereafter.[40]

The Newcastle Commission, set up in 1858 to '. . . inquire into the present state of Popular Education in England . . .',[41] investigated both civilian and military education, and as part of its evidence adopted the Wooley report. The Commission published its findings in 1861 and was especially critical of the training hulks or 'Harbour ship schools' as it called them:

> The educational arrangements for the Navy present a marked difference to those in force for the Army. The organisation is inferior, and the Admiralty does not appear to take an equal interest with the War Office in promoting it. The necessity of education for the Navy is acknowledged, but little earnestness is displayed in carrying it out.[42]

Such forthright criticism stung the Admiralty into action, its Order in Council dated 26 April 1862 admitting that the education of boys and seamen in the Royal Navy had not '. . . advanced in proportion to that given in schools generally under Government inspection or that of Your Majesty's land forces'.[43]

For civilian schools, the Newcastle Commission had proposed the development of the pupil–teacher system (as per Kay-Shuttleworth's scheme of 1846), and the Admiralty latched on to this, supplementing its existing pool of teachers by selecting pupil teachers. In the aftermath of the 1870 Education Act it was decided in 1875 that pupil–teachers, selected between the ages of 15 and 16 would receive six year's training before being rated 'Naval Schoolmaster' and gaining the certificate of the Education Department. Their training was broad, including such subjects as reading, writing, mathematics, geography, history, music, school management and teaching.

By 1883 most of the deficiencies exposed by Newcastle had been rectified, and by 1884 there were five clearly established and co-ordinated establishments (training hulks) for new entry boy seamen: *Impregnable* (the hulk that had drawn Wooley's criticism in 1857) and *Lion* at Devonport, along with *Ganges* at Falmouth, *Boscawen* at Portland and *St Vincent* at Portsmouth. In total, there were some 3,125 boys under training, who had entered as 2nd Class Boys at age 15–16½ and were rated 1st Class at age 16 (and on passing an examination) and Ordinary Seaman (2nd Class) at 18. They studied reading, writing, arithmetic, geography and religious knowledge, along with their naval subjects. *Impregnable* became a celebrated part of the Plymouth scene (and home of the curious expression 'nozzer', an alternative to the more familiar 'sprog' to describe a new entry rating), its three constituent hulks moored conspicuously in the Hamoaze, and its training in 1911 said to consist of seamanship, wireless training, gunnery, mechanical training, navigation and gymnastics, in addition to the academic studies.[44]

Cambridge, the other Devonport training establishment criticised by Wooley, also flourished as a result of the response to the Newcastle criticism. In 1857 she had been at Plymouth for little under a year, moored on the south side of the harbour and consisting of the hulks *Windsor Castle* and *Calcutta*. *Cambridge* served for many years as a Diving School, but it was her role as Gunnery School which brought her fame and recognition as a centre of training excellence. In the aftermath of Newcastle, standards rose steadily, surviving students' notebooks from the era revealing an enormous attention to detail in the taking of notes and drawing of diagrams. Instructions and explanations in those notebooks have a certain engaging charm, as the *Gunner's Instructions* of 1866–67 reveal:

> Article 4. He is to examine very carefully into the state of the magazine, that he may be certain of its being properly fitted and properly dry before the powder is received on board, but if he should

find in it, any appearance of dampness: he is to report it immediately to the Captain, that it may be properly dried, this may be ascertained by placing in the magazine a piece of sponge, which has been dipped in a solution of salt and water, and afterwards dried; should it become heavier if the magazine is damp.[45]

Examination questions at *Cambridge* in the late 1860s included such as 'From what guns may red hot shot be fired?', and 'What projectile do the howitzers throw?',[46] but the steady pace of technological advance ensured that the *Cambridge* courses became increasingly complex. By 1897 up to 300 Boy Seamen came on board *Cambridge* each day for drills from the training hulks *Lion* and *Impregnable*, the function of the establishment being then described as:

> . . . the training of officers and seamen in the theory and practice of gunnery, and in small arms and cutlass exercises, the handling of muzzle and breech loading guns of every kind in use, the ammunition in use in the Service, rifle, cutlass, and pistol exercise, field and machinegun and infantry battalion drills.[47]

Cambridge has survived into the modern Navy as 'Gunnery School' (Fig. 19.9), though since 1940 it has been situated ashore at Wembury in the site of a one-time holiday camp (the establishment at Wembury was officially commissioned as HMS *Cambridge* in 1956).[48] The movement ashore followed the general pattern of abandoning training afloat in hulks, although a measure of the tenacity and longevity of this old (if not always satisfactory) tradition was the survival at Devonport into the post-1945 era of the two dreadnought battleships which together comprised HMS *Imperieuse* – the 'Stokers' Training Establishment', as it was known. Here, a twelve-week course prepared Junior Ratings for their tasks at sea as 'stokers' in the engine rooms of Royal Navy warships.[49] Likewise, a contemporary of the old *Cambridge* was HMS *Defiance*, another of the well-known Tamar hulks, situated, as the *Navy and Army Illustrated* explained in August 1897, at '. . . the entrance to the St German's River, just below Saltash suspension bridge . . . with the smaller hulks *Perseus* and *Flamingo* ahead of her . . .'.[50] Like *Cambridge*, *Defiance* became a seemingly timeless and permanent part of the local environment (the Great Western even named a railway halt after it) and, like the Gunnery School, was a specialist training establishment, teaching signalling and giving instruction in the theory and practice of torpedoes, for which purpose she had allocated 'tenders' (a gunboat, torpedo boats, and a destroyer) which carried out exercises in Whitsand Bay. Today, however, again like *Cambridge*, HMS *Defiance* is a modern establishment ashore (in Devonport Dockyard), though her task is now that of a fleet maintenance base.

The Dockyard School

Part of the Admiralty's response to the need for technical education, and indeed predating the Newcastle criticisms but contemporary with the emergence of the 'schools of design', was the foundation of the Royal Dockyard Schools in the principal naval towns. Devonport Dockyard School was opened in 1843, its purpose being to provide an education for dockyard apprentices (civilians), men who would be employed subsequently as draughtsmen and '. . . subordinate dockyard officers . . .', together with shipwrights, fitters, boilermakers, coppersmiths, patternmakers and the like.[51] Over the years the syllabus expanded gradually to encompass such things as mathematics, engineering drawing, physics, metallurgy, electrics and naval architecture. From the beginning there were close links with the training of uniformed personnel. Many dockyard apprentices went on to become naval artificers or engineer officers, others joining the Corps of Naval Constructors, and the Dockyard School itself on occasions undertook the instruction of naval personnel. As early as 1868, for example, a limited number of boys (sons of Royal Marines) who had been attending the Marines' 'Divisional School' at Plymouth were given the opportunity to enter as dockyard apprentices on the understanding that they would subsequently enlist for limited service in the Artificer Companies of the Royal Marines.[52] Later, in the 1880s, the Dockyard School undertook the instruction of Keyham students.

The Dockyard School acquired an enviable reputation, being described in 1916 as '. . . entirely British in origin, and its character is in keeping with the present democratic age'.[53] Following the complete removal of the Royal Naval Engineering College to Manadon, the Dockyard School moved into the old Keyham buildings (which were demolished finally in 1985), its name by now having been updated to Dockyard Technical College, and retained its independent existence until 1971, when it was merged into the newly-formed College of Further Education.

Philip Payton

Marine Training

The Royal Marines trace their ancestry back to the formation of the Duke of York and Albany's Maritime Regiment of Foot in 1664, raised specifically for service at sea during the Second Dutch War. From their beginnings, the Marines were associated with Devon, frequently being quartered in Plymouth during the Dutch Wars and with garrisons established from time to time at Plympton, Stonehouse, Ridgeway and Exeter, as well as across the Tamar at Cawsand, Millbrook and Saltash in Cornwall. There were certainly many Devon Marines involved in the seige and capture of Gibraltar in 1704/5, the only battle honours carried on today's Royal Marines Colours, representing all subsequent achievements.[54]

In 1755 the permanent Marine Corps was established, with a total of 5,000 men in the three Grand Divisions of Chatham, Portsmouth and Plymouth. Initially, the Plymouth Marines were billetted around the Barbican, using the Hoe as their parade ground, moving subsequently to Devonport (where they were used to police the dockyard, before their release to fight in the American wars) and finally in December 1783 to their new, purpose-built barracks at Stonehouse (Fig. 19.10). From 1802 the Marines Corps was officially styled 'Royal Marines', and two years later Royal Marines Artillery companies were formed, one of which was stationed in Plymouth. Within Plymouth, the introduction of the celebrated Lee Enfield rifle during the Crimean War of 1854 meant that the musketry range in the Citadel was unsuitable, so that the Mount Batten range on the eastern side of Plymouth Sound was employed instead. It was also at this time that the training potential of Dartmoor was first appreciated, with its challenging terrain and arduous conditions so conveniently close to Plymouth. By the middle of the nineteenth century, therefore, Plymouth had emerged as an important centre for both the garrisoning and training of Royal Marines, reflecting of course the port's long-established role as a major naval base.

At the same time the Plymouth Division provided detachments of Marines to complement HM Ships at Devonport, taking part in campaigns as far distant as the Maori Wars of 1845, the Crimean War, the Indian Mutiny of 1857 and the later China Wars. It was in the Crimea that Corporal John Prettyjohn, from Dean Prior, Buckfastleigh, won (at Balaclava on 2 November 1854) the first Victoria Cross awarded to a Royal Marine. A further aspect of Royal Marines activity was the creation of their band service. In 1766 the Plymouth Division had conceived the idea of a 'Band of Musick', heralding the formation of the Royal Marines Bands which served to provide ceremonial music for the Royal Navy, and anticipating the establishment in 1903 of the Royal Naval School of Music (in Portsmouth). The Plymouth Band developed as an integral part of Devon life, performing concerts within the City and beyond in addition to its military functions, and amongst a string of celebrated Plymouth Divisional Directors of Music was Major F H Ricketts (1930–44), who composed such famous marches as 'Colonel Bogey', 'The Standard of St George', and 'HM Jollies'.

In the First World War a Plymouth Battalion formed part of the Royal Marine Brigade which saw service ashore at Ostend, Dunkirk and Antwerp, and later as part of the Royal Naval Division at Gallipoli and on the Western Front. Meanwhile, Marine detachments from Plymouth saw action in all the theatres of the naval war, from the Falkland Islands to Jutland, and a Plymouth Company distinguished itself in the heroic if futile raid on Zeebrugge on St George's Day 1918. After the war, Marine detachments continued to serve afloat in their traditional manner, but a new role was developed and formalised: that of 'Combined Operations'. This role proved to be of vital importance in the Second World War, and it is significant that much of its attendant development and training occurred within Devon. Vast stretches of the Devon coastline, such as the infamous Slapton Sands in the south and Braunton Sands and Appledore in the north, were well suited for the rehearsal of amphibious landings. Barnstaple Bay and the Taw estuary, in particular, afforded secluded venues for the trials of newly-developed landing craft, locations unlikely to be molested by enemy action.

Pressure on training facilities in the southeast of England also encouraged the Royal Marines to expand their sphere of activities further within Devon. As early as 1938, Exton, between Exeter and Exmouth, was earmarked as a possible major training camp, a competing site at Tankerton on the north Kent coast having been discounted because of its lack of suitable adjoining training areas of the calibre of Dartmoor.[55] By August 1939 the Admiralty had given the order for work to start at Exton, on a site on the Nutwell Court Estate, close to the Exe estuary.[56] The proximity to the river gave scope for amphibious training, and the site had good road and rail communications. Dubbed the Royal Marines Reserve Depot, the Exton camp was intended to accommodate the Royal Marines Specialist Reservists. Designed originally to hold 900 officers and men, Exton received its first intake of 320 Marines on 22 February 1940. With the implementation of the National Service (Conscription) Act 1940, the tempo increased and Hostilities Only squads (forty strong) began to join Exton twice weekly. In its first year until December 1940 approximately 4,000 Royal Marines had passed through Exton. In 1941 the figure rose to about 7,400, increasing to some 8,600 in 1942, and in the eleven months to November 1943 it climbed to 11,500. In all, it was estimated that by March 1944 51,500 recruits had trained at Exton, while training elsewhere in the Corps had accounted for only 7,900 Royal Marines and 750 Bandsmen. Devon had become the principal home of Royal Marine training.

Indeed, the outbreak of hostilities had led to the creation of a plethora of

19.10   The Royal Marine Barracks, Stonehouse, in the late nineteenth century. (*F Frith*)

19.11   Street fighting drills at Dalditch Camp during the Second World War. (*RMCTC, Lympstone*)

Royal Marine camps across Devon – Plasterdown Camp (near Tavistock), Hartford Bridge, Blerrick (just across the border in Cornwall), South Brent, Stoke Gabriel, Thurlestone (which became for a time the Royal Marines Military School and Officer Cadet Training Unit) and Teignmouth, where the Royal Marines Boom Patrol Detachment (forerunners of the Special Boats Section) set up their headquarters in the Courtney Hotel. On the River Dart, further arrangements were made for the training of Royal Marines landing craft flotillas.

Of particular importance was the camp that sprang up at Dalditch, on common land near East Budleigh. Designed to accommodate 5,000 officers and men in its five constituent sub-areas – 'Frying Pans', 'Triangle', 'Wheathill', 'Hayes' and 'Tuckers' – Dalditch had 648 Marines under canvas by the end of May 1941. In due course more permanent accommodation was offered in the form 378 semi-circular corrugated Nissen huts (along with an additional 107 for offices, stores and other facilities), with Dalditch developing its principal role as an infantry training centre (which recruits joined after their initial training at Exton), and also serving when required as temporary accommodation for Royal Marines brigades and battalions (Fig. 19.11). At times the camp hosted Army regiments, as in May 1942, when 268 men of the North Irish Horse arrived complete with tanks, and as the war years passed so Dalditch's activities diversified still further. Royal Marine Engineers were trained in the camp, and in the preparations for D-Day the camp was used for forming up several Royal Marines battalions destined for the Normandy invasion. Amongst the camp's many and varied inmates, the 88 Marines on the camp staff were, it is interesting to note, liberated and repatriated Prisoners-of-War from Stalag VIIIB. This was a reminder that many Devon Marines had seen service in the war, including those lost in *Prince of Wales* and *Repulse* in 1941, and their survivors, who teamed up with the depleted Argyll & Sutherland Highlanders in Singapore to form the 'Plymouth Argylls'.

The end of the war, however, brought this frenetic activity to a close. By September 1945 the barbed-wire surrounds at Dalditch had already been removed, and in December 1946 the regimental journal *Globe and Laurel* announced dramatically that 'Dalditch camp is no more!'. Most of the other temporary camps in Devon were abandoned at about this time, the notable exception being Exton, which survived in a new incarnation as 'Lympstone', becoming the Commando Training Centre and specialising in the training of new-entry Royal Marines Officers and men – the role that it performs today. The demise of the temporary camps was offset, however, by the opening in April 1946 of the Royal Marines Infantry School, Bickleigh, which re-emphasised the continuing importance of Devon to the Corps.

Situated near Roborough, to the north of Plymouth, Bickleigh was close to Dartmoor, and an added advantage was that an embryonic camp existed already in the form of an establishment used variously during the war to house Free French and Polish servicemen, the Canadian Fire Fighting Service and the Civil Defence.

On 1 April 1946 an Infantry Training Cadre was set up at Bickleigh as part of the Royal Marines Training Group (Devon), soon developing as a full Infantry Training School with, for example, a Commando School and a Cliff Assault Wing (based at St Ives in Cornwall). In 1950 Bickleigh was redesignated the Commando School Royal Marines, which it remained until 1960, when the function was concentrated at Lympstone, but it was also involved in operational activity on occasions. During the Korean War, when the Government decided to deploy a small specialist Marine force, 41 (Independent) Commando Royal Marines was formed at Bickleigh, and in 1954 42 Commando was based at Bickleigh as an operational nucleus before becoming the first Commando unit to embark in a Commando Carrier, HMS *Bulwark*, in March 1960. The decision to move the Commando School to the redeveloped Lympstone in 1960 allowed Bickleigh to become the home for the newly-reactivated 41 Commando, which was replaced in turn by 42 Commando in 1971, the unit that still occupies the camp today. Bickleigh has thus remained of vital operational importance to the Royal Marines, not least during the Falklands conflict in 1982, when the camp saw the departure of its occupants for the South Atlantic.

Against the background of this intense activity, with the rise of Exton (later Lympstone) and Bickleigh and the bewildering spread of temporary wartime facilities, the Stonehouse Barracks in Plymouth have continued

19.12   Obstacle training at RMCTC Lympstone in the 1980s. (*RMCTC, Lympstone*)

throughout to house various Royal Marines formations. It has acted, too, as the focus of the Corps in the Plymouth area, and is presently the home of the staff of Headquarters 3 Commando Brigade. The staff of the Major General Royal Marines, Commando Forces is close by in Hamoaze House. Seaton Barracks at Crownhill and Coypool have also been occupied by various Royal Marines units since 3 Commando Brigade withdrew from the Far East in 1970. Indeed, the close proximity of all of these facilities to Devonport Dockyard and to the various naval establishments in the Plymouth area has ensured the closest co-operation and integration between Royal Marines and Royal Navy in the realms of amphibious warfare, with Devon as their stage. Although the Royal Marines are also active elsewhere in Britain, for example at Eastney near Portsmouth, at Taunton, and at Arbroath in Scotland, Devon remains their principal home.

Derek Oakley

Devon in the 1990s

The training developments that have been described reflect both the evolving needs of the Navy and advances in civilian education (and particularly technical and scientific education) at both elementary and higher levels. Although a considerable proportion of naval education and training came to be focussed upon Portsmouth, Chatham, and later Rosyth (together

with other locations such as Greenwich), Devon achieved an early prominence, particularly in the realms of officer education and training. Dartmouth, Keyham and Manadon afforded Devon a special status within the field of naval education and training, a position that still obtains today despite the plans to close the Royal Naval Engineering College, Manadon. Although specialist rating training has become increasingly concentrated in the Portsmouth area (most notably at *Sultan* and *Collingwood*), a wide range of rating training is nonetheless centred upon HMS *Raleigh*, on the Cornish side of the Tamar. *Cambridge* continues its role as Gunnery School, and elsewhere in the Plymouth area are significant elements of naval education and training, soon to be augmented in the late 1990s when the Flag Officer Sea Training staff move their 'work-up' operation from Portland to Devonport. For officers and men of the Royal Marines commando training is centred at Lympstone on the Exe Estuary (Fig. 19.12).

The Devon of the 1990s is set to remain, therefore, a principal focus of Royal Navy education and training. However, as in earlier times, the process of education and training will continue to be subject to ceaseless evolution and review, and – as ever – its development will continue to be determined by the requirements of the Fleet at sea and the pace of technological advance, but with increasing Treasury pressures upon the defence budget also affecting the difficult choices that have sometimes to be made.

19: Naval Education and Training in Devon

1 S J Curtis and M E A Boultwood, *An Introductory History of English Education Since 1800* (4th edn., 1966), 282.
2 I Morrish, *Education Since 1800* (1970), 93.
3 D R Jones, *The Origins of Civic Universities. Manchester, Liverpool and Leeds* (1988).
4 P W Musgrave, *Sociology, History and Education. A Reader* (1970), 143.
5 Morrish, *Education Since 1800*, 95; J Lawson and H Silver, *A Social History of Education in England* (1973), 346.
6 *Navy List* (1842), 157.
7 F G D Bedford, 'Life on Board The *Britannia*', *Boy's Own Paper*, (1890), 572; see also *Britannia Magazine*, (summer 1979), 37.
8 H L Hitchins, 'HMS *Britannia* in 1899', *Britannia Magazine*, Easter 1949, 42.
9 Bedford, 'Life on Britannia', 574.
10 Bedford, 'Life on Britannia', 572, 589, 590, 622.
11 *The Times*, 26 July 1867. See also E P Statham, *The Story of the Britannia. The Training Ship for Naval Cadets* (1904), 76.
12 NMM, LVG 3, letters from Osbert G Leverson-Gower, Joining Instructions, 1903–4.
13 NMM, LVG 3, letter, Leverson-Gower, 31 Jan. 1904.
14 Hitchins, '*Britannia* in 1899', 42.
15 Portsmouth Naval History Library, 254, Memorandum – Captain M P O'Callaghan, 28 Feb. 1901.
16 NMM, LVG 3, Leverson-Gower, letter, 25 June 1904.
17 *Navy and Army Illustrated*, VII, 3 Dec. 1898, 354.
18 Archibald S Hurd, 'Naval Engineers and their Training', *Windsor Magazine*, October 1897.
19 Quoted in Rupert Nichol, 'The Royal Naval Engineering College, Keyham, 1880–1960, Part 1 – The Nineteenth Century', *Journal of Naval Science*, VII, Jan. 1981, 18.
20 Nichol, 'Royal Naval Engineering College', 16–21. For general histories of the Royal Naval Engineering College, see Rupert Nichol and Alan York, *RNEC 1880–1980* (Plymouth, 1980); and Geoffrey Penn, *HMS Thunderer: The Story of the Royal Naval Engineering College, Keyham and Manadon* (Emsworth, 1984).
21 Penn, *Thunderer*, 27–8.
22 *Navy and Army Illustrated*, VII, 3 Dec. 1898, 253.
23 Penn, *Thunderer*, 46.
24 *Navy and Army Illustrated*, VI, 23 July 1898, 418.
25 *Page's Magazine*, 1904, 81.
26 E A Hughes, *The Royal Naval College, Dartmouth* (n.d., c.1950), 22.
27 F B Sullivan, 'The Origin and Development of Education in the Royal Navy From 1702 to 1902' (unpublished PhD thesis, University of Reading, 1975), 379.
28 *Hansard*, Vol. 122: 158, 160–2, 183.
29 Julian S Corbett, 'Lord Selbourne's Memorandum', *Monthly Review*, February–March 1903.
30 Hughes, *Royal Naval College*, 56. For general histories of the Britannia Royal Naval College, Dartmouth, see also S W C Pack, *Britannia at Dartmouth* (1966); and E L Davies and E J Grove, *Dartmouth* (Portsmouth, 1980).
31 Board of Education, *Report of an Inspection of the Royal Naval College, Osborne, and of the Royal Naval College, Dartmouth, May 1912* (1912).
32 A H R York, 'The Royal Naval Engineering College, Manadon: Part 2 – Into the Twentieth Century', *Journal of Naval Science*, VII, Jan. 1981, 23; Penn, *Thunderer*, 86.
33 *Question Papers of the Examination for Entrance to the Royal Naval College, Dartmouth, held in June 1952* (1952).
34 'The Training of Engineer and Air Engineer Officers', *British Machine Tool Engineering*, XXVII, Jan–June 1945, 45.
35 L Le Bailly, *The Man Around the Engine. Life below the Waterline* (Emsworth, 1990), 34.
36 For a general history of artificer training, with particular reference to HMS *Indus* and HMS *Fisgard*, see Philip Payton, *The Story of HMS Fisgard* (Redruth, 1983).
37 *Industrian*, summer 1918, quoted in Payton, *Fisgard*, 15–6.
38 *Industrian*, summer 1918.
39 Portsmouth Naval History Library, 750/85. Early days at HMS *Raleigh* – an account by Captain R Williamson-Jones, 1, 8–9.
40 Sullivan, 'Origin and Development of Education in the Royal Navy', 231.
41 Morrish, *Education since 1800*, 14.
42 *Newcastle Commission Report*, 1861, Vol. I, 415.
43 Sullivan, 'Origin and Development of Education in the Royal Navy', 240.
44 *Impregnable*, April 1912, 6.
45 Portsmouth Naval History Library, 431/83 6.9.3. Naval Gunnery as Taught on Board HMS *Cambridge*, 1866–67, 13.
46 Naval Gunnery as Taught on Board HMS *Cambridge*, 88–9.
47 *Navy and Army Illustrated*, III, 14 May 1897, 324.
48 HMS *Cambridge. Information Handbook*, (Worcester n.d.).
49 'The Technical Training of Stoker Ratings', *British Machine Tool Engineering*, XXVII, Jan.–June 1945, 7–16.
50 *Navy and Army Illustrated*, IV, 20 Aug. 1897, 210.
51 G A Baxendall, *The Admiralty Method of Training Dockyard Apprentices* (1916) 4; *Report of the Committee on Dockyard Schools* (1894), 1.
52 Royal Marines Archives, Eastney, DAGRM, Confidential Letter Book 1849–78, Circular of 16 Sept. 1868.
53 Baxendall, *Admiralty Method*, 10; Terry J Bickford, 'Royal Dockyard School', in Alston Kennerly, ed., *Notes on the History of Post-School Education in the 'Three Towns', 1825–1975* (Plymouth, 1976).
54 For a general history of the Royal Marines Corps, see J L Moulton, *The Royal Marines* (1972).
55 *Exmouth Journal*, 29 July 1939.
56 *Exmouth Journal*, 12 Aug. 1939.

20 *Devon and the Navy in the Second World War*

Ian Skinner

The outbreak of war in 1939 saw Devonport prepared to adopt a similar role to that which it had played in the First World War: as guardian of the Western Approaches and provider of repair and refit facilities in the naval dockyard. Within a year, however, Plymouth found itself also reverting to its original role as the main western base against an enemy directly across the Channel. The Germans occupied the French naval bases developed in the seventeenth and eighteenth centuries for a war against Britain, and the ethos behind the original strategic role envisaged for Plymouth, untested operationally since 1815, was put on trial in modern warfare.

Plymouth and the Defence of Atlantic Trade

Western Approaches Command, 1939-41

In 1939 the key to the security of the worldwide network of maritime trade upon which Great Britain was dependent lay in the defence of the South-West Approaches, through which some seventy ships of over 1,600 tons passed daily to and from British ports.[1] In 1917 the great volume of commercial traffic concentrated in this focal area had proved vulnerable to submarine attack, and in 1939 it came under renewed threat from the resurgent German U-Boat fleet. Responsibility for the defence of Atlantic trade against this menace rested with Western Approaches Command, established at Plymouth in 1938 under Admiral Sir Martin Dunbar-Nasmith, KCB,VC.

The strategic location of Plymouth at the entrance to the English Channel, combined with the operational facilities at Devonport and the Mount Batten flying-boat base, made it a natural site for Western Approaches Command Headquarters. Its importance had been accentuated in 1938, when Britain relinquished the naval base at Berehaven as a political gesture of goodwill to Eire, despite protests at the loss of facilities for warships operating in the Approaches.

Western Approaches Command prepared to counter the submarine threat with the convoy system that had proved the undoing of the U-Boat campaign in 1917 and which, with the added benefit of Asdic, was confidently expected to defeat any similar offensive in 1939.[2] These plans were implemented when the Admiralty construed the sinking of the liner *Athenia* to herald the onset of unrestricted submarine warfare, and convoys began sailing on 7 September 1939. The organisation of convoys in overseas ports took longer to arrange, however, and in the meantime the Approaches were full of independent shipping arriving from abroad. Western Approaches Command broadcast daily dawn rendezvous for British ships entering the Approaches, and patrolled the designated 'controlled routes' with destroyers and aircraft to afford some protection against the U-Boats preying on this vulnerable traffic.[3]

Most of the early casualties were stopped in daylight by a U-Boat surfacing nearby and were then sunk by gunfire or torpedo. Few merchantmen could outrun a surfaced U-Boat, and their best hope lay in an aircraft responding swiftly to their distress signal. The demands upon Coastal Command's limited resources meant, however, that 15 Group at Plymouth had only two squadrons of Sunderlands with the range to reach the principal U-Boat hunting grounds. To supplement these meagre forces and extend aerial cover further into the Approaches, two aircraft carriers, *Courageous* and *Hermes*, were assigned to Devonport.[4]

The few aircraft that could be maintained on patrol over the broad expanses of the outer Approaches could offer only limited returns for the risk to which their parent ships were exposed. Lacking the weapons to inflict fatal damage on U-Boats, the most they could achieve was to force submarines in their vicinity to remain submerged. The risks were also compounded by the practice of sending destroyers from the escort screen to hunt reported U-Boats. On 17 September 1939, only two of *Courageous*' four escorts were present when she was sunk by the U-29

20.1 Warships at the Keyham Extension, Devonport, 3 October 1939. The battleship *Warspite* and the cruiser *Effingham* are in No.5 Basin, with the aircraft carrier *Hermes* and two destroyers moored outside. Photographic reconnaissance practice is under way with the start of a smokescreen to cover the Dockyard. (*Devonport Dockyard Museum*)

20.2 HMS *Courageous* sinking after being torpedoed by U-29, 17 September 1939. (*Imperial War Museum*)

(Fig. 20.2). *Hermes* was immediately withdrawn from such operations.

The first month of the war saw a rapid influx of warships into Plymouth from other areas as Western Approaches Command was reinforced to meet patrol and escort commitments. Its twenty-one destroyers on strength at the outbreak of war had increased to fifty-seven by 27 September 1939.[5] By October the convoy system was in full swing, and the demand for escorts continued to grow. Shortages led to some faster shipping being sailed in unescorted groups, but this policy was abandoned after U-Boats intercepted two such groups and sank five ships.[6] More escorts were withdrawn from the Mediterranean, and the French took over escort work on the Gibraltar route.

The convoy system cut losses considerably by reducing the flow of vulnerable independent shipping through the Approaches. Nevertheless, the U-Boats continued to exact a toll amongst ships that did not come within the parameters of the system, convoy stragglers and shipping sailing beyond the point where escorts dispersed their outward-bound charges before meeting an incoming convoy. This point was gradually moved westwards as far as 15° West, but the U-Boats followed into the outer extremities of the Approaches. Deprived of facilities at Berehaven, escorts had to waste precious time and fuel in transit between Plymouth and the principal U-Boat hunting grounds, more than 250 miles away. Unfortunately, the strain upon the escorts was exacerbated by Western Approaches Command's efforts to deploy destroyers in independent strike forces to hunt down reported U-Boats, despite the failure of such 'offensive' tactics in the First World War. A submarine was unlikely to linger at the scene of an attack until a hunting group could arrive, and the chances of locating a target in the open ocean were remote.

The reluctance to adhere to 'defensive' convoy work ignored the basic precept that U-Boats had to attack the convoys to cause significant disruption to British trade, and in so doing expose themselves to counterattacks by escorts. In 1939, 3,532 ships sailed in 201 ocean convoys, and only four were sunk whilst under the protection of their naval escorts.[7] In the same period, nearly 120 vessels that had sailed independently or in unescorted groups succumbed to U-Boat attacks. Whilst hunting groups accounted for three U-Boats during this period, nine were sunk by convoy escorts.[8] The effort devoted to the 'offensive' strategy would have been better directed towards extending the convoy system to encompass shipping that continued to run the gauntlet of the Approaches without the benefit of naval escort.

In March 1940 all U-Boats were withdrawn from the Atlantic to take part in the invasion of Norway, and Western Approaches Command enjoyed a respite from U-Boat attacks until mid-May 1940. However, the demands of the Norwegian campaign also reduced the trade protection forces, so that by that time some convoys in the South-West Approaches were sailing without escorts. Any hopes that the Command would soon be restored to its former strength were dispelled by the heavy losses incurred off Norway and the Allied collapse in France. Troop evacuations took precedence over the defence of trade, and British and French destroyers were withdrawn in large numbers to take part in the Dunkirk evacuations.

No sooner had these operations been completed than Admiral Dunbar-Nasmith had to commit his forces to Operation Aerial, the withdrawal from the Biscay ports. The use of ocean liners relieved the pressure on destroyers as makeshift troop transports, but it enhanced their role as escorts to evacuation traffic in potentially dangerous waters. In the event the anticipated U-Boat intervention failed to materialise, but the threat of their presence contributed to the loss of the liner *Lancastria*, which was bombed whilst waiting in the Loire estuary for a convoy to Plymouth. Over 3,000 lives were lost.[9]

The evacuations deprived Western Approaches Command of some of its most experienced escorts just as the U-Boats resumed their Atlantic offensive. The shortage of escorts not only resulted in more independent shipping sailing the Approaches, but also encouraged U-Boats to attack weakly-escorted convoys. The situation was exacerbated by Western Aproaches Command's continued adherence to the outmoded strike force concept. Although most convoys were escorted by just one corvette, the few available destroyers were deployed in hunting groups which achieved nothing. Whilst U-Boats were able to develop their tactics and skills, the lone convoy escorts and destroyer hunting groups gained little experience in the teamwork so essential to convoy defence.

The Allied defeat in France thrust Devon into the front line of the naval war and transformed the role played by Plymouth. On 4 July 1940 convoy OA178 was badly mauled by Luftwaffe dive bombers near Portland, and four days later the Admiralty conceded that German air power would make the South-West Approaches untenable to merchant traffic by diverting all Atlantic shipping north of Ireland. Western Approaches Command escort forces were withdrawn north, although operations staff initially remained at the established Plymouth headquarters to avoid a disruptive transfer at this critical juncture in the war, with invasion imminent and shipping losses escalating. This delay was only temporary, as staff needed to be in closer contact with their forces, and on 18 February 1941 Western Approaches Command moved into new headquarters at Liverpool.

By this stage, the South West had acquired a new role in the defence of Atlantic trade as the Germans developed French bases such as Brest, Lorient and St Nazaire for surface vessels and U-Boats engaged in commerce raiding in the Atlantic. New boundaries were drawn to create Plymouth Command as a separate entity, with 19 Group Coastal Command providing maritime air support, and responsibility for operations against the German transit routes in the Bay of Biscay immediately devolved upon the new Command.

Plymouth Command and the Surface Raider Threat

Before the summer of 1940 the German surface effort against Atlantic commerce had been limited by the restricted access to and egress from North Sea bases. The acquisition of the French Atlantic coast then transformed the strategic situation and enabled the Germans to employ more of their surface fleet as Atlantic commerce raiders. This manifested itself on 27 December

20.3 A Sunderland flying boat of 10 Squadron RAAF taking off from RAF Mount Batten. (*Imperial War Museum*)

1940, when the cruiser *Admiral Hipper* arrived at Brest after a cruise which included a brief skirmish with the escorts of a troop convoy.

The task of observing and containing German raiders on the Biscay coast was frustrated by German defences, the vagaries of the weather and the limited reconnaissance forces available in the South West. Scant intelligence on raider movements in the Atlantic meant that there was little prospect of intercepting raiders before they reached the coast and, although the RAF maintained a daily watch on their activity in port, the Germans enjoyed the advantage of initiative in sending their warships to sea. Patrols failed to locate *Hipper* when she sank eight ships in a brief foray in February 1941 and set off for Germany on 16 March 1941.

The arrival of the battlecruisers *Scharnhorst* and *Gneisenau* a few days later acted as a stimulus to naval operations from Plymouth. Specialist minelayers and minelaying destroyers attempted to pen the battlecruisers in Brest, and the Fifth Destroyer Flotilla also patrolled off the port before being transferred to the Mediterranean in April 1941.

Whilst the battlecruisers remained operational they posed a major threat to Atlantic trade, but their relative proximity to British bases also exposed them to intensive air attack. Both Bomber Command and Coastal Command maintained a major bombing and mining offensive against Brest, and on 6 April 1941 Fg Off K. Campbell of 22 Squadron from St Eval won a posthumous Victoria Cross for torpedoing *Gneisenau* in Brest harbour. Damage to the battlecruisers consistently prevented them operating in the Atlantic, and this factor weighed heavily in Hitler's decision to withdraw them through the Channel in February 1942. The German squadron was fortunate in evading detection by the waiting submarine and air patrols off Brest, and had escaped Plymouth Command waters before the alarm was raised.

The usefulness of French bases to German surface raiders was reduced if they could be denied the necessary repair facilities. The only dry dock on the French Atlantic coast capable of accommodating the powerful battleship *Tirpitz* was the dock at St Nazaire designed for the liner *Normandie*. On 28 March 1942 a force assembled and trained at Falmouth under the auspices of Plymouth Command raided St Nazaire. The old destroyer *Campbeltown*, prepared in Devonport Dockyard, was rammed into the dock gates, which were completely destroyed when explosives hidden in the vessel blew up later that day.

The Anti-submarine Offensive in the Bay of Biscay

Whilst the surface raider threat proved to be a passing phenomenon, the U-Boat menace emanating from Biscay bases was more critical. The regular flow of U-Boats traversing the Bay of Biscay between their bases and the Atlantic convoy routes represented a vital target for the naval and air forces controlled by Plymouth ACHQ. A submerged U-Boat could make only slow progress in 24 hours, and had to surface for about five hours in that time to recharge its batteries. If the requisite distance was covered by aircraft, a U-Boat would have to expose itself to attack. Even by forcing the U-Boats to cross the Bay submerged, and so waste valuable time and fuel in transit, an aerial campaign could make a valid contribution to the defence of Atlantic trade, and 19 Group began a limited offensive with the few available aircraft in April 1941.

Despite some initial promise, the offensive began to wane because U-Boats exploited the lack of an effective airborne searchlight or flare to make good progress on the surface at night and then remain submerged by day. Without long-range aircraft, 19 Group could also do nothing to prevent U-Boats travelling on the surface beyond 12° West.

The Navy contributed to the offensive at the beginning of 1942, when *Manxman* and *Welshman* operated from Plymouth and Milford Haven to lay minefields on the 100-fathom line in the Bay. Although no U-Boats were sunk by these fields, they placed considerable strain on the German minesweeping services and encouraged U-Boats to remain surfaced inside this line, reducing the mine risk but increasing the chances of aerial detection.

In June 1942 the balance swung back in favour of 19 Group when 172 Squadron from Chivenor, in Devon, began operating with Wellington bombers equipped with Leigh Lights, powerful searchlights which could illuminate a radar contact during the attack approach. More powerful depth charges also gave aircraft a real chance of inflicting decisive damage on U-Boats. Faced with the prospect of being surprised on the surface at night, most U-Boats reverted to surfacing by day, when lookouts could give advanced warning of an impending attack. Sightings in the Bay soared (Fig. 20.4), and reinforcements were sent from Bomber to Coastal Command to maintain the impetus during the fine summer weather. The Biscay offensive was a major bone of contention between the two RAF Commands, as both needed heavy bomber squadrons for their respective tasks. The loan was a compromise which enabled 19 Group to maintain a small scale of penetration into the Outer Bay, although Bomber Command crews were not trained in maritime warfare.

The number of aerial combats over the Bay mounted in 1942 as the Germans transferred long-range fighters from other fronts to operate against the antisubmarine patrols and 19 Group responded with its own fighter patrols. By the autumn the Germans had produced search receivers capable of picking up radar transmissions from searching aircraft, and U-Boats reverted to surfacing by night. Between October 1942 and January 1943 inclusive, an average of only one sighting was achieved for every 385hr airborne over the Bay.[10]

The introduction of a new type of radar and the release of more long-range aircraft from the Atlantic gave 19 Group the initiative once more in the spring of 1943. In the last ten days of March the ratio of sightings to hours airborne improved to 1 in 60.[11] In April, U-Boats were equipped with heavy anti-aircraft armament and remained surfaced to fight back against attacking aircraft. Aircraft casualties increased, but U-Boats made poor gun platforms and their defences were countered with increased aircraft firepower.

In June the Germans adopted group sailings as a means of passing their U-Boats through the Bay. Group transits made U-Boats more difficult to locate, improved their lookout capability, gave them denser concentrations of firepower and made fighter protection easier. These tactics were thwarted by the transfer of surface hunting groups from the Atlantic to Plymouth to operate in the Bay. American aerial reinforcements began arriving in the South West, where the airfields were crammed to capacity, and the Biscay offensive reached its peak. Once located, U-Boats either dived, in which case they were attacked by the assembling aircraft, or held them off with their guns, only to be faced by warships summoned to the scene. Sixteen U-Boats were sunk in the Bay between 2 July and 2 August 1943.[12]

In August U-Boats began squeezing along the Spanish coast to confuse their radar returns with echoes from fishing boats and the mainland. The naval hunting groups had to be withdrawn westwards after the Luftwaffe had sunk HMS *Egret* and damaged HMCS *Athabaskan* with glider bombs. U-Boat activity also decreased as the Germans gathered their strength to meet the expected invasion of Europe. Nevertheless, the offensive continued, preparing 19 Group for the forthcoming anti-submarine effort in support of the invasion, persistently hounding the U-Boats in the Bay and instilling in their crews a morale-sapping dread of aerial attack.

Plymouth Command and the Defence of Coastal Waters and Trade

The Threat of Invasion, 1940

By the time Plymouth Command was created in 1941, the South West was already embroiled in a local conflict with the German forces across the Western Channel, the opening exchanges of which arose out of the threat of invasion in the autumn of 1940.

Plymouth was strategically situated within striking distance of the probable landing beaches in the eastern Channel, and commanded the approaches to southern Eire. Had the Germans seized Ireland, the Atlantic convoy routes would certainly have been severed, whilst the commitment of British troops to a campaign in Eire would have depleted the defences on the Channel coast. Naval forces at Devonport thus became an important factor in forestalling German ambitions in that direction, and also operated along the French coast to hinder the German build-up of barges and landing craft in the Channel. These offensive operations culminated in Operation Medium on 10 October 1940, when the battleship *Revenge* and the Fifth Destroyer Flotilla bombarded the port of Cherbourg.[13]

The big operations headquarters, dockyard and deep-water anchorage, and the greater distance from German airfields compared with other anti-invasion bases, meant that Plymouth was the only Channel port to receive cruiser and battleship reinforcements. Nevertheless, the threat of air attack caused considerable concern, as few anti-aircraft guns could be spared to supplement the existing defences, whose weakness reflected Plymouth's previous immunity to air attack. Great Britain's air defence system had been outflanked and, although 10 Group, Fighter Command, was created in July 1940 to extend fighter cover to the South West, the area remained weakly defended compared with the South East. The fighter defences of Plymouth initially included Gladiator biplanes. In the event, however, the crucial aerial battles were fought further east and only minor raids were mounted against the warships at Devonport.

The German Fifth Destroyer Flotilla moved to Brest in September 1940 to mine and cover the approaches to the western flank of the projected invasion, but the indefinite postponement of Operation Sealion released them for offensive operations against British trade. The threat posed by these destroyers to Atlantic shipping was countered by the creation of Force F at Plymouth, comprising the cruisers *Newcastle* and *Emerald* and the modern destroyers of Lord Louis Mountbatten's Fifth Flotilla. On 17 October 1940 the German destroyers endeavoured to attack shipping in the Western Approaches but were intercepted by Force F and forced into headlong retreat (Fig. 20.5). German destroyers would always run the risk of being located and cut off from France by forces from Plymouth if they strayed too far into the South West Approaches, and the Germans never repeated the attempt.

Minelaying and gun sweeps under cover of darkness in the Channel proved more effective employment for the German destroyers in the winter of 1940, despite patrols from Plymouth by Mountbatten's destroyers to counter their raids. On 28 November 1940 the German destroyers sank a tug and a barge off Start Point before being intercepted by the Fifth Destroyer Flotilla. In a brief engagement, German torpedoes blew the bow and stern off *Javelin*, leaving the centre section to be towed back to Plymouth to undergo a thirteen-month reconstruction (Fig. 20.6). At this stage in the war, however, targets were scarce in the western Channel and the German destroyers also suffered from constant mechanical trouble, so that their operations never amounted to a sustained offensive. Their numbers gradually decreased as they were withdrawn to Germany for refits, and the last destroyer left the western Channel in March 1941.[14]

Defence of Coastal Trade against Air Attack

Once the opportunity for invasion had been lost in the autumn of 1940, the Germans prepared for a more prolonged struggle against Britain. By the spring of 1941 many Luftwaffe bomber squadrons were ready to join the offensive maintained by the U-Boats and KG40, a specialist anti-shipping bomber unit. The Luftwaffe also turned its attention on the western ports as the Germans sought to impose an aerial blockade on maritime trade, and Plymouth was devastated by a series of heavy raids between 20 March and 29 April 1941 (Figs. 21.8, 9).

Coastal shipping played a vital role in the Devon and wider southern economy by bringing in essential supplies of coal, so relieving the pressure on the overland transport systems. Whilst some supplies could be shuttled across the Bristol Channel from Wales, the capacity of the northern ports and the difficulty in transporting goods overland to the big towns on the south coast restricted this method of supply. Shipping therefore sailed from Wales to the south coast ports, giving the Germans ample opportunity to attack and dislocate this link in the supply and distribution network.

In March 1941 an unprecedented scale of attack was unleashed on shipping in West Country waters, carried out by bombers flying singly or

20.4 U-71 being attacked by a Sunderland of 10 Squadron RAAF in the Bay of Biscay on 5 June 1942. (*Imperial War Museum*)

in pairs mainly at dawn or dusk. Most attacks were concentrated in the Bristol and St George's Channels and their approaches. Patrols over these areas by 10 Group were ineffective, as the fighters had no contact with the shipping below and little support from an underdeveloped radar network. Consequently 10 Group was reinforced with additional squadrons and more effective deployment was made possible by increased co-operation with the Navy. Stricter control was enforced over shipping movements by Plymouth Command, which liaised with 10 Group to provide specific fighter support on a scale relative to the importance of the ships concerned.

Although fighter escorts were an essential response to the Luftwaffe campaign, the key to keeping merchant losses down lay in improving ship defences. By using cloud cover or approaching at sea level, intruders invariably avoided fighter escorts until they had released their bombs. Bombers could also fly at night or in weather conditions which grounded single-seat fighters. Much therefore depended on the provision of improved anti-aircraft defences by Plymouth Command.

Merchant vessels were initially sailed in escorted groups, but the lack of suitable escorts in Plymouth Command meant that only one armed trawler or motor launch could be assigned to each group. Requests for reinforcements were finally heeded after six tankers, escorted by one trawler, were attacked in the Bristol Channel on 1 April 1941. Two were sunk and three damaged. 'Hunt' class escort destroyers were assigned to Plymouth and the Command reduced independent sailings to a minimum, introducing convoys on a regular three-day cycle between Dartmouth and the Bristol Channel on 29 April 1941. These were supplanted by the PW/WP convoys, which ran between South Wales and Portsmouth from July 1941.

The coastal convoy system enabled a greater concentration of firepower against attacking aircraft and made the provision of fighter escort a simpler task. It also enabled the extension of the Anti-Aircraft Guard Scheme into South West waters. Naval gunners and their weapons sailed aboard ships in a convoy for the duration of the voyage, transferring to a returning convoy at the terminal port. Additional guns were fitted aboard merchant ships, and their crews trained in gunnery. Emphasis was placed on the need for constant vigilance against air attack, for effective defences not only benefited crew morale but also deterred aircraft from pressing home attacks.

Suffering increased losses in the face of more effective defences in April and May 1941, the Luftwaffe increasingly turned to night operations. The weight of attack against Plymouth Command also fell off as the Luftwaffe probed elsewhere for weaker defences. The invasion of Russia in June 1941 drew many Luftwaffe squadrons away from the Western Front, and by December 1941 the scale of attack in the 10 Group area had fallen below that experienced before the campaign began.

Anxious to conserve the small bomber force retained in France, the Luftwaffe introduced fighter-bombers into the anti-shipping role in March 1942, and coastal shipping and towns such as Dartmouth, Torquay and Salcombe soon became the principal targets for their hit-and-run raids. These attacks caused little material damage, but were unnerving for the local population, tied down several RAF squadrons in defensive operations, and released anti-shipping bomber units for operations in the Mediterranean and Arctic. Attacks began to peter out in 1943 as the fighter-bomber units were returned to interceptor duties to counter American daylight bomber raids. Thereafter, the Luftwaffe abandoned any sustained effort against coastal targets and concentrated largely on reconnaissance, reflecting the growing German concern with the threat of invasion.

E-Boat Operations against Coastal Trade in Plymouth Command

A new menace appeared in the western Channel in July 1942, when German E-Boats arrived at Cherbourg. Plymouth Command initially failed to act upon the implications of their presence, with the result that convoy WP183 was surprised by eight E-Boats on 8 July. Five merchant ships and the escort trawler HMS *Manor* were sunk in the attack, and another vessel was lost in a follow-up strike by Luftwaffe fighter-bombers at dawn. Although the larger coastal convoys on the East Coast remained the Germans' principal target, the attack on WP183 established the western Channel as a worthwhile target area. Henceforth, the Germans exploited the potential to keep British defences at full stretch by switching forces between the two areas, using seasonal weather and light conditions to their advantage.

The threat posed by the E-Boats presented Plymouth Command with the problem of maintaining almost constant vigilance against intermittent torpedo and minelaying incursions along a long and exposed convoy route. Coastal waters watched by Luftwaffe reconnaissance offered no prospect of evasive routeing, whilst adjustments to convoy schedules to avoid vulnerable areas at night entailed an unacceptable reduction in the frequency, and hence the volume, of coastal trade. The onus therefore lay with Plymouth Command to provide effective defences to counter the E-Boat raids.

Radar cover extending to seaward of the convoy routes was essential in order to give warning of approaching E-Boats and to facilitate control of countermeasures from the shore. The WP183 disaster exposed the inadequacy of the Plymouth Command network and, although it was swiftly supplemented with new and temporary radar stations, high-power equipment was not available until mid-1943. Information from shore radar had to be interpreted and relayed to naval forces swiftly and correctly, but effective plotting of E-Boat movements amongst the myriad of other contacts and spurious echoes posed constant problems. Plymouth Command was frequently criticised for delays in communicating, often in inadequate or misleading form, the available information on approaching E-Boats. The problem highlighted the difficulty faced by the Admiralty in providing the Home Commands with sufficient staff of the calibre necessary to deal with the demands of controlling a fast-moving action from the shore.

At sea, the defences were divided between convoy escorts and Coastal Forces interception patrols, which were introduced in July 1942 to intercept and engage E-Boats away from any direct commitment to convoy defence. The Coastal Forces patrols were handicapped by poor visual and radar range, but were expected to intercept larger, faster and better protected opponents. Nevertheless, the policy held considerable sway with successive Commanders at Plymouth,

20.5 The cruiser HMS *Newcastle* in action against German destroyers, 17 October 1940. (*Imperial War Museum*)

20.6 The destroyer HMS *Javelin* towed into Plymouth after losing her bow and stern in action with German destroyers off the Lizard on the night of 24–25 November 1940. (*Imperial War Museum*)

even though the E-Boats invariably avoided unnecessary skirmishes by using their superior speed to escape. Despite the considerable effort devoted to Coastal Forces defensive patrols by Plymouth Command, the Germans consistently broke through to the convoy routes without ever incurring serious damage to an E-Boat.

Aircraft offered a viable alternative to surface patrols, because altitude gave them the advantages of a clear radar picture and excellent visual range on clear nights, and their speed enabled them to close swiftly on reported E-Boat activity. The task required radar-equipped aircraft capable of manoeuvring at low speed near sea level to engage the agile E-Boats, but not presenting too large a target to their anti-aircraft defences. Swordfish proved ideal, and the institution of regular patrols from St Eval and Exeter in the spring of 1943 caused significant disruption to E-Boat operations. Although it proved difficult to sink E-Boats by bombing, the constant aerial harassment and damage incurred through strafing forced the Germans to abandon operations on moonlit nights, and to fit armour against air attack. Any E-Boats that failed to regain their bases by dawn or ventured out in daylight also exposed themselves to air attack by 10 Group fighter-bombers. An attack in August 1943 sank one E-Boat and inflicted such damage on another six that two flotillas were out of action for a month.[15]

In the last resort, the fate of a convoy under E-Boat attack depended on the strength and handling of the naval escort. The varying demands made upon Plymouth Command's limited resources meant that it was rarely possible to set aside time for training in anti-E-Boat tactics or to maintain an escort group system to ensure that escorts were experienced at working with one another. Destroyers, in particular, were in short supply, and it was not until reinforcements were sent to Plymouth and Portsmouth in May 1943 that more than one could regularly be included in the escorts.

The war against the E-Boat in the western Channel reached its lowest ebb between October 1942 and May 1943, when a sustained German offensive repeatedly exposed deficiencies in Plymouth Command plotting and communications organisation. Admiralty reports criticised the failure to provide convoys with adequate warning of attacks, and on two occasions British forces were vectored on to and engaged one another.[16] Armed trawlers, which bore the brunt of the attacks in their exposed positions on convoy flanks, suffered heavy casualties, and two valuable destroyers were sunk on convoy escort duty.

The introduction of more destroyers, better radar cover and improved convoy organisation all bolstered the Plymouth Command naval defences in the late spring of 1943. Air patrols by 19 Group also began to affect E-Boat

Table 20.1

Losses to E-boat attack in the Western Channel, 1942–1943

Date	Convoy	Merchant ships (tonnage)	Escort trawlers	Destroyers	Others
9.7.42	WP183	5 (12,934)	1		
2.10.42	PW226		1		
18.11.42	PW250	3 (3,528)	1		
1.12.42	PW256		1		
3.12.42	PW257	1 (389)		HMS *Penylan*	
27.2.43	WP300	1 (4,858)	2		1 LCT
14.4.43	PW323	1 (1,742)		HMS *Eskdale*	

operations, which were increasingly disadvantaged by the lack of support from their own air force. Bereft of reconnaissance information, the E-Boats were forced into dangerous and often fruitless searches for targets. This, coupled with the onset of shorter hours of darkness in which to operate, forced the Germans into a greater emphasis on minelaying in the summer of 1943. Plymouth Command was able to monitor these operations by tracking E-Boats on radar and listening to their inter-boat radio communications. Minefields could then be identified on these plots and convoys re-routed whilst minesweepers cleared the danger areas of mines, which posed few sweeping problems. No merchant ships were sunk by E-Boat minefields in the Plymouth Command.

The increased level of Allied naval and air activity in the Channel, and the associated expectation of an invasion, forced the Germans to deploy their E-Boats on defensive duties in the autumn of 1943. Torpedo operations against the Plymouth Command did not resume until December 1943, but, with the Channel convoys then being used extensively to transport invasion equipment, and amphibious training exercises about to begin on the south Devon coast, the threat they posed was greater than ever. This was demonstrated on 6 January 1944, when WP457, without a destroyer escort because Plymouth Command had assumed the area to be safe, was attacked near Mount's Bay and lost four ships. The action exposed similar plotting and communications weaknesses to those that had plagued Plymouth Command in the previous E-Boat torpedo offensive. The failure to rectify these inadequacies and develop more effective methods of combating E-Boats in the intervening period had disastrous consequences.

The Slapton Sands Disaster

In November 1943 the War Office began to prepare the south Devon coast for amphibious assault exercises by the American troops preparing for the invasion of Europe.[17] By 20 December 3,000 local residents had been moved out of the requisitioned area between Torcross, Blackpool Sands and Blackawton. Exercises began in January 1944 (Fig. 20.7) and proceeded without interference by German forces until April, when an American convoy taking part in Exercise Tiger suffered one of the worst disasters in Devon's maritime history.

Convoy T.4, comprising eight LSTs carrying the troops and equipment of the 1st Engineer Special Brigade, assembled off Brixham on the morning of 27 April 1944. The convoy was to sail a circuitous route in Lyme Bay before arriving off the 'beachhead' at Slapton Sands the following morning. The escort consisted of the destroyer *Scimitar* and the corvette *Azalea*,

20.7 American troops practising landing at Slapton Sands during Exercise *Tiger*, 26–29 April 1944. (*Muriel & David Murch*)

neither of which had any experience of E-Boat warfare. This should be compared with the escort given to a typical coastal convoy in the western Channel, averaging about fifteen small colliers, of two destroyers and five armed trawlers. Experience had shown that underprotected convoys were extremely vulnerable and that two destroyers were necessary to counter massed E-Boat attacks. Armed trawlers also played a vital role in marshalling the convoy and defending its perimeter.

Additional defences against E-Boat attack were provided by the covering forces of Plymouth Command. The approaches to Lyme Bay were covered by four destroyers, deployed in two separate patrols, and five MTBs which were also organised into two patrol groups. The subsequent comment by the Deputy Director of the Admiralty Operations Department on the value of these patrols is fully borne out by the history of E-Boat operations in the Western Channel:

> The system of patrol lines which looks so solid and comforting on a chart is in fact an ensnaring myth of security yet one in which a sublime faith is invariably put. Naval history abounds with examples of attacking forces slipping through these thin almost skeleton lines, but scarcely an instance of patrols intercepting and completely driving off and breaking up the attackers.[18]

The potential vulnerability of convoy T.4 was exacerbated when *Scimitar* was involved in a collision during the early stages of the exercise. The destroyer put into Plymouth to effect temporary repairs and refuel, but was not permitted to return to sea because of the damage she had sustained. For over nine hours staff at the Plymouth headquarters remained under the erroneous impression that the Senior Commanders at sea were aware of the situation, and the convoy failed to query the absence of its principal escort. Further lapses in communications meant that another six hours elapsed between the realisation at Plymouth that something was amiss with the escort of T.4 and a reinforcement being dispatched.[19]

In the meantime, nine German E-Boats of the 5th and 9th Flotillas had sailed from Cherbourg on an offensive sweep across the Channel. Soon after midnight two of these E-Boats were involved in a fleeting engagement with the destroyer *Onslow*, but used their superior speed to disengage. This was the only inward-bound interception achieved by the patrols in which Plymouth Command had placed such unwarranted faith.

As it became apparent that E-Boats were heading into the area another convoy, codenamed Obstacle, was ordered to reverse course near Start Point, but T.4 received no specific warning or new orders from Plymouth Command. The inadequacy of the communications system is highlighted by the fact that the Obstacle convoy never received the order. Neither convoy acted on its own initiative in response to the general E-Boat reports issued

by Plymouth Command, and both continued to sail into the danger area. The flow of information from Plymouth also ceased as the central plot was thrown into confusion by the rapidly developing events.

Without any trawlers to help maintain a close formation, convoy T.4, arranged in line ahead as opposed to the more compact double column employed by the PW/WP convoys, had straggled over several miles. *Azalea* was stationed ahead of the convoy, and the E-Boats were able to close on its exposed flanks and launch a devastating attack, sinking LST 507 and LST 513 and badly damaging LST 289. Losses might have been even greater had the Germans not initially failed to identify their targets as shallow-draughted vessels, several torpedoes passing underneath LSTs as a result. The E-Boats then disengaged and passed back through the alerted interception patrols, narrowly missing another engagement with the Obstacle convoy, without suffering any losses.

Survivors spent many hours in the water before being rescued, and the final toll of killed and missing from T.4 was 639, considerably in excess of the losses incurred in the assault on Utah beach on D-Day.[20]

Offensive Operations by Plymouth Command against German Trade

The victories of 1940 enabled the Germans to develop maritime trade along 1,600 miles of coastline from the North Cape to the Spanish border, relieving the pressure on the European railway network and opening hitherto inaccessible overseas markets, particularly through the French Atlantic ports. Ships could import iron ore and other contraband from Spain and Portugal, whilst others had direct access to the Atlantic and beyond to the markets of the Far East. It was the responsibility of Plymouth Command to contribute to the war of economic attrition waged against Germany by attacking and disrupting this trade in the coastal waters between Cherbourg and Ushant, around the heavily fortified Channel Islands and further afield in the Bay of Biscay.

The Bay of Biscay

The most regular merchant traffic in the Bay was the iron ore and contraband trade between the Iberian countries and Bayonne. This trade was conducted in a fleet of small coastal traders, supplemented by a few larger ships which took their cargo to the Gironde. They were difficult to attack because the German ships hugged the coast and completed most of their journeys under cover of darkness at extreme range from 19 Group airfields. Minelaying by aircraft and the submarine *Rubis* caused some disruption, but it was not until May 1944 that significant losses were inflicted, when the submarine *Sceptre* sank two of the large ships off the north Spanish coast.

The most important ships operating in the Bay, however, were the blockade runners sailing between occupied Europe and the Far East. This trade became essential to Germany and Japan once the trans-Siberian railway link was cut in 1941, as their respective economic strengths were in many respects complementary to one another's needs. Plymouth became the centre of the anti-blockade-runner effort because the Bay was the one focal area where reasonable opportunities for interception existed.

In the spring of 1942, when blockade running first attained serious proportions, 19 Group and Plymouth Command were poorly equipped to deal with the problem. The destroyers based at Plymouth did not have sufficient endurance to patrol the approaches to the Bay, and the few 19 Group aircraft with the requisite range were vulnerable to anti-aircraft fire from their targets. The Germans made the most of poor weather conditions to evade air patrols, and blockade runners often sought refuge in Spain to escape pursuing forces. Numerous problems also arose in identifying and shadowing ships and then homing air strike forces on to their targets at such long range. Submarines were introduced into the Bay in October 1942 but had no success, and HMS *Unbeaten* was sunk in error by a 19 Group anti-U-Boat patrol.

The odds swung in favour of Plymouth Command at the beginning of 1943, when a cruiser was allocated to Plymouth to operate in the Bay and the Command was given centralised control of anti-blockade-runner operations.[21] Aircraft could be switched from the antisubmarine patrols when blockade runner activity was suspected, and home specialist anti-shipping air strikes and surface forces directed to their targets. The Germans responded by transferring destroyers from Norway to the Biscay ports to provide escorts for the blockade runners in the Bay in March 1943. This forced Plymouth Command to provide cover for convoys passing in the vicinity and made air attacks more difficult in the face of heavy anti-aircraft fire.

The battles fought around successive blockade runners in the Bay reached a peak in December, 1943, when *Osorno* reached France in spite of heavy air attacks. *Alsterufer*, however, was sunk by 19 Group before meeting her escorts, which were then intercepted by HMS *Glasgow* and HMS *Enterprise* from Plymouth on 28 December 1943. The cruisers pursued the ten German destroyers and sank three. Faced with insuperable odds in the Bay of Biscay, Hitler ordered that surface blockade running be abandoned on 18 January 1944, and thereafter the trade was reduced to a trickle carried in converted submarines.

The Western Channel
Coastal Forces began regular anti-shipping sweeps from Dartmouth in July 1942, when Plymouth Command was reinforced by the 8th MGB Flotilla in response to the attack on WP183. Such operations forced the Germans to withdraw E-Boats from their offensive to supplement existing defensive patrols and exposed them to the risk of interception by MGBs lying in wait off their own bases. The offensive by Plymouth Command Coastal Forces was limited, however, by the distances involved and the type and number of boats available. Operations were subject to weather conditions, whilst the strain on engines and hulls required lengthy spells in maintenance. The considerable effort devoted to fruitless anti-E-Boat patrols also detracted from the MGBs' offensive potential.

The targets available in the western Channel also posed problems for Coastal Forces. The only regular merchant traffic was that between the Channel Islands and the French mainland, but these convoys were small and their journeys were short and under strong escort. The most important targets were merchant and naval shipping on passage between Cherbourg and Brest, but these forces were too powerful to be tackled by the Coastal Forces craft. ULTRA decrypts of German cypher traffic, supported by aerial reconnaissance by 10 Group fighters, gave Plymouth Command some indication of German activity, and destroyers were occasionally diverted from defensive duties to support Coastal Forces or operate independently against important targets.[22] These operations achieved some success, notably the destruction of the armed merchant raider *Komet* by a combined force of destroyers and MTBs on 14 October 1942.

The 'Hunt' Class destroyers of the 15th Destroyer Flotilla based at Plymouth were designed for defensive escort duties, and their relative lack of hitting power exposed them to the risk of serious damage in close-range duels with German escorts. Although Plymouth Command could not afford to lose its precious destroyers to the dockyards, the Flotilla and the 1st Destroyer Flotilla at Portsmouth provided the mainstay of the destroyer sweeps in the Channel until September 1943. Plymouth Command then began to employ the larger warships based at Devonport primarily for operations in the Bay of Biscay on a regular offensive sweep known as Operation Tunnel. It was envisaged that the cruisers and destroyers could pick up targets at greater range and rapidly overwhelm them with heavy gunfire.

Operation Tunnel required a high degree of teamwork and nightfighting experience to counter the threat posed by E-Boats and torpedo boats in waters covered by German shore radar. Plymouth Command learnt this lesson when surprised by German torpedo boats on 23 October 1943. The cruiser *Charybdis* and the destroyer *Limbourne* were both torpedoed and sunk. The only cross-Channel sweeps mounted by Plymouth destroyers for the remainder of 1943 were covering patrols in support of Coastal Forces minelaying operations.

As the Allies built up their naval strength in the Channel in preparation for Operation Overlord, Plymouth Command was finally availed of the means to escalate its offensive and so wear down the German forces liable

to oppose the invasion. Operation Tunnel was revived, using a trained strike force based around the cruisers *Bellona* and *Black Prince* and the 10th Destroyer Flotilla. The value of these operations remains questionable because of the risks to which the valuable warships were exposed. In March 1944 German torpedo boats unsuccessfully attacked the 10th Destroyer Flotilla without being sighted and, in May 1944, U-Boats were sent into the Western Channel to attack the British warships off the French coast. The operation was abandoned before any attacks could be mounted.

The main success achieved by Operation Tunnel in 1944 was the destruction of T 29 in a battle with the 4th Torpedoboat Flotilla off the Ile de Bas on 26 April 1944. Two days later, ULTRA intelligence enabled Plymouth Command destroyers to intercept the two survivors of this action en route to Brest. T 27 was driven ashore under heavy fire from HMCS *Haida*, but the dangers of such operations were again brought home by the loss of HMCS *Athabaskan*, which was torpedoed during the chase. The grounded torpedo boat was subjected to air attacks by 10 Group and was finally destroyed by Dartmouth MTBs on 6 May 1944.

Plymouth Command and the Invasion of Europe

Operation Overlord
Plymouth Command worked in close co-operation with American shore authorities to load and dispatch the US forces bound for Utah beach from Torquay, Brixham (Fig. 20.8), Dartmouth, Salcombe (Fig. 20.9) and Plymouth. On 6 June 1944 it was able to report that this force had sailed according to plan, and by 1800hrs that evening 21,328 men, 1,742 vehicles and 1,695 tons of stores had been landed on Utah beach.[23] The Command then provided administrative, repair, salvage and replenishment facilities to effect the quick turnaround of shipping during the subsequent build-up as the Allies sought to secure a firm lodgement in France.

Operation Neptune
The Allied invasion depended not only upon the success of the initial assaults, but also on the subsequent build-up of supplies and reinforcements. The Germans were expected, therefore, to make great sacrifices to repel the invasion or cause sufficient losses and disruption to the build-up to ensure victory on land. The U-Boat and E-Boat forces located to the west of the invasion beaches had a wealth of experience in raiding and infiltration tactics, whilst the destroyers based on the Biscay coast posed a major threat. Plymouth Command and 19 Group played a key role, therefore, in securing their flank of the invasion against German naval intervention.

The Germans began allocating U-Boats to anti-invasion duties in February 1944, resting and training crews and equipping some submarines with schnorkels that enabled them to draw in fresh air and expel exhaust fumes whilst submerged. The Allied defences against this force were based on Operation Cork, which was designed to saturate the western approaches to the English Channel with 19 Group aircraft patrols, so that U-Boats risked almost certain detection if they surfaced. Plymouth Command was reinforced with Naval Support Groups from Western Approaches Command, so that any U-Boat attempting the passage to the Channel had to run a daunting gauntlet of sea and air patrols.

By midnight on D-Day, thirty-five U-Boats had sailed on anti-invasion duties. Nine schnorkel-equipped boats were bound for the central Channel, eight non-schnorkel boats were ordered to patrol west of Start Point, and the remainder were stationed off the Biscay coast to guard against further Allied landings.[24] Operation Cork took an immediate toll on the first night as U-boats surfaced to make their best possible speed under cover of darkness, and was so successful that by the evening of 10 June 1944 only six of the original seventeen U-Boats sent to attack the invasion supply lines were still making their way up the Channel. The entire group bound for the patrol line in the western Channel had either been sunk or forced back to port with damage, and only the schnorkel-equipped submarines had made any progress.

The constant air and surface patrols by 19 Group and Plymouth Command also ensured that any submarines which did succeed in advancing towards their target area did so at a tortuously slow pace. The U-Boats were

20.8 American LCTs loading at Brixham in preparation for D-Day. (*Torquay Museum*)

forced to remain constantly submerged, not even using their schnorkels in daylight in case the wake and trail of exhaust fumes betrayed their position. The resulting drain on their batteries forced U-Boats to bottom and conserve their energy during adverse tides and restricted their rate of advance to about 1.5 knots. Thus, it was not until 15 June 1944 that the only U-Boat from the first wave actually to reach its designated operational billet successfully attacked an invasion convoy. Hounded by escort forces, U-621 only succeeded in sinking one small landing craft before embarking on the return passage to Brest.

By 30 June, more than 4,250 vessels had sailed to the invasion beachheads in convoy. From this huge morass of shipping the U-Boat offensive claimed just five transports (30,994 tons) and a 250-ton landing craft sunk and one ship damaged. Four escorts had also been sunk or damaged beyond repair in clashes with the U-Boats, but these slender achievements had cost the Germans dear. Of the twenty-five U-Boats sent to operate in the central Channel, seven had been sunk, three had aborted after being damaged in action and another five had had to abandon the attempt. At the end of the month, only two of the four U-Boats that had succeeded in reaching the target area remained in position and another six were still heading for the Channel. Uncertain as to the progress of its forces but fearful of heavy losses, the U-Boat Command suspended further operations against the cross-Channel shipping lanes on 1 July.

Plymouth Command and 19 Group then went on to the offensive by mounting Operation Dredger, in which Escort Groups were sent into the Bay of Biscay to operate in the approaches to the U-Boat bases. The Germans proved powerless to prevent these forces ranging as far south as the Gironde as attempts by the Luftwaffe to intervene soon fell away after

fighter escorts inflicted heavy losses. Thus, although U-Boat operations were resumed in early July, the initial success achieved by Plymouth Command and 19 Group in defeating the U-Boat offensive that might have caused so much disruption to the invasion supply lines was maintained, and the cross-Channel shipping lanes were only subjected to weak and intermittent U-Boat activity.

Plymouth Command forces also bore the responsibility of ensuring that the German destroyers based in the Bay of Biscay were denied access to the Channel. ULTRA proved to be a key factor, and Plymouth Command was able to dispose its forces to counter German intentions even before they had left port. Although the destroyers survived heavy attacks by Coastal Command Beaufighters from Davidstowe Moor whilst on passage to Brest, further westward progress was prevented by the waiting 10th Destroyer Flotilla off the Ile de Bas on 9 June 1944. Two of the German destroyers attempting to reach Cherbourg were sunk, and the surviving destroyer and a torpedo boat were forced to return to Brest. They played no further part in the anti-invasion effort. Coastal Forces and destroyers from Plymouth Command also played an important role in the numerous actions fought against the E-Boats based at Cherbourg. The German effort waned as losses and damage incurred in constant operations restricted availability and torpedo supplies at the port ran low. E-Boat operations were soon concentrated against the eastern flank of the invasion from Le Havre.

Offensive Operations after D-Day

As the German naval effort against the invasion weakened, Plymouth Command was able to commit more of its forces to the offensive against German sea communications between Cherbourg, the Channel Islands and

St Malo. The German dependence on sea transport grew as overland communications succumbed to air attack and the Allied advance. Patrols by 10 Group fighter-bombers ensured that no German shipping ventured out of port in daylight, setting the scene for numerous night actions as the Germans attempted to move supplies and equipment by sea under cover of darkness.

MTBs were employed to good effect in Channel Islands coastal waters to hinder the build-up of supplies there and prevent any wholesale transfer of the 30,000-strong garrison to join the fighting on the mainland. The craft were ideal for operations in confined and rocky waters covered by shore batteries, and could penetrate close inshore to carry out their attacks. The principal limitation was the dependence on surprise, for alerted convoys were generally successful in holding their protagonists at bay with starshell and gunfire.

Plymouth Command destroyer operations also began to have a significant impact, particularly as the German convoys no longer enjoyed torpedo boat protection. On 14 June 1944 the Germans were forced to abandon regular passages around Cap de la Hague after HMS *Ashanti* and ORP *Piorun* sank one minesweeper and seriously damaged another four attempting to take torpedoes to the E-Boat base at Cherbourg. Nevertheless, the actions were not all one-sided, for the German minesweeper and trawler escorts were difficult targets, and destroyers exposed themselves to damage from their powerful armament in a close-range fight. HMS *Eskimo* was badly damaged by an armed trawler in one action, and an American PT Boat was sunk by German convoy escorts off Jersey in August 1944.

Forces from Plymouth Command and 19 Group also waged an offensive against the German forces attempting to transfer supplies and equipment south from Brest and Lorient to escape the Allied land advance. By day, the Strike Wings assigned to 19 Group swept the coast and inflicted fearsome casualties on German shipping. Their victims included the last two destroyers on the Biscay coast, which were sunk at Le Touquet on 24 August 1944. German attempts to run the gauntlet under cover of darkness fared little better, as cruiser and destroyer sweeps from Plymouth penetrated close inshore to intercept their targets. Shoals and coastal artillery provided intermittent protection for the small convoys, but several were caught and annihilated by the naval patrols. The U-Boats that joined the southern exodus from the northern ports in the Bay were also subjected to constant harassment by air and naval forces controlled from Plymouth, and eight of the sixteen submarines that attempted the passage were sunk.[25]

Offensive operations from Plymouth reached their conclusion when the German garrison at Cezembre surrendered in September 1944, although the Command helped monitor German activity in the Channel Islands until they were liberated by forces from Plymouth in May 1945.

The U-Boat Campaign in Plymouth Command Coastal Waters, 1945

Although the Germans had been driven back from the French coast and their surface forces cleared from the Channel, the reopening of the Channel to ocean convoys in September 1944 ensured that Plymouth continued to play an active role in the naval war. There was no immediate large-scale response from the Germans, who were withdrawing their submarines

Table 20.2
German surface losses in the Bay of Biscay, August 1944

Causes	Warships (tonnage)	Merchant ships
Naval forces	13 (7,336)	3 (666)
Air strikes	17 (30,817)	3 (1,347)
Mines	6 (1,996)	5 (768)
Bombed in port	21 (34,163)	8 (23,720)

from the beleaguered Biscay bases to Germany and Norway and were then hindered by the ensuing pressure on the dockyards there. By the end of 1944, however, the Germans were able to develop a limited offensive against the shipping converging on the coastal waters of the Plymouth Command.

U-Boat operations were inhibited by the need for the vessels to remain submerged in transit to and from North Sea bases to avoid aerial detection, which curtailed the time available in the target area. U-Boat Command also received little feedback on operational conditions because captains were reluctant to remain surfaced long enough to establish radio contact. The flow of instructions emanating from Germany also declined with the demise of pack operations, as independent patrols required less central control. This meant that some of the benefits bestowed by ULTRA on the conduct of anti-submarine operations were lost, placing the onus on the air and naval forces at the disposal of Plymouth Command to establish the whereabouts of U-Boats in local waters and hunt them to destruction.

The aircraft of 19 Group continued to play an important role in anti-submarine operations, but the schnorkel and improved radar equipment aboard the U-Boats meant that sightings were rare. Nevertheless, the incessant patrolling activity by 19 Group exerted a vital influence on U-Boat operations, forcing them to spend long periods bottomed on the seabed to conserve energy and avoid detection. This restricted their offensive potential and caused U-Boats to miss opportunites to attack shipping in their vicinity, as they failed to make visual or hydrophone contact in the prevailing conditions in coastal waters.

20.9 American landing craft moored at Salcombe in preparation for the D-Day landings. An RAF Air Sea Rescue launch (one of four stationed at Salcombe) is in the foreground. (*Muriel & David Murch*)

By December 1944 the anti-submarine forces assembled in the Plymouth Command for the invasion had long since dispersed, leaving a heterogenous assortment of warships to form the Plymouth Escort Force, which was reinforced with Naval Support Groups from Western Approaches Command. The latter bore the brunt of the anti-submarine campaign, remaining almost constantly at sea in their allotted section of the convoy route and only returning to Plymouth to refuel and refit.

Both sides derived some advantages from the fact that the campaign focused on inshore waters. The shallow coastal waters with their tide rips and density layers offered the U-Boat some protection against detection, and the sea bed was close at hand to enable it to lie low or repair damage that would have meant certain destruction in the open ocean. It also proved difficult for escorts to locate their targets amongst the myriad of bottom contacts, although Plymouth Command compiled a checklist of known false contacts. Naval patrols and escorts also benefited from the overview provided by shore radar and the proximity of the operational headquarters and base facilities. Anti-submarine minefields were sown in some danger areas in April 1945 to hinder U-Boat operations and release Support Groups to patrol other sections of the convoy route.

Conclusion

The naval forces commanded from Plymouth faced the most diverse responsibilities of all the Home Commands in the Second World War. Plymouth was the nerve centre for anti-submarine operations during the formative stages of the Battle of the Atlantic before the Allied collapse in France transformed the strategic situation. The opposing forces in the Western Channel then occupied bases that had originated in the eighteenth century in pursuance of basic objectives that still held true over 150 years later: denying the enemy access to maritime communications whilst preserving the freedom of one's own. Neither side, however, was either prepared or equipped for a close-quarters conflict across the Western Channel which, owing to the mobility of modern naval and air power, also extended into the Bay of Biscay.

Thus the Plymouth Command had to develop the strategy and tactics required to defend coastal shipping in its waters against the unexpected threat of air and E-Boat attack with limited resources. It also had to fulfil offensive commitments that ranged from operations against surface raiders, U-Boats and blockade runners in the Bay of Biscay to naval sweeps across the English Channel. Ultimately, it played a decisive role in repelling German attempts to intervene in the Western Channel in June 1944, and in the subsequent strangulation of German maritime communications from Cherbourg to the Spanish coast.

The final stages of the war effectively saw the operational role of the forces based in the South West complete a full circle as their primary function reverted to the defence of merchant shipping against U-Boat attack.[26]

20: Devon and the Navy in the Second World War

1 PRO, ADM 199/2365.
2 Asdic was an anti-submarine detection device developed in the interwar period.
3 PRO, ADM 186/802.
4 The aircraft carrier HMS *Ark Royal* was also deployed on anti-submarine duties west of the Hebrides. On 14 September 1939 U-39 narrowly missed the carrier with a salvo of torpedoes and was subsequently sunk by her destroyer escorts.
5 PRO, ADM 199/124.
6 These losses were sustained in KJF3 and HG3. Their inclusion in some accounts as convoy losses is not strictly accurate, as the ships in question were sailing in unescorted groups and not convoys, which are defined as receiving warship protection.
7 PRO, ADM 186/804.
8 Details of all U-Boat losses are available in V E Tarrant, *The U-Boat Offensive 1914–45* (1989).
9 Some estimates of the losses sustained aboard the liner are as high as 5,000, but no record of the numbers embarked was kept.
10 PRO, AIR 41/48.
11 PRO, AIR 41/48.
12 A detailed account of the Bay Offensive at its height is available in Norman Franks, *Conflict over the Bay* (1986).
13 Operation Medium was originally planned as a diversion for Operation Lucid, a plan to send fireships into Calais harbour. Two of the old tankers allocated for this purpose were prepared at Devonport, but the operation was abandoned after several aborted attempts.
14 In five operations in the Western Channel between September 1940 and February 1941, German destroyer torpedoes and mines accounted for one destroyer seriously damaged and six naval auxiliaries, four merchant ships and six smaller vessels sunk.
15 S121 was sunk in this attack. The only other E-Boat sunk in the Western Channel before D-Day was S141, sunk by Plymouth Command destroyers on 12 May 1944.
16 The convoy escort of PW226 opened fire on a Coastal Forces patrol in October 1942. (PRO, ADM 199/785). On 29 May 1943 three British forces engaged one another in an action which an Admiralty report attributed to 'an inefficient communications organisation in the Command, involving long delays and/or corruption of signals'. (PRO, ADM 199/536).
17 Whilst the main assault exercises were conducted on the Channel coast, some training also took place in North Devon.
18 PRO, ADM 199/261.
19 At 0137 HMS *Saladin* was sent to join T.4, but could not reach the convoy until after the E-Boat attack. A full account of the sequence of events is to be found in PRO, ADM 199/261.
20 There were 197 American casualties on Utah beach.
21 There was a high turnover in cruisers based at Plymouth, and cruisers in transit between England and Gibraltar also came under Plymouth Command Control.

22 Allied success in breaking the German Enigma cypher machine proved to be a major advantage, although use of information had to be carefully controlled to avoid compromising the source.
23 J Rohwer, *Chronology of the War at Sea, Vol. 2*, (1972).
24 PRO, AIR 41/74.
25 PRO, AIR 41/74.
26 This chapter is based on the following sources:
    Primary (PRO, Kew, London).
    Western Approaches and Plymouth Command War Diaries ADM 199/371–2, 633, 655, 422, 1393, 1442.
    Western Approaches 1939–1940 and Creation of Plymouth Command ADM 186/799, ADM 199/2057, ADM 199/2074–2077, AIR 15/34, ADM 199/124, ADM 186/802, ADM 234/67–68, ADM 116/4479, ADM 1/11346.
    Operations against Surface Raiders and U-Boats in the Bay of Biscay AIR 15/19, AIR 15/758, ADM 199/2437, AIR 41/47–48, ADM 199/1693, ADM 199/2021, ADM 1/12644, ADM 205/13.
    The Threat of Invasion ADM 199/2057, ADM 199/667.
    Aerial Blockade AIR 41/47–48, ADM 199/2093, ADM 205/11, AIR 16/639, ADM 199/673.
    E-Boat Operations in the Plymouth Command ADM 219/13, ADM 219/220, ADM 179/260, ADM 199/536, ADM 199/541, ADM 199/261, ADM 223/28, ADM 1/16068, ADM 199/784–785.
    Offensive Operations in the Bay of Biscay AIR 15/535–536, AIR 15/539, AIR 15/542, AIR 15/545, AIR 15/549, ADM 219/88, ADM 1/14955, ADM 199/1693–1694, AIR 41/47–48.
    Offensive Operations in the Western Channel ADM 234/352, ADM 199/532, ADM 199/536, ADM 199/782, ADM 199/1036, ADM 116/5059–5061.
    Plymouth Command and the Invasion of Europe ADM 199/1644, ADM 199/262, AIR 41/74, ADM 234/68, ADM 223/28, ADM 223/311–312, ADM 199/1620, ADM 199/1576, ADM 199/1692, ADM 199/471, ADM 199/1563–1565, AIR 15/612, ADM 179/455.
    U-Boat Campaign in South-West Coastal Waters AIR 41/74, ADM 1/17589.
    Secondary
    M Brice, *Axis Blockade Runners* (1981).
    E Brookes, *Destroyer! German Destroyers, 1939–45* (1962).
    N Franks, *Conflict Over the Bay* (1986).
    R Hill, *Destroyer Captain* (1975).
    E P Hoyt, *The Invasion Before Normandy* (New York, 1985).
    N Lewis, *Channel Firing: The Tragedy of Exercise Tiger* (1989).
    J Rohwer, *Chronology of the War at Sea* (1972).
    S W Roskill, *The War at Sea*, 4 vols., (1954–61).
    V E Tarrant, *The U-Boat Offensive 1914–45* (1989).
    J Terraine, *Business in Great Waters. The U-Boat Wars 1916–1945* (1989).
    D E G Weymuss, *Relentless Pursuit* (1955).

21 *The Dockyard in the Local Economy*

Peter Hilditch

Patterns of change, 1801–1914

DEVONPORT'S POSITION AS THE INDUSTRIAL COLOSSUS, not just of Devon but also of the entire South West, became glaringly apparent in the second half of the nineteenth century as the region declined in national economic importance.[1] The 1851 Census, which ranked employers by workforce-size, showed that for the 'South Western Division' (Devon, Cornwall, Somerset, Wiltshire and Dorset) only 43 out of 10,313 enterprises employed more than 100 workers (0.4 per cent), including nine with 350 employees and upwards (0.1 per cent). This latter group comprised seven textile mills, the largest two employing 1,600 and 1,079 respectively, and two silk makers each with 500. Amongst the 58 recorded private shipyards, the largest fell within the range of 50-74 men. The only other substantial industrial enterprises comprised an engine/toolmaker with between 200–249 employees and a toolmaker with between 150 to 199 employees. The Dockyard with *c*1,400 men therefore had a comparable workforce to the largest of the region's private employers, and after the Keyham development certainly contained a greater range of modern technical skills. Although comparable statistics are not available, by the early twentieth century the Dockyard was certainly by far the most important industrial enterprise within Devon. The Dockyard's 12–14,000 employees, just before the First World War, can be compared with the county's leading private establishments such as Heathcotes textile mill at Tiverton, with approximately 1,000 workers, the silk glove factories of Great Torrington with 500, and the Great Western locomotive repair works at Newton Abbot, employing about 400. In the 1911 census 85.5 per cent of those employed in Devon in shipbuilding, and 58.1 per cent of those employed in metal fabrication and engineering, resided in the three towns of 'Greater Plymouth' (Devonport, East Stonehouse and Plymouth).[2] Nothing in the South West remotely compared with the Dockyard's output of sixteen steel battleships between 1898 and 1914, culminating in the giant 30,600-ton *Warspite* (1913) and 29,150-ton *Royal Oak* (1914).

Some indication of the Dockyard/naval impact on Greater Plymouth is provided by Fig. 21.1. Devon's relative decline meant that its population increased by barely 95 per cent between 1801 and 1901 (as against the national 247 per cent), and Exeter's 171 per cent increase reflected the slow growth of southern county towns in a period of generally rapid urbanisation. Plymouth's increase of 345 per cent, however, was closer to industrial urban trends and easily maintained it as the second largest West Country town behind Bristol (439 per cent growth).[3] It is Greater Plymouth's decennial fluctuations in growth, however, that most clearly reflect the Dockyard/naval impact. These fluctuations differed in both timing and size from the trends shown in both Exeter and Bristol.

In 1801 Greater Plymouth stood as the ninth largest town in Great Britain (excluding London). The extent to which it owed that position to the Dockyard can be shown from the fact that Devonport, which had scarcely existed 100 years before, numbered 23,747 of the three towns' total 43,514 population. Still known as 'Dock', it was already by itself the largest town in Devon. Fig. 21.1 shows the impact of increased Dockyard employment and naval activity during the Napoleonic Wars on Greater Plymouth's dramatic growth rate between 1801 and 1811 and its collapse during the ensuing decade when the wars ended. The two decades from 1821 saw Greater Plymouth reflect the regional urban pattern of Bristol and Exeter, and saw

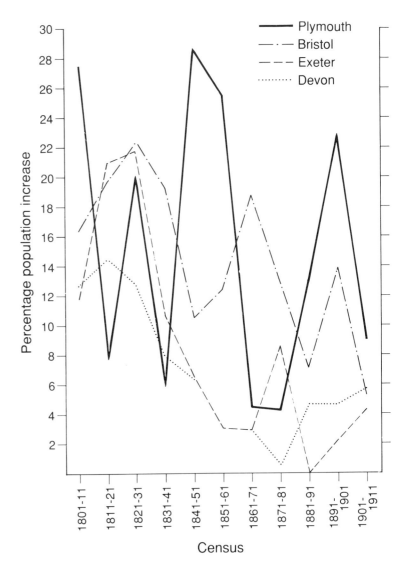

21.1   The populations of Plymouth, Bristol, Exeter and Devon, 1801–1901

Plymouth town overtake Devonport (so named in 1824) on the back of the growth of its commercial port and residential development, while naval development suffered marked contraction.[4] Greater Plymouth then swung wildly away from the Bristol-Exeter trend between 1841 and 1861 in a massive expansionist surge. In part, this can be accounted for by the arrival of the railway and its extension via the Saltash bridge into Cornwall, which greatly expanded Plymouth's function as a regional communications and services centre, but it also reflects the establishment of long-term naval service in 1853, which necessitated the accommodation of large numbers of naval ratings awaiting ship, and the construction of the Keyham Steam

21.2   Fore Street, Devonport's main commercial street, looking east. A print by
Francis Frith, *c*1890. (*City of Plymouth Museums and Art Gallery*)

Yard, which opened in the same year. *Slater's Directory* for 1852–3 declared
that, 'The Dockyard . . . may be considered as the primary source of the
increased extent, wealth, and population of the whole port'.[5]

Greater Plymouth's last major boom before the First World War began
earlier, reached a far higher peak than either Bristol or Exeter, and drew into
the conurbation by 1911 nearly a third of Devon's population. This reflected
a combination of both civil and naval factors. The depression in agriculture
and in Cornish tin mining produced a drift to the three towns. Plymouth
began to develop or expand a diverse range of industries including
chemicals, brewing and printing, while construction and service sectors
including transport (ports, railways and tramways) and retailing recorded
significant increases. Yet in 1908 a Board of Trade report maintained that
while

> To some extent an industrial place altogether apart from the
> Dockyard, [Plymouth] is nevertheless not a great industrial centre,
> nor do its surroundings help it become one, for Devonshire is not in
> any sense of the word an industrial county.[6]

Emphasis was still placed on the Dockyard/naval contribution to Greater
Plymouth's growth, and justifiably so. The naval arms race initiated by the
Naval Defence Act of 1889, the great expansion of numbers of naval seamen,
and the build-up of the Dockyard labour force associated with the
construction and opening of the Keyham extension (see Table 21.1) are all
reflected in the Census for 1911. This recorded 48,707 civilian male
employees in Greater Plymouth, of whom approximately half worked in
manufacturing industry. The Dockyard's 9,000 workmen therefore represented nearly one-fifth of the male workforce and two-fifths of the male
manufacturing workforce. The Census further recorded 18,157 seamen and
officers in port or ashore in Plymouth and Devonport out of a total male
occupied population of 63,765. Significant numbers of sailors and marines
would also have been in East Stonehouse, but these were not enumerated
separately. There was, in addition, an army garrison guarding the naval
base, so that dockyard and defence employment within the three towns
accounted for around half of the total male occupied population in Greater
Plymouth and approximately one-third of all employment.

The Dockyard and economic growth in Devon to the First World War

The growth of Greater Plymouth and the scale and modernity of the
Dockyard industrial complex stand in stark contrast to the general economic
decline of Devon, and the question arises as to why the Dockyard did not
fulfil a greater role in pulling the rest of the Devon economy along with it.
Even Plymouth, fast as it grew, failed to match the dramatic urban growth

Table 21.1
Numbers of workmen in principal royal dockyards in selected years 1890–1930

Year	Portsmouth	Devonport	Chatham	Pembroke	Rosyth	Total
1890	7,616	5,206	5,670	2,092	–	20,584
1900	10,044	8,456	8,599	2,790	–	29,889
1910	10,471	9,443	8,303	2,043	–	30,260
1914	13,117	12,290	10,003	2,478	–	39,888
1916	14,182	14,035	10,473	3,348	2,944	44,982
1918	16,576	15,803	11,494	3,479	6,687	54,039
1920	16,164	13,631	10,778	2,968	5,779	49,320
1925	14,808	12,919	10,313	1,109	2,765	41,914
1930	13,345	11,670	8,827	52	476	34,370

Sources: BPP, 1890–91, LII, 375; BPP, 1901, XLII, 209; HCD, 5 March 1924, Cols.
1421–22; 19 March 1935 Cols. 1013–4.

rates of the industrial Midlands and North, and slipped back from ninth
largest town in 1801 to twentieth in 1901.[7] In some respects it can be argued
that the Dockyard actually played a role in reinforcing Devon's peripheral
status.

The breakdown of Greater Plymouth's occupational structure shown in
Table 21.2 indicates some of the wider spin-offs of the Dockyard/naval
presence to its economy. Besides the relatively greater importance of defence
(i.e. uniformed servicemen) and shipbuilding/metalworking, there was also
greater employment in construction, transport, food, drink and tobacco
relative to Britain as a whole. The construction sector benefited from the
expansion of the Dockyard, fortifications, barracks, training facilities and
hospitals, whilst transport, food, drink, and tobacco employment must have
benefited from the massive flow of sailors through the three towns. (Figs.
21.2, 3)

Adverse effects were also felt, however, particularly in Devonport, whose
former town clerk, Thomas Woolcombe, told a House of Commons'
Committee in 1858 that, 'It is quite clear that had Devonport been free for
commercial enterprises without any interference from the government at all
there must have been very much larger development of ad hoc commercial
capabilities than there is at the present moment.'[8] Woolcombe instanced the
recently-introduced Post Office steam packet service to Southern Africa,
which abandoned Devonport after a very short trial owing to problems in
transferring mail to the main-line railway. The Admiralty had both
prevented the main line coming to Devonport and made continuous
objections to the use of anchorages and waterfront space for shipping and
port development in the town. Woolcombe complained that Devonport
could have surpassed Bristol or Southampton as a commercial port owing to
its favourable geographic position and deep-water harbour.

The Select Committee had been set up to consider the near-total
exemption of crown property (including the Dockyard and all naval and
army establishments) from local rates. This exemption clearly hindered
Devonport's ability to make civic improvements, and the Admiralty's failure
to contribute to the social welfare of the town contrasts strongly with the

Table 21.2
Principal groups of male employment, 1911
(%)

	Plymouth and Devonport	Exeter	Rest of Devon	Great Britain
Defence	30.0	2.6	6.2	1.7
Agriculture	0.9	3.2	26.4	11.1
Metals/engineering	6.1	7.7	3.7	12.8
Shipbuilding	6.7	0	0.6	1.2
Transport	11.3	17.3	9.0	11.2
Construction	7.4	11.0	8.1	3.3
Food, drink, tobacco	7.0	10.4	7.6	6.2

Source: Census of the population, 1911; C H Lee, *British Regional Employment
Statistics 1814–1971* (1979).

so-called 'company towns' dominated by a single employer in the industrial north. For example, Palmer's Shipbuilding & Iron Company, which dominated Jarrow, sponsored in the 1860s a building society for its workers. By 1900 over half of the town was owned by them. Charles Palmer, Jarrow's first mayor and MP, financed the building and staffing of the town hospital and supported a social club, canteen and brass band.[9]

The type of social welfare provision offered by firms such as Palmer's was often made to attract and retain workers (especially skilled workers) to areas where such provision was non-existent or inadequate. In a southwestern labour market glutted by the decline of the regional economy, the Admiralty had less need to go to such lengths to attract labour. Besides, it had its own alternative attractive system through the Establishment. Part of the Dockyard labour force was traditionally granted 'Established' status, virtually guaranteeing continuity of employment, a privilege not given to even the most skilled of private shipyard workers. Additional benefits included a pension on retirement at sixty, equivalent to two-thirds of the final three years' average pay after forty years' service, half pay and free medical attendance if injured at work, compensation if permanently incapacitated and a widow's pension if killed on duty. Established workmen tended to be skilled workers, and in particular shipwrights, but not exclusively so. Of the 5,500 Established men in the Royal Dockyards in 1893, 1,929 were shipwrights, 121 boilermakers, 452 skilled labourers and 112 ordinary labourers.[10]

Although the proportion of Established to the remaining workforce fell steadily in the late nineteenth century, from 53.7 per cent in 1870-3 to 22.1 per cent in 1890–93, as the Admiralty met the expansion of the dockyards with hired workmen, and although hired workmen had no security of employment (a point emphasised by the annual firing and re-engagement of the entire hired workforce), the expansion of the dockyard system did lead to the development of an effectively permanent hired workforce. Hired workers were also eligible for half pay and free medical treatment if injured at work. They did not receive a pension, but if made redundant (except through misconduct) would receive a gratuity equal to one week's wages per year of service. At the Admiralty's discretion, the widows of hired men killed on duty might receive a small pension. Promotion in the dockyards for both hired and Established men was granted through competitive examination, both groups having increasingly equal earning opportunities as the proportion of Established workers declined.

The evidence given to the 1893 Royal Commission on Labour suggests that although none of these individual benefits were unique to the dockyards, the range of benefits provided by the Admiralty combined with the continuity of employment for a proportion of the workforce was unusual compared with private industrial employers, especially within shipbuilding. The Admiralty did not base its labour policies on the principle of benevolence, but upon finance. Any attempt to match private sector employers in boom conditions would have proved extremely expensive and consequently would have attracted fierce outside criticism. Wage costs would have to be increased for all the groups likely to be attracted to the private yards, including individuals within those groups who had little or no intention of actually moving, and regardless of length of service. The particular dockyard payment system described above had the virtue of rewarding individual loyalty whilst keeping actual costs relatively low and predictable.[11]

The consequence, however, was that the Admiralty failed to make a positive contribution to the social amenities of the dockyard towns, the expense of which had to be met by the wider community. Its contribution was made instead through the purchasing power of its labour force. Wage rates of skilled Dockyard workers were among the best for 'blue collar' occupations in Devon and Cornwall in the late-nineteenth and early-twentieth centuries. The 1906 standard rate for Dockyard shipwrights exceeded that of agricultural labourers by 80–100 per cent. In contrast to national trends, Dockyard workers received higher pay than comparable private shipbuilding workers in the two counties or even within Plymouth. In 1893 standard pay rates for Dockyard shipwrights were 11–13 per cent higher than for private shipwrights in Plymouth and 41–80 per cent higher than in Brixham (Table 21.3).[12]

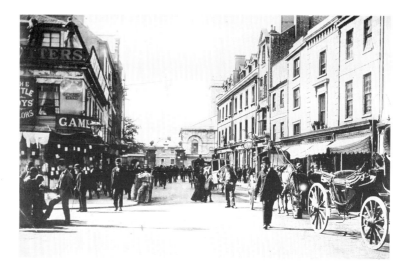

21.3 Fore Street, Devonport, looking west to the main gate of the South Yard of the Dockyard, c1891–4. All of this area was absorbed into the Dockyard after the Second World War. From a print by Francis Frith. (*City of Plymouth Museums and Art Gallery*)

Nevertheless, Dockyard workers agitated almost continually that their standard rates of pay were lower than those of comparable workers in the leading private shipbuilding regions. For example, between 1881 and 1890 Devonport shipwrights' weekly wages were 40 per cent below those on the Thames, the highest wage area for shipbuilding and engineering, and 13–31 per cent below those at Barrow, the Mersey, Clyde and Tyne, the other principal rivers on which warshipbuilding was practised (Table 21.3).

Did the Admiralty therefore make an inequitable contribution to the Devon economy by paying its workers lower than national wage rates? In fact, research by Price and Reid has suggested that the 1906 Board of Trade statistics, which are used by Hobsbawm and others to identify skilled private-sector shipbuilding workers as labour aristocrats, are seriously misleading. Price has highlighted the exclusion from analysis of men who failed to work a full 54-hour week. The difficulty of organising an even flow of work, partly owing to the varying proportions of particular trades required as construction progressed, combined with the practice of skilled men taking time off work, meant that it was very common to work for less than the standard hours. Reid's detailed study of Clydeside riveters' earnings indicates that, in contrast to the Board of Trade average of 55s per a week, most men in this occupation were taking home around 30s, and almost 30 per cent were earning less than this (*i.e.*, they may have been earning less than the dockyard standard rate of 32s 6d–34s 6d). Moreover, the notorious boom and slump cyclical pattern of shipbuilding output meant that some of this income was not available for immediate consumption, with men working hard to pay off debts incurred during the last spell of unemployment and building up reserves for the next. For the years between 1902 and 1914, unemployment amongst unionised private shipyard workers averaged 11 per cent but fluctuated between 8.2 per cent (1902), 14 per cent (1904), 7.7 per cent (1906), 23 per cent (1908), and 3.1 per cent (1913). Because of the Establishment, the dockyards were not subject to such violent fluctuations, and the spending power of Devonport workers was regular and not greatly disproportionate to that of other shipbuilding areas.[13]

It may be that the Dockyard helped limit the purchasing power of the Devon community in another way; in failing to provide an example of organised trade unionism capable of being imitated by private employees in what had become a low-waged county. The naval dockyards should have been fertile ground for the development of modern trade union organisation in the second half of the nineteenth century. They contained some of the largest and most concentrated groupings of skilled industrial workers in Britain, with a tradition of sporadic but sometimes fierce labour militancy, and they had a grievance in their apparently low wage rates compared with those of private yards. Trade unionism in private yards was unusually

Table 21.3
Selected comparisons of dockyard, private shipbuilding and other pay rates and earnings

A Shipwrights' average earnings 1881–1890

Thames	42s
Clyde	34s 1d
Mersey	39s 6d
Tyne	36s 11d
Devonport Dockyard	30s 3d

B Shipwrights' weekly time rates 1893

Devonport Dockyard	31s–34s
Plymouth	27s–30s
Appledore	24s
Dartmouth	25s
Brixham	20s–24s

C Shipbuilding weekly standard time/piece and average earnings 1906

Shipwrights' Standard Time

Devonport	32s 6d–34s 6d
Plymouth	30s–33s
Dartmouth	28s
Falmouth	24s

Average Earnings Working Full Week

Shipwrights (time)

Tyne, Wear, Tees	39s 11d
Clyde	37s 5d
South East/South West and Wales	34s 9d
UK	36s 4d

Riveters (piece)

Tyne, Wear, Tees	58s 1d
Clyde	54s 4d
South East/South West and Wales	46s
UK	55s 7d

Platers (piece)

Tyne, Wear, Tees	82s
Clyde	63s 1d
South East/South West and Wales	66s 9d
UK	71s 3d

D Various industries standard time weekly rates 1909

Engineers (turners/fitters)

Devonport and Plymouth General	36s
Naval	38s
Redruth	24s

Police Constables minimum – maximum

Devonport	23s 6d–34s 8d
Barnstaple	21s–26s

Lithographic printers

Devonport and Plymouth	33s–40s

Ordinary agricultural labourers

Devon (including in kind)	17s 1d

Ironfounders

Devonport	36s
Exeter	28s

Sources: A, BPP, 1873–4, Royal Commission on Labour Minutes of Evidence Group A, V c–6874, (1893) – VII 463–4; B, BPP, 1894, LXXXI, Report on Wages and Hours of Labour, Part III Standard Time Rates, Board of Trade; C, BPP, 1911, VI, Earnings and Hours Inquiry, Metal, Engineering and Shipbuilders Trade in 1906. Report by Board of Trade, 109–117; D, BPP, 1909, LXXX, Standard Time Rates, Board of Trade, 47–117.

strong, especially following the replacement of wood by iron and later steel. The Boilermakers Society in particular, founded in 1834, became one of the most powerful, best organised and most militant unions in Britain, and claimed to have organised 95 per cent of eligible skilled and semi-skilled workers in private yards by the early 1890s. Formal dockyard labour organisation, however, was characterised by its apparent relative weakness and late development, and by an almost total absence of significant industrial disputes.

Within the dockyards, two overlapping types of labour organisation emerged in the late nineteenth century; one of unions, associations, and societies specifically and exclusively representing government employees, and the other of trade unions with a majority of private-sector members. The first began in the 1880s after unionism was already well established in private shipbuilding, and largely paralleled the development of 'new unionism', *i.e.* the industrial organisation of unskilled and semi-skilled workers within the national economy. The most important was the Ship Construction Association, representing shipwrights, founded in 1884 and accounting for between half and two-thirds of total union membership in the dockyards in the 1890s and early 1900s. Unlike most dockyard labour organisations, it had significant membership in all the yards. However, from a peak of 2,400 in 1892 it declined to 540 in 1907, and in the following year merged with the dominant private sector union, the Associated Shipwrights Society, which had over 20,000 members. The successful 1889 London Docks strike provided the initial impetus for the organisation of dockyard labourers. Branches of the Dockyard Labourers Protection League, begun at Chatham in 1889, were formed at Devonport and Sheerness in 1890 and joined together in the Chatham-based Federated Council of Government Employees in 1891, subsequently including Portsmouth labourers and various small groups of semi-skilled men such as sawmill workers, hand-drillers and enginemen. However, the Federation's membership of 1,300 men in 1897 had only expanded to 1,550 by 1910, and it was declining in Devonport. [14]

The majority of dockyard labour organisations were much smaller (Table 21.4) and often short-lived. The Devonport and Keyham Ship Joiners (founded 1889), the Devonport Sailmakers (1901), the Devonport Royal Wood Caulkers branch (1906) and the Devonport Hammermen (1909) all subsequently disappeared.

The most important private-sector shipbuilding unions all had some members in the dockyards, but only the Associated Shipwrights Society achieved a significant base before the First World War. The Society opened a branch in Devonport in 1889, subsequently organising in other yards. Total dockyard membership topped 1,000 in 1891, but still represented less

Table 21.4
Significant dockyard trade unions (peak membership 100 and over) 1891–1910

	Year formed	Membership Peak	Year	1910
Ship Construction Association	1884	2,400	1892	(A)
Ship Joiners, Chatham	1886	125	1910	125
Ship Smiths, Chatham	1888	105	1909	100
Government Labourers, Chatham	1889	608	1909	593
Ship Joiners, Devonport	1889	150	1906	130
Government Labourers, Sheerness	1890	430	1909	400
Dockyard Ship Riggers	1890	250	1896	(B)
Government Labourers, Devonport	1890	430	1909	400
Royal Dockyard Iron and Steel Shipbuilders	1891	109	1906	98
Chatham Hand Drillers	1892	120	1895	98
Government Labourers, Portsmouth	1894	270	1910	270
Boilermakers Helpers, Chatham	1896	150	1910	150
Engine Drivers, Stokers, Chatham	1896	117	1910	117
Sail Riggers, Portsmouth	1906	102	1906	89
Hammermen, Devonport	1909	113	1910	113

(A) Merged with Associated Shipwrights Society in 1908.
(B) Dissolved 1899.
Sources: (BPP, LXXIII, 1900, 124–5). Report on Trade Unions 1899; (BPP, XLVII, 1912–3, 72–5). Report on Trade Unions 1908–1910.

than a fifth of potential recruits. Alexander Wilkie, the Society General Secretary, complained in 1892 that if the dockyard shipwrights ' . . . refuse or fail to join in with their fellow shipwrights and retain their present isolated and, in some respects, selfish position then they will have none but themselves to blame'. Despite increases in membership, neither the Shipwrights nor any other organisation was formally recognised by the Admiralty before the First World War, and they could not therefore engage in the type of collective bargaining well established in the private sector.[15]

Several factors inhibited such a development. Waters and Casey have stressed the impact of the Establishment system in tying a core of dockyard workers to the government, and the system of promotion by competitive examination on Civil Service lines which encouraged individual achievement rather than collective action. Yard labour organisations also had to deal with a single employer, normally dominant in the local labour market. By contrast, in times of high demand the private shipbuilding unions could exploit differences between competing employers on leading rivers such as the Clyde, which contained numerous yards. Following the closure of Woolwich and Deptford, the remaining dockyards were all situated in areas with low trade union densities and little tradition of sustained labour militancy.[16]

On the other hand, dockyard labour organisation adopted a clear strategy of using political rather than industrial pressure to exploit the favourable situation resulting from increased naval expenditure in the late nineteenth century. This was a means open to them, since the government was their employer, and they were also likely to attract wider support from its political opponents. Dockyardmen could express their grievances by means of petitions presented through the hierarchy of subordinate officers and the chief constructor to the Lords of the Admiralty. Before the 1880s these petitions were generally formulated by *ad hoc* shop-floor meetings or committees. Local MPs raised grievances in the House of Commons, often relating to individual workmen. The Conservative MP Sir John Gorst moved a motion accepted by the Liberal government for better pay and conditions in 1893. The Royal Commission on Labour of the same year was bombarded with dockyard grievances. Dockyard workers did receive significant wage increases in the early 1890s, probably as a result of this campaign. Their working hours were also reduced from fifty-four to forty-eight in 1894, a concession not generally granted to private sector engineering and shipbuilding workers, despite fierce agitation, until 1919-20. Devonport Dockyard workers played a leading role in this campaign, organising a Government Employees Eight Hours Committee, petitioning the Admiralty, organising mass meetings and sending deputations to Parliament.[17]

Workers in private yards did not have such ready methods of channelling grievances, but their effect was to isolate dockyard workers and to tie them to the dockyard system. In a Devon already weak in trade union organisation, their type of labour organisation and means of redress set them totally apart.

There were undoubtedly other significant reasons for the low level of trade unionism and the low level of wages in Devon besides the failure of the main industrial centre, Devonport Dockyard, to provide an imitable example. The small and scattered nature of business activity and the generally depressed state of the economy were major factors. In these matters, the failure of the Dockyard to do more to sustain either business activity or the wider Devon economy was more fundamental.

The limited impact of defence spending upon civilian manufacturing employment in Devon might seem surprising. Shipbuilding is essentially an assembly industry, with a high proportion of output accounted for by materials and components brought in from outside. The increasing complexity of ships, especially warships, reinforced this characteristic. For example, in 1913–14 material accounted for £1.429 million of the £3.708 million which the Admiralty spent in Royal Dockyards on new construction.[18] Devonport's shipbuilding output was at its peak leading up to the First World War (Figs. 21.5, 6), so the potential for outside suppliers in Devon was at its greatest. However, an analysis of several hundred contracts placed by the Admiralty between 1909 and 1913 suggests both the relatively small scale of Admiralty purchasing in the county and that its principal impact was in reinforcing the existing economic structure rather than providing much potential for growth. The Admiralty Contracts

21.4 Workers in the ship-fitting shop, main factory at Keyham, 1898. (*Devonport Dockyard Museum*)

Department placed thirty-four orders with Devon companies. Fifteen went to Plymouth and Devonport, seven were granted to the long-established Buckfastleigh-Ashburton woollen industry, and eight were for various types of woodwork. Engineering products are conspicuous by their absence (Table 21.5).

Table 21.5

Admiralty contracts placed in Devon, 1909–13

Type of contract/company	Location	Number of contracts
Serge		
Hamlyn	Buckfastleigh	4
J. Berry	Ashburton	3
Mattresses/pillows		
Graves	Devonport	2
Rundle, Rodgers & Brooke	Plymouth	2
Hides/leather		
Baker	Colyton	2
Vicary	Newton Abbot	2
Firebricks		
Martin	Plymouth	2
Candy	Newton Abbot	1
Candles		
New Patent Candle	Plymouth	3
Cabinet making, joinery, other woodwork		
Bartlet	Bideford	1
Claridge	Exeter	1
Graves	Devonport	2
Spooner	Devonport	1
Snawdon	Plymouth	1
H. Berry	Crediton	2
Upholstery		
Graves	Devonport	1
Knife lanyards		
Combs	Devonport	1
Horse and cart hire		
Cleave	Devonport	(running contract)
Timber		
Bayley	Devonport	3

Source: Board of Trade Journal, 1909–13.

21.5 Workers boarding the battleship HMS *King Edward VII*, 17,500 tons, under construction at Devonport in 1903. (*Devonport Dockyard Museum*)

The relative lack of civilian shipbuilding and engineering employment in Devon suggests that local industry also did not achieve significant benefits from using Dockyard-trained labour. The early development of private iron and steel steamship building shows many examples of men trained in one yard subsequently starting their own business. The mature industry continued to be characterised by the geographical mobility of labour between yards.

Three main factors served to limit linkages between the Dockyard and the local economy: technological change, the centralisation of decision making away from the Dockyard, and the distinctive culture of the Dockyard organisation. In the days of sail the Admiralty relied on outside contractors for basic raw materials such as timber, hemp, sailcloth, iron and copper.

21.6 Shipwrights cheer the launching of the battlecruiser HMS *Lion* from No.3 slip, South Yard, in 1912. Of 29,700 tons, with 8 × 13.5in guns, she was Admiral Beatty's flagship in the battles of Dogger Bank, 1915, and Jutland, 1916. (*City of Plymouth Museums and Art Gallery*)

The Dockyards maintained their own manufacturing capacity for hulls, masts, rope, sails, anchors, chains and copper sheeting, but, especially in wartime, made extensive purchases of the majority of these items. However, technological change tended to reduce the reliance placed on smaller suppliers. For example, between 1802 and 1806 the Admiralty installed a 12hp steam-powered block mill at Portsmouth, operating forty-five machines which initially supplied all the Navy's needs and put out of business three workshops which made blocks by hand in Plymouth and two in Devonport. The establishment of the Royal William Victualling Yard at East Stonehouse during 1835 provides another example of the consequences of the Navy's drive for self sufficiency and centralisation. Built at a cost of £2 million, the yard provided a wide range of mechanised facilities. A 40hp steam engine powered twenty-five pairs of millstones capable of grinding 1,000 bushels of corn in ten hours. Other facilities provided for the simultaneous slaughtering of seventy to eighty head of cattle, brewing beer, and baking bread and biscuits.[19] The Victualling Yard seldom worked at maximum capacity, and its potential in time of war, plus the extensive storehousing, designed to hold up to three years' supply of many items, meant that commercial suppliers could no longer hope for periodical windfall profits from the Navy. Canned food, encouraged by the Navy, and refrigeration also contributed to this greater self-sufficiency.

During the later part of the century, with the introduction of the steam ironclad, the Admiralty became more dependent on outside suppliers for a wide range of metalware including armour, gun mountings, engines and anchors. In some cases the dockyards had never developed sufficient capacity to meet their need, in others they had stopped manufacture, an example being the rolling of iron plates in the dockyards, which ceased in 1883. The Admiralty actively encouraged the growth of the private armaments industry, which developed into a very strong and sometimes seemingly incestuous relationship. The areas surrounding the principal dockyards lacked a general commercial engineering tradition and suffered from poor access to basic raw materials including coal and iron ore. They were further disadvantaged by the increasing centralisation of dockyard purchasing, culminating in the appointment of a Director of Contracts in 1869. By the late nineteenth century local dockyard officials had virtually no power to negotiate their own contracts.

Research indicates that branch factories controlled from outside a region are less likely to develop intra-regional supplier linkages than comparable locally-based enterprises. A local business will have a greater interest in sustaining the local economy. The Admiralty controlled in the royal dockyards one of Britain's major national manufacturing enterprises – collectively second largest in the country around 1907 and still eighth in 1935.[20] It took a wider national, rather than local, economic view in running them.[21]

The third factor inhibiting linkages between Devonport Dockyard and the local economy was the dockyard tradition in manufacture, which bred a distinctive culture of its own. Dockyards, at least until the introduction of commercial management, did not produce profits. Any financial gain from increased efficiency flowed back into central government funds. The supreme function of the dockyard, as repeatedly defined by the Admiralty, was its reliable and efficient operation in war, rather than considerations of peacetime manufacturing efficiency. Its manning levels always had to keep in mind the possibility of a sudden expansion of activity through war, as much as immediate work in hand. The Navy, as customer for its own products, specified work of high standard, and the dockyard culture was therefore to place an unusual and often overriding stress on quality over such other considerations as cost and delivery date. As Rear Admiral Pasley, Admiral Superintendent at Devonport, observed in 1860: 'The object of the Admiralty is not to have cheap ships, but good ones; and I have no doubt whatever of the superiority of quality of work done in the dockyards over private yards'.[22] It is not argued here that the emphasis on quality and the absence of a profit motive made Devonport Dockyard inherently more or less efficient than commercial enterprise. However, it is suggested that these characteristics, when combined with the diminishing freedom of action of local officials, made the skills developed in the Dockyard less transferable to local industry. In a wider context, the domination of the Dockyard in the local economy of Plymouth provided a cushioned, long-term security that did not encourage the development of competitive, risk-taking entrepreneurship in the community.

Those from outside the dockyard towns, who supported a shift of work to private yards on the grounds that state institutions could not by definition be efficient, were sometimes sceptical of the real economic benefit which the dockyards brought the local communities. Patrick Barry, a leading advocate of private warshipbuilding in the 1860s, protested:

> Why should society be taxed for the benefit of a handful of landlords in the dockyard towns, who in many cases have provided only wretched hovels for the shelter of the labourer and mechanic? The dockyard towns are in the main the filthiest in England.[23]

Imperfect though they may be as a measure, the ratable values in Table 21.6 suggest that Barry might have had a point in the case of Devonport.

It can be argued that both the lack of major private local wealth producing enterprises and the general preoccupation with the Navy as the main employer contributed to the long-term failure of Plymouth, the largest conurbation west of Bristol, to obtain a reasonable share of private or public (*e.g.* regional administrative centres) infrastructural investment. The growth of the Navy and the growth of Plymouth up to the First World War masked these failings. Naval retrenchment after the war revealed the inherent problems starkly.

Table 21.6
Rateable values per head 1874 and 1894

	1874	1894
England and Wales	4.6	5.2
Devon	4.2	5.0
Devonport	1.5	2.2
East Stonehouse	2.3	2.8
Plymouth	2.4	3.8
Newton Abbot	4.5	5.3
Exeter	4.1	5.5
Other Dockyard towns		
Portsmouth	2.5	4.0
Commercial ports		
Bristol	4.1	7.3
Liverpool	7.5	11.8
Southampton	3.5	4.6
Shipbuilding towns		
Barrow-in-Furness	–	4.4
Hartlepool	3.5	3.9
South Shields	2.7	3.9
Sunderland	2.8	3.8

Source: (BPP, 1895, LXXXIV). Local taxation returns.

The Interwar Period

The First World War added to the prewar expansion of the Dockyard workforce another 50 per cent increase to about 20,000 male and female employees. Demobilisation in 1918-19 inevitably produced contraction, but this was extended by the pressing need to economise on government expenditure after the enormous costs of the war, by the ending of the naval arms race with the elimination of the European threat, and by the subsequent great economic depression. Dockyard employment fell back to 15,803 in 1918. For a while the Admiralty sought to maintain numbers by short-time working, but reversion to full hours in August 1921, followed by the notorious 'Geddes Axe' on the naval estimates and the ten-year moratorium on capital ship construction in the Washington Naval Treaty of 1922, saw the workforce decline remorselessly to a low of 10,804 by 1933. The main burden of these cuts fell upon the hired workforce, but their extent was shown in 1926-7 when the first reduction of Established workers were made. No longer was the Admiralty able to sustain the core of Established skilled workers in each main dockyard, whatever the particular level of naval spending.

21.7 Dockyard workers leaving the Fore Street Gate at the noon lunch break, 1930. (*Devonport Dockyard Museum*)

The royal dockyards as a whole suffered less than the commercial naval shipbuilders, as the unemployment figures for 1932, the worst interwar year, demonstrate. Plymouth's 20.6 per cent unemployed contrasted to Newcastle's 26.7 per cent, Glasgow's 30.7 per cent and Barrow's 34.2 per cent. Unemployment in the Plymouth area throughout the interwar period tended to fluctuate around the national average, but was above that for Devon as a whole.[24] Nevertheless, an unemployment level in the early 1930s representing one in five of the working population presented major economic and social problems for the now consolidated city. Whilst Devon's overall population showed a minor increase, that of Plymouth stagnated around its 1921 level of 210,000, and in the following decade it was overtaken by Cardiff as second largest West Country city.

Although fluctuations in employment in the Dockyard were not unusual, the length of the economy drive, combined with moves towards international disarmament, led to a more fundamental questioning of the future of Plymouth and the Navy. Leslie Hore Belisha, the Liberal MP for Plymouth, declared that the 'naval towns [are] faced with disaster', while J H Moses, the Labour MP for Devonport and a former Dockyard worker, raised the issue of 'the Dockyard's continuance as a government establishment or – what nobody considers possible – its complete transfer to civilian control'.[25]

The three major dockyards took less of the burden of cuts than smaller or less well-established yards, although the decision to put Rosyth and Pembroke Dock on a care and maintenance basis from 1926 caused problems for Plymouth through the transfer of 300 of their Established men to Devonport. This accelerated the rate of discharges in Devonport's own workforce and also aggravated the already serious housing problem in the Plymouth area. The Admiralty replied to protests from local MPs that it was in the first instance the local authorities' function to provide suitable accommodation. The Navy continued to distance itself from the local economic and social consequences of its policies.[26]

A number of suggestions were made to the Admiralty and the government, from the Colwyn Committee appointed by the Admiralty in 1919 to local MPs and the City authorities in the early 1930s, as to ways that the Dockyard might be used to relieve Plymouth's unemployment problem. One suggestion was to transfer part of the Dockyard's labour force and facilities to a commercial employer. The Admiralty always set its face resolutely against this, and as far as private shipbuilding was concerned it was supported by the Colwyn Committee, which pointed to the difficulty of subdividing facilities and the Navy's need for priority use, as well as the 'fruitful source of discontent between the two bodies of men in disparity of wages and conditions of employment'.[27] The Colwyn Committee did, however, recommend the redevelopment of part of the Dockyard as a passenger terminal port, and in 1930 it was again proposed to turn part of the south yard into a commercial port. In rejecting the latter proposal the Admiralty argued that the facilities, even if currently underused, could not be given up because they might perform an essential role in the future, and it again stressed the problems of Admiralty and civilian labour, over whom it had no direct control, working in close proximity. The Admiralty argued that Plymouth had little advantage to attract traffic away from Southampton, a view backed in 1919–20 by the Board of Trade, which pointed to the lack of a thriving population or industrially developed hinterland to support such a port. Since such a port was intended to create these, this was a classic 'Catch 22' situation.[28]

The Admiralty was more willing to consider (though only as a temporary expedient) a second type of proposal: to use dockyard labour and facilities to do commercial work under the Admiralty's control.[29] However, it proved notably unenthusiastic about implementation. Between October 1919 and April 1920 Devonport received requests to build a 5,150dwt cargo steamer and seven smaller coasters and trawlers, and to recondition two Cunard passenger liners. Of these it only accepted the cargo steamer and a small collier, both for Plymouth owners. Subsequently, in 1922, it completed a 5,680grt tanker for Anglo-Saxon Petroleum, but these were the sum total of the yard's commercial construction. Devonport did undertake a significant amount of merchant repair and refitting work in the 1920s, but much of this was of reconversions from war purposes.[30] The Admiralty was loath to depart too far from the yard's basic functions. The rising tide of unemployment at the end of the decade increased pressure on the government to develop alternatives to naval work, but the Dockyard's own proposal, to construct a tunnel under the Tamar or to manufacture tanks and other mechanical parts for the Army, or aircraft parts, were rejected by the Admiralty on grounds of practicability and lack of long-term value because of the need for specialised plant and labour skills.[31]

More fundamentally, the Admiralty remained unconvinced about whether it had any specific responsibilities to maintain employment in the dockyard towns, and was more concerned to conserve the wider stock of national shipbuilding resources against its future needs. Walter Bridgeman, First Lord of the Admiralty in Baldwin's Conservative government, responding to pressure from dockyard town MPs in 1927, declared: 'The question of giving employment cannot be looked upon as a local matter and employment should be as widely distributed as possible'. Bridgeman followed the general line common to governments of all parties, that the commercial shipbuilding areas had a greater claim to help from limited governmental resources because they suffered greater unemployment.[32]

Despite the decline in Dockyard employment during the 1920s, Plymouth remained critically dependent on the Navy. The 1931 census shows that 40 per cent of the occupied population actually in employment fell into two groups 'Public Administration and Defence' and 'Shipbuilding and Marine Engineering', compared with 11 per cent for the country as a whole. The number directly engaged upon defence was 17,200, or 21 per cent of the occupied population in work. The interwar period did see some industrial development, but the overall employment structure remained largely the same as in the late nineteenth and early twentieth centuries. Rearmament in the 1930s helped employment but further increased the importance of the Navy in the local economy, with shipbuilding and marine engineering classified as the fastest growing manufacturing sectors between 1923 and 1937. The Nuffield Social Reconstruction Survey carried out in the early part of the Second World War noted:

> All Plymouth's industrial and commercial port activities taken together were a very small matter before the war by comparison with the employment provided directly and indirectly by the services.[33]

Although the Admiralty's reluctance to take measures actively to boost employment in the dockyard towns conformed to mainstream political opinion of the period, it is nevertheless surprising in the context of its traditional desire to maintain a core of workers who would be available for any emergency. In the longer term, lack of employment opportunities in all the dockyard towns could only encourage the type of depopulation evident at Pembroke Dock when that yard was closed. An underlying motive for opposing alternative development seems to have been a desire to maintain the Admiralty's domination of the dockyard towns' physical and labour resources. Throughout the period of retrenchment the Admiralty never lost

21.8   Frankfort Street in flames during the blitz on Plymouth, March 1941. (*Crispin Gill*)

hope of future expansion, but its desire to keep its opportunities open put a blight on alternative courses for the local economy. During the Second World War that policy might have seemed to have paid off from the Admiralty's viewpoint, but when retrenchment returned after the war that policy proved disastrous for the former town of Devonport.

The Dockyard and the Navy in Postwar Plymouth

Between 1945 and the early 1980s employment within Devonport Dockyard did not dramatically collapse. Rather, it generally subsided from over 20,000 to 14,000. The level of employment in the late 1970s and early 1980s remained substantially above that of the interwar years. However, it was now clear that the Navy and defence no longer offered any real prospect of sustained growth such as that which occurred between the mid-nineteenth century and 1914. Major investments in physical facilities, including the new frigate complex, formally opened in 1977, a submarine refit complex opened in 1980, and the greater area occupied by the postwar yard, served to increase efficiency and preserve the yard's future, but these and other developments did not create jobs in the same way as the establishment of the Keyham Steam Yard and its subsequent extension. Moreover, because the Dockyard still employed large numbers, the potential for the economic collapse of the local economy remained, underlining the need for industrial diversification already recognised in the 1920s and 1930s. If Plymouth and Devon were to lose their peripheral status, then economic growth had to come from elsewhere.

As in the 1920s and 1930s, the Admiralty showed little enthusiasm for using the Dockyard facilities for non-naval purposes. In 1948 only 2,000 men in all the royal dockyards were so employed. At Devonport, commercial work was mostly of a very minor nature, such as the installation of wiring on local housing estates and the manufacture of simple coal-cutting machinery. The two most important private repair jobs carried out after the war were to the 8,258-ton US liner *American Farmer* and a Norwegian tanker.[34]

Commercial work in the Dockyard virtually ended with the start of the Korean War in 1950, and never increased beyond a negligible proportion of Devonport's workload whilst the Dockyard remained under direct naval management. The issue of using dockyard facilities and labour for civilian purposes but under Admiralty control never became important after 1945, largely because of the long period of relatively stable employment in the Dockyard. The emphasis on the need for diversification of employment away from the Dockyard instead shifted the focus towards land use and the role of the Navy in shaping the city's postwar urban structure.

21.9 The ruins of George Street, the main shopping thoroughfare of Plymouth, after the blitz, March 1941. (*Crispin Gill*)

The intensive bombing raids of March and April 1941 are the most obvious harmful economic and social consequences of Plymouth's connection with the Dockyard. The raids destroyed the central part of the prewar city, leaving 1,500 houses beyond repair and a further 1,500 damaged. (Figs. 21.8, 9) Yet there was also economic and social opportunity in this disaster, and Plymouth was urged to plan 'boldly and comprehensively' by Lord Reith, the Minister of Buildings and Works, who visited the city in July. The result was the *Plan for Plymouth* completed in 1943 by Patrick Abercrombie, Professor of Town Planning at London University and President of the Town Planning Institute, and James Paton Watson, the City Engineer and Chief Surveyor.[35]

In the preparation of the *Plan* the ambivalent position of the Dockyard as both the mainstay of, and a deadweight on, the city's economy quickly became apparent. The *Plan* itself noted, 'In all seaport and ship-building towns a reservoir of labour is always desired and industries likely to compete for this reservoir are not especially encouraged'.[36] Far more immediately damaging was the way in which the Admiralty saw the devastation of large areas around the Dockyard as a good opportunity to obtain land cheaply and expand, so as to develop the Dockyard's internal layout on less congested lines to increase operating efficiency and reduce the future danger of extensive bomb damage among closely concentrated buildings. In 1942 the Admiralty set its extra requirements at not less than 150 acres, increasing this to 250 acres in 1945. This was a demand that the city council felt unable to resist. Abercrombie remarked after one meeting, 'The council (mainly retired men on pensions or of modest means) were naturally sensitive to any proposals involving an increase on the rates but were determined to put nothing in the way to prevent the retention of the Navy at Devonport or the extension of the Dockyard'.[37]

Increased rates would result from loss of income owing to reduced commercial development because of the proposed extension. Traditionally the Admiralty made a 'contribution' to the local authority which was always less than comparable business and commercial rates.[38] However, at the meeting the Admiralty warned that 'if no extra land could be acquired then the importance of the yard would necessarily decrease'. Given the Dockyard's long-standing and still-existing central place in the city's economy, that could not be contemplated. Even Abercrombie and Watson complacently accepted the continuing dominance of the Dockyard in their *Plan*, making only a few proposals for new small locally-controlled firms, and stating

In one way Plymouth has an easier task in preparing for its future than some other places: her destiny in the national economy is not and never has been uncertain . . . so long as the British Navy exists, Plymouth's principal occupation remains.[39]

Plymouth's urban structure, however, would be different, and the immediate casualty was the Navy's own offspring, the former town of Devonport. In 1942–5 the Admiralty planned an expanded Dockyard sufficient to maintain a Navy to defend the Empire. In the next two decades that Empire disintegrated before its eyes and the Dockyard's space requirements came down along with it. By 1957 it was asking for only 51.5 acres,[40] but in the meantime planning blight had befallen the area earmarked for its expansion (Fig. 21.10). An Admiralty report in 1945 admitted,

At Devonport, land which was offered to us (the only land suitable to us as it was contiguous to the Dockyard) was to have been the site of the new civic centre and the whole of the town planning was related to that fact.[41]

The result was that the focus of administrative, commercial and business development shifted decisively away from Devonport towards central Plymouth in the critical early period of reconstruction, while industry moved north and west of the city. Devonport's shops now serve only a local function, and all indicators including employment, housing, and social amenities demonstrate the relatively inferior status of Devonport within the city.[42] Having risen in 100 years from nothing to being the largest town in Devon, 150 years later its urban destiny was destroyed through the actions of its own creator.

At the end of the Second World War the government continued the policy of its predecessors in giving priority to reviving industry in formerly depressed areas. Hugh Dalton, President of the Board of Trade, privately doubted in 1943 'whether Plymouth or Devonport will number high or even not at all in areas for special consideration'.[43] In the event it was left to the City Council from an early stage to encourage industrial diversification to a much greater extent than that planned by Abercrombie and Watson or contemplated by successive governments. The first Development Plan in 1956 explicitly declared its desirability.[44] This policy was already under way with the establishment of the first industrial estates.

The first new firms arrived in 1946, and by the early 1980s over 65 new factories had been set up, providing over 10,000 jobs. Sixteen of the new factories were American owned, and electronics was strongly represented. Successive governments' attitudes to encouraging new industry became more positive with the provision of financial assistance between 1958 and 1961, and after 1969.[45] The policy of industrial diversification has achieved some significant success. For example, by 1984 high-technology industries such as electronics provided 3,265 jobs in the Plymouth travel-to-work area, representing 2.9 per cent of the total employment (UK average 2.7 per cent).[46] However, the structural problems of the local economy have not been completely solved, since the major beneficiaries of the new industries have been women and other workers not normally employed by the Dockyard. Indeed, Hurst asserts that, 'Many firms found a shortage of skilled labour in Plymouth as they considered ex-Dockyard workers of long employment unsuitable due to their attitude to work'.[47] The City Council's opposition to further cuts in the dockyard labour force during the 1980s was also based partly on the experience of the late 1970s recession, when some of the factories established after the war, with their decision-making located outside the region, closed or reduced their workforce.[48] By contrast, the Dockyard provided greater stability, allowing Plymouth to avoid the problems of de-industrialisation found in other major industrial cities. Plymouth was actually the only one of Britain's twenty largest cities not to experience population decline between the 1971 and 1981 censuses.[49]

The Dockyard's major contribution to the local economy continued to lie in terms of wages and salaries, which in 1984/85 totalled £150 million. Dockyard purchases from the local economy remained small, totalling approximately £1.5 million out of £90 million.[50] The City Council, when considering the introduction of commercial management into the Dockyard, did urge that preference should be given to locally based consortia which would achieve the greatest benefit to the local economy, but DML, led by American multinational Brown & Root, won the contract.[51]

The mid 1980s saw a shift in emphasis by the City Council towards encouraging development of small businesses, which have a greater propensity to purchase local goods and services, and of tourism. These

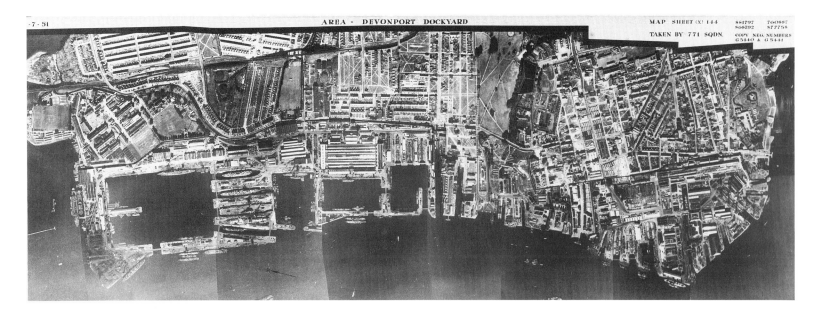

21.10   The full extent of Devonport Dockyard, shown in a photographic reconnaissance survey by 771 Squadron RAF in 1951. (*Devonport Dockyard Museum*)

developments in part reflected national policy, and in part the urgent need to replace Dockyard jobs. The closure of the Dockyard at Chatham, and the sharp contraction of activities at Portsmouth, have allowed and encouraged the development of naval-related tourism to a much greater extent than at Plymouth. The 1988 celebration of the defeat of the Spanish Armada marked the start of a much more vigorous effort to promote Plymouth's historical naval attractions.[52]

The evidence suggests that Plymouth's new private manufacturing industry (in common with similar branch factory type developments elsewhere) shares the traditional Dockyard characteristics of lack of linkages with local industry.[53] Therefore, in respect of its vulnerability to external decision-making and the low level of inter-industry linkages, the local economy appears little different at the start of the 1990s from that in the nineteenth century. However, in two other respects the local economy is changing significantly. First, defence manufacturing is developing for the first time outside the Dockyard. A 1986 survey of high-technology industry in Plymouth found that 71 per cent of the sample sold products to the Ministry of Defence, with 14 per cent selling more than 40 per cent of the output of the MoD. This development is completely unrelated to Plymouth's traditional defence role (the defence dependence of Bristol's much larger high-technology sector was found to be very similar), but is related to the high national orientation of high-technology industry (especially electronics) towards defence. The employment provided remains well below that still provided in the Dockyard, but the factors which discouraged private defence manufacture in the nineteenth century, such as access to raw materials, are no longer relevant in the age of missiles and electronic warfare. Secondly, the new commercial management of the Dockyard began with the specific objective of increasing the proportion of non-defence work in the yard, a reversal of the Admiralty's traditional policy of seeing such work, at best, as a temporary stop-gap. The 1990s and beyond may therefore see increasing defence-related employment outside the Dockyard, combined with in-creased non-defence-related work within the yard.

Despite the efforts at diversification, the Dockyard and the Navy continued to dominate the local economy into the late 1980s, with shipbuilding and repair accounting for 43 per cent of manufacturing employment in the Plymouth travel-to-work area, compared with 56 per cent in 1961, 41 per cent in 1971 and 49 per cent in 1981. Between 1987 and mid-1993 employment within the Dockyard more than halved to about 5,500 men, and is set to fall further, as is the number of uniformed personnel in the Navy. Some of the problems experienced due to the undeveloped local economy are reflected in research carried out on the fates of dockyard workers made redundant during the late 1980s. It was found that a significant number of workers classified as skilled manual within the Dockyard had taken unskilled employment in a diverse range of occupa-tions. Some office and administrative workers also moved into unskilled manual employment. The two groups which experienced the highest rates of unemployment comprised former managerial staff and former unskilled manual workers. Overall, Plymouth continued to experience unemployment rates higher than general in the UK; hence the intensive and successful political lobbying to secure the contract to refit Trident submarines at the dockyard in 1993.[55]

Conclusion and prospect

The Admiralty Dockyard/naval base presence in Greater Plymouth over the last century and a half has taken on something of a Jekyll and Hyde character in its contribution to the economic and social life of city and county. While all of its rivals were closed or downgraded, Devonport's strategic situation has ensured its survival as Britain's premier dockyard and the biggest naval base in Western Europe. The Dockyard remains Plymouth's major employer, while the City Council admitted to the House of Commons Defence Committee in 1985 that its policy of economic diversification had achieved 'only a limited degree of success. The creation of new jobs has not reduced unemployment but only prevented the problem becoming worse'.[56]

In this, the major emerging deadweight from the continuing naval presence is its hold on land. A report by Peat Marwick & Co for the City Council in 1984–5 showed that the extensive use of land by the Navy, including the 330–acre Dockyard site, had reduced the scope for industrial development given the shortage of suitable sites elsewhere in a Plymouth hemmed in by the Sound, Tamar, Plym and Dartmoor and surrounded by environmentally sensitive neighbours.[57] The way in which Portsmouth's flagging economy has been turned round by industrial and commercial use of land released by the Navy is an example which will inevitably fuel a continuing tension between naval and civilian needs. A mutually acceptable balance has still be be achieved.[58]

21: The Dockyard in the Local Economy

1 See G Finch. 'The Experience of the Peripheries in an Age of Industrialisation. The Case of Devon 1840–1914' (unpublished D. Phil. thesis, University of Oxford, 1984).

2 Census of the Population, 1851, 1911; *Kelly's Directory* of Devon, 1914.

3 B R Mitchell and P Deane, *Abstract of British Historical Statistics* (Cambridge, 1971), 20–7.

4 W G Hoskins, *Devon* (1954), 530, 532; William White, *White's Devon* (1850; reprinted Newton Abbot, 1968), 633.

5 *Slater's Directory 1852–3*, 111.

6 *Accounts and Papers*, (BPP, 1908, CVII. 743). The Cost of Living of the Working Classes: Report by the Board of Trade.

7 Mitchell and Deane, *Abstract*, 24–7.

8 *Select Committee on Public Establishment* [Exemption from Rates] (BPP, 1857–8, XI, 40).

9 R Fitzgerald, *Business Labour Management and Industrial Welfare in the Industrial Revolution 1841–1939* (1988), 167.

10 *Accounts and Papers* (BPP, 1893–4, LV). Statement of the Classes of Workers in Employment at Home.

11 *Royal Commission on Labour* (BPP, 1893–4, XXXII(3), 158–71, 478–86).

12 BPP, 1893–4, LXXXI.

13 S Price, 'Riveters' Earnings in Clyde Shipbuilding 1883–1913', *Scottish Economic and Social History*, 2 (1981), 42–65; A Reid, 'The Division of Labour in the Shipbuilding Industry, 1888–1920, with Special Reference to Clydeside' (unpublished PhD thesis, University of Cambridge, 1980), 90–2.

14 N Casey, 'An Early Organisational Hegemony. Methods of Social Control in a Victorian Dockyard', *Social Sciences Information*, 23 (1984), 671–700.

15 D Dougan, *The Shipwrights* (Newcastle, 1975), 74.

16 M Waters, 'A Social History of Dockyard Workers at Chatham, Kent, 1860–1914' (unpublished PhD thesis, University of Essex, 1979). Devonport nevertheless produced one of the most prominent and successful trade union leaders of the late nineteenth century in Robert Knight, General Secretary of the Boilermakers Society, 1871–99. See J Bellamy and J Saville, eds, *Dictionary of Labour Biography* (1982) vi, 152–6.

17 *HCD*, Vol. IX, 4th series, Col.310, 24 Feb. 1893.

18 *Accounts and Papers* (BPP, 1914–16, XL, 11–12). Dockyard Expense Account, 1913–14.

19 *White's Devon*, 647.

20 C Shaw, 'The Largest Manufacturing Companies of 1907', *Business History*, XXV (March 1983), 42–60; L Journham, 'The Largest Manufacturing Companies of 1935', *Business History*, (April 1986), 226–45.

21 *Accounts and Papers*. (BPP, 1886, XIII, 137). Report of the Committee to Inquire into Dockyard Administration and Economy; P Gripaios, P Bishop, R Gripaios and C Herbert, 'High Technology Industry in a Peripheral Area. The Case of Plymouth', *Regional Studies*, 23 (April 1989), 151–8.

22 *Accounts and Papers* (BPP, 1860, XLIII). Observation of the Superintendents and Officers of the Dockyards on the Report of the Committee on Dockyard Economy.

23 P Barry, *Dockyard Economy and Naval Power* (1863), 20.

24 M P Fogarty, *Prospects of the Industrial Areas of Great Britain* (1945), 31–3, 373.

25 *HCD*, 24 July 1927; *Western Morning News*, 11 Dec. 1929.

26 *HCD*, Vol. 193, Col.966, 22 March 1926. G Dicker, *A Short History of Devonport Royal Dockyard* (Devonport, n.d.), 18, points out that the Admiralty eventually relented and sponsored a new street, named Pemros Road, of 174 houses in St Budeaux for the transferees from Pembroke and Rosyth.

27 *Accounts and Papers* (BPP, 1920, XXI, 2). Report of the Committee Appointed to consider how far it may be possible to use the Royal Dockyards for the Construction of Merchant Shipping.

28 PRO, BT 65/2, 1919–20; BT 56/7, 311. 'Admiralty View on the Development of Devonport as a Terminal Port', 10 Feb. 1930.

29 PRO, BT 65/2. Admiralty Memorandum to the Cabinet, Dec. 1919.

30 *Shipping and Shipbuilder Record*, 20 May 1920; K V Burns, *The Devonport Dockyard Story* (Liskeard, 1984), 85.

31 Burns, *Devonport Dockyard Story*, 93; *HCD*, Vol. 230, cols. 1294, 1567, 24, 26 July 1929.

32 *HCD*, Vol. 203, col. 1802, 14 March 1927; Vol. 221, cols. 1567–1571, 26 July 1929.

33 Fogarty, *Prospects of the Industrial Areas*, 374.

34 Burns, *Devonport Dockyard Story*, 100; *HCD*, Vol. 448 col. 967, 8 March 1948.

35 Western Morning News, *The Plymouth Blitz* (Plymouth, n.d.); J Goodridge, 'No Half and Half Affair. The Plan for Plymouth' in W M Brayshay *Post War Plymouth. Planning and Reconstruction* (Plymouth, 1983), 9.

36 J P Watson and P Abercrombie, *A Plan For Plymouth* (1943), 25.

37 PRO, ADM 1/17810. 'Plymouth's Post War Reconstruction and Development'. Minute of Conference at Admiralty with Abercrombie and Watson.

38 *Western Morning News*, 14 June 1988.

39 *Plan for Plymouth*, 2.

40 PRO, ADM 1/17810. 'Plymouth's Post War Reconstruction'; Burns, *Devonport Dockyard Story*, 101.

41 PRO, ADM 1/19056. Royal Dockyard Policy, Memorandum from the First Lord to the Prime Minister, 1945.

42 D J Maguire, W M Brayshay and B J Chalkley, *Plymouth in Maps. A Social and Economic Atlas* (Plymouth, 1987), 26–79.

43 PRO, BT 64/3217. 'Enquiry about Postwar Reconstruction at Plymouth', Letter from L Hore-Belisha to the Board of Trade and reply, 1943.

44 Plymouth City Council, *City of Plymouth Development Plan* (Plymouth, 1956), 53.

45 *City of Plymouth Local Plan. Report of Survey* (Plymouth, 1980), 40.

46 P Gripaios *et al*, 'High Technology', 151–8.

47 R L Hurst, *The Devon and Cornwall Economy* (Plymouth, 1984), 11.

48 Bishop, 'Dependence and Diversification in the Local Economy', 169–76.

49 Maguire *et al*, *Plymouth in Maps*, 26.

50 House of Commons Sessional Papers, 1984–85, HC 453, 4th Report from the Defence Committee 1984–85, 'The Future of the Royal Dockyards', 71, 75.

51 'Future of the Dockyards', 75.

52 Bishop, 'Dependence and Diversification in the Local Economy of Plymouth', 175; Maguire *et al*, *Plymouth in Maps*, 37; J Bradbeer and G Moon, 'The Defence Town in Crisis. Paradox of the Tourism Strategy' in Bateman and Riley, eds, *The Geography of Defence*, 82–99.

53 Gripaios *et al*, 'High Technology', 155.

54 P Bishop, 'Defence, the Dockyard and Diversification' in B Chalkely, *et al*, eds, *Plymouth: Maritime City in Transition* (1991), 128.

55 P and R Gripaios, 'Post Redundancy Experience: The Case of Devonport', *Defense Analysis*, 8 (1992), 321–4.

56 House of Commons Sessional Papers, 1984–85, HC 453, 4th Report from the Defence Committee 1984–85. Supplementary Memorandum from Plymouth City Council.

57 See n.56; Devon County Council, *Devon Structure Plan 1979* (Exeter, 1979), 168.

58 The author gratefully acknowledges the assistance of Michael Duffy and Todd Gray in the preparation of this chapter.

22 Ocean Liners at Plymouth

CRISPIN GILL

FOR OVER A CENTURY Plymouth was a port of call for all the famous ocean liners of the world. In this century alone, since 1900, 6,120,820 passengers landed or were embarked from Millbay Docks, an average (figures are missing for the years 1937–46) of 15,487 a year. This includes the thin years of World War One and the final years when the trade was running down (see Table 22.1). In the great years between 1926 and 1936 the yearly total never fell below 30,000.

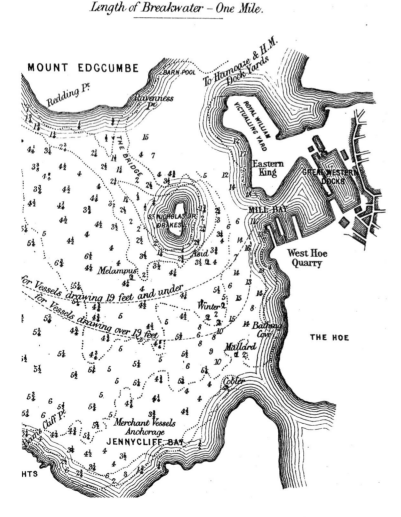

22.1 A chart of Plymouth Sound, 1877. (*Thubron*, Docks of Great Britain *[1881]*)

Plymouth was never a terminal port, like Liverpool, London or Southampton, but in the days before air travel a whole day could be cut from travelling time by landing at Plymouth and going on to London by Ocean Mail express train, instead of sailing up-channel to Southampton. Politicians, diplomats, soldiers, film stars, the great and the good and the jet set of the age, everyone in a hurry, came ashore at Plymouth. As many as 800 at a time would come ashore from one liner. Millions of mailbags were handled, too, from the first days, when mail contracts were given to steamers, to the last days, when air travel took over. The dawn of the trade came within forty years of the first commercial steamers in the world.

In 1812 Bell's steamship *Comet* started a regular service on the Clyde. In 1824 Abraham Cunard & Son had a British Admiralty mail contract for a steamer service between Halifax, Boston and Bermuda.[1] In 1825 the Plymouth and Portsmouth Steam Packet Company had two steamers in service, *Sir Francis Drake* and *Brunswick*.[2] In 1831 *Cape Breton* made the first east-west crossing of the Atlantic using steam, from Plymouth to Sydney, Nova Scotia.[3] In 1832 an American, Dr Junius Smith, took fifty-seven days crossing the Atlantic under sail and resolved that there must be a quicker way.[4]

He was not alone in his idea. In 1833 Cunard's son, Samuel, already chairman of the Quebec and Halifax Steam Navigation Co, sent *Royal William* across the Atlantic on the first passenger-carrying Atlantic voyage using steam.[5] In 1835 I K Brunel proposed to the Great Western Railway (GWR) directors that they should build steamers as well as railways, and take their western terminus from Bristol across to New York.[6] In the same year Smith formed the British and American Steam Navigation Co.

Both Smith's company and the Great Western began building, and when it became clear that the railway's *Great Western* would be ready first, Smith hired the paddler *Sirius* from an Irish company and just beat *Great Western* into New York.[7] That was in April 1838. That year the British Admiralty offered a contract for carrying mail across the North Atlantic, by steamer. On her second return from New York *Sirius* landed passengers and about 3,000 packets of mail at Plymouth, anchoring in the Cattewater.[8] But not until 1840 was the Atlantic mail contract awarded, and it went to Samuel Cunard's British & North American Royal Mail Steam Packet Co, formed with Scottish capital and sailing out of Liverpool.[9]

Plymouth Ambitions

A Plymouth entrepreneur, Thomas Gill, first Mayor of Plymouth under the Municipal Reform Act of 1835, MP for the town 1841–6, and owner of lime kilns and a soap factory at Mill Bay, saw new opportunities. He was already chairman of the railway company which had Brunel survey a line from Exeter to Plymouth in 1836. In 1839 he announced plans to build a new pier at Mill Bay,[10] capable of taking the largest steamers afloat, with J M Rendel as the engineer. In fact, the *Great Britain* berthed alongside on her passage back from London to Bristol in 1845.[11]

Southampton had already been more enterprising. When, in 1840, commissioners were examining the rival merits of the Channel ports as potential mail packet stations, Southampton already had the Royal Pier, an established railway link with London, and had started building the first tidal dock. In 1842 the Peninsula & Oriental Steam Navigation Company was using the dock, and in the same year the Royal Mail Steam Packet Company

Table 22.1
Ocean mail & passenger traffic, Millbay Docks, Plymouth, 1879–1963

Year	Homeward bound			Outward bound		Totals			Passengers to Continent
	No. of vessels	passengers	specie	No. of vessels	passengers	No of vessels	passengers	mailbags	
1879							3,538		
80							3,706		
81							4,399		
82							8,816		
83							9,139		
84							9,315		
85							8,781		
86	6,484				2,784		10,268		
87	6,090				3,234		9,324		
88	6,898				2,316		9,204		
89	8,012				2,406		10,418		
1890	9,022				1,825		10,847		
91	8,788				1,678		10,466		
92	8,457				1,710		10,167		
93	8,351				1,319		9,670		
94	9,164				1,327		10,491		
95	9,693				1,828		11,521		
96	12,796				1,822		14,618		
97	15,485				1,829		17,314		
98	8,579				1,402		9,981		
99							11,556		
1900							12,467		
1	342			102		444	12,919		
2	359			105		464	15,466		
3	404			106		510	18,421		
4	422			91		513	17,146		
5	375			69		444	15,482		
6	391			85		476	19,300		
7	440			106		546	21,181		
8	428			94		522	18,841		
9	421			67		488	18,287		
1910	442			41		483	20,796		
11	452			39		491	24,213	187,231	
12	457			40		497	27,334	187,411	
13	469			44		513	30,841	219,691	
14	391			57		448	30,291	178,997	
15	209			31		240	25,705	111,374	
16	164			52		216	19,609	87,572	
17	65			47		112	7,257	97,664	
18	20			50		70	4,185	64,595	
19	188			75		263	21,622	95,675	
1920	221		£623,134	64		285	18,022	84,439	
21	284		£761,000	66		350	16,496	200,224	
22	448		£301,465	79		527	23,094	302,025	
23	471		£848,872	69		540	23,215	267,721	
24	444			68		512	24,938	249,893	
25	486		£1,368,297	60		546	28,817	235,481	
26	570			68		638	31,159	277,901	
27	615			61		676	34,929	282,247	1,444
28	637			71		708	37,027	325,412	1,882
29	667			77		744	39,086	317,594	1,560
1930	682			106		788	41,130	307,912	1,942
31	606			101		707	32,859	222,914	1,940
32	536			86		622	29,233	226,255	1,619
33	500			92		592	27,941	207,362	1,691
34	500			96		596	34,141	231,466	1,590
35	471			33		504	33,294	233,314	1,234
36	478			20		498	30,873	206,812	873
1947				66			3,589	112,996	
48				109			5,769	355,365	
49				127			7,960	437,295	
1950				162			10,977	202,026	
51				182			15,945	256,685	
52				145			15,097	128,266	
53				166			18,824	130,456	
54				185			24,669	68,053	
55				187			29,038	39,552	
56				177			25,832	39,558	
57				154			20,446	50,405	
58				172			18,286	16,798	
59				113			13,386	10,006	
1960				93			12,572	8,103	
61				104			12,345	4,074	
62				82			6,425	2,872	
63				—			—	—	

Note: Some Chamber of Commerce reports survive from pre-1936 years, but figures are not quite identical with Dock records. Dock records have been used for these years, although Chamber of Commerce Tables also give numbers of vessels and total vessel tonnages.

When no figures are given, none are available.

Sources: 1879–1936, MSS vols. in Dock Manager's Office, Millbay. 1947–1963, Plymouth Chamber of Commerce Annual Reports.

was using Southampton as the terminus of its West Indies service.[12] Not until 1850, with its railway link with London completed and the outer basin of Millbay Docks finished, did Plymouth receive its first mail contract, for the Cape of Good Hope mails.

Although passengers ultimately became the vital factor in ocean liner traffic, it was the mail contracts which first made the business economic, and which determined the timing, the regularity, and even to some extent the kind of ship employed. Not for nothing did older Plymothians, up to the end of the traffic, call these mighty vessels the 'mail boats'. Later mails could be embarked at Plymouth, courtesy of the railway, instead of at London or Southampton, and homeward-bound mail landed at Plymouth could be in London long before the ship even reached Southampton. In the fullness of time this was realised by passengers, too.

Mail-Packet Station

Monday 16 December 1850 was a great day in Plymouth. 'The Corporations of Plymouth and Devonport [then a separate town] conveyed the first dispatch of Cape Mails from the Post Office in grand procession through the town to the screw steamer *Bosphorous*, waiting to receive them'. It was a grand procession: three military bands, sailors from HMS *Bellerophon*, twenty carriages and an omnibus drawn by four white horses containing the Post Master of Plymouth and with the mail bags piled on top.[13] The General Screw Steamship Co had the contract, and in 1852 Plymouth also became the packet station for the Australian mail, awarded to the Australian RMSNC.[14]

General Screw also extended its services to Australia, but problems with the ships, the cost of coal at distant coaling stations and the inadequate mail subsidy soon had the company in difficulties. It went out of business in 1856, and in 1857, after a brief spell with another company, the Cape contract was awarded to the Union Line. In September 1857 *Dane* sailed from Southampton, picked up the mail at Plymouth, and made Cape Town in forty-four days. On her return voyage she landed 10,867 letters and 3,671 newspapers at Plymouth on 6 January 1858. A monthly service was launched, by 1861 it was fortnightly, and the Union Line became the most successful of its day, beating even Cunard for regularity.

Table 22.2
Lines of Royal Mail steamers calling at Plymouth, 1882–3

Name of line	Service	Owners	Local Agents
Colonial Line	Australia		Weekes, Phillips & Co
Castle Line	Cape of Good Hope	Castle M1.Pkt.SSCo	Smith, Sundius & Co
Direct Line	Demerara		Fox, Sons & Co
Holt Line	New York		JT Wright & Co
Monarch Line	Australia	J Patton, jun & Co	
Orient Line	Cape of Good Hope and Australia	Anderson, Anderson & Co	JT Wright & Co
P and O Line	China, India and Australia	Peninsula & Oriental SN Co	Fox, Sons & Co
Royal Mail Line	West Indies	Royal M1.S.Pkt Co	Fox, Sons & Co
Queensland Royal Mail	Australia		Weekes, Phillips & Co
South African Line	Cape of Good Hope	Tower Hill SS Co Ltd	Weekes, Phillips & Co
West African Line	West Coast Africa	African S Ship Co	H J Waring & Co
West African Line	West Coast Africa	British & African Steam Nav Co	H J Waring & Co
Union Line	Cape of Good Hope	Union Steam Ship Co	H J Waring & Co
Hamburg American Line	New York and Hamburg	Hamburg American Steam Ship Co	Smith, Sunduis & Co
British India Line	Australia	British India SN Co	Weekes, Phillips & Co

Source: Eyre Brothers Post Office Plymouth, and Devonport District Directory, 1882–3.

Dartmouth Competition

In 1872 Donald Currie started his rival Castle Line from Dartmouth, operating on alternate weeks with the Union Line so that a weekly mail service was provided. Mail could go by his ships if one marked the envelope 'By private steamship - - - - - - Castle', 'by Donald Currie Line', or 'by

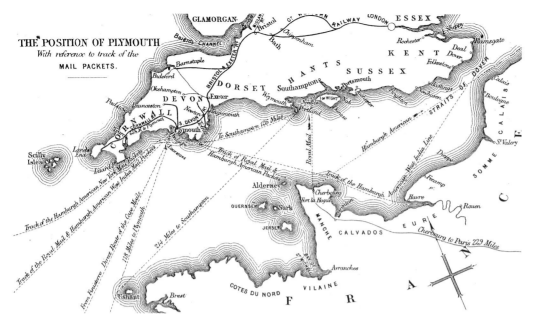

in the Sound and embarking or discharging mail and passengers by tender. At first these tenders were hired, but when the railway companies took over the dock in 1873 they built their own tender. By 1882 there were four. In that year, when the prestigious P&O began its regular call, conditions in Millbay Dock were considerably improved. Instead of passengers having to take cabs to Millbay Station, trains of carriages and luggage vans were brought into the dock and passengers could emerge from the Customs shed and go straight to their compartment. This facility, which continued as long as liners used the port, was also made available to the Union, Royal Mail, Castle and Orient lines, as well as the foreign companies.[25] Both Custom House and waiting rooms were enlarged, and the Duke of Cornwall Hotel opened a refreshment room. The

Dartmouth ship of 22nd instant'. His ships were faster, his postage rates were lower because private ships did not have to guarantee the fixed times of the Royal Mail steamers, and by 1876 Donald Currie was sharing the mail contract with the Union Line. In 1891 Castle ships abandoned Dartmouth in favour of Southampton, landing the homeward mail at Plymouth, and in 1900 the two amalgamated as the Union-Castle Line. This brought an end to the Plymouth call, although it was revived in 1922.[15]

Competition was great in the Australian run, with various companies, including Houlder and Money Wigram,[16] competing and making Plymouth calls both ways. Eventually the route around the Cape was taken over by the Orient Line, which in 1877 began calls at Plymouth outward and homeward,[17] and the Peninsula and Oriental Line, which had the contract for the Far East mail via Suez, followed suit in 1882 (before the canal opened in 1869 the mail was carried overland across the isthmus). Orient won part of the contract for the Australian mail in 1883, and henceforth made all its voyages via Suez.[18] In time the two companies merged, but the Plymouth call remained. In 1880 Shaw Savill & Albion began Plymouth calls on its New Zealand service both outward and homeward, a service taken over in 1884 by White Star ships under Shaw Savill management.[19]

Atlantic Traffic

If the earlier liner trade at Plymouth is associated with the Cape and Australian runs, it was not long before the Atlantic crossing came into the picture. Royal Mail, serving the West Indies and South America, began a homeward call at Plymouth in 1860, and in 1869 the German Hamburg-America ships from New York began an eastbound call at Plymouth instead of Southampton.[20] But within a year the Franco-German war broke out and Hamburg-America's *Holsatia*, with five other German ships, was trapped in Plymouth with French frigates hovering outside the port.[21] With the end of the war the Plymouth call was resumed, and the Colonial Line, which later became the Temperly Line, operating between London and Montreal, began a Plymouth call which continued until the line fell to the North Atlantic competition in 1879.[22]

The liner trade was becoming international. The Compagnie Generale Transatlantique, commonly called the French Line, began a both-ways call at Plymouth in 1875, and its *Amerique* caused some stir, for she was the first ship in the world to be lit by electricity.[23] The Eagle Line of Germany began calling homeward-bound from New York to Hamburg in 1873, but the loss of *Schiller* with over 300 lives in the Isles of Scilly in 1875 brought the company to an early end.[24]

Beginning of the Boom

Ships were getting too large to berth in Millbay, and were now anchoring

Table 22.3
Liners calling at Plymouth, 1885

Date service started	Company	From	For	Calls in weeks	
				Outward	Homeward
1867	Royal Mail	London	Panama	–	2
1869	Hamburg-America	Hamburg	New York	–	1
1873	Union Co	London	Natal	2	2
1875	Donald Currie	London	Natal	–	2
1878	British & African	Hamburg	West Coast	2	–
1879	Orient	London	Sydney	2	2
1881	British India	London	Sydney	4	4
1881	Money Wigram	London	Australia & New Zealand	Occasional	
1882	S Africa Line	London	S Africa	4	–
1883	P & O	London	India, China & Australia	–	1/2
1883	New Zealand SC	London	NZ, Aus.	4	4
1884	Shaw Savill Albion	London	NZ, Aus.	4	4
1884	National (British)	London	New York	2	2
1885	British India	London	India	–	2

Note: Inglis' dates do not always agree with those in text, but are according to his paper.

Source: J C Inglis, 'Harbour Accommodation in the West', *Transactions of the Plymouth Institution*, IX, 154, paper delivered 18 December 1884.

hotel was built by the directors of the railway and the docks in 1862 to serve the new traffic, and was quickly followed by the Albion and the Continental (now one hotel) and in 1880 by the Grand on the Hoe.[26] An 1882 directory lists fourteen lines as calling at Plymouth.[27]

The year 1882 saw the traffic doubled, to 8,800 passengers compared with 4,400 the previous year. The figure passed the 10,000 mark in 1886 and reached 17,000 in 1897. London was *en fête* that year for the Queen's Diamond Jubilee, in Paris *la belle epoque* was at its height, holiday traffic between the United States, Britain, France and Germany was growing at great speed, and bigger and better liners were being produced. In 1897 the Norddeutscher Lloyd's *Kaiser Wilhelm der Grosse*, the fastest and biggest ship in the world, called homeward-bound on her maiden voyage.[28] Two years later the Hamburg–America company began calling both ways. Germany was challenging Britain's supremacy at sea. She had captured the blue riband for the fastest crossing of the North Atlantic and had held it since 1881. For several years the battle was between the two rival German companies, with Cunard and the White Star competing from Liverpool, and the French Line and the American Line also in the battle for profits.

The Railway Battle

There was also competition ashore. The London and South Western Railway (LSWR), owner of Southampton Docks, achieved its ambition of nearly half a century when in 1890 it opened its own line to Plymouth. It had a goods branch line from Devonport Station to Stonehouse Pool, and in 1904 it obtained a contract from the American Line to handle its passengers at Plymouth. A station was rapidly built at Ocean Quay, the terminus of this Stonehouse Pool line, and the LSWR brought one of its Southampton–Jersey ships down to act as tender. The first ship handled was *St Louis*, on 9 April 1904, and fifty-seven passengers were at Waterloo in 4hr 22min. The GPO still insisted on the GWR handling the mail, so two tenders had to serve the liner. The Ocean Mail trains which met the tenders were racing to London along their different routes, a race which in time led to the GWR's *City of Truro* reaching a record 102.3mph on one journey.[29] Racing ended with the crash in 1906 of an LSWR Ocean Mail in Salisbury Station with the death of twenty-four passengers.[30] From then on the LSWR concentrated on comfort, and in 1910 the competition ended.

The GWR, encouraged by the start of a cross-Channel service to Brest to handle the Breton strawberry crop in 1896, started a regular passenger service to Brest in 1908, extending it to Nantes in 1910. The LSWR resented any rivalry to its cross-Channel services, and in the co-operative atmosphere of 1910, when both companies were ironing out competition on various routes, compromise was reached over Plymouth. The LSWR gave up its liner business and sold its tender *Atalanta* to the GWR, and next year the GWR ended its Brest–Nantes service.[31] Ocean Quay was an expensive luxury, only used by some small companies apart from the American Line. On at least one occasion a steamer from West Africa actually docked there.[32]

Traffic was steadily growing. In 1901, 102 steamers called outward bound and 342 homeward bound, with 12,919 passengers handled (see Table 22.1). In 1908 two new tenders came into service, in 1910 Holland–America started a weekly mail call both ways,[33] and the next year the Booth Line began to call on its Liverpool–South America service. From 1907 to 1911 some White Star liners from New York, *Adriatic*, *Majestic* and *Oceanic*, called regularly homeward bound for Cherbourg and Southampton.[34] In 1913 the outward-bound calls were down to 44, probably as a result of the fall-off in the emigration traffic, but homeward-bound calls were up to 469, with 30,841 passengers. Nor did the war years end the traffic through the port, though it was drastically reduced, down to 70 calls in 1918 and only 4,185 passengers. The end of the war saw an immediate leap upwards, with 263 calls in 1919 and 21,622 passengers. The GWR and the shipping agents set up a signal station on Rame Head, with good visibility to the west, so that telephone calls could report the imminent arrival of liners and tenders could be waiting for them in the Sound. This replaced the formerly-used Watch Tower on Plymouth Hoe, near Smeaton's Tower. There were some ten shipping agents in the port, with men known the world over such as Frank Phillips, Harry Clear (who died a centenarian in 1969), W T Leaman and George Scantlebury.[35]

The Interwar Years

The year 1919 also saw Cunard move its base from Liverpool to Southampton, partly to shorten the railway journey to London, but even more to replace the now-vanished German lines.[36] With this move came Cunard calls at Plymouth inward-bound, with famous ships such as *Mauretania* and *Aquitania* and the ex-German

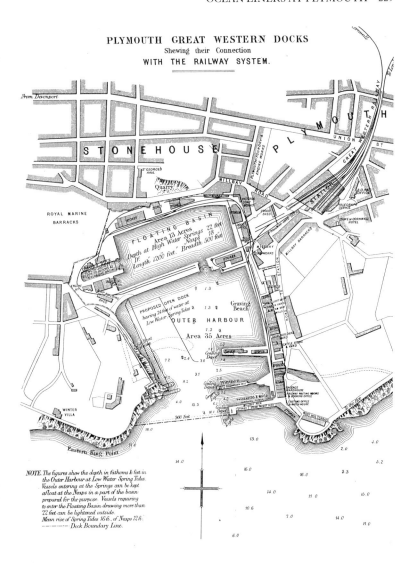

22.3 An 1877 plan of Millbay Docks, before the West Wharf was built. (*Thubron, Docks of Great Britain [1881]*)

22.4 The procession carrying the first dispatch of mails for the Cape of Good Hope from the General Post Office to Millbay Docks, passing the Royal Hotel, Plymouth, 16 December 1850. (Illustrated London News)

Table 22.4
A typical Saturday in Plymouth Sound, 1910

Saturday 6 August

2 am	*Akabo* (British & African) from Calabar etc, Sierra Leone landed 50 passengers, 106 bags of mail, specie
4.15 am	*Ormuz* (Orient) from Brisbane, Sydney, Melbourne & Adelaide, 35 passengers, mails landed Naples
6 am	*Arabia* (P&O) from Bombay, landed 44 passengers
9.18 am	*Marathon* (Aberdeen Line) from Brisbane etc, landed 97 passengers, gold
9.58 am	*Philadelphia* (American Line) from New York, landed 40 passengers and 1,617 bags of mail
2.35 pm	*Friedrich der Grosse* (Norddeutscher Lloyd) from New York, landed 22 passengers, 51 bags of mail, embarked 444 passengers, 48 bags of mail for Germany
8.40 pm	*Kaiserin Auguste Victoria* (Hamburg-America) from New York, landed 93 passengers, 164 bags of mail, embarked 74 passengers for Germany.
11.20 pm	*Tongariro* (New Zealand SC) from London for New Zealand.

Source: *Western Morning News*, shipping intelligence, Monday 8 Aug. 1910.

Table 22.5
A typical week in Plymouth Sound, August 1932

Saturday 6 August

5.15 am	*Oxfordshire* (Bibby) from Rangoon for London, landed 15 passengers. Agents Weekes Phillips
7.30 am	*Aurania* (Cunard) from Montreal for Havre, landed 81 passengers and mails. Cunard
8.50 am	*American Trader* (American Merchant) from New York for London, landed a few passengers and 1,284 bags of mail. Weekes Phillips
12.30 pm	*Stuyvesant* (Royal Netherlands) from Demerara for Amsterdam, landed 38 passengers, 9 bags of mail. Bellamy
3.40 pm	*Rotterdam* (Holland America) from New York for Continent, landed 172 passengers, 80 bags of mail, embarked 13 passengers. Bellamy
11.45 pm	*Baradine* (P&O Branch), from London for Australia, embarked 26 passengers. Weekes Phillips

Sunday 7 Aug

10.30 pm	*Morvada* (British India) from Calcutta for London, landed 8 passengers (sailed 7am Monday). Weekes Phillips

Monday 8 Aug

11.45 am	*Cuba* (French Line), from Havre for West Indies, embarked 56 passengers. Haswell

Tuesday 9 Aug

5 am	*Mauretania* (Cunard) from New York for Cherburg and Southampton, landed 261 passengers, 945 bags of mail. Cunard

Wednesday 10 Aug

evening	*Champlain* (French) from Havre for New York, landed some passengers, embarked 150. Haswell
evening	*President Harding* (US Line) from New York for Cherburg and Bremen, landed 72 passengers, 1,680 bags of mail

Thursday 11 Aug

12.45 pm	*Moolton* (P&O) from Australia for London, landed 51 passengers, including Governor of Gibraltar (taken ashore in C-in-C's barge), and some mail. Cory Strick

Friday 12 Aug

12 noon	*Landaff Castle* (Union-Castle), from London for Port Said & East Africa, embarked military details. Travellers Ltd

Expected on Saturday 13, *France, Ile de France, Lafayette* (all French Line). *Veendam* (Holland America), *Leviathan* (US) and *Manhattan* (US) on maiden voyage.

Imperator, now renamed *Berengaria*. It was followed in 1922 by the French Line with *Paris* and *France*, joined in 1927 by *Ile de France* on her maiden voyage. In 1929 the Germans were back, North German Lloyd bringing into service *Bremen* and *Europa*. *Mauretania* had long held the blue riband, but in 1929 *Bremen* beat her with an average speed of 27.83 knots.[37] Plymouth's peak year in the trade was 1930, with 106 outward calls, 682 homeward, 41,130 passengers landed and 307,912 bags of mail. There were even 1,940 passengers to the Continent.

Competition continued right through the 1930s, with *Normandie* of the French Line making her maiden voyage in May 1935 and returning to Plymouth with an average of 30.35 knots behind her.[38] Cunard's answer was *Queen Mary*, which made 30.63 knots in 1936, only to have *Normandie* steam into Plymouth in November 1936 with a vast blue riband streaming from her foremast for an average speed of 30.99 knots. These were halcyon days, with these 80,000-ton giants sweeping to and fro across the Atlantic in just four days with all the celebrities of the day – statesmen, film stars and those of the fashionable world all making news. In these pre-jet days it was the fastest way to travel, and because these people were in a hurry they always landed at Plymouth. One Plymouth shipping reporter, Walter Taylor, remembered interviewing Lloyd George, Clemenceau, General Allenby, Mary Pickford and Douglas Fairbanks, Ben Lyon and Bebe Daniels.[39] Another, Rufus Endle, recalled Anna Pavlova, General Pershing, Helen Keller, Pierre Laval, Maurice Chevalier, Marlene Dietrich, General Smuts, Winston Churchill, Bernard Shaw, H G Wells and the young John

Notes: During this week Jim Mollison was preparing for his double Atlantic flight.
On the Wednesday a seaplane was catapulted from the *Europa* (Norddeutscher Lloyd) 500 miles to the west and landed in the Hamoaze to refuel, an early attempt to speed the mails.

Source: *Western Morning News*, shipping intelligence, Monday 8 to Saturday 13 Aug. 1932

22.5   The French liner *Amerique* entering Plymouth, 1875. (*Plymouth Local History Library*)

Kennedy.[40] Rufus's father, Martin Endle, the most renowned of all Plymouth shipping reporters, could even recall walking up and down Plymouth Hoe with Cecil Rhodes while he waited for his train, listening to his dreams of Empire-building.[41] *Queen Mary* made nine Plymouth calls in 1937, and *Normandie* four.[42] In 1938 it was claimed that one passenger in nine reaching the United Kingdom by sea entered through Plymouth.[43]

Enter Air Travel

Records do not survive for the war years, and wartime developments in air travel were already sounding the death knell of passenger traffic by sea. Pan-American and Imperial Airways had launched the first regular transatlantic passenger flights in 1939, and during the war there was a regular Britain–Canada air service.[44] In 1947 the Post Office was issuing no new mail contracts to shipping lines; they were going to airlines. For a few years Plymouth did handle more mails than ever before, reaching a peak of 437,295 bags in 1949. The number of passengers grew to a maximum of 29,038 in 1955, touching the regular 30,000 of the 1930s (see Table 22.1), but passengers in a hurry were no longer going by sea, so the Plymouth disembarkation was not so important. The great liners began cutting out the Plymouth call, and *Queen Mary* or *Queen Elizabeth* would only come in when there was labour trouble at Southampton. *Ile de France* called at Plymouth in 1958 on her last voyage, and in 1961 *Liberté* made the last call by the French Line.[45] This call was symbolic, for the *Liberté* was *Europa*, sistership of *Bremen*, taken over from the North German Lloyd after the war by the French. P&O-Orient, which could trace its links with Plymouth back to the 1850s, was tempted back in 1962 with its Australian ships, but they, too, stopped the next year, with the call of *Orion* on her way into retirement.[46]

The final death knell sounded when jet aircraft began flying the Atlantic in 1958 and could cut out the delaying refuelling calls at Shannon and Gander. By 1962 the number of passengers using Plymouth was down to 6,425, but this was falsely inflated by cruising ships which used Plymouth

as their base. That spring it was announced that the last surviving tender would be withdrawn in the autumn, and Plymouth closed to passenger liners.[47]

The Tenders and Millbay Docks

The tender fleet indeed sums up the history of the passenger liner trade at Plymouth. The first purpose-built vessel, *Sir Francis Drake*, came into service in June 1873. There were two by 1876, three by 1883, four or five from the 1890s until 1939, three in 1947, two in 1953, one in 1962 and she, *Sir Richard Grenville*, was sold in September 1963. In the heyday of the traffic the big liners required two tenders, and in the 1930s the tender fleet could carry 2,460 passengers and were often all in service at one time.[48]

The history of Millbay Docks also reflects the rise and fall of the liner trade. It was within a few months of *Sirius* landing that first mail from the United States in the Cattewater that Thomas Gill announced his plans for Millbay Pier. Mill Bay had served the port in the siege years of the Civil War, when Royalist guns denied the use of the Cattewater to the Parliamentary shipping. When Gill started his pier there was just the small Union Dock in the northeast corner of the bay, running up to Millbay Road and with one arm reaching down the line of the present Phoenix Street towards Union Street.[49] The clubhouse of the Royal Western Yacht Club was on the northern shore, the Royal Marines Barracks reached to the western shore, and on the eastern side was Gill's soap factory and a cove where Mrs Kingdom hired out bathing machines.[50]

There were great plans for the railway link and a full dock system. Gill sold his pier to the Plymouth and Great Western Dock Company in 1846, the Outer Dock was completed by 1848, and the South Devon Railway had an extension line from Millbay Station (opened 1849) to the pier by 1850. The complex was completed with the inner lock basin by 1856. The company was heavily in debt, however, and was bailed out by the South Devon, the Bristol & Exeter and the Great Western railway companies. In 1874 the dock company still owed the railways £30,000, and in 1875 the

22.6 The *Queen Mary* entering Plymouth Sound for the first time, 15 March 1937. Note the tender, left, coming to meet her. (*Crispin Gill*)

22.7   A Plymouth reporter, Walter Taylor, interviewing Lloyd George in 1922 on his return from a holiday just before the General Election. He was more anxious to question the reporter about home news than to answer questions. (*Crispin Gill*)

docks were transferred to them, though they had been in effectual management for a year or two already. When in 1875 the Great Western swallowed the other two companies it took over the docks as well, buying out all the warehouse owners around the quays.[51] Within five years West Wharf was built as a deep water berth, taking ships up to 21½ft draught.[52]

But the pattern was already established. By anchoring in the Sound, with tenders waiting, a liner could embark or disembark passengers and mail in a couple of hours and be on its way, far quicker than coming into dock. The railways built the tenders, and dock improvements were concentrated on improving handling arrangements for the tenders. A pontoon, believed to be one used by Brunel in building the Royal Albert Bridge at Saltash, was used to provide extra berthing (it still lies derelict in the Outer Basin), and in 1893 a covered way was built from the pontoon to the Customs shed. Trinity Pier was added and in 1902 extended by 100ft. In 1903, with the expected introduction of the American Line calls, the pontoon was replaced by another jetty extending from the stump of the Princess Royal Pier, again covered, and available like Trinity Pier at all states of the tide.[53] Millbay was not, of course, only concerned with the liners. Plymouth was still the sixth busiest provincial port in England until the 1870s,[54] and Millbay shared this trade with Sutton Harbour and Stonehouse Creek, and from the 1870s with the new wharves at Cattedown.

Plymouth's commercial port has always suffered from railway infighting. The LSWR not only competed with Millbay at Ocean Quay, but in the 1870s

22.8   Passengers aboard a tender in Plymouth Sound, with ocean liners in the background. (Western Morning News)

had lines to Cattedown and in 1897 to Turnchapel on the southern side of the Cattewater. This led to plans to develop the Cattewater right up to Laira Bridge, with extensive docks from Queen Anne's Battery as well as on the Turnchapel side, capable of taking ocean liners. This was killed by the Admiralty, whose Dockyard interest has always impeded Plymouth's commercial ambitions.[55] Since then there have been schemes for other liner quays, under Jennycliff on the eastern shores of the Sound, and even a breakwater from the mouth of the Yealm to the Mewstone, with deep-water berths at Wembury. This last scheme, in 1909, was deliberately set outside the Dockyard Port limits to avoid Admiralty interference.[56]

Casualties

There were casualties in the Plymouth calls. The start of the Australian RMSN Co's mail service to Australia in 1852 had its problems. *Australian* struck the pier so heavily on leaving Millbay that she had to go into the Dockyard for repairs, *Melbourne* was delayed a fortnight for bad weather repairs and then fouled two hulks on leaving Millbay, which held her up another two days, and *Adelaide* had to go into Devonport for a new rudder to be fitted.[57]

In 1856 *London* (Money Wigram) foundered in the Bay of Biscay after embarking passengers at Plymouth, with the loss of 230 lives,[58] and in 1875 *Schiller* (Eagle Line) was Plymouth-bound when she struck in the Isles of Scilly and was lost with over 300 lives.[59] A fire in the cargo of *Gothic* (Shaw Savill) in 1906 led to her being beached in the Cattewater.[60] In 1912 *Lapland* brought 167 survivors from the *Titanic*'s crew into Plymouth.[61] The Orient Line's *Orsova*, torpedoed off the Eddystone when trooping in 1917, was beached off Cawsand and later taken into the Dockyard for repair.[62] The French Line's *Paris* left Plymouth in thick fog and struck the Eddystone rocks, returning to Plymouth.[63] In 1955 the cruise liner *Venus* (Fred Olsen) dragged her anchors in Jennycliff Bay and went up on the rocks under Mount Batten, but was salvaged.[64]

Gold

Gold, too, has played its part. In the 1850s Australian-bound ships were embarking prospective gold miners. In the 1870s specie, over 300,000 dollars at a time, was being brought ashore from the United States,[65] and in 1904 *Kronprinz Wilhelm* (North German-Lloyd) landed bullion, United States payment to France for the Panama Canal.[66] This, incidentally, travelled to London on the celebrated *City of Truro* run. Gold and specie from Australia, the Cape and West Africa, also arrived in Plymouth from 1857 onwards.[67] In the 1930s, with the steady flow of gold out of London into Fort Knox, it was commonplace to see stacks of gold bars on the quayside at Millbay awaiting shipment by tender to the liners, with only a solitary unarmed policeman on guard.[68]

Brittany Ferries

Millbay today is handling far more passengers than it did in the great days. Under pressure from the Breton farmers in the late 1960s, the French government put up finance for the building of a huge fruit and vegetable market outside Morlaix, a new roll-on roll-off (ro-ro) dock near Roscoff a few miles away, and a shipping company to ferry lorry-loads of European produce into England. The British Transport Dock Board (which had taken over from the railway on nationalisation) built a landing facility in the northwest corner of Millbay Outer Dock, and Brittany Ferries began their service on 1 January 1972, to take advantage of Britain entering the Common Market on that day.[69] In no time private cars were using the ferries, and in June 1974 this traffic was formalised with the opening of a passenger terminal in Millbay.[70] The following year the original 14,000 passengers had increased tenfold, with 28,491 cars carried.[71] Between 1978 and 1991 the number of passengers to Roscoff increased threefold to 555,079, and the cars fourfold to 142,620. Only the lorry traffic fell, from 14,954 vehicles in 1989 to 10,142 in 1991. In 1978 a service to Santander in Spain was started, also by Brittany Ferries, and by 1991 it was carrying 151,096 passengers, 51,695 cars and 5,493 lorries.

Thus, in 1991, Britanny Ferries conveyed more than seventeen times the number of passengers carried by the liner trade in its peak year of 1930. This business is still growing, and in 1993 the company introduced the 31,000-ton *Val de Loire*, its biggest ferry, to the Plymouth routes. The service to Roscoff for the summer months was doubled.

The Changing Scene at Millbay Docks

Changes have inevitably resulted at Millbay Docks. Millbay Station was closed in 1939, and the last rail to the docks went in 1971.[72] The dock was privatised again in 1980 and sold to Associated British Ports. After nationalisation the Docks were at various times much under the thumb, ironically enough, of their old rival, Southampton. The northwestern end of the Inner Dock was progressively filled in to make car parks for the ferry, Willoughby's dry dock has disappeared in the same way, and in spring 1986 a second ro-ro facility was installed.[73] Brittany Ferries is now the only commercial user of Millbay Docks, apart from the occasional cruise liner which can be fitted into the ferry timetable and lie alongside West Wharf. Otherwise, the dozen or so cruise liners which call each summer anchor in the Sound, although a few have been taken up to Cattedown Wharves. The historic buildings on Millbay Pier, and the old waiting room, Custom shed and adjacent warehouses, have all been demolished and replaced by a complex of houses and flats, with a marina in front. Only the original octagonal watch tower survives, now used as Plymouth Lifeboat's base.

Yachting, of course, provides employment, as does Brittany Ferries. At its height the liner trade made work for five tenders, say fifty men, possibly another fifty in the shipping offices, work for the railways, Post Office, Customs, waiting room and refreshment staffs. As a guess it gave employment to about 250.

The days of the great liners calling at Plymouth were truly remarkable days. On one evening alone, in or about 1930, there were five liners anchored in the Sound, all of them having left New York on the same day. They were *Paris*, flagship of the French Line, the veteran White Star liner *Olympic*, Holland–America's *Rotterdam*, Norddeutscher Lloyd's *Columbus*, and *President Harding* of the United States Line. *Paris* blazed with lights. Some 2,000 passengers who were not landing at Plymouth were dining or dancing, and most were in evening dress.[74] The liner traffic at Plymouth was prestigious, romantic and exciting for the century or more years that it lasted, with ships arriving from every corner of the globe and bringing in amongst their passengers the great and the good, the famous and glamorous people of the day, as well as thousand upon thousand of less exotic but still worthy folk.

22: Ocean Liners at Plymouth

1 T W E Roche, *Samuel Cunard and the North Atlantic* (1971), 12
2 R N Worth, *History of Plymouth* (Plymouth, 2nd edn, 1890), 341.
3 P W Brock & Basil Greenhill, *Steam and Sail. In Britain and North America* (Newton Abbot, 1973), 13.
4 N R P Bonsor, *North Atlantic Seaway* (Prescott, 1955), 5.
5 Bonsor, *North Atlantic*, 3.
6 Adrian Ball and Diana Wright, *SS Great Britain* (Newton Abbot, 1981), 5.
7 Bonsor, *North Atlantic*, 5–6.
8 *Plymouth, Devonport & Stonehouse Herald*, 21 July 1838.
9 Roche, *Cunard*, 12–15.
10 Worth, *Plymouth*, 332.
11 Ball and Wright, *Great Britain*, 23.
12 Bernard Knowles, *Southampton. The English Gateway* (1951), 52–3.
13 *Illustrated London News*, 28 Dec. 1850.
14 J M Maber, *North Star to Southern Cross* (1967), 46.
15 M Murray, *Union Castle Chronicle* (1957).
16 Maber, *North Star*, 73, 157.
17 Maber, *North Star*, 100.
18 Maber, *North Star*, 103.
19 Maber, *North Star*, 138.
20 Bonsor, *North Atlantic*, 113.
21 *Western Morning News*, (hereafter *WMN*) 23, 25 July 1870.
22 Bonsor, *North Atlantic*, 223.
23 Bonsor, *North Atlantic*, 210.
24 Bonsor, *North Atlantic*, 319.
25 Report on Millbay Dock 1882, Forbey's MSS in Millbay Docks office.
26 Crispin Gill, *New History of Plymouth*, Vol.II, (Newton Abbot, 1979), 135.
27 *Eyre Bros Post Office Plymouth & Devonport District Directory*, 1882–3.
28 Bonsor, *North Atlantic*, 187.
29 *Railway Magazine*, XIV May 1904, 353, 383, 522; and *Devonia*, III (1905), 94.
30 David St J Thomas, *Regional History of the Railways of Great Britain, I. The West Country* (1960), 174.
31 J H Lucking, *Great Western at Weymouth* (Newton Abbot, 1971).
32 Rufus Endle, 'Here's to the Grand Old Man of Plymouth', *Western Evening Herald*, (hereafter *WEH*), 1 Oct. 1968.
33 Bonsor, *North Atlantic*, 298.
34 Bonsor, *North Atlantic*. 736
35 Letter from Jack Hurrell, shipping agent, in author's possession.
36 Bonsor, *North Atlantic*, 25–6.
37 Bonsor, *North Atlantic*, references under Index of Ships.
38 Bonsor, *North Atlantic*, 216.
39 Walter Taylor, interviewed by author.
40 Rufus Endle, *WEH*, 11 May 1966.
41 Martin Endle, in conversation with author.
42 F L Booker, *The Great Western Railway* (Newton Abbot, 1977), 149.
43 Frank Sandon, 'An Introduction to a Statistical Review of Plymouth', *Transactions of the Plymouth Institution*, 18 (1939), 112.
44 *Penguin Dictionary of Twentieth-Century History*, 6.
45 Bosnor, *North Atlantic*, 653.
46 *Lloyd's List*, 24 July 1963.
47 *Lloyd's List*, 23 April 1963.
48 Grahame Farr, *West Country Passenger Steamers* (Prescott, Lancs, 2nd edn, 1967), 186–7; Duckworth and Langmuir, *Railway & Other Steamers* (1948).
49 Worth, *Plymouth*, 332.
50 Crispin Gill, *Sutton Harbour*, (Plymouth, 1970), 6.
51 E T MacDermott, *History of the Great Western Railway*, II (1927), revised by C R Clinker (1964).
52 Forbey MSS, Millbay Docks office.
53 Millbay Docks Annual Reports, held in Docks office.
54 Annual Reports, Plymouth Chamber of Commerce.
55 Gill, *Sutton Harbour*, 40.
56 Papers held in Plymouth Chamber of Commerce Office.
57 Maber, *North Star*, 42–3.
58 Maber, *North Star*, 73.
59 Bonsor, *North Atlantic*, 319.
60 Maber, *North Star*, 142.
61 John Easton and Charles Haas, *Titanic. Triumph and Tragedy* (1986).
62 Maber, *North Star*, 108.
63 Walter Taylor, interviewed by author.
64 *WMN*, 24 March 1955.
65 *WMN*, 5 June 1870, 9 Oct. 1871, 5 Aug. 1872.
66 St J Thomas, *West Country Railways*, 173.
67 *WMN*, shipping intelligence, various dates.
68 Personal recollections of author.
69 *WMN*, 8 Nov. 1972.
70 *WMN*, 5 June 1974.
71 *WMN*, 1 Sept. 1976.
72 *WMN*, 1 July 1971.
73 *WMN*, 24 March 1987.
74 Rufus Endle, *WEH*, 11 May 1966.

23 Devon's Port Industry since 1914

MARK PORTER

THE ECONOMIC SIGNIFICANCE OF PORTS has generally been understated by students of the maritime dimensions of history. Concerned above all with trade flows and shipping, many maritime historians have afforded the port an essentially passive role in the transport system, viewing it merely as a point of trans-shipment, a convenient interface between land and sea. This is far from the truth, and has been since the earliest attempts were made to improve berthing and cargo-handling facilities at sites of loading and discharging, as well as access thereto. The port, in fact, has long been an active agent in the communication network, a business developed and operated to cater for, and derive income from, the receipt and despatch of goods and people.[1] It is as part of a specific industry, the port industry, that the harbours and havens of Devon will be considered in this chapter.

At the national level, the port industry has experienced substantial change since 1914. Shifting patterns of demand (the volume and nature of traffic and the type of vessels utilised) and supply (the provision of facilities), together with developments in other forms of transportation, have combined to alter the character and location of the industry, especially since the 1960s. Estuarial sites, such as those at Avonmouth, Seaforth and Tilbury, have been developed, while North Sea oil ports such as Sullom Voe, ferry termini like Dover and Folkestone and container bases such as Felixstowe have experienced rapid growth in recent times.[2] On the other hand, the great Victorian and Edwardian dock complexes of 'inner-city' Liverpool, London, Glasgow and other major ports have closed, to be 'regenerated' in the 1980s by the property developer or the heritage business. Typically, change has been less dramatic in Devon. Yet even here modern methods of freight handling have been adopted, most notably in the roll-on, roll-off ('ro-ro') facility at Plymouth, while traces of 'gentrification' and 'museumification' have recently appeared in quayside areas across the county. Indeed, though the level of business handled by the county's ports has formed a small and generally declining part of the nation's seaborne traffic, many of the factors governing twentieth-century port development can be discerned in Devon's port industry. It is therefore hoped that this chapter, which examines the fluctuating levels of traffic and investment – of demand and supply – at the county's ports, and considers the influences underlying these patterns, will reveal something of the forces which have shaped the British port industry since 1914.

Demand and Supply

In 1972 the National Ports Council identified thirty-two sites in Devon that were 'used by ships from time to time' (see Table 23.1). This list included twenty-five 'ports' and 'shipping places' between the Axe and the Tamar on the county's south coast, and a further seven, from Clovelly to Lynmouth, in North Devon. The list clearly exaggerated the extent of Devon's port industry, however, for many of the locations cited were of little or no significance as trading bases, some, such as Beer, Brixham and Budleigh Salterton, being classified as fishing harbours, and others, such as Paignton, Salcombe and the Yealm River, having received or discharged neither goods nor passengers since 1965.[3]

In reality, the county's port provisions were largely concentrated, as they had been in the nineteenth century,[4] in the Customs Head Ports of Bideford, Dartmouth, Exeter, Plymouth and Teignmouth, though Exmouth and

Table 23.1

Devon's Customs Ports, associated port authorities and shipping places, 1972

Customs Port and port authorities	Shipping places within Customs Port
Exeter	
City of Exeter	Axmouth, Beer, Budleigh Salterton,
The Exmouth Dock Co	Exmouth, Lyme, Lympstone, Sidmouth, Topsham
Teignmouth	
Teignmouth Harbour Commission	Paignton, Torquay
Teignmouth Quay Co Ltd	
County Borough of Torbay	
Dartmouth	
Brixham Urban District Council	Brixham, Hope Cove, River Dart,
Dartmouth Harbour Commission	Salcombe, Totnes
River Dart Navigation Commissioners	
Plymouth	
British Transport Docks Board	Cattedown, Cattewater Harbour,
Cattewater Harbour Commission	Devonport, Millbay Docks, Sutton
Sutton Harbour Improvement Co	Harbour, Victoria Wharf, River Yealm
Bideford	
Borough of Barnstaple	Appledore, Barnstaple, Bude, Clovelly,
Borough of Bideford	Fremington Quay, Ilfracombe, Lynmouth
British Railways Board	
Bude and Stratton Urban District Council	
Ilfracombe Urban District Council	

Source: *Digest of Port Statistics 1973* (National Ports Council, 1973), 215–6.

Barnstaple each possessed a cargo-handling capacity.[5] Essentially, these were small ports. Even Plymouth, with its superior natural harbour and its massive naval base, only ranked at best as a medium-sized port, as it had done before the Second World War when the high profile hustle and bustle associated with the regular visits of the great transoceanic liners had given the port the illusory appearance of a major commercial base.[6] As small-scale operations, the various units of Devon's port industry have generally struggled to prosper in the changing and often difficult commercial environment of the twentieth century. This is reflected both in the levels of traffic handled and in the range of facilities provided.

Traffic Levels

The business handled by Devon's ports has fluctuated considerably since 1914. At the aggregate level, as Fig. 23.1 indicates, the depressions in activity rates caused by the two world wars have been succeeded by slow and modest recoveries. In the interwar years the volume of shipping entering and clearing the county's ports increased gradually, as Table 23.2 and Fig. 23.2 imply, but failed to reach the levels evident in the pre-1914 era. Likewise, growth was sluggish in the 1950s and 1960s, though, as Tables 23.2 and 23.3 suggest, the early 1970s witnessed a marked rise in both coastal and overseas trade, with exports increasing appreciably. This

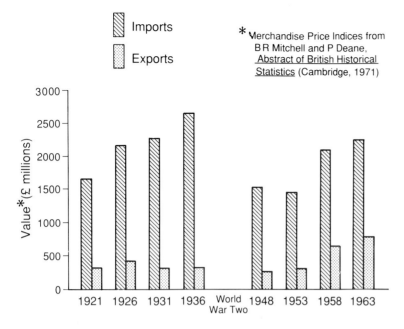

23.1 Devon's foreign seaborne trade, 1921–63, by value.

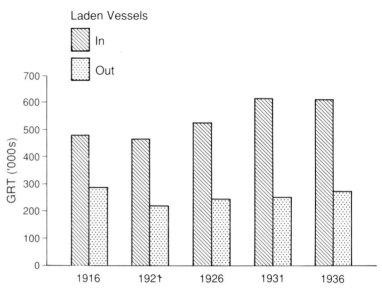

23.2 Devon's coastwise trade, 1916–1936, by tonnage.

buoyancy was not evenly spread, however, for this period witnessed the virtual cessation of activity at Bideford, Dartmouth and Exeter, all of which were relegated to the status of 'other ports' in the official port statistics.[7] It was also shortlived, the mid-1980s heralding a decline in the volume of Devon's seaborne trade, which had peaked in 1984 as a consequence of the rise in coal imports during the protracted miners' strike.[8] This contraction was highlighted by the closure of Exmouth Dock on 1 January 1990, though it is probable that much of its business, which had increased from 101,000 to 585,000 tonnes between 1970 and 1987,[9] will be diverted to Plymouth and Teignmouth, now the principal surviving units of Devon's port industry.

Table 23.2
Devon's foreign trade, 1901–1975, by tonnage of principal bulk commodities
('000 tons)

	1901	1921	1937	1946	1961	1975
Imports						
Foodstuffs	122	61	125	8	99	242
Timber	*	*	86	47	77	81
Fuel	19	149	207	212	183	14
Exports						
Clay	49	22	53	41	235	486

* Incompatible data for these years

Source: *Annual Statements of Trade and Navigation.*

In terms of the character of the trade channelled through Devon's ports, it appears that many of the patterns apparent in the nineteenth century persisted after 1914. Thus, the predominant flow of trade has been inwards, with imports exceeding exports throughout the period. Coastal commerce has eclipsed foreign trade; bulky, low-value cargoes have proved to be the most significant type of commodity handled; and Plymouth, serving the most productive and populous hinterland in the West Country, has dealt with much of the county's seaborne trade.

This trading profile has changed in certain respects during the twentieth century. While the value of goods imported into Devon from overseas has declined in relative terms, from 0.4 to 0.15 per cent of the national aggregate between 1900 and 1980, the county's contribution to the United Kingdom's exports has increased, especially during the 1946–80 period, when a rise from 0.04 to 0.15 per cent by value occurred. Accordingly, Devon's

Table 23.3
Devon's coastwise trade, 1965–1980, by tonnage
('000 tons)

		1965	1968	1971	1974	1977	1980
Foodstuffs	in	3	10	19	17	4	6
	out	0	0	0	0	0	0
Basic	in	1	1	6	5	0	8
Materials	out	123	77	121	115	76	267
Manufactured	in	52	25	54	15	20	25
goods	out	4	1	1	2	18	3
Fuel	in	1,087	923	1,211	891	795	754
	out	0	0	0	3	4	0
Total	in	1,143	959	1,290	928	819	793
		127	78	122	120	98	270

Source: *Digest of Port Statistics* (National Ports Council, 1965–1980).

pronounced negative balance of foreign trade has been reduced. Whereas in the interwar period approximately 85 per cent of the county's overseas commerce by value consisted of imports, the equivalent figure for 1980 was just 55 per cent.[10] Rising clay exports from Plymouth and Teignmouth were largely responsible for this shift. As this commodity exhibits a low value-to-bulk ratio, moreover, the proportion of the county's exports by volume (a key measure of port activity) passing through Devon's ports was much higher than the value figures suggest. In 1965, for instance, the county's exports represented only 0.04 per cent of the national total by value, but 1.42 per cent by volume.[11]

More significantly, the twentieth century has witnessed the contraction of coastwise trade at Devon's ports. This decline has been a nationwide phenomenon, of course, though its impact has been felt especially by the minor ports, such as those in Devon, whose commercial viability has often depended upon coastwise business.[12] Having expanded considerably in the late nineteenth century to reach a peak in the Edwardian period, the level of Devon's coastal traffic fell sharply during the First World War. This was so in relative terms, with the county's ports handling only 0.8 per cent of the United Kingdom's cargo-carrying coasters in 1917, against 2.5 per cent in 1913. It was also true in absolute terms, with coastal entrances declining to just a third of the 1913 level in 1918, and clearances to less than a fifth.

The volume of coastal shipping handled at Devon's ports did not recover

23.3 Millbay Docks, 1926. (*British Rail*)

to pre-1914 levels in the interwar period. Thus, in 1929, when incoming traffic reached its peak for the 1919–39 period, it represented only 60 per cent of the tonnage entering the county's harbours in 1913. The decline in coastal traffic departing Devon was even steeper, failing to exceed half of the 1913 figure during the entire interwar period. Contraction was also evident in relative terms after the First World War. Thus, Devon's share of Britain's coastal traffic remained below 2 per cent in each of the interwar years, having regularly exceeded 4 per cent in the Edwardian era. This trend continued after 1945, the county's ports handling 1.1 per cent of all freight transported coastwise in the United Kingdom during 1965, a figure which had fallen still further, to 0.8 per cent, by 1980.[13]

Devon's coastal trade therefore diminished both absolutely and relatively since 1914. The contraction of this, for centuries the most important branch of the county's seaborne commerce, has inevitably exerted a depressive influence on Devon's port business. Accordingly, the supply of factors into the various units comparing this industry has tended to decline during the course of the twentieth century.

Port Facilities

During the nineteenth century, authority over Britain's ports was vested in a miscellany of individuals, private companies and public and municipal bodies. Since 1918, and more particularly since the Second World War, some rationalisation has occurred in the organisation of the port industry, with central and local government generally assuming more control over 'shipping places'. Thus, by the 1960s it was possible to classify ports according to four types: nationalised ports, administered by the British Transport Docks Board, the British Railways Board, the British Waterways Board or the Admiralty; public trust ports; local authority ports; and privately-owned ports. Each of these variants operated in Devon. For instance, Millbay, formerly owned by the Great Western Railway, was administered by the British Transport Docks Board, while Dartmouth and Cattewater were public trust ports controlled by Harbour Commissions, Exeter and Bideford were run by their respective local authorities, and private enterprise was represented by Exmouth Docks Company, Teignmouth Quay Company and Sutton Harbour Improvement Company.[14] In addition, as Table 23.1 indicates, bodies such as the Teignmouth Harbour Commission, Brixham and Ilfracombe Urban District Councils, and British Railways Board (at Fremington Quay) also held interests in Devon's ports.

This organisational picture continues to evolve, as the privatisation of Millbay and the changes in ownership at Teignmouth during the 1980s readily attest. Whatever their ilk, however, Devon's port authorities have faced the common problem of operating loading and discharging facilities while traffic levels, and therefore income, have been subject to fluctuation. Against this background, capital investment in the county's port industry has been relatively limited in the twentieth century. This can be seen from various perspectives. At the general level, for instance, the post-1914 era contrasts sharply with the second half of the nineteenth century, in that no new ports have been established in Devon. Whereas the 1850s witnessed the opening of the Great Western Docks at Millbay, Plymouth, and the 1870s saw the creation of Exmouth Dock, such major additions to the local industry's capital stock have been lacking in the twentieth century. Moreover, the friction between port users and harbour authorities, fostered by the rising volume of trade, which was widely apparent in Devon during the nineteenth century – leading to the formation of the Sutton Harbour

Company and Dartmouth Harbour Commission, for instance – has rarely surfaced since the First World War.

In the interwar period Devon's port authorities largely concentrated on the maintenance of the infrastructure created in Victorian times, though some investment was made in the provision of specialised facilities, such as oil jetties. Accordingly, the fabric of the county's port industry in the 1940s was largely indistinguishable from that at the turn of the century. Since 1945 a number of relatively large-scale investments have been undertaken. At Exmouth, for instance, the late 1960s saw the implementation of a £35,000 scheme to provide more waterfront storage space and to widen the entrance to the Dock to allow vessels of up to 1,000 tons to enter.[15] In more recent years, Teignmouth's cargo- and ship-handling provisions have been enhanced by the extension of the quay frontage and the replacement of warehouses.[16]

However, the most important improvements to Devon's port structures have taken place at Plymouth. In the immediate postwar years the facilities available at Cattedown were extensively modernised, while the Sutton Harbour Improvement Company built new warehousing for local firms and improved the amenities used by the port's fishing industry.[17] Although the industrial development of Millbay was given some priority in the plans for the postwar reconstruction of Plymouth,[18] major investment in the dock area was slow in coming. This moved one observer to note with disappointment in 1945 that, 'the Great Western Railway did not propose to improve Millbay's facilities'.[19] Indeed, in subsequent years, falling passenger numbers helped persuade British Railways to switch the focus of Plymouth's rail network from Millbay to the more central North Road site.

Having passed to the control of the British Transport Docks Board, Millbay did receive an injection of capital in the late 1950s and early 1960s. This investment was intended to speed up cargo-handling operations and improve the general efficiency of the site. It entailed the expenditure of £61,000 on resurfacing quays and the provision of open storage space, and a further £90,000 on cranes, transit sheds and extensions to the port's road system.[20] More significant developments were to follow at Millbay with the establishment of a cross-Channel ferry terminal in 1972. First mooted in 1965, this plan came to fruition with the construction of a £1 million 'ro-ro' facility by Brittany Ferries. The success of the cross-Channel operation, initially intended for freight users but quickly gaining popularity as a passenger service, led to the opening of a second berth at a cost of £4.5 million in 1986, with Plymouth now linked with Roscoff, Santander and Bilbao.[21]

23.4 One of the ferries running from Plymouth to Roscoff in Brittany or Santander in Spain, seen in Millbay Docks with the wartime silo behind. The ferry is virtually the only commercial use now made of Millbay. (Western Morning News)

century, but has been falling since the 1930s. The 1901 census indicates that Devon's port workers numbered 832, with a further 392 men identifying themselves as bargemen and lightermen, some of them presumably in the service of the ports. By 1931 more than 1,000 Devon men were employed as dockers, the total halving over the next twenty years and reaching its nadir in 1961, at 240 employees. Subsequently, a slight increase in the size of the labour force occurred, though it was not proportionate to the expansion of trade in the 1970s owing to the adoption of more efficient cargo-handling practices such as palletisation and the 'ro-ro' system.

Despite such developments, there has been a net reduction in the extent of Devon's port facilities in the post-1945 period, especially since the 1960s. A number of sites have closed to commercial traffic. In 1969, structural deterioration, coupled with a declining level of trade, led to the official closure of Baker's Quay and Rolle Quay at Barnstaple. Similar reasons were advanced for the sudden termination of trading activity at Exmouth Dock in 1990. Elsewhere in South Devon, significant areas of the region's ports are now utilised by recreational, rather than commercial, craft. Marinas with up to 540 berths now occupy much of the water space at Sutton Harbour and the outer basin at Millbay, as well as the outer harbours at Brixham and Torquay. Yachts, dinghies and motor cruisers proliferate on the Dart, the Exe and Salcombe River, once the province of merchant ships (see Chapter 26). Likewise, to landward, former quay areas such as those at Exeter and Barnstaple have been developed for residential purposes in recent years. As a consequence of these changes in the utilisation of harbour space, it is probable that in the 1990s Devon's port industry has less capacity to handle commercial shipping than it has had at any time since the 1850s.

This shrinkage is reflected, and to some degree measured, in the changing labour requirements of Devon's port industry. As Fig. 23.7 indicates, direct employment at the county's harbours increased during the early twentieth

Dock work has remained a male preserve at each of Devon's ports during the twentieth century. There have been differences between sites, however, in terms of employment practices. Millbay alone of Devon's ports has operated within the Dock Labour Scheme, a result of the transfer of the railway ports to the state following the Second World War. At some ports dockers have worked for privately-owned stevedoring companies, while at others the harbour authority has employed dock labour. The significance of dock work to the local labour market has also varied between Devon's ports. At Plymouth, the largest centre of dock employment in twentieth-century Devon, stevedoring has proved to be a relatively important source of work, especially in the interwar period. For example, 805 men, over 1 per cent of the city's working male population, were employed in Plymouth's docks in 1921. Dock work featured less prominently in the local economies of Devon's other ports, the notable exception being Teignmouth, where the Dock Company has been the town's single largest employer for much of the post-1945 period.[22]

The port industry has also stimulated employment in various businesses dependent to some degree on seaborne trade and shipping operations. Such linkages exist with a range of activities, from closely-related industries such as ship repair and chandlery to import processing – flour milling, timber merchanting and oil refining, for instance – to tourism, with docks having amenity value as examples of living industrial archaeology. Calculating the extent of employment in these port-associated industries is difficult, but it is evident that ship support services have declined in the twentieth century. Sailmakers, ropemakers, and mast, spar and blockmakers could be found at all of the county's ports in Edwardian times,[23] but with the decline of the sailing ship these craft operations have either closed or turned to other, non-maritime markets. Moreover, ship repair activity within the commercial ports has slowly diminished. At Millbay, for instance, Willoughby Brothers, the last of the three major ship repair and general engineering concerns that had served Plymouth in 1900, closed in 1969. The graving dock which had formed the base of the firm's business was filled in to become a car park in 1973.[24] The fate of this facility, which was constructed in 1857, when Devon's port industry was expanding, was indicative of the contraction apparent in the county's ports and port-related activities a century or so later. A multiplicity of factors underpinned this adaptation.

Devon's Ports in a Changing Commercial Environment

The long-term, uneven contraction of Devon's port industry in the twentieth century can be attributed largely to falling levels of demand, to the declining volume of trade passing through the county's docks and harbours. Seaborne trade, in turn, has been conditioned by various factors, chief amongst which have been the levels of production and consumption in the port hinterlands, changing traffic flows, competition from other forms of transportation and a range of political influences.

23.5 Victoria Wharves, Plymouth, at low tide, with coal in the foreground and a ship loading china clay in the dock. The rocky point behind the dock, Queen Anne's Battery, is now a yacht marina. (Western Morning News)

Such determinants have operated to differing degrees on the various branches of Devon's maritime commerce. The development of the county's economy, for instance, has not proved conducive to the growth of foreign trade in the twentieth century. While its primary and secondary sectors have experienced only limited development, tertiary activities, particularly in the field of tourism and retirement, have gone from strength to strength. These growth industries may have brought income and employment to Devon, but they have offered little for the conventional freight-handling business of the county's ports. Accordingly, the commodity mix of Devon's foreign imports and exports has diverged little from that evident in Victorian times, with foodstuffs, agricultural supplies and timber the principal cargoes arriving from abroad, and primary products – grain, fish and, most particularly, clay – consistently forming the basis of Devon's overseas exports.[25]

In contrast, the secondary, or manufacturing sector, as in the nineteenth century, has provided relatively little business for Devon's ports. Even the much vaunted growth of manufacturing in the county during the 1950s and 1960s, dubbed a 'minor industrial revolution',[26] failed to stimulate demand for local port services, arguably because of the general lack of linkages and integration between incoming new industry and the existing Devon economy.[27] Thus, imports of raw materials for industry have remained inhibited. The papermaking industry alone provided a regular bulk import trade, but even this activity declined in the twentieth century owing to the steady fall in the number of operational paper mills in Devon. The remnants of this once flourishing trade were conducted through Teignmouth before 1914, through Plymouth in the interwar years, and through both Plymouth and Exeter after 1945. Exports of manufactured goods likewise reflect the relatively unproductive character of the Devon economy. Apart from the output of the shipyards in the Dart and the Torridge, which hardly stimulate port activity, the county's manufactured exports have been limited to the products of the chemical and machine tool industries, both of which expanded in Plymouth during the 1970s and 1980s.

Only two other foreign trades of any note have developed in Devon during the twentieth century. The shipment of waste products for recycling overseas has formed a consistent export trade since the First World War. Before the advent of natural gas in the 1960s, tar, pitch and coke from Devon's gasworks and power stations had been exported in some quantity. In the 1970s a further waste business developed in Plymouth and Exeter, with a substantial volume (50,000 tons in 1980) of scrap exported to the iron and steel producing ports of Spain, Italy and Holland.

Of greater significance was the import of refined petroleum products, the only new bulk trade to alter appreciably the nineteenth-century pattern of Devon's foreign trade. At the turn of the century small quantities of barrelled oil were being imported, but with demand increasing rapidly, and 'tanker' technology proceeding apace, oil imports burgeoned. The First World War enhanced demand, and Devon's imports of petroleum products rose to 300,000 tons, over fifteen times the volume arriving in 1900. Although this level declined markedly after the war, the increasing energy requirements of both domestic and industrial consumers, notably the electricity industry, led to a steady expansion, 200,000 tons of refined petroleum being landed at Devon's ports in 1937. After the Second World War, however, this trade declined as the national campaign to reduce expensive imports led to the displacement of direct imports of refined oil by crude oil from the Middle East delivered to home refineries. As none of the major refineries were built in Devon, the county's port industry lost a valuable branch of its foreign import business, though this was mitigated to some degree by the consequent

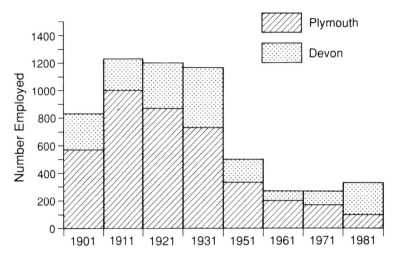

23.6 Men employed as dockers in Devon ports, 1901–81. (*Census, Occupation Tables*)

increase in the volume of home-refined products delivered coastwise.

Such re-routeing was a persistent feature of Britain's foreign trade in the twentieth century. Generally, it served to disadvantage the smaller ports, for it was part of the centripetal process, apparent since the 1840s, by which overseas commerce became increasingly concentrated at the nation's major ports. In Devon this was reflected in the negligible volume of manufactured imports reaching the county directly from overseas. Most of these goods, in fact, were discharged at Liverpool, London or another of the larger ports and transported to Devon by rail, coaster or road, emphasising the extent to which the great entrepots had penetrated the hinterland of local ports. Re-routeing has also acquired an international dimension in recent years, with the development of a European trans-shipment network. This has effectively undermined Plymouth's function as the regional entrepot for the South West. Whereas imports of commodities such as bulk grain at one time entered Plymouth to be redistributed in coasters to other southwestern ports, latterly they have been offloaded at Rotterdam or Antwerp into relatively small, efficient vessels and carried directly to the South West's lesser harbours.

Competition from other forms of transportation has had little impact on the scale and character of Devon's overseas freight traffic, but it has changed the county's role in the movement of passengers. Thus, the rapid growth of transatlantic air services after the Second World War effectively brought an end to the liner trade which had generated much activity in Plymouth in the 1920s and 1930s.[28] To some degree this lost business has been replaced by the continental ferry services established at Millbay in 1972. This trade has also been affected by the development of other arms of the transport system, though in a complementary rather than a competitive sense, for the expansion of Plymouth's ferry traffic has largely depended on the major

23.7 Bideford Quay in the early 1970s, with a motorship from Cyprus alongside. (Western Morning News)

improvements effected to the port's road links by the construction of the A38/M5 trunk route in the mid 1970s.

The coastal trade, in contrast, suffered greatly from the competition of the rail and road industries in the twentieth century. Frequently aided by state regulation and investment, these landward modes of transportation have exacerbated the deficiencies in demand for port services apparent in areas such as Devon. The First World War marked a clear turning point in the fortunes of the British coastal trade. Having expanded consistently and considerably throughout the Victorian and Edwardian eras, coastwise commerce was adversely affected by the conflict. While the supply of vessels and labour was inevitably disrupted, seriously reducing the volume of home trade, it was the improved competitive position of the railways, benefiting from a state-sanctioned system of subsidised rates, which proved most detrimental to coastal transport in the long term.[29] Henceforth, railway companies were able to engage successfully in the market for low-value, bulk freight, traditionally the preserve and the base of the coastal trade.

In Devon, mainly at Plymouth and Teignmouth, the First World War saw the railways compete vigorously for the cargoes of clay normally carried coastwise. This competition intensified in the interwar years, with the result that a major source of business was diverted away from the county's ports, though the increasing volume of clay shipped to foreign markets offered much compensation in the long run. However, it was the incursions made by the railways into the coal trade which critically impaired coastal shipping activity in the ports of Devon and most other maritime districts. For centuries, the import of coal from northeastern England and South Wales had formed the backbone of the county's seaborne trade. The diversion of much of this traffic to the railways during the First World War set a trend which has persisted ever since, encouraged, it would seem, by the periodic intervention of the State. Its impact upon Devon's port industry was immediate. For instance, at Bideford, where this trade dominated commercial freight handling activity, 10,000 tons of coal were imported in 1918, just half of the quantity landed in 1910.

Demand for coastal coal deliveries was partially sustained in the interwar years by the expanding consumption of the gas and electricity industries. Rationalisation in production favoured large, cheaply supplied production plants. In Devon, these power stations and gas works were sited on estuaries to take advantage of coastal coal supplies. Approximately 40,000 tons of coal were landed annually at Sutton Harbour to supply the Prince's Rock power station alone,[30] while new coal berths were constructed to handle coastally delivered coal for the expanded Torbay power generating facilities at Torquay.

In the Second World War some of the county's ports enjoyed an increase in coal imports, for once benefiting from government traffic directives, but after the war the decline in coastal coal landings, particularly at ports primarily engaged in handling domestic house coal, gathered pace. In the early postwar years coastwise trade in general was restricted, as the export drive combined with congestion at major ports to reduce the supply of shipping for coastal work and the availability of cargoes for coastal delivery. However, the coal trade was further disrupted by State regulation. With industry being afforded priority, ports serving the more developed industrial

hinterlands were favoured with a greater allocation of coal. Thus, small ports primarily handling house coal, such as Bideford, found coastwise trade activity much reduced in the late 1940s. The reduction of Bideford's seaborne summer allocation of house coal from only 250–350 tons per week to 100 tons in July 1948 brought protests to the Ministry of Fuel from the united front of the port authority, the port employers and the port's coal merchants. The ministry replied that the heavy northeast demand for Yorkshire coal was at the root of the problem, but expressed the hope that normal supplies would soon be re-established. In November 1948 Bideford's allocation of seaborne house coal was cut even more drastically. Port interests were further antagonised by the State-directed transfer of some of the lost allocation to the railways.[31]

As supply conditions for coal became more fluid, the coastwise coal trade began to expand. Imports to the Taw-Torridge estuary increased considerably with the opening of the East Yelland power station in 1953, and the establishment of Bideford as the delivery point for the North Devon and North Cornwall coal requirements of the South West Gas Board. At Plymouth the substantial coal demands of the Prince's Rock Power Station and the various gasworks ensured that large quantities of coal were handled at the harbour facilities. By 1962 245,000 tons of coastally transported coal were landed at Plymouth.[32]

In the mid-1960s the coastal coal trade of Devon's ports suffered a series of setbacks as the railways further penetrated the coal market. After Beeching had signed a coal by rail contract with the Ministry of Power in 1964, the Western Region of British Rail approached the National Coal Board (NCB) to increase coal supplies to the South West by rail. A year earlier Bideford had been negotiating with the NCB to establish a sea-supplied coal depot at the port, but this bid foundered as British Rail's counter-proposal of a merry-go-round hopper train service to ferry half a million tons of East Midlands coal annually to the South West found favour. This prompted A H C Wreland, secretary of the Devon and Cornwall Seaborne Coal Traders Association, to predict that 'the loss of coal trade could finish small West ports'. According to Wreland, the competition of rail for seaborne coal supplies for industrial use was being extended to the delivery of house coal to the South West. Before 1964, east of a line joining Bideford and Teignmouth only coastal areas were supplied with house coal by sea, while to the west virtually all the peninsula's domestic coal demand was met by coastwise delivered coal. However, he argued, British Rail's agreement with the NCB would change this pattern, threatening the commercial viability of small ports in the South West.[33] His forecast proved accurate. Whereas more than 300,000 tons of coal were imported coastwise into Devon in 1965, within three years the trade had been halved, only Plymouth retaining a substantial interest.[34]

Competition from the railways was an important factor in the decline of other Devon coastal trades. Cement offers one such case. Stimulated by the construction boom, cement imports had burgeoned in the interwar years, providing Devon ports with an important source of business and revenue, especially since scheduled harbour rates for landing cement were commonly six times the rate charged for coal. After 1945, however, the export drive meant that much of Britain's cement output was channelled through

23.8 Exmouth Dock, September 1988, with the pilot boat standing by a ship under way. In January 1990 this dock closed to commercial traffic. (Western Morning News)

Thamesside wharves, while there was mounting pressure to distribute domestic supplies by rail. In 1950 this culminated in the decision of the government-controlled Cement Marketing Company to transport all cement by rail. Builder's Merchant Associations in the South West bitterly criticised this policy. Disaster was predicted, and it was claimed that rail-delivered cement was far more likely to spoil and that British Rail would be unable to handle the 150,000 tons of cement supplied annually to Devon and Cornwall. The Chairman of the Devon Builder's Merchant Association considered that, in view of the existing, well-established infrastructure for seaborne supply, the decision must have been 'purely political . . . designed to make their wretched railways pay'.[35] Be that as it may, the county's coastwise imports of cement had all but ceased by the late 1960s, Plymouth, the only port left in the trade, receiving a mere 4,000 tons of cement in 1974.

In the interwar years, much of the cement handled by Devon's ports had been conveyed in coastal liners. Such vessels, which operated according to regular schedules, also carried the lion's share of the general merchandise which had long formed an important part of coastwise trade. In Plymouth the firm of Coast Lines, based at Victoria Wharves, Cattedown, operated weekly sailings to Liverpool, Swansea, Cardiff, Falmouth, Poole, South-ampton and London, while the Clyde Shipping Company, working from the Glasgow berth at Millbay, linked Plymouth with Waterford and Glasgow. Likewise, Bideford was a port of call for the Bristol Channel liner services. By the Second World War, however, these long-established communication routes were already in decline, and many were discontinued after the war. The Harbour Authority at Bideford, aware of the importance of this trade to the commercial fabric of the South West's smaller ports, sought forlornly to revive the Bristol Channel liner services, but on approaching Coast Lines in 1954 the authority met with a response that encapsulated the dilemma which had afflicted the coastal trade and the smaller ports since 1945. It was informed that the company did not possess the appropriate vessels and 'in view of the present operating costs' it would not be possible to 'compete with road and rail rates'.[36]

Nevertheless, there have been pockets of growth in Devon's coastal trade since the Second World War. For instance, landings of sand and gravel by licenced dredging companies increased in the 1950s, notably at Bideford and Barnstaple, where the business provided revenue through charges for cranage and weighbridges in addition to harbour and tonnage dues. Much more significant was the increase in coastwise deliveries of refined oil from the late 1940s, a development which contributed to, and partly compensated for, the decline in coal imports. Oil depots were established at Plymouth, Exeter, and at East Yelland on the Taw-Torridge estuary. Here cargoes of oil refined in other parts of the country, chiefly on the Solent and the Mersey, were discharged and distributed to domestic and industrial consumers, large quantities, for instance, being piped from Cattedown to the Prince's Rock power station. Plymouth, echoing its entrepôt role of earlier times, emerged as the region's leading distribution centre for coastwise-supplied petroleum products, its imports peaking at over one million tons in 1971. The oil crises of the 1970s depressed this trade, however, and by 1980 less than 700,000 tons of refined oil were landed at Plymouth. Since then, this activity has been further depleted by the transfer of oil carriage from coasters to the roads, a reflection of the great improvement that the extension of the motorway network (again, a direct consequence of government transport policy) has made to landward communications in the South West.

While falling demand levels largely explain the decline in Devon's twentieth-century port business, supply-side factors have also contributed to the industry's contraction. To some extent this had been inevitable, for the income of port operators ultimately depends on the charges levied on vessels using the facilities provided. As the volume of traffic shrinks, so the earnings of the port authority declines, impairing its financial viability and leading to the deterioration or loss of its capital assets – the very ship- and cargo-handling facilities which it requires to attract business. This intract-able, self-perpetuating problem has faced many West Country ports in the twentieth century, the plight of Bridgwater, succinctly described in an official report of 1930, offering a good example:

of recent years the tonnage handled has much diminished due . . . to

the severe competition from road and rail transport, which has resulted in a considerable loss of revenue and consequent lack of funds to prevent silting up of the channel and approaches, and to maintain or improve the facilities of the port.[37]

Such 'vicious circles' developed at Devon's smaller ports. In the 1920s, for example, the lock gates at Exmouth Dock needed repair, but the Dock Company lacked the necessary funds and was obliged to remove the gates, rendering its dock a tidal harbour. Meanwhile, Teignmouth Harbour Commission, unable to pay for the river to be dredged properly, was placed in an even more precarious financial position when damages had to be paid to owners of vessels such as ss *Coombe Dingle*, which fell foul of obstructions in the channel.[38]

Cures for such financial crises were generally sought in short-term internal measures such as rate reductions designed to generate traffic, or in manpower reductions aimed at cutting costs. In most cases, however, solutions could only be found in an infusion of capital from external sources. Thus, Teignmouth's fortunes revived in the 1930s and again in the 1980s when 'outside' funds were injected into the Quay Company, though on both occasions a more dynamic management team accompanied the investment.[39] Similarly, port operations at Millbay have always relied to some degree on external funding, either from the 'parent' railway companies which owned the site or from outside firms such as Brittany Ferries.

Underlying the question of capital resources has been the limited scale of most of Devon's port operations. In itself, this has posed a problem, for the country's harbour authorities have frequently lacked the political weight to influence the decision-making process. In a broad sense this was apparent in the failure of the small ports as a whole to arrest the general demise of the coasting trade, the bedrock of their activity, in the face of powerful competition from the rail and road lobbies. It was likewise evident in the various attempts of local port operators to collaborate with 'big business'. In the interwar period, for instance, the harbour authority at Bideford, the Town Council, endeavoured to extend its quay facilities, but schemes to build a new quay along land belonging to the Southern Railway Company foundered as the firm shunned all approaches from the council. Similarly, the authority made an unsuccessful attempt to acquire part of the quay extension being constructed for Concrete Products Ltd at Northam in the mid-1930s. After the war, Bideford and other port authorities in the South West, recognising the prospects for arresting flagging trade, approached oil companies with a view to accommodating depots for the coastwise distribution of petroleum. However, in a buyer's market, the oil giants could choose from a range of prospective sites, and despite protracted negotiations in 1953–4 Bideford Council failed to convince BP and Shell Mex to invest in a discharging facility at the port.[40]

Devon's port authorities have also suffered at the hands of local vested interests. At Plymouth, for instance, the need for deep-water facilities was identified in the mid-1960s by the Association of Industrial Consultants for the West Economy, which cited the ports' inability to take vessels of over 20,000 tons as a key constraint on its development. Although the Association recommended that the Admiralty should be requested to release deep-water sites, and though the issue was central to the campaign of the Labour candidate, Peggy Middleton, in the Tavistock Division election of March 1966, the necessary facilities remained in State control. Teignmouth's port interests also experienced local difficulties at this time. In 1962, proposals submitted by the 'pro-port, pro-clay' trade lobby to ease traffic congestion in the town met with stiff resistance. Councillor Harry Pike for one felt that the ball clay producers exaggerated their case for improved road links with the docks, feeling that they wanted 'the route cleared and sanded for a Royal Procession of lorries, but we have other people to think of'.[41] Three years later, with the port working to its limit, it was proposed that new quays should be built on the west foreshore, using land leased from the Crown Estate. But the plans to increase the capacity of the port, including the removal of the bar at the entrance to the harbour, were frustrated by the opposition of the groups interested in the local holiday industry, which were concerned that an expansion of port activity would lead to further industrial development, impairing Teignmouth's attractiveness as a resort. As a consequence, major investment in the port was delayed until the 1980s.

Nevertheless, Teignmouth's role as a port was only marginally impaired by these parochial tensions. Its continuing viability, and that of Plymouth, stand in marked contrast to Devon's other 'shipping places' where rail and road competition have combined with wider influences to undermine the coastal trade, rendering much of the Victorian legacy of port capacity redundant. Plymouth and Teignmouth have avoided such a fate because of a number of factors. Both have benefited from injections of 'external' capital; both serve relatively productive hinterlands, handling notable quantities of locally-won clay; and both have developed overseas rather than coastal links, exchanging clay for a range of foreign goods, with Plymouth boasting an extra dimension to this business in the form of its cross-Channel ferry trade. In short, both Plymouth and Teignmouth have succeeded in adapting to the changing commercial environment of the twentieth century.

23: Devon's Port Industry since 1914

1 See G Jackson, *The History and Archaeology of Ports* (Tadworth, Surrey, 1983).
2 See *Port Statistics 1987* (Department of Trade and British Ports Federation, 1968), v.
3 *Digest of Port Statistics 1973* (National Ports Council, 1973), 205–13.
4 See Chapters 3 and 4.
5 Bideford was the sole Customs Port in North Devon from 1928, when it regained the distinction from Barnstaple. However, there were still occasions when Barnstaple was erroneously classified as a Customs Port, a throwback to the rivalry and confusion which had clouded the issue since the late eighteenth century. For instance, see *Digest of Port Statistics 1966* (National Ports Council, 1966), 81.
6 This is intimated in the findings of the Rochdale Committee. *Report of the Committee of Enquiry into the Major Ports of Great Britain* (BPP, 1962).
7 In 1987, for instance, Bideford's trade was grouped with Watchet, Dartmouth's was considered under Teignmouth, and Exeter's under Exmouth. See *Port Statistics 1987*, 159–60.
8 *Port Statistics 1987*, 15; See H Trump, *Teignmouth. A Maritime History* (Chichester, 2nd edn, 1986), 123.
9 *Port Statistics 1987*, 15.
10 *Annual Statments of the Trade of the United Kingdom.*
11 *Annual Statement of the Trade of the United Kingdom, 1965.*
12 See P Ford and J A Bound, *Coastwise Shipping and the Small Ports* (Oxford, 1951).
13 *Annual Statements of the Trade of the Union Kingdom; Digest of Port Statistics*, 1966 and 1980.
14 *Digest of Port Statistics 1966*, 2–3.
15 E Delderfield, *The Exmouth Docks Company. 100 Years of Progress and History, 1865–1975* (1965), 6.
16 Trump, *Teignmouth*, 123.
17 C Gill, *Sutton Harbour* (Plymouth, n.d.), 42.
18 J P Watson and P Abercrombie, *A Plan for Plymouth. The Report Prepared for the City Council* (Plymouth, 1943).
19 *Western Morning News*, 4 May 1945.
20 *Western Morning News*, 9 May 1963.
21 M Langley and E Small, *Millbay Docks* (Exeter, 1987), 26, 38.
22 Trump, *Teignmouth*.
23 For instance, see *Kelly's Directory of Devonshire*, 1910.
24 Langley and Small, *Millbay Docks*, 7.
25 For instance, see C B M Sillick, 'The City Port of Plymouth. An Essay in Geographical Interpretation' (Unpublished PhD thesis, University of London, 1938).
26 D Spooner, 'Industrial Movement and Rural Peripheries. The Case of Devon and Cornwall' in *Regional Studies* 6, 197–215.
27 See P Gripaios, ed., *The Economy of Devon and Cornwall. Papers from a Conference Held At Plymouth Polytechnic* (South West Papers in Geography, Occasional Series, 9, 1984).
28 See Chapter 22.
29 D H Aldcroft, 'The Eclipse of British Coastal Shipping, 1913–21' *JTH*, VI (1963–4), 24–36; and P S Bagwell, *The Transport Revolution from 1770* (1974).
30 Sillick, 'City Port of Plymouth'.
31 NDRO, Borough of Bideford, Minutes of Committees, 1948.
32 Gill, *Sutton Harbour*.
33 *Western Morning News*, 1 Feb. 1964.
34 *Digest of Port Statistics*, 1965–8.
35 *Western Morning News*, 6 Jan. 1950.
36 NDRO, Borough of Bideford, Minutes of Committees, 1953–4.
37 *Port Facilities Committee of the United Kingdom Chamber of Shipping* (2nd Report, 1930). Cited in Trump, *Teignmouth*, 98.
38 Trump, *Teignmouth*, 99.
39 Trump, *Teignmouth*, 104, 122–3. See Chapter 26.
40 NDRO, Borough of Bideford, Minutes of Committees, 1953–4.
41 *Western Morning News*, 22 Jan. 1962.

24 Devon's Fishing Industry, 1880–1990

MARK PORTER

IN THE CLOSING DECADES OF THE NINETEENTH CENTURY, Devon's fishing industry continued to play an important role in the county's coastal economy. Fishing provided considerable employment for men working the county's fishing vessels, and also for those engaged in supporting activities ashore. However, by the First World War the 'Golden Age' of Devon's fishing industry was rapidly becoming a distant memory.

Whereas Brixham's fleet of first-class trawlers had once been a model for the world in terms of technology and efficiency, the failure to adopt steam or motor propulsion left the diminishing sailing fleet as an ailing, if quaint, anachronism. The First World War added impetus to the contraction of the county's fishing industry, unravelling and undermining its established form. The war took away men and vessels, many of which did not return to the fishing after the war. Similarly, support activities lost labour, and with capital shortages maintenance work was held indefinitely in abeyance.

In the interwar years, in contrast to the rise and rise of the East Coast fleets, Devon's fleets struggled to recover and modernise. Some commentators have speculated that the ownership and reward structures associated with the majority of Devon's fleets were inappropriate for the realisation of the necessary scale of reinvestment to furnish a fleet to compete with the principal East Coast fishing stations.

Annual fish landings at Devon's fishing ports showed some improvement in the interwar years, but remained well below those of the late nineteenth century. Furthermore an increasing proportion of the catch was contributed by the 'intruding' East Coast vessels as some of Devon's deep-water boats were driven to tougher grounds in the Bristol Channel to make a living. Direct and indirect employment in the industry continued to dwindle.

The impact of the Second World War was by no means as devastating as that of the First. Once again vessels and labour were lost to the war effort, but these were substituted by an influx of fishing vessels and fishermen fleeing occupied Europe, particularly at Brixham.

In the first two decades of the postwar years the industry reached a base level of capital, effort and employment. But significant reorganisation and reinvestment in some facets of the industry arrested the decline and heralded a second 'Golden Age' at the principal wet fish stations of Plymouth and Brixham and at the shellfish stations in the vicinity of the Dart. At Plymouth this resurgence has proved less easy to sustain, being initially founded upon huge but unreliable harvests of mackerel.

The postwar loss of distant-water fishing grounds, the extension of territorial waters to twelve miles, and the entry into the European Economic Community (EEC) have all had significant effects upon the county's indigenous fishing industry. However, no simple conclusions about the positive or negative effects of specific events on Devon's industry are sustainable. For example, with the loss of Icelandic fishing grounds, some of the East Coast distant-water fleet in desperation turned its attentions to the English Channel and Western Approaches, arguably driving out local fishing effort. However, the summer visitation of large numbers of 'foreign' vessels (i.e. foreign to Devon) boosted the income of Devon's fish markets, ports and support services. Similarly, the home advantage gained for Devon's fishing industry with the extension of the limit of territorial waters from three to twelve miles was offset by the fishing quotas imposed consequent upon Britain's entry to the EEC. But EEC entry has had its positive side for the local fishing industry, not the least of which has been the EEC as a new source of grants for major new capital projects.

Grants from the EEC and the British government, through the Ministry of Agriculture, Fisheries and Food, have been channelled into large-scale investment in the shore stations, most notably in new storing, discharging and market facilities at the county's two principal fishing centres, Plymouth and Brixham. However, the provision of new market facilities has, in the eyes of many commentators, achieved little in correcting the fundamental problem that has dogged the development of Devon's fishing industry in the twentieth century – the constricting marketing practices that particularly bedevil fishing activities in the South West peninsula. In the 1970s the instant success of the fishing co-operative – Brixham and Torbay Fish Ltd – seemed finally to have laid this ghost to rest, but cash-flow problems in the 1980s have demonstrated that the problem remains.

Fish Landings in Devon

Brixham and Plymouth have continued to dominate Devon's wet fish landings over the twentieth century. The species of fish landed at these two stations and the grounds from which the fish are taken have overlapped only to a limited extent, remaining essentially distinct throughout the century. The quantity of fish landed at Plymouth has been greater than at Brixham for all but the 1950s and 1960s (See Table 24.1). However, fish landings at Plymouth have been dominated by pelagic species that have commanded a much lower price in the market than the 'prime' demersal species that constituted most of the catch landed at Brixham.

The grounds yielding the richest harvest of herring, pilchards, sprats and mackerel, landed at Plymouth, have been the grounds to the west in Falmouth Bay and Mounts Bay. Demersal fish landings at Plymouth have predominantly been of lemon sole, monk fish and hake, with the richest local takings being in the vicinity of Eddystone.

The late-nineteenth-century tradition of the larger Brixham trawlers being

24.1 After the auction. Brixham at the end of the nineteenth century. (*Torquay Natural History Museum*)

Table 24.1
Fish landings at Devon's ports, 1886–1988
('00 tons)

	1886	1901	Average for Years					
			1919 to 1928	1929 to 1938	1952 to 1961	1962 to 1971	1972* to 1981	1982 to 1988
Brixham	24	29	30	17	23	16	45	73
Plymouth	71	97	75	47	6	9	292	93
Other	35	11	13	9	7	12	3	**
Devon	130	137	118	73	36	37	340	166†
UK	3,206	4,324	6,300	7,415	5,982	5,086	6,725	8,084
Devon/UK (per cent)	4.1	3.2	1.9	1.0	0.6	0.7	5.1	2.1

* Before 1977 figures for all landings exclude shellfish
** No data for fish landings at other ports
† Figure for Devon is the total of landings at Brixham and Plymouth

Source: Board of Agriculture and Fisheries, Sea Fisheries Statistical Tables; Ministry of Agriculture and Fisheries, Sea Fisheries Statistical Tables; Ministry of Agriculture, Fisheries and Food, Sea Fisheries Statistical Tables; Devon Sea Fisheries Committee Report, 1977

absent from the home grounds for most of the year has persisted in the twentieth century. However, the activities of all but the largest Brixham vessels have been concentrated on the home grounds between Start Point to the west and Portland to the east. The principal grounds within this area were reported by W Garstang[1] to be so distinct that dealers at the Brixham market could identify which fish had been caught on which grounds. The most significant grounds were given names by the Brixham men, with 'Spion Kop'[2] and the deeper-water 'Biscuit Dust' providing rich takings of plaice, sole and rays. The richest ground in this area was reported to be 'The Corner', located on the southern edge of the Biscuit Dust, which has yielded large quantities of sole, lemon sole, plaice, dabs and highly-priced turbot.

Table 24.1 shows that, before the spectacular mackerel landings at Plymouth in the late 1970s, the quantity of fish being landed at Devon's fishing stations was in a steady and protracted decline that many contemporary observers interpreted as terminal. Whereas at the end of the nineteenth century annual landings in excess of 13,000 tons were recorded, between 3 and 4 per cent of the UK's total landings, in the early 1960s annual landings had fallen to less than 4,000 tons.

At its nadir there seemed no future for Devon's fishing industry; a stark and ironic contrast to the booming state of the East Coast industry founded upon the success of the distant-water fleet. However, in the late 1960s landings at Devon's ports started to recover. The exceptional 1977 mackerel season at Plymouth, with 67,000 tons of mackerel being landed there, saw Devon's annual fish landings approaching 90,000 tons. Quotas and the associated reduction in the fishing effort dedicated to harvesting mackerel have seen annual landings fall a long way below the 1977 mark, but nonetheless landings remained above 10,000 tons throughout the 1980s.

One of the more contentious and emotive explanations offered by fishermen for the prolonged slump in the county's fishing industry has been that foreign vessels have driven local boats from their own grounds. The evidence of fish landings from foreign fishing boats at Devon's ports in general does not support such an argument. In the interwar years landings from foreign fishing vessels rarely exceeded 100 tons at Brixham and 300 tons at Plymouth. The exceptional years of the Second World War resulted from the granting of fishing permits to vessels seeking sanctuary from occupied Europe. The vast majority of the 250 fishing vessels fleeing Belgium resettled in Brixham. Of course, landings in Devon from foreign fishing boats are likely to be the tip of an incalculable iceberg of the fish actually taken by foreign vessels and landed elsewhere.

While there is no clear evidence of the quantities of fish being 'poached' by foreign vessels in the postwar years, it is clear that Devon fishermen have become increasingly exasperated at the believed poaching activities. In his

submission to the Brixham hearing of the Expenditure Committee's[3] investigations into the UK's fishing industry, Mr Williams, Secretary of the Devon Sea Fisheries Committee, expressed the view that, whereas Devon fishermen had once been prepared to turn a fraternal blind eye to the activities of foreign vessels on Devon grounds, increasingly they were now willing to report them to the Fishery Protection Service (FPS). Plymouth has witnessed the bringing in of arrested vessels by their FPS captors from time to time, but there is some dispute as to whether these sporadic events highlight the deterrent value of the service or its inadequacies.

Perhaps of greater concern to Devon fishermen than the activity of genuinely foreign fishing vessels has been the competition of UK vessels 'foreign' to Devon. Early in the century local observations recorded in the Annual Report of the Sea Fisheries Industry frequently made reference to large numbers of East Coast vessels fishing on Devon's home grounds, causing 'the large smacks to leave for the Bristol Channel early in the year'.[4] The Brixham vessels that did fish the relatively uncongested Bristol Channel grounds often sent their catches overland by rail to the Brixham market.

Following the loss of the distant-water fishing grounds, the annual summer invasion of large, better equipped and more efficient vessels from elsewhere in the UK restarted. These vessels, which came to harvest the mackerel, came in such numbers that all of Plymouth's port facilities were called into use for the landing of fish that were not being sold directly to the anchored Eastern Bloc 'klondykers' or factory ships.

The impact of fishing on this scale upon the local fishing industry is difficult to calculate. With the scale of catches forcing the local price of mackerel down, industrial fishing for mackerel (i.e. mackerel for fishmeal) was only sustainable by the large, efficient non-Devon vessels. However, the scale of the mackerel activity brought revenue to industries supporting the fishing and prompted new investment in local fish processing activities.

Fishing Effort

Table 24.2 shows that, in the period of the extended decline in Devon's fish landings, the size of Devon's registered fishing fleet was also rapidly diminishing. The table also shows that the fleet underwent a belated transition to motor propulsion, and in the postwar years diversified away from the trawler that had for so long dominated the Devon fishing scene. In particular, specialised 'liners' started to appear along with vessels with greater catching system flexibility. Of the 145 vessels on the registers at Brixham and Plymouth in 1926, only seven used lines as the main system of fishing. By 1956 62 of the 119 registered vessels were liners, compared with only 43 trawlers.

The failure of the Devon fleet to maintain its position at the forefront of fishing innovation by embracing mechanical propulsion earlier has been cited as one of the crucial issues in the pedestrian development of the county's fishing industry in the twentieth century. At the outbreak of the First World War, Devon's fleet was dominated by the sail-powered trawler. Twenty-one of these vessels were still on Devon registers at the outbreak of

24.2 East Coast herring drifters at Sutton Pool in the 1930s. (*Muriel Sillick*)

Table 24.2
Brixham and Plymouth fishing fleets in transition, 1926–1956

	1926	1936	1946	1956
Sail trawler	108	21	0	0
Steam trawler	2	1	1	0
Motor trawler	19	20	27	43
Motor liner	7	3	1	62
Motor trawler/drifter	3	4	0	0
Motor – others	6	3	0	14
Total	145	52	29	119

Sources: Board of Agriculture and Fisheries, Sea Fisheries Statistical Tables; Ministry of Agriculture and Fisheries, Sea Fisheries Statistical Tables; Ministry of Agriculture, Fisheries and Food, Sea Fisheries Statistical Tables.

the Second World War. In contrast to the rapid movement to more contemporary technologies at the East Coast fishing stations, sail-powered trawlers were being built at Brixham until as late as 1927, when the 70ft *Ruby Eileen* was launched. These refined hybrid ketch-rigged vessels had epitomised Brixham in the heady colonising days of the eighteenth and nineteenth centuries.

The largest class of these vessels, the 'dandies', varied in size from 34 to 60 tons and were crewed by four to six. These vessels, which had introduced the beam trawl to fishing 150 years before, numbered in excess of 200 in 1913. Medium-sized trawlers, locally referred to as mules, varied between 24–34 tons, and in every respect were scaled-down versions of the large trawlers and carried a crew of three. A third, smaller class of trawler, the 'mumble bees', stayed resolutely at home throughout, fishing Brixham's local inshore grounds.

The persistence of the sail trawler was more marked at Brixham than at Plymouth, where there apeared to be a greater willingness to embrace the age of mechanical propulsion. The first steam trawler on the port's register, *Reginald*, appeared in 1896, and was owned and operated by Chant & Paddon. In the following ten years Chant & Paddon increased their Plymouth fleet to ten. However, this was an isolated example of early transition at Devon's fishing stations.

Concern for the tardy conversion from sail to motor propulsion in Devon was expressed as early as 1908, and was the subject of a Ministry enquiry in 1913. The Devon and Cornwall Fishing Committee brought the relatively backward state of South West fishing technology to the attention of the Board of Agriculture and Fisheries with a request for a £10,000 grant from the Development Commission to fund a modernisation scheme for fishing vessels in the South West. The local fisheries committee envisaged a scheme whereby loans of £5–£500 would be available at an interest rate of 2½ per cent in an attempt to encourage the fitting of engines.

The investigating Committee found that, at some of the fishing stations visited in Devon, 'the industry is carried on under conditions that are almost incredibly hard'.[5] However, in general the committee found that the need for conversion to motor propulsion was more pressing in Cornwall than in Devon. Furthermore, in the instance of Brixham the committee recorded the opinion that the need for motorisation was markedly less pressing. This opinion was expressed even though it was not fully understood how Brixham

24.3   Though Brixham and Plymouth have dominated Devon's twentieth-century fishing industry, other bases have engaged in the business. Here, fishing vessels are seen at Beer, in East Devon, shortly after the First World War, when motors had been introduced but sails and oars were still in everyday use. (*Basil Greenhill*)

24.4 The Scottish mackerel fleet in Plymouth in the 1970s. (*Plymouth Local History Library*)

succeeded in maintaining its 'fine fleet of sailing trawlers in the face of steam competition'.[6]

A part explanation of this riddle must be that Brixham's home fishing grounds were within easy reach of the port. Furthermore, a local by-law existed at Brixham that gave some protection to the Brixham fleet in its prohibition of trawling within three miles of the coast by any other vessel than those propelled by sail or oar.[7]

The reservations expressed by the committee about Devon's need relative to Cornwall did not hinder the acceptance of the need for a scheme for encouraging conversion. It was recommended that the scheme for funding the purchase and fitting of modern technology take the form of loans, not grants, and that these loans should be made to co-operative groups or societies of fishermen rather than to individual fishermen. A total of £3,000 was to be made available for Devon's fishing industry, with a further £2,000 for research into engining Brixham boats.[8]

The scheme as operated in Devon does not appear to have been an overwhelming success. The exigencies of the war had prompted some trawlermen in Devon to fit engines. At Brixham eight vessels acting as guards to convoy fishing vessels were fitted with 60–80hp engines, giving a stimulus to the engining of other large vessels. M W Straight, in his 1935 report of the Brixham fishing industry, found that there were only three converted trawlers working in Brixham, *Prevalent*, *Resolute* and *Toreador*, of which only *Prevalent* was entirely motor propelled.[9] The overheads of these vessels were obviously higher than for their sail equivalents, but their earnings were proportionally higher and, furthermore, fluctuated less, because the vessels were less constrained by the weather. An additional advantage of the converted vessels was that they continued to fish from Brixham in the summer, whereas the sail-powered large trawlers in the interwar years fished Mounts Bay out of Newlyn.

The Board of Agriculture and Fisheries Report of the 'Fisheries in the Great War' singled out the pioneering South West scheme for motor installation for particular attention.[10] The report found that, where Development Commission loans had been made to fishermen, their vessels were capable of landing two or three times as much fish. The problem with the scheme was not the engineering problem of fitting engines to vessels designed to be propelled by sail, but the wariness fishermen exhibited towards engines and even more towards debt.

This failure to convert to mechanical propulsion clearly restricted the development of the county's fishing industry in the interwar years, but what are less certain are the factors that inhibited the adoption of motor propulsion. Both the 1913 and 1919 Reports emphasised the unwillingness of conservative Devon fisherman to place themselves in the position of

debtors. In general, fishermen in the South West were not conversant with, and were generally suspicious of, borrowing.

However, Straight suggests that this reluctance of Devon fishermen to assume the position of debtors was only one facet of the fishing industry's problems in the interwar years. Straight identifies the interwar decline of the industry with several related factors, all of which tended to limit expectation of return from new investment in the fishing industry.

Firstly, war losses of vessels exceeded new buildings, and in the years following the war prices of new and secondhand vessels increased considerably. Thirty-five Brixham smacks were sunk by U-Boat activity in the First World War. In the absence of comprehensive insurance schemes the owners struggled to replace these vessels. Sir Felix Pole's enquiry considered various proposals to establish a system for remuneration for war and war-related losses of fishing vessels and equipment, but all of the suggested solutions foundered upon the refusal of the government to contribute towards replacement or repair.

While many of the larger vessels on the East Coast were company owned, the predominant pattern of ownership in the South West was of owner-operated vessels. The increased capital cost of vessels made them unattractive and often unobtainable investments for the owner/operator in Devon. This was particularly so in view of the depressed returns of poor fish prices that most commentators viewed as resulting from the restrictive marketing practices specific to many South West fishing stations. For many this has been the central factor in the failure of Devon's fishing industry in the twentieth century, and it is discussed in some detail below. The third, related, factor identified by Straight as contributing to the industry's decline in Devon was the seepage of younger men from the industry. This, too, is discussed below.

Thus, by the outbreak of the Second World War Devon's fishing fleet was only a shadow of that of former years. Shrunken and outdated, the fleet desperately needed investment in new vessels and modern equipment. The first evidence of such new investment was at Brixham, with the arrival of several large new trawlers (80–90ft) owned and operated by Torbay Trawlers Ltd. Ironically, Brixham, the port that had established large-scale fishing on the East Coast, was now the beneficiary of East Coast investment, Torbay Trawlers Ltd being a subsidiary of a large East Coast fishing company.

This outside investment was, however, relatively rare. As government grants and loans became available, Devon men started to acquire new vessels or re-engine and re-equip their old ones. The tendency was to purchase secondhand vessels, rather than commission the building of new vessels. After the Second World War a good source of secondhand vessels was the sale of Admiralty Motor Fishing Vessels (MFVs). Similarly, with the extension of territorial waters to twelve miles from three miles in 1965, several Continental fishing vessels came on to the market.

The reorganisation of fish marketing at Brixham under the auspices of the fishermen's co-operative Brixham and Torbay Fish Ltd (BTF) brought greater stability to the markets, along with higher and more reliable returns to the fishermen. This, in turn, spawned more confidence in investment in vessels and equipment, with the co-operative offering the structures for financing investment. Fishing methods employed in the Devon fishing industry started to diversify away from the ubiquitous trawler. Liners became more popular, particularly with the advent of automatic baiting and stripping systems. Liners were able to fish rougher grounds and provide better-quality fish. Plymouth-based vessels such as *Pescato II* started to experiment with mid-water trawls. Another important development in the postwar years has been the investment in highly capitalised crabbers, several vessels capable of working 300–400 pots being on the registers of the UK's leading shellfish stations, in the vicinity of Kingswear, by the late 1970s.

However, this investment in vessels and equipment still left the Devon fishing industry, with its secondhand technology, limping along behind those of most other areas, in the view of many Devon fishermen. At the Brixham hearing of the 1977 House of Commons Expenditure Committee several witnesses representing Devon fishermen referred to their envy of outside fishermen with their 'much more expensive equipment and much more efficient crews'.[11] Some skippers even stated that they would not fish areas where outsiders were fishing because they were embarrassed by their inferior equipment.

Labour

Table 24.3 shows that in 1891 some 2,600 men listed fishing as their occupation in Devon. This figure represented only 1.3 per cent of Devon's total working male population, but locally at many fishing stations fishing dominated employment. The slump in the numbers of fishermen to 1,725 in 1911 emphasises the decline in the industry that predated the First World War. The continued decline in the fishing industry in the interwar years, coupled with a gradual increase in efficiency of fishing operations, saw the number of full-time fishermen in Devon reduced to 340 by 1961, less than 0.2 per cent of Devon's working male population. The upturn in Devon's fishing industry saw men returning to fishing in the 1970s, such that between 1971 and 1981 the number of fishermen all but doubled to 600.

Table 24.3
Fishermen in Devon, 1891–1981

	1891	1901	1911	1921	1931	1951	1961	1971	1981
Fishermen	2,600	2,028	1,725	1,705	1,356	641	340	350	600

Source: Census occupation tables, 1891–1981

24.5 A fine catch of sprats, Brixham, 1959. (*Torquay Natural History Museum*)

In the major period of employment contraction, at the beginning of the century, the wage return to fishermen was too inadequate to compensate for the hard and dangerous work when easier, better-paid employment beckoned. Straight was particularly concerned at the loss of young men from fishing, viewing this as robbing the industry of its vitality and future. Deflated fish prices reduced the crew's share of boat income, once the boat and owner's share had been taken. The share fishing practices prevalent at most Devon fishing stations, notably Brixham's antiquated stock-a-bait system, could not sustain a wage high enough to keep the younger men in the industry.

These men were attracted to alternative careers ashore, but Straight also found that significant numbers preferred to use their undoubted seamanship skills as professional crew aboard the yachts of gentlemen. Summer employment crewing yachts could be supplemented by a winter of drawing the dole.[12] This assistance was not available to all Devon fishermen. As mainly share fishermen they were effectively self-employed, and thus disqualified from the benefits accruing to the waged.

The gradual seepage from the industry early in the century turned into a flood in the First World War. Nationally, 49 per cent of full-time fishermen were engaged in the wartime naval service, and a further 41 per cent of part-time fishermen. Inevitably these were the younger men in the industry, pushing up the overall age of those remaining. Large numbers of fishermen returning from the war found that the 'industry could no longer support them' and sought alternative employment.[13]

Not only could the industry not support them, but many of the returning men had no interest in returning to the hardships and privations of fishing. Paradoxically, the war service had shown the Devon men that work conditions need not be so harsh. As before the war, some men found work ashore, but increasingly there were opportunities on the sea quite apart from the marine services and yachting. The interwar development of the major fishing stations as tourist centres brought the opportunity of work as boatmen for pleasure trips and charter angling parties. The Reverend Appleyard in the 1927 *Brixham Official Guide* stated that those 'who desire to witness deep-sea trawl fishing will find no difficulty in getting a skipper to take them to sea'.[14] The importance of such leisure activities to fishing station employment in the postwar years is evident in the high proportion of registered vessels that were engaged in conveying angling parties and other recreational activities. In 1977 it was estimated that at least two-thirds of the 600 vessels on Devon registers were engaged in such activities.

The twentieth-century experience of employment in ancillary and support activities is difficult to ascertain. However, some idea of the centrality of the fishing industry to the local economy is evident in a 1977 estimate that 1,500 people in Brixham were dependent upon the fishing industry, approximately 20 per cent of the working population.[15]

However, over the century as a whole it seems likely that fishing-related employment ashore declined. Certainly with the end of sail the numbers of boatbuilders, sailmakers and spar makers fell. With the advent of mass production techniques and synthetic fibres the county's numerous rope-walks disappeared. Devon has never carried a great tradition of large-scale fish processing beyond the curing and packing of pilchards, sprats, herring and mackerel. Even the huge landings of mackerel in the 1970s did not herald the establishment of large-scale fish processing plant, the fish being processed on the Eastern Bloc factory ships or dispatched to processing plants in Hull or on the Continent. The unreliability of the catch prompted caution amongst would-be investors in Devon-based processing plant.

Shellfish processing has provided considerable employment in the postwar years, with large plants at Plymouth and Brixham. Tamar Fish Processor's crab processing plant at Lockyer Quay, for example, employed eighty people in the 1970s, and the UK Foods Ltd's (part of BTF) troubled plant at Brixham employed forty in the 1980s.

Fish Distribution and Marketing

Historically, it is the problems of distribution and marketing that have been identified as the root of the ills of Devon's fishing industry. The coming of the railway to the South West in the mid-nineteenth century had opened up

24.6 Trading at the Brixham Fish Market, December 1986. (Torquay Herald Express)

24.7   A Brixham trawler at sea, August 1988. (Torquay Herald Express)

distant markets to the peninsula's relatively isolated fishing stations. Those investigating Devon's fisheries in the early part of the twentieth century tended not to find fault with the quality of the rail service. The increasing proportions of catches dispatched to markets in London and elsewhere supports the view that rail provided a reliable and rapid distribution service for this particularly perishable cargo. By 1901 99 per cent of the fish landed at Brixham was being transported from the port by the Great Western Railway (GWR). A greater proportion of Plymouth's landings found local markets or was exported through the port, but nonetheless in 1901 the GWR and London South Western Railway transported 6,810 tons of fish from the port, 70 per cent of the total catch.

However, although the rail service appears to have been adequate in logistical terms, investigators tended to identify high rail rates for fish carriage as a fundamental problem in providing Devon fishermen with a sufficient return.[16] Local quayside auction prices reflected the quality and size of fish, the cost of transferring fish to their ultimate markets, and, overridingly, the market demand for fish. What the quayside did not reflect was the cost of production.[17]

Thus transport costs were only one factor depressing quayside prices. Fishermen throughout the history of Devon's fishing industry have felt that they were not being dealt with fairly, either in selling their fish or in the purchase of fishing supplies. Certainly the evidence tends to suggest that the shore-side structures of the industry have tended to operate against the fishermen receiving a workable return from their activities.

24.8   Trawlers at Brixham, January 1991. (David J Starkey)

This was clearly illustrated by the partial success of the Torbay Fisherman's Co-operative Society, formed in 1919, in remedying some of the problems and highlighting the nature of others through its activities. Formed by Charley Scott (a Brixham salesman and merchant) and others, the co-operative had the broad aim of undermining the power that the local vested interest of suppliers to the fishing industry and fish sellers/buyers had in dictating prices to the fishermen. Thus the co-operative's aim was essentially to provide a fairer deal for the fishermen.[18]

At its high point in 1931 the co-operative had control of thirty boats and Scott reckoned to have paid £10,000 back in dividends to the Society's members, although this claim has to be seen in the light of the fact that, by the 1930s, the co-operative was no longer in a financial position to pay dividends. The co-operative was particularly successful in reducing the cost of supplies to the fishermen. Straight cites the example of the Gourock Rope Company being forced to reduce the price of its boat rope from 144 shillings per cwt to only 90 shillings as a result of the co-operative's success in providing rope to the fleet at a comparable cost. Overall, Straight calculated that the co-operative successfully cut costs to fishermen by a third.[19]

The co-operative was markedly less successful in attempts at marketing fish. The fishermen's fundamental distrust of the fish buyers/sellers and their desire to waive the profits of these middlemen led to various attempts at direct marketing of fish, both within untapped local rural markets and in more distant urban markets. These attempts failed, the failure being due, in part, to the irregularity of fish supply. This irregularity was related to the shortage of powered-fishing vessels that would have been capable of providing a regular supply.[20]

In 1923 the co-operative started to buy fish on the market as well as sell. Immediately the entrenched local vested interests of fish buyers sought to smash this marketing move and rapidly achieved success, the co-operative being forced to withdraw from the market to avoid crippling losses. For their part, the buyers rapidly recovered their losses by restricting competition through agreed market shares.[21]

Thus the co-operative became a successful supplier to the fishermen but failed to provide the marketing structure that had been envisaged at the outset. Furthermore, the financial difficulties of the co-operative left it unable to provide capital for major changes to the fleet. It had been hoped that the co-operative, through the establishment of a capital fund, would be able to provide an alternative source of loans to the established mortgagees. Mortgage agreements with the latter frequently contained conditions limiting vessel owners to dealing with certain suppliers and fish sellers.

Thus, with the demise of the 1919 co-operative, the operation of Devon's fisheries returned to their former unsatisfactory structures. This situation pertained until the 1960s, when two new fishing co-operatives were formed, heralding a new age of good and stable returns for Devon's fishermen. Mr Williams, the Chief Fishing Officer of the Devon Sea Fisheries District, claimed in his 1977 report that the resurgence within Devon's fishing industry in the previous decade

> can to a major degree be attributed to the Brixham and Torbay Fish Ltd and the Devon Shellfishermen's Association, two co-operative organisations whose officials and members have investigated and procured markets which hitherto had not been exploited, and in the process acquired favourable terms of sale for catches.[22]

The creation of these two co-operatives seemed at last to have solved the marketing problems of Devon's fishermen. The growth of the BTF was rapid, and by 1986, the year in which BTF was first reported to be facing a serious cash flow crisis, it was reckoned that 700 trawlers were on the co-operative's books and 16,000 jobs were directly linked to BTF's activities.[23]

By this time the co-operative's activities had diversified well beyond the running of Brixham market and supplying Brixham fishermen. By 1970 the closure of Brixham's direct rail link had instigated the development of a road haulage wing by BTF, fresh fish being transported to Billingsgate and other leading English markets daily. Increasingly BTF developed overseas markets, so that by 1977 it was reported that 60 per cent of the co-operative's turnover took the form of exports.[24] Ironically, it was the overseas links forged through this export activity that proved to be central to the demise of BTF in the late 1980s.

BTF also, somewhat inauspiciously, diversified into the field of fish processing, and in 1985 a fish processing plant was opened at Brixham. However, the stench of boiled crabs issuing from the plant immediately incensed large sections of the local populace, who engaged in vociferous and organised protest. A public enquiry in 1986 ordered the introduction of improved scrubbing systems for the fish factory's emissions.[25]

The early success of the co-operatives in stabilising Devon's fishing industry ended the Torbay County Borough Council's prevarication over upgrading and extending facilities at the port. In 1969 the £380,000 contract placed by the local authority, in its role as the port authority, for the extension of the fish jetty and the building of a new market was completed.[26] This was soon followed by a further £125,000-worth of improvement work. This was undertaken with substantial grant aid both from the British government and the European Economic Community.

This investment represented the first major investment in Brixham's facilities since the belated completion of the breakwater in 1916. Brixham now had up-to-date market and handling facilities with nine deepwater berths. In addition, a privately owned ice-making plant was constructed at the end of the extended wharf.

Evidence of the local authority's continued confidence in Brixham's fishing operations can be seen in the widening of the Market Pier and the provision of a new ice plant, an extension costing £3 million completed in 1986. However, this concrete evidence of confidence appears grossly mistimed with hindsight, as it coincided with the first rumours of BTF's difficulties.

The rumours of severe cash-flow problems first surfaced in the press in 1986. The substantial bad debt of BTF's French twin concern, Pecheries de la Manche, were reported to be at the core of the crisis.[27] Bankruptcy beckoned, and in 1987 it was reported that BTF owed £2 million. Although the co-operative members successfully raised £200,000 over a weekend in July 1987 to keep the company operating, their bank maintained that BTF's problems stemmed from the structural limitations of its operating as a co-operative, and called for the re-formation of BTF as a limited company.

BTF struggled on as a co-operative, but by the end of 1987 its twenty-two-year monopoly of the Brixham fish auctions was ended. In early 1988 the situation had deteriorated to the position that BTF was cancelling auctions, a harbinger of its imminent collapse. However, from the ashes rose a new consortium of Brixham trawlermen. Starting from the same position as the 1965 co-operative, this consortium immediately organised auctions, with the first in February 1988.[28] These auctions were successful from the start, heralding a new era of co-operative effort at Brixham.

Fishing and Tourism in Devon

Over the twentieth century, fishing in Devon has recovered from a prolonged slump to something approaching an extended boom. In the process, the fish catching vessels and the methods employed have become increasingly efficient and the structures for marketing the product have developed to offer a more reliable return to the fishermen. Towards the end of the twentieth century, fishing remains an important element of Devon's economy.

However, this significance is not as direct as in the 1890s, when Devon's fishing industry provided employment for substantial numbers of local men. In 1990 far fewer are involved in the fishing industry. Now, however, fishing has come to play an important new role as a tourist attraction. Fishing activities at stations such as Plymouth and Brixham provide the instant theatre of others' working lives. The Reverend Appleyard in the 1927 Brixham Official Guide established a marketing tradition for Devon in drawing attention to the possibility of viewing offshore activities. This tradition has continued. For example, a 1982 guide to Plymouth invites visitors to 'wander around Sutton Harbour and watch the fishermen at work in the bustling fish market'.[29]

At Brixham the interplay between tourism and the fishing industry was clearly exhibited in the incorporation of a public viewing gallery in the new fish market. Local authority planners have increasingly been aware of the importance of the relationship between the fishing industry and tourism. Torbay Council has acknowledged that whilst Brixham 'is the mother of the trawl fisheries, it is also a holiday resort. As the Borough Council we have always got to balance these interests.'[30] Generally, in seeking this balance, fishing has achieved more success than other less favoured industrial sectors in Devon.

24: Devon's Fishing Industry, 1880–1990

1 W Garstang, *Report on Trawling and Other Investigations Carried Out in the Bays on the South-east Coast of Devon during 1901 and 1902* (Devon Sea Fisheries Committee, 1905).

2 'Spion Kop' was so called because of a fancied resemblance of promontaries of the coast in the area to a Natal battlefield in the Boer War.

3 *House of Commons Expenditure Committee (Trade and Industry Sub-committee), The Fishing Industry,* (hereafter *HCEC*) Evidence taken at Brixham, 11 Nov. 1977 (BPP, 1977–8, XXXII, 473).

4 *Annual Report of the Sea Fisheries of the United Kingdom. Board of Agriculture and Fisheries* (BPP, 1908, XIII, 105).

5 *Board of Agriculture and Fisheries, Report of the Committee, The Devon and Cornwall Local Fisheries Committee Application for Grants for Development for Assisting Fishermen to Install Motor Power in their Boats* (BPP, 1913, XXIV, 6).

6 *Board of Agriculture and Fisheries, Devon and Cornwall Local Fisheries Committee Application* (BPP, 1913, XXIV, 6).

7 *Board of Agriculture and Fisheries, Devon and Cornwall Local Fisheries Committee Application* (BPP, 1913, XXIV, 8).

8 *Board of Agriculture and Fisheries, Devon and Cornwall Local Fisheries Committee Application* (BPP, 1913, XXIV, 19).

9 M W Straight, *A Report on the Brixham Fishing Industry* (1935).

10 *Board of Agriculture and Fisheries, Report of Fisheries in the Great War* (BPP, 1920, XVI, 643).

11 *HCEC*, 11 Nov. 1977, (BPP, 1977–8, XXXII, 473).

12 Straight, *Brixham Fishing Industry*.

13 Straight, *Brixham Fishing Industry*.

14 Rev J Appleyard, *The Brixham Official Guide* (Brixham, 1927).

15 Estimate included in the Torbay County Borough Council's submission to *HCEC*, 11 Nov. 1977, (BPP, 1977–8, XXXII, 473).

16 This, for example, was the finding, as early as 1913, of the Board of Agriculture and Fisheries investigating committee, *Board of Agriculture and Fisheries, Devon and Cornwall Local Fisheries Committee Application* (BPP, 1913, XXIV, 6).

17 The White Fish Authority in 1952 reported that this was a problem common to many of the UK's lesser fishing stations. *White Fish Authority's Annual Reports and Accounts, 1952* (HMSO, 1953), 13.

18 For a detailed history of the early days of Brixham fishing co-operatives see Straight, *Brixham Fishing Industry*.

19 Straight, *Brixham Fishing Industry*, 65.

20 Straight, *Brixham Fishing Industry*, 69.

21 Straight, *Brixham Fishing Industry*, 65.

22 Devon Sea Fisheries Committee, *Devon Sea Fisheries District, 1977 Report* (1977).

23 *Western Morning News*, (hereafter *WMN*), 'Co-operative in Trouble', 5 Dec. 1986.

24 BTF evidence to *HCEC*, 11 Nov. 1977 (BPP, 1977–8, XXXII, 473).

25 *WMN*, 13 March 1986.

26 Details of expenditure are to be found in the Torbay County Borough Council's submissions to *HCEC*, 11 Nov. 1977 (BPP, 1977–8, XXXII, 473).

27 *WMN*, 15 Dec. 1986.

28 *WMN*, 11 Feb. 1988.

29 Plymouth Marketing Bureau, *Plymouth, the Real Maritime Centre* (1982).

30 Torbay County Borough Council's submission to *HCEC*, 11 Nov. 1977 (BPP, 1977–8, XXXII, 473).

25   Devon Seaside Tourism since 1900

N J MORGAN

THE LAST TWO DECADES have seen the study of seaside tourism in Britain become an accepted field of research, and the pattern of its development within Devon from the mid-eighteenth century to the end of the nineteenth century has been discussed in various works (see Chapter 13).[1] By 1900 the pattern of Devon's modern tourist industry was already well established. Those towns which were to dominate the trade in the twentieth century were recognised watering places at its beginning. This pattern of resort development was in line with that of the majority of British resorts. Whereas in continental Europe many resorts evolved after the First World War, only a handful of the modern British resorts were little more than villages at the time of the 1911 census.[2]

The period from 1870 to 1940 was the high point of the British seaside resort.[3] In these decades the trip to the seaside, along with professional league football, the music hall and, later, the cinema, became so much a part of the remodelled working-class culture shaped by technological innovation and the rise of consumer capitalism that it was soon considered a 'traditional' leisure form. However, whilst the emergence of this commercially-orientated 'mass' leisure market has attracted a great deal of attention, the period beyond 1914 has been somewhat neglected.[4] Yet these years witnessed vast changes in leisure patterns and, in the sphere of tourism, moves towards 'mass' participation in holidaying. By 1938 Roland Robinson, MP for Blackpool, was able to make the boast (although it was somewhat of an exaggeration) that 'the summer holiday, so recently a privilege of a minority has become the prerogative of the million'.[5]

The Devon seaside tourist industry differs from the general pattern of British seaside tourism development in that the county's geographical distance from the main centres of urban population delayed its popularisation until the interwar period and beyond. The experiences of its resorts thus differed widely from those of, for instance, Lancashire or the North East.[6] The factor of distance meant that those resorts with a controlling interest favouring the attraction of a select clientele were able successfully to pursue exclusionist policies. This was the case, for example, in Sidmouth, Budleigh and, to a lesser extent, in Torquay. At the beginning of the twentieth century all the major Devon resorts were 'select' and 'respectable', and, whilst social gradations did exist, they ranged only from middle class Ilfracombe to the more genteel Torquay.[7] Such were the massive social and economic changes of the ensuing decades that, although the basic spatial pattern of the industry remained largely unaltered, the nature of the county's tourist trade was quite different by the latter years of the century. The advent of the motor car opened up previously inaccessible areas of the county, and legislation such as the 1938 Holidays with Pay Act combined with rising living standards to bring the holiday habit to increasing numbers of people. The period 1918–78 witnessed huge increases in holidaymaker numbers, with Devon becoming the prime destination within a British context, capturing 20 per cent of the domestic market by the mid-1960s.[8]

Expanding throughout this century, the holiday industry has assumed a huge importance to Devon's economy. Indeed, tourism and leisure enterprises, although often characterised by seasonal employment and low wages, have partially offset the decline of Devon's traditional maritime activities of shipping and trade. By 1973 tourists were spending almost £100 million in the county each year, a figure which had increased to £370 million by 1987, over a third of this figure being retained as income to Devon

residents.[9] Yet the industry has also brought problems to the county. The oddly-balanced economy has meant that seasonal unemployment has been a major concern throughout the twentieth century, and the industry's benefits of improved retailing and leisure facilities have to be weighed against disadvantages such as traffic congestion and higher property values and living costs. Tourism has also increased pressure on the environment and public utilities such as water and sewage services, hindered economic diversification, and drained labour and capital from other areas of investment.[10] The benefits and drawbacks of the industry have been concentrated in certain areas within the county throughout the period, and this itself has caused problems in Devon.

The spatial pattern of the county's tourist industry owes much to its early development. Although the emergence of the resorts predates the railway age, it was the pattern of railway development which dictated much of the evolution of those seaside holiday towns which became the mainstay of Devon's tourism industry as a whole. Even with the dominance of the motor car in recent decades, tourism accommodation remains coastally-based, concentrated in the Victorian rail resorts (see Map 25.1). The influence of the railways can be seen in that, with the exception of the Kingswear branch and the Kingsbridge line opened in 1893, both of which were sited too far up the estuaries to create seaside resorts in the Victorian mould, they never reached the south Devon coast west of Brixham, and therefore the coastal communities here did not develop into traditional resorts.[11] The nature of the coastline itself has also played a role in determining the siting of the modern resorts. From Dartmouth to Plymouth, for example, the coastline is wild, with no towns and few beaches, although from Bigbury to Plymouth the more accessible coast serves local trippers. Tourists in numbers are attracted to sandy beaches, and thus they concentrate at Saunton, Woolacombe, Northam and Instow on the North Devon coast and Bigbury-on-Sea, Dawlish Warren, Exmouth and the Torbay resorts in the south. It is noticeable that there are no family resorts between Budleigh and Lyme Regis because of the lack of safe sandy beaches.[12]

Undoubtedly it is the sea which holds the attraction for the modern tourist, and in the late 1960s over 90 per cent of all main holidays which included a stay in Devon were spent in seaside resorts.[13] The inland areas of Devon – the two moorlands of Dartmoor and Exmoor and the broad sweep of farmland north of Dartmoor; the South Hams south of the moor; and inland east Devon – have never attracted great numbers of tourists. Even in summer the moors are used surprisingly little by visitors, serving more as a recreational resource for local people, and whilst the two main urban centres of Plymouth and Exeter attract their share of tourists as historic cities and facility and retailing centres, the coastline remains the focus of holidaying.[14]

This coastal concentration of tourist activity particularly intensified after 1945. By the mid-1960s the peak-season visitor numbers seen in Table 25.1 translated into over 4,500 tourists per mile of coastline between the Exe and the Dart estuaries.[15] Torbay and Ilfracombe have suffered from the greatest visitor pressure, although the South Hams and the Exmouth and Seaton areas were experiencing considerable congestion by the late 1970s.[16] Composed of the three communities of Brixham, Paignton and Torquay, Torbay is Devon's main resort and accommodated 1.4 million or 40 per cent of the county's total visitors each year by the late 1970s. Together with

Plymouth, it had the vast majority of the county's amusement facilities, although Ilfracombe retained several entertainment facilities as the main north coast resort.[17]

Table 25.1
Estimated peak holiday populations in Devon, 1964

Devon region	Estimated peak holiday population
Exe Estuary–Dart Estuary	125,000
North Devon Coast	38,000
Exe Estuary–Dorset Border	30,000
Dart Estuary–River Plym	18,650
Plymouth	8,000
Dartmoor	7,000
Rest of Devon	3,000
Exeter	2,000

Source: South West Economic Planning Council, *Region With a Future* (1967), 53.

The County Council policies formulated during the 1980s recognised this concentration of visitors and advised discouraging development in both the saturated and the unspoilt areas, whilst channelling development in target areas such as Exmouth and Seaton. The resorts thus remain the focus of development, with efforts being made to extend their seasons and improve their accommodation and facilities. To be fully effective, policies of containment have to be accompanied by the promotion of areas targeted for expansion. Above all, the tourism planners have urged resorts to adopt policies of specialisation, 'with each resort integrating its attractions with those of the surrounding area rather than each attempting to provide everything for the holidaymaker.'[18] Here, the policy planners of the late twentieth century are advocating the continuance of policies which have long been followed in the county's tourist industry.

Establishing an Image: 1900–1939

The years 1900–1939 saw far-reaching changes in British society, reflected in the nation's holiday industry. Although the conflict of 1914–18 proved a notable interruption, these four decades witnessed the consolidation of the modern British seaside industry. The expansion of the railways had created many of the seaside resorts, and their dominance of the transport networks until the 1920s preserved the early pattern. Even with the coming of age of road transport and the massive increase in the numbers of holidaymakers between the wars, tourism development was still concentrated mainly on the outskirts of existing resorts, although newer forms of accommodation, such as holiday camps, did appear, Brixham and Seaton being among Devon's more popular sites for camps.[19] Nevertheless, the increasing prevalence of the car among the middle classes accelerated the trend away from the lodging-house-single-centre-type holiday to the increased mobility offered by motoring holidays, although the accommodation still tended to be resort-based. Indeed, evidence suggests that as early as the 1930s the market for traditional seaside holidays was stagnating in the larger, more popular resorts such as Blackpool, where the numbers of landladies stopped increasing and the building of new boarding houses ceased.[20]

The holidaymaking patterns established in the late nineteenth century continued in the early decades of the twentieth. Even after the Second World War, when the numbers coming into Devon increased still further, the growth was channelled along familiar lines and traditional accommodation remained at the centre of the 'resort package'. Throughout much of the cen-

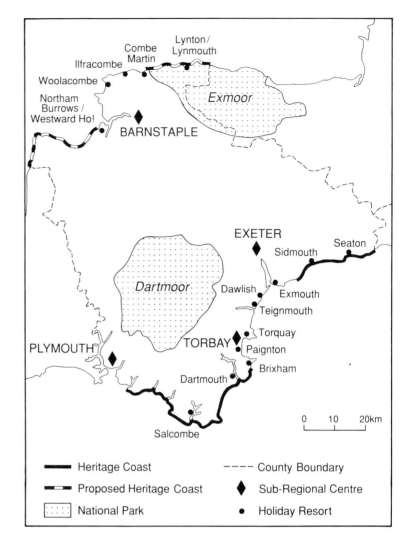

Map 25.1 Holiday Resorts identified by the Devon Structure Plan of 1979 in relation to major Landscape Conservation Areas.

25.1 Passenger steamers approaching Ilfracombe, c1900. (*Ilfracombe Museum*)

25.2   Tourism facility provisions: Torquay Pavilion, *c*1914. (*Torquay Library*)

tury these patterns were unaltered, especially amongst the working class, and visitors often returned each year to the same resort, even to the same guest house, spending their leisure time with their neighbours and workmates. As John Walton has written, 'the working-class holiday habit,' firmly rooted in the communal life of the street and factory culture, 'took on a cosy conservatism which lasted beyond the Second World War and has only recently come under serious attack'.[21]

Yet the First World War and its aftermath brought radical social transformation to Britain, and despite the years of depression the interwar period saw people indulge in the modern forms of leisure on an unprecedented scale. The growth rate in the mass entertainment sector between 1931 and 1939 was 49 per cent, a figure far exceeding the rate for other areas of the economy. Indeed, of all the economic sectors, sport and entertainment experienced the third greatest increase in numbers employed

between 1931 and 1937.[22] Britain's seaside resorts boomed, spending an estimated three to four million pounds annually on seafront improvements in the 1930s. Blackpool, which alone spent £3 million on schemes for its parks, promenade and Winter Gardens in these years, was merely the most prominent example of a trend to be seen all around the British coast.[23]

The burgeoning of seaside development was reflected in the increased quantity and quality of publicity in the interwar decades. It seems that the years from 1870 to 1940 mark the period when most resort images, popular or fashionable, were established, and this is clearly the case in Devon.[24] Between 1905 and 1913 both the Torquay and Ilfracombe Councils established their publicity machinery on a more professional footing. These achievements were consolidated in the interwar period, and consummated in the high-quality publicity material of the 1920s and 1930s, produced in conjunction with the railway companies.[25]

The expansion of municipal involvement in advertising and in the provision of entertainment in this period was facilitated by two pieces of legislation: the Health and Pleasure Resorts Acts of 1921 and 1936. The first of these quite modest enactments allowed local authorities to fund advertising from beach undertakings and admission charges from attractions, while the second allowed them to draw upon the rates up to the product of one and one-third penny rate for the same purpose. Together they provided the 'major breakthrough in seaside promotion' during the interwar period.[26] Although some resorts, including Sidmouth in Devon, preferred to rely on the activities of their Chambers of Commerce and publicity associations until after the Second World War, many more resorts quickly took advantage of the Acts.[27] Certainly many of the initiatives of the Joint Advertising Committees of Torquay and Ilfracombe were built upon the foundations they provided, allowing the former to further promote itself as 'The Queen of the English Riviera'.[28]

The interwar period truly witnessed the establishment of Devon as a prime holiday area in the popular mind. The greatest population growth in the county at this time was along the coastal belt, reflecting the importance of the holiday industry as well as the influx of retired individuals which these communities were already attracting. Furthermore, much of the interwar capital investment in Britain's seaside tourism industry occurred in Devon. Almost 20 per cent of the county's medium-sized hotels extant in 1970 were built during the 1930s.[29] The most intensive investment occurred in Torquay, where the middle classes sought seclusion, having been driven out of the less select, more populous resorts elsewhere in Britain.[30] This was a crucial period in Torquay's development, seeing the demise of the 'gentry' era, the end of its existence as a select watering place and its rise as a modern resort.[31] One interesting feature of Torquay's development is that, owing to its communications networks, its diversity of functions and the policies of the local authority, it was able to achieve a 'popular fashionability', rejecting both the selectivity of Sidmouth and the popularity of Paignton. Drawing its clientele from a broad economic and geographic range, but concentrating on prosperous regions with rising real incomes, such as the South East and the Midlands, the resort was able to ride out the vicissitudes of the depression.[32]

This was not the case in Ilfracombe, the leading North Devon resort and Torquay's

25.3   The beach at Seaton in the 1920s. Working fishing boats are making more money taking 'freights' of holidaymakers round the bay than with their nets and traps. (*Postcard*)

25.4 The sea front at Ilfracombe, *c*1925. Dominated by the new Pavilion Theatre, walled gardens and the bandstand, this area was thronged with visitors throughout the summer months. (*Ilfracombe Museum*)

greatest rival. In close proximity to the Welsh coast, Ilfracombe had long been heavily reliant on trippers from South Wales and Bristol. The distress in these key catchment areas of the Welsh valleys and coastal belt communities, devastated by the interwar depression, was mirrored in Ilfracombe by seasonal unemployment and a population stagnating at just over 9,000. Although eased by the increased traffic from the beneficiaries of new industries in the Midlands, the 1930s brought mixed seasons to North Devon, with the trough of the Channel tripper trade, as measured by the Ilfracombe pier receipts, located in the mid-1930s.[33]

This is not to imply that Ilfracombe's tourism trade was negligible. In the peak summer months of the 1930s over 45,000 resident visitors flooded into the resort each week, amounting to about half a million visitors a year. In a town of some 9,000 inhabitants this represented a 300 per cent population increase, even excluding the seasonal workers who came to the town in search of work each year, a few thousand arriving from South Wales alone.[34] The Ilfracombe Urban District Council strove to maintain and boost this tourism trade. Indeed, it was probably Devon's most active local authority during these years. An expert on the Devon holiday trade noted, 'The Municipality [did] everything in its power to organise entertainments and to encourage others to organise them privately', providing a Pavilion, concerts, bands, theatres, bowling and putting greens and swimming pools.[35] It is worth noting that Ilfracombe's most ambitious interwar project, the laying-out of the Victoria Pleasure Grounds and the building of the Concert Hall during 1922–8, was a Council initiative.[36]

Other resorts in Devon which followed similar policies to those of Ilfracombe included Paignton and Exmouth. In the interwar period, Paignton, with its wide expanse of sandy beaches, established a reputation as a family resort. These natural attractions were enhanced in the years before the Second World War by Council investments of over £54,000 in improvements to Goodrington Sands, including new cliff gardens, promenades, putting greens and a boating lake.[37] Exmouth was also a very popular resort, with a large tripper dimension to its holiday trade, many of them drawn from nearby Exeter. During the 1930s the trippers numbered many thousands, whilst between July and mid-September resident visitors doubled the town's population to about 32,000. Here, the local authority was also keen to encourage the tourist trade and provided municipal entertainments, bands, beach kiosks on a large scale, bowling greens, tennis courts, mini-golf and a swimming pool.[38]

At the other extreme in terms of municipal involvement were resorts such as Sidmouth and Budleigh. Sidmouth, in particular, provided an excellent example of a resort where the controlling groups within the community consciously pursued policies designed to exclude certain types of tourist; policies which achieved a high degree of success. A sizeable resort with a population over half that of Ilfracombe, Sidmouth differed significantly from the North Coast resort. Its Bank-Holiday tripper trade was minimal and the average number of resident visitors was kept down 'by supreme effort' to 'about 3,000'. This policy of exclusion maintained by the Council and the holiday trades' pressure groups was seen in operation in 1933, when the local authority used town boundary changes to secure powers to prevent nuisances such as touting and street advertising and, more significantly, to scotch plans to develop a holiday camp scheme at nearby Salcombe Regis.[39] Whilst the Urban District Council did invest in tourism-related facilities, opening a new esplanade in 1926 and the Connaught pleasure gardens in 1934, municipal activity was limited.[40] During the period the Council declined to organise any entertainments, the life-blood of resorts such as

Ilfracombe and Torquay, and minimal sums were spent on resort promotion, the authority preferring to rely on the initiatives of the town's score of quality hotels.[41]

Reconstruction, Consolidation and Reorientation: 1945–78

This period saw the Devon, like the British, holiday industry initially expand hugely and peak in terms of tourist numbers in the late 1970s. Thereafter decline set in with the growth of competition from foreign destinations (see Fig. 25.7). The three postwar decades were characterised by increasing affluence and a more economically powerful working class. Further trends impacting on patterns of tourism included the delayed effects of the statutory holidays introduced in 1938, and rising levels of car ownership. Between 1950–56 the numbers of private cars in Britain grew from 2.2 to 3.9 million, rising by a further 4 million by 1960.[42]

These changes boosted the seaside holiday industry in Devon as elsewhere. The numbers of visitors to the county doubled during the 1950s and 1960s, while main holidays taken in the South West region as a whole increased from 3.5 to 8 million between 1951 and 1965, constituting a rise from a 14 to a 20 per cent share of the domestic market.[43] The success of the region's seaside resorts meant that from 1939 to 1964 the previous century's trend of population loss was reversed. In these years the population of the South West increased by 24 per cent, a figure twice that of the national average.[44] In Devon the larger coastal resorts grew rapidly, absorbing an eighth of new dwellings built in the county between 1965 and 1975. In the 1960s and 1970s the population increases in Ilfracombe, Torbay and Sidmouth were almost entirely due to their growing populations of retired people, whilst the small resorts of Dartmouth, Lynton, Salcombe and Woolacombe remained virtually static.[45]

Although this period witnessed substantial shifts in holidaying patterns, holidaymaking behaviour remained remarkably traditional, retaining much of its interwar character. Even in the late 1970s, 'it would seem that the British holidaymaker [was] "tied" either by tradition or institutional factors such as "wakes weeks" to the week or fortnight holiday period',[46] The major changes in patterns tended to be merely the acceleration of previously identifiable trends in accommodation and in transport. Perhaps the most significant shift was the decline in traditional accommodation. Caravan and tent sites proliferated in the postwar decades and high concentrations developed around Brixham, Dawlish Warren and Seaton and in the rural areas of Bigbury Bay, and on the north coast at Westward Ho!. The numbers of static and mobile caravans in the county leapt from just over 1,000 to almost 12,000 between 1949 and 1959, 84 per cent of them located on the coast.[47] By 1977 the traditional accommodation sector of the market had decreased to only 45 per cent, although it remained popular in South Devon.[48]

The other significant trend in the period 1945–78 was the increased importance of the motorist in Devon tourism. By the 1960s over 80 per cent of Devon and Cornwall's holidaymakers arrived by car, the numbers arriving by this means having risen rapidly during the 1950s and stabilised in the early to mid-1960s, although it still represented a higher proportion of tourist arrivals than in any other region, probably due to the suitability of the area for car-centred holidays.[49] This pattern cushioned the effects of the loss of rail links in the period. In the early 1960s Seaton, Sidmouth and Budleigh Salterton all lost their connections, and Ilfracombe Station closed in 1970.[50]

Although the period 1945–78 was one of seemingly uninterrupted growth in the British tourist industry, it also held the seeds of its own decline in the late 1970s. The Second World War and its aftermath brought difficulties to an industry which in many respects was still in its infancy. The war meant that many resorts needed an urgent injection of investment to renovate dilapidated facilities. Yet whilst central government regarded tourism as a depressed industry, little aid was forthcoming in an age of austerity. Any postwar progress was achieved by private and municipal enterprise, often in spite of central government opposition on economic grounds.[51] Thus it was with little financial support or planning that tourism expanded into an industry of huge significance in the 1950s, becoming a major foreign-currency earner.[52] The tourism boom in the 1960s and 1970s, however, masked the need to improve and update the domestic holiday product. Opportunities were missed, and although 'a lot of money was made . . . little was ploughed back. Facilities became jaded and badly maintained. Very few new ideas were introduced and standards were assumed to be high enough. Heads were buried in the golden sand.'[53] This situation made the British holiday trade, vulnerable to the rivalry of sunny foreign beaches, easy prey to such competition, and between 1951 and 1965 the numbers of Britons holidaying abroad increased from 1.5 to 4.9 million.[54]

In the South West the postwar picture was very similar. Although the holiday industry expanded, there were increasing signs that the resorts were ailing as the affluent turned to Continental destinations. In the 1960s both the average income of holidaymakers and their average level of expenditure fell, except in a few select resorts. Although the South West's visitor numbers continued to rise, topping 7 million by 1970, the previous uninterrupted increase gave way to fluctuations which reflected the general economic climate.[55] In 1969 the British Tourist Authority urged the region to place less emphasis on passive sun and sand-orientated holidays and concentrate on raising standards of accommodation and facilities in order to compete with package holidays.[56] Yet investment took the form of consolidation rather than innovation, and although there was more investment in certain urban areas in the early 1970s, evidence suggests that the smaller resorts could not sustain large enough units to cover capital costs.[57] In Ilfracombe, for example, amenities were closed or converted without being replaced by facilities of an adequate standard.[58] Even resilient Torquay suffered. The change in its fortunes plunged the town's commercial heart into decline, 'Ugly amusement arcades, charmless souvenir shops and garish fast-food places' opened near the harbour, while cheap bed and breakfast establishments sprang up to cater for the growing market of Midlands holidaymakers able to reach the resort far more easily with the opening of the M5 motorway.[59]

An Industry on Shifting Sands: 1978–1993

During the 1960s and 1970s the Devon seaside tourist industry, in common with that of Britain as a whole, experienced virtually continuous expansion. But between 1979 and 1982 it was hit by the recession which struck the national economy, a crisis which was exacerbated by a succession of poor summers. Annual visitors to the county fell from a peak of 3.5 million in 1978 to under 3 million in 1982 (see Table 25.2). During this period there was a county-wide shift away from the familiar resorts, reflected in the declining share of the Devon market experienced by the Torbay and Teignbridge Districts, areas dependent on the resorts of Torquay, Paignton, Brixham, Teignmouth and Dawlish. Although Torbay was still Devon's most popular holiday area, its share of the county market fell from 39 per cent in 1975 to 32 per cent in 1987, with visitors falling below the 1 million mark in 1983[60] (see Fig. 25.8). In spring 1988 winter unemployment in Torquay, at 18 per cent, was the highest in Devon. Although it was the county's most prominent resort, at the end of the 1980s it faced severe problems, in common with many of Britain's resorts. In a report produced in 1991 on the problems of small seaside resorts, the English Tourist Board highlighted the 'legacy of neglect' created by 25 years of market decline. The continuous loss of visitors over a quarter of a century has resulted in the closure of hotels and traditional attractions, the consequent low levels of confidence and investment accelerating the physical decay in the resorts and further undermining their appeal.[61]

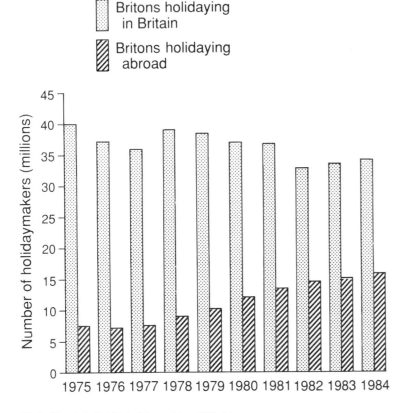

Britons holidaying
in Britain

Britons holidaying
abroad

25.5   Trends in British holidaymaking, 1975–84.

Table 25.2
Resident visitors to Devon, 1974–1987

	Tourists	Annual change	
1974	2,938,300		
1975	3,181,250	+242,950	+8.3%
1976	3,386,500	+205,250	+6.5%
1977	3,421,000	+ 34,500	+1.0%
1978	3,485,100	+ 64,100	+1.9%
1979	3,407,350	− 77,750	−2.2%
1980	3,292,450	−114,900	−3.4%
1981	3,044,300	−248,150	−7.5%
1982	2,903,900	−140,400	−4.6%
1983	3,077,400	+173,500	+6.0%
1984	3,095,250	+ 17,850	+0.6%
1985	3,195,380	+100,130	+3.2%
1986	2,960,075	−235,305	−7.4%
1987	3,034,370	+ 74,295	+2.5%

Source: Devon County Council, *Devon Tourism Review* (1987).

Despite these difficulties, Torquay has been more successful than many resorts in attempting to reposition itself in the changing leisure market of the late twentieth century. Moreover, whilst the investment of the late 1980s in the British tourism industry has become retrenchment and restraint in the early 1990s, when tourism spending has to be seen against economic recession and a lack of business confidence, the prospects for the domestic tourism industry may begin to improve. In 1988 a £25 million upgrading and refurbishments programme repaid Butlins with a boom in demand, whilst Holiday Club Pontins reported a 60 per cent increase in the luxury end of its market. In that year over £2.5 billion was invested in Britain's tourist facilities in an attempt to attract more domestic visitors. These efforts were assisted by the Department of Employment and the tourism promotion bodies, which tried to encourage people to holiday at home, a campaign backed by the Minister for Tourism.[62]

Tourism and leisure investment programmes were also instituted in Devon in the late 1980s. In 1987 the County Council reported that, in the north of the county, 'expectations are rising . . . with the advent of the North Devon Link Road and Barnstaple Relief Road' and the major County Council initiative of the Tarka Project which seeks 'to develop appropriate recreation, tourism and conservation opportunities, within an overall framework of benefitting the natural beauty, character and economic well-being of North Devon'.[63] The resort of Ilfracombe, in seemingly irreversible decline in recent decades, was also targeted for investment, and whilst a marina development there still seems unlikely, the town has been boosted by a multi-million-pound urban regeneration project. Launched in 1986, the Ilfracombe Project, which co-ordinates the initiatives of local authorities, national agencies and voluntary bodies, continues to be instrumental in progressing environmental enhancements and improvements to the physical fabric of the resort.[64]

In Torbay, recent improvements in the town's retailing and leisure facilities have been even more extensive. The success of the Imperial Hotel, one of Torquay's leading establishments since it opened in 1867, bears witness to the resilience of the resort in the current recession. The lines of Jaguars and Rolls-Royces in its car parks and its insistence on male diners wearing a jacket and tie suggests that people do not holiday there because they cannot afford to go abroad. For two decades the Hotel maintained its old-fashioned standards whilst the town became somewhat shabby. Yet now there is a revival in prospect for such a market. Torbay's tourism officer predicts that the days of the town's more seedy outlets are numbered. 'Torquay's brave new future is to be built not on deck chairs, buckets and spades or candy floss – but on shopping malls, a conference centre and a marina.' The Pavilion, the once popular theatre opened in 1912, has been converted into a fashionable retailing complex, a 460-berth yachting marina has been built and the multi-million-pound English Riviera Centre, an impressive conference, exhibition and leisure facility, opened in 1987 (see Map 25.2). One of the later phases in this project was based on the concept of 'leisure-oriented shopping', £35 million being invested in the Fleet Walk shopping development which incorporates a covered mall, car parking provision and a large Winter Gardens rotunda at its heart. Such projects illustrate that the resort sees the future in terms of the all-year-round money earners of the conference and the short-break businesses, rather than that of the traditional holiday fortnight.[65]

Much of the impetus for the revitalisation of Torbay at the end of the 1980s was provided by an English Tourist Board report on the resort published in 1982. It signalled the beginning of a major Torquay Tourist Board advertising initiative spearheaded by eye-catching guide covers and poster designs. Incorporating the controversial new palm image and Torbay's own colours of blue, yellow, white and jade green, the designs market Torbay as an image, not as a location, skilfully blending traditional and modern images, creating an impression of a sophisticated resort capable of providing old-fashioned service and elegance together with modern facilities.[66]

The repositioning of Torbay's image in the 1980s typifies the present trends in the British tourism industry. During the later 1970s holidays in the UK declined in the face of foreign competition, increasing personal mobility, higher expectations of facilities and amenities, and a gradual change in the appeal of the traditional seaside holiday as tourists became increasingly sophisticated. The industry responded by turning to newer areas of profit: activity holidays, conferences, language schools and foreign visitors. Second holidays and weekend breaks, made easier by improved transport links,

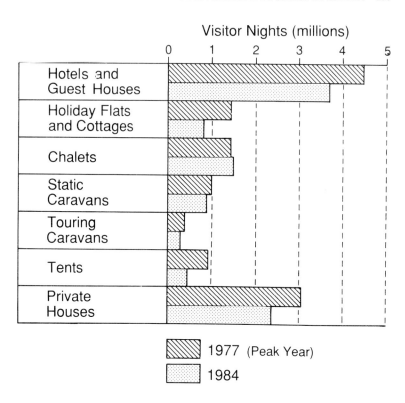

25.6   Shifts in Torbay visitor numbers and accommodation patterns, 1977 and 1984 (*Torbay Borough Council*, The English Riviera 2000 *[1985]*)

proved a major growth area in the late 1970s and the 1980s, when spending on short holidays increased by 32 per cent in real terms between 1974 and 1982. In the 1990s this market continues to be a prime target for resorts.[67]

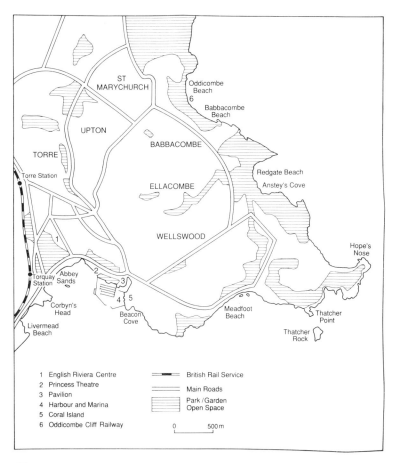

Map 25.2   Torquay's beaches and major tourism facilities.

Conclusion

It is apparent that Torquay has been one of the more successful of the Devon resorts in adapting to the changing tourism patterns of the later twentieth century. As a large resort it has been able to sustain more than one character and has achieved a 'popular fashionability'. Other resorts, however, have been uncertain of their desired image or have tried to be more than one thing and failed. Clearly, this overview of Devon's tourism industry highlights the importance of resort specialisation; 'the most successful resorts' in the county 'seem to be those which have set out, intentionally or perhaps accidentally, and succeeded in appealing to a particular section of the market'.[68] Teignmouth, for instance, has long targeted family holidaymakers: in the late 1950s over 80 per cent of its visitors were in family groups.[69] Thus in the late 1980s Teignbridge District Council's commitment to 'maintain the character of the area as one suitable for family holiday enjoyment' continued a long-term trend.[70] Further down the coast, Salcombe, physically isolated by land and unsuitable for industrial use, but with a good sheltered harbour, concentrated on sailing and other forms of boating. Here, appeal to a particular part of the market or 'market segmentation', has led to an economically satisfactory result. Budleigh has developed its function as a limited quiet resort, providing essentially for a resident retired population. 'The result seems to be a social organisation based on retired leisure, which older people find very satisfying', and economically the town has prospered although growth has been limited by the need to preserve the secluded atmosphere.[71]

Sidmouth, with its very sheltered position and Georgian townscape, provides perhaps the best example of resort specialisation. Catering for a specific market which it has cultivated over the twentieth century, Sidmouth has a very large number of high-quality hotels for a modest-sized resort. As at Budleigh, no caravan or chalet sites have been allowed to develop and the market targeted requires a quiet, expensive holiday. Almost 65 per cent of Sidmouth's tourists are drawn from the ABC1 socio-economic group, a higher proportion than any other East Devon coastal resort. The town draws much of its clientele from the Midlands, London, the South and the West Country; particularly those aged over 55, a market with high living standards and disposable incomes and an increasingly large leisure-time budget.[72]

Since the early 1960s the main problem for the British tourism industry has been the continental package holiday. However, the Mediterranean sun-oriented holidays are under threat as the teenage market, the main consumer of this type of holiday, fell by 20 per cent between 1983 and 1993.[73] The growth sectors of the holiday market are now the young childless professionals and young retired holidaymakers. These market changes, together with the appropriate response by the tourism sector, could promise a revival in the recession-hit British trade. The key to any recent successes in a sector dominated by changing consumer demand has been the branding and aggressive marketing of the 'holiday product' which is typified by the strategies of the Torbay Tourist Board. Moreover,

> Just how successful these new skills have been can be demonstrated most clearly in the recent up-turn in the traditional holiday centre. Instead of being perceived as a cheap alternative for those who cannot afford to go abroad, the holiday centre is increasingly seen as a force to be reckoned with.[74]

The mid-1990s promise further changes in the tourism scene, not least of which is the advent of 'green tourism'.[75] Above all, the 1990s will be the decade when UK leisure becomes truly European, building on the creation of a single (west) European market, and awaiting the opening of the Channel Tunnel. Devon is well located geographically to capitalise on these initiatives, and it has the natural environment to attract the 'Euro-Tourist', with a high proportion of Britain's European Blue Flag beaches in the county.[76] Whether it has the imagination and will to respond positively to the challenges posed by the new market opportunities of a restructured Europe remains to be seen.

25: Devon Seaside Tourism since 1900

1 See J A R Pimlott, *The Englishman's Holiday. A Social History* (1947); J Walvin, *Beside the Seaside. A Social History of the Popular Seaside Holiday* (1978); J K Walton, *The English Seaside Resort. A Social History 1750–1914* (Leicester, 1983); H J Perkin, 'The Social Tone of Victorian Seaside Resorts in the North West', *Northern History*, 11 (1975), 187–94; M Huggins, 'Social Tone and Resort Development in North East England. Victorian Seaside Resorts Around the Mouth of the Tees', *Northern History*, 20 (1984), 187–206; and J Lowerson and J Myerscough, *Time to Spare in Victorian England* (1977). On the early development of the seaside tourist industry in Devon, see J Travis, 'Lynton in the Nineteenth Century. An Isolated and Exclusive Resort', in E M Sigsworth, ed., *Ports and Resorts in the Regions* (Hull, 1980), 152–67, 'The Rise of Holidaymaking on the Devon Coast with Special Reference to Health and Entertainment' (unpublished PhD thesis, University of Exeter, 1988), and *The Rise of the Devon Seaside Resorts* (Exeter, 1993); F B May, 'The Development of Ilfracombe as a Resort in the Nineteenth Century' (unpublished PhD thesis, University of Wales, 1978), 'Victorian and Edwardian Ilfracombe', in J Walvin and J K Walton, eds, *Leisure in Britain 1780–1939* (1983), and 'The Rise of Ilfracombe as a Seaside Resort in the Nineteenth Century', in H E S Fisher, ed., *West Country Maritime and Social History* (Exeter, 1980).

2 N Yates, 'Selling the Seaside', *History Today*, XXXVIII (1988), 20–7.

3 Yates, 'Selling the Seaside', 20.

4 See P Bailey, *Leisure and Class in Victorian England. Rational Recreation and the Contest for Control 1830–1885* (1978); and A Briggs, *Mass Entertainment. The Origins of a Modern Industry* (Adelaide, 1960). Few serious academic works venture beyond 1914, but see S Jones, 'Sport and the State in Interwar Britain', *Society for the Study of Labour History Bulletin*, 50 (1985), 7, *Workers at Play: A Social and Economic History of Leisure 1918–1939* (1986), and 'State Intervention in Sport and Leisure in Britain between the Wars', *Journal of Contemporary History*, 22 (1987), 163–82.

5 Quoted by Pimlott, *Englishman's Holiday*, 237.

6 See K Parry, *The Resorts of the Lancashire Coast* (1983), and Huggins, 'Social Tone and Resort Development'.

7 This was one of Travis' conclusions, see Travis, 'The Rise of Holidaymaking on the Devon Coast'.

8 South West Economic Planning Council (hereafter SWEPC), *Region with a Future* (1967), 20.

9 Devon County Council (hereafter DCC), *Devon County Structure Plan* (Exeter, 1979), 107; and *Devon Tourism Review* (Exeter, 1987), 15. For more details of the development of the industry in the twentieth century see N J Morgan, 'Perceptions, Patterns and Policies of Tourism: The Development of the Devon Seaside Resorts During the Twentieth Century With Special Reference to Torquay and Ilfracombe' (unpublished PhD thesis, University of Exeter, 1991).

10 See *Structure Plan*, 108; SWEPC, *Economic Survey of the Tourist Industry in the South West* (1976); and *Region with a Future*, 3–4, 47; 'All Eyes on Ilfracombe', *Planning*, 841, 20 Oct. 1989, 30–1; and Devon Alliance of Amenity Societies, *Report of a Survey on the Effects of Tourism in Devon* (Exeter, 1978).

11 F M M Lewes et al, *The Holiday Industry of Devon and Cornwall* (1970); and 'The Holiday Industry', in F Barlow ed., *Exeter and its Region* (Exeter, 1969), 244–58.

12 Lewes, 'Holiday Industry', 244.

13 Lewes, 'Holiday Industry', 245–6; and British Travel Association, *South Western Counties Tourist Study, Interim Report* (Exeter, 1967), ix.

14 DCC survey of 1966, quoted in Lewes, 'The Holiday Industry', 202–3, 245–6. The continued strength of coastal tourism in the 1990s is demonstrated in the latest figures produced by the domestic tourist boards, which show that in 1992 44 per cent of all holiday tourism nights were spent at the coast: English Tourist Board, Scottish Tourist Board, Northern Ireland Tourist Board, Wales Tourist Board, *The UK Tourism Statistics, 1992* (1993).

15 National Parks Commission, 'The Coasts of South West England', Report of the Regional Coastal Conference held in Exeter in 1966 (Exeter, 1967), 37.

16 SWEPC, *Economic Survey of the Tourist Industry*, 20.

17 Lewes, *Holiday Industry of Devon and Cornwall*, 131; and DCC, *Devon in Figures* (Exeter, 1977), 159.

18 DCC, *Structure Plan*, 25, 34–5; and SWEPC, *Economic Survey of the Tourist Industry*, 8.

19 Lewes, 'The Holiday Industry', 244–5.

20 J K Walton, 'The Social Development of Blackpool 1788–1914', (unpublished PhD thesis, University of Lancaster, 1974); and Parry, *Resorts of the Lancashire Coast*, 92.

21 Walton, 'Social Development of Blackpool', 224.

22 Walvin, *Seaside*, 107; and W Beveridge, *Full Employment in a Free Society* (1944), 63, quoted in Jones, *Workers*, 43.

23 Walvin, *Seaside*, 117.

24 Yates, 'Selling the Seaside', 20.

25 *Ilfracombe Chronicle*, 23 Mar. 1910; Ilfracombe Urban District Council Joint Advertising Committee Minutes, 21 Jan. 1913 and 2 Dec. 1913; and Torquay Chamber of Commerce Annual Reports, 1906 and 1912. See also R Burdett Wilson, *Go Great Western: A History of GWR Publicity* (1970).

26 Yates, 'Selling the Seaside', 23.

27 Yates, 'Selling the Seaside', 23; and Pimlott, *Holiday*, 244–6.

28 Torquay Municipal Borough Council Minutes and Official Guides, 1918–39.

29 Lewes, *Holiday Industry of Devon and Cornwall*, 92.

30 Walvin, *Seaside*, 117; and J R Pike, 'Studies in Local History', unpublished material on Torquay held in Torquay Library.

31 Pike, 'Studies'.

32 The ability of Torquay to ride out the depression is apparent in the reports of the interwar seasons in the local press of the town, notably the *Torquay Times*.

33 DRO, R2458 A (2/3), R1–9, Ilfracombe Urban District Council Pier Accounts Books, 1928–1940.

34 PRO, HLG 82/49 and 82/46. Devon Industries (with special reference to South Devon), Nuffield College Social Reconstruction Survey, May 1941; and The Devon Tourist Trade, Nuffield College Social Reconstruction Survey, May 1944.

35 DRO, 430GM/01–9, Papers of the Rev Dr J McIntyre, compiler of Nuffield College Social Reconstruction Surveys on Devon Industries and Tourism, 1941–3.

36 DRO, R2458A/(2/3) C57–63, Ilfracombe Urban District Council Committees' Minutes, 1908–27; and *Ilfracombe Chronicle*, 14 May and 9 July 1921.

37 PRO, AN 17/2, British Rail, Western Region Holiday Guide, 1949.

38 DRO, R7/4/C92–96, Papers of the Rev McIntyre; and Exmouth Urban District Council Foreshore and Pleasure Grounds Committee Minutes, 1919–1938.

39 Nuffield, 1944.

40 DRO, R7/7/C137, Sidmouth Urban District Council Pleasure Grounds Committee Minutes, 1923–1935.

41 DRO, R7/7/C139, Sidmouth Urban District Council Publicity Committee Minutes, 1928–1957; DRO, R7/7/C140, Sidmouth Urban District Council Entertainments and Publicity Committee Minutes, 1957–1962.

42 A Good, 'Coastal Resorts', in DCC, *Coastlines of Devon* (1980), 87–95, 91; L J Lickorish and A G Kershaw, *The Travel Trade* (1958), 179; T Barker, 'The International History of Motor Transport', *Journal of Contemporary History*, 20 (1985), 3–19; and T L Burton. 'Holiday Movements in Britain', *Town and Country Planning*, 33 (1965), 118–23.

43 Lewes, *Holiday Industry of Devon and Cornwall*, 4; and SWEPC, *Region with a Future*, 20.

44 SWEPC, *Region with a Future*, 14.

45 DCC, *Structure Plan*, 23–5.

46 SWEPC, *Economic Survey of the Tourist Industry*, 30.

47 DCC Planning Department, *A Survey of Mobile Caravanning and Tented Camping in Devon* (Exeter, 1959).

48 DCC, *Devon in Figures*, 85; and *Structure Plan*, 112; and SWEPC, *Economic Survey of the Tourist Industry*, 28.

49 SWEPC, *Economic Survey of the Tourist Industry*, 21.

50 SWEPC, *Region with a Future*, 55. See also Ilfracombe Urban District Council files on reduced fares for resorts, 1956, and DRO, R2458A/(2/3) C134–5, the closure of Barnstaple–Ilfracombe railway line, 1966–1968.

51 For example between 1945 and 1953 Ilfracombe fought the Department of Transport over the renovation of the Ilfracombe Pier. See DRO, R2458A/(2/3), Ilfracombe Urban District Council Committee Minutes, 1945–53.

52 Lickorish and Kershaw, *Travel Trade*, 116.

53 D Waterman, 'Seaside Resorts to a Theme for a Dream', *Town and Country Planning*, 53 (1984), 104–6.

54 R Farley, 'The British Seaside Resort – Can it Survive?', *Hotel and Catering Review*, (July 1967), 12–15.

55 SWEPC, *Region with A Future*, 108; and Lewes, *Study of Tourism and Holiday Facilities*, 217.

56 British Travel Association, *South Western Counties Tourist Study. Interim Report* (Exeter, 1967), vi.

57 Lewes, *Holiday Industry of Devon and Cornwall*, 139.

58 For instance, 1964 saw the conversion of the Gaiety Theatre into flats, and in 1970 the bandstand was removed.

59 *Independent*, 26 Aug. 1989.

60 DCC, *Tourism and Recreation*, 1981, 1983 and 1984; and *Devon Tourism Review*, 1987.

61 *Guardian*, 9 Mar. 1988; and Building Design Partnership, Victor Middleton, and Tony Wright for the English Tourist Board, 'The Future for England's Smaller Seaside Resorts', (1991), quoted in PA Cambridge Economic Consultants, 'Prospects for Coastal Resorts – A Paper for Discussion', for the Wales Tourist Board (Cardiff, 1992).

62 H Wright, 'At Home or Abroad?', *Leisure Management*, 9 (1989), 29–30; and *Daily Telegraph*, 9 Mar. 1989. In 1992 the highly successful 'Seaside Campaign' was developed and co-ordinated by the English Tourist Board to improve the image of resorts; see P Travis. 'The Seaside Fights Back', *Insights*, (1992), 9–17.

63 DCC, *Tourism Review* (1987), 45 and 37.

64 'All Eyes on Ilfracombe', 30–1; Civic Trust, *New Heart for Ilfracombe. A Profile of the Ilfracombe Project*, (1990); and B Hall, 'Seaside Resorts: A Case Study of Ilfracombe', Paper Presented to the Civic Trust Conference, 'Regenerating Welsh Communities.' (Cardiff, 1992).

65 *Independent*, 26 Aug. 1989. For detailed policy statements, see Torbay Borough Council, *The English Riviera 2000. An Integrated Tourism Strategy for Torquay, Paignton and Brixham* (Torbay, 1985); and *The English Riviera 2000. Tourism Development Action Programme. Tourism Position Statement* (Torbay, 1986).

66 English Tourist Board, *Torbay Tourism Study* (1982); Devon County Council, *Devon County Structure Plan*, 108; and 'Tourism in East Devon: A Report of a Set of Surveys conducted in East Devon, June 1986–June 1987'. East Devon Action Project (Totnes, 1987), 12.

67 Wright, 'At Home or Abroad?'. The importance of these new markets is highlighted in the marketing strategies of the domestic tourist boards; see, for example, Wales Tourist Board, *Tourism 2000: A Strategy for Wales* (Cardiff, 1994), and English Tourist Board, *Annual Report* (1993).

68 Lewes, *Holiday Industry of Devon and Cornwall*, 200–1.

69 DCC. *Teignmouth: A Survey of Holidaymakers*, 1957 (Exeter, 1958).

70 Teignbridge District Council, *Teignmouth, Shaldon and Dawlish Structure Plan* (1987), 19–20.

71 Lewes, 'Holiday Industry', 200.

72 'Tourism in East Devon', 4, 15.

73 Wright, 'At Home or Abroad?'; and R Pickering, 'The Changing Face of Leisure Trends' *Baths Service and Recreation Management* (Jan–Feb. 1990), 6–11.

74 Wright, 'At Home or Abroad?'.

75 J Montgomery, 'Social Tourism Approach Indicates the Last Resort', *Planning*, 853, 26 Jan. 1990, 39; and G Turner, 'Tourism and the Environment: The Role of the Seaside', *Insights*, Mar. 1993, 125–31.

76 B Martin and S Mason, 'The Spirit of a New Decade', *Leisure Management*, 10 (1990), 30–3; European Tourism Year Newsletter, 3 (autumn 1989), 1.

26 *Towards the Twenty-first Century*

JOHN CHANNON, CRISPIN GILL, ALSTON KENNERLEY, TONY REDFERN and DAVID J STARKEY

DEVON'S MARITIME INTERESTS REMAIN STRONG in the late twentieth century. If this is implicit in the County Council's choice of a ship for its emblem, it is clearly evident in the wide range of sea-related activities which currently generate income and employment for Devon residents. Seaside tourism, fishing, shipbuilding and port operation are notable features of Devon's economy, while the Navy's significant presence is apparent in the various educational and training establishments it has located in the county, as well as in the naval base and the recently privatised Dockyard at Devonport. Similar generalisations, of course, might be applied with equal validity to the late nineteenth (or even the late eighteenth) century. However, recent decades have witnessed both absolute and relative change in every facet of Devon's maritime economy. Thus, in line with the national experience, the service industries associated with the safety and recreational exploitation of coastal waters have expanded rapidly, while activity deriving from the transportation function of the sea – the shipping, shipbuilding and port industries – has generally contracted.

This chapter, which comprises a number of short contributions, considers some of these modern developments and speculates as to the future course of Devon's wide-ranging relationship with the sea. Attention is initially focussed on the safety of the seas adjacent to Devon, a theme explored in Chapter 1 of this volume, with Tony Redfern discussing the salient advances which have occurred in navigational techniques since the 1950s. Alston Kennerley then examines the changing character of the search and rescue services provided for those in peril in the waters off the southwest peninsula. In both respects, it seems reasonable to assume that in the twenty-first century technological innovation, especially with regard to position fixing and communications at sea, which has markedly improved safety standards during the last fifty years, will continue to temper the immense natural and man-made hazards inherent to man's use of the sea and which so much handicapped mariners in earlier times.

Advances in Coastal Navigation since 1950

In 1987 the *Admiralty Manual of Navigation* related, 'the last thirty years has seen great advances in navigational techniques [but] the principles of navigation remain unchanged'.[1] With respect to transoceanic voyages, the most significant developments have been the introduction of the lattice charts and transmitting stations which comprise the 'Omega' system, and the growing use of satellite navigation. While these innovations have reduced the navigator's dependence on the long-established use of sextant and stars for position fixing, 'Omega' lacks the accuracy, and satellites the continuity, required for coastal navigation. The new satellite-based system, Global Positioning, promises to rectify these inadequacies, once the United States' satellite launch programme is completed and navigational charts are amended on the basis of universal geodetic data.

Nevertheless, many improvements in coastal navigation have taken place in recent years. Visual terrestrial observations were the standard means of position fixing when coasting in the early 1950s. In clear weather, by day, ships would close the shore to make identification of charted features more certain. This, in turn, made vessels of all sizes and trades a common sight from Devon headlands. From Prawle and Start Points, and from Bolt Head and Tail, a steady stream of ships could be seen seemingly inching their way up Channel or out into the Atlantic, while the Bristol Channel ports generated a similar scene for watchers from Hartland and Bull Points. These vistas have since changed. The Bristol Channel ports have declined in importance, while to the south, vessels on international voyages sail mid-Channel, well clear of the coast, leaving the previously busy coastal waters to yachtsmen, inshore fishermen and the occasional small coastal-trading vessel.

Navigators of the 1950s developed an empathy towards the land and its unknown inhabitants, brought about through a familiarity with small white buildings illuminated by the Mediterranean sun, with clusters of Scandinavian timber

26.1   The bridge of MV *Agapenor*, *c*1950 – a layout typical of the period. (*Alston Kennerley*) (*Far left*)

26.2   Fixing position by Decca Navigator. (*Media Services, University of Plymouth*)

houses by the still water's edge, and with prominent hills on foreign soil given English names, such as Asses Ears. Closer to home, the China clay spoil tips on Dartmoor's southern slopes, appearing strangely snow-clad even in mid-summer, were features well known to sailors who had never set foot in Devon.

In reduced visibility, and by night, ships would stand further off shore to improve the margins of safety. Even then, the night-time offshore breeze would often carry the evocative smell of the land – wood smoke and seaweed – out to the watchkeeper on the ship's bridge.

In well-surveyed areas the use of soundings for position fixing was not uncommon. Hand and deep-sea sounding leads are recessed at the base. The recess may be filled with tallow before use, a process known as arming the lead, so that a sample of the sea-bed can be obtained. The 1947 edition of the *Channel Pilot* advised,

> the bottom in the western approaches appears mainly to consist of fine or coarse sand, a great deal of broken shell, occasional patches of pebbles, gravel, small stones and now and then yellow mud. The sand is mostly white though in many places it is yellow with black specks. The greater proportion of yellow sand lies south of the parallel of 49° 30′N and that of black specks north of that line. This distribution is so marked, especially between 9° 40′W and 7° 30′W . . .[2]

It is doubtful whether many readers of the *Channel Pilot* ever took bottom samples, but where depth contours vary significantly over a small distance – the Hurd Deep, off the Channel Islands, and the Devil's Hole, 100 miles from the Firth of Forth, are two such bathographical features – soundings provided, and still provide, useful position lines for the navigator.

The Second World War saw the evolution of radio navigational aids for military use, chiefly in the air, and in the postwar years these systems were further developed, extended, and made available for use by shipping. The first aid to navigation of this kind was 'Gee', in which a position line was obtained by measuring the time interval between reception of signals from two land-based transmitters. Special charts were produced on which the hyperbolic position lines so generated were overprinted as lattices. By 1950, forty-four such charts were available, including those covering the approaches to the English Channel using the South Western Chain set up in 1945. Users had to carry special radio receivers, but continuous position fixing, by day or night regardless of visibility, was feasible within the coverage area. A similar system, 'Loran', a mnemonic for Long Range Navigation, had been developed in America, and in 1950 there were fourteen Admiralty Loran lattice charts available. Unfortunately the South West approaches to the English Channel were outside the system's coverage area. Loran has further developed and extended to cover most of the North Atlantic and North Pacific, and although there are now over a hundred Loran charts published by the Hydrographic Department, the approaches to the English Channel are still outside the full coverage area.

In the early 1950s 'Gee' was already being replaced by the Decca Navigator system. Decca was first used operationally during the Normandy landings in 1944, and in 1950 two chains, the English and the Danish, were being commercially operated by the Decca Navigator Company. Non-military users could rent but not buy Decca receivers, and the costs of operating the system were met by hire charges. The inducement to hire increased as the availability of the facility widened, and by 1988 there were forty-two chains in service, giving full cover in the waters around Western Europe, and area cover off Canada, Japan, India, Australia, South and West Africa, while a chain provided earlier in the Persian Gulf fell victim to the Gulf War. The master transmitter of the South West British chain is located at Bolberrow in Devon, with slave stations in the Bristol Channel, the Channel Isles and Scilly. The story of Decca exemplifies the progress of land-based marine navigation systems over the past thirty years. Although the transfer of receiver readings to lattice chart remains the standard means of using Decca, alphanumeric rather than meter readout is now commonplace. And the track plot, devised to give the user a continuous record of position on a paper printout, is being replaced by full-colour video presentation, in which the picture on the screen can replace the paper chart. These last two facilities are particularly favoured by fishermen, nowhere more so than off the coasts of Devon, as means of planning, monitoring and recording the precise navigation required to make their fishing operations profitable.

26.3   Port control radar picture, Plymouth Sound. (*AQHM, Devonport*)

The carriage of Decca, or any radio navigation aid other than direction finding, remains entirely at the discretion of the owner of the vessel. This is not the case with radar, which performs the dual functions of collision avoidance and coastal navigation aid. It is the collision-avoidance applications of radar that have made its carriage a statutory requirement aboard merchant vessels of 1,600grt and over. Similarly, where it is necessary for a vessel to be fitted with radar, it is also a requirement that all watchkeepers are trained in its proper use.

Radar, being independent of land-based transmitters, may be used for coastal navigation anywhere in the world. Despite this apparent advantage, great skill is often needed by the navigator in relating the picture on his radar screen to the charted representation of the same coastal area. As an aid to positive target identification, use is increasingly being made of radar responder beacons known as 'Racons'. One such beacon was installed on the Eddystone lighthouse in 1981, so the question 'which of those echoes are fishing vessels and which is Eddystone?' no longer arises.

Hydrographic Survey

It will surprise many to learn that in 1993 the information used to chart more than half of the United Kingdom continental shelf is derived from surveys carried out before 1935. Much of this information results from two centuries of random observations, some of dubious merit, but in general terms the adequacy of such surveys has been proved by the continuing safe passage of vessels in well-frequented waters.

Before 1935 charted depths depended on lead-line soundings taken in spot positions up to several miles apart. The intervals between soundings reduced where navigational hazards were located, but surveys using this method could easily fail to detect shoals rising close to the surface of the sea. The echo sounder was widely used in surveys from 1935 onwards, permitting continuous lines of soundings to be obtained, though typically these were some 250m apart and shoals could still remain undetected. It is only from surveys carried out since 1975 that we can be reasonably certain that all underwater features within an area have been detected, and their positions fixed to within 10m or so. The introduction of sidescan sonar, supplemented by use of divers, has ensured the location of rocks and shoals, while the use of precise fixing-systems has guaranteed the accuracy of their charted positions. Nevertheless, only about 20 per cent of the United Kingdom continental shelf has been fully surveyed to these modern standards.

The primary task of the Hydrographer of the Navy is to meet naval requirements, though in recent years increased emphasis has been placed on civil needs and commercial charting services. Therefore, whether an area has been fully surveyed or not will be coloured by a combination of naval and commercial factors. The draughts of naval surface vessels have changed little over the past thirty years, but during the same period merchant ships, particularly oil tankers, have increased greatly in size and draught. The risk of such vessels grounding on uncharted shoals, spilling their cargoes and causing environmental pollution is of public concern, and the areas through which such vessels pass have been extensively surveyed.

Off the coasts of Devon, for instance, the areas traversed by deep-laden tankers using Lyme Bay for transshipment of oil have been surveyed to modern standards, as have the approaches to Dartmouth and most of the approaches to Plymouth. That the latter two areas are well surveyed is partly a product of training exercises carried out by the Royal Navy Hydrographic School, which moved from Chatham to Devonport in 1964. At the other extreme, with a few exceptions such as Barnstaple Bay, the charts of the North Devon coastal areas are based on old hand-lead surveys. This reflects the absence of a pressing commercial need for modern surveys in the area. Thus in 1957 just under 400 vessels, totalling 45,000 tons deadweight, visited Bideford, the most active port on the North Devon coast, and by 1972 the number had dropped to 134, the largest being only some 1,000 tons.

Lack of deep water prevents development, a fact borne out by noting that Ilfracombe, described in the *West Coast of England Pilot* as 'having one of the most accessible harbours on the southern shore of the Bristol Channel',[3] dries out when the tidal height is one metre. With the little commercial, and no naval, incentive, to survey the port's approaches, the Ilfracombe chart is based on an Admiralty survey carried out in 1893, supplemented by aerial photography in 1971. In contrast, full surveys of the northern shores and approaches to the Bristol Channel have been carried out to ensure the safe passage of large vessels using the deep-water ports of Milford Haven and Port Talbot. The limits of full survey are now being extended southwards and westwards in patchwork fashion, towards the North Devon coast, when facility permits, fuelled by the possibility of mineral resources being discovered in the Celtic Sea.

Charting

Charts in the 1950s often appeared as much examples of the copper-plate engravers' art as working documents. In making up topographical detail, extensive use was made of contour lines and hachuring to give an indication of the appearance of the land, while a wide range of symbols was employed to depict features that would be visible from seawards to the human eye. Apart from magenta flashes to distinguish lighthouses and other lit marks, no colours were used in the printing of non-lattice charts. Soundings were in fathoms, or, in shallow water, fathoms and feet. Charts of this type would not have been unfamiliar to Captain Cook.

In 1974 a modernisation process began. Land masses were printed in yellow, and gone were hachures and heavy contouring. Soundings were given in metres, and shallow areas high-lined in blue. The colours were overlapped to produce green in the tidal areas between the land and shallows. Some symbols disappeared, while others were introduced to make the charts more suitable for use when navigating by radar and other modern aids. Such updating is a lengthy process, but by 1987 some 1,700 charts of the Admiralty series had been metricated, and the halfway point in the programme was passed.

The needs of small-boat owners are being recognised increasingly, a policy of particular relevance to Devon's coastal waters. In 1942, military activity before the Normandy landings initiated a survey of the River Dart up to Dittisham Mill Creek. Beyond that point the river was uncharted until 1980, when a survey of the upper reaches to Totnes was conducted. Similarly, until 1984, Admiralty charting of the Tamar terminated at Cargreen, but the replacement chart has been extended to include the lower reaches of the Lynher and Tavy, and the Tamar as far as Gunnislake with good detail to Calstock. A further touch is the addition of special symbols of interest to small craft, one for toilets, another for car parks and so on, thus marrying Landranger Ordnance Survey to chart.

Buoyage

Buoys have long been used to mark navigable channels and warn mariners of dangers, but until the 1970s no common international system of buoyage existed. The combinations of buoy shapes, colours and topmarks adopted by maritime states varied widely and were often in conflict with each other, giving rise to serious risk of confusion. In 1971 disaster struck off Dungeness in the Dover Straits. The wreck of the *Texaco Caribbean*, properly marked by Trinity House, was struck by the *Brandenburg*, whose German crew had misread the buoys. The *Brandenburg* sank, but within a short time the combined wrecks, now marked by a wreck-marking vessel and many buoys, were hit by the *Niki*, which also sank. Fifty-one lives were lost in total, and the shock of this disaster intensified attempts to evolve a single world-wide system of buoyage. In the event this has not been possible, but the International Association of Lighthouse Authorities (IALA) has achieved great success in reaching agreement on two parallel and largely identical schemes, IALA A and IALA B. IALA B will apply to the Americas, Japan, Korea and the Philippines, the rest of the world adopting IALA A.

Lateral marks are used in conjunction with a conventional direction of buoyage to indicate the port and starboard sides of channels to be followed. Under IALA A port-hand buoys are can-shaped and red in colour, while starboard-hand are conical and green. Cardinal marks are used in conjunction with the compass to indicate where the mariner may find the best navigable water. A wide range of cardinal and lateral marks are used in Plymouth Sound to warn the mariner of hazards and indicate the deep-

26.4   The start of the second single-handed Transatlantic Race in Plymouth Sound, 1964. To port of the motor boat in the foreground is Colonel 'Blondie' Haslar in his junk-rigged *Jester*, surrounded by spectator craft. (*Crispin Gill*)

26.5 Torquay Harbour, with the Marina in the background. (*Andrew Besley*)

A pilot station one mile off the port would have been a long journey for the crew of the Teignmouth boat in 1950, but not today. The advances in navigational techniques in the intervening years constitute an equally long journey.

Tony Redfern

Modern Search and Rescue Provision[6]

Reinforcing the improvements in navigation to provide greater safety at sea has been the growing sophistication of search and rescue techniques. During the twentieth century, state funding and voluntary interest have continued to provide for the needs of maritime casualties, with the Coastguard and the Royal National Lifeboat Institution (RNLI) responsible for most aspects of search and rescue at sea. Devon has retained its

water route inwards from the sea, and Plymouth Hoe offers the landsman an unrivalled vantage point from which to view IALA buoyage in operation.

Traffic Management

There are many focal areas around the coasts of the world where high traffic density increases the risk of collision. By adopting traffic separation schemes – dual carriageways of the sea – the incidence of head-on collisions is reduced, since all traffic should either be going in the same direction or crossing, as if from side roads. Such a scheme exists to the south of Devon, close to the median line between England and France. Regrettably, even within formal traffic separation schemes, collisions still occur.

During the last thirty years the potential for positive maritime traffic control has greatly increased. In the 1950s harbour authorities were only able to communicate with vessels entering and leaving port by hailing or by using visual signals. On the South Devon coast there was a Lloyds Signal Station on Prawle Point, and another on Berry Head, through which vessels could report using a signal lamp. High-intensity light signals, visible by day as well as by night, are still used at Dover and other ferry ports, but radio telephony on VHF radio has now become the standard means of short-range ship-to-shore communication.

The second element of traffic management is the provision of radar coverage, perhaps backed up by closed-circuit television and automatic direction-finding equipment, through which harbour control can maintain awareness of all shipping movements in the area for which they have responsibility. The monitoring and communication facilities required for positive control are now available, but with few exceptions the service provided remains advisory, and masters retain navigational command of their ships. Indeed, although traffic management services doubtless increase navigational safety in the areas where they are provided, their primary function often appears to be to increase the operational and commercial efficiency of the port area they serve.

The general intensity of shipping activity in Devon's ports does not justify the installation of expensive control facilities, the Port of Plymouth being the exception. Here, shore radar and closed-circuit television facilities have recently been provided to assist in the safe operation of the port. Port radio stations, however, are now commonplace. The captain of a ship visiting Teignmouth in 1950 would have read in the Pilot Book that 'pilots board from a small rowing boat with the pilot flag painted on the bow'.[4] The captain of today's ship is advised:

Ships should send their expected time of arrival and request pilots . . . by VHF RT to Teignmouth pilots. Pilots board from a vessel with a black hull and orange superstructure one mile off the port.[5]

prominent role in this national system, though significant organisational changes have occurred in recent years. In the regional structure of the Coastguard before 1982, the Divisional Rescue Headquarters for the Southern Division was at Brixham, and Hartland in North Devon was a Rescue Headquarters within the Western Division. The latter was closed following a restructuring of coastguard services in 1988/89. The opening of the Coastguard Maritime Rescue Co-ordination Centre at Falmouth, with responsibility for the eastern Atlantic Ocean area, has absorbed the functions carried out at Brixham. This has reinforced the communications and co-ordination role of the Coastguard for civilian marine casualties, and it is now responsible for calling out the service most appropriate for a particular incident. The RNLI still maintains voluntarily manned and supported boats at three locations in North Devon and four in South Devon, in 1987, for instance, launching a major appeal for a new boat for its Plymouth Station. Local involvement is also maintained by the Coastguard through membership of the part-time Auxiliary Coastguard.

The demands placed upon these organisations have increased over the last fifty years. Although the Coastguard has long been responsible for the co-ordination of the removal of wreckage, including cargoes washed ashore from ships, it was the stranding of the *Torrey Canyon* in 1967 which clearly placed coastal pollution within its orbit. Communications relating to the spread of oil and the cleansing operation were handled by the Coastguard. The south coast of Devon, particularly, has been at risk of major pollution through one of the very large oil tankers becoming a casualty in any part of the English Channel, as the case of the *Amoco Cadiz*, which stranded on the coast of Brittany in 1978, demonstrated. For some years transfer operations from large tankers to smaller ones have taken place in Lyme Bay, and this has heightened the threat.

Further pressure on Devon's search and rescue services has been occasioned by the expansion of the county's seaside holiday industry. As early as 1933 it was apparent to the Coastguard that the number of incidents it was handling was increasing, and that the main element in this was the growth in marine recreation. This foreshadowed the much greater expansion which occurred after the Second World War, and was reflected in the number of incidents handled by the Coastguard, which had trebled, compared with prewar figures, by the late 1960s. Of these, about half concerned small recreational craft. This upward trend has continued in line with the growth of marine recreational activity in Devon. Consequently the rescue services in the county have been obliged to service increasing numbers of small craft casualties. The RNLI has met this need by introducing small, light and fast inshore rescue boats, capable of working off beaches, for summer duty. Moreover, concern for small-boat safety led to a government sponsored publicity and educational campaign, and to an extended system of voluntary education, training and qualification for boat owners, operated by the Royal Yachting Association for the Department of Transport.

Training has long been important for members of the rescue services. Whether full-time or volunteer, rescuers have always needed to be thoroughly familiar with their equipment and boats, and moulded into teams, to achieve fast and effective responses to distress calls. Most training was undertaken locally, but the increase in incidents, the greater complexity of equipment and an increasingly professional service led to the establishment of a Coastguard Training School at Brixham in 1971. This provided short courses for initial entrants to the service and regular updating courses for established staff at all levels of seniority. The range of subjects of which coastguard personnel need some knowledge has been extended by the expanding role of the service. To communications, seamanship, navigation and cliff rescue have been added meteorology, foreshore protection and pollution control. The School was moved out of Devon, to Bournemouth in Dorset, in the 1980s.

The twentieth century has also seen facilities provided by other organisations added to the search and rescue services of the Coastguard and the RNLI. The installation of wireless telegraphy equipment in ships – compulsory for vessels of 1,600 tons or over from 1933 – meant that emergency calls could be picked up by a network of coastal radio stations, and provided a communications link between the rescue services and vessels in distress. The RAF has provided assistance in the form of launches belonging to its Marine Branch, which had a base at Mount Batten from 1918 until 1987. Although principally engaged in training aircrews, the Branch fulfilled a rescue role, particularly during the Second World War. Perhaps most important has been the use of aircraft in search and rescue roles. Searches over extensive areas of sea have become possible, and the use of helicopters has added another and very effective rescue capability. The Coastguard now contracts for air coverage, but many of the aircraft services are provided by the Royal Navy, in this area from the Royal Naval Air Station at Culdrose in Cornwall and from the Royal Air Force station at Chivenor in North Devon. Searches over large areas of the seas are undertaken by fixed-wing aircraft, first Shackletons and then Nimrods, from RAF St Mawgan in Cornwall. Search and rescue for military casualties at sea was handled through the Rescue Co-ordination Centre at Mount Wise in Plymouth until its closure in the summer of 1993. It also assisted with civilian incidents, such as the foundering of the *Herald of Free Enterprise* outside Zeebrugge in 1987, when Service personnel helped in the rescue.

While improvements in communications and rationalisation exercises have combined to reduce Devon's part in the co-ordination of maritime search and rescue operations in recent years, the county still contributes significantly to the provision for maritime casualties, not least in the work of the Coastguard and the voluntary efforts of local RNLI stations. With the waters off the southwest peninsula used ever more intensively for recreational purposes, fishing and as a seaway, it is clear that Devon will continue to perform this important role in the forseeable future.

Alston Kennerley

Improved navigational aids and better safety provisions have been among the factors facilitating the rapid expansion of recreational seafaring in the late twentieth century. In turn, the growth of the marine leisure industry has not only intensified and altered the demands placed upon the search and rescue services, but has also had a direct and major impact on many of Devon's estuaries and havens. With the county's recreational sailors far outnumbering its professional seafarers, large areas of Devon's ports are now given over to yacht marinas and sailing dinghy parks. This transition from commercial to recreational usage has aroused opposition from various quarters. Environmentalists argue that the proliferation of leisure craft spoils the natural beauty of estuaries such as those of the Dart and Salcombe rivers, while marina development can only add to the pollution problems facing busy harbours such as those at Brixham and Teignmouth. Other port users also see marinas as a threat to their established concerns. Witness the case of Brixham in the late 1980s. Here, the local fishing interest headed opposition to the construction of the Prince William marina by Marina Developments plc. That this campaign was ultimately unsuccessful attests

to the strength of the pro-marina lobby, which included many local parties keen to exploit the commercial potential of such establishments. Quite simply, as Crispin Gill points out below, the marine leisure industry is now a vital feature of Devon's maritime economy, bringing work to boatbuilders, repairers, and to marine suppliers as well as providing business for local retailers, taverns, and other service traders. How far this shift towards the recreational utilisation of the sea can proceed (there are some signs in the early 1990s that saturation point may not be far off) is uncertain, for the maritime leisure business, like the leisure industry at large, is ultimately conditioned by changing levels of prosperity and work patterns in the national economy.

Yachts, Marinas, and the Maritime Leisure Industry[7]

With people having more money to spend and more time for leisure, and the cheaper mass production of small boats, there are more yachts around the coast than ever before. The port of Plymouth, for instance, has four marinas with over 1,000 berths, and three of them have three-figure waiting lists. Two or three more marinas are planned. The Port of Plymouth Sailing Association has eighteen affiliated clubs. The Royal Western Yacht Club of England, which in 1989 opened a new clubhouse at Queen Anne's Battery overlooking the new marina, has about 1,500 members who between them own some 440 craft. On the south coast of Devon all told there are nearly 4,000 marina berths and moorings. Adapting Parkinson's Law, it is as if the number of yachts grows to fill the marina berths available.

Cynics observe that about a third of the craft in marinas never move, and if they do the sails remain unfurled. In contrast, there are many enthusiastic cruising people. The Channel and Biscay coasts of Brittany are familiar playgrounds for the cruisers. Some owners cross the Channel half-a-dozen times in a season. Racing is also very popular. On any of the Sunday-morning series of meetings in Plymouth Sound there are sixty to eighty yachts crossing the line, in five classes. Sometimes, up to sixty dinghies race in the Sound as well. Nearly 500 people must be out racing each Sunday, and the local cruising types still have their Sunday potter out to Cawsand Bay.

But racing is no longer around the buoys. The 1989 programme of the Port of Plymouth Sailing Association included thirteen coastal passage races, not counting jaunts to the Yealm, or singlehanded around the Eddystone, and eight offshore races, some of which, like the Fastnet, are really ocean races. The Royal Western has been described as the cradle of ocean racing in Britain. The first Fastnet Race in 1925, originally called the Ocean Race and the first fixture of this kind organised in Britain, was sailed under the Royal Western flag. Ever since, the race, which starts in the Solent and follows a course around the Fastnet Rock off the southern tip of Ireland, has finished in Plymouth. Indeed, while the last yacht home in that first Fastnet was approaching the port, the Ocean Racing Club, later the Royal Ocean Racing Club, was being formed in the dining room of the Royal Western.

When Blondie Haslar and Francis Chichester had the madcap idea of a singlehanded 'uphill' race across the Atlantic, from east to west and so against the prevailing winds, it was to the Royal Western that they turned. Six yachts competed in that first 1960 race from Plymouth, and it has been repeated every four years since. There were 200 entries in 1976, of whom 125 started, but now the field is limited to 100. In 1966 the club organised the first two-handed race around Great Britain, starting and finishing in Plymouth. A month later Francis Chichester left the port for his famous solo voyage around the world. His finish at West Hoe was an international news event, and soon afterwards he became commodore of the club.

Today the Royal Western, the Royal Plymouth Corinthian and the Royal Naval Sailing Association share the organisation of these coastal and offshore races, as well as the series of races in the Sound. The programme starts in March and ends with a Boxing Day Regatta run by the Mayflower Sailing Club.

The Mayflower is one of the leading dinghy clubs in the country, having organised thirty-two national, one international and five board championships between 1978 and 1988. In that time the Plymouth Corinthian has run six national, one international, and four regional championships. In

1959 there were 232 boats entered in the Firefly class championship. The late 1950s and early 1960s were boom years for dinghy sailing. Subsequently it declined, although the late 1980s has seen a revival, largely owing to the extensive youth training programme run by local clubs.

The dinghy boom was fired by the development of marine plywood and synthetic resin glues, which not only made the craft cheaper but also made do-it-yourself construction feasible. The demand for parking space became intense, and the city created a large dinghy park between Fisher's Nose and the Mayflower Pier, on either side of the Mayflower club house. Other clubs created their own parks, and there was talk of making up to 1,500 boat parking spaces in the city.

But the same cheap construction methods, and the use of glassfibre, made yacht building cheaper, too. George Hurley started building small and cheap cabin cruisers in the old Grand Theatre, the beginning of assembly-line factory methods of boat building. The business grew fast and came to grief, but another company, Marine Projects, was founded in a small Stonehouse shed in 1959. By 1985 it was Britain's biggest boatbuilder, and by 1989 it was the third largest in Europe, employing 1,150. Its yard filled the Stonehouse side of the creek from the bridge to Whitehall, and it was the third largest employer in Plymouth. It had always concentrated on the most expensive kind of motor yacht, the first to be hit by recession. By the end of 1992 its peak workforce of 1,500 had been halved, though in 1993 it seemed to be weathering the storm.

The dinghy boom had given way to the cruiser boom. This was partly due to the racing men growing older and preferring the comforts of cruisers, partly, in Plymouth at any rate, to the proliferation of classes of dinghies, which introduced unsatisfactory handicap racing, and partly to the appeal to youngsters of the new high-speed wind surfers. The demand now was for yacht berths rather than small boat parks, and marinas began to grow instead.

The Plymouth story can be told of most other yachting stations. If Plymouth has been called a miniature Solent, then Torbay could challenge that title. With the opening in 1989 of the Prince William Marina at Brixham, Torbay has more marina berths than Plymouth. There are two yacht clubs and two sailing clubs in the bay itself, with another four clubs just around the corner on the Dart. The Royal Torbay Yacht Club runs the biggest inter-club regatta in the West Country, as well as the three-day Torbay Admiral's Cup event which attracts teams from well outside the region. The Royal Torbay also has a fine fleet of Dragons, the class made famous by the Duke of Edinburgh's *Blue Bottle*.

In some of the smaller estuaries, such as Salcombe with its 300 moorings and the Yealm with its 500, yachting seems to have completely taken over life both ashore and afloat. Salcombe also has the important Island Cruising Club, which is a power in the land. Its training facilities, for everybody from the dinghy novice to the deep-sea man, are second to none, and in its fleet is the *Provident*, the last surviving Brixham sailing trawler.

Something has been lost in the growth. Multihulls get bigger and bigger, and more like electronic racing platforms than yachts. They dominate all the major long-distance events and, with the sponsorship from commercial firms and the advertising that has crept in, have created a new kind of professional yachtsman. No longer do the J-class yachts recruit their paid hands from the Essex longshoremen, or the cruisers from the Brixham and Plymouth fishermen. Sponsorship depends on success, and a cut-throat attitude has replaced the old amateur spirit of the gentleman amateur. The big events have ballyhoo and bring in all kinds of non-sailing people.

For all that, yachting in Devon is in good health. More local people are taking part in the various sides of the sport than ever before. With modern craft and new navigations aids the West is no longer isolated from the Solent by the perils of Portland Bill and West Bay. In some ports the yachts have completely replaced the old commercial vessels. This has happened in Plymouth in the northern end of Sutton Harbour and on the eastern side of Millbay Docks. Exmouth Docks closed to commercial traffic in 1990, but the intention of turning it into a marina and holiday village is still held up by planning wrangles.

The employment which all of this gives to designers, builders, sailmakers, yacht chandlers and even the book and clothing shops is enormous. It is

26.6 The covered shipyard at Bidna, Appledore. (Appledore Shipbuilders Ltd)

estimated that 2,000 are employed in yacht building and servicing in Plymouth alone. Marine Projects is still a major employer in the city. Around Sutton Harbour there are seven yacht-related firms, with more at Queen Anne's Battery and Ocean Quay. Devonport Dockyard built the dozen identical yachts for the 1992–3 round-the-world British Steel Race, which originally was planned to start and finish in Plymouth until the sponsors insisted on Southampton. An 80ft yacht has been built at Totnes for the Whitbread Round-the-World Race.

The owner of one of the smallest cabin cruisers estimates that it costs £1,000 a year to maintain his craft, and there are already a thousand yachts of this size and larger in the Plymouth marinas alone. That is £1 million a year, and there must be £20 million represented in capital outlay in the craft in these marinas. The 1988 Plymouth Boat Show attracted 35,000 visitors and orders worth £4 million. Yachting is now big business.

Crispin Gill

The British economy in the final quarter of the twentieth century has been marked by an expanding service sector and contracting primary and manufacturing production. These trends, together with the further development of road and air transport, have generally brought depression to the British shipping industry and its dependents, the shipbuilding and port industries. Such a pattern can be detected in Devon. Here, the dynamic sector of the twentieth-century maritime economy has been the seaside holiday and leisure business, essentially a service activity which provides little stimulation, and indeed some rivalry, for the 'traditional' maritime activities. With the county's still significant farming and manufacturing sectors being attracted to the highly competitive road and rail transport provisions, the county's once extensive shipping industry has very largely disappeared, and, with it, much of the demand which sustained numerous local shipbuilding enterprises in the nineteenth century. Harbour authorities, too, have been adversely affected by the shift in the modern orientation of Devon's economy, with many experiencing falling traffic levels, some to the point of closure or conversion to recreational usage, since the 1960s. Exacerbating this trend has been the decline of seaborne imports of coal, once the mainstay of the county's maritime trade, as a consequence of long-sustained railway competition and the emergence of oil as the leading fuel of the modern era. Although delivered in some quantitiy to local ports from the 1920s to the 1960s, oil is now largely carried by road. The fleets that now supply Devon are fleets of petrol tankers penetrating most areas of the county via the M5 motorway and its various tributaries.

However, some 'traditional' maritime activity persists, indeed flourishes, within the county owing to the exploitation of particular comparative advantages and the application of commercial realism. In the passages which follow, David J Starkey discusses the innovatory production techniques underlying the recent success of Appledore Shipbuilders, while Crispin Gill

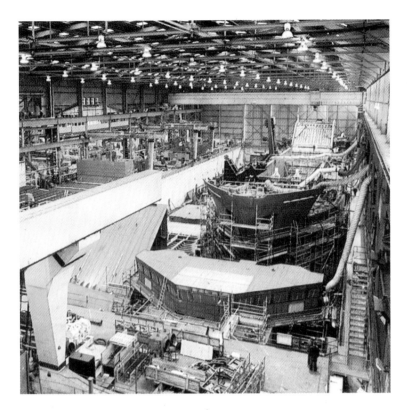

26.7 Vessels under construction inside the covered shipyard, Bidna, Appledore. (*Appledore Shipbuilders Ltd*)

examines the continuing prosperity of the port of Teignmouth, a port which has handled a growing volume of business based largely on the export of locally-won ball clay. Although both of these enterprises are limited in scale, they are significant in that both have run counter to national as well as local trends, consolidating their market position as other British shipbuilders and ports have experienced absolute, even terminal, decline.

Appledore Shipbuilders[8]

Ships have been built and repaired at Appledore, on the banks of the Torridge, for at least 200 years. Many different firms have engaged in this local industry over this time. Although some were shortlived ventures, others endured for long periods as founding fathers were followed into the business by their heirs and successors. From the 1790s to the 1860s, for instance, William Clibbett and his son, William jr, were engaged in shipbuilding at the port, while the enterprise established by Robert Cock in 1858 was pursued by his sons James and Frank until its collapse in 1932. Likewise, P K Harris & Sons passed through three generations between the early twentieth century and the 1960s, the descendants of Philip Kelly Harris maintaining a strong interest in the concerns which succeeded this archetypal family firm. Continuity has also been evident in the sites utilised for vessel construction and repair in the town. The Richmond Yard, though not so named until the mid-nineteenth century, was used successively by the Clibbetts, the Cocks, and the Harris's, while the New Quay Yard was occupied by numerous firms between 1852 and 1908, when it passed into the hands of P K Harris & Sons, remaining in that company for over fifty years.

Naturally, Appledore's shipbuilding trade has experienced considerable change since the days of William Clibbett sr. Two particular developments stand out as turning points in the long course of the industry. The first of these climacterics occurred in 1901-2, when Frank and James Cock equipped the Richmond Yard for the construction and repair of steel ships. In the wider context of the contemporary British shipbuilding industry, this investment was limited, late, and of marginal significance. Yet locally it was to prove of great importance, for the ability to build and repair steel vessels

provided the lifeline – lacking in most West Country ports – by which Appledore's shipbuilders survived the generally depressed interwar years, aided by the repair business generated by North Devon's declining, but still active, wooden fleet. The second decisive break came in the 1960s with the demise of P K Harris & Sons and the acquisition of Appledore's shipyards (consolidated by now into one venture) by successive large-scale industrial concerns. Although much uncertainty surrounded the town's shipbuilding interest during these years, the net result was an infusion of capital which permitted the newly-established Appledore Shipbuilders Ltd to undertake investment on a scale which has probably guaranteed the viability of shipbuilding in the Torridge into the twenty-first century.

At the heart of this latter watershed lay the expansionary policies of Court Line Ltd. A conglomerate with major interests in the shipping, aviation, and leisure industries, Court Line acquired Appledore Shipbuilders Ltd for £200,000 in 1965. This represented a good deal for the vendors, a local consortium which had purchased from the Official Receivers the assets of Seawork Ltd, the successor to P K Harris & Sons, for £40,000 just fifteen months earlier. It also proved to be one of Court Line's more successful acquisitions, the profits of the subsidiary increasing steadily between 1966 and 1974, when the parent company collapsed spectacularly. During this period Appledore Shipbuilders expanded considerably. The Durrant House and Seagate Hotels were purchased in 1967-8 with the express purpose of providing suitable accommodation and hospitality for the shipyard's clients, such facilities not being readily available in the area during the summer holiday season. Six years later the company ventured further into the property market, acquiring R Harris & Son Ltd, one of North Devon's largest building firms. Most significantly, however, Appledore Shipbuilders added considerably to their Torridge-side shipbuilding capacity. It had become apparent that the Richmond dry dock (built in 1855) and the New Quay dry dock (built in 1860) were inadequate for the needs of the late 1960s. With a 'virgin' waterside site available at Bidna Farm, funds supplied by the parent company and a government keen to support the generally ailing shipbuilding industry, the company constructed a new covered yard, the first of its type in Europe.

Opened in 1970, the Bidna yard permitted work to proceed in controlled conditions, regardless of the weather, with ships of up to 10,000dwt tons – chiefly coastal tankers, dredgers, small product carriers and tugs – constructed in sections and moved down what was effectively a factory production line. This innovation was deemed a considerable success by all parties. Profits before tax increased from £192,000 in 1969 to £1,375,000 in 1973, while in 1972 contracts worth £10 million filled the order books. The company was honoured with a Queen's Award for Technological Innovation, while the directors of Court Line were so encouraged by the Appledore experience that plans were devised to build a much larger 'ship factory' on Weirside. Analysts of the British shipbuilding industry highlighted Appledore's excellent delivery record and marketing strategies. Moreover, the government investigation into the failure of Court Line found that the Appledore concern did not in any way contribute to the collapse, the firm's profitability and success standing in sharp relief to the parent company's much larger investments in Sunderland Shipbuilders and its disastrous over-expansion in the holiday trade.

With the demise of Court Line, Appledore Shipbuilders passed into state ownership, to be reprivatised, by sale to Langham Industries, in 1989. Since its initial success in the early 1970s the firm has continued to produce a range of vessels at a profit, in marked contrast to many larger British shipbuilders, despite the hightly volatile nature of the market. Competition has intensified, with foreign builders, notably in the Far East, adopting on a much larger scale the flow production methods pioneered by Appledore and 'exported' by its associated consultancy firm, A & P Appledore.[9] Whether the firm can withstand the commercial pressures which have put paid to much larger operations on the Clyde and in the North East is an open question. However, throughout the last 200 years Appledore's shipbuilders have adapted to many fundamental changes in the industry. If this flexibility and willingness to innovate continues, perhaps another two centuries of shipbuilding lies ahead for the port.

David J Starkey

The Port of Teignmouth in the 1990s[10]

In brick vaults at the back of Teignmouth Quay, where giant yellow fork-lift trucks rattle around like demented Daleks, the beams on which salt cod from Newfoundland once hung can still be seen. The brickwork is crumbling and the ironwork still rotting from the salt. The quay was built in the 1880s for the schooners which brought the cod in, one of Teignmouth's oldest trades, and took the ball clay out, as vessels had done for two centuries past. Teignmouth in the 1990s is likely to remain the only working port between Poole and Plymouth, thanks largely to the clay deposits around Bovey Tracey, ten miles up the valley, and to vigorous management. It is a river port with a long quay which it would like to double in length, and the largest employer in the town. It has handled twenty-six ships in a week, moves over half a million tons of cargo a year, and could handle more with greater wharfage and more storage facilities. It is a present-day success story.

The only small port in Devon with a similar volume of trade was Exmouth, but in 1990 the dock closed to commercial vessels, a victim of its inability to take bigger ships, and proposals emerged to turn it into a marina and yachting village. Bideford handles a small amount of clay each year and not much else.

Plymouth, not really a big port but a collection of small ports all under different control, is changing. Millbay Docks is given over to roll-on roll-off ferries (see Chapter 22), with all the eastern side now a yachting village and marina. Stonehouse Pool, which once had its own improvement company, is yachting. Pottery Quay is now ship repairs. Sutton Harbour is yachting and fishing, the latter set to benefit from the biggest reshaping of the harbour since East and West Piers were built in the 1790s, and the Barbican fish market was constructed on reclaimed land in 1895. Starting this development in 1993, the Sutton Harbour Company installed lock gates across the entrance to the harbour, filled in the head of Coxside Creek, and extended Bayly's Wharf over the former low tide beach behind the eastern pier to provide the site for a new fish market.

Only Cattedown is a conventional commercial port, handling 1.25 million tons of cargo in 1988, including 220,000 tons of roadstone shipped out by Pomphlett for the Kentish roadbuilding programme behind the Channel Tunnel. But it is the existence of clay on Dartmoor which gives the port its staple export. In 1988 Victoria Wharves handled 210,000 tons of china clay, though then the trade was in danger from a subsidised deal between British Rail and English China Clays to move the clay to the Cornish ports of Fowey and Par. In spite of this, Victoria Wharves was still exporting clay in 1993, while the grain trade, which had begun to build up in 1988, had considerably expanded. The wharf, put up for sale by Inchcape UK in 1993 as a going concern, has been bought by Mark Gatehouse of Queen Anne's Battery marina.

Cattedown Wharves, the oldest and still the largest port facility in the Cattewater, is berthing bigger and bigger ships, up to 20,000-ton tankers. All of the petroleum products for Plymouth and the hinterland pass over its wharf, amounting in 1992 to nearly a million tons. Cattedown was also handling fertilisers, animal feeds, imported coal (between 5,000 and 15,000 tons a year), salt and shot grit for the Dockyard and other engineering works. All told, in 1992 the Cattewater Commissioners coped with 691 ships and 1,389,000 tons of cargo. At the moment they control just the Cattewater, but the Navy is anxious to shed its overall control of the port and transfer the commercial authority of the Queen's Harbourmaster to the Cattewater harbourmaster.

But Teignmouth, handling less than half the tonnage of Cattewater alone, is doing well. It owes not a little to its being a non-registered port, outside the Dock Labour Scheme, able to employ casual labour. Its peak year was 1984, the year of the coal strike, when cargoes normally handled by registered ports moved to Teignmouth and the year's total was 700,000 tons. By 1988 that figure had settled at 575,000 tons, but it is significant that the ball clay, though handled in the same quantities, now amounts to only 50 per cent of the total trade when once it was 95 per cent.

Western Quay was built a century ago, and for most of its life Devon Trading Company held a controlling interest in the Quay Company. In 1968 it sold out to United Builders Merchants (UBM), although neither company

26.8 An aerial view of Teignmouth Docks in the late 1980s, with china clay loading in the foreground. (*Teignmouth Quay Co Ltd*)

was much inclined to spend money on the port, which just ticked over. Then in 1979, when UBM grew tired of its operation, the Quay Company was taken over in what was then the biggest management takeover in Britain. The new owners were Jeff Boyne, who had grown up in the company's service, and Ken Dunn, who owned inland storage capacity. It cost the pair £1 million, and they promptly borrowed more money from the bank to begin modernising facilities. They scrapped the derelict old sheds and built new. Because the ships entering the port were small vessels increasingly designed to penetrate up rivers and under bridges, and did not have their own cargo-handling gear, the company invested in its own loading equipment, and now owns twenty big fork-lift trucks, six cranes, five conveyor sets, two loading shovels and two weighbridges, all self-maintained. Some £4 million has been spent in the last seven years. The railway had made difficulties about the shunting involved in bringing clay into the quay sidings, so the transfer to road transport was made. Clay can now be loaded at a rate of 800 tons an hour, and the record is 6,000 tons in a ten-hour shift. In 1985 the Old Quay Inn was demolished and a new office block built on the site. In 1988 234,000 tons of clay went out, along with 6,000 tons of roadstone and 20,000 tons of barley. Imports, which at about 246,000 tons made nearly half the total cargoes, include newsprint, chip board, woodpulp, timber, plywood, animal feed, fertiliser, steel, cement and coal.

In 1988, because of problems over the partnership, Teignmouth Quay Company was sold to Associated British Ports (whose policy is not to divulge cargo details 'because it yields information to rivals'!). But relationships with the new owners are good. Jeff Boyne remains general manager and has had no interference with his handling of affairs. ABP is willing to invest in the port. The two current problems are shortage of storage, because the inland facilities were lost when the partnership dissolved, and berthing spaces. Present-day ships are up to 100m in length and longer, and in 1989 only two could be berthed at one time. So two indented docks, which were too small to take the bigger vessels, were filled in and piled across, and the eastern quay re-piled. There were plans to extend the waterfront out into the river, and to make the quay twice as long, reaching up to a point nearly 200m south of Shaldon Bridge. This would have enabled four 100m ships to berth at one time, and provided room to increase storage space by 30 to 40 per cent. The Quay Company claimed that this would have expanded the port's trade and increased employment from fifty to seventy-five.

Strong local environmental opposition killed the scheme, and the company has had to be content with lesser improvements, and modernising and enlarging its storage capacity.

Teignmouth is in many ways an archetypal small port of the West Country. For centuries it has been the home of small shipowners, builders, chandlers, bargemen, fishermen, deep-sea men; all living in a tight community. It has given investment opportunities and employment to the villages and towns in the hinterland. It has been fortunate in having clay as a staple trade. Now, in the past century and a half, it has expanded into the holiday trade and attracted retired people. Since the war, road improvements have cut up the old communities, the holiday trade has declined into rather tawdry attractions and the old hotels have been divided into self-catering flats. But, almost out of sight, the port has gone on. Shipowners, bargemen and shipbuilders have disappeared, but the trade has survived through thick and thin. Today Teignmouth is a real success story, and deserves to prosper.

Crispin Gill

Shipbuilding at Appledore and Teignmouth's port industry both seem set to continue into the twenty-first century, and so, too, will the tottering giant of Devon's traditional maritime economy of the last 300 years, the naval presence at Plymouth. The same sort of recapitalisation in modern infrastructure, plant, and technology which has been the salvation of Appledore and Teignmouth has been applied by the State on a much greater scale at Devonport Dockyard in the frigate and submarine complexes. The naval presence is now contracting to this modernised core, with the Royal William Victualling Yard and parts of South Yard being abandoned during the 1990s, but the contraction is nowhere so severe as at Britain's other naval bases and, indeed, the strategic shift resulting from the apparent ending of the Cold War is likely to enhance Plymouth's pre-eminence. It is the northeast base of Rosyth, built to watch the threat from Germany and then Russia, that now faces the reduction of status suffered by Portsmouth, if not the extinction visited upon Pembroke and Chatham. As the threat from the east subsides, so British naval activity is more likely to focus on its world role

26.9 A lorry-load of ball clay being transferred to a ship at Teignmouth Docks in the mid-1980s. (*Nicholas Horne*

to the south and westward, a shift clearly signalled by the conflicts in the Falklands and the Gulf. This was the role that Plymouth performed before the threat from the east emerged and which Plymouth, as the largest, best situated and best equipped British naval base, remains capable of sustaining into the twenty-first century, now as a commercial enterprise run by Devonport Management Ltd. The Dockyard's £120-million, two-and-a-half-year refit of the aircraft carrier *Invincible* in the late 1980s, and subsequently that of *Illustrious*, demonstrated its continuing ability to maintain the largest units of the Navy – a capacity which will embrace the maintenance of the Trident nuclear-missile submarines well into the twenty-first century. Uncertainties still remain as to the size of dockyard workforce that any cost-conscious government is willing to maintain (through substantial refit orders) to keep the present capacity in constant readiness, but there is little doubt that Plymouth will remain Britain's (and Western Europe's) premier operational naval base.

Equally assured seems Devon's role in naval training, especially since the 1993 decision to move sea-training from Portland to Devonport. Nevertheless, naval manpower needs continue to diminish, so that officer training at Dartmouth and marine training at Lympstone may contract with them, while changing policy towards technical education has condemned the Royal Naval Engineering College at Manadon to closure.

Ever since the eighteenth century the Royal Navy has been the most significant instigator of maritime activity in Devon, only rivalled in more recent times by the seaside tourist industry, the most dynamic element of Devon's maritime economy over the last half-century or more. This, too, will doubtless remain significant in the forseeable future, though it faces considerable challenges. In the following section, John Channon discusses the importance of the holiday business to Devon's economy and isolates one issue – pollution – which currently threatens its long-term prosperity.

Seaside Tourism: The Pollution Problem

Devon's holiday industry, largely a function of the natural beauty and amenities of the county's coastlines, has formed an increasingly important part of the county's economy since the eighteenth century.[11] In recent times, indeed, it has occupied a critical position, for

> in no other field would it appear that Devon has so good a comparative advantage . . . and it would seem that a reasonable rate of growth of the holiday industry and continuing development to meet changing demands will be needed to retain the prosperity of the county.[12]

Tourism is of both direct and indirect significance to the local economy. Its main contribution lies in the expenditures made by holidaymakers during their stay in the county. In 1987, for instance, visitors spent around £370 million, approximately £135 million of which remained as income to Devon residents.[13] Indirectly, seaside tourism benefits the local population in multifarious ways, generating business for service activities as diverse as the motor repair trade and the water supply industry, thereby providing much employment. However, various problems are associated with this holiday business. It is highly seasonal, the majority of tourists visiting the county between Easter and the end of September, with a marked concentration in July and August. While this leads to traffic congestion during the summer and uneven demands on local services, exacerbating the South West's now seemingly annual water stringencies, for instance, it also entails high levels of unemployment in winter. Moreover, the benefits of seaside tourism are poorly distributed throughout Devon, the industry being chiefly located adjacent to the sandy beaches between the rivers Exe and Dart on the south coast, and between the towns of Braunton and Ilfracombe on the north coast.

A further difficulty arises from the uncertain nature of year-by-year demand in the seaside holiday industry. Various factors – boom or recession in the national economy, the vagaries of the weather, the attractiveness and cheapness of holidays abroad in sunnier climes, the development of inland 'activity' holidays – can affect the numbers of tourists visiting Devon's seaside resorts. While many of these factors are beyond the control of the local holiday industry, some adverse influences can derive from the quality of the product offered. In recent years, one such determinant has attracted particular attention: the pollution of Devon's beaches and coastal waters.

The problem of pollution[14] arises from two main sources, the spillage of oil at sea and inadequate local sewage disposal facilities. While the former may deter would-be tourists (witness the impact of the highly-publicised *Rose Bay* disaster on South Devon's holiday trade in May 1990[15]), its incidence is extraneous to local authority and generally of shortlived significance. Sewage pollution, on the other hand, is a product of long-term deficiencies in the local infrastructure and therefore a particularly intractable problem, and potentially very expensive to overcome. Recognition of this issue has spawned a series of campaigns to encourage seaside resorts to improve the condition of their beaches and inshore waters. In 1987, for instance, the national Clean Beaches Award Scheme was launched in conjunction with the 'Keep Britain Tidy Better Beaches' campaign, while European 'Blue Flags' were awarded to beaches which complied with the comparatively strict European Community standards. Since then, these awards have become a regular feature of the holiday season, their announcement being attended with much comment and publicity.

Resort competition, of course, underlies such schemes, with resorts standing to gain much favourable media coverage from the acquisition of awards. For example, thirty-one British beaches were contenders for the 1988 'Blue Flag' award, including those at Seaton, Sidmouth, Exmouth, Dawlish Warren, Teignmouth and eight beaches in Torbay. With six of these local entrants – the Torbay beaches of Oddicombe, Anstey's Cove, Corbyn, Paignton, Broadsands (considered a 'model' beach) and Meadfoot – amongst the seventeen successful British beaches, it would seem that Devon fared well in this contest. However, some clear problems were highlighted. Godrington failed on the quality of its water, Breakwater was considered too small with poor facilities, while Dawlish Warren withdrew its application because dogs are permitted on the beach and the judges did not even bother to visit Teignmouth owing to the poor state of its bathing water. Moreover, residents of Meadfoot, near to a successful entrant beach, actually questioned the award, claiming that the beach was full of rubble, scrap metal and broken bottles. Sundry well-publicised reports of sightings of sewage, and other flushed waste matter, floating in the water off Torre Abbey Sands,

and the paraphernalia of drug takers being found on Paignton beach, and at Salcombe and Exmouth, did little to advance Torbay's carefully cultivated 'English Riviera' image.

Such poor publicity, together with growing concerns about man's impact upon the marine environment, has prompted some corrective action. More stringent tests on sea water quality are now conducted by the National Rivers Authority, while piecemeal material improvements, such as the construction of screening plants at notorious outfalls, have given way to a major regional investment programme initiated in 1991 by the newly-privatised South West Water plc. Styled 'The Clean Sweep', this £900-million scheme is designed to improve the South West's essentially nineteenth-century sewage system so that it can cater for the needs of the twenty-first century. Whether this ambitious project will succeed remains to be seen. In the meantime, the quality of Devon's coastal and estuarial water, and its suitability for bathing and other recreational pursuits, is very much a live issue as the twentieth century draws to a close.

John Channon

As this group of discussions of Devon's maritime involvement in the late twentieth century indicates, there is justification for the belief that Devon is still very much a maritime county. Furthermore, these contributions support yet again the view that the county's maritime activities, as with maritime activity in general, should be regarded as organic, exhibiting ever-present sectoral growth, adaptation and decline, in response to such factors as the play of technological change, the competition of other areas, and the changes in demand arising from continuing income growth and increasing leisure in the wider British economy and society.

It might be interesting to speculate how our descendants in 100 years' time, say, will write about *their* maritime Devon. And also, perhaps to consider how they, from their perspective, would view this long story of transition and change, this saga of challenge and endeavour, that makes up Devon's maritime history over the centuries. Of one thing we can be sure. While the economy may change, the seas themselves will ensure that there will still be ships and seafarers, the continuing link between Devon's past, present and future.

26: *Towards the Twenty-first Century*

1 Ministry of Defence (Navy), *Admiralty Manual of Navigation* (1987), VI, 1.

2 Admiralty Hydrographic Department, *Channel Pilot* (13th edn, 1947), I, 3.

3 Admiralty Hydrographic Department, *West Coast of England Pilot* (10th edn, 1960).

4 *Channel Pilot* (1947), I, 141.

5 Admiralty Hydrographic Department, *Channel Pilot* (1st edn, 1971).

6 This account is based on O Warner, *The Lifeboat Service. A History of the Royal National Lifeboat Institution, 1824–1974* (1974); W Webb, *Coastguard. An Official History of HM Coastguard* (1976); and A Redfern, 'Radar Simulator Training for Effective Search and Rescue' (unpublished Ph.D thesis, Plymouth Polytechnic, 1987). Also see Chapter 1.

7 This account is partly based on material supplied by Peter Harvey, secretary of the Port of Plymouth Sailing Association, and Cmdr L R R Foster RN (retd), past Commodore of the Royal Western Yacht Club.

8 This account is based on *British Shipbuilding 1972. A Report to the Department of Trade and Industry by Booz-Allen & Hamilton International BV* (1972); the *Interim Report on Court Line Limited* (1975); the *Final Report on Court Line Limited* (1978); G Farr, *Shipbuilding in North Devon* (1976); and L Harris, *A Two Hundred Year History of Appledore Shipyards* (Combe Martin, 1992). Much useful information was kindly supplied by Michael Guegan.

9 P Hilditch, 'The Decline of British Shipbuilding since the Second World War' in S Fisher, ed., *Lisbon as a Port Town, the British Seaman and other Maritime Themes* (Exeter, 1988), 137–8.

10 This account is based on information supplied by Jeff Boyne, managing director of Teignmouth Quay Company; Cmdr A Dyer RN (retd), the Harbour Master, Cattewater Commissioners; Lionel Stribley, managing director, Cattedown Wharves; Michael East, manager of Victoria Wharves; and Brittany Ferries. The main secondary work consulted was H J Trump, *Teignmouth. A Maritime History* (Chichester, 1986).

11 See Chapters 13 and 25.

12 F M M Lewes, A J Culyer and G Brady, 'The Holiday Industry', in F Barlow, ed., *Exeter and its Region* (Exeter, 1969), 257.

13 *Devon Tourism Review* (Devon County Council, 1987).

14 This section is largely based on reports in the *Western Morning News, Exeter Express and Echo*, and *Torquay Herald Express*, April 1987 – May 1993.

15 The *Rose Bay*, a Liberian-registered, 250,000-ton 'supertanker', collided with the Brixham-based trawler *Dionne Marie* twelve miles south of Start Point on 12 May 1990. A large quantity of oil leaked from the tanker and was subsequently washed up on the beaches of Bigbury Bay. Local hoteliers complained that the intense media coverage which ensued served to depress bookings for the summer holiday season.

Epilogue: The New Maritime History of Devon and The Maritime Aspects of History

BASIL GREENHILL

The close of these two volumes may be a good place to reflect on the reasons for preparing and publishing this contribution to the history of Britain. This book appears at an especially important time in the development of the study of the maritime aspects of history. It is a time when we are faced with a great dislocation.

Merchant and naval shipping has completely changed in nature in the last generation. There are fewer and larger merchant vessels. They are designed in every way to make the maximum of modern technology. They bear little resemblance to their forbears. They berth in docks equipped with specialised automated cargo-handling gear tending in their turn to be situated further and further away from the centres of population, so that merchant shipping, once part of the lives in one way or another of millions, now scarcely enters into the consciousness of most people in Europe and North America, except briefly in an occasional short trip in a roll-on roll-off ferry or when some much publicised disaster occurs. Similarly navies, their equipment ever more secret, their capital ships more and more submersibles, operating unseen, whose working environments are almost as exotic as those of vehicles for space travel, become more and more remote from citizens' experience.

Where contact with maritime reality is rare, romance tends to take over. The 'Romance of the Sea' (and especially of sailing ships) has been exploited by journalists, novelists, the poets and by television to an almost extreme degree. Devon is a county many people associate with maritime activities, but only too frequently romantic mythology is substituted for even more interesting fact. In examining thoroughly the maritime element in Devon's history, complex and varied as it is, we hope we have created something of a model which may be followed, and no doubt much improved upon, in other counties. It is doubtful that the British were ever a 'seafaring nation', whatever that much misused term was meant to mean. Britain was and is a trading nation, its prosperity rested much on trade with other nations in modern times, but it was never as dependent on participation in the world's carrying trade, for example, as were the Norwegians, or the Swedish-speaking population of coastal Finland, or at one time the New Englanders and eastern Canadians.

This is perhaps one of the reasons why the seafarer has never enjoyed high social status in Britain, which has perhaps in its turn been one of the complex causes for the frequent neglect of the maritime dimensions of our history. But seafaring has been all-absorbing for the communities of the coastal fringe of North Devon and the communities around the sheltered harbours of South Devon, while the development of the naval dockyard is almost the *raison d'etre* for the growth of Plymouth. Thus Devon's history has a strong maritime element which is intrinsically worth examining.

Of course, so-called maritime history is, as we hope the preceding pages have demonstrated, more than just ships and seafarers. It is also about trade and merchants, shipbuilders, financiers, fishing and fishermen, naval enterprise and, in more recent years, seaside tourism and other sea-related leisure activities, and always about people and the ways in which they lived. It is not so much a subject in its own right as one which has an important bearing on other fields of study such as economic, social or political history. We of the Editorial Board hope that these volumes will lead, not to the further development of a specialised sub-branch of historical studies, but to

an awareness among mainstream historians of the all-pervasiveness of the maritime dimensions of history and a respect for and an understanding of it, for the future of so called maritime history lies in its absorption into the mainstream of historical studies.

In the past, maritime historical studies have all too often been marginalised in historical perception if perhaps less so in popular perception. They should be considered an essential component in the study of the many activities which affect society, influencing and being influenced by all manner of wider economic, social and political developments. Moreover, marginalised as they have been, maritime historical studies have been fragmented by compartmentalisation into mercantile and naval history. To a degree this has been the consequence of the use of separate sources. In the past naval and mercantile affairs have all too often been treated as separate branches of historical study, but in reality they are inextricably mingled and integral to the mainstream of British development, and to divide them into specialisms is to make a limiting and artificial distinction.

The ship is a powerful symbol, and without ships and boats there would be no maritime history, but she was only one part of a complex of activities, commercial, industrial, political, strategic. Her development and her movements were the end product of human activity reaching deep into the structure of society. There has in the past perhaps been a tendency in maritime historical (but not archaeological) studies to look too much to the history of ships in isolation from all the activities which go with them.

Nevertheless, some understanding of the ship and her people, her technology and their psychology, is essential to the sort of study we have sought to achieve. It is essential for the understanding of the maritime aspects of history that this kind of study should continue, and, as it is the role of universities to absorb the maritime element into historical studies of all kinds, so it is the role of maritime museums to keep alive understanding of the ship and her ways, how she developed, how she was built, how she was navigated, and the rich terminology which grew up around her, so much of which has entered into everyday usage. As long ago as 1925, Sir Alan Moore, in a book which represents the very best of the old school of educated dilettante writing on boats and ships, put this point in words which are still very relevant:

> The square sail has been an element in history comparable with the use of the horse. It has been the instrument of war, commerce and discovery, activities of which no man has not felt the consequences; and yet, so much apart is the life of the seaman, and so little is his art known, that in ages when men saw symbols everywhere and regarded the hilt of a sword even beyond the blade, they missed the emblem of the mast and crossed yard. And what escaped medieval imagery has largely eluded modern interest.
>
> There are signs that this indifference is passing, now that sails are passing too; but it will be long before the forms of sails command as much attention as the shapes of arches. Yet they are at least equally important to the student of mankind.[1]

Epilogue.

1 A Moore, *Last Days of Mast and Sail* (Oxford, 1925) 84–5.

Index